Fifth Edition

THROUGH WOMEN'S EYES

An American History

WITH DOCUMENTS

Ellen Carol DuBois
UNIVERSITY OF CALIFORNIA,
LOS ANGELES

Lynn Dumenil
OCCIDENTAL COLLEGE

With Contributions by

Sharla M. Fett
OCCIDENTAL COLLEGE

bedford/st.martin's
Macmillan Learning

Boston | New York

For Norman, as always; for Arnie

For Bedford/St. Martin's
Vice President, Editorial, Macmillan Higher Education Humanities: Edwin Hill
Program Director for History: Michael Rosenberg
Senior Program Manager for History: William J. Lombardo
History Marketing Manager: Melissa Rodriguez
Director of Content Development: Jane Knetzger
Developmental Editor: Kathryn Abbott
Senior Content Project Manager: Gregory Erb
Senior Workflow Project Supervisor: Joe Ford
Production Supervisor: Robin Besofsky
Senior Media Project Manager: Michelle Camisa
Assistant Editor: Stephanie Sosa
Copyeditor: Nancy Benjamin
Composition: Lumina Datamatics, Inc.
Indexer: Sonya Dintaman
Cartography: Mapping Specialists, Ltd.
Permissions Manager: Kalina Ingham
Permissions Researcher: Arthur Johnson
Photo Editor: Sheena Goldstein
Photo Researcher: Naomi Kornhauser
Director of Design, Content Management: Diana Blume
Cover Design: William Boardman
Cover Images: Cathy Murphy/Hulton Archive/Getty Images (Huerta); Smith Collection/Gado/Getty Images (Tape); National Portrait Gallery, Smithsonian Institution (La Flesche); Photo12/Universal Images Group/Getty Images (Parks); Terry Ashe/The LIFE Images Collection/Getty Images (Ginsberg)
Printing and Binding: LSC Communications

Manufactured in the United States of America.

1   2   3   4   5   6   23   22   21   20   19   18

For information, write: Bedford/St. Martin's, 75 Arlington Street, Boston, MA 02116
   (617-399-4000)

ISBN 978-1-319-10493-1 (Combined Edition)
ISBN 978-1-319-15625-1 (Volume 1)
ISBN 978-1-319-15627-5 (Volume 2)

PREFACE FOR INSTRUCTORS

Each new edition of *Through Women's Eyes: An American History with Documents* provides an opportunity to revisit and refine our vision for this textbook. Our original goal was to create a U.S. women's history that combined an inclusive and diverse narrative with primary-source essays — a comprehensive resource to aid instructors and encourage student engagement and analysis. We have been thoroughly delighted that this book has resonated with instructors and students alike and were gratified to hear from one instructor that it is "the single best textbook in U.S. women's history." Our belief that U.S. women's history is U.S. history and vice versa continues to fuel our approach to this book, and we are pleased that *Through Women's Eyes* is the number one choice for U.S. women's history.

◆ NEW TO THIS EDITION

In this new edition, we have paid particular attention to the theme of women and health, as well as the connections among women activists from the nineteenth century to the present. Recent developments in scholarship and reviewer requests also prompted the addition of new material on slavery; Native American women; Western history; popular culture; environmentalism and ecofeminism; lesbian and transgender history; twentieth-century feminism; and women in contemporary politics, with particular emphasis on the 2016 election and its aftermath.

Of the thirty-four primary-source features, four are new and two have been substantially revised. New essays include "Mothering under Slavery," "Female Labor in the Gold Rush Economy," "Representing Native American Women in the Late Nineteenth Century," and "Women's Lobbying in the 1920s." New documents on witchcraft have been added to Chapter 2's "By and About Colonial Women," and a new selection by Judith Sargent Murray has been added to Chapter 4.

New "Reading into the Past" documents include a woman's account of her escape from slavery in Chapter 3; an account of the Bear Flag Revolt told by a Californiana in Chapter 5; labor activist Genora Johnson Dollinger on the 1936–37 Flint sit-down strike in Chapter 9; Esther Peterson on the President's Commission on the Status of Women in Chapter 10; an account of forced sterilization in Chapter 11; an excerpt from Lakota activist LaDonna Brave Bull Allard that provides historical context for the opposition to the Dakota Access pipeline, and a piece on Ilhan Omar, the first Muslim Somali American lawmaker, both in Chapter 12. Also new to the fifth edition, the "Reading into the Past" documents now include "Questions for Analysis."

We have also heard reviewer calls for end-of-chapter pedagogy and have added chapter reviews to the narrative section of every chapter. The review includes key terms and people, narrative review questions, and a synthetic "Making Connections" question.

We are also very excited to welcome Sharla M. Fett as a contributor to this edition. Fett brings her expertise on American slavery and the history of women's health. She has helped to revise Chapters 1–6 for the fifth edition.

Finally, with the fifth edition, we once again offer *Through Women's Eyes* as split volumes (Volume 1, Chapters 1–7; Volume 2, Chapters 6–12) in addition to the combined comprehensive volume with all chapters. We also continue to include the option to purchase a low-cost e-book version of *Through Women's Eyes*. For a list of our publishing partners' sites, see **macmillanhighered.com/ebookpartners**.

◆ APPROACH AND FORMAT

Through Women's Eyes: An American History with Documents challenges the separation of "women's history" from what students, in our experience, think of as "real history." We treat all central developments of American history, always through women's eyes, so that students may experience the broad sweep of the nation's past from a new and illuminating perspective. *Through Women's Eyes* combines in-depth treatment of well-known aspects of the history of women, such as the experiences of Lowell mill girls and slave women, the cult of true womanhood, and the rise of feminism, with developments in U.S. history not usually considered from the perspective of women, including the conquest of the Americas, the role of women in war and the military, post–World War II anticommunism, the civil rights movement, and the increasingly visible role that women have played in recent politics. Our goal of **a full integration of women's history and U.S. history** is pragmatic as well as principled. We recognize that there may be some students who read *Through Women's Eyes* who have little background in U.S. history and that they will be learning the nation's history as they follow women through it.

At the same time that we broaden the conception of women's and U.S. history, we offer **an inclusive view of the lives of American women and their historical experiences**. We continue to decenter the narrative from an emphasis on white privileged women to bring ethnic and racial minorities and wage-earning women from the margins to the center of our story. In providing an integrated analysis of the rich variety of women that includes ethnic and racial diversity and class, immigrant status, geographical information, and sexual orientation differences, we have also explored the dynamics of relationships between women. Examples of sisterhood emerge from our pages, but so too do the hierarchical relations of class and race and other sources of tensions that erected barriers between women.

Just as many of our students hold preconceived notions of women's history as an intriguing adjunct to "real history," they often equate the historian's finished product with historical "truth." We remain determined to reveal **the relationship between historical scholarship and original sources** to show history as a dynamic process of investigation and interpretation rather than a set body of facts and figures. To this end, we divide each of our chapters into narrative text and primary-source essays. Written sources range from diaries, letters, and memoirs to poems, newspaper accounts, and public testimony. Visual sources include artifacts, engravings, portraits, photographs, cartoons, and television screen shots. Instructors often tell us that these essays are their favorite aspect of the book. "The primary-source essays are an outstanding way for students to explore topics more in-depth," one instructor wrote, "and students really connect to the individual stories."

Together, the sources reveal to students the **wide variety of primary evidence** from which history is crafted. Our documentary and visual essays not only allow for focused treatment of many topics — for example, the experience of Native American women before and after European conquest, the higher education of women before 1900, women's use of cosmetics in the context of a commercialized beauty culture, women's roles in World War II, women's activism in the civil rights movement, and gender in the military — but also provide ample guidance for students to analyze historical documents thoughtfully. Each essay offers advice about evaluating the sources presented and poses questions for analysis intended to foster students' ability to think independently and critically. Substantive headnotes to the sources and plentiful cross-references between the narrative and the essays further encourage students to appreciate the relationship between historical sources and historical writing.

◆ FEATURES AND PEDAGOGY

We are proud as well of the pedagogical features we provide to help students enter into and absorb the text. Each chapter opens with a **thematic introduction** that starts with a particular person or moment in time chosen to pique students' interest and segues into a clear statement of the central issues and ideas of the chapter. An **illustrated chapter timeline** alerts students to the main events covered in the narrative and relates women's experience to U.S. history by visually linking key developments. At the close of each narrative section, an **analytic conclusion** revisits central themes and provides a bridge to the next chapter. New to this edition, we have included a chapter review, containing a list of key terms and people, as well as review questions that will encourage students to reread and think about what they've learned throughout the chapter.

Beyond the visual sources presented in the essays, **102 historical images and 10 maps and charts** extend and enliven the narrative, accompanied by **substantive captions** that relate the illustration to the text and help students unlock the image. Also animating the narrative while complementing the documentary essays are **25 primary-source excerpts, called "Reading into the Past," drawn from classic texts** featuring women such as Anne Hutchinson, Catharine Beecher, Sojourner Truth, Margaret Sanger, and Mary McLeod Bethune. At the end of each chapter, we provide **plentiful endnotes** and a **bibliography** that gives students a myriad of opportunities for reading and research beyond the boundaries of the textbook.

In addition, we open the book with an **Introduction for Students** that discusses the evolution of women's history as a field and the approach we took in capturing its exciting state today. An **extensive Appendix** includes not only tables and charts focused on U.S. women's experience over time but also the Seneca Falls Declaration of Sentiments and Resolutions and annotated extracts of Supreme Court cases of major relevance to U.S. history "through women's eyes."

◆ RESOURCES FOR INSTRUCTORS

Bedford/St. Martin's offers a wide variety of teaching resources for this book and for this course, including presentation materials, lecture strategies, and suggested in-class activities. All can be downloaded or ordered at **macmillanlearning.com /catalog/history**.

Instructor's Resource Manual. Both experienced and first-time instructors will find useful teaching suggestions for the U.S. women's history course in the *Instructor's Resource Manual.* The available resources include suggested assignments and sample term paper topics and in-class exams, as well as teaching tips, lecture strategies, recommended films and television shows, tips for teaching with visual sources, and test bank questions.

Guide to Changing Editions. Designed to facilitate an instructor's transition from the previous edition of *Through Women's Eyes* to this new edition, this guide presents an overview of major changes as well as changes in each chapter.

Online Test Bank. This test bank includes a mix of carefully crafted multiple-choice questions for each chapter. All questions appear in Microsoft Word.

Maps and Images in PowerPoint and JPEG formats. Instructors can access all of the maps from the book and selected images, some in color, from the visual essays.

The Bedford Lecture Kit Presentation Slides. Be effective and save time with *The Bedford Lecture Kit.* These presentation materials are downloadable individually from the Instructor Resources tab at **macmillanlearning.com/catalog/history**. They include fully customizable multimedia presentations built around chapter outlines that are embedded with maps, figures, and images from the textbook.

◆ PACKAGE AND SAVE YOUR STUDENTS MONEY

For information on free packages and discounts up to 50%, visit **macmillanlearning .com/catalog/history**, or contact your local Bedford/St. Martin's sales representative.

The Bedford Digital Collections for U.S. Women's History. Instructors looking for digital packaging options can package *Through Women's Eyes* with the Bedford Digital Collections, an online repository of discovery-oriented primary-source projects that they can easily customize and link to from their course management system or Web site. See **macmillanhighered.com/launchpadsolo/ bdcwomen/catalog** for more information.

Bedford Series in History and Culture. The more than 100 titles in this highly praised series include a number focused on women's history and combine first-rate scholarship, historical narrative, and important primary documents for undergraduate courses. Each book is brief, inexpensive, and focused on a specific topic or period. For a complete list of titles, visit **macmillanlearning.com /Catalog/discipline/History/TheBedfordSeriesinHistoryCulture**.

Trade Books. Titles published by sister companies Hill and Wang; Farrar, Straus and Giroux; Henry Holt and Company; St. Martin's Press; Picador; and Palgrave Macmillan are available at a 50% discount when packaged with Bedford/St. Martin's textbooks. For more information, visit **macmillan.com/tradebooksforcourses**.

A Pocket Guide to Writing in History. This portable and affordable reference tool by Mary Lynn Rampolla provides reading, writing, and research advice useful to students in all history courses. Concise yet comprehensive advice on approaching typical history assignments, developing critical reading skills, writing effective history papers, conducting research, using and documenting sources, and avoiding plagiarism — enhanced with practical tips and examples throughout — has made this slim reference a best-seller.

◆ ACKNOWLEDGMENTS

Textbooks are for learning, and writing this one has taught us a great deal. We have learned from one another and have enjoyed the richness of the collaborative process. But we have also benefited immensely from the opportunity to read and assess the works of literally hundreds of scholars whose research and insights have made this book possible. For this volume specifically, we thank Susan E. Gray, Arizona State University; Katarina Keane, University of Maryland; Renee LaFleur, University of Tennessee at Martin; Holly L. Masturzo, Florida State College at Jacksonville; Georgina M. Montgomery, Michigan State University; Louise M. Newman, University of Florida; and Kimberly Welch, University of Redlands. Since the first edition, we have received assistance from numerous colleagues, former students, researchers, and archivists, who graciously answered phone and e-mail queries. For the fifth edition, we would like to specifically thank Tarah Demant, Deena Gonzalez, Ann D. Gordon, Diana Mara Henry, Karla Mantilla, Gloria Orenstein, Chaitra Powell, Pamela Stewart, Kevin Terraciano, and Mir Yarfitz. Thanks also to Sarah Pirpas-Kapit and Serena Zabin for help with the bibliography. Sharon Park provided exceptional research assistance for one of the document essays in this edition, not only finding rich material but also offering excellent analysis that shaped the interpretation of the essay.

We have a great deal of admiration for the people at Bedford/St. Martin's who worked so hard to bring all five editions of this book to fruition. We would specifically like to thank editorial director Edwin Hill, publisher Michael Rosenberg, senior executive editor William Lombardo, freelance developmental editor Kathryn Abbott, marketing manager Melissa Rodriguez, and assistant editor Stephanie Sosa. Naomi Kornhauser and Sheena Goldstein researched and cleared images;

Kalina Ingham supervised the clearance of text permissions; Nancy Benjamin copyedited the manuscript; William Boardman designed the cover; and Gregory Erb oversaw the production process.

We viewed the first edition of *Through Women's Eyes* as an exciting new departure, and the wide adoption and warm reception of reviewers and adopters have confirmed our aspirations. The revisions for this new, fifth edition benefited significantly from the comments of instructors who have used the textbook in their classes and who weighed in specifically on the primary-source essays. We continue to acknowledge the pioneering work of Mary Ritter Beard, *America through Women's Eyes* (1933), and also note that this book would not have been possible without the dynamic developments and extraordinary output in the field of U.S. women's history since Beard's book appeared. In 1933 Beard acknowledged that the "collection, editing, sifting and cataloguing of sources dealing with women's work and thought in the making of civilization" was ground as yet uncultivated.[1] We have been fortunate to reap a rich harvest from the scholarly literature of the last forty years, a literature that has allowed us to express the diversity of women's lives and to conceive of U.S. history from a gendered perspective.

Ellen Carol DuBois
Lynn Dumenil
Sharla Fett

1. Mary Ritter Beard, ed., *America through Women's Eyes* (New York: Macmillan, 1933), 9.

BRIEF CONTENTS

CONTENTS

photos: Chapter 1, Beinecke Rare Book and Manuscript Library, Yale University; Chapter 2, Abby Aldrich Rockefeller Folk Art Museum. The Colonial Williamsburg Foundation

xi

**CHAPTER 3
Mothers and
Daughters of the
Revolution,
1750–1810   *102***

Chapter 7
Women in an Expanding Nation: Consolidation of the West, Mass Immigration, and the Crisis of the 1890s   356

photo: File 12017/37232 for Leong Lee, Chinese Departure Application Case Files, 1912–1943, San Francisco District Office, Immigration and Naturalization Service, Record Group 85, National Archives and Records Administration—Pacific Region, San Bruno, CA

photo: Library of Congress, 3a42473

Chapter 12
U.S. Women in a Global Age, 1980–Present *688*

SPECIAL FEATURES

INTRODUCTION
FOR STUDENTS

I N READING THIS TEXTBOOK, you will encounter a rich array of source materials and a narrative informed by a wealth of scholarship, so you may be surprised to learn that women's history is a comparatively new field. When Mary Ritter Beard, the founding mother of women's history in the United States, assembled *America Through Women's Eyes* in 1933, she argued that an accurate understanding of the nation's past required as much consideration of women's experience as of men's. But so limited were the sources available to her that she had no choice but to present the first women-centered American history as a spotty anthology of primary and secondary writings by a handful of women writers. Not until the 1970s, with the resurgence of feminism that you will read about in Chapter 11, did researchers start to give extensive attention to women's history. In that decade, history, along with other academic disciplines such as literature and sociology, underwent significant change as feminist scholars' desire to analyze as well as to protest women's unequal status fueled an extraordinary surge of investigation into women's experiences. Feminist theorists revived an obscure grammatical term, "gender," to distinguish the meaning that a particular society attaches to differences between men and women from "sex," or the unchanging biological differences between men and women. Because gender meaning varies over time and among societies, gender differences are both socially constructed and subject to change.

The concept of gender and the tools of history go together. If we are to move past the notion that what it means to be a woman never changes, we must look to the varying settings in which people assume female and male roles, with all their attendant expectations. Definitions of femininity and masculinity, family structures, what work is considered properly female or male, understandings of motherhood and of marriage, and women's involvement in public affairs all vary tremendously across time, are subject to large forces like economic development and warfare, and can themselves shape the direction of history. As historian Joan Scott forcefully argues, gender can be used as a tool of historical analysis, to explore not only how societies interpret differences between women and men but also how these distinctions can work to legitimize other hierarchical relations of power.[1]

This textbook draws on the rich theoretical and historical work of the past fifty years to present a synthesis of American women's experiences. We begin with a discussion of the many meanings of "America" and end with a chapter that examines the issues women face in the twenty-first century. In between we highlight both the

---

1. Joan Wallach Scott, "Gender: A Useful Category of Historical Analysis," *American Historical Review* 91, no. 5 (December 1986): 1067.

broad patterns of change concerning women's political, economic, and family lives and the diversity of American women's experiences.

As its title suggests, however, *Through Women's Eyes: An American History with Documents* aims for more than an account of U.S. women's history. Beyond weaving together the wealth of scholarship available to U.S. women's historians, we seek to fulfill Mary Beard's vision of a text that covers the total range of the nation's history, placing women — their experiences, contributions, and observations — at the center. We examine major economic developments, such as the emergence of slavery as a labor system, the rise of factories in the early nineteenth century, the growth of an immigrant labor force, and the shift to corporate capitalism. We explore major political themes, from reform movements to political party realignments to the nation's many wars. We look at transformations in family and personal life, the rise of consumer and mass culture, the racial and ethnic heterogeneity of the nation's peoples, and shifting attitudes about sexuality. And we analyze international developments, beginning with the interrelationship of the Americas, Europe, and Africa in the Atlantic world of the sixteenth and seventeenth centuries and ending with contemporary globalization. But as we do so, we analyze how women experienced these national developments and how they contributed to and shaped them.

◆ THE HISTORY OF WOMEN'S HISTORY: FROM SEPARATE SPHERES TO WOMEN'S DIVERSITY

When the field of U.S. women's history began to take off as a scholarly endeavor in the 1970s, one particular form of gender analysis was especially influential. The "separate spheres" paradigm, as historians termed it, focused on the nineteenth-century ideology that divided social life into two mutually exclusive arenas: the private world of home and family, identified with women, and the public world of business and politics, identified with men. In a second phase, as scholarship on women of color increased, the primacy of the separate spheres interpretation gave way to a more nuanced interpretation of the diversity of women's experiences.

Separate Spheres and the Nineteenth-Century Gender System

Women's historians of the 1970s found in the nineteenth-century system of separate spheres the roots of the gender distinctions of their own time. They observed that although ideas about separate spheres had been of enormous importance in the nineteenth century, these ideas had received little to no attention in historical accounts. The approach that women's historians took was to re-vision this nineteenth-century gender system through women's eyes. They found that, although women's lives were tightly constricted by assumptions about their proper place within the family, expectations of female moral influence and a common sense of womanhood allowed women collectively to achieve a surprising degree of social authority.

The separate spheres paradigm proved a valuable approach, but it hid as much as it yielded about women's lives. Early on, historian Gerda Lerner observed that it was no coincidence that the notion of women's exclusive domesticity flourished just as factories were opening up and young women were going to work in them.[2] Because adherence to the ideology of separate spheres helped to distinguish the social standing of middle-class women from their factory-working contemporaries, Lerner urged that class relations and the growth of the female labor force be taken into account in understanding the influence that such ideas held. Subsequent historians have observed that the idealization of women within the domestic sphere coincided exactly with the decline of the economic importance of family production relative to factory production; and that just as class inequality began to challenge the nation's democratic self-understanding, American society came to define itself in terms of the separate spheres of men and women.

Additional problems emerged in the reliance on the separate spheres paradigm as the dominant basis for nineteenth-century U.S. women's history. Historian Nancy Hewitt contends that whatever sense of female community developed among nineteenth-century women rarely crossed class or race lines. On the contrary, hierarchical relationships — slave to mistress, immigrant factory worker to moneyed consumer, nanny to professional woman — have been central to the intricate tapestry of the historical female experience in America.[3] Even among the middle-class wives and mothers who did not work outside the home and whose family-based lives made them the central focus of separate spheres ideology, Linda Kerber urges historians not to confuse rhetoric with reality, ideological values with individual actions.[4] The lasting contribution of the historical exploration of separate spheres ideology is the recognition of the vital impact of gender differentiation on American history; the challenge posed by its critics is to develop a more complex set of portraits of women who lived in, around, and against these notions. As it matures, the field of women's history is able to move from appreciating the centrality of gender systems to accommodating and exploring conflicts and inequalities among women.

Toward a More Inclusive Women's History: Race and Ethnicity

The field of U.S. women's history has struggled to come to terms with the structures of racial inequality so central to the American national experience. As Peggy Pascoe observes, modern scholars have learned to think about race and gender in

2. Gerda Lerner, "The Lady and the Mill Girl," *Midcontinent American Studies Journal* 10 (1969): 5–15.

3. Nancy Hewitt, "Beyond the Search for Sisterhood: American Women's History in the 1990s," in Vicki Ruiz and Ellen Carol DuBois, eds., *Unequal Sisters: A Multicultural Reader in U.S. Women's History*, 3rd ed. (New York: Routledge, 2000), 1–19.

4. Linda K. Kerber, "Separate Spheres, Female Worlds, Woman's Place: The Rhetoric of Women's History," *Journal of American History* 75, no. 1 (June 1988): 9–39.

similar ways, no longer treating either as unchanging biological essences around which history forms but as social constructions that change meaning and content over time and place.[5] Building on a century-long scholarly tradition in African American history, black women scholars started in the 1980s to chart new territory as they explored the interactions between systems of racial and gender inequality or what they called "intersectionality." Analyzing the implications of the denial to late nineteenth-century black women of the privileges granted white women, Evelyn Brooks Higginbotham observes that "gender identity is inextricably linked to and even determined by racial identity."[6]

Other scholars of color, especially Chicana feminists, advanced this thinking about racial hierarchy and its intersections with the structures of gender. They made it clear that the history of Chicanas could not be understood within the prevailing black-white model of racial interaction. The outlines of a multivocal narrative of U.S. women's history that acknowledges women's diversity in terms of race, class, ethnicity, and sexual orientation are advanced by *Unequal Sisters: A Multicultural Reader in U.S. Women's History,* coedited by Vicki Ruiz and one of the authors of this text, Ellen Carol DuBois. This anthology of pathbreaking research pays particular attention to the historical experiences of Western women, noting that "the confluence of many cultures and races in this region — Native American, Mexican, Asian, Black, and Anglo" — required "grappling with race" from a multicultural perspective.[7] By using her own southwestern experience, Gloria Anzaldúa added the influential metaphor of "borderlands" to this approach to suggest that the division between different communities and personal identities is somewhat arbitrary and sometimes shifting.[8] This new approach took the logic of the historical construction of gender, so important to the beginning of women's history, and pushed it further by emphasizing an even greater fluidity of social positioning.

◆ APPROACHING HISTORY THROUGH WOMEN'S EYES

How then to bring together a historical narrative told from such diverse and at times conflicting viewpoints? All written histories rely on unifying themes to organize what is otherwise a chaotic assembly of facts, observations, incidents, and people. Traditionally, American history employed a framework of steady national progress, from the colonial revolt against England to modern times.

---

5. Peggy Pascoe, "Gender," in Richard Wightman Fox and James Kloppenberg, eds., *A Companion to American Thought* (Cambridge, MA: Blackwell, 1995), 273.

6. Evelyn Brooks Higginbotham, "African American Women's History and the Metalanguage of Race," *Signs* 17, no. 2 (Winter 1992): 254.

7. Ellen Carol DuBois and Vicki L. Ruiz, eds., *Unequal Sisters: A Multicultural Reader in U.S. Women's History* (New York: Routledge, 1990), xii. This reader has three later editions (1994, 2000, 2008) that include substantially different articles.

8. Gloria Anzaldúa, *La Frontera/Borderlands: The New Mestiza* (1987; repr., San Francisco: Aunt Lute Books, 1999).

Starting in the 1960s, the writing of American history emphasized an alternative story line of the struggles of workers, slaves, Indians, and (to some degree) women, to overcome enduring inequalities. Initially, women's history emphasized the rise and fall of the system of separate gender spheres, the limits of which we suggest above. In organizing *Through Women's Eyes,* we employ another framework, one that emphasizes three major themes that shaped the diversity of women's lives in American history — work, politics, and family and personal life.

Work and the Sexual Division of Labor

The theme of women's work reveals both stubborn continuities and dramatic changes. Women have always labored, always contributed to the productive capacity of their communities. Throughout American history, women's work has taken three basic forms — unpaid labor within the home, chattel slavery, and paid labor. The steady growth of paid labor, from the beginning of American industrialization in the 1830s to the present day (women now constitute essentially half of America's workforce), is one of the fundamental developments in this history. As the female labor force grew, its composition changed, by age, race, ethnicity, and class. By the mid-twentieth century, the working mother had taken over where once the working girl had predominated. We have also followed the repeated efforts of wage-earning women to organize collectively in order to counter the power of their employers, doing so sometimes in conjunction with male workers and sometimes on their own. Always a small percentage of union members compared to men, women exhibited unanticipated militancy and radicalism in their fight with employers over union recognition and fair wages and hours.

Most societies divide women's work from men's, and America has been no exception. Feminist scholars designate this gender distinction as the "sexual division of labor." Yet the content of the sexual division of labor varies from culture to culture, a point made beginning with the discussion of Native American communities in the precolonial and colonial eras and of African women's agricultural labor in their native lands. When women first began to take on paid labor in large numbers, they did so primarily as servants and seamstresses; the nature of their work thus generally followed the household sexual division of labor. The persistence of sex segregation in the workforce has had many sources of support: employers' desire to have a cheap, flexible supply of labor; male workers' control over better jobs and higher wages; and women's own assumptions about their proper place.

The division between male and female work continued, and with it the low wages and limited opportunities on the women's side of the line. This was true even as what counted as women's jobs began to expand, and teaching and secretarial labor, once securely on the male side of the line, crossed over to become "*feminized*" job categories. American feminism in the late twentieth century was committed to eroding this long-standing principle that work should be divided into male and female categories. As historian Alice Kessler-Harris puts it, feminists "introduced the language of sex discrimination onto the national stage, casting a new light on seemingly natural patterns of accommodating sex difference."[9] The degree to which the sexual division of labor has been substantially breached — whether it is half achieved or half undone — we leave to our readers, who are part of this process, to determine.

Gender and the Meaning of Politics

The theme of politics in women's historical experience presents a different sort of challenge, for it is the *exclusion* of women from formal politics that is the obvious development in U.S. women's history, at least until 1920 when the Nineteenth Amendment granting woman suffrage was ratified. While the story of women's campaign for the vote plays an important role in our historical account, we have not portrayed the suffrage movement as a monolithic effort. Rather, we have attended to the inequalities of class and race and the strategic and ideological conflicts that ran throughout the movement. We have also stressed the varying political contexts, ranging from Reconstruction in the 1860s to the Populist upsurge in the 1890s to Progressivism in the 1910s, within which women fought for their voting rights. Finally, we have traced the significance of voting in U.S. women's history after the right to it was formally secured, following women's efforts to find their place — as voters and as officeholders — in the American political system.

U.S. women's historians have gone beyond the drama surrounding the vote, its denial and its uses, to a more expansive sense of the political dimension of women's historical experience. Feminist scholars have forged a definition of politics that looks beyond the formal electoral arena to other sorts of collective efforts to change society, alter the distribution of power between groups, create and govern important institutions, and shape public policy. Women's historians have given concrete substance to this broad approach to female political involvement by investigating the tremendous social activism and civic engagement that thrived among women, especially through the long period during which they lacked formal political rights. "In order to bring together the history of women and politics," writes Paula Baker, "we need a more inclusive definition of politics . . . to include any action, formal or informal, taken to affect the course or behavior of government or the community."[10]

From this perspective, the importance of women in the realm of politics reaches back to the Iroquois women who elected chiefs and participated in decisions to go to war and the European women colonists who provided the crucial support necessary to sustain pre-Revolutionary boycotts against British goods in the struggle for national independence. Just a small sampling of this rich tradition of women's civic activity through the nineteenth century includes the thousands of

9. Alice Kessler-Harris, *In Pursuit of Equity: Women, Men, and the Quest for Economic Citizenship in 20th-Century America* (New York: Oxford University Press, 2001), 245–46.

10. Paula Baker, "The Domestication of Politics: Women and American Political Society, 1780–1920," *American Historical Review* 89 (June 1984): 622.

New England women who before the Civil War signed petitions against slavery and Indian removal; the campaign begun by Ida B. Wells against the lynching of southern blacks; the ambitious late nineteenth-century national reform agenda of Frances Willard's Woman's Christian Temperance Union; and Jane Addams's leadership in addressing problems of the urban immigrant poor and on behalf of international peace. "Women's organizations pioneered in, accepted and polished modern methods of pressure-group politics," observes historian Nancy Cott.[11]

Indeed, this sort of extra-electoral political activism extended into the twentieth century, incorporating women's challenges to the arms race of the post–World War II era and the civil rights leadership of women such as Ella Baker of the Southern Christian Leadership Conference in the 1950s and Dolores Huerta of the United Farm Workers union in the 1960s. This inclusive sense of what constitutes "politics" has not only enriched our understanding of women's history but generated a more complex understanding of the nature of political power and process within U.S. history in general.

Given the theme of politics as one of the major frames for this book, what is the place of the politics of feminism in the tale we tell? There are many definitions of feminism, but perhaps the clearest is the tradition of organized social change by which women challenge gender inequality. The term "feminism" itself arose just as the woman suffrage movement was nearing victory, but the tradition to which it refers reaches back to the women's rights movements of the nineteenth century. Historical research has unearthed a great deal of breadth and diversity in the many campaigns and protests through which women from different groups, in different times and places, dealing with different challenges, expressed their discontent with the social roles allotted to them and pursued their ambitions for wider options, more individual freedom, and greater social authority.

Feminism and women's history are mutually informing. Feminism is one of the important subjects of women's history, and history is one of feminism's best tools. Knowing what the past has been for women, doing the scholarship that Anne Firor Scott calls "making the invisible woman visible," is a necessary resource in pressing for further change.[12] But feminism is also a method by which historians examine the past in terms of women's efforts to challenge, struggle, make change, and sometimes achieve progress. Like so many of the scholars on whom the authors of this text rely, we have worked from such a perspective, and the passion we have brought to this work has its roots in a feminist commitment to highlighting — and encouraging — women's active social role and contribution to history. For us, however, a women's history informed by feminism is not a simple exercise of celebration, but a continuing and critical examination of what we choose to examine in the past and the methods we use to do so.

---

11. Nancy Cott, *The Grounding of American Feminism* (New Haven: Yale University Press, 1987), 95.

12. Anne Firor Scott, "Making the Invisible Woman Visible: An Essay Review," *Journal of Southern History* 38, no. 4 (November 1972): 629–38.

The Role of Family and Personal Life

The third integrating category of *Through Women's Eyes* is the theme of family and personal life. In contrast to the categories of labor and politics, which have been recognized in all narratives of the nation's past, women's historians took the lead in bringing family and personal life into the mainstream of American history. Indeed, one of the fundamental contributions of feminist scholarship has been to demonstrate that kinship and sexuality have been not static elements of human nature but elements with their own complex histories. We try to make this clear by discussing the variety of family patterns evident among Native Americans, immigrants, African Americans, white middle-class Americans, and other ethnic groups.

Over the span of American history, family life has gone from the very center of political power and economic production in the seventeenth and eighteenth centuries to a privileged arena of emotional life in the early twenty-first century. As we write this introduction, issues relating to family life — who can marry whom, what forms of sexuality and gender identity should be tolerated, who should care for children and how — have become topics of intense public contest and political positioning. Thus concepts and experiences of family and sexual life, once viewed as the essence of women's separate sphere, are increasingly understood as a major connection between private concerns and public issues.

The histories of both motherhood and female sexuality reveal this connection. Motherhood not only has been central to women's individual family lives but also has served larger functions as well. Within slave communities, mothers taught their children how to survive within and fight against their servitude. Among middle-class women in the nineteenth and early twentieth centuries, motherhood became an effective way to claim female public authority. In the 1950s, at the start of the Cold War between the United States and the former Soviet Union, radical women subverted intense anti-Communist interrogations under the cloak of motherhood, thus trumping one of the decade's most dramatic themes with another. The social significance of motherhood has been used for conservative political purposes as well, with claims about the centrality of women's maternal role to social order providing the fuel of the antifeminist backlash of the 1970s and through it the emergence of a new political right wing.

When it comes to the subject of sexuality, historians have proved particularly innovative in learning to read through the euphemisms and silences that obscure women's sexual lives even more than men's. They have delved into documents left by guardians of sexual propriety about prostitutes and by lascivious masters about slave women, in order to imagine how the objects of these judgments themselves experienced these encounters. When historians set aside modern attitudes toward sexuality and reexamined the lives of seemingly prudish nineteenth-century middle-class women, they found, as Linda Gordon demonstrates, the origins of the American birth control movement and all the radical changes in women's lives that flowed from it.[13] No longer content to portray the history of female sexuality as a

---

13. Linda Gordon, *The Moral Property of Women: A History of Birth Control Politics in America* (1976; repr., Urbana: University of Illinois Press, 2004).

simple move from repression to freedom, historians have examined the changing understandings of female sexuality and its shifting purposes in the twentieth century, as it played a major role in advancing new standards of consumerism, and in modernizing — though not necessarily making more egalitarian — relations between men and women.

Perhaps historians of women have been most creative in learning to look beyond the heterosexual relations that traditionally have defined sexuality to explore the intimate, romantic, and ambiguously sexual relations among women themselves. Carroll Smith-Rosenberg pioneered in demonstrating how common romantic friendships among women were in the nineteenth century, describing them as "an intriguing and almost alien form of human relation, [which] flourished in a different social structure and amidst different sexual norms."[14] Historical work on what has come to be called "homosociality" has deepened understandings of sexuality overall. Thus, as with the concepts of gender and race, women's history has led us to view sexuality itself as socially constructed, not as biologically prescribed.

Sexuality has been an especially important site for historians to locate the intersections of race and gender. Middle-class white women's historical prominence rested in considerable part on the contrast between their reputed sexual innocence and propriety and the supposedly disreputable (and titillating) sexuality of women of color on the margins, such as black slaves, so-called Indian squaws, and Asian prostitutes. This intersection between sexuality and race has also been investigated from the position of women who found themselves on the other side of the vice-virtue divide. As historian Paula Giddings argues, the rising up of recently freed African American women against their reputations as sexually available and that of African American men as sexually predatory helped to generate the creation of a black middle class and "a distinctive mix which underlined Black women's activism for generations to come."[15]

These and other discoveries in the field of U.S. women's history have made this textbook possible. The rich body of scholarly literature developed over the past decades has also enabled us to achieve our goal of integrating women's history into U.S. history, of showing how material once separated as "women's history" contributes to a broader understanding of the nation's history. In *America Through Women's Eyes,* Mary Beard insisted that women be rendered not as the passive objects of men's actions but as makers of history themselves; and that their history not be removed from the historical flow into a separate narrative but be understood as part and parcel of the full range of national experience. This has been our guiding principle in writing this textbook — and the reason we have titled it an American history "through women's eyes."

---

14. Carroll Smith-Rosenberg, "The Female World of Love and Ritual," *Signs* 1 (1979): 1–29.

15. Paula Giddings, *When and Where I Enter: The Impact of Black Women on Race and Sex in America* (New York: William Morrow, 1984), 50.

Fifth Edition

THROUGH WOMEN'S EYES

An American History

WITH DOCUMENTS

12,000 B.C.E.	Archaeological evidence indicates human habitation in the Americas
300 B.C.E.	Anasazi settle in the North American Southwest
600 C.E.	**Pueblo cultures emerge, establishing a matrilineal system**
1100–1400	Mississippian cultures develop
1444	First African slaves in Spain and Portugal
c. 1450	Iroquois Confederacy formed
1479–1504	**Reign of Isabella of Castile**
1492–1504	Christopher Columbus's voyages
c. 1502	**Malintzin born near the Gulf of Mexico**
1502	First African slaves in Caribbean
1513	Spanish explorers land in Florida, bringing disease
1517	Protestant Reformation begins
1519	Hernán Cortés arrives in Mexico
1519	**Malintzin and nineteen other Indian women are presented to Cortés**
1520	First epidemics of Old World diseases occur in North America
1525	First recorded African slave shipment to Hispaniola
1533	**Princess Elizabeth born to Anne Boleyn and Henry VIII, king of England**
1534	Jacques Cartier's first voyage down the St. Lawrence

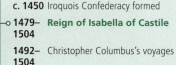

1

America in the World

TO 1650

PEOPLE WHO LIVE IN THE UNITED STATES OFTEN refer to themselves as Americans and to their nation as America. From this perspective, "America" includes the places, peoples, and economic systems that eventually became the single national entity of the United States. But there are other meanings of "America" to consider. "America" is the name given to the entire hemisphere by the Europeans who accidentally encountered it in the late fifteenth and early sixteenth centuries. "America" is also the term that eventually devolved on the northern continent of that hemisphere; there, many European empires vied for control before England prevailed. The indigenous peoples of North America had many names for themselves that translated as "men" or "the people," but Europeans called them "Americans" or "American Indians." Finally, colonists of European descent came to refer to themselves as Americans, to distinguish themselves from their Old World predecessors. Modern Americans have inherited all of these meanings of "America."

To begin American history, more and more historians are looking beyond (or before) the English establishment of the thirteen Atlantic colonies. Using a multicultural lens, we can reconfigure early American history as the intersection of and conflict between several distinct histories — Native American, European, and African. In addition, each of these groups contained many different societies. With this approach, we can reach back before the traditional starting events, the first English settlements that proved to be permanent on the North American continent — Jamestown in 1607 and Plymouth in 1620 — to important and shaping processes in the 1500s. These include the developments among Native peoples; the impact of the initial sixteenth-century contact between Native peoples and Europeans, including disease, trade, and conquest; the powerful Spanish empire in the New World that preceded, inspired, and competed with the later-arriving English; the invention of transatlantic slavery and the plantation agriculture system that it served; and political, economic, and religious upheavals in Europe from the late Renaissance through the Protestant Reformation.

To view these beginnings of American history through women's eyes requires creativity. Although our cherished national myths emphasize the family origins of seventeenth-century New England immigration, the first century of European incursions in the western hemisphere was overwhelmingly male. So was the introduction of African slaves to the Americas in the sixteenth century, because enslaved women were held back in Africa, where they were valued, even as enslaved men were worked to death in the Americas. But Native women and European and African men encountered each other, willingly and unwillingly, across a divide of massive cultural difference that has been described as "an epochal cross-roads of gender."[1]

For much of their national history, Americans have preferred to think of their country as exceptional, different from the other nations of the world, set apart by geography, democratic traditions, and Christian heritage. In our own age of airplanes and the Internet, in a thoroughly multicultural and multireligious society, faith in American exceptionalism and superiority seems outdated. America in the twenty-first century is situated thoroughly in a global system of culture, economics, power relations, and human migration.

But America was in and of the world in other periods as well. From the 1500s on, people, ideas, natural materials, and manufactured goods went back and forth between the Old World and the New, including the horse, an animal that dramatically changed the culture of Native peoples, and the maize plant, first developed in what is now Mexico, then imported to Europe to become an important staple crop. As one historian has put it, "America was international before it was national."[2]

◆ NATIVE AMERICAN WOMEN

With at least two hundred languages spoken in North America on the eve of European conquest, the world of Native Americans defies simple generalization. Historians usually analyze Native Americans in the context of region and economic activities. Thus, in the Southwest lived agricultural peoples, the Pueblos. In California lived hunter-gatherers, for example, the Chumash; in the Northwest, the fishing Nootkas; and in the Great Plains, hunters such as the Crows, the Sioux, and the Blackfeet. In the Great Lakes region, groups such as the Ojibwas emphasized hunting. In the eastern woodlands, the Iroquois lived inland west of the Hudson River, and Algonquian-speaking peoples populated the Atlantic Coast from what is today Maine to the present Carolinas. Both the Iroquois and coastal Algonquians engaged in agriculture (see Map 1.1).

The diversity of Native peoples extended to their gender systems. Here, as in all of the history that went into creating America, this fundamental fact stands out: the divisions between the worlds of men and the worlds of women, the distinctions that we call gender, were omnipresent but infinitely varied. In horticultural societies, where people depended on corn and other crops, lineage was generally traced by matrilineal descent, or through the mother's line. In hunter-gatherer societies, lineage was often determined by patrilineal descent, that is, through the father's line. Women's experiences after marriage depended on whether they were expected to live among their husband's people (patrilocal marriage) or whether their husbands came to live with them (matrilocal). Indigenous women's daily work varied according to where they lived and what foodstuffs were available. For example, women planted and tended corn in both the Northeast and the Southwest, but southwestern women spent more time irrigating their crops. Women also had different degrees of status and autonomy in their societies. No matter what specific tasks were included, roles related to economic activities were a powerful determinant in Native women's lives.

Indigenous Peoples before 1492

Archaeological evidence indicates that at least fourteen thousand years ago (and probably much earlier), Native Americans migrated across a land bridge that once united Siberia and Alaska. Historians believe that by the fifteenth century, between 7 and 12 million people lived in the area that is now the United States. Although popular images of Native Americans depict them primarily as hunter-gatherers or nomadic hunters, a significant number engaged in farming, along with fishing or hunting. The Cahokia settlement in present-day Illinois, for instance, featured large cornfields around a residential and ceremonial center. In these agricultural communities, women fulfilled crucial roles in planting, harvesting, and processing food. Before the arrival of Europeans, some indigenous groups hunted bison on the Great Plains by using fires to stampede the animals over cliffs. It was not until Native groups living on the borders of the plains—like the Comanches, Arapahos,

ARCTIC OCEAN

INUIT

ALEUT

INUIT
(ESKIMO)

DENE

TLINGIT

DOGRIB

HAIDA TSIMSHIAN

CHIPEWYAN

CREE

BLACKFEET

SALISH

NOOTKA KOOTENAI ASSINIBOINE

PACIFIC
OCEAN

NEZ PERCE CROW

CHEYENNE

PAIUTE SHOSHONE

POMO

YOKUT

UTE

COCHIMI

PAPAGO
APACHE

PIMA

ZACATEC

TOLTEC

NAHUATL
(AZTEC)

MIXTEC

ZAPOTEC

COCHIMI COAHUILTEC

INUIT

NASKAPI

MONTAGNAIS

BEOTHUK

MICMAC

CREE ALGONQUIAN

ABENAKI
PASSAMAQUODDY

OJIBWA
(CHIPPEWA)

IROQUOIS

DAKOTA
(SIOUX) SAUK

NARRAGANSETT
PEQUOT

PAWNEE POTAWATOMI SUSQUEHANNOCK
DELAWARE

IOWA

POWHATAN

ILLINOIS

ARAPAHO SHAWNEE

TUSCARORA

KIOWA

CHEROKEE

NAVAJO
HOPI

COMANCHE CHICKASAW

ATLANTIC
OCEAN

CREEK

CHOCTAW

CALUSA LUCAYO
SEMINOLE

Gulf of
Mexico

CIBONEY SUB TAINO

TAINO

Caribbean Sea

MAYA

MISKITO

CUNA

GUAYMI

N
W E
S

Dominant Economic Activity

Agriculture
Hunting
Hunting-gathering
Fishing

0   500   1,000 miles
0   500   1,000 kilometers

◆ **Map 1.1 Native American Peoples, 1492**

By the time of Columbus's arrival, Native American peoples populated the entire western hemisphere. Among those groups who practiced intensive agriculture, both men and women farmed. Among groups who practiced both hunting and agriculture, men were primarily the hunters while women did most of the farming. Among tribes engaged primarily in hunting, women hunted smaller game, gathered wild plant foods, and processed the meat and skins of the larger animals killed by men.

◆ **Effigy Bottle from Cahokia Mound (c. 1200–1400)**
The people of Cahokia were part of a large group whom historians call Mississippians, who lived in the Mississippi and Ohio Rivers' watersheds from roughly 1000 to 1730. Distinguished by the large earthen mounds they built for ceremonial, political, and residential purposes, they apparently had a highly stratified social structure and complex culture. Artifacts recovered from the mounds reveal a wide variety of artisanal crafts, including pottery and stonework, some of which may have been produced by women. This meticulously carved ceramic bottle in the shape of a nursing mother was presumably not for everyday use but for ritualistic or symbolic purposes; perhaps it was placed in a grave for use in the afterlife. What insight into Mississippian women's lives and into the larger meanings of motherhood in their culture does the image offer? *St. Louis Museum of Science & Natural History, Missouri, USA/Photo © The Detroit Institute of Arts/Bridgeman Images.*

Cheyennes, and Sioux—had access to horses that significant numbers migrated to the Great Plains and became nomadic bison hunters. In all groups that emphasized hunting, men killed big game while women skinned the animals and prepared the meat.

Wherever they lived, indigenous Americans were not a static people, frozen in time waiting for Europeans to "discover" them. Historians have mapped out an amazing array of Indian trails that crisscrossed the continent. Trading in shells, furs, agricultural products, pottery, salt, copper, and slaves, communities of Native Americans had contact with and knowledge of many other groups with whom they shared the continent. Although trade was peaceful, Native Americans sometimes warred with one another over land and resources. This violence had special meaning for women since they and children were often taken captive and forcibly integrated into the societies of their captors. Both warfare and ecological pressures such as drought prompted significant migration, the merging of communities, and the rise and fall of powerful Indian nations. Although we have virtually no documents written by the women themselves, a cautious reading of European eyewitness accounts of the Native communities they encountered has provided historians with insights into Native American lives. (See Primary Sources: "European Images of Native American Women," pp. 35–45.)

In many Indian nations, women had more power and sexual choices than most European women of their time did, albeit in the context of clear distinctions between the labor and responsibilities of men and women. In other words, in traditional Native societies, relations between the sexes were characterized simultaneously by difference and by a degree of equality. The following examination of two well-documented groups reveals the diverse lives of Native American women and their cultures.

The Pueblo Peoples

Perched on cliffs in present-day New Mexico and Colorado are the remains of prehistoric dwellings of the Native people called Anasazi, who settled in the area as early as 300 B.C.E. From their distinctive multistoried, mud-plastered buildings came the generic name "Pueblos," which the Spanish gave to Anasazi descendants such as the Zuñi, Hopi, Acoma, and similar peoples who were living in the American Southwest (New Mexico, Arizona, Colorado, and Utah) by 1250 C.E. When the Spanish arrived in the region in the mid-sixteenth century, there were close to 250,000 Pueblo people living in more than one hundred towns and villages. The Pueblo peoples encompassed seven language groups, and undoubtedly customs and rituals varied from tribe to tribe, despite many points of similarity. Like many other Indian peoples, the Pueblos apparently experienced much social disruption in the years preceding conquest. The hostile incursions of more nomadic Apaches from the Great Plains into their region may have been one of the causes for significant Pueblo migration and change in the region during the thirteenth and fourteenth centuries.

By the 1500s, the Pueblos were already practicing intensive agriculture, growing corn, squash, and beans. As in other societies, labor was divided by sex. Men traded goods and provided defense; they also tended the corn crop. Men collected and placed the timbers for the construction of their homes, but women plastered the walls. Women's work centered on what went on within those walls, the "inside" of the community. They created pottery, made moccasins and blankets, and, most crucially, prepared the food. Grinding the dried corn was women's work, a task that daughters and mothers shared. Women viewed their food production as vital to their people, as something spiritual, a point reinforced by the Acoma Pueblo origin story (see Reading into the Past: "Two Sisters and Acoma Origins").

In addition to its association with corn and the earth's fertility, women's spirituality — and men's — was tied to their sexuality. Intercourse often held ritualistic and religious meanings. It was not only the source of life but also a means of taming bad spirits in nature and of integrating outsiders into the tribe. It helped to maintain the cosmic balance. Pueblo ideology thus recognized women's sexual power, a factor that, like women's role in food production, contributed to relatively egalitarian relationships between the sexes.

The matrilineal system, tracing ancestry and control of land through the female line, consolidated women's position in their communities. As with most Native American peoples, among the Pueblos land and households were occupied communally by particular families and, in their case, passed through the

READING INTO THE PAST

Two Sisters and Acoma Origins

According to the Acoma Pueblo Indians' origin story, the first women in the world were two sisters, born underneath the ground and sent above by Tsichtinako (Thought Woman). She first taught them to plant corn, tend and harvest it, grind it for food, and use fire to cook it. What follows is an excerpt from one such story told in 1928 by residents of the Acoma and Santa Ana pueblos to anthropologist Matthew W. Stirling. Native peoples' oral traditions, recorded by ethnographers, have become the source of much knowledge of Native history.

Tsichtinako spoke to them, "Now is the time you are to go out. You are able to take your baskets with you. In them you will find pollen and sacred corn meal. When you reach the top, you will wait for the sun to come up and that direction will be called ha'nami [east]. With the pollen and the sacred corn meal you will pray to the Sun. You will thank the Sun for bringing you to light, ask for a long life and happiness, and for success in the purpose for which you were created." Tsichtinako then taught them the prayers and the creation song, which they were to sing. . . .

They now prayed to the Sun as they had been taught by Tsichtinako, and sang the creation song. Their eyes hurt for they were not accustomed to the strong light. For the first time they asked Tsichtinako why they were on earth and why they were created. Tsichtinako replied, "I did not make you. Your father, Uchtsiti, made you, and it is he who has made the world, the sun which you have seen, the sky, and many other things which you will see. But Uchtsiti says the world is not yet completed, not yet satisfactory, as he wants it. This is the reason he has made you. You will rule and bring to life the rest of the things he has given you in the baskets." . . . Tsichtinako next said to them, "Now that you have your names, you will

female line. Control of the land was tied to its use, not to some abstract concept of ownership. In addition to being matrilineal, Pueblos were matrilocal, meaning that men left their mothers' homes to marry and moved in with their wives' families. In Pueblo society, men and women could leave their marriages and choose new partners without stigma, an arrangement in accord with the understanding that an individual's primary identity was defined by his or her mother's identity, not a marital bond. Older women were therefore particularly influential members of the community. While men dominated the "outside" realm — trade, pray with your names and your clan names so that the Sun will know you and recognize you." Tsichtinako asked Nautsiti which clan she wished to belong to. Nautsiti answered, "I wish to see the sun, that is the clan I will be." The spirit told Nautsiti to ask Iatiku what clan she wanted. Iatiku thought for a long time but finally she noticed that she had the seed from which sacred meal was made in her basket and no other kind of seeds. She thought, "With this name I shall be very proud, for it has been chosen for nourishment and it is sacred." So she said, "I will be Corn clan." . . .

When they had completed their prayers to the sun, Tsichtinako said, "You have done everything well and now you are both to take up your baskets and you must look to the north, west, south, and east, for you are now to pray to the Earth to accept the things in the basket and to give them life. First you must pray to the north, at the same time lift up your baskets in that direction. You will then do the same to the west, then to the south and east." They did as they were told and did it well. And Tsichtinako said to them, "From now on you will rule in every direction, north, west, south, and east."

SOURCE: Matthew W. Stirling, *Origin Myth of Acoma and Other Records* (Washington, DC: Smithsonian Institution, 1942), 3–5.

QUESTIONS FOR ANALYSIS

1. What are the advantages and disadvantages of oral traditions recorded by outsiders as a source of historical knowledge?

2. What does this origin story tell you about the importance of corn to Acoma Pueblo identity and to Pueblo gender roles, especially for women?

defense, and war — women dominated the world inside the pueblo walls they had constructed.

The Iroquois Confederacy

Far away from the southwestern Pueblos, the Iroquois Confederacy — initially consisting of the Seneca, Cayuga, Onondaga, Oneida, and Mohawk people — constructed another version of Native life. In the forests of what became New York

◆ **Huron Women**
In 1615, Samuel de Champlain, French founder of Quebec City, lived for a time with the Hurons. He was both impressed and disturbed by Huron women's responsibilities. He wrote: "[They] till the soil, sow the Indian corn, fetch wood for the winter, strip the hemp and spin it, and with the thread make fishing-nets for catching fish, . . . have the labour of harvesting the corn, storing it, preparing food, and attending to the house." In contrast, the men "do nothing but hunt deer and other animals, fish, build lodges and go on the warpath."[3] (Figure "E" is Champlain's depiction of a Huron warrior.) Champlain also drew Huron women in several of their roles. Figure "F" is an adult woman, holding a child in one hand and a stalk of corn in the other. Figure "G" is a young girl, both provocative and modest, dressed for a ritual dance. Figure "H," wrote Champlain, depicts "how the women pound the Indian corn." *Private Collection/Bridgeman Images.*

State and Ontario, Canada, an estimated twenty to thirty thousand people lived in perhaps ten villages at the turn of the seventeenth century. The Iroquois were unique among Native peoples for their Great League of Peace and Power, thought to have been founded in 1451, which linked them in an elaborate confederation. The chiefs of the Iroquois Confederacy were always men, but they were chosen by the women and could be deposed by them. The distinctive political power of Iroquois women was also reflected in how families were organized. The Iroquois matrilineal system emphasized women's importance for establishing identity and rights to the use of land in each clan. Several families lived together in longhouses, large bark-and-log dwellings, which were supervised by the clans' elder women.

The sexual division of labor reinforced women's dominance in the village. Men prepared fields for planting, but their major duties took them to the forests, where they hunted, conducted trade, and warred with hostile tribes. Women's responsibilities centered in the village, where they raised crops (corn, beans, and squash); gathered mushrooms, berries, and nuts; prepared food; distributed the results of men's hunting; and made baskets, pottery, and other implements. They worked hard but communally. This gendered division of labor continued even after European colonization began. Mary Jemison, a British captive who married and raised a family among the Seneca in the eighteenth century, later explained: "In order to expedite their business, and at the same time enjoy each other's company, they all work together in one field, or at whatever job they may have on hand." In the spring, Jemison continued, "they choose an older woman to be their driver and overseer, when at labor, for the ensuing year. She accepts the honor, and they consider themselves bound to obey her."[4]

Women also had a significant voice in religious activities. According to Jemison, Seneca women formed Chanters of the Dead, a group that interpreted dreams and participated in numerous rituals. In other ways Iroquois women influenced what might be termed the political side of life. Because they controlled food supplies — both current crops and the food they had carefully preserved and stored — they provisioned warriors and thus had a say in plans for raids and wars. They also determined adoptions into a clan — a means of integrating captives and minimizing losses due to disease and warfare — and could call for the avenging of deaths in their own families, thus initiating raids and warfare. Iroquois women's political power impressed European observers. Father Joseph-François Lafitau, a French Jesuit missionary in Canada, noted as late as 1724 that "nothing, however, is more real than this superiority of the women. . . . The land, the fields and their harvest all belong to them. They are the souls of the Councils, the arbiters of peace and of war. They have charge of the public treasury. To them are given the slaves. They arrange marriages. The children are their domain, and it is through their blood that the order of succession is transmitted."[5]

Native Women's Worlds

Pueblo and Iroquois women lived far apart. Their economic systems and their environments varied dramatically, as did their social structures. Iroquois women had more formal power than Pueblo women. But the similarities in their lives provide a starting point for sketching a few broad generalizations about indigenous women of North America in the era of European conquest. What were their economic roles? What can we know of their sexual lives? What political and religious influence did they exert within their communities?

Women's economic significance was a common denominator most indigenous peoples shared. Starting with Christopher Columbus, who observed in 1493 that "the women seem to work more than the men," the productive role of women was an object of much commentary. European men reacted as if their own women were entirely freed from hard labor, which they certainly were not. Among the coastal Algonquians, women not only tended crops but also participated in the fishing vital to their people's survival. They fashioned mats and baskets and other essential artifacts of daily life. Among the groups that emphasized hunting, like the Ojibwas of the Great Lakes region or the Apaches of the southern plains, men's role as hunters was complemented by women's labor of curing meat and dressing skins. Women also gathered feathers from birds, fashioned moccasins, and sometimes bartered in the increasingly important fur trade. In 1632, a French cleric, Paul Le Jeune, observed of the Iroquois: "The women know what they are to do, and the men also; and one never meddles with the work of the others." As one Iroquois man reported to Le Jeune, "To live among us without a wife . . . is to live without help, without home, and to be always wandering."[6]

All indigenous groups had strict moral codes within their own cultural norms. European observers tended to view Native American sexual practices through a pejorative lens, giving the impression that Native women were promiscuous. It is also difficult to untangle the effects of intimate relations across cultural borders, notably in fur-trading regions, on sexual mores. In some cases, European men projected their own desires onto Native women. In others, women entered into liaisons with fur traders so that these outsiders could be incorporated into the community. Europeans were also shocked by some groups' polygyny, whereby a man might have multiple wives who were often sisters. Another factor that seemed to give Native women more sexual freedom than their European counterparts, especially in matrilineal societies, was that women did not need to stay in unhappy marriages for economic security. According to a French observer of a group of Algonquians, "A Young Woman, say they, is Master of her own Body, and by her Natural Right of Liberty is free to do what she pleases."[7]

To early Europeans, one of the most striking aspects of Native American sexuality was the existence of individuals who crossed the gender line and lived the lives of the opposite sex. Later anthropologists used the word "berdache" for such a person. Male-to-female transgendering was present in virtually all Native American societies, but female-to-male crossing was by no means unknown. Modern feminist theory contends that the possibilities of gender extend beyond two categories, and evidence for this is striking in several traditional Native American societies. In the 1520s on Mexico's northern frontier, Cabeza de Vaca recorded, "I saw one man married to another . . . , and they go about dressed as women, and do women's tasks, and shoot with a bow, and carry great burdens . . . and they are huskier than the other men and taller."[8] The explanations, and probably the causes, of transgendering were multiple. Some men may have been responding to desires to play the female role, although there is evidence of male homosexuality in Native cultures that took other forms. In some cases, the berdache was an especially spiritual person whose path across the gender divide was dictated by a youthful vision quest.

Despite their relative sexual freedom and the importance of their economic contributions, most Native American women held no formal political power. The Iroquois matrons were one exception; another was the few Algonquian women—like Weetamoo, a sachem (chief) of the Wampanoag people of New England, or Cockacoeske, female sachem of the Pamunkey Indians of Virginia. Informally, however, women's influence was often significant, especially in the many Native communities that emphasized consensus in decision making and allowed the voices of women, particularly older ones, to be heard. As one historian has noted, speaking of the Indians of the East Coast, "The women's power normally operated more covertly, though often no less effectively than the men's, for they were the acknowledged guardians of tradition and peace in societies whose survival depended in large measure on both."[9] In religious matters, women's access to high-status roles varied from group to group. In some groups they might be healers, crucial to the well-being of their people, while in others they were religious leaders.

Whatever their roles in their societies, Native American women, like men, faced extraordinary challenges in the wake of the European invasion. Historians often describe the interaction of the two worlds of indigenous peoples and Europeans in the context of a "Columbian exchange." Enslaved Africans and European settlers were the human part of the exchange. From the Americas, the Europeans took gold and silver, furs, fish, and crops such as corn, potatoes, and tobacco. To the Americas, they brought disease, Christianity, and new technology. The meanings of this complex process of conflict and contact varied for indigenous peoples. But overall these changes would have specific—and usually damaging—effects on Native women.

◆ EUROPEANS ARRIVE

Europe in the sixteenth century was a continent undergoing dramatic change, not all of which constituted "progress" for European women but much of which had an impact on American history. On the one hand, this was the age of European queens, powerful, educated, politically savvy women, two of whom—Isabella of Castile and Elizabeth of England—presided over the beginnings of the two major European empires in the Americas. The Protestant Reformation, starting with Martin Luther in Germany in 1517, challenged the hierarchical control of the Catholic clergy and eventually led to important changes in women's status. Yet processes that two centuries later would lead to enhanced education and greater independence for women had the immediate impact of limiting their possibilities. Conflict between Catholics and Protestants restrained and even eliminated female religious orders that had permitted some women education, spiritual authority, and alternatives to family life. One historian has called the sixteenth century "the zenith of the patriarchal family" in Europe, as women were newly confined to wifehood and motherhood.[10] Similarly, as the foundations of modern European capitalism unfolded, women found themselves in subordinate positions, rarely controlling the production of goods for market and always earning less than men for their labors.

Early Spanish Expansion

In the century before the English settlement of America began in earnest, Spanish America flourished. As every American schoolchild knows, the Italian explorer Christopher Columbus "discovered" the Indies of the West, while traveling in search of the Indies of the East, under the sponsorship of King Ferdinand and Queen Isabella of Spain. However, the funds for Columbus's journey came not, as the story goes, from the queen's jewels, but from the confiscated wealth of the Jews, whom the royal pair was expelling from Spain and Portugal along with the Moors (Muslims), to cleanse the Iberian Peninsula of non-Christian influences. Queen Isabella was devoted to the triumph of the Catholic faith against all competitors. Her support for Columbus's oceanic adventure was also shaped by her desire to spread what she understood as the one true faith. When it became clear that the lands Columbus claimed in her name were not the East Indies but a "new" world, Isabella showed considerable concern for the souls of the indigenous peoples there, rejecting, for instance, a gift of seized Native American slaves. Her death in 1504 removed one important obstacle to Spanish conquistadores' exploitation of Native labor and the natural resources found on Native lands. Forty years later, the Spanish Dominican priest Bartolomé de Las Casas passionately pleaded the case of indigenous Americans, arguing that men and women alike were enslaved under horrific conditions, but by then their cause was virtually lost.

Las Casas documented the catastrophic collapse of Native populations as European diseases ran rampant among peoples with no immunity to them. The first places to be devastated were the Caribbean islands of the Columbian expeditions, Hispaniola and Cuba especially. This process of disease, death, and conquest happened over and over in the New World, with European microbes often preceding European settlement. The first Spanish incursion into Florida in 1513, for example, failed to establish a permanent settlement, but the Spaniards' brief visit spread disease and by the time the next Spanish landed there, twenty-five years later, the population had already fallen precipitously; the pathogens had spread farther, all the way to the Mississippi River. Two and a half centuries later, when the Spanish finally settled northern California, the same process occurred again, as the population of Native peoples plummeted, female fertility suffering in particular, leaving the very foundations of the community and culture in tatters and the way opened for thorough occupation and conquest. Although historians are still debating the actual numbers of human beings living in the Americas in 1500, it is likely that the population losses during the first century after Columbus, which varied from group to group, ranged from 60 to 90 percent.[11]

In the initial phases, the Spanish invaders of the Americas were almost entirely male and focused on the wealth to be gained, first from the booty of existing cultures, then from the resources of the land, and finally from the labor and tribute of the Natives, in a system known (in Spanish) as the *encomienda*. In 1519, Hernán Cortés, who had participated in the Spanish conquest in the Caribbean, made his way to the east coast of Mexico. As he moved inland, the indigenous Aztec empire he found there was notable not only for its incredible wealth but also for its high

◆ **Queen Isabella and King Ferdinand Reconquer Granada**
Many of the images of Queen Isabella show her at prayer or surrounded by religious icons that testify to her intense devotion to Catholicism. This 1520–1522 image, however, a carved relief of wood, depicts her in an explicitly political role. Here, with their army in the background, Isabella and her husband, King Ferdinand, are shown entering Granada after having reclaimed it from the Moors in 1492. The image speaks both to Isabella's militant defense of Catholicism and to her role in consolidating the power of Spain. *Capilla Real, Granada, Spain/Bridgeman Images.*

level of political organization. Cortés's success in subduing the Aztecs colored all subsequent Spanish exploration, including that into North America. Other adventurers followed rumors and legends of cities of gold and Natives easily subjugated elsewhere on the continent. But only in Peru, where silver deposits flowed into Spanish coffers, were these aspirations for wealth met.

The virtually all-male character of the first phases of the Spanish invasion resulted in patterns of intimacy between Native women and European men that shaped American history until European women began to appear later in the sixteenth century. As we shall see, this distinguished the gender relations of Spanish America from those of British America, a century later, in which official, legitimate marriages across cultural, racial, and religious barriers were frowned upon. In Spanish America, cross-cultural conjugal relationships took various forms and have been the subject of much scholarly controversy, especially turning on the role and volition of the Native women involved. Many of these relations were coercive, best described as rape and/or sexual and domestic slavery. In others, Native women determined that attaching themselves to European men would bring benefits to themselves, their children, and their people. No doubt, as with all such relationships, some of these connections involved genuine affection.

Many of the individual Native women whose names we know from these early years were involved in such intimate relationships and played important diplomatic and political roles as bridges between the Native and European communities of the Americas. Of these, the first and most controversial was Malintzin, known to history as Malinche. Originally one of twenty female captives given by the Native people to the Spaniards as a gift, she became Cortés's interpreter and the mother of his son. Her language skills aided Cortés in communicating with the Nahuatl-speaking Aztecs. After the conquest of Tenochtitlan, Malintzin took a lower-ranking Spanish husband, and continued to work with Cortés. Among subsequent generations of Mexicans, Malintzin has been both revered as the mother of their race and reviled as the first to betray Native peoples to Europeans. In the 1970s, Chicana feminists sought to understand her, not merely as a victim of Europe and of men, but as a woman seeking to act in a swiftly changing historical environment and to find a way between cultures and to the future (see pp. 639–640). Regardless of her controversial legacy, these words from a translated sixteenth-century Nahuatl song offer insight into Malintzin's possible response to her difficult position as an enslaved concubine: "Hey mother, I am dying of sadness here in my life with a man. I can't make the spindle dance. I can't throw my weaver's stick."[12]

By the middle of the sixteenth century, Spanish women in the New World were increasing in number, although they never exceeded more than a third of the immigrants in any one decade. The pressure from crown and clergy to curb the violence of womanless men and to facilitate permanent settlement in the Americas encouraged wives to come to join their husbands and unmarried daughters to marry unattached male colonials. A pattern was for women to marry men much older than they were, making widowhood a common experience. Spanish property law (in contrast to English) allowed widows to inherit easily, and this made widows

◆ Malintzin and Cortés

Prior to the arrival of the Spanish, the indigenous people of Mexico recorded their culture and history in pictorial form; they continued to do so after the conquest. This image comes from a painting on cloth that records the experience of the Tlaxcalan people, who remained independent of the Aztec empire and became Spain's most important Indian allies. Malintzin occupies the center of the frame, indicating the central importance of her role in the encounter/conquest. She is wearing Native dress and is depicted as unmarried, with her hair unbraided. She is interpreting for Cortés, who sits beside her, in a conversation with people from a community called Xaltelolco, to whom she points. The name of the community is written in the Roman alphabet above the traditional place glyph, which depicts a sandy hill, the community's own name and representation for itself. The people from Xaltelolco are offering tribute to Cortés, his soldiers, and the Tlaxcalan warriors in the form of food. *Universal History Archive/UIG/Bridgeman Images.*

attractive candidates for remarriage. Women immigrants congregated in the great cities of Mexico City and Lima. Throughout the Spanish empire, the wealth that the Americas promised, plus the presence of Native women as servants to do most of the domestic labor, elevated Spanish women beyond the class from which they had come. Maria de Carranza encouraged her sister-in-law in Seville to give up "the poverty and need which people suffer in Spain" and hurry to immigrate to "a land where food is plenteous."[13] Life on the northern frontier of Spanish America was more difficult for women; amid continuing warfare between colonists and Natives, the threats of kidnapping and Indian captivity shadowed their sex. Fewer women immigrated to the northern frontier voluntarily, and more were recruited to strengthen settlement.

One unusual Spanish woman in Mexico about whom we know something is Marina de San Miguel, who came to Mexico as a child in 1547. After her profligate father squandered his American riches, she dedicated herself to religious life, serving as a teacher of Native girls and a sort of freelance religious advisor and spiritual counsel to her community. She earned enough from her labors to buy her own home in Mexico City. Her spiritual independence and economic success, unusual for Spanish women outside of marriage, drew her to the attention of Spanish authorities. In these years, church and royal authority combined to bestow enormous power on the Inquisition, an institution for the detection and rooting out of all forms of heresy from the Catholic faith. In Spain, the Inquisition particularly concentrated on cleansing the faith and the country of Moors and former Jews suspected of superficial conversion to the Catholic faith. In 1601, finding Marina de San Miguel guilty of spiritual arrogance and sexual misconduct, the Mexican wing of the Spanish Inquisition subjected her to community humiliation and the termination of her vocation.

The history of these New World women points to their changing options in the context of Protestant/Catholic conflicts in Europe. Reformation-era pressures to cleanse the Catholic Church of corruption bore down particularly hard on women, whose allegedly unruly sexuality seemed to threaten religious purity. Starting in the middle of the century, the church placed religious sisterhoods under male supervision, strictly cloistered them, and prohibited their efforts in education and social service. In 1540, the first American convent, Nuestra Señora de la Concepción, opened under these conditions in Mexico City under Franciscan supervision. Most of the women who lived there were Spanish and of high birth, but Native women were occasionally admitted: two of the granddaughters of Aztec ruler Montezuma became sisters of la Concepción.

In the sixteenth century, the Spanish made several incursions north, into what would eventually be the United States. These lands, much more sparsely populated than those of Mexico and Peru, offered no great Indian empires to conquer and loot. The coast of northern California was explored and mapped but not opened to settlement until the eighteenth century. In 1565, the Spanish established St. Augustine in what is now Florida; formed to protect Spanish Cuba from French marauders and pirates, it is the longest continually occupied colonial settlement in the United States, founded four decades before the English established permanent settlements to the north. None of these excursions, however, uncovered great empires or elaborate cities, stores of gold or mountains of silver. Indeed, the only valuable commodity of these early frontier efforts was the Native people, who were seized and sold as slaves. For an overwhelmingly male population of soldier-colonists, Native women were particularly valuable as sexual partners (willing or not), as mothers of their children, as laborers, and as a bridge between indigenous and colonial men.

Spain's Northern Frontier

The northern territories in which the Spanish were most active in the sixteenth century were the lands occupied by the Pueblo peoples. In 1540, a group of Spaniards from central Mexico led by Vásquez de Coronado ventured into the land of one of these peoples, the Zuñis. Frustrated at failing to find the gold they had expected, Coronado's men seized food, blankets, and women. The Spaniards' relationship to and treatment of Native women lay at the root of this first and formative disastrous encounter on Mexico's northern frontier. Some Native men traditionally exchanged women to cement treaties with former enemies. What the Pueblos saw as the gift of a marital alliance, Spanish men saw as their patriarchal right. When the Spanish kept demanding tributes and women's bodies without offering appropriate exchanges, the Pueblos' anger mounted. The Zuñis drove Coronado back to central Mexico. Evidence of his failure to find great wealth and news of his brutal treatment of the Indians created such controversy that the Spanish made no further attempts to subdue the northern territories for another six decades.

In 1598, when the Spanish returned to the Pueblos' lands, they did so under another guise. Instead of soldiers in search of gold and tribute, Franciscan missionaries led the way, in search of souls and Christians. Less openly violent than the military men of the 1540s, Spanish Christians nonetheless wreaked their own kind of havoc on Native cultures. Franciscan friars pressured the Pueblos to participate in Catholic rites and suppressed traditional religion. The church tried to impose a patriarchal system on Native women by attempting to restructure a division of labor consistent with European notions of proper gender roles. They urged men to take over building and farming tasks that formerly had been women's work. The friars also called for Natives to enter into monogamous, lifelong marriages and for women to emulate European notions of female modesty and reserve.

To ensure that the events of the 1540s were not repeated, the friars required that the soldier-settlers who accompanied them be married men. Even so, and although their purpose was to "pacify" the Natives under Spanish and Catholic authority, violence soon broke out, as it had a half century earlier. Accounts differ. The Native men objected to the arrogance with which the soldiers seized their women. Not recognizing the complex rules and rituals surrounding Pueblo sexuality, the soldiers believed that the women were making themselves sexually available. Modern scholars point to the very different ways in which the Natives and the soldiers conducted their sexual relations and the violent turn that these differences could take under conditions of abrupt cultural clash. What the women thought, we do not know. In 1598, in response to the rape of one of their women, Native men killed a dozen soldiers, in retaliation for which the Spanish massacred eight hundred Natives. Most of those slaughtered must have been men, because the survivors who were rounded up and punished by enslavement were overwhelmingly women and children.

The important tasks of converting and educating Native Americans were left largely to male priests. How might the first contacts between Europeans and Native Americans have been affected if colonial women had also been representatives of the Christian faith? Would the sexual tensions surrounding conversion efforts have been defused? Would the traditional sexual/spiritual role of Pueblo women have found more room to survive? Or would colonial women have been as immune to Native American concerns as Spanish men were?

In New Mexico, Spanish rule proceeded along two lines: the physically violent, economically exploitative, military-led version of the conquistadores and the spiritually driven, culturally and morally coercive version of the priests. Both undermined and profoundly altered Pueblo societies. At the beginning of the seventeenth century, then, European invasions had already established a century-long legacy of invasion, disease, military conflict, religious coercion, and enslavement, contributing to a precipitous decline in the numbers and integrity of Native cultures and the position of women in them.

Fish and Furs in the North

While the Spanish achieved uncontested rule over Mexico and much of South America, other European powers, eager to find their own sources of profit and global power, looked to the north. For much of the sixteenth century, the French, English, and Dutch presence in North America was informal. The crucial process was trade, and the crucial commodities were fish and fur on one side, European manufactured goods, including ironware and guns, on the other. Women were active in this process as both producers and consumers. As in Spanish America, sexual contact and disease accompanied and complicated trading relations. Permanent settlements of European men and women developed later, in the first years of the seventeenth century (see Chapter 2).

Hundreds of European ships yearly fished the waters from Newfoundland to Massachusetts, drawn by an inexhaustible supply of cod, the source of protein at the base of the Western European diet. By the middle of the sixteenth century, more than half the cod consumed in Europe came from North American waters. Men cast the nets, but in European coastal cultures women sold their catch on the streets. Fishwives, as these market women were called, impinged on the disreputable, all-male culture of the wharves and the ships, and the term outlived the occupation, becoming synonymous for any foul-mouthed, quarrelsome female.

By the 1580s, fur had overtaken fish as the primary source of European wealth gained in North America. Beaver fur in particular was a luxury commodity, the North American equivalent of Mexican gold. It was warm and, when properly tanned, waterproof, and thus highly prized. Men were still the fashionable gender in Europe in the sixteenth century and sported most of the large, jaunty beaver hats of the age. Pocahontas was one of the few women to be pictured in such a hat (see Figure 1.10, p. 45). Most women wore lesser furs as collars and cuffs on their gowns. The French dominated trade. Native men were the hunters, while women were responsible for scraping, tanning, and preparing the skins. The European commodities that Native people received in exchange fell along gendered lines, as women got beads, metal needles, and iron kettles to use in fur preparation, while men received guns and knives, as well as alcohol. Both male and female Natives got and valued cloth and clothing.

The fur trade with the French affected family and gender relationships. Instead of hunting communally for larger animals such as moose and caribou, men trapped in small groups for beaver. Hunting and trapping for the market left men with less time and energy for subsistence activities. Thus, Native societies demanded more and more trade goods, including clothing and food. As the hunt for fur intensified, men had to travel farther and farther away from home to satisfy the demands of the market, intensifying intertribal warfare. Looking over this process from the perspective of the late nineteenth century, ethnologist Lewis Henry Morgan, writing about the Iroquois, hypothesized that the rise of capitalist economies was responsible for the subordination of women.

Native women played another role in the fur trade, especially in the Great Lakes region, through their marriages with European men. Although some fur traders formalized their marriages to Native women, most of these relationships were what the French called *mariage à la façon du pays* (marriage in the custom of the country, that is, without formal church recognition). Begun in the late sixteenth century, this practice flourished over the next two centuries until significant numbers of European women arrived. These so-called country marriages were markedly different from the interracial liaisons in Spanish America, because they tended to accept European men into Native culture rather than Native women into European culture. Native wives gave their French husbands, in the words of one historian, "an entrée into the cultures and communities of their own people. In this way, Indian women were the first important mediators of meaning between the cultures of two worlds."[14] The children of these liaisons formed a mixed, or *métis*, society along the trade routes of rivers and lakes deep into the North American heartland.

Early British Settlements

The British were slow to follow the Spanish and Portuguese in settling the Americas. During the first half of the sixteenth century, the British ignored America in favor of subduing and occupying Ireland, a promising colony much closer to home. In 1558, the half-century reign of Elizabeth I began, and England's interest in the other side of the Atlantic grew. Elizabeth wanted to challenge the legacy of Isabella of Spain, who had established her country's control of the seas and access to the New World's wealth.

In contrast to the highly religious Spanish queen, Elizabeth was a thoroughly worldly monarch. She abjured the Catholic Church in favor of heading the Church of England, more as a source of political than spiritual identity and authority. Elizabeth brilliantly maneuvered through the difficulties of being a female monarch by refusing to marry, having no children, and maintaining a reputation for chastity. She did, however, have numerous male "favorites." To one of these favorites,

◆ **Queen Elizabeth I**

In 1588, the Spanish navy, or Armada, attempted to invade England. This epochal event was commemorated in this extraordinary portrait by George Gower. Elizabeth is encased in symbols of royal and imperial power, including pearls from the New World. The channel storm that helped the English defeat the much larger and better-armed Spanish is depicted on the upper right as a sign of England's divine destiny as ruler of the seas. The globe in the lower left is turned to show the Americas, and Elizabeth's hand rests on the continent's northern lands, above New Spain, which were to become British North America. The defeat of the Spanish Armada helped to clear the way for England's growth as a transatlantic power. *Woburn Abbey, Bedfordshire, UK/Bridgeman Images.*

Sir Walter Ralegh, she granted dominion over the large, undefined American territory north of the Spanish lands that Ralegh named Virginia to honor not the Virgin Mary but the Virgin Queen.

Unlike the Catholic settlers, the Protestant English had few structures for and little interest in converting the Natives to Christianity. While the Spanish and French created "frontiers of inclusion" by liaisons between European men and Native women, the English created "frontiers of exclusion," bringing in white women very early. Instead of integrating themselves into Native American society, they pushed out Native Americans to make room for their own exclusively English settlements.

The initial effort at British colonization of the American mainland was a famous failure. In 1587 more than a hundred British emigrants (including seventeen women and nine children) sailed across the Atlantic to the island of Roanoke, on the North Carolina coast. They were following an earlier expedition composed entirely of men, during which the English had launched a surprise attack on the Native inhabitants and had murdered women and children as well as warriors. The inclusion of English women this time may have been an attempt to signal a less confrontational approach.

The head of this effort at settlement was John White, who had accompanied the first expedition as official painter. Many of his extraordinary drawings from that trip focused on Native women (see Figures 1.4 and 1.6, pp. 39 and 41). In addition to providing a kind of ethnographic record of Native women's labors, these images suggest the English men's fascination with the physical appearance of Native women: their beauty, strength, and of course partial nudity.

On the 1587 expedition, however, White was traveling not as an observer but as Ralegh's replacement. The symbol of British hopes for establishing a fully English society on American soil and the centrality of families to that effort was the birth, barely a month after landing, of White's granddaughter, Virginia Dare. Imagining this series of events through women's eyes leads us to wonder about the experience of Virginia's mother, nineteen-year-old Eleanor White Dare, pregnant during the grueling two- to three-month transatlantic journey. Who aided her in the birth? Perhaps it was a Native American woman, recognizing the commonality of female experience with this otherwise strange being from unknown places.

As food and other necessities dwindled, John White sailed back to England to replenish the community, leaving most of the other colonists behind. White did not return to Roanoke until 1590, only to discover that the entire settler community — including his own daughter and granddaughter — had disappeared. Current hypotheses are that most of the surviving settlers moved north and lived among the Indians. Rumors circulated for many years of Indian children with blond hair and blue eyes, presumably the product of intermarriage with English men and women. Groups of North Carolina Indians continue to regard themselves as descendants of the Roanoke community.

Twenty years later, the British attempted another settlement along the more sheltered banks of the Chesapeake Bay, naming the community after the new British monarch, James. This time, British investors provided greater support and Jamestown survived, though just barely. As in Roanoke, the first shipments of settlers were all male, heavily biased toward adventurous gentlemen, and singularly unprepared to provide the labor to survive. Recognizing that settlers had to be committed to permanent lives in the new land, subsequent groups of emigrants included significant numbers of unmarried English women meant to become settlers' wives. For women who were servants back in England, Virginia, for all its trials, may have promised a step up in the world. However, women never constituted more than about 20 percent of the population in the early years. Married couples received larger land grants and both men and women worked hard in the tiny community, but by the winter of 1609, the inability of the settlers to feed themselves became lethal, and more than three-quarters died. Recent archaeological research suggests that the settlers may have resorted to cannibalism to survive.

It was the agricultural productivity of the women of the surrounding peoples, the Algonquian-speaking Powhatans, that made the difference between life and death for the surviving few. As in so many Indian communities, women planted, harvested, and controlled the crops that were the core of their diet. English observers recorded with considerable astonishment and unconcealed disdain that, unlike in their home cultures, here in the New World, women were the primary agriculturists. To them, women's labor in the fields made them drudges and their husbands lazy and uncivilized, and yet this female labor kept the colonists from total starvation. It was Native women who delivered foodstuffs regularly in the first few years.

Certainly the most well-known woman in the first years of permanent British settlement on the Virginia coast was Pocahontas (see Figures 1.9 and 1.10, pp. 44 and 45). She was the daughter of one of the many wives of the powerful paramount chief, Powhatan. The British appreciated Native American structures of power and chieftainship. From a very young age, Pocahontas had the authority to serve as an intermediary between her people and the English settlers. Had she never become involved with the English settlers of Jamestown, she might have become a powerful female leader in her own right.

The legend of Pocahontas as it has come down through history follows suspiciously close to the lines of a typical European romance, with the young girl (no more than thirteen at the time) saving Jamestown leader John Smith from death at the hands of her father out of personal passion for the dashing Englishman. This version comes from Smith, who published it upon returning to England several years later. A more likely explanation is that Pocahontas was participating in a Powhatan ritual by which Smith was being absorbed into the community by some sort of adoption process, as was often the case with valuable captives of war.

Several years later, Jamestowners kidnapped Pocahontas, and she remained as part of their community for the rest of her short life. She was treated as a woman of noble birth, converted to Christianity, renamed Rebecca, and married in a church ceremony to gentleman planter John Rolfe. It is possible that she took on the role of cultural intermediary out of her sense of service to her people and her father's need to know more about the newcomers. Several portraits of her survive because in 1616 Pocahontas, along with her husband, her son, and a considerable Native entourage, sailed to England, where they were presented to the royal court as evidence of the promising future of the colonial experiment in Virginia. Interestingly, Pocahontas's role as Indian foremother for British America brought her historical praise from her adopted people, rather than the reputation of traitor, as in the case of Malintzin a century before in Spanish America. Pocahontas never returned to Virginia, dying at the age of twenty-one of unknown causes.

One final detail of Pocahontas's life bears emphasis: with her help, John Rolfe became Virginia's first European cultivator of tobacco, the next in a long line of valuable commodities, beginning with sugar, produced in America and traded around the world. Tobacco cultivation allowed for the development of market-based plantation agriculture in Virginia, which was critical to the wealth and power of the British Empire. Tobacco cultivation also encouraged the development of African slavery in North America, and to this we now turn.

◆ AFRICAN WOMEN AND THE ATLANTIC SLAVE TRADE

The first Africans to be recorded in Virginia arrived in 1619, forty-three years before the Virginia legislature passed the initial laws establishing African chattel slavery. Nonetheless, the origins of this institution, with its incalculable significance for American history, lie in the Atlantic slave trade developed long before British settlement of North America. In what has been called the triangle trade, Europeans brought goods to Africa to trade for slaves, slaves to the New World to trade for slave-grown agricultural commodities such as sugar and tobacco, and these commodities to Europe for consumption. The roots of North American slavery can be found in the European trade of African slaves during the fifteenth and sixteenth centuries, in the understandings that Europeans used to classify Africans as inferior, and in the development of a commercial plantation economy in the eastern Atlantic and Brazil. In each of these, the ideologies of gender roles were important dimensions.

Women in West Africa

West African women were productive, independent, sometimes truly powerful members of their societies. They were agriculturalists, with responsibilities for cultivating major foodstuffs, such as yams and rice, and innovating new agricultural methods. They produced textiles, spinning and weaving cloth. In towns and along trading routes, women were often the local traders, an economic practice that West African women have maintained to this day. Though productive and family roles were divided by gender, women could cross over into male roles under exceptional

Tom. 4 . pag. 37 .

Audiance du Vice Roy d'angole a la Reine Anne Zingha.

◆ Queen Njinga

Njinga was undoubtedly one of the most politically and diplomatically skilled monarchs of the early modern period. She expertly used her father's royal lineage and manipulated gender roles to move with authority among powerful African and European men. She led armies against the Portuguese, required her soldiers to view her as a man, and dressed her husband and male concubines in women's clothing. This late seventeenth-century image portrays Njinga's 1622 negotiations with the Portuguese governor of Luanda. Faced with the governor's humiliating suggestion that she sit on the floor, Njinga ordered one of her female attendants to serve as her human chair. Behind her is a large, imposing view of the Angolan landscape. How does the image convey Njinga's authority in relation to both the Portuguese and her own subjects? *Widener Library, Harvard University.*

◆ **Female Clothing Styles, Gold Coast, Late Seventeenth Century**
John Barbot, an agent of the Royal African Company, provided detailed descriptions of Gold
Coast men and women that accompanied his sketches. Note the varying forms of dress for
different ranks of women, such as "A Country Girl," and "A Merchant's Wife." Why might
Barbot, a slave trader for the English crown, be interested in the social hierarchies of West
African societies? What messages about African women did these illustrations convey to
European readers? *David M. Rubenstein Rare Book & Manuscript Library, Duke University.*

circumstances. In the internal slave trade, discussed in the following section, some
African women bought female slaves so that they could have their own "wives" and
through them augment their families' wealth.

Just as this was a period of female monarchs in Europe, so too in Africa. In
the middle of the sixteenth century, Queen Amina, a renowned warrior, ruled the
Hausa Zazzau peoples in what is now northern Nigeria. More is known about
Queen Njinga. Born to the Ndongo king and his favored concubine in what is now
Angola, Njinga rose to power just as the Portuguese attempted to expand their

colonial rule and slave trading. Njinga's strategies for consolidating power shifted from fighting the Portuguese and sheltering runaways to Catholic conversion and peace negotiations in her later years. An astute ruler and military strategist, Njinga interacted with both African and European officials; in 1660, she even corresponded directly with Pope Alexander VII, who addressed her as "our Daughter Anna Queen Nzinga."[15] Her legacy, like that of Malintzin, has shifted over time toward a recuperation of her agency and courage.

In contrast to Queen Njinga's exceptional story, most African women in the sixteenth and seventeenth centuries lived rich but ordinary lives grounded in the collective identities of their lineage groups. Young West African girls were likely to come of age learning skills of cultivation, harvesting, and pottery from their mothers and other older women. As they entered puberty, many African girls underwent specific initiation rituals with other girls of similar age. In the Upper Guinea region of West Africa, for example, older women initiated younger generations into the secret female society *Sande*. During their training, young girls received ancestral knowledge about healing, sexuality, maternity, and other responsibilities of adult womanhood. In these societies, motherhood served as a central institution that could elevate a woman's social status and even lead to political authority.[16]

However, European records of sixteenth-century encounters with sub-Saharan Africans record little of this. Early European slave traders dealt primarily with African men. When they did come across women, they mainly noticed their sexuality and their maternity; comments focused on their nakedness and the way they carried and breastfed their children. Writing in 1555 of his voyage to Guinea, the Englishman William Towerson was astonished that both men and women went about unclothed. He particularly noticed the women's breasts — indeed, he could not take his eyes off them — though not because he thought they were beautiful: "In the most part be they very foule and long, hanging down like the udder of a goate."[17] Such comments likening black mothers to animals laid the groundwork for racial distinctions between African and European women that provided an ideological defense of New World slavery.

The Early Slave Trade

Trading in African slaves predates the involvement of Europeans. Long-standing slaving practices in Africa allowed victors to keep captives taken in war or, more likely, sell them to trans-Saharan caravans trading them elsewhere on the continent. Within Africa, women were more desirable as slaves than men because they could provide both agricultural labor and offspring. They could be absorbed by marriage and motherhood as inferior members of the kin structures of the peoples who acquired them.

Beginning in the mid-fifteenth century, European slavers on the west coast of Africa developed working relationships with indigenous African slave traders, who supplied them with people from inland Africa. The European slave trade drew primarily from the West African coast south of the Sahara, initially from the

Upper Guinea area and shifting to the region south of the mouth of the Congo River. The growing demand among Europeans for African labor drove the internal African slave trade to new heights. For all the European nations involved, the slave trade became the source of immense wealth, both because of the profit involved in buying and selling human beings and because of the fruits of slave labor in the commercial enterprises of the New World.

The Iberians were the first Europeans to trade in African slaves. At first, the Spanish and Portuguese brought their black captives to their own countries, where they served as domestic and personal servants. Unused to slave trading, common people in Spain and Portugal were at first horrified, but they soon accommodated themselves to the sight of human beings sold on wharves along with other African commodities, crying children being pulled from weeping mothers, husbands and wives clutching each other as they parted. By the turn of the sixteenth century, there were as many as ten thousand Africans in Lisbon and almost that number in Seville.

Within two decades, captured black Africans were being shipped off the mainland to Spanish and Portuguese settlers on a small group of Atlantic islands midway between the Iberian Peninsula and the Guinea coast. On Madeira, São Tomé, and the Canary and Cape Verde islands, displaced Africans formed the labor force of a new form of large-scale, commercially oriented agriculture. This was the beginning of the plantation system, which, along with chattel slavery, eventually flourished in the Americas, including the British North American colonies. On these sixteenth-century plantations, mostly male and some female African slaves cultivated and processed crops meant for sale around the known world. Sugar set the pattern later taken up by tobacco: it was a luxury product, not meant for local consumption and indeed irrelevant to the subsistence of the people who grew it, of interest instead to people far away with disposable wealth and cosmopolitan tastes.

In the late sixteenth century, sugar cultivation crossed the Atlantic, arriving in the massive Portuguese colony of Brazil and the Spanish island colonies of Hispaniola (now Haiti and the Dominican Republic) and Cuba. There, the gradual shift to an African slave-labor force in the late sixteenth century was the ironic consequence of the protests by Las Casas and others against the mistreatment and high death rates of American Native peoples. Already exposed to the diseases carried by Europeans during more than a century of trade, Africans seemed hardier than the American Natives. Thus one tragedy, the near eradication of the Native population of the Americas, was compounded by a second one, the development of a brutal traffic in human beings, brought from Africa to work in the fields of America for crops to be consumed largely in Europe. By one estimate, at the end of the sixteenth century, there were 150,000 African slaves in the Spanish West Indies and 50,000 more in Portuguese Brazil (see Map 1.2).[18]

The transatlantic slave trade was much larger and more violent than the intra-African slave trade that preceded it. Instead of domestic service, enslaved Africans were employed in a modern, commercial, globally oriented form

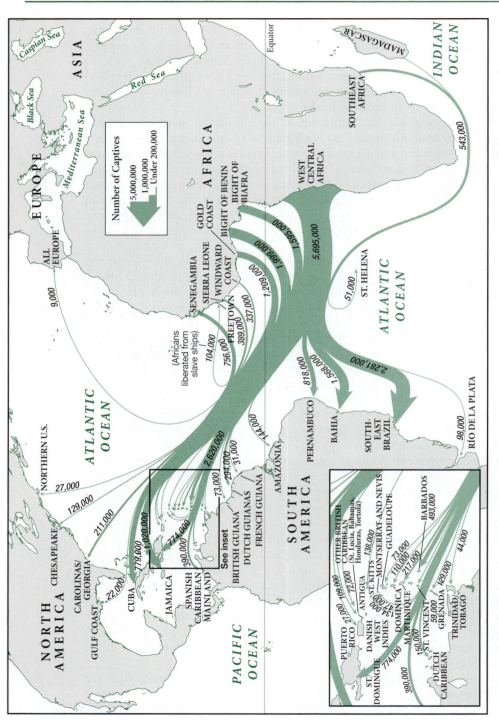

◆ **Map 1.2 Major Trends in the Atlantic Slave Trade**

A global team of scholars headed by historian David Eltis have compiled records of specific slave ship voyages in a ground-breaking project on the history of the Atlantic slave trade. According to *Voyages: The Trans-Atlantic Slave Trade Database* estimates, slavers forcibly carried 12.5 million captive Africans into the Americas. Millions died, but 10.7 million survived the brutal Middle Passage. While 200,000 of these survivors were intercepted at sea by naval patrols during the nineteenth-century era of abolition, 10.5 million were purchased by New World slaveowners. Spanish and Portuguese slavers dominated the transatlantic slave trade in the sixteenth century. The entry of first Dutch and then British and French slave traders in the mid to late 1600s, however, caused a sharp increase in the numbers of trafficked Africans. By 1837, all slaving nations had abolished the transatlantic slave trade, but a vigorous illegal trade nonetheless transported another 1.2 million captive Africans into slavery, primarily to Brazil and Cuba. *Eltis & Richardson,* Atlas of the Transatlantic Slave Trade *(2010), Yale University Press.*

of production. Far from home, surrounded by strangers, they had no means of escape. Unlike the intra-African slave trade, which was mostly female, the majority of Africans taken across the Atlantic to be slaves were men. And in the Americas, slaves were distinguished from their masters by the highly visible difference of their African blackness.

Racializing Slavery

Long before European colonists to the Americas solidified the legal status of black Africans and their offspring as lifelong slaves, skin color differentiated black Africans from other categories of unfree labor. The long history of prior slave systems rested on various sorts of difference, such as kinship, religion, or geography. The Spanish and Portuguese were particularly experienced with distinctions of religion, as they were busy cleansing their society of Jews and Moors at the same time as they were inventing the transatlantic slave trade. But these other systems of differentiating and relegating people to slavery allowed for some individuals to cross over to freedom, by conversion for instance, or by adoption and marriage.

A new, far more inescapable form of human categorization was emerging in connection with the enslavement of Africans in Europe and the Americas, that of "race." Nothing could make a black person white. The "science" of racial classification and hierarchy was not fully formed until the nineteenth century. But the idea of an ineradicable and unbridgeable difference inscribed on the face and the body of the potential slave was already beginning to appear in the sixteenth century. The profitable prospect of enslavement encouraged debasing, dehumanizing images of Africans. Europeans' contempt for black Africans as closer to animals than themselves encouraged enslavement. The two worked hand in hand.

African women were fundamental to this development. Although sexually intrigued by the nakedness and exoticness of African women, Europeans were rarely interested in domesticating or "civilizing" them through marriage or conversion to Christianity — unlike their attitude toward Native Americans. On the contrary, once the idea of the inherited differentiation called "race" hardened, African women became crucial to the development of permanent and inherited enslavement. At the point that transatlantic slavery shifted away from working Africans to death and toward a system of slavery that could reproduce its own labor force, the reproductive capacity of African women's bodies was the key.

African Slavery in the Americas

By the middle of the sixteenth century, 25 percent of the people who came across the Atlantic to the New World were African. By the first half of the eighteenth century, that percentage had risen dramatically to 75 percent. With regard to gender, transatlantic slavery in its first century was the mirror image of the intra-African slave trade: it was preponderantly male. Even so, women had a significant presence in this early period. The sparse evidence for gender ratios on known slave ship voyages indicates an average of 41.5 percent female captives in the period between 1525 and 1700 compared to 34.7 percent female captives after 1700.[19] Although the great majority of Africans shipped to the pre-nineteenth-century Americas as slaves were men, African women constituted a significant majority of nonnative women there. Put another way, although men outnumbered women in the slave trade, African women outnumbered European women in early migration to the New World. Unlike virtually all other female immigrants in this period, African women were not sent to America as wives or daughters within male-headed family systems.

The daily work of African women on the plantations of the sugar islands also differed from European patterns of gendered labor. Unlike the way that most human societies arranged their work patterns, plantation society did not distinguish African workers by gender in the labor they performed. African women, in a perverse version of their agricultural roles in their own lands, were incorporated alongside men into gangs of workers on the sugar plantations of the Caribbean and South America. Sugar was a grueling crop to raise, cut, and process. Slave women seem to have had special responsibility for the dangerous work of guiding the freshly cut cane between millstones. According to one historian, the pace at which sugarcane was brought into the mills and ground down was so furious that "in northeastern Brazil slave women with a missing arm were a common sight."[20] These grim conditions repeated themselves as the plantation economy spread to the British Caribbean by the 1640s and Barbados came to rival Brazil as the world's leading sugar producer.

As a result of brutal working conditions, violence, and poor health, African women in early New World slavery had very low fertility rates. In fact, both African men and women in Brazil and the Caribbean were generally worked to death, because it was less costly to replace them than to sustain them. There is also some evidence that slave women turned to Native contraceptives and abortifacients to keep from giving birth to children whom they would then lose to slavery. Yet, even in the early seventeenth century, before all the laws of inheritance and bondage had been written, English slaveowners began to use a language of "breeding" and "increase" in wills and other legal documents that indicated their awareness of the potential of enslaved women's childbearing. In the British colonies, racialized ideas about black women's reproductive capacity proved foundational to a system of chattel slavery where children would inherit their slave status from African-descended mothers.

Not until the turn of the eighteenth century did the use of enslaved African labor for plantation production take off in the North American colonies. By this time, the Dutch and the British had overtaken the Portuguese and Spanish as the major powers in the transatlantic slave trade. African slavery as it matured in its North American form in the late eighteenth century finally became self-reproducing: more people were born into slavery in North America than were imported into the institution from abroad. The consequences of this shift became clearer over the next century: even though less than 4 percent of Africans traded into the New World ended up in British North American colonies, the population of African Americans emancipated after the U.S. Civil War comprised the largest population of freedpeople anywhere in the western hemisphere.[21]

The climate in most parts of mainland North America did not favor sugar, so other crops became the focus. In the Carolinas, rice was a challenge to grow and difficult to mill, yet cheap to ship. In the Senegambian region of West Africa, cultivating and milling rice were women's tasks, and numerous legends on either side of the Atlantic suggest that the first rice crops in America came from seeds that enslaved women hid in their hair, perhaps to remind themselves of their homeland, or in the hair of the children sold away from them, to make sure that they would be properly fed. But for international commerce, the crucial plantation crop grown by African slaves in British North America starting in the early seventeenth century was the Indian medicine that Pocahontas's widower, John Rolfe, was the first to cultivate: tobacco.

◆ CONCLUSION: Many Beginnings

The beginnings of all nations are difficult to identify, even a nation as relatively young as the United States. Our cherished national narratives tell us that our roots were in the wilderness. By contrast, in this account, the beginnings of America are set in the wide world: in the diverse cultures of the Americas of course, but also in those of western sub-Saharan Africa and of Europe. The distinctions between the two American continents had not yet hardened, except that the southern one offered riches and conquests that the northern one did not. Perhaps most surprisingly, the history of the American nation reaches back at least a full century before the first permanent European settlements, not only in the British Atlantic colonies but also in Spanish incursions into Florida, the Southwest, and the lower Mississippi River valley.

Of all these conflicting and intersecting cultures, only Native American societies involved men and women from the same society in approximately equal numbers, living together in family and kin groupings, engaged in complementary productive tasks and varying political roles as determined by their communities. The others, the Europeans who came freely and the Africans who did not, were mostly men. Their women would not arrive in significant numbers for another hundred years. Thus, many of the interactions between men and women in sixteenth-century America were also between peoples largely unknown to each other, and many of the cross-cultural contacts that characterized the New World of the 1500s were accomplished via relations between men and women, the inequalities of culture intersecting with those of gender.

CHAPTER 1 REVIEW

KEY TERMS AND PEOPLE

Terms
Ojibwas
Algonquians
Pueblo people
Apaches
Iroquois Confederacy
berdache
"Columbian exchange"
encomienda

Nuestra Señora de la
    Concepción

People
Isabella of Castile
Christopher Columbus
Bartolomé de Las Casas
Hernán Cortés
Malintzin

Marina de San Miguel
Elizabeth I
Virginia Dare
Njinga

REVIEW QUESTIONS

1. Compare the economic roles of Iroquois and Pueblo women. In general, across North America, how did women's economic contributions shape their political and social roles within their communities?

2. How did the fact that early European invaders of the Americas were mostly male influence the way they interacted with Native American societies and Native women in particular?

3. How did the demography of the slave trade and the conditions of early plantation societies affect African women's experiences of work and motherhood?

4. **Making Connections** How did European, African, and Native American women meet at the "crossroads of gender" in early colonial America? Compare and contrast experiences of family and sexuality, gendered divisions of labor, and opportunities for female authority among these three large groups of women.

PRIMARY SOURCES

European Images of Native American Women

In exploring the lives of early Native American women, historians rely on the images and narratives produced by Europeans eager to describe the peoples they encountered in what they viewed as the New World. How does this essay on European images of Native women reveal the advantages and limitations of such sources in conveying women's lives accurately and clearly?

Europeans' representations of Native American women tell us about European perceptions of their conquest of the Americas. However, depending on the artist, and with careful critical tools, we can also learn about the women depicted. Figure 1.1 uses allegory, a device common in Western European art — employing the female form to symbolize a country or abstract qualities such as virtue or

Americen Americus retexit, & Semel vocauit inde semper excitam.

AMERICA.

◆ **Figure 1.1** Theodor Galle, *America* (c. 1580)
Private Collection/The Stapleton Collection/Bridgeman Images.

liberty. Images of America represented by an idealized Native American woman were highly popular in Europe. The illustration here, titled *America*, is an engraving created around 1580 by Flemish engraver Theodor Galle, based on a drawing from around 1574 by Jan van der Straet. The striking image represents Amerigo Vespucci, the Italian explorer whose name was eventually given to the land mass he first explored in 1499,° as he "awakens" America. The animal at bottom right is a sloth, and in the background naked people are roasting a human leg on a spit, indicating the widespread belief that American Natives were uncivilized, barbaric, and cannibalistic. The engraving projects America as a bountiful land, but with savage peoples. The phrase in Latin may be translated in two ways: "Amerigo rediscovers America; he called her once and thenceforth she was always awake" or "Amerigo laid bare America; once he called her and thenceforth she was always aroused." How might these different translations elicit different interpretations of the engraving? What is the significance of Vespucci's being clothed and standing while the woman representing America is largely naked and reclining? Why would Europeans choose to depict America as a woman? What does the engraving reveal about European society and values?

More helpful to us in understanding the reality of indigenous women's lives are the illustrations and descriptions made by Europeans who encountered them in the sixteenth and seventeenth centuries. Often these accounts aimed to promote enthusiasm and funding for exploration, colonization, or missionary activity, so they presented Native American peoples in ways that would appeal to their readers. But they also reflect their artists' ethnographic intentions to record, with more or less accuracy, the appearance and ways of strange new peoples. Publications such as Theodor de Bry's multivolume *Great Voyages* (1590) provided texts with illustrations detailing geography, information about flora and fauna, and accounts of Native peoples. A native of Flanders, de Bry had a fervent interest in promoting the colonization schemes of Protestant nations on a continent where the Catholic French and Spanish had already established a foothold. His depiction in Figure 1.2 must be analyzed with his point of view and purpose in mind. The image is based on the work of artist Jacques Le Moyne de Morgues, who had spent time in Florida when the French had an outpost there. The drawing purports to describe the Timucua, a Muskogean-speaking people. Timucuas were a matrilineal, agricultural people who raised corn, beans, and squash. Scholars believe that details in this image such as the dress, the baskets, and the sticks used to punch holes in the ground for planting may be accurate, but the straight rows are apparently modeled after the plowed fields of Europe, and the hoes depicted are Flemish tools. The bodies of the women themselves reflect European ideas of classical beauty (female nudes were common in European painting). What does this image suggest about the Timucuas' sexual division of labor?

° Historians dispute the exact year of Vespucci's arrival in the Americas.

◆ **Figure 1.2** **Indians Planting Corn, from Theodor de Bry, *Great Voyages* (1590)**
Beinecke Rare Book and Manuscript Library, Yale University.

A much later depiction of women's work (Figure 1.3) appeared in *Moeurs des Sauvages Amériquains* (1724) by Joseph-François Lafitau, a Jesuit missionary in the region of Montreal, Canada. It is included here because there are no such depictions of Iroquois women's traditional work in the Great Lakes area from the sixteenth century. Accompanying his illustration of Canadian Iroquois women making maple sugar, Lafitau wrote, "The women are busy going to get the vessels which are already full of the sap which drips from the trees, taking this sap and pouring it into the kettles which are on the fire. One woman is watching over the kettles while another one, seated, is kneading with her hands this sap which is thickening and in condition to be put in the shape of sugar loaves. Beyond the camp and the woods appear the fields as they look at the end of winter. We can see the women busy putting the fields into shape for the first time and sowing their corn."[22] What does this drawing and description suggest about the work patterns of these Iroquois women? What are the similarities and differences with Figure 1.2?

Undoubtedly the most comprehensive set of sixteenth-century North American illustrations are those of John White, who was not only the most prolific and accomplished European artist of the New World but also governor of Roanoke, the first English attempt at settlement on the North American continent (see pp. 21–25). Sir Walter Ralegh commissioned White to illustrate plant and animal life and the Native peoples encountered in the three Roanoke

◆ **Figure 1.3 Canadian Iroquois Women Making Maple Sugar, from Joseph-François Lafitau, *Moeurs des Sauvages Amériquains* (1724)**
Beinecke Rare Book and Manuscript Library, Yale University.

voyages of 1584–1590. White's extraordinary watercolors, such as Figure 1.4, appear to have been accurately painted from his careful observations of the coastal Algonquians, who lived on the Outer Banks of today's North Carolina. Among most Algonquian peoples, men and women ate separately, although these Carolinians seem to have had different practices. Who may have made the mat on which the couple sits? "They are very sober in their eatinge, and drinkinge, and consequentlye verye longe lived because they doe not oppress nature," Thomas Harriot wrote in the accompanying text.[23] How is White's admiration for these people portrayed visually?

◆ **Figure 1.4** John White, *Theire sitting at meate* (c. 1585–1586)
The Granger Collection, New York.

Theodore de Bry modified White's drawings when he published them in 1590. In White's version (Figure 1.4), the only dish the couple is eating is boiled maize. De Bry's version (Figure 1.5) adds nuts, a fish, and corn; there is also a gourd, a pipe, and a shell. What are the other differences between the two versions of the image *Their sitting at meate*? Why might de Bry have changed White's original drawing?

White's detailed depiction of clothing and ornamentation is particularly valuable. Why might the English have been so interested in such details? Figure 1.6, *A Chief Lady of Pomeiooc and Her Daughter*, features the wife of the chief in an Algonquian town in what is now North Carolina. Although not clear from the drawing, the accompanying text indicates that the marks on the woman's arms and face are "pounced," or tattooed.[24] In what other ways has the woman decorated herself? Her fringed skirt is made of skins and covers her front only, not her back. She is wearing a three-strand necklace, probably made of pearls and/or copper, hanging to her waist. Her daughter also wears a beaded necklace and, though it is hard to see, a skin covering her genitals. She carries a doll — a

◆ **Figure 1.5** Theodor de Bry, *Their sitting at meate* (1590), based on a drawing
by John White
Courtesy of the John Carter Brown Library at Brown University.

European one, dressed in Elizabethan clothing. A similar illustration that
appeared in a de Bry engraving in 1590 adds a background landscape and shows
the girl holding both the doll and an armillary sphere—a globelike ornament
commonly used to depict the earth and its heavens. What is the significance of
the inclusion of these European items?

More than a century later, when British colonization had been well established, the Virginian Robert Beverley reproduced an altered version of *A Chief
Lady of Pomeiooc and Her Daughter*. In this image, *A Woman and a Boy Running
After Her* (Figure 1.7), the doll and armillary sphere have been replaced with
an "Indian rattle" and an ear of corn and the daughter has become a boy. Historian Joyce Chaplin observes, "It is as if the English had initially been eager to
place European objects in native hands, but later they were just as eager to take
these things away."[25] What shifts in European views of American Indians might
these newly substituted items represent? What is the significance of the text
labels added to the later image? Why might the eighteenth-century version have
changed the gender of the child?

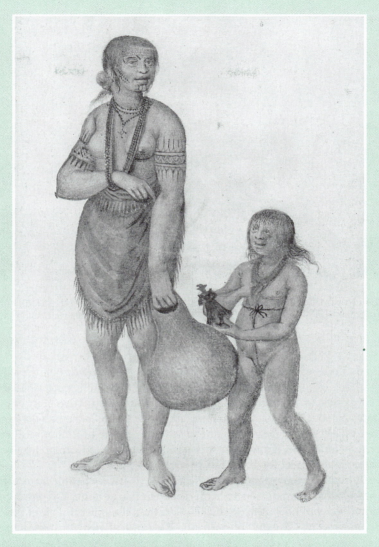

◆ **Figure 1.6** John White, *A Chief Lady of Pomeiooc and Her Daughter*
© *The Trustees of the British Museum/Art Resource, NY.*

While most of White's paintings focus on the Atlantic Coast Algonquians with whom he met and lived, a small part of his work focused on Aleutian Islanders. The British explorer Martin Frobisher sailed in search of a Northwest Passage to Asia in the 1570s and landed in what is now Baffin Island, northern Canada, between Greenland and Quebec Province. He brought back two captives with him,

◆ **Figure 1.7   Robert Beverley, *A Woman and a Boy Running after Her* (1705)**
Documenting the American South, University Library, The University of North Carolina at Chapel Hill.

one man and one woman. White either sailed with Frobisher or met these Indians in London in 1577. In either case, White's attention to detail is once again evident. Figure 1.8 is that of a woman in a sealskin dress and distinctive high boots. Her face is tattooed, but what is most striking about the image is the baby's face visible inside her hood. Why did White paint yet another image of Indian motherhood? What other similarities, if any, does this woman bear to the women near Roanoke that White painted a decade later?

Pocahontas of the Algonquian-speaking Powhatan people in Virginia is perhaps the most famous Native American woman. Figure 1.9 represents the well-known story of how she convinced her father, the powerful chief Powhatan, to spare the life of Captain John Smith. An unidentified illustrator prepared this image for Smith's account of his adventures, published in London in 1612. As Smith recounted it (writing about himself in the third person), "At last they brought him to Meronocomo, where was Powhatan their Emperor. Here more than two hundred of those grim Courtiers stood wondering at him, as he had beene a monster; . . . having feasted him after their best barbarous manner they could, a long consultation was held, but the conclusion was, two great stones were brought before Powhatan; then as many as could laid hands on him, dragged him to them, and thereon laid his head, and being ready with their clubs, to beate out his braines, Pocahontas the Kings dearest daughter, when no intreaty could prevaile, got his head in her armes, and laid her owne upon his to save him from death."[26] What is Smith suggesting about Pocahontas and about

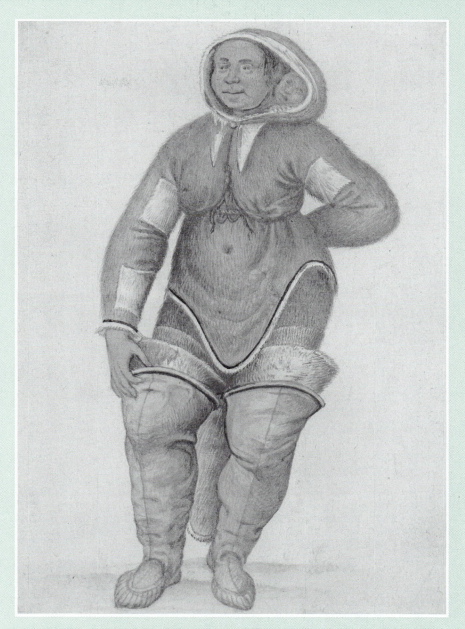

◆ **Figure 1.8** John White, *Eskimo Woman* (1577)
© *The Trustees of the British Museum/Art Resource, NY.*

King Powhatan comands C. Smith to be slayn his daughter Pokahontas beggs his life his thankfullness and how he Subiecled 39 of their kings reade & histor

◆ **Figure 1.9** *Pocahontas Convinces Her Father, Chief Powhatan, to Spare the Life of Captain John Smith*, from John Smith, *Generall Historie of Virginia* (1612)
Beinecke Rare Book and Manuscript Library, Yale University.

himself by this story? What other possible interpretations of the events depicted here can you suggest?

Other images of Pocahontas come from her brief, celebrated trip to England, where she was presented as Native American royalty and as proof of the promise and success of the Jamestown settlement and of the eventual transplantation of English culture in the New World. Figure 1.10, a 1616 portrait engraved shortly before her death, represents her as John Smith later described her: "a gracious lady" with a "very formall and civill . . . English manner."[27] The Virginia Company, which

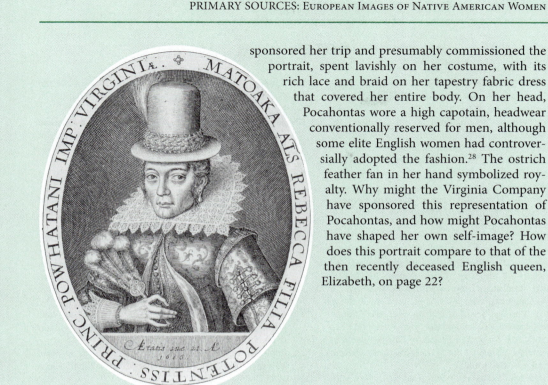

sponsored her trip and presumably commissioned the portrait, spent lavishly on her costume, with its rich lace and braid on her tapestry fabric dress that covered her entire body. On her head, Pocahontas wore a high capotain, headwear conventionally reserved for men, although some elite English women had controversially adopted the fashion.[28] The ostrich feather fan in her hand symbolized royalty. Why might the Virginia Company have sponsored this representation of Pocahontas, and how might Pocahontas have shaped her own self-image? How does this portrait compare to that of the then recently deceased English queen, Elizabeth, on page 22?

◆ **Figure 1.10 Simon Van de Passe, *Pocahontas* (1616)**
Beinecke Rare Book and Manuscript Library, Yale University.

QUESTIONS FOR ANALYSIS

1. This visual essay features European images of early Native American women and cautions that we must "read" these images carefully in using them to understand indigenous women's lives. What limitations do these images have as historical sources?

2. What commonalities do you find among the different representations here of Native American women? What differences?

3. One important characteristic of Native societies was the sexual division of labor. In what ways do these images depict women's economic participation in their communities?

NOTES

1. Mary P. Ryan, *Mysteries of Sex: Tracing Women and Men through American History* (Chapel Hill: University of North Carolina Press, 2006), 21.

2. Karen Kupperman, "International at the Creation," in Thomas Bender, ed., *Rethinking American History in a Global Age* (Berkeley: University of California Press, 2002), 105.

3. Samuel de Champlain, *The Works of Samuel de Champlain*, 6 vols., ed. H. P. Biggar (Toronto: The Champlain Society, 1922–1936), 136–37.

4. Judith K. Brown, "Economic Organization and the Position of Women among the Iroquois," *Ethnohistory* 17, nos. 3–4 (Summer–Fall 1970): 159.

5. Ibid., 153.

6. Ibid.

7. Richard White, *The Middle Ground: Indians, Empires, and Republics in the Great Lakes Region, 1650–1815* (Cambridge: Cambridge University Press, 1991), 63.

8. Ramón A. Gutiérrez, *When Jesus Came, the Corn Mothers Went Away: Marriage, Sexuality, and Power in New Mexico, 1500–1846* (Stanford, CA: Stanford University Press, 1991), 34.

9. James Axtell, ed., *The Indian Peoples of Eastern America: A Documentary History of the Sexes* (New York: Oxford University Press, 1981), 142.

10. William Monter, "Protestant Wives, Catholic Saints, and the Devil's Handmaid," in Renate Bridenthal and Claudia Koonz, eds., *Becoming Visible: Women in European History* (Boston: Houghton Mifflin, 1977), 207.

11. John Huxtable Elliott, *Empires of the Atlantic World: Britain and Spain in America 1492–1830* (New Haven: Yale University Press, 2007), 64.

12. Camilla Townsend, *Malintzin's Choices: An Indian Woman in the Conquest of Mexico* (Albuquerque: University of New Mexico Press, 2006).

13. Susan Migden Socolow, *The Women of Colonial Latin America*, 2nd ed. (Cambridge: Cambridge University Press, 2014), 194–95.

14. Clara Sue Kidwell, "Indian Women as Cultural Mediators," *Ethnohistory* 39, no. 2 (Spring 1992): 97.

15. Linda Heywood, *Njinga of Angola: Africa's Warrior Queen* (Cambridge, MA: Harvard University Press, 2017), 210.

16. Kathleen Sheldon, *African Women: Early History to the 21st Century* (Bloomington: Indiana University Press, 2017), 1–34.

17. Jennifer Lyle Morgan, *Laboring Women: Reproduction and Gender in New World Slavery* (Philadelphia: University of Pennsylvania Press, 2004), 27.

18. Elliott, *Empires of the Atlantic World*, 100.

19. Voyages: The Trans-Atlantic Slave Trade Database, http://www.slavevoyages.org.

20. David Brion Davis, *Inhuman Bondage: The Rise and Fall of Slavery in the New World* (Oxford: Oxford University Press, 2006), 108.

21. David Eltis and David Richardson, *Atlas of the Transatlantic Slave Trade* (New Haven: Yale University Press, 2010), 17.

22. Father Joseph-François Lafitau, *Customs of the American Indians Compared with the Customs of Primitive Times*, ed. and trans. William N. Fenton and Elizabeth L. Moore (1724; Toronto: Champlain Society, 1977), 2:8.

23. Thomas Harriot, *A Briefe and True Report of the New Found Land of Virginia*, reprint of the 1590 de Bry edition (New York: Dover, 1972), 50.

24. John White, *The First Colony*, reprinted in *The Roanoke Voyages, 1584–1590*, vol. 1 (London: The Hakluyt Society, 1955), 430.

25. Joyce E. Chaplin, *Subject Matter: Technology, the Body, and Science on the Anglo-American Frontier, 1500–1676* (Cambridge, MA: Harvard University Press, 2001), 36.

26. Captain John Smith, *The Generall Historie of Virginia, New England & the Summer Isles, Together with the True Travels, Adventures and Observations, and a Sea Grammar*, vol. 1 (1607), Library of Congress, American Memory, "The Capital and the Bay: Narratives of Washington and the Chesapeake Bay Region, ca. 1600–1925," http://docsouth.unc.edu/southlit/smith/smith.html.

27. Karen Ordahl Kupperman, *Indians and English: Facing Off in Early America* (Ithaca, NY: Cornell University Press, 2000), 199.

28. Camilla Townsend, *Pocahontas and the Powhatan Dilemma* (New York: Hill and Wang, 2005), 152.

SUGGESTED REFERENCES

America in the World, to 1650: Overview

James Axtell, *Beyond 1492: Encounters in Colonial North America* (1992).

Thomas Bender, *America's Place in World History* (2006).

J. H. Elliott, *Empires of the Atlantic World: Britain and Spain in America, 1492–1830* (2007).

Peter C. Mancall and James H. Merrell, eds., *American Encounters: Natives and Newcomers from European Contact to Indian Removal, 1500–1850*, 2nd ed. (2006).

Philip Morgan and Molly A. Walsh, *Early North America in Global Perspective* (2013).

Mary P. Ryan, *Mysteries of Sex: Tracing Women and Men through American History* (2006).

Native Lives and Encounters

James Axtell, *The Indian Peoples of Eastern America: A Documentary History of the Sexes* (1981).

Karen Olsen Bruhns and Karen E. Stothert, *Women in Ancient America*, 2nd ed. (2014).

Carl J. Ekberg, *Stealing Indian Women: Native Slavery in Illinois Country* (2013).

Matthew Jennings, *New Worlds of Violence: Cultures and Conquests in the Early American Southeast* (2011).

Andrew Lipman, *The Saltwater Frontier: Indians and the Contest for the American Coast* (2015).

Karen Vieria Powers, *Women in the Crucible of Conquest: The Gendered Genesis of Spanish American Society, 1500–1600* (2005).

Daniel K. Richter, *The Ordeal of the Longhouse: The Peoples of the Iroquois League in the Era of European Colonization* (1992).

Spanish America

Mary Giles, *Women in the Inquisition: Spain and the New World* (1998).

Ramón Gutiérrez, *When Jesus Came, the Corn Mothers Went Away: Marriage, Sexuality, and Power in New Mexico, 1500–1846* (1991).

Susan Migden Socolow, *The Women of Colonial Latin America*, 2nd ed. (2014).

Lisa Sousa, *The Woman Who Turned into a Jaguar, and Other Narratives of Native Women in Archives of Colonial Mexico* (2017).

Roanoke and Jamestown

James Horn, *A Kingdom Strange: The Brief and Tragic History of the Lost Colony of Roanoke* (2010).

Camilla Townsend, *Pocahontas and the Powhatan Dilemma* (2005).

African Women and the Atlantic Slave Trade

Judith Carney, *Black Rice: The Origins of Rice Cultivation in the Americas* (2009).

David Eltis and David Richardson, *Atlas of the Transatlantic Slave Trade* (2010).

Linda M. Heywood, *Njinga of Angola: Africa's Warrior Queen* (2017).

Herbert Klein, *The Atlantic Slave Trade* (2010).

Jennifer Lyle Morgan, *Laboring Women: Reproduction and Gender in New World Slavery* (2004).

Sowande' M. Mustakeem, *Slavery at Sea: Terror, Sex, and Sickness in the Middle Passage* (2016).

Claire C. Robertson and Martin A. Klein, eds., *Women and Slavery in Africa* (1997).

2

Colonial Worlds

1607–1750

IN 1690, HANNAH SWARTON'S VILLAGE, LIKE MANY other communities on the New England frontier, was raided by Indians angered by the incursions on their lands. The Abenaki warriors, following the practices of their people, took the surviving men, women, and children back to their home villages as captives, there to be adopted, kept as slaves, or ransomed. Swarton's children were taken from her, and she was given as a slave to an Abenaki family. For the next eight months, she lived and traveled and ate and dressed as a Native woman. She was hungry, cold, exhausted, and terrified of being killed. Arriving in French Canada, her Indian master sold Swarton to local Catholics, who dressed her in European clothes, gave her a bed to sleep in, and fed her relatively well. But now that Swarton's outer self was saved, she felt that her inner self was endangered. As a Protestant, Swarton had been taught to view Catholics as papists, or people who mindlessly followed the pope, and to view Catholic practices and beliefs such as the veneration of Mary and the saints as idolatry. Now Swarton was pressured to convert to Catholicism: "[T]he Lady, my mistress, the nuns, the priests, the friars, and the rest set upon me with all the strength of argument they could." Yet she held on to her Protestant faith for four long years, until intercolonial negotiations permitted her to return to New England.[1]

Hannah Swarton's story, which we know because the renowned Puritan cleric Cotton Mather published it to teach the power of faith, shows modern readers that colonial North America was home to a wide range of cultures and societies, close geographically yet far apart in lifeways and expectations for women. These different

photos: top, The Newport Historical Society (53.3); middle, The Granger Collection, New York; bottom, © Collection of the New-York Historical Society, USA/Bridgeman Images peoples, not just "Europeans," "Africans," and "Indians" but French, English, Spanish, Mbundu, Igbo, Pueblos, Iroquois, Hurons, and Ojibwas, just to name a few, knew each other as neighbors, trading partners, allies, and enemies. Women rarely fought, but they were caught up in these conflicts. Hannah Swarton was unusual in crossing not just one boundary but two, the first between English and Indian America and the second between Indian and French America. Her experience, first as a free woman and then as a captive and slave, reminds us that slavery in North America took many forms before it became synonymous with African origins. Her religious devotion and her family attachments link her to other women whose stories reveal the history of seventeenth- and early eighteenth-century North America through women's eyes.

◆ A NATIVE NEW WORLD

After the first century of contact, North American Indians entered a long period of trade, exchange, and conflict with European invaders. For some, their changed new world meant merging shattered communities and rebuilding new identities. Many Native peoples survived by migrating as a group and reestablishing new territory. Along the Eastern Seaboard, the growing population of English families, like Hannah Swarton's, caused the most harmful Native dispossession and displacement during the seventeenth and early eighteenth centuries. Elsewhere, in the Great Lakes, Great Basin, interior plains, and southwest, indigenous societies continued to exert and, in some cases even expand, their sovereignty effectively.

Although the political economies of Native American peoples varied widely, one historian tells us, "all of them governed and defended bounded, sovereign domains."[2] American Indians established their borders in various ways, including strategic assignment of place names, tree markings, and passport systems. Rather than imagining the expansion of European colonists across a blank North American map, we must understand that European newcomers continually bumped up against Native American boundaries (see Map 2.1). In the resulting interactions, many Indian women gradually lost political and economic

49

1. Klallam	19. Chinook	37. Yuki	55. Halchidhoma	73. Houma
2. Cowichan	20. Tlatskanai	38. Pomo	56. Mohave	74. Chitimacha
3. Quileute	21. Tillamook	39. Wappo	57. Walapai	75. Acolapissa
4. Quinault	22. Alsea	40. Coast Miwok	58. Havasupai	76. Biloxi
5. Twana	23. Siuslaw	41. Costano	59. Hopi	77. Mobile
6. Sanpoil	24. Coos Bay	42. Salina	60. Zuni	78. Alabama
7. Kalispel	25. Chastacosta	43. Chumash	61. Hidatsa	79. Apalachee
8. Klikitat	26. Takelma	44. Wintun	62. Mandan	80. Hitchiti
9. Spokan	27. Klamath	45. Washoe	63. Arikara	81. Yuchi
10. Coeur D'Alene	28. Karok	46. Miwok	64. Menominee	82. Cusabo
11. Walla Walla	29. Shasta	47. Tubatulabal	65. Winnebago	83. Tuscarora
12. Wishram	30. Tolowa	48. Kawaiisu	66. Omaha	84. Pamlico
13. Tenino	31. Hepa	49. Gabrielino	67. Missouri	85. Powhatan
14. Umatilla	32. Yurok	50. Luiseno	68. Kiowa-Apache	86. Nanticoke
15. Cayuse	33. Wiyot	51. Cahuilla	69. Karankawa	87. Metoac
16. Molala	34. Wailaki	52. Kamia	70. Chakchiuma	88. Mohegan
17. Chehalis	35. Achomawi	53. Yuma (Quachan)	71. Tunica	89. Massachuset
18. Kwalhioqua	36. Yana	54. Maricopa	72. Natchez	90. Pennacook

◆ **Map 2.1 American Indian Claims to Sovereignty, c. 1600**
While most maps of the North American colonial era depict Indian names floating above
a blank continent, this map attempts to outline the bounded domains of Native nations.
Although it is dated c. 1600, the Native peoples depicted here in the continent's interior and
west retained their claims and sovereignty well into the 1700s. Imagine this map overlaid
on Map 2.2 and consider the zones where conflict arose between these indigenous claims of
sovereignty and the territorial claims of European nations.

power relative to men in their groups. Where war erupted with Europeans or other Native American groups, Indian women (and children) bore the brunt as captives, hostages, and slaves. Yet women also played a crucial part in rebuilding their societies and mediating culture exchange. The dilemmas of negotiation and survival faced by singular women like Malinztin and Pocahontas (see Chapter 1) spread to Native women across North America as they encountered colonists with their own gender ways. Nowhere was this more urgently the case than in the regions of British settler colonialism.

◆ SOUTHERN BRITISH COLONIES

Although colonists came from many European nations, the English dominated the Eastern Seaboard region, which eventually formed the political foundation of the United States as the thirteen English colonies. English cultural values were particularly influential in shaping early American assumptions concerning women's proper place. The male-headed family was the primary unit of society. Women's work was expected to be confined to household production, even though prevailing notions concerning the sexual division of labor were not always met, particularly among the poor. Both Protestant religious values and English law, especially as it related to property, reinforced women's subordination to men.

Ideas about women's roles framed the experiences of the Englishwomen who came as settlers to Britain's southern colonies as well as the African women who came bound as slaves. But the special circumstances of the New World also powerfully shaped migrant women's lives. The chronic shortage of marriageable (read English) women put them under irresistible pressure to marry quickly but also gave them some leverage in choosing a husband. The economic goals that dominated the plantation societies of the South not only created potential class conflict among whites but also led to the institution of a new form of chattel slavery and the evolution of a distinct African American culture.

British Women in the Southern Colonies

As noted in Chapter 1, the English finally succeeded in establishing a permanent beachhead in North America at Jamestown in 1607. Crucial decisions affecting the Virginia colony came initially from the Virginia Company of London, whose merchant directors hoped that they would reap a fortune from trade with Native Americans. Their economic hopes for Virginia shifted in 1613, when the colonists began raising tobacco in mass quantities for the European market. Plantation-grown export crops became crucial to the economies of the other southern British colonies: tobacco in Maryland (1634), rice and certain varieties of cotton in the Carolinas (1663) and Georgia (1732) (see Map 2.2).

Once they shifted to these marketable crops, merchants who sought to exploit the potential wealth of North America needed a steady supply of laborers to make

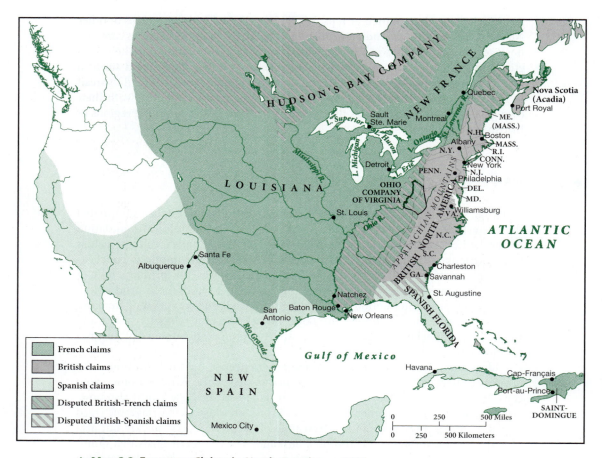

◆ **Map 2.2** **European Claims in North America, c. 1750**
Of the four European nations that had permanent colonies along the Eastern Seaboard of
North America in 1650, only England had substantial numbers of colonists. Approximately
twenty-five thousand British subjects lived in New England, and another fifteen thousand
lived in the Chesapeake region. Europeans in the interior, particularly Dutch and French
fur traders, established diplomatic relationships with Indian peoples, bringing with them
European trade goods and diseases.

their ventures successful. A population explosion in England and rising levels of
poverty facilitated the recruitment of thousands willing to make the hazardous
journey across the Atlantic. The first settlers were overwhelmingly male. To redress
this imbalance, in 1620 and 1621 the Virginia Company imported approximately
150 "tobacco brides" — "respectable" young women whose passages were paid for
with 120 pounds of tobacco by men eager to acquire wives who could serve not
only as sexual partners but also as another pair of agricultural hands. The disap-
pearance of most of these women from historical records suggests that many died,
some from disease and starvation in the hardship years of 1622–1623, others in the

1622 uprising of Powhatan's brother Opechancanough. Thus the imported brides made hardly a dent in improving the balance between the sexes. Women continued to immigrate in small numbers compared to men (in 1635, only 14 percent of the 2,010 settlers arriving from London were women), and the lack of marriageable women was a constant complaint among English men. Maryland, founded in 1634 to provide refuge for Catholics, had an even greater disproportion of men to women: in the colony's first decade, men outnumbered women by 6 to 1. In Maryland and Virginia, it was not until after 1700, when the numbers of European women migrants increased and subsequent American-born generations began to reproduce, that the sex ratio came into balance.

Even so, mortality rates remained exceptionally high in the Chesapeake region throughout the seventeenth century as a result of harsh conditions and diseases such as malaria and dysentery. Men's average life span was forty-eight years; women's was thirty-nine. (The hazards of childbirth caused the disparity; women who survived their childbearing years lived much longer than men.) The death of a spouse, usually an older husband, often cut marriages short; in Maryland, for example, only one in three couples could expect their marriage to last ten years. Widows, especially with inherited wealth from first husbands, remarried quickly, creating complicated households of stepsisters and stepbrothers.

The circumstances of the Chesapeake colonies made it difficult to reestablish as strong a patriarchal system as the one that flourished in England. While colonial political and religious leaders insisted upon formal marriages, their authority was limited, especially in the backcountry, and many couples cohabited without legal sanction and separated and created new relationships that ignored the law. The many children who came to adulthood with just one living parent had unusual freedom from parental oversight in their marriage choices. In the scattered homesteads of the southern colonies, with little communal oversight given to young couples, premarital sex was undoubtedly common. The availability of land and the uncertainty of life induced many Chesapeake fathers to leave land to their daughters as well as to their sons.

Married women, however, generally were just as subordinate to their husbands as in England. Under the English common law of coverture, which the Chesapeake colonies followed, a married woman became a *feme covert* (meaning her legal identity was absorbed into that of her husband). Naming practices by which a married woman took her husband's family name embodied this system. Without any separate legal identity, married women could not sue or be sued, hold public office, or vote. Their husbands had legal control over their property, their children, and even their bodies. When a married woman was brought before the court for an offense, her husband was held responsible. Further, given that a wife's sexual services were the property of her husband, he could be found guilty if she committed the crime of adultery.

Upon her husband's death a widow did receive a portion — a dower right, which was at least one-third of the estate — for the duration of her lifetime. Those few women who remained single or who remained widowed had the status of *feme sole*, which gave them some individual rights before the law. Chesapeake widows also had decent opportunities to improve their circumstances by remarrying well. Husbands often left their wives more than the accustomed one-third dower rights — perhaps because they were so uncertain that their children would live to adulthood — and even made wives executors of their estates. Thus, astute women could amass wealth and achieve a degree of economic autonomy. Elizabeth Digges, the widow of the former governor of Virginia, had an estate valued at 1,100 pounds, which was the largest in York County.

The most famous Chesapeake woman who acted independently was not a widow, but someone who never married. Margaret Brent, a well-connected English Catholic, came to Maryland in 1638. Both she and her sister Mary acquired substantial landholdings that they managed independently. Margaret Brent actively exercised her *feme sole* rights, making contracts, appearing in court to reclaim debts, and conducting her business freely. Her business acumen, her status as a large landholder and English gentlewoman, and the fact that she was not burdened by a husband with political entanglements led the governor of Maryland, Lord Calvert, to name her as his executor. When Calvert died in 1647, Maryland had recently experienced a local rebellion, and the troops that had put it down had yet to be paid. The responsibility of bringing order to the colony fell to Brent. The Maryland assembly resolved that "the colony was safer in her hands than any man's in the Province and she rather deserves favor and thanks from your Honour for her so much concerning for the public safety."[3] Despite this show of trust and respect, the assembly refused in 1647 to honor Brent's novel demand that she be given two votes in the assembly, one based on her role as landowner and another on her role as representative of her male clients. Although Brent's story illustrates the fluid circumstances in the seventeenth-century Chesapeake colonies that allowed women to have unusual economic power — and in rare cases even limited political power — it is clearly an exceptional one.

In contrast to Brent, the vast majority of the early white immigrants to the Chesapeake — male and female — came as indentured servants. In Virginia and Maryland, and later in the Carolinas and Georgia, a system of "bound" labor predominated. Impoverished young people, seeking opportunities unavailable in Europe, bound themselves via a legal document (an indenture) to masters for fixed periods of time — usually between four and seven years — exchanging their labor for their passage to the colonies. Recognizing the importance of women in creating a stable colony, the Virginia Company eagerly recruited young women by using propaganda that assured them that they would be treated well and would find it easy to marry at the conclusion of their service. Although the company also promised that indentured women would not be "put into the ground to worke, but occupie such domestique imployments and housewifery as in England," this was often not the case.[4]

As many as three-quarters of the women who migrated to the Chesapeake colonies in the seventeenth century were indentured. Despite the promises of the colonies' promoters, indentured women servants found life harsh (see Primary Sources: "By and About Colonial Women," pp. 81–91). They carried out their responsibilities for food preparation and housekeeping in meager circumstances in small dwellings. In the early years, the zeal to produce a cash crop overrode the English sensibilities about proper gender roles. Instead of concentrating on domestic production, women servants often were sent into the tobacco fields — planting seedlings, hoeing, weeding, and, at harvest, stripping and processing the leaves for market.

Other conditions of their servitude added to the hardships of indentured women. Prohibited from marrying while servants, they were subject to sexual exploitation. When they became pregnant — and an estimated 20 percent of indentured women did — they were punished with a public whipping and a fine. Those unable to pay the fine had their time of servitude extended, usually by one to two years. A servant who claimed that her master was the father of her child was not released from service, for fear that if a "woman got with child by her master should be freed from that service it might probably induce such loose persons to lay all their bastards to their masters."[5] Rather, a pregnant servant's indenture was transferred to a new master, who paid the county for her services.

Because of the indenture system, most young white women who came to the Chesapeake colonies married relatively late, at age twenty-four or twenty-five. Marriage helped to mark a woman's freedom from bound labor, but it did not necessarily lighten her load. Some women married "up" — and found themselves the mistress of servants — but others married men less well off than their former masters. Until the legal codification of perpetual slavery for Africans in the later 1600s, many of them married enslaved African men. In addition to the responsibilities of childbirth and child care, in poorer families wives worked in the fields. In middling families, women conducted business and trade in their husbands' absences. Wives' contributions to the household economy were valued, but as elsewhere in the English world, married women lived highly circumscribed lives.

Discontent among indentured servants, female as well as male, played a major role in Bacon's Rebellion. In 1676, a rebel faction of the Virginia colony's elite, led by Nathaniel Bacon, recruited white indentured servants and African slaves to protest the high-handed rule of the royal governor. These men protested the governor's control over land and trade. They also argued that his policies shielding the lands of Native Americans from seizure and sale interfered with colonial men's ability to establish their own economic independence. They especially resented the shortage of English women to marry. Women also joined the ranks of protesters. Sarah Drummond, the wife of one of Bacon's closest advisors, famously defied royal authority by declaring, "I fear the power of England no more than a broken straw."[6] After six months of hostilities, authorities in London constrained the local governor and allowed greater mobility to the lower ranks of free white men.

Although the rebels had forced an unprecedented crisis in Virginia affairs, the resolution of the rebellion taught the ruling powers of the colony how to quell cross-class conflicts among Englishmen and thus stabilize their own leadership. The colony's rulers went to great lengths to forestall any future alliance between white servants and black slaves, and they made it easier for land-hungry whites to seize treaty-protected territory from Native Americans. Colonial legislators also lifted restrictions on the enslavement of Native Americans. In the next half century,

English captors sold between thirty thousand and fifty thousand Indian people into slavery either in the mainland southeast or to the British Caribbean colonies.[7]

At the same time, economic and political power remained in the hands of large plantation owners, who continued to acquire not only the best land but also more and more slaves. They began to build large, elegant mansions for themselves, conspicuously displaying their wealth and social prominence. Women of the planter class, aided by a large retinue of slaves for household tasks, were able to devote time to such leisurely pursuits as studying French, playing music, writing letters, and doing needlework. Wealthy women also began to participate in a growing consumer economy, importing gowns, china, silver, and furniture. Privileged white women's attention to hospitality and fashion, as well as to domesticity and maternal duties, eventually became essential elements in the ideal of the genteel lady that reinforced southern patriarchal culture.

African Women

Whether plantation mistresses or wives of yeomen, white women in the southern colonies were inextricably tied up with slavery. Until the mid-seventeenth century, relatively few Africans had been imported into North America, and the historical records on them are spotty. One of the first African women was "Mary," who arrived in Virginia in 1622 and ended up at the same plantation as "Antonio a Negro." Eventually the two won their freedom, married, adopted the surname Johnson, and became modest landowners, even owning slaves. The couple's experience points to an important fact about early African servitude: initially the system was a fluid one that allowed some blacks opportunities for freedom and created a small nucleus of free blacks in the region. By the end of the seventeenth century, however, chattel slavery had become a nearly inescapable status for those of African descent.

The harshness of African women's American existence began when they were kidnapped or sold into the Atlantic slave trade, which had passed from the Iberians to the Dutch and the English. Of those captured in Africa, 10 to 20 percent died in transit, a figure that was no respecter of gender. The numbers of women, men, and children being bought, shipped, and sold increased significantly as the scale of the transatlantic trade grew. Of the estimated 1 million Africans forcibly shipped to the British American colonies as slaves between 1650 and 1750, some 39 percent were female, including girls as well as adult women.[8] Female captives made the Middle Passage in gender-segregated quarters, stripped naked and terrorized by crew members who routinely abused them. Olaudah Equiano struggled for words to describe his Atlantic passage after being abducted from his Nigerian home: "The shrieks of the women, and the groans of the dying, rendered the whole a scene of horror almost inconceivable."[9] When African women arrived in the mainland colonies in the late 1600s, they found a new system of chattel slavery emerging that relied on both their field labor and their childbearing.

Begun as an institution that was similar to the indentured servitude of poor white immigrants, slavery began to shift toward a unique lifelong and inherited status starting in the middle of the seventeenth century. Scholars have pointed out that African slave women were particularly crucial to this shift. Virginia's laws reveal the steps by which perpetual slavery was institutionalized. A 1643 law placed a tax on the labor of African women, putting them in the same category as paid male (European and African) labor. White women were exempt from this tax, under the assumption that whatever work they might do in the fields was temporary and would eventually give way to their return to domestic concerns. By making a sharp distinction between black women's and white women's labor, the law thus contributed to the view of Africans as fundamentally distinct from Europeans. Eventually, the increased use of African men and women in the fields allowed the reinstitution of traditional English gender roles for white women. By 1722, Virginian William Beverly could write that "slaves of both sexes are employed together in tilling and manuring the ground" while "a white woman is rarely or never put to work in the ground."[10]

This first law distinguishing between black and white women was followed by others. Particularly important was the 1662 law known as *partus sequitur ventrem* that made bondage an inherited condition, derived only from the mother. Enslavement now extended beyond an individual's lifetime and was passed to offspring through the female parent, a major break with traditional English patrilineage. The principle of *partus sequitur ventrem* increased slave women's vulnerability to rape, even though the 1662 law imposed stiff penalties on whites who had sexual intercourse with blacks. Sexual relations between white female servants and black male slaves, which had once been quite common, were now deemed illegal. By contrast, sexual relations between white men and black women were largely ignored by the law. Indeed, should a master get his slave pregnant, the child's birth only added to his wealth in slaves. Laws that centered on women and their bodies illustrate the intersection of gender, sexuality, and reproduction in differentiating between free and enslaved, white and black.

Most African slaves were initially sent to the Chesapeake Bay colonies of Maryland and Virginia. In 1650 there were only 300 enslaved Africans in all of Virginia; by 1700 there were 13,000, and by 1750 there were 150,000. The majority of these slaves cultivated and processed tobacco. Tobacco could be raised on small farms as well as on large plantations; thus, slaveholding was widespread in the Chesapeake region. On small farms white and black, master and slave, and male and female worked together to bring in a crop, with African women performing both field work and domestic tasks, including spinning and weaving. On the great plantations, by contrast, all the labor of most slaves, women and men alike, went to cultivating tobacco; only a minority, again men as well as women, worked in domestic and personal service. Women's production in field work was notable. The records of planter Robert Parnafee indicate that the value of his female slaves' tobacco crop was 1,140 pounds, a figure nearly equal to his male slaves' production.

Because of the initially skewed sex ratio, the low fertility rates of African immigrant women, and the practice inherited from the West Indies of working slaves to death, Africans living in the Chesapeake region did not have enough children to offset their deaths until the 1720s. The change was the result of better nutrition and

◆ *Virginian Luxuries*

This early nineteenth-century painting by an unknown artist was hidden on the back of another painting. The title is key to the meaning. The term *luxuries* satirically links slave-holders' sexual exploitation of their female slaves with their beating of the male (and female) slaves. Both practices are equated in their violence and their perverse attraction for the slaveholding class. *Abby Aldrich Rockefeller Folk Art Museum. The Colonial Williamsburg Foundation.*

declining disease rates. Even so, the hard labor and poor living conditions meant that African women's fertility rates remained lower than those of English women. The gradual creation of family units among North American slaves changed not only the history of the slave institution but also the lives of African Americans. For women, the birth and survival of their children was a powerfully mixed blessing, as surviving children could be and were often sold away from their mothers.

By the early eighteenth century, second- and third-generation slaves were form-ing a composite African American culture, adapted from multiple African origins but also including both English and Christian elements. Slaves whose parents and grandparents spoke different languages began to evolve a pidgin language, a mixture of English and African words. While many African religious practices continued,

African Americans also incorporated elements of Christianity as it began to spread among them in the 1740s, with the beginning of the First Great Awakening (see p. 104). Women seem to have been especially responsible for transferring and adapting medicines, foods, and some cultural and religious practices. For example, they led the call-and-response songs that accompanied ecstatic ring shouts and made quilts following African patterns of decoration.

In addition to the development of African American culture, communities of free blacks began to develop throughout the British mainland colonies as small numbers were freed by their masters or bought their own freedom. By one estimate, in some Virginia counties in the 1660s, free blacks made up as much as one-third of the black population.[11] Overall, a disproportionate number of free black colonial households were headed by women, reflecting African traditions of matrilocality as well as the legal restrictions that made it difficult for marriages with black women to be recognized as legitimate. The intensification and growth of slavery affected free blacks for the worse. They were, in the words of one historian, "an anomaly in a society committed to racial slavery," and their very presence was taken as incitement to slave rebellion.[12] Denied the rights of free persons, black men could not vote or carry guns. Despite the efforts of the legislature, however, some white servant women continued to bear children by African American fathers. These interracial relationships were the major factor in the increase of the free African American population well into the eighteenth century.[13]

A substantial proportion of the early African population of North America was reimported from the British colonies of the Caribbean. This was particularly true of the Carolinas, which began virtually as a colony of the wealthy sugar island of Barbados. One of the earliest slave women in the Carolinas — we know her only as "Sara" — came in 1678, with no family of her own, accompanying her master for reasons about which we can only speculate. In South Carolina, slave importation was so dramatic after 1700 that Africans formed a majority of the population. "A fruitful woman . . . is very much valued by planters, and a numberous Issue esteemed the greatest Riches in this country," an observer wrote in 1737.[14]

African women were particularly involved in the Carolinas' two major export crops, one of which was the indigo plant, the source of a valuable blue-black textile dye. The other, rice, was South Carolina's most important and valuable product, in large part because African women had useful knowledge about its cultivation. They used African techniques for processing the rice, but with a critical difference. Women in Africa had spent a small part of their day pounding rice for their families; African women in America spent whole long days shelling rice for distant markets.

After two centuries of English colonization, tobacco, indigo, and rice plantations that were sustained by slave labor had created a distinctive economy and culture in the Chesapeake and Carolinas. Slaves could be found elsewhere in North America, too — an active African slave trade helped define port cities such as New York, Boston, and Newport, for example — but only in the southern British colonies did slavery constitute the primary source of labor or wealth.

◆ **Hulling Rice in West Africa**
Southern white slaveowners drew on the tools of African women's traditional work as agriculturists. African women's contributions to the technology of southern rice cultivation were particularly notable. They were responsible for introducing methods for processing harvested rice. They usually did the backbreaking work of hulling and polishing the rice, pounding open the outer shell and then scouring out the inner germ. Their tools were fashioned according to those they remembered from Africa. Using a hollowed-out log and a pine branch, they pounded away in a method that required prolonged movement and tremendous strength. This engraving is an eighteenth-century depiction of women's work in West Africa. *Library of Congress.*

◆ NORTHERN BRITISH COLONIES

Despite their common English origins, the colonies of New England differed dramatically from the Chesapeake and Carolina settlements. Although climate and geography accounted for some of the differences — the land there did not offer possibilities for commercially oriented agriculture — at the center of the distinctive quality of New England was religion.

The people who founded the colonies of Plymouth (1620), Massachusetts Bay (1630), Connecticut (1635), and New Hampshire (1638) were Puritans, dissenters from the established Church of England. Puritans believed that the Anglican Church, despite the English Reformation, retained too many vestiges of Catholicism. Calling for a more thorough "purification" of Christian worship and ecclesiastical, hierarchical organization, they emphasized religious conversion as a deeply personal experience. Each church stood as an autonomous congregation of baptized saints who could testify to their conversion, as well as children and others who still awaited the conversion experience. While not the moralistic prudes of popular stereotype, the Puritans did strive to reverse what they saw as England's moral, including sexual, degeneracy and closely monitored the behavior not only of other Puritans but also of the larger community. Given all these characteristics, Puritans placed great emphasis on the family as a "little commonwealth," the essential foundation of reformed churches and a virtuous and orderly community.

Puritanism acknowledged women's spiritual equality before God. Nonetheless, both the little commonwealth of the family and the greater one of the community were male-headed, and women's role in Puritan society was definitely subordinate. The contradiction between Puritanism's religious radicalism and its social conservatism helps to account for some of the contradictions in women's experience in the northern colonies. While the majority accepted and lived the Puritan "goodwife" ideal, a minority followed the word of God into unconventional behaviors or were accused — as witches — of female responsibility gone horribly awry.

Subject to religious persecution and inspired by the idea of creating a harmonious Christian commonwealth in the New World — what Puritan leader John Winthrop described as "a city on a hill" that would be a model for all peoples — nearly fifty thousand Puritans arrived in North America between 1620 and 1640. Dedicating themselves to a righteous and disciplined life based on a covenant with God, they established a society in which church and state, while officially separate, were in reality intertwined, giving the religious and moral values of Puritanism the force of law. Whereas in the South commercial agriculture and slavery were the defining factors shaping women's lives, in New England religion served as the major force constructing gender roles and framing women's experiences. In a different way, the Quaker religion shaped the lives of women in the settlement of the Pennsylvania colony.

The Puritan Search for Order: The Family and the Law

In contrast to virtually all other groups of Europeans who settled on the North American continent, the Puritans did not send men alone: nearly three-quarters of Puritan migrants to New England came in family groups that included wives and daughters. Puritan notions of marriage combined mutuality and hierarchy. Husband and wife had reciprocal responsibilities, were enjoined to recognize their mutual dependence, and were charged with creating social order and community virtue together through their domestic conduct. As one historian puts it, they were "sturdy mates and fellow travelers on the road to salvation."[15] At the same time, male headship characterized their families, and wives were clearly secondary to their husbands. Indeed, female deference to male authority was the Puritans' model for humanity's relation to God.

New England women married early and had an astonishingly high childbirth rate, considerably more than women in England or the Chesapeake colonies. First-generation Plymouth women bore an average of 7.8 children, the majority of whom lived to adulthood. Within Puritan ideology, the family stood as a lynchpin of social order, a value that was magnified by the frontier conditions of the New World. Although Puritans encouraged love and respect within the family, each person's role was clearly delineated by gender and age. So crucial was the family unit to social order that single adults were required to live with a family to ensure their righteous behavior.

Religion also shaped New England laws governing marriage and women's status. The Massachusetts colonies followed the English principle of *feme covert*. However, Puritans, in keeping with Protestant Reformation theology, viewed marriage as a civil contract rather than as a religious sacrament; thus they permitted divorce, offering women more legal options than they had in England. Nonetheless, remarriage was rarely allowed and women were still legally subordinate. A woman might be released from marriage to a husband who abandoned his family completely, but while married, she had to obey her husband's decisions, even if those decisions included abusive behavior.

The Puritan moral code, at least in the early years of settlement, punished both men and women—though not equally—for sexual crimes such as intercourse outside of marriage. Despite popular notions of Puritans as sexually repressed, they valued sexual pleasure for men and women within marriage, though they viewed extramarital sexuality as damaging to social order and Christian piety. Puritan religious leaders in both Europe and New England sought to reform the indulgent sexual culture of their times, but with mixed success. In New England, premarital pregnancy was fairly common: records for the 1690s in New Haven County, Connecticut, for example, reveal that 19 percent of women were already pregnant at the time of their marriage.[16] For the most part, neither men nor women were harshly condemned as long as the couple married, but an unmarried woman giving birth was pressured to name the father so that he could care for her and the child, preventing them from becoming burdens on the community. A liaison between a married man and an unmarried woman was a less serious offense than that between a married woman and an unmarried man. The former crime was deemed "fornication," while the latter was given the much more serious label of "adultery." As Puritan William Gouge put it, a woman's crime created "greater infamy before men, worse disturbance of the family, more mistaking of legitimate, or illegitimate children."[17] Similarly, the rape of a married woman was regarded, in the words of one historian, as "not the offense against the woman but the offense against her husband."[18]

Women's subordination to men was evident throughout Puritan society. Although the New England colonies mandated that all children be taught to read so that they could study the Scriptures (and women did have a high literacy rate), few girls attended school. Not surprisingly, few women wrote diaries or books. (See Primary Sources: "By and About Colonial Women," pp. 81–91.) Only four women authors were represented in the 911 books produced in seventeenth-century New England. Of these, the most famous was Anne Bradstreet, whose works included *The Tenth Muse, Lately Sprung Up in America* (1650) and the posthumously published *Several Poems Compiled with Great Variety of Wit and Learning* (1678).

Bradstreet's brother, the pastor Thomas Parker, wrote to Bradstreet, "Your printing of a Book, beyond the custom of your sex, doth rankly smell."[19]

Mary Rowlandson's *A True History of the Captivity and Restoration of Mrs. Mary Rowlandson* (1677) was also one of the most important books authored by a North American woman. Rowlandson, who had emigrated from England in 1639, wrote powerfully about her captivity and enslavement during the brutal colonist/Indian conflict known as King Philip's War (1675–1676; King Philip was the colonists' name for the Wampanoag leader Metacom). During this conflict, which coincided with Bacon's Rebellion in Virginia and reflected the Indians' growing desperation at the hands of whites, one thousand white colonists and three thousand Nipmucs, Wampanoags, and Narragansetts were killed. Half the towns of Massachusetts were attacked, including Lancaster, where Rowlandson and her minister husband lived. Rowlandson's tale of her captivity includes her interactions with her mistress, Weetamoo, Metacom's sister-in-law and a powerful woman in her own right. Among other things, Rowlandson survived by sewing shirts and stockings for her Indian captors, who appreciated her skill with a needle. Eventually she was ransomed by Massachusetts authorities. When the conflict ended, both Metacom and Weetamoo were killed, and their families sold into slavery in the West Indies. King Philip's War was a watershed in the history of New England. In the aftermath of the war, Native American survivors looked for safety by adopting English customs while others joined distant relatives in Canada or west of the

◆ Esther Wheelwright

Esther Wheelwright (1696–1780), who was born into a Puritan family in Maine, became an Ursuline nun after being captured and adopted by a Catholic Wabanaki family. When New England soldiers retaliated, the Wabanaki band who raised Esther took shelter in mission towns near Quebec. Esther lived as a Wabanaki girl from ages seven to twelve and then enrolled as a student at a nearby Ursuline convent school in 1709. In later life, she became Mother Superior of the convent. This oil painting was most likely painted by a sister artist, as the Ursulines were known for their fine brushwork. Her biographer notes that "across every political, religious, and linguistic border, Esther was surrounded by communities of women."[20] How do her experiences of religion in the northeastern colonial borderlands compare with those of Mary Rowlandson and Kateri Tekakwitha, also discussed in this chapter? *Massachusetts Historical Society, Boston, MA, USA/Bridgeman Images.*

Hudson River. Rowlandson viewed her own survival and rescue as a sign of God's blessing on the Puritan community.

While Puritan leaders valued Rowlandson for her pious example, they drew clear rules to discipline women who presumed to offer their own doctrinal interpretations. Even though Puritan women shared with men the right to be members of the church once they satisfactorily testified to their salvation, the clergy and other male community leaders periodically punished or banished heretical women who challenged male authority.

Disorderly Women

In the 1630s, Massachusetts leaders faced a major controversy regarding both religious orthodoxy and gender assumptions: the case of Anne Hutchinson. Hutchinson, a midwife, arrived in the colony with her merchant husband in 1634 and began her religious proselytizing among women only. She believed that people were "saved" by a direct infusion of God's spirit and contended that the Puritan ministers were wrong in preaching that salvation came from earthly obedience to Puritan laws. Her provocation went even deeper than her theological notions; she also contested the status of women in the Puritan religious world, if only by her assertion of religious authority. Hutchinson began holding informal religious meetings in her home that included both men and women. Although male leaders worried that her radical religious views were heretical and posed a threat to the colony, their court proceedings focused on her behavior as a woman: in their view, Hutchinson had "rather been a Husband than a Wife and a preacher than a Hearer; and a Magistrate than a Subject."[21] Trial records indicate that Hutchinson ably defended both her religious ideas and her right as a woman to expound upon them. However, after days of unrelenting interrogation, she made the mistake of openly claiming to have received direct revelation from God. The Puritan magistrates used this statement as evidence that she was "delusional." Excommunicated and banished, she moved first to Rhode Island, established in 1636 as a haven for the growing number of refugees from Massachusetts orthodoxy, before finally settling in New Netherland, where she died during an indigenous attack on the Dutch settlement (see Reading into the Past: "Trial of Anne Hutchinson").

The Hutchinson controversy represented not just a theological position that attracted men and women but also an undercurrent of female rebelliousness that community leaders felt compelled to repress. In the aftermath of Hutchinson's trial, churches began to drop the requirement that women make their conversion statements publicly. Instead they could relay their experience to their ministers who, in turn, would convey their words to the congregation. Moreover, one historian has found that during this crisis the percentage of female defendants brought before the courts rose significantly. Either women were becoming more assertive or the magistrates were becoming more determined to discipline them.

The most dramatic kind of disorderly act associated with women was witchcraft. Of the 344 people accused of being witches in the colonial period, 80 percent were female; of the men accused, half were relatives of accused women. Two major witch hunts occurred in New England: one during the period 1647–1663, in which seventy-nine people were accused and fifteen hanged, and an even larger episode in 1692, in Salem, Massachusetts, in which over two hundred were accused and nineteen were hanged.

Witchcraft was a complex crime. Sometimes women associated with heresy were charged with being Satan's servants. Many of Anne Hutchinson's critics, for example, hinted that she was a witch. For others, it was less their religious positions than their *maleficia*, or malicious actions against their neighbors, that brought such women to trial. Did milk sour, an animal die, a child take sick? Did a midwife assist at — or perhaps cause — a deformed birth? Did young girls have fits and see an unpopular village woman in spirit form? Did men believe themselves sexually ravaged by a neighbor woman with supernatural powers? (See Primary Sources: "By and About Colonial Women," pp. 81–91.)

The finger often pointed at an older, poor, and powerless woman. She might have a reputation for being argumentative, discontented, or prideful. She might also be suspected of causing abortion, committing infanticide, or, if she were a midwife, using her healing power for ill instead of good. Another major category of witches — more evident in the Salem cases — were those with some measure of authority or prestige. For example, a widow engaged in a dispute with her husband's heirs over property rights was a likely candidate for suspicion. Indeed, as the frenzy escalated in Salem, some elite men and women were accused by young women who claimed the witches had "possessed" them. The young women's accusations gave them an unprecedented opportunity to influence community affairs and to exercise a degree of power, thus complicating the gendered dimensions of the incidents. Indeed, the clergy and the magistrates quickly lost control of the situation and ceased to support the prosecutions. Eventually, the governor of Massachusetts interceded and brought the trials to a halt in 1692.

What accounts for these tumultuous outbursts of witchcraft accusations? Most historians believe that societal tensions laid the groundwork. Many Salem residents were refugees from violent Indian wars on the southern Maine frontier. The Salem cases suggest a link between the community's susceptibility to believing in the malevolent power of witches among them (and those witches' ability, for example, to aid the "heathen" Indians in massacring the Christian colonists) and the insecurities of living near the frontier at a time of heightened Indian resistance to colonial encroachment. In addition, by the 1690s the stability of New England's Puritan order was being eroded by the growth of trade, an influx of immigrants, and the inroads of secularism and materialism. These tensions were compounded by a rise in population that put pressure on available land, which in turn created intergenerational tensions as young people chafed at the older generation's control of family property. While these anxieties help to explain the dynamics of witchcraft accusations, they do not fully explain why the witch hunts had such a strong gendered component. Whatever the source of the frenzy, the accused women had seemingly violated their prescribed gender roles.

READING INTO THE PAST

Trial of Anne Hutchinson

This excerpt from the published transcript of the 1637 trial of Anne Hutchinson (1591–1643) before a panel of Massachusetts Bay colony judges headed by Governor John Winthrop can only begin to suggest the theological intricacies of the interrogation. Hutchinson's religious crimes were several. Not only did she act in the male role of a religious teacher, but she compounded this crime by ministering to men as well as women. She was further accused of preaching various doctrines contrary to Puritan teaching. Not reflected in this excerpt is an intricate debate between Hutchinson and Winthrop about whether she diverged from the Protestant belief in salvation by God's grace to advocate the doctrine of salvation by "works," that is, human effort.

GOV.: Why do you keep such a meeting at your house as you do every week upon a set day? . . .

MRS. H.: I conceive there lyes a clear rule in Titus [Titus 11:3–5], that the elder women should instruct the young and then I must have a time wherein I must do it. . . . If any come to my house to be instructed in the ways of God what rule have I to put them away? . . .

GOV.: But suppose that a hundred men come unto you to be instructed will you forbear to instruct them? . . .

MRS. H.: No Sir for my ground is they are men. . . .

GOV.: You must shew your rule to receive them.

MRS. H.: I have done it.

GOV.: I deny it because I have brought more arguments than you have.

MRS. H.: I say, to me it is a rule. . . .

GOV.: . . . [W]e must therefore . . . restrain you from maintaining this course. . . . We are your judges, and not you ours and we must compel you to it. . . .

Women's Work and Consumption Patterns

Only a small minority of women were involved in the dramatic events connected to mid- to late seventeenth-century witch hunts or religious dissent. Most New England women led ordinary, work-filled lives. Wealthier women's labor was less physically demanding than poorer or rural women's, but all women's work was valued for its contribution to the family economy. The division of labor followed

MRS. H.: It is one thing for me to come before a public magistracy and there to speak what they would have me to speak and another when a man comes to me in a way of friendship privately there is difference in that. . . . [I]f you do condemn me for speaking what in my conscience I know to be truth I must commit myself unto the Lord.

MR. NOWEL [ASSISTANT TO THE COURT]: How do you know that that was the spirit?

MRS. H.: How did Abraham know that it was God that bid him offer his son . . . ? . . . So to me by an immediate revelation. . . .

DEP. GOV.: How! an immediate revelation. . . .

MRS. H.: By the voice of his own spirit to my soul. . . .

GOV.: . . . [T]he ground work of her revelations is the immediate revelation of the spirit and not by the ministry of the word, and that is the means by which she has very much abused the country that they shall look for revelations and are not bound to the ministry of the Word, but God will teach them by immediate revelations and this hath been the ground of all these tumult and troubles. . . . [T]he sentence of the court you hear is that you are banished from out of our jurisdiction as being a woman not fit for our society. . . .

SOURCE: Mr. [Thomas] Hutchinson, *The History of the Province of Massachusets-Bay, From the Charter of King William and Queen Mary in 1691, Until the Year 1750,* vol. 2, 2nd ed. (London: Printed by J. Smith, 1828), 484–87, 489, 508, 513, 520.

QUESTIONS FOR ANALYSIS

1. How does Hutchinson threaten ministerial authority when she claims to receive a direct revelation from God?

2. What does Winthrop's last comment here reveal about his central criticism of Hutchinson and her spiritual errors?

English patterns: men's duties concentrated outside the home in farming, fishing, or trade; women's duties centered within the home around food preparation, childbearing, and childrearing. Goodwives, as hard-working married women were called, tended domestic animals and vegetable gardens, and fashioned meals with the few cooking utensils available. They produced their own candles, soap, thread, cloth, and clothing.

Women created networks of female friends and relatives to help with their tasks. Since few women were mistresses of all necessary household trades, they usually bartered among themselves for necessities, especially in more remote areas where women's lives were harder and their time more constrained. Women trained their own daughters in wifely responsibilities and often took in daughters of neighbors to apprentice them in exchange for their household labor. And for another form of distinctly female labor—childbirth—women came together in close communion, often spending days at a prospective mother's home, giving practical assistance and emotional comfort during a time when almost one in ten New England women died during childbirth or of related complications.

Midwives were central figures in the New England world of women; their existence demonstrates that women could and did engage in work beyond their own homes. They generally were highly respected and often tended to other ailments with herbal remedies. Their assistance was rewarded with payment in kind—chickens, eggs, cloth, sugar, and so on—or with coin from more prosperous citizens. Occasionally other women, too, moved outside the sexual division of labor. If her husband was away hunting, serving in the militia, or trading, a wife could conduct family business or represent her husband in legal matters. Widows, who as *femes sole* could act on their own, ran taverns, inns, or printing establishments. Many took pride in their abilities to manage their estates. Bostonian Ann Pollard reported that "[by my] own proper gettings by my Labour and Industry [the estate of my husband] is Considerably Advanced and bettered."[22]

As the colonies' commerce increased, mercantile cities such as New York, Philadelphia, Boston, and Charleston grew in size and importance. At the same time, King William's War (1689–1697) and Queen Anne's War (1702–1713), European conflicts that also played out in the American colonial empires, created a dramatic rise in widows, who with their children often moved to urban centers like Boston, where widows represented 16 percent of the population by 1725. Poorer town women, encouraged to work by community leaders eager to keep them off the charity rolls, found employment as seamstresses and in other trades that drew on their wifely skills. Shopkeeping was another avenue for urban women, and historians estimate that between 1740 and 1775, more than ninety Boston women operated commercial enterprises.

In addition to urban/rural distinctions, other divisions were growing in New England. Approximately 3 percent of working women in eighteenth-century New England were African slaves. Northern slaveholders tended to have small numbers of slaves (one or two) and to buy and sell them frequently in response to labor demands, making it difficult for slaves to form families. Most northern slaves lived in the cities, where they worked as domestic servants and contributed to the leisure of their white mistresses, usually the wives of merchants, professionals, and craftsmen. For these prosperous women and their daughters, increased free time contributed to changes in their daily lives. Some took up activities like fancy needlework that demonstrated their genteel feminine skills. Well-to-do women increasingly bought what they needed instead of making it themselves, and imported goods were especially popular. Boston milliner and merchant Elizabeth Murray offered satin gloves, ebony fans, and ermine muffs. Although this kind of opulence was unusual, it pointed to the emergence of a consumer culture in urban areas.

This consumer culture was part of a broad pattern of economic change evident in New England life, especially after 1700. High childbirth rates and immigration from numerous nations meant that the population of the four New England colonies (Massachusetts, Connecticut, Rhode Island, and New Hampshire) doubled every twenty-five years—in 1775 it was 345,000. As urban areas and commerce grew and class distinctions increased, men, increasingly focused on economic success, moved away from religion, leaving women to predominate in most churches; thus began a distinctive association of women with moral and spiritual matters that deepened over time (see pp. 130–33). Puritans' political control slipped as well, as the British Crown revoked the Massachusetts charter in 1684. In a new charter of 1692, the influence of the Puritan church was greatly reduced when property holding, not church membership, became the basis for freeman—and voting—status.

Some scholars argue that the breakdown of the Puritan commonwealth also eroded the power of the patriarchal family, giving women a greater degree of freedom. Certainly new prosperity and urban growth stimulated female education and opened increased economic opportunities for some women. Changes in church membership patterns gave women more voice in the religious sphere of life, but at a time when church influence was declining. Perhaps the most significant change toward the end of the colonial period in New England was the increased diversification in women's lives—the continued hard labor on the farms, the variety of work in the cities, the increased presence of female slaves as servants, and new goods for consumption for prosperous urban women. These patterns pointed to the segmentation of women's communities that would persist throughout the course of American history, in New England and beyond.

Dissenters from Dissenters: Women in Pennsylvania

Although the Puritans had come to North America to be able to practice their own religion free from persecution in England, they did not tolerate dissent in their own midst. Another group of dissenting English Protestants, the Quakers, who did not rely on an institutionalized clergy (and thus allowed for a much greater religious role for women), were banned in Massachusetts. Mary Dyer, a follower of Anne Hutchinson, was hanged in Boston in 1660 when she returned from exile as a Quaker. In 1681, Quaker William Penn received a charter from the British king giving him authority to establish a colony in the lands west of the Delaware River that had once been part of New Netherland. Pennsylvania was thus founded as a haven for the beleaguered Quakers.

Quaker women had no distinctive economic privileges, yet religious values made their society unusually egalitarian. The Quakers believed that "the Inner Light of Christ" was available equally to all. This experience stressed the individual's direct relationship with God and deemphasized ceremony and sermonizing. Among American Quakers, a number of women, such as Elizabeth Norris of Philadelphia, were noted for articulating the idea that women should not be subordinate to men. In contrast

READING INTO THE PAST

JANE FENN HOSKENS
Quaker Preacher

Jane Fenn Hoskens (1694–1764) emigrated from England to Philadelphia in 1712. She spent a brief time in debtor's prison after refusing to sign indenture papers that contradicted her agreement with the man who paid her passage, but she was rescued by Quakers, to whom she became indentured as a teacher. She eventually became a Quaker, but was often tormented by religious doubts. Her account of her experiences, published in 1771, was the first spiritual autobiography written by an American Quaker woman. Hoskens became a religious teacher and traveled throughout the eastern colonies and to Britain speaking at Quaker meetings. Here she describes how powerfully she was affected by Elizabeth Lewis's preaching.

I had not appeared in public for a great while, nor felt any motions that way; but was very slow in my mind, and being got in a dark spot, had again almost lost hope, and thought impossible but that I should fall a sacrifice to the temptations of the grand enemy, who still followed me; however it happened that friend Lewis came to visit Haverford meeting, where I then was; after some time of silence she stood up, and (speaking in the authority of truth) so effectually laid open my present state, that I could heartily subscribe to the truth of the testimony; the power that attended her ministry reached the witness of God in my heart; a zeal was begotten in me for the honor of the good cause; and I was filled with love to the instrument through whom I had thus been favoured. — Hope was

to the Puritan effort to suppress women's religious speech, Quaker women were often respected religious teachers, in part because religious ministry was not ordained or institutionalized among them (see Reading into the Past: "Quaker Preacher").

Quaker institutions reflected women's high status. In Pennsylvania, women's local monthly groups sent representatives to quarterly meetings, which in turn sent representatives to the annual convocation in Philadelphia. Created "for the better management of the discipline and other affairs of the church more proper to be inspected by their sex," the meetings monitored family life in the community.[23] In particular they forwarded petitions that determined whether a betrothed couple embraced appropriate Quaker values. By formalizing the responsibility of some Quaker matrons to monitor the behavior of other women, Quaker practice offered an additional degree of religious authority to women.

again renewed in me, that by virtue of the word preached, the Lord would still continue his wonted favours to me, in preserving me from the snares of the wicked one. — After meeting she took kind notice of me, and said, I came here to day through the cross, the Lord knows for what end; it may be for thy sake: I was so overcome I could not speak, but wept much, and esteemed it as a blessing she had taken notice of me. — I went home rejoicing in spirit, because I had met with divine refreshment which I was in much need of. As it pleased the Almighty to visit me in a wonderful manner, by the renewing of pure love, I made covenant that if he would be with me in the way I should go, he should be my God, and I would serve him forever. And as this disposition increased, I felt the unity of the one spirit to his dear hand-maid, and in that we became near and dear to each other, and in process of time we joined as companions in the work of the gospel, as I shall here-after have occasion to mention in the course of this account.

SOURCE: *The Life and Spiritual Sufferings of That Faithful Servant of Christ Jane Hoskens, a Public Preacher among the People Called Quakers* (1771), 17, Digital Commons, University of Nebraska, Electronic Texts in American Studies, http://digitalcommons.unl .edu/etas/24.

QUESTION FOR ANALYSIS

1. How does this selection about Quaker female spiritual leadership contrast with the document concerning Anne Hutchinson's trial (pp. 66–67)?

Pennsylvania Quakers' relation to African slavery was complex. On the one hand, British Quakers were among the first to develop a full-fledged critique of slavery as a violation of God's law. On the other hand, the leadership of the Quaker community in Pennsylvania was made up of wealthy merchants, for whom traffic in slaves was an important element of their trade. As a result, about 20 to 30 percent of Pennsylvania's labor force before 1750 consisted of slaves and at least 10 percent of Philadelphia Quakers were slaveowners. A combination of religious objections and the migration of Germans and other immigrants to work as indentured servants in Pennsylvania's fertile farmlands led to a gradual decline in dependence on African slavery. Sometime after 1760, a slave woman named Margaret, already married to a free black man, secured her freedom; though in her forties, she began to have children, knowing they would be free. Her son James Forten became leader of the strongest free black community in British America.

◆ BEYOND THE BRITISH SETTLER COLONIES

Despite the growing size and strength of the British colonies, the North American continent continued to be the site of other European nations' expansionist hopes, and Native American persistence. As with North America's indigenous peoples, European groups too had their differences. Cultural variation went hand in hand with different economic purposes and gender patterns in colonial endeavors. For example, the Dutch, though also Protestant, competed fiercely with England in matters of trade. In addition, both the Spanish and the French kept their agricultural and settlement projects to a minimum, concentrating, especially in the French case, on trade. Thus their need for female labor and family formation were considerably less and their toleration for marriages with Native Americans much greater. Native Americans incorporated new European goods into their economies and, where possible, developed new strategies of defending their borders.

New Netherland

The Dutch sojourn in North America was the briefest, lasting only from 1614 to 1664. The center of New Netherland was the port town of New Amsterdam (later New York City). In 1647, the stern reformer Peter Stuyvesant was brought in to administer the colony; he relinquished his post when the British laid claim to it in 1664.

Women's lives in New Netherland differed from those in the British colonies. Although both societies paid a great deal of attention to proper domestic arrangements, Dutch women had more legal rights and economic authority. In contrast to the British concept of *feme covert*, Dutch women could choose a form of marriage in which women were considered their husband's partners and maintained their independent legal identities. Husband and wife viewed their possessions as community property and usually constructed a mutual will, in which each left the estate to the other, postponing the children's inheritance until both died. Married women could and did own property and manage their own businesses.

Margaret Hardenbroeck perfectly exemplified a New Netherland businesswoman. She immigrated to North America in 1659 and established herself as a successful trader who represented other merchants as well. When she married her first husband, she maintained her business and at his death became even wealthier. In her second marriage, the couple drew up a marriage contract that delineated her control over her own property and ensured that she would be able to continue her commercial activities. Husband and wife were highly successful traders and partners in their own shipping enterprise, often acting as each other's agent in business matters and in court.

In part because of the prominent role that the Dutch played in the slave trade, New Amsterdam was home to many enslaved Africans, and substantial numbers of slaves were shipped through the port. African men worked on the wharves, and African women were domestic servants to wealthy families. (Stuyvesant himself owned forty slaves.) Concentrated in one city, slaves could develop explosive discontent, and there were at least two slave uprisings in New Amsterdam in the seventeenth century. In 1991, an excavation of an African burial ground in lower Manhattan unearthed the remains of a twenty-two-year-old woman with a musket ball lodged near her ribs, a likely casualty of one of these upheavals.[24]

The great growth in the New York slave population occurred under the British, and most of it was urban. By the middle of the eighteenth century, 20 percent of New York City's population was black and half of the households in the cities owned slaves. Thus most slaves were isolated in white households, separated from partners and children. Unlike black men, who frequently learned skilled crafts

◆ **_Nieu Amsterdam_ (c. 1670)**

This late seventeenth-century copper engraving displays New Amsterdam, its bustling trade, and diverse population in panoramic view. In the foreground, a well-dressed European man displays the tobacco leaves soon to be shipped to Europe in the barrel immediately behind him. He calls the viewers' attention to the productivity of the well-dressed European woman holding a basket of agricultural goods. In the background, a very early Manhattan skyline signals the industry of the port. Analyzing these buildings, scholars have dated the scene portrayed to around 1642. What does the prominence of African men and women laboring in the background suggest about the relationship between Dutch prosperity and the slave trade? Compare the depiction of the African woman to the Dutch woman. What gendered divisions of labor are suggested by the image, and how have early ideas about race shaped these gendered divisions? _From The New York Public Library._

from their masters, slave women did common household labor. A 1734 ad for the sale of a twenty-year-old slave woman emphasized that "she does all sorts of house-work, she can brew, bake, boil soft soap, wash, iron and starch and is a good dairy woman, she can card and spin at the great wheel."

New Amsterdam was also the home to some of the first Jews to arrive in North America. Many European Jews, expelled from Spain and Portugal, had migrated to the Netherlands. Some went on to Dutch colonies in the New World, where toler-ance was considerably less. Among the first Jews to arrive in North America were twenty-three people, including six women and thirteen children, who had been driven out of another Dutch colony, Recife, Brazil, in 1654. Jews suffered under the haughty anti-Semitism of Peter Stuyvesant but were determined to remain and re-create their community. Miriam Israel Levy, the widow of one of the men in the original group, followed the Dutch practice of serving as executor of her husband's estate.[25] Even after the Dutch lost control of the colony to the British, Dutch Jews continued to migrate to New York, sometimes intermarrying with British colonists.

When the English conquered New Netherland, they decreed that Dutch inheritance laws could be sustained and Dutch contracts honored. However, as more English people settled in New York, they implemented English common law practices that circumscribed married women's property rights. Dutch women gradually became less visible in the public sphere. In Albany, for example, forty-six women were listed as traders before the British conquest, but by the turn of the eighteenth century, there were none. Women's names also became less preva-lent in the rosters of skilled artisans and proprietors — brewers, bakers, and the like — and women were less likely to appear in court representing themselves or others. Margaret Hardenbroeck continued her business ventures, but when she bought land in New Jersey, her husband had to make the purchase for her. In 1710, the New York assembly passed a law that placed married women in the same legal category as minors and people of unsound mind. All these people presumably were not capable of acting on their own. Perhaps the reversal of women's property rights contributed to making New York the birth place of American women's fight for equal economic rights in the nineteenth century.

New France

New France was a large territory, covering almost as much of North America as the lands claimed by the British. Beginning in 1608 with the small settlement of Quebec, traders and missionaries spread south and west through the Great Lakes region and down the Mississippi, ultimately founding the city of New Orleans in 1718. Lightly populated and barely supported by the French Crown, New France was organized as a series of small communities closely linked to Indian villages. Although some farming took place, the major focus was trade, not agricultural set-tlement. Emigration from France was almost entirely made up of single men until between 1663 and 1673, when almost eight hundred marriageable women, known as *filles du roi* ("the king's daughters"), were shipped to Quebec; the families they formed with French men grew rapidly. Still, by 1700, the population amounted to less than 20 percent of British America's and included a substantial portion descended from the liaisons of French men and Native women.[26] Native wives of French traders along with the French religious women who worked to convert these *métis*, or mixed-race, families to Catholicism were important historical actors in the growth of New France.

The fur traders who moved into the upper Great Lakes and Illinois territories learned quickly that connection to a Native woman through the practice of country marriage (see p. 21) was the most important resource a French man could have on the frontier. Ojibwa, Huron, Illini, Missouri, and Osage women had excellent fur-preparation skills, could act as translators, and, most important, connected European traders to the Indian societies that provided them their wares. Native women retained their relatively easy rights of divorce and the ability to retreat back into their birth families. At the same time, country marriages gave Native women more direct access to trading goods, such as the prized European cloth most frequently exchanged for Indian furs. Native wives gave their European husbands, in the words of one historian, "an entrée into the cultures and communities of their own people. In this way, Indian women were the first important mediators of meaning between the cultures of two worlds."[27]

By the eighteenth century, however, increasing numbers of these French/Native alliances were undertaken with the blessings of the church. Native women seem to have been more attracted to Catholicism than their menfolk were. Some historians see conversion as providing Native women with external resources as they became major conduits for the expansion of Catholicism into Native lands. Others argue that Catholic conversion, with its encouragement of female submission, destroyed these women's traditional sources of strength and independence. Either interpretation can be sustained by the experience of the Kaskaskia woman Aramapinchue, renamed Marie Rouensa. When her father urged her to marry a dissolute French trader in 1694, she was reluctant; already a convert, she turned to her priest, who supported her, telling her parents that "she alone was mistress" of her own life and decisions. In the end, Aramapinchue agreed to the marriage on the condition that her parents convert to Catholicism. Was this her assertion or her concession to the church's priorities?[28]

French Catholic women exerted influence in France's efforts to convert American Indians. Particularly important in this regard were the Ursulines, a religious order with a special commitment to the education of women. Marie de l'Incarnation, a woman with great energy and organizational gifts, came from Rouen, France, in 1639 to establish the first Ursuline community in New France. Although she was successful in establishing a community of Ursuline sisters in Quebec, she did not convert as many young Huron women as she had hoped would spread the faith among the Native population. The second Ursuline convent in North America was more successful in its educational mission. It opened in New Orleans in 1727, charged by French authorities with helping to clean up the chronically disorderly and raucous port city. The girls who boarded at the convent school included Europeans, free blacks, enslaved Africans, and Indians. Marie Charlotte, a mulatto, was sent to the sisters by the terms of her dead father's will. An unnamed Osage young

◆ **Kateri Tekakwitha**
Kateri Tekakwitha exemplified the attraction Catholicism held for many Native women whose lives were upended by violence and Old World diseases. Daughter of an Algonquian mother and Mohawk father (both of whom died of smallpox), Kateri arrived at a Jesuit mission near Montreal in 1677, already a convert. She developed a following of Native women who physically tortured themselves to demonstrate their faith. After her death in 1680, she became associated with miracles and healing, heightening the veneration she is still accorded today (she was canonized in 2012). This 1690 painting of Kateri, by Father Chauchetière, hangs in the St. Francis-Xavier Church in Kahnawake, Quebec, Canada.
AP Photo/Alessandra Tarantino.

woman was also entrusted to the convent by her owner upon his death. Although distinctions of race and hierarchies of class certainly existed in the New Orleans Ursuline community, the sisters succeeded remarkably well in creating, in the words of its historian, "a shared femininity that cut across disparate geographic origins."[29]

New Spain

In 1608, the same year in which the French established Quebec City, the Spanish established Santa Fe in the heart of Pueblo territory (see pp. 19–20) as a center for their soldiers, administrators, and merchants. Throughout the seventeenth century, tensions were building both among and between Natives and colonists. Priests and soldier/settlers had very different ideas about how to absorb Indians—as a tributary labor force or as converted Christians. The Pueblos' resentment over their economic and physical exploitation and the failure of the Spanish god to protect them from disease and abuse led to what became known as the Pueblo Revolt. In 1680, only a few years after both King Philip's War in New England and Bacon's Rebellion in Virginia, Pueblo peoples drove the Spanish out of New Mexico. In the aftermath, the revolt's leaders did all they could to rid the Pueblos of Christianity and return to the traditional religions exemplified by the corn mothers who had given birth to the world as they once knew it (see pp. 7–9).

One of the most important areas of Native restoration was with respect to women, marriage, and gender roles. Spanish priests had sought to impose monogamous marriages on the Pueblos, angering Pueblo men and helping to spark the revolt. It is not clear to what extent Native women welcomed back their indigenous spiritual and sexual powers, nor is it known how much they missed the new kinds of protection that Catholicism and the Spanish military presence had offered them. After twelve years, colonial forces retook Santa Fe and killed or enslaved the Native rebels, including four hundred women and children. From this point on, Spanish control over the colony went largely uncontested.

Native Grounds of the North American Interior

In the continent's heartland, neither French nor Spanish colonists succeeded in controlling terms of engagement with Native groups. In the Arkansas River Valley (present day Arkansas, Oklahoma, and Kansas), for example, Quapaws who had newly migrated to the valley in the mid-seventeenth century used alliances with French traders to establish their own sovereignty. Rather than being conquered or mounting a war of resistance, the Quapaws incorporated French traders into their political networks. Quapaw women, however, contributed essential agricultural goods used in gift-exchange rituals that forged interdependent relations with Europeans and other Indian groups. The ability of Quapaw society to retain relative control over their "native ground," may have been rooted in their patrilineal rules of descent.[30] In contrast to Algonquian matrilineal practices, the Quapaw patrilineal system meant that mothers and children of such unions would no longer belong to Quapaw society. French priests may have encouraged intermarriages for purposes of cultural assimilation and conversation, but Quapaws rejected these suggestions to guard their political strength well into the eighteenth century.

To the west and south of Quapaw native ground, Comanches used the upheaval of the early colonial period to create a new equestrian empire on the grassy plains between 1700 and 1750. Indigenous groups living in the New Mexico mountains appropriated horses, guns, and metal goods left behind when the Spanish retreated after the Pueblo Revolt. From a small, relatively egalitarian group of hunter-gatherers, the Comanche grew in population, centered their culture around equestrian prowess and bison hunting, and intensified their trading relations with markets in New Mexico. Their military strength proved highly significant in preventing French and Spanish colonists from setting up permanent posts in a wide swath of land stretching from present-day eastern New Mexico to northern Texas.

Women's labor — free and enslaved — proved central to Comanche expansion. The increased emphasis on warfare heightened the cultural value of the male lineage head, whose prestige came from raiding and hunting exploits. Masculine respect and honor rested on a Comanche man's "ability to protect and expand his kinship network."[31] Women and child captives of raided Apache, Pawnee, and Navajo towns could be incorporated into Comanche lineages or sold as slaves to the Spanish. At the same time, Comanche women and girls also grew skilled in horse riding, as entire families traveled on horseback. To traditional female skills of food gathering and child care, women now added care of horses, leather skills for making harnesses and halters, and curing of bison hides, all critical to Comanche trade relations. Without women's skills and the exchange of female captives, the Comanche people could not have taken and held their sovereign ground.

◆ *Comanche Village, Women Dressing Robes and Drying Meat*
George Catlin, riding with the U.S. dragoons, painted this image in 1835 when his unit encountered a Comanche encampment near the Wichita Mountains. Although he portrayed the Comanche empire at a later phase of its history, the work of processing bison meat and hides belonged to women, even in the eighteenth century. *Smithsonian American Art Museum, Washington, DC/Art Resource, NY.*

◆ CONCLUSION: The Diversity of American Women

As diverse as the lives of North American women were in the seventeenth and eighteenth centuries, there were some commonalities. All women operated within a fairly rigid sexual division of labor, although the actual tasks assigned to them varied from culture to culture. Most women's roles included childbearing, childrearing, and food preparation. Within their communities, women tended to form strong bonds with other women in similar circumstances — whether grinding corn in the Pueblo communities, planting it in Iroquoia, bartering in female networks in New England, or forming supportive communities of slave women in the southern British colonies. With some exceptions, women shared an exclusion from direct political participation. They also shared the burdens — which varied widely — of adjusting to the new societies created by both contact and conflict in North America.

Despite these commonalities, the differences among women of this period were striking. With the emergence of transgenerational chattel slavery, the legal significance of African women's childbearing veered sharply away from that of European and many Native American women. Not only were there significant variations among Native American, African, and European women, there were also differences within each group. Native American women encompassed perhaps the richest cultural variety. But Africans as well represented various linguistic, religious, and political backgrounds. Among European women, too, distinctions emerged. Between first- and second-generation settlers, there were major differences in quality of life, especially in the southern colonies. Beyond that, ethnic, religious, and regional differences proved powerful determinants of women's legal and economic circumstances. And by the mid-eighteenth century, class — both in growing cities and in the plantation regions of the South — had become as important as any other factor that shaped women's experiences.

Earlier generations of historians tended to see the colonial period as a monolithic one in which women's lives were static. Reading back from nineteenth-century middle-class gender roles, which relegated women firmly to the private world of the home, the white colonial women's participation in a preindustrial household economy can be seen as empowering. A similar tendency to romanticize the hard life of Native American women contrasted their freedom and influence with the patriarchal structure within which European women lived. Although comparisons are perhaps inevitable, they can obscure the complexities of women's lives — both the diversity that characterized them and the points of common ground they shared. Such comparisons also deflect attention from the historical changes that shaped these women's lives: the challenge to Native American sovereignty, the importation and enslavement of Africans, the massive migration of Europeans, and the economic and political maturation of the British colonies.

CHAPTER 2 REVIEW

KEY TERMS AND PEOPLE

Terms
"tobacco brides"
feme covert/feme sole
Bacon's Rebellion
partus sequitur ventrem
Puritans
Salem witch trials
Quakers

filles du roi
Ursuline sisters
Pueblo Revolt
Comanche empire

People
Hannah Swarton
Margaret Brent

Mary Rowlandson
Esther Wheelwright
Anne Hutchinson
Margaret Hardenbroeck
Kateri Tekakwitha

REVIEW QUESTIONS

1. Compare the information offered by Maps 2.1 and 2.2. How did the expansion of European colonization in the Americas create a "new world" for Native Americans and, in particular, Native American women? How would the answer to this question vary depending on the perspective of Powhatan, Iroquois, Comanche, and Pueblo peoples?

2. How did laws passed in seventeenth-century Virginia related specifically to African women serve to institutionalize a system of chattel slavery?

3. How did the lives of planter-class women differ from indentured European and enslaved African women?

4. How did Christianity shape northern free women's identity and family relations? How did both church and state respond to women who were considered "disorderly"?

5. **Making Connections** Given the wide diversity of women in colonial North America, can you name any similarities in women's experiences across cultures and nations? What major historical developments most changed women's lives between 1607 and 1750? How does geographic location matter in your answer to these questions?

PRIMARY SOURCES

By and About Colonial Women

Little material written by American women in the seventeenth century is available to historians. Even in New England, where literacy was prized and most women were taught to read, relatively few women could write, as historians who have examined the signatures on deeds and other legal documents have discovered. In seventeenth-century New England, women produced only two of the fifty-seven surviving diaries from that period. More records exist from the mid-eighteenth century, when educational opportunities for women expanded slightly. But for most of the period from 1600 to 1750, men wrote much of the material we rely on to learn about women's experiences. Even our knowledge of a famous and knowledgeable woman such as Anne Hutchinson comes from accounts written by men, such as ministers like John Cotton and John Winthrop. Yet historians have managed to mine the historical record imaginatively to capture the voices of at least some women of the era.

LAWS ON WOMEN AND SLAVERY

Although slave women of this period left behind no written documents, references to them do appear in newspapers and in their owners' letters and diaries; property inventories also provide clues that historians use to determine something of slave women's environment. More impersonal, but vital to understanding slaves' experiences, are the laws that, taken together, created the system of perpetual slavery.

In the southern colonies, the laws that created boundaries between slave and free and black and white were added in a piecemeal fashion. One of the first legal distinctions between blacks and whites concerned the labor of women. Instead of taxing land, Virginia taxed planters according to the numbers of the laborers who worked in their tobacco fields.

In this first sentence of a 1643 statute designed to support the colony's ministers, the assembly refers specifically to taxing ("tithing") the labor of "negro women." Although white women worked in the tobacco fields, they are not mentioned here. What does the presence of black women and the absence of white women in this law suggest about the distinctions being made between the two?

Laws of Virginia (1643)

Be it further enacted and confirmed That there be tenn pounds of tob'o. per poll & a bushell of corne per poll paid to the ministers within the severall parishes of the collony for all tithable persons, that is to say, as well for all youths of sixteen years of age as upwards, as also for all negro women at the age of sixteen years.

Source: William Waller Hening, ed., *The Statutes at Large, Being a Collection of All the Laws of Virginia* (Charlottesville: University Press of Virginia, 1969), I:242, II:170.

AN EVEN MORE DRAMATIC INDICATION of the hardening of lines between black and white is the short 1662 law that assigned the child of a black woman and a white man to the status of the mother. The statute also assigned penalties for interracial sex. The use of the term "christian" was common, to distinguish English people from Africans, who were considered heathens. What are the implications of this act for the institutionalization of slavery?

Laws of Virginia (1662)

WHEREAS some doubts have arrisen whether children got by any Englishman upon a negro woman should be slave or free, Be it therefore enacted and declared by this present grand assembly, that all children borne in this country shalbe held bond or free only according to the condition of the mother. And that if any christian shall committ fornication with a negro man or woman, hee or shee soe offending shall pay double the fines imposed by the former act.

Source: William Waller Hening, ed., *The Statutes at Large, Being a Collection of All the Laws of Virginia* (Charlottesville: University Press of Virginia, 1969), I:242.

LEGAL PROCEEDINGS

ALTHOUGH IN ENGLISH AND BRITISH COLONIAL LAW, married women as *femes covert* had no legal identity, women appear frequently in legal documents. Unmarried women and widows could act for themselves, and even some married women successfully petitioned the courts for *feme sole* rights in order to conduct a business — usually in the absence of their husbands. They sued and were sued, sold and bought property. Women appeared as beneficiaries or as servants and slaves in men's wills. Women were also brought to court as defendants, on trial for sexual offenses, slander, theft, infanticide, and witchcraft. The documents offered here are from courts in the Chesapeake and New England regions, but they have many similarities to those from other British colonies.

SLANDER AND THE COURTS

Slander cases were common throughout the colonies, revealing the way in which individuals in small communities placed great store on their reputations; when their neighbors engaged in gossip accusing them of inappropriate behavior, many victims turned to the court for satisfaction. In analyzing defamation cases from seventeenth-century Maryland, historian Mary Beth Norton has discovered that while women participated in only 19 percent of the colonies' civil cases, they appeared in over 50 percent of the slander cases.[32] Cases that men brought against their defamers tended to concern questions of business and honesty, while those by women focused on sexual irregularities, although witchcraft was another common accusation. While some women came to court to protect their reputations, others were summoned for having spread rumors.

The following case featuring Michael Baisey's wife revolves around issues of sexuality and paternity. What does women's gossiping indicate about their role in the community? What does this suggest about privacy in colonial towns?

Michael Baisey's Wife (1654)

Richard Manship Sworne Saith that the wife of Peter Godson related . . . that Michael Baiseys wifes Eldest Son was not the Son of Anthony Rawlins her former husband, but She knew one at Maryland that was the father of him, but Named not the man, and that the Said Michael Baisey's wife was a whore and a Strumpett up and Down the Countery, and Said that Thomas Ward of Kent tould her Soe.

Elizabeth Manship Sworne Saith the Same.

Margaret Herring Sworne Saith that the wife of Peter Godson affirmed that Anthony Rawlins

Son was not his Son but the Son of another man at Maryland. . . .

Whereas Peter Godsons wife hath Slandered the wife of Michael Baisey & Saying She was a whore & a Strumpet up and Down the Countery, It is ordered that the Said Godson's wife Shall be Committed into the Sheriffs hand untill She Shall find Security for the behaviour which the plfᵗ [plaintiff] is Satisfied with as he hath declared in Court. . . .

Whereas Mrs Godson was bound in a bond of Good behaviour from the 21st of October till the 5th of December towards the wife of Michael Baisey, and none appearing to renew the Said Bond, It is ordered that she be remitted from her Bond of Good behaviour.

SOURCE: *Archives of Maryland Judicial and Testamentary Business of the Provincial Court*, 1649/50–1675, ed. William Hand Browne (Baltimore, 1887), 10:399.

WOMEN "JURORS"

Other court cases reveal the ways in which women could expand their limited public power. When women were accused of witchcraft, the court might ask a group of women, which usually included a midwife, to examine the defendant's body for telltale signs of witchcraft. They might also be called to duty in cases in which it was crucial to determine whether a woman had given birth.

In the following complex murder accusation, the court officially termed the group of women a "jury." What does the case suggest about women's access to authority in their communities?

Judith Catchpole (1656)

At a Generall Provinciall Court Held at

Putuxent September 22th

Present Capt William ffuller, m^r John Pott Present

    m^r Richard Preston: m^r Michael Brooke

    m^r Edward Lloyd

Whereas Judith Catchpole being brought before the Court upon Suspicion of Murdering a Child which She is accused to have brought forth, and denying the fact or that She ever had Child the Court hath ordered that a jury of able women be Impannelled and to give in their Verdict to the best of their judgment whether She the Said Judith hath ever had a Child

Or not . . .

The Names of the Jury of women Impannelled to Search the body of Judith Catchpole . . .

Rose Smith	m^rs Cannady
m^rs Belcher	m^rs Bussey
m^rs Chaplin	m^rs Brooke
m^rs Brooke	Elizabeth Claxton
m^rs Battin	Elizabeth Potter Dorothy Day

SOURCE: *Archives of Maryland Judicial and Testamentary Business of the Provincial Court*, 1649/50–1675, ed. William Hand Browne (Baltimore, 1887), 10:456–58.

We the Jury of Women before named having according to our Charge and oath Searched the body of Judith Catchpole doe give in our Verdict that according to our best judgment that the Said Judith Catchpole hath not had any Child within the time Charged.

Whereas Judith Catchpole Servant to William Dorrington of this Province of Maryland Was apprehended and brought before this Court upon Suspicion of Murthering a Child in her Voyage at Sea bound for this Province in the Ship Mary and ffrancis who Set forth of England upon her intended Voyage in or about october Last 1655 and arrived in this Province in or about January following, and her accuser being deceased and no murther appearing upon her Examination denying the fact; was Ordered that her body Should be Searcht by a Jury of able women, which being done the Said Jury returning their Verdict to this Court that they found that the Said Judith had not had any Child within the time Chargd[.] And also it appearing to this Court by Severall Testimonies that the party accusing was not in Sound Mind, whereby it is Conceived the Said Judith Catchpole is not Inditable, The Court doth therefore order that upon the reasons aforesaid, that She the Said Judith Catchpole be acquitted of that Charge unless further Evidence appeare.

A PRENUPTIAL AGREEMENT

Court records are a vital source of information about property holding. Through wills and property settlement documents, we can determine the range of goods that people owned and make distinctions between rich and poor; we can discover patterns of slave ownership and servant holding; and we can acquire some information about women's economic circumstances.

The following is a prenuptial settlement by Ralph Wormley, a wealthy man, on a widow, Mrs. Agatha Stubbings, whose first husband had been a successful merchant. How does it shed light on the economic advantages widows in early Virginia might have experienced? What clues does the reference to black "servaunts" give us about African Americans' circumstances in early Virginia?

Mrs. Agatha Stubbings (1645)

To All to whom these presents shall come I Ralph Warmley [sic] of the Parrish and County of Yorke in Virginia gentleman send Greeting etc. Knowe Yee, That I the sayde Ralph Wormley For and in consideration of the unfayned love and affection That I beare unto Mrs. Agatha Stubbings late the wife of Luke Stubbings of the County of Northampton gentleman deceased, And especially in Consideration of Matrimony intended presently (by gods grace) to bee solemnized betweene the sayde Ralph and the sayde Agatha doe by these presents give graunt confirme and endow, And by these presents have given graunted and in nature of a Free Joynture endowed unto Nathaniell Littleton Esquire and Phillip Taylor gentlemen . . . in trust For and on the behalfe of the sayde Agatha six Negro servaunts . . . Fower Negro men, and Two women, To say Sanio, and Susan his wife, and greate Tony, and his wife Dorothis, Tony the younger, and Will, Tenn Cowes, six Draught Oxen, two young Mares, two Feather Bedds and Furniture, six paire of sheetes of Holland, two Dyaper table cloathes, two dozen of Napkins and Cubboard Cloath to it, two dozen of Napkins, Twelve pewter dishes, one dammaske table cloath, one Dozen of Napkins and cubboard Cloath to it, To have and to hold, the said Recited promisses and every parte thereof, unto her the sayde Agatha, and the heyres [heirs] Lawfully ingendered between mee the said Ralph Wormley and shee the sayde Agatha whether Male or Female or both to bee equally devided after his decease Provided alwayes that the same and every parte thereof graunted as aforesaid shalbe and Remayne to the only use benifitt and behoofe of mee the said Ralph Wormley during my naturall Life, And in case I the said Ralph shall happen to depart this lyfe without issue begotten betweene mee the said Ralph and shee the said Agatha as aforesayde, Then the said demised promisses and every parte thereof with the proceeds and increase thereof shalbe and Remayne to the only use benifitt and behoofe of the sayde Agatha her heyres Executors or Administrators And For the true and reall performance of this deede and every parte and parcel thereof in manner and Forme aforesaid I the said Ralph Wormley doe bynde over unto the said Nathaniell Littleton Esquire and Phillip Taylor gentlemen the said Six Negroes and Six other Negroes, the sayde Tenn Cowes and other tenn Cowes, the sixe Oxen and other sixe Oxen, one plantation and houses whereon I now live scituate at Yorke aforesaid Conteyning Five hundred Acres more or lesse according to the purchase lately made by mee of Jefery Power to bee all Lyable and Responsable For the full Assurance of makeing good the abovesaid Joynture for the use of the said Agatha her heyres Executors or Administrators as aforesaid In Witnes whereof I the sayde Ralph Wormley have hereunto sett my hand and Scale the second day of this instant July Annoque Domini 1645.

Ralph Wormeley
The Seale

SOURCE: Susie M. Ames, ed., *County Court Records of Accomack-Northampton, Virginia 1640–1645* (Charlottesville: University Press of Virginia, 1973), 433–34.

WITCHCRAFT TESTIMONY

The Salem witch trials of 1692 (see pp. 64–66) brought women into the courtroom not only as defendants, but also as plaintiffs and witnesses. The first three witnesses below accused Sarah Bibber (known also as Vibber) of malevolent behavior. Notably, Bibber also swore testimony against Sarah Good (who was executed for witchcraft less than one month later). The accusations against Bibber are followed by testimony from the accused "Goody" Mary Bradbury and her husband, Thomas Bradbury. The seventeenth-century spellings can be difficult to decode but if you read the passages out loud, their meaning will be clearer. According to her accusers, how did Sarah Bibber appear to have violated the norms of Puritan motherhood? How does Thomas's testimony compare with Mary's defense of herself? What ideals of Puritan womanhood can you see in these statements? Bradbury, whose husband was well connected, received a guilty verdict and a death sentence, but managed to evade execution. Little is known about Bibber's life beyond her testimony.

Testimony of John Porter and Lydia Porter v. Sarah Bibber (June 29, 1692)

The Testimony of John Porter: And Lidia Porter These The Testimony of John Porter, who Testifieth & sayth that Goodwife Biber Somtime living amongst us I did observe her to be a woman of An unruly turbulent Spirit; And shee would often fall into strange fitts; when shee was crost of her humor: Likewise Lidia Porter Testifieth, that Goodwife Bibber And her Husband would often quarrel & in their quarrels shee would call him, very bad names, And would have strange fitts when she was crost, And a woman of an unruly turbulent spirit, And double tongued[.]

Testimony of Joseph Fowler v. Sarah Bibber (June 29, 1692)

The Testimony of Joseph fowler, who Testifieth that Goodman Bibber & his wife, Lived at my house, and I did observe and take notice, that Goodwife Bibber was a woman, who was very idle in her calling And very much given to tatling & tale Bareing making mischeif amongst her neighbo'rs, & very much given to speak bad words and would call her husband bad names & was a woman of a very turbulent unruly spirit[.]

Testimony of Thomas Jacobs and Mary Jacobs v. Sarah Bibber (June 29, 1692)

The testymony of Thomas Jacob and mery his wife doth testify and say that Good Bibbor #[and] now that is now counted aflicketed parson she did for a time surgin in our hous and Good Bibber wood be very often spekeking against won and nother very obsanely and thos things that were very falls. and wichshing very bad wichchis and very often and she wichs that wen hor chill fell into the rever that she had never pull #[out] hor chilld out and Good Bibbor yous to wich ill wichches to horselfe and hor chilldren and allso to others: the nayborhud werr she liveued amonkes aftor she bered: hor fust housbon hes told us that this John Bibbor wife coud fall into fitts as often as she pleased[.]

Answer of Mary Bradbury (September 9, 1692)

The Answer of Mary Bradbury in the charge of Witchcraft or familliarity with the Divell I doe plead not guilty.

I am wholly inocent of any such wickedness through the goodness of god that have kept mee hitherto) I am the servant of Jesus Christ & Have given my self up to him as my only lord & saviour: and to the dilligent attendance upon him in all his holy ordinances, in utter contempt & defiance of the divell, and all his works as horid & detestible; and accordingly have endevo'red to frame my life; & conversation according to the rules of his holy word, & in that faith & practise resolve by the help and assistance of god to contineu to my lifes end:

for the truth of what I say as to matter of practiss I humbly refer my self, #[my selfe,] to my brethren & neighbors that know mee and unto the searcher of all hearts for the truth & uprightness of my heart therein: (human frailties, & unavoydable infirmities excepted) of which i bitterly complayne every day:

Mary Bradbury

Testimony of Thomas Bradbury for Mary Bradbury (July 28, 1692)

Concerning my beloved wife Mary Bradbury this is that I have to say: wee have been maried fifty five yeare: and shee hath bin a loveing & faithfull wife to mee, unto this day shee hath been wonderfull laborious dilligent & Industryous in her place and imployment, about the bringing up o'r family (w'ch have bin eleven children of o'r owne, & fower grand-children: shee was both prudent, & provident : of a cheerful Spiritt liberall Charitable: Shee being now very aged & weake, & greived under her affliction may not bee able to speake much for herselfe, not being so free of Speach as some others may bee: I hope her life and conversation hath been such amongst her neighbours, as gives a better & more reall Testimoney of her, then can bee exprest by words.

own'd by mee
*Tho: Bradbury

Source: Essex County Court Archives, Salem, Massachusetts.

NEWSPAPER ADVERTISEMENTS

ANOTHER SOURCE THAT ALLOWS US to recapture women's voices are newspaper ads appearing in colonial publications. While men predominate among those offering services and goods for sale, as the eighteenth century wore on, women's names appeared with greater frequency. What does this ad suggest about the expansion of women's economic roles in urban colonial America?

South Carolina Gazette, Charleston, October 22, 1744

This is to give Notice, to all Persons inclinable to put their Children to board, under the Care of the Subscriber [illegible], that she has noow Vacancies; where there is taught, as usual, Writing, and all sorts of fine Needle work. Masters likewise attend to teach Writing, Arithmetick, Dancing, and Musick, if required. Mary Hext.

Oᴛʜᴇʀ ᴀᴅᴠᴇʀᴛɪsᴇᴍᴇɴᴛs ᴏꜰꜰᴇʀᴇᴅ sʟᴀᴠᴇs for sale or slaves or servants for hire. What clues do the following ads give about these women's experiences?

South Carolina Gazette, Charleston, December 23, 1745

To be hired out a home born Negro girl about thirteen or fourteen years of age who has been for some years past kept employed at her needle and is a handy waiting maid. Enquire at the Printer [illegible].

Boston Gazette, April 28, 1755

A likely Negro woman, about 25 years of age, has had the smallpox, and been in the country ten or twelve years, understands all household work, and will do either for town or country.

Boston Gazette, June 20, 1735

A white Servant Maids Time to be disposed of for about four years and a half; she is a Scotch woman that can do all sorts of Household Business and Knit, and thoroughly honest. Enquire of The Publisher.

LETTERS

Lᴇᴛᴛᴇʀs, ᴛʜᴏᴜɢʜ ʀᴇʟᴀᴛɪᴠᴇʟʏ ʀᴀʀᴇ, are a major source for exploring early colonial women's experiences. The following examples offer insight into very diverse southern women's lives, those of the prosperous Eliza Lucas Pinckney and a desperate indentured servant, Elizabeth Sprigs.

Eliza Lucas Pinckney (1722–1793), a South Carolinian woman, left numerous records detailing her life among her colony's elite. Daughter of a wealthy planter and invalid mother, Eliza Lucas ran the large household, supervised her father's estates in his lengthy absences, experimented with new crops, and was instrumental in introducing indigo to the region. She made good use of her father's legal library and not only represented her family in court but neighbors as well. Lucas married a much older man, the recently widowed Charles Pinckney, and became a devoted wife and energetic mother. At her husband's death, she again employed her business skills to run the complex estate of her family. Pinckney's letters and diaries reflect on the privileged life of an elite woman in the mid-eighteenth-century South, with slaves and servants at her disposal. As you read these letters, consider the factors in early South Carolinian life that shaped her opportunities and limits.

In the following passage from a letter to a Miss Bartlett, Pinckney is unusual in her concern for teaching her slaves to read, but typical of wealthy plantation women in how she spends her time.

Eliza Lucas Pinckney
To Miss Bartlett

In general then I rise at five o'Clock in the morning, read till Seven, then take a walk in the garden or field, see that the Servants are at their respective business, then to breakfast. The first hour after breakfast is spent at my musick, the next is constantly employed in recolecting something I have learned least for want of practise it should be quite lost, such as French and short hand. After that I devote the rest of the time till I dress for dinner to our little Polly and two black girls who I teach to read, and if I have my paps's approbation (my Mams I have got) I intend [them] for school mistres's for the rest of the Negroe children — another scheme you see. But to proceed, the first hour after

dinner as the first after breakfast at musick, the rest of the afternoon in Needle work till candle light, and from that time to bed time read or write. 'Tis the fashion here to carry our work abroad with us so that having company, without they are great strangers, is no interruption to that affair; but I have particular matters for particular days, which is an interruption to mine. Mondays my musick Master is here. Tuesdays my friend Mrs. Chardon (about 3 mile distant) and I are constantly engaged to each other, she at our house one Tuesday — I at hers the next and this is one of the happiest days I spend at Woppoe. Thursday the whole day except what the necessary affairs of the family take up is spent in writing, either on the business of the plantations, or letters to my friends. Every other Fryday, if no company, we go a vizeting so that I go abroad once a week and no oftener.

SOURCE: *The Letterbook of Eliza Lucas Pinckney 1739–1762*, ed. Elise Pinckney (Columbia: University of South Carolina Press, 1997), 34, 35, 38.

OTHER LETTERS FROM PINCKNEY show the energetic businesswoman at work. In the following excerpt from a 1740 letter to a friend, she explains her plans for one of her father's plantations, which she clearly considers her property.

Wont you laugh at me if I tell you I am so busey in providing for Posterity I hardly allow my self time to Eat or sleep and can but just snatch a minnet to write to you and a friend or two now. I am making a large plantation of Oaks which I look upon as my own property, whether my father gives me

the land or not; and therefore I design many years hence when oaks are more valueable than they are now — which you know they will be when we come to build fleets. I intend, I say, 2 thirds of the produce of my oaks for a charity (I'll let you know my scheme another time) and other 3rd for those that shall have the trouble of putting my design in Execution. I sopose according to custom you will show this to your Uncle and Aunt. "She is [a] good girl," says Mrs. Pinckney. "She is never Idle and always means well." "Tell the little Visionary," says your uncle, "come to town and partake of some of the amusements suitable to her time of life." Pray tell him I think these so, and what he may not think whims and projects may turn out well by and by. Out of many surely one may hitt.

IN STARK CONTRAST to the lives of elite southern women like Pinckney were the lives of their servants. Details about the thousands of European women who came to the colonies as indentured servants in the seventeenth century are largely lost to historians because such women left few written records.

The following is a rare document, a letter written by a distressed servant in Maryland to her father. We cannot know what she had done to so displease her parent, but what does her letter indicate about the hardships facing indentured servants in America?

ELIZABETH SPRIGS

To Mr. John Sprigs White Smith in White Cross Street near Cripple Gate London

Maryland Sept'r 22'd 1756.

Honred Father

My being for ever banished from your sight, will I hope pardon the Boldness I now take of troubling you with these, my long silence has been purely owing to my undutifullness to you, and well knowing I had offended in the highest Degree, put a tie to my tongue and pen, for fear I should be extinct from your good Graces and add a further Trouble to you, but too well knowing your care and tenderness for me so long as I retaind my Duty to you, induced me once again to endeavour if possible, to kindle up that flame again. O Dear Father, belive what I am going to relate the words of truth and sincerity, and Ballance my former bad Conduct [to] my sufferings here, and then I am sure you'll pitty your Destress[ed] Daughter, What we unfortunat English People suffer here is beyond the probability of you in England to Conceive, let it suffice that I one of the unhappy Number, am toiling almost Day and Night, and very often in the Horses druggery, with only this comfort that you Bitch you do not halfe enough, and then tied up and whipp'd to that Degree that you'd not serve an Annimal, scarce any thing but Indian Corn and Salt to eat and that even begrudged nay many Negroes are better used, almost naked no shoes nor stockings to wear, and the comfort after slaving dureing Masters pleasure, what rest we can get is to rap ourselves up in a Blanket and ly upon the Ground, this is the deplorable Condition your poor Betty endures, and now I beg you have any Bowels of Compassion left show it by sending me some Relief, C[l]othing is the principal thing wanting, which if you should condiscend to, may easely send them to me by any of the ships bound to Baltimore Town Patapsco River Maryland, and give me leave to conclude in Duty to you and Uncles and Aunts, and Respect to all Friends

Honred Father

Your undutifull and Disobedient Child

SOURCE: Nancy Cott, ed., *Root of Bitterness: Documents of the Social History of American Women* (New York: E. P. Dutton, 1972), 89–90. Original source: Isabel Calder, ed., *Colonial Captivities, Marches, and Journeys* (New York: Macmillan, 1935), 151–52.

QUESTIONS FOR ANALYSIS

1. What evidence do these documents offer about the diversity of women's experiences in colonial America? What are some of the hardships or challenges that women encountered? In what ways did women of this period seek control over their lives?

2. What do these documents suggest about societal expectations for white elite women's roles? About the roles of servants and slave women?

3. How do legal documents allow us to understand the experiences of women who left no personal writings behind? What insights can descriptions of property give about the social circumstances of colonial women? How do the court cases concerning slander and witchcraft portray women and expectations about their behavior?

PRIMARY SOURCES

Depictions of "Family" in Colonial America

In the varied cultures of seventeenth- and eighteenth-century North America, "family" meant different things—different groupings of people, different relations of affection, different hierarchies, and different implications for the larger society. One of the only characteristics that all these different meanings of "family" had in common was male dominance. Visual sources can convey relationships of power within the family in ways that written sources cannot.

The period explored in this chapter predates the sentimental ideal of the nuclear family that characterized nineteenth-century middle-class American society (see pp. 157–66). Nonetheless, family relations were, if anything, more crucial to daily life in the seventeenth and eighteenth centuries, because family was a system not only of emotions and kinship but of economics and production. While some of the family bonds illustrated here may seem unusual to modern Americans, they were nonetheless deeply felt and fundamental to the people who lived them.

Although family paintings were a luxury of the wealthy, American painters were struggling artisans more than they were purveyors of high culture. In these earlier years, we do not even know the names of the artists; scholars identify them by the families who patronized them rather than by their own reputations. Traveling from place to place and looking for commissions, American painters, unlike their British counterparts, were usually not formally trained.

One of the earliest family group paintings from colonial British America was the 1674 portrait of Elizabeth Clarke Freake (b. 1641) and child shown in Figure 2.1. By 1674, Freake had already borne six children, and although tradition identifies this baby as a girl, in fact infant boys and girls were dressed exactly alike, so it is difficult to distinguish them. This portrait is part of a series that includes a separate painting of the husband and father, Boston merchant John Freake. Painted as standing and facing toward his left, John Freake's portrait was probably meant to hang alongside that of his wife and child. John Freake died just a year after the painting was completed, and his widow—like so many other New England women—went on to remarry.

Art historians have discovered that this version of Elizabeth Freake and child was painted over a previous portrait created three years earlier. The major difference is that, in the later version, the mother's right arm is around her child, whereas in the earlier version, it was crossed in front of her chest. Why do you think, after three years, the painter was asked to make this change? What aspects of the painting convey Elizabeth Freake's piety? What details suggest her wealth and social

◆ **Figure 2.1 Elizabeth Freake and Child**
The Granger Collection, New York.

standing? How do these two dimensions come together in the overall portrait of mother and child?

Joint portraits of husband and wife from this period are very rare. Family portraits were meant to illustrate intergenerational family descent, not conjugal affection. Art historians are not sure who painted the example in Figure 2.2, but it is generally attributed to John Watson, a Scots immigrant who arrived in the colonies in 1714. A traveling artist in New Jersey, Pennsylvania, and New York, Watson is one of the first generation of painters working in America whose name is known to us. His style is much more refined than that of the anonymous painter of Elizabeth Freake and child in Figure 2.1.

Figure 2.2 records the alliance through marriage of two of the wealthiest Dutch American families in New York State, the Schuylers and the Wendells. Both were located in Albany and began to accumulate their wealth in the late seventeenth

◆ **Figure 2.2 Johannes and Elsie Schuyler**
© *Collection of the New-York Historical Society, USA/Bridgeman Images.*

century through trade with the Mohawks and through extensive agricultural hold-ings. The husband, Johannes Schuyler, was an Albany merchant and later became the city mayor. The wife, Elsie Staats Wendell, also a member of a founding Dutch American family, was a decade older than her husband and already quite wealthy from her father and her first husband. A widow, she had given birth to nine chil-dren before she married Schuyler. Their first child was born eight months after their marriage and together they had three more. How do the details of this mar-riage help to explain the Schuylers' decision to commission a joint portrait? Notice that she chose to be pictured with papers and books in her hands; what might she be trying to indicate about her tastes and activities? What other aspects of this portrait signal the Schuylers' social status?

We have no paintings of black families, slave or free, from the early eighteenth century. Indeed, African migrants were just beginning to live long enough to

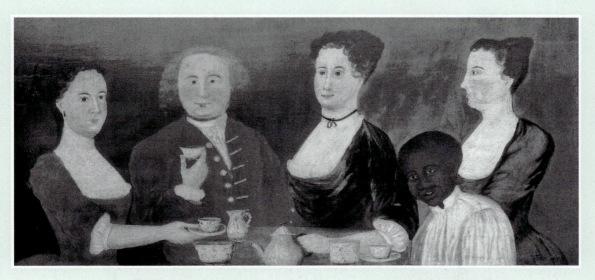

◆ Figure 2.3 **The Potter Family**
The Newport Historical Society (53.3).

establish multigenerational kinship ties. However, some portraits of white families included a black domestic slave or servant among the family grouping.

The group portrait of the Potter family of southern Rhode Island in Figure 2.3 was painted around 1740 by an unknown artist. The Newport Historical Society identifies the white male head of household as John Potter, a wealthy land- and slaveowner who later became a Quaker and freed his slaves. The Potters lived near Narragansett Bay, on one of several large plantations in the area whose land had been seized from Native people. Included in the picture are three unidentified women, no doubt Potter's wife, their daughter, and probably a collateral relative or friend of his wife. But what draws our modern attention is the young black boy holding a tea tray. Newport, Rhode Island, was the center of New England slave trading, and Potter was both a slave trader and slaveholder. Unlike most of Potter's slaves, who worked in the fields, this young child was likely a full-time domestic servant. How does the picture itself signal this information? Curiously, this slave child and Mr. Potter are portrayed as looking directly at the viewer, while the three women look slightly away. Why might the painter have chosen to do this?

Why do you think that the Potters made the deliberate decision to include this child in the painting of their family grouping? The painting was permanently installed over the family's mantelpiece. How might it have affected master, mistress, and slave to see themselves together in the portrait day after day? Remember that the slave, in addition to being a worker, was also a marker of wealth: the Potters owned many. What else about the portrait suggests their wealth?

Figures 2.1, 2.2, and 2.3 are portraits of particular families, each with its own intentions, relationships, and personalities. All are products of Protestant New England and New Netherland societies, which revered domestic life and parent/child and husband/wife relations. Spanish America grew out of a very different religious and artistic tradition. Like the artists of Catholic Europe, most of its painters concentrated on religious themes. Undoubtedly the family they painted most frequently was Mary, Joseph, and the baby Jesus.

Casta paintings were a genre unique to New Spain and represent a distinct pictorial approach to family relationships. The collective term *castas* — in English, "castes" — refers to the intricate system, part racial and part economic, that constituted the social and political hierarchy of New Spain. Among English colonists, racial inequality was enforced by legal prohibitions against interracial marriage and a system in which only two racial identities were available: white and nonwhite. By contrast, in New Spain, interracial marriage within the church was encouraged, as a means to "civilize," absorb, and ultimately eliminate nonwhite populations. This racial system, although different from the Protestant English one, was also hierarchical and white-dominated. The goal was to move up the racial scale, toward the apex of whiteness.

The *castas* system was a kind of taxonomy, or system of classification, and the paintings themselves contained indicators of that system. Most *casta* paintings consisted of sixteen different categories, painted on either a single canvas or separate canvases. The paintings depicted highly stylized categories rather than real people, and each family's racial composition was inscribed on the canvas. The artists painted their fantasy family groupings in beautiful colors and wearing exquisite clothes, so as to convey a sense of beauty, opulence, and wealth. Both as idealizations of interracial families and as depictions of New World wealth, the *casta* paintings were a kind of advertisement for the wonders and possibilities of New Spain. But scholars also suggest that the emphasis on hierarchical categorization indicates anxiety about the potential disorder of racial mixing and may have been "intended as reminders to the Spanish Crown that Mexico was still a rigidly structured society."[33]

The actual lives of interracial families, and their experience of racial inequality and hierarchy, bore little relationship to the depictions of the *casta* paintings. *Castas* were usually painted in the urban centers of Mexico City and Lima, but we can be confident that the images they purveyed and the system they represented would have been familiar on the northern borders of Mexico, among the colonists who came to Santa Fe and El Paso, for whom interracial liaisons and difficult living conditions were major factors of life.

The elaborate depiction of interracial combinations and offspring in Figures 2.4, 2.5, and 2.6, dated about 1715 and attributed to Juan Rodríguez Juárez, conveys the abstract and idealized quality of the *castas* genre. The two family combinations in Figures 2.4 and 2.5 are *español/India/mestizo* and *español/negra/mulatto*. *India/mestizo* here means Christianized, urbanized people of mixed Spanish and Indian descent. Note that in both these paintings, the man is European and white and the woman is not. Significantly, according to the *castas* system, Indian blood,

◆ **Figure 2.4**
Mestizo Family
*Breamore House,
Hampshire, UK/
Bridgeman Images.*

◆ **Figure 2.5**
Mulatto Family
*Breamore House,
Hampshire, UK/
Bridgeman Images.*

INDIOS BARBAROS

◆ **Figure 2.6**
Indian Family
*Breamore House,
Hampshire, UK/
Bridgeman Images.*

in contrast to black blood, could be redeemed (Christianized and civilized) by admixture with Spanish blood. Figure 2.6 portrays an *India Barbara*, an Indian family unredeemed by any Spanish blood. What are the differences between the three images that suggest the hierarchical *castas* system? Why does each family unit consist only of mother, father, and child, rather than the much more diverse and numerous family units depicted in the Protestant portrait tradition?

QUESTIONS FOR ANALYSIS

1. In what different ways is male headship of family life depicted in these paintings?
2. What do these images tell us about women's roles in family relations?
3. What similarities and differences do you see among the women portrayed in these images?

NOTES

1. Cotton Mather, *A Narrative of Hannah Swarton Containing Wonderful Passages Relating to Her Captivity and Deliverance*, in Puritans among the Indians: Accounts of Captivity and Redemption, 1676–1724, ed. Alden T. Vaughan and Edward W. Clark (Cambridge, MA: Belknap Press, 1981), 153.

2. Juliana Barr, "Borders and Borderlands," in Susan Sleeper-Smith et al., *Why You Can't Teach United States History without American Indians* (Chapel Hill: University of North Carolina Press, 2015), 10.

3. Sophie H. Drinker, "Women Attorneys of Colonial Times," *Maryland Historical Magazine* 56, no. 4 (December 1961): 350.

4. Paula A. Treckel, *To Comfort the Heart: Women in Seventeenth-Century America* (New York: Twayne, 1996), 37.

5. Carol Berkin and Leslie Horowitz, eds., *Women's Voices, Women's Lives: Documents in Early American History* (Boston: Northeastern University Press, 1998), 16.

6. Kathleen M. Brown, *Good Wives, Nasty Wenches, and Anxious Patriarchs* (Chapel Hill: University of North Carolina Press, 1996), 166.

7. James D. Rice, "Rethinking the 'American Paradox,'" in Susan Sleeper-Smith et al., *Why You Can't Teach United States History without American Indians* (Chapel Hill: University of North Carolina Press, 2015), 51.

8. *Voyages: The Trans-Atlantic Slave Trade Database*, http://www.slavevoyages.org/.

9. Olaudah Equiano, *The Interesting Narrative of the Life of Olaudah Equiano, or Gustavus Vassa, the African. Written by Himself* (London, 1789), Documenting the American South, University Library (University of North Carolina at Chapel Hill, 2001), 79.

10. Peter Kolchin, *American Slavery, 1619–1877* (New York: Hill and Wang, 1993), 51.

11. Philip D. Morgan, *Slave Counterpoint: Black Culture in the Eighteenth-Century Chesapeake and Lowcountry* (Chapel Hill: University of North Carolina Press, 1998), 12.

12. Brown, *Good Wives, Nasty Wenches, and Anxious Patriarchs*, 214.

13. Paul Heinegg and Henry B. Hoff, "Freedom in the Archives: Free African Americans in Colonial America," *Common-Place* 5, no. 1 (October 2004), http://www.common-place.org/vol-05/no-01/heinegg-hoff.

14. Morgan, *Slave Counterpoint*, 100.

15. Laurel Thatcher Ulrich, *Good Wives: Image and Reality in the Lives of Women in Northern New England, 1650–1750* (New York: Vintage Books, 1991), 115.

16. Richard Godbeer, *Sexual Revolution in Early America* (Baltimore: Johns Hopkins University Press, 2002), 228.

17. Treckel, *To Comfort the Heart*, 145.

18. Mary Beth Norton, *Founding Mothers and Fathers: Gendered Power and the Forming of American Society* (New York: Alfred A. Knopf, 1996), 351.

19. Lyle Koehler, *A Search for Power: The "Weaker Sex" in Seventeenth-Century New England* (Urbana: University of Illinois Press, 1980), 31.

20. Ann M. Little, *The Many Captivities of Esther Wheelwright* (New Haven: Yale University Press, 2016), 4.

21. Norton, *Founding Mothers and Fathers*, 359.

22. Vivian Bruce Conger, "'If Widow, Both Housewife and Husband May Be': Widows' Testamentary Freedom in Colonial Massachusetts and Maryland," in Larry D. Eldridge, ed., *Women and Freedom in Early America* (New York: New York University Press, 1997), 249.

23. Treckel, *To Comfort the Heart*, 175.

24. Michael L. Blakey, "The New York African Burial Ground Project: An Examination of Enslaved Lives, a Construction of Ancestral Ties," *Transforming Anthropology* 7, no. 1 (1998), http://www.huarchivesnet.howard.edu/0008-huarnet/blakey1.htm.

25. Leo Hershkowitz, "Original Inventories of Early New York Jews (1682–1763)," *American Jewish History* 90 (December 2002): 239–322.

26. Alan Taylor, *American Colonies* (New York: Viking, 2001), 368.

27. Clara Sue Kidwell, "Indian Women as Cultural Mediators," *Ethnohistory* 39, no. 2 (Spring 1992): 97.

28. Richard White, *The Middle Ground: Indians, Empires, and Republics in the Great Lakes Region, 1650–1815* (Cambridge: Cambridge University Press, 1991), 72.

29. Emily Clark, *Masterless Mistresses: The New Orleans Ursulines and the Development of a New World Society, 1727–1834* (Chapel Hill: University of North Carolina Press, 2007), 82.

30. Kathleen DuVal, *The Native Ground: Indians and Colonists in the Heart of the Continent* (Philadelphia: University of Pennsylvania Press, 2006), 73, 84.

31. Pekka Hämäläinen, *The Comanche Empire* (New Haven: Yale University Press, 2008), 52.

32. Mary Beth Norton, "Gender and Defamation in Seventeenth-Century Maryland," *William and Mary Quarterly*, 3rd ser., 44 (January 1987): 4–5.

33. Ilona Katzew, "Casta Painting: Identity and Social Stratification in Colonial Mexico," *Laberinto* 1, nos. 1–2 (Fall 1997), https://acmrs.org/sites/default/files/sites/default/files/laberinto_v1.pdf.

SUGGESTED REFERENCES

General Works

James Axtell, ed., *The Indian Peoples of Eastern America: A Documentary History of the Sexes* (1981).

Beryl Lieff Benderly and Hasia R. Diner, *Her Works Praise Her: A History of Jewish Women in America from Colonial Times to the Present* (2003).

Ira Berlin, *Many Thousands Gone: The First Two Centuries of Slavery in North America* (1998).

Sharon Block, *Rape and Sexual Power in Early America* (2006).

Elaine Forman Crane, *Witches, Wife Beaters, and Whores: Common Law and Common Folk in Early America* (2011).

Richard Godbeer, *Sexual Revolution in Early America* (2002).

Darlene Clark Hine, ed., *Black Women in American History: From Colonial Times through the Nineteenth Century* (1990).

Peter C. Mancall and James H. Merrell, eds., *American Encounters: Natives and Newcomers from European Contact to Indian Removal, 1500–1850*, 2nd ed. (2006).

Mary Beth Norton, *Founding Mothers and Fathers: Gendered Power and the Forming of American Society* (1996).

Marylynn Salmon, *Women and the Law of Property in Early America* (1986).

Nancy Shoemaker, *A Strange Likeness: Becoming Red and White in Eighteenth-Century North America* (2004).

Alan Taylor, *American Colonies* (2001).

Women in the Southern Colonies

Kathleen M. Brown, *Good Wives, Nasty Wenches, and Anxious Patriarchs* (1996).

Patricia Cleary, *Elizabeth Murray: A Woman's Pursuit of Independence in Eighteenth-Century America* (2000).

Kirsten Fischer, *Suspect Relations: Sex, Race, and Resistance in Colonial North Carolina* (2002).

Gunlog Für, *Nations of Women: Gender and Colonial Encounters among the Delaware Indians* (2011).

David Barry Gaspar and Darlene Clark Hine, eds., *More Than Chattel: Black Women and Slavery in the Americas* (1996).

Catherine Kerrison, *Claiming the Pen: Women and Intellectual Life in the Early American South* (2006).

Cynthia A. Kierner, *Beyond the Household: Women's Place in the Early South, 1700–1835* (1998).

Allan Kulikoff, "The Beginnings of the Afro-American Family in Maryland," in Aubrey Land, Lois Green Carr, and Edward C. Papenfuse, eds., *Law, Society, and Politics in Early Maryland* (1977).

Gloria L. Main, *Tobacco Colony: Life in Early Maryland, 1650–1720* (1982).

Ben Marsh, *Georgia's Frontier Women: Female Fortunes in a Southern Colony* (2007).

Jennifer L. Morgan, *Laboring Women: Reproduction and Gender in New World Slavery* (2004).

Philip D. Morgan, *Slave Counterpoint: Black Culture in the Eighteenth-Century Chesapeake and Lowcountry* (1998).

Mary Beth Norton, "Gender and Defamation in Seventeenth-Century Maryland," *William and Mary Quarterly* 44 (January 1987).

John Ruston Pagan, *Anne Orthwood's Bastard: Sex and Law in Early Virginia* (2002).

Theda Perdue, *Cherokee Women: Gender and Cultural Change, 1700–1835* (1998).

Darret B. Rutman and Anita H. Rutman, *A Place in Time: Middlesex County, Virginia, 1650–1750* (1984).

Carole Shammas, "Black Women's Work and the Evolution of Plantation Society in Virginia," *Labor History* 26 (1985).

Terri L. Snyder, *Babbling Women: Disorderly Speech and the Law in Early Virginia* (2003).

Lorena S. Walsh, "'Till Death Us Do Part': Marriage and Family in Seventeenth-Century Maryland," in Thad W. Tate and David L. Ammerman, eds., *The Chesapeake in the Seventeenth Century: Essays on Anglo-American Society* (1979).

Monica C. Witkowski, *Women at Law in Early Colonial Maryland* (2012).

Peter H. Wood, *Black Majority: Negroes in Colonial South Carolina: From 1670 through the Stono Rebellion* (1974).

Women in the Northern Colonies

Linda Briggs Biemer, *Women and Property in Colonial New York: The Transition from Dutch to English Law, 1643–1727* (1983).

Ava Chamberlain, *The Notorious Elizabeth Tuttle: Marriage, Murder, and Madness in the Family of Jonathan Edwards* (2012).

Michelle Coughlin, *One Colonial Woman's World: The Life and Writings of Mehetabel Chandler Coit* (2012).

Cornelia Hughes Dayton, *Women before the Bar: Gender, Law, and Society in Connecticut, 1639–1789* (1995).

John Demos, *A Little Commonwealth: Family Life in Plymouth Colony* (1970).

Carol F. Karlsen, *The Devil in the Shape of a Woman: Witchcraft in Colonial New England* (1987).

Lyle Koehler, *A Search for Power: The "Weaker Sex" in Seventeenth-Century New England* (1980).

Ann M. Little, *Abraham in Arms: War and Gender in Colonial New England* (2006).

M. Michelle Morris, *Under Household Government: Sex and Family in Puritan Massachusetts* (2012).

David E. Narrett, "Men's Wills and Women's Property Rights in Colonial New York," in *Women in the Age of the American Revolution*, ed. Ronald Hoffman and Peter J. Albert (1989).

Deborah A. Rosen, "Women and Property across Colonial America: A Comparison of Legal Systems in New Mexico and New York," *William and Mary Quarterly* 60 (April 2003).

Mary Beth Norton, *In the Devil's Snare: The Salem Witchcraft Crisis of 1692* (2002).

Rebecca Tannenbaum, *A Healer's Calling: Women and Medicine in Early New England* (2002).

Teresa A. Toulouse, *The Captive's Position: Female Narrative, Male Identity, and Royal Authority in Colonial New England* (2006).

Laurel Thatcher Ulrich, *Good Wives: Image and Reality in the Lives of Women in Northern New England* (1991).

New Spain, New France, and Native America beyond British Settler Colonies

Karen Anderson, *Chain Her by One Foot: The Subjugation of Native Women in Seventeenth-Century New France* (1993).

Stephen Aron, *American Confluence: The Missouri Frontier from Borderland to Border State* (2005).

Julianna Barr, *Peace Came in the Form of a Woman: Indians and Spaniards in the Texas Borderlands* (2007).

James Brooks, *Captives and Cousins: Slavery, Kinship, and Community in the Southwest Borderlands* (2002).

Emily Clark, *Masterless Mistresses: The New Orleans Ursulines and the Development of a New World Society* (2007).

Natalie Zemon Davis, *Women on the Margins: Three Seventeenth-Century Lives* (1995).

Kathleen DuVal, *The Native Ground: Indians and Colonists in the Heart of the Continent* (2006).

Allan Greer, "Colonial Saints: Gender, Race, and Hagiography in New France," *William and Mary Quarterly* 57 (April 2000).

Ramón A. Gutiérrez, *When Jesus Came, the Corn Mothers Went Away: Marriage, Sexuality, and Power in New Mexico, 1500–1846* (1991).

Pekka Hämäläinen, *The Comanche Empire* (2008).

Susan Sleeper-Smith, *Indian Women and French Men: Rethinking Cultural Encounter in the Western Great Lakes* (2001).

Jennifer Spear, *Race, Sex, and Social Order in Early New Orleans* (2009).

Richard White, *The Middle Ground: Indians, Empires, and Republics in the Great Lakes Region, 1650–1815* (1991).

Michael Witgen, *An Infinity of Nations: How the Native New World Shaped North America* (2012).

3

Mothers and Daughters of the Revolution

1750–1810

Y EARS AFTER THE AMERICAN REVOLUTION ENDED British colonial rule in 1783, Sarah Osborn applied for a widow's pension from the U.S. government. In her 1837 deposition, she described not only her husband's service as a soldier but also her contributions to the war effort. During one battle she took "her stand just back of the American tents, say about a mile from the town, and busied herself washing, mending, and cooking for the soldiers, in which she was assisted by the other females. . . . She heard the roar of the artillery for a number of days."[1] Osborn's account of life close to the fighting suggests a significant break from notions of women's traditional place at the hearth. But that she performed domestic work for her husband and his fellow soldiers also reveals that, even in the disruptive context of war, women's customary domestic roles prevailed. Osborn's experiences were hardly universal, yet her deposition underscores a crucial point. Even though the dramatic events of the second half of the eighteenth century centered on political and international concerns — which were customarily viewed as exclusively male terrain — women actively participated, albeit usually in distinctly gendered ways, in the American Revolution and the founding of the United States of America.

photos: top, Library of Congress, LC-USZ62-12711; bottom, The Granger Collection, New York.

Historians vigorously debate the long-term impact of the American Revolution on women's lives. Some scholars argue that while white men enjoyed expanded legal and political rights in the postrevolutionary period, women's relative status declined. Others contend that women developed a new consciousness that led to improved education and increased opportunities to influence public life. These historians also point out that the religious revival that preceded the Revolution, the First Great Awakening, similarly offered women a greater voice in the world beyond their homes. Neither scenario, however, neatly fits the experience of all women. Free black women strove to make a living and build communities as full citizenship became increasingly tied not only to being male, but also to being white. Women of many Indian nations faced a newly empowered, expanding U.S. republic and a transforming continent. This chapter emphasizes the ways in which women participated in the Revolution and traces the complex changes the revolutionary era brought to their lives. Although traditional expectations about women's roles were challenged, they were rarely overturned.

◆ BACKGROUND TO REVOLUTION, 1754–1775

For two centuries North America was the site of contending colonial powers, with France, Spain, and Britain struggling with Native peoples and each other to dominate the continent's land and resources. The transformation by which the region came to be controlled largely by Britain, and later the United States, was rooted in the French and Indian War of 1754–1763 and further consolidated by the American Revolution of 1776–1783. A number of factors led to the outbreak of the Revolution. Social changes from the First Great Awakening and new ideas introduced during the Enlightenment loosened the strict hierarchy that had defined social relations up to the eighteenth century. Further, British attempts to recoup the economic losses incurred by colonial wars led to a tightening of economic and political controls on the settler colonists in North America, leading to colonial resistance that brought about the American Revolutionary War.

photos: top, The Granger Collection, New York; middle, Library of Congress. From *Memoir of Jemima Wilkinson*, 1844; bottom, The Granger Collection, New York

Social Change in the Eighteenth Century

Two important social factors paved the way for rebellion against imperial power in the eighteenth century. The first was the evangelical revival known as the First Great Awakening (1730–1770). Waves of Protestant revivalism began as early as the 1730s and 1740s, inspired in part by English minister George Whitefield's preaching tours throughout the British colonies. Outpourings of evangelical fervor reached their greatest intensity between the 1750s and the 1770s, especially in the South, where revivalism touched both blacks and whites. Evangelical worshippers gathered outside at camp meetings, in fields and pastures, where their religious joy could have physical expression. The First Great Awakening split established churches and created increasing numbers of converts to new denominations, such as the Baptists and the Methodists, whose evangelicalism emphasized an emotional spiritual rebirth and validated the religious experience of ordinary people.

In challenging religious authority and church hierarchy, the First Great Awakening promoted a leveling of the social hierarchies that cut across gender, class, and race. Evangelicals within the Methodist and Baptist churches, especially the Separate Baptists in the South, reached out to the poor and uneducated, generally welcoming black converts. A few churches explicitly condemned the institution of slavery, and some slaveholders, moved by the evangelical message, freed their slaves or at the least encouraged their slaves to become Christians. This set of evangelical revivals, in which women were prominent participants, promoted a rough egalitarianism that many scholars think fostered political unrest as well.

In addition to the religious awakening, the onrushing crisis with Britain led some colonists to examine closely not only their relationship to the Crown but also their conceptions of the existing social order and government itself. Among educated elites, the ideas of the Enlightenment had a powerful impact. This European intellectual movement emphasized the rights of individuals, the role of reason, the promise of social progress, and the importance of the scientific method. In America, it contributed to the questioning of the British Crown's authority and to an appreciation for the rights of the individual. Particularly influential was the seventeenth-century political philosopher John Locke, whose *Two Treatises of Government* was widely circulated in the colonies.

These public debates occasioned by the British efforts to control the colonies more tightly in the latter half of the eighteenth century were conducted almost exclusively by men. Although many addressed the questions of hierarchical structures within the British Empire and within the colonial governments, few questioned the hierarchy embedded in their gender system. Despite societal assumptions that the weighty considerations of government, diplomacy, and the economy were outside the realm of women's concerns, many women from diverse groups actively participated in the events surrounding the revolutionary conflict. But while many women found themselves acting in novel ways, for the most part their activities followed the traditional lines of household production and family obligation.

The Growing Confrontation

In the British colonies, settlers on the frontier experienced the events leading up to the Revolution as part of an ongoing struggle over colonial freedom from British intervention. During the early years, colonists had enjoyed a high degree of freedom from British intrusion in their domestic affairs. But the French and Indian War, in which British and colonial troops conquered New France, brought dramatic changes. It was a costly war, and Britain insisted that the colonials pay their share through increased taxation, a burden that women, as consumers, often experienced firsthand. Moreover, the victory had opened up more land for British settlement: by the terms of the Treaty of Paris that ended the war, the French yielded their vast lands in North America to the British, who now claimed all the territory east of the Mississippi River (see Map 3.1). The war also drew in various Native American peoples, who sided and fought with whichever European power they thought most likely to honor individual tribal claims to territory. Usually this was the French, who, unlike the British, had learned to live with Native Americans rather than drive them off their lands. The British victory imperiled Native Americans in part because they could no longer play off European powers against one another, and in part because of the avidness with which British colonists eyed the newly acquired territories.

◆ **Map 3.1 British Colonies in North America, 1763**

Following the French and Indian War, the Treaty of Paris gave Britain control over all of New France east of the Mississippi and all of Spanish Florida. At the same time, Britain imposed the Proclamation Line of 1763, which prohibited white settlement west of the Appalachian Mountains. Subsequent legislation designated most of the western lands reserved for Indians. This western policy angered settlers hungry for land and land speculators eager to make a profit, and it contributed to the crisis in the British colonies that eventually led to the American Revolution.

The promise of land won during the war accelerated European emigration. Irish, Scots, Ulster Scots, German, and English peoples expanded the population of the British colonies, which counted almost 2 million settlers by 1765. Cities grew, but so did the population of the backcountry. Pressured for years by a scarcity of good, affordable land, settlers as well as land speculators coveted Native American lands along the frontier. The British, hoping to put an end to the recurring Indian wars, issued the Proclamation of 1763, which temporarily closed the land west of the Appalachians to settlement. Expansion-minded colonists resented (and often ignored) the Proclamation Line, thus fomenting conflict with Native Americans and creating tension between the colonies and the mother country.

Other British efforts to exert more control over the American colonies included a series of fiscal and administrative reforms. The Revenue Act of 1764 (known as the Sugar Act) lowered duties on sugar but firmly established the means of enforcing their collection. Designed to defray the cost of keeping British troops in North America, the Sugar Act was followed by the 1765 Stamp Act, which required the use of embossed paper for legal documents and other printed matter. Forced to rescind the Stamp Act because of colonial protests, the British Parliament in 1767 passed the Townshend Act. By placing new duties on tea, coffee, and other items of household consumption, the Townshend Act directly affected women's domestic responsibilities and consequently heightened their political consciousness. At the same time, the British increased their bureaucratic presence in the colonies — the number of Crown officials doubled during this period — and sought to limit the autonomy of the colonies' governing assemblies.

As tensions between Britain and the colonists took center stage in the years after the French and Indian War, waves of social and economic problems roiled the colonies. Seaport towns and cities suffered an economic downturn after the war boom, and the colonists, especially those indebted to English creditors, became all the more resentful of British taxation. Tax-related unrest prompted the British occupation of Boston, where a 1770 clash between colonists and British soldiers resulted in the death of five colonists; this "Boston Massacre" set off a wave of anti-British sentiment and propaganda. Hard times widened the gap between rich and poor in the colonies, deepening dissatisfaction. Extraordinary unrest in the backcountry regions of the southern and middle colonies — where poor farmers went on rampages against Native Americans and resisted the authority of colonial elites on the seaboard — also promoted the desire for change. While perhaps resenting the wealthy colonial merchants and landed gentry who controlled so much of the economic and political life of the colonies, in some areas, especially the mid-Atlantic colonies, poor people diverted much of their anger toward British authority and its efforts to bring the American colonies more tightly into the imperial fold.

Liberty's Daughters: Women and the Emerging Crisis

Women made critical contributions to settler colonists' resistance to the new British policies. When the colonists resisted the new taxes by boycotting British goods, women were necessarily involved. Where colonists had formerly relied on imported cloth, they now proposed to make their own cloth. Even though most textile production was women's work, initial reports of the substitution of homespun cloth for imported fabric often ignored women's contributions. In 1768, the *Providence Gazette* commended one man for the large quantities of cloth and yarn "spun in his own house," without reference to the women who were doing the work. But male patriots (as colonials who protested British domination were called) quickly realized their dependence on women's efforts, and northern newspaper reports of patriotic women's production of homespun cloth escalated.[2] In New England, spinning bees for manufacturing the yarn for homemade cloth were particularly popular.

Southern white women also produced homespun, but because they lived on farms and plantations often widely separated from one another, they rarely did so in the large groups typical in the North. Nor was there much publicity for their work, and indeed the southern press tended to criticize women for their extravagant taste in clothes and to suggest that men would have to persuade their wives to provide the necessary assistance.[3] Although free white women did provide assistance, masters of large plantations bought equipment and set groups of slave women to spinning. Robert Carter of Virginia had his overseer "sett a part, Ten black Females the most Expert spinners . . . — they to be Employed in Spinning, solely."[4] This method of using slaves to produce cloth continued through the Revolutionary War, allowing some slave women to acquire new skills.

While enslaved black women had little choice in the matter of assisting their masters in their boycotts against the British, free white women could and did see themselves as acting in a patriotic cause, and many called themselves "Liberty's Daughters." Their spinning bees may not have resulted in a large amount of cloth, but their efforts took on symbolic importance and reinforced their importance as consumers — or nonconsumers — in the boycott. The spinning bees were, says one historian, "ideological showcases" that demonstrated women's contribution to the colonial struggle.[5]

Beyond producing homespun, women practiced all sorts of economies as they spurned a wide variety of British goods. Tea became the focus of boycotts in the early 1770s, especially after 1773, when the British instituted new regulations designed to undercut the colonials' illegal importation of non-British tea. Some women substituted herbal teas and coffee and engaged in collective efforts to encourage other women to do the same. In Edenton, North Carolina, Penelope Barker declared, "We women have taken too long to let our voices be heard." She organized fifty-one women who signed a proclamation acknowledging their "duty" to support the nonimportation resolutions passed by the First Continental Congress in 1774 (see Figure 3.1, p. 135).[6] Women boycotters were roundly applauded in the press for their sacrifice. Presbyterian leader William Tennent III told women that "you have it in your power more than all your committees and Congresses, to strike the Stroke, and make the Hills and Plains of America clap their hands."[7]

Articles attributed to women appeared in both northern and southern newspapers. Whether these were actually written by women or by men using female pseudonyms, they helped to legitimate the idea of women as authors with valuable

READING INTO THE PAST

HANNAH GRIFFITTS

The Female Patriots, Address'd to the Daughters of Liberty in America

The controversy over the Townshend Act led women to use not only their consumer power as a political voice, but also their pens. In this extract of a 1768 poem, Philadelphia Quaker Hannah Griffitts wittily expresses defiance toward the British consumer taxes, including those on paper and dyes. The stanzas below urge women to refuse to buy tea. "Grenville" refers to Lord George Grenville, chancellor of the British Exchequer and author of the hated taxes. First circulated among Griffitts's literary women friends, the poem was later published in the Pennsylvania Gazette, *a newspaper that often praised women's contribution to the colonials' cause.*

Since the Men from a Party, on fear of a Frown,
Are kept by a Sugar-Plumb, quietly down.
Supinely asleep, and depriv'd of their Sight
Are strip'd of their Freedom, and rob'd of their Right.
If the Sons (so degenerate) the Blessing despise,
Let the Daughters of Liberty, nobly arise,
And tho' we've no Voice, but a negative here,
The use of the Taxables, let us forbear,
(Then Merchants import till yr. Stores are all full

insights to impart. Some women wrote poems denouncing tea drinking[8] (see Reading into the Past: "The Female Patriots, Address'd to the Daughters of Liberty in America"). Others produced thoughtful essays, such as one that appeared in 1774 in the *Virginia Gazette*, which was edited and published by Clementina Rind. The essay explained that American women "will be so far instrumental in bringing about a redress of the evils complained of, that history may be hereafter filled with their praises, and teach posterity to venerate their virtues."[9]

Despite the widespread sense that politics was not a woman's affair, participation in the boycotts and in the production of homespun did bring women to the margins of political action and encouraged them to see themselves as part of a larger American whole. Even someone as young as thirteen-year-old Anna Green Winslow wrote in her diary in 1771, "As I Am (as we say) a daughter of liberty, I chuse to wear as much of our own manufactory as possible."[10] Another young girl, Betsy Foote, recorded her daily labor at spinning and carding, and reported that

May the Buyers be few and yr. Traffick be dull.)
Stand firmly resolved, and bid Grenville to see
That rather than Freedom, we'll part with our Tea
And well as we love the dear Draught when adry,
As American Patriots, — our Taste we deny . . .

. . . .

Join mutual in this, and but small as it seems
We may jostle a Grenville and puzzle his Schemes
But a Motive more worthy our patriot Pen,
Thus acting — we point out their Duty to Men,
And should the bound Pensioners, tell us to hush
We can throw back the Satire by biding them blush.

SOURCE: *William and Mary Quarterly*, 3rd ser., 34 (1977): 307–8. Noted as from the Commonplace Book of Milcah Martha Moore, but *The Cambridge Guide to Women's Writing in English* (1999) identifies the author as Griffitts.

QUESTIONS FOR ANALYSIS

1. What does the author mean by the phrase "And tho' we've no Voice, but a negative here"? What action does the poem call for?
2. In what ways does Griffitts suggest that women are better American patriots than men?

she "felt Nationly into the bargain."[11] Women wrote of duty, of civic virtues, of freedom, and of sacrifice. However, despite the centrality of women's contributions to the success of the Americans' resistance, their efforts were extensions of their roles within the home — as goodwives and consumers — and, as such, the potential challenge to the gender order was minimized.

◆ WOMEN AND THE FACE OF WAR, 1775–1783

Colonial resistance escalated from boycotts and protests to armed conflict in April 1775, when British troops marched on Lexington and Concord, Massachusetts, in an effort to put down the growing rebellion. Although colonial leaders did not issue the Declaration of Independence until July 1776, the Revolution had begun. A struggle between imperial Great Britain and its colonies, the American

Revolution was also a civil war in which British subjects fought one another and former friends and neighbors became enemies. While many colonists tried to avoid taking sides, historians estimate that about one-fifth of the white population were loyalists (that is, loyal to Britain and opposed to the Revolution), also called Tories by their enemies. Probably two-fifths were patriots, supporters of the Revolution. Native Americans and African Americans, too, became embroiled in the conflict on both sides of the fence. A wide spectrum of Americans, both male and female, thus faced profound disruptions and complex decisions.

Choosing Sides: Native American and African American Women

Native American communities confronted particularly weighty choices. In part because their experiences with land-grabbing settlers had been so negative, many Indian nations opted to side with the British — who had made some efforts to control the colonists' encroachment into Indian territory — and they waged war against the patriots and their Indian allies throughout the backcountry. In many of the Indian nations, including the Iroquois and the Cherokee, women traditionally exerted significant influence over the decision to go to war; the causes were often linked to the desire to avenge deaths of loved ones killed by enemies. As Native Americans became enmeshed in European and American conflicts, the rationale for warfare shifted from kinship issues, and women's role may have diminished. Nonetheless, when some of the Iroquois peoples (the Mohawks, Cayugas, Senecas, and Onondagas, but not the Oneidas and Tuscaroras) decided to ally with the British, they announced that the "mothers also consented to it," and some well-known Native American women were highly visible in the war effort. Molly Brant, the Mohawk wife of Sir William Johnson, a British official on the frontier, followed the path of many Native American women who had married white men and then mediated between the two cultures (see p. 21). After Johnson died, Brant returned to her people and enjoyed unusual wealth and status. She so actively engaged in revolutionary era diplomacy on the side of the British that one officer claimed that her influence among her tribe was "far superior to that of all their Chiefs put together."[12]

Black women's choices in the Revolution were of a completely different nature. Although small communities of free blacks existed throughout the colonies, the Revolution affected slaves far more profoundly. For example, scarcities of foodstuffs and clothing were particularly hard on slaves, whose owners gave their needs a low priority. However, wartime labor shortages and political circumstances gave slaves more room for maneuvering in their relations with their masters. Southern whites repeatedly complained about slaves' insolence and intractability. Slaveowners were particularly worried about the prospects of insurrection and flight, especially after November 1775, when Virginia's royal governor offered freedom to rebels' slaves who agreed to fight for the British. His goal was twofold: to acquire troops and laborers, and to pressure white slaveholders to stay within the loyalist fold. His offer led to a massive flight of slaves, including men expecting to serve as soldiers and also women and children.

Throughout the war, slave men and women pondered their choice: Could they make it safely to the British lines? Would the British be true protectors? Would the British or the rebels win? An estimated fifty-five thousand southern slaves escaped during the Revolution. Some made their way to the British; others, like Mary Willing Byrd's slaves in Virginia, had the British come to them. When the British left after occupying Byrd's home, forty-nine slaves went with them. Many other slaves simply escaped, looking for freedom independent of the British. Those who went over to the British often did so in groups, frequently with family members. Historians estimate that one-third of those who fled were women, a much higher proportion of runaways than before the Revolution. With nearby British troops offering sanctuary, women with children were willing to take the risk.

Escape from an owner, however, did not mean escape from danger and hardship. Former slaves were forced to work for the British, often at the most disagreeable tasks. When the British occupied Philadelphia, for example, they formed a "Company of Black Pioneers." This group of seventy-two men, fifteen women, and eight children were to "assist in Cleaning the Streets and Removing all Newsiances being thrown into the Streets."[13] Living conditions were harsh. In the British camps, many former slaves succumbed to smallpox and other diseases. In 1781, the British general Alexander Leslie reported that "about 700 Negroes are come down the River in the Small Pox." In an eighteenth-century version of germ warfare, he decided to "distribute them about the Rebell Plantations."[14] This callous attitude toward the black men and women under his care underlines the fact that most British officers viewed the slaves seeking freedom as pawns in the imperial struggle. Despite the unsettled conditions of wartime, black men and women fought an uphill battle to escape to freedom and survive.

White Women: Pacifists, Tories, and Patriots

White women also had to make decisions about the war, but of a very different sort than those of black slave women. The war created a painful situation for Quaker women, whose pacifism was a tenet of their religion. Patriots were often suspicious of Quakers, and Quakers themselves clearly struggled with their political identity. Margaret Morris, a Quaker from New Jersey, was concerned about the welfare of soldiers on both sides, yet she was critical of the patriots' rowdy and aggressive efforts to capture loyalists and proudly recounted her success in hiding a friend from a group of armed men who appeared at her door. At the same time, she described General George Washington's troops as "our side."

American or British, patriot or Tory: Did a woman's political identity follow her husband's? To whom would the wife of a Tory man show allegiance? Women whose loyalist husbands had been exiled or who had gone to fight with the British were subject to ostracism. They sometimes found their land and personal goods plundered. State laws permitting the confiscation of land of known Tories differed slightly regarding the rights of the wife or widow of an "absentee." Massachusetts, for example, acknowledged her dower rights in the estate only if she had remained in the state and not followed her husband. Most generally, states presumed that a woman's allegiance followed her husband's, in accordance with the assumptions of *feme covert*. Significantly, most states did not require the loyalty oaths of women that they required of men, an indication that women were not viewed as political actors.

Not all women followed the allegiance of their husbands. A few took up the patriot cause despite their husbands' loyalty to the British Crown. Florence Cook of Charleston, South Carolina, attempted to regain her family's dispossessed property after the war. In her petition, she described herself as a "Sincere friend to her Country," who taught her daughter "the love of Liberty and this her Native Country." Jane Moffit of Albany, New York, was protected from expulsion despite her husband's political sentiments because, said city leaders, she "has always been esteemed a Friend to the American Cause."[15]

In case after case, decisions about the fate of wives were based on the assumption that wives could not act independently of their husbands, but they also reflected the reality that some women directly aided the loyalist cause. Many women who remained behind when their loyalist husbands left did serve as couriers and spies or in other ways assisted the British. In Albany, thirty-two women were brought to the attention of the New York State Commissioners for Detecting and Defeating Conspiracies in 1780. Some, like Lidia Currey and Rachael Ferguson, were jailed for hiding loyalists in their homes. Others smuggled messages to British troops. In Philadelphia, Margaret Hutchinson carried "Verbal Intelligence, of what, she had seen of their [the Rebels'] different Movements" to British spies. While in absolute numbers such daring women were not numerous, they were considered so serious a threat that patriot committees of safety sought the help of "discreet Women, of Known attachment to the American Cause" to search for contraband and hidden letters on the persons of suspected female Tory couriers.[16]

Maintaining the Troops: The Women Who Served

Service to one's country during wartime often becomes a defining moment of citizenship. Sacrifices become emblems of civic virtue and worthiness. Since the ultimate signs of service are bearing arms and risking death, women's contributions are frequently less valued than men's. During the Revolution, few women actually fought in combat. But the exceptions are notable. In South Carolina, one woman joined her son-in-law to resist 150 British soldiers who were trying to destroy a cache of ammunition. Pennsylvanian Mary Hays McCauley, perhaps the inspiration for the legendary Molly Pitcher, routinely carried water to troops in battle. When her husband fell at the Battle of Monmouth, New Jersey, in 1778, she took his place, keeping a cannon loaded in the face of enemy fire, for which she later received a pension from the state of Pennsylvania "for services rendered in the revolutionary war." Deborah Sampson, later Gannett, was one of a handful of female cross-dressers in the Revolution. Donning men's clothing and enlisting as Robert Shurtleff in the Fourth Massachusetts Regiment, she served eighteen months from

1782 to 1783 and was wounded twice before her sex was discovered and she was discharged. Another woman attempted to enlist in 1778 at Elizabethtown, New Jersey. A suspicious officer required that she submit to a physical exam, and the following day, "ordered the Drums to beat her . . . Threw the Town with the whores march."[17]

More generally, women's role in the military was one they had historically taken in warfare: the so-called camp follower. Some who attached themselves to the patriots' Continental Army under George Washington's command were prostitutes, but more were soldiers' wives. While officers' wives did make protracted visits to encourage their husbands and to participate in entertainments, most women who followed the army were poor men's wives. Their presence may have signaled

◆ Joseph Stone, *Deborah Sampson* (1797)

In 1797, Herman Mann commissioned Joseph Stone to paint this image for the frontispiece of his book on Deborah Sampson's life, titled *The Female Review: or Memoirs of an American Lady.* Sampson had come of age as an indentured servant in Middleborough, Massachusetts. When her period of indenture concluded at age eighteen, she became a masterless woman, an unusual status in the colonial era, having neither husband, father, nor a master to whom she was bound. This gave her rare freedom for a woman, and she moved from town to town, working sometimes as a teacher, sometimes as a weaver. After her service and honorable discharge from the Fourth Massachusetts Regiment (see pp. 112–13), she married and had three children. With the help of her friend Paul Revere, she obtained a small military pension from the U.S. Congress. Although in later statements, she appeared at times apologetic for her "uncouth actions," she also pronounced, "I burst the tyrant bonds which held my sex in awe and clandestinely or by stealth, grasped an opportunity which custom and the world seemed to deny, as a natural privilege."[18] *The Granger Collection, New York.*

a patriotic fervor to aid the cause, but more probably it indicated their desire to attend to their husbands' welfare as well as their inability to function on their own financially. Camp followers, often with their children in tow, faced extraordinary challenges, risking disease, injury, and death. Living under primitive conditions with scanty provisions, some even gave birth in army camps.

But camp followers did provide valuable services. Some were "sutlers," merchants who sold provisions to the troops. More commonly, women such as Sarah Osborn, whose story opens this chapter, did laundry or worked as cooks. Women served as nurses, both in the fields and at the general hospitals for the sick and wounded where conditions were primitive. While male doctors and their assistants performed the skilled work, female nurses were assigned "to see that the close-stools or pots are emptied as soon as possible after they are used . . . they are to see that every patient, upon his admission into the Hospital is immediately washed with warm water, and that his face and hands are washed and head combed every morning."[19] The sexual division of labor relegated women to menial tasks, and no matter how important this work was, women's compensation was small.

Thus, although camp followers lived and worked in the very midst of war, drawing on a physical fortitude associated with male activities, they did not break down traditional expectations about women's proper role. Their presence with the army was for the most part a reflection of their dependence. Women continued to be controlled not only by their husbands but also by what one historian terms "that most male of institutions, the military."[20] Their activities were extensions of women's traditional household work. Although many undoubtedly took pride in their patriotic contributions, they did not exhibit a new sense of independence.

Some women did not follow the armies but did observe the fighting as it came to them. Occupying armies commandeered homes for quartering soldiers, and women frequently bore the brunt of their demands for food and firewood. In September 1777, Elizabeth Drinker, alone with her children in Philadelphia, found herself the unwilling hostess to a British officer: "Our officer mov'd his lodging from the bleu Chamber to the little front parlor, so that he has the two front parlors, a chamber up two pair of stairs for his bagge, and the Stable wholly to himself, besides the use of the kitchen."[21] Catherine Van Cortlandt, a Tory woman, wrote disparagingly to her husband about the patriot troops who commandeered her house in New Jersey and complained that "the farmers are forbid to sell me provisions, and the millers to grind our grain. Our woods are cut down for the use of their army, and that which you bought and left corded near the river my servants are forbid to touch, though we are in the greatest distress for the want of it."[22] Women caught in the crossfire worried about their personal safety and that of their children. While reported rapes were infrequent, British soldiers were brutal on occasion. More commonly, women had to adjust to being alone and to handling the day-to-day affairs of running a farm or managing a business in a husband's prolonged absence. Their independent management proved to be one of their most significant roles in the revolutionary era.

A small group of patriot women, reminiscent of the Daughters of Liberty who had organized spinning bees in the early stages of the Revolution, carved out more public ways of participating in the war effort by raising funds for the beleaguered Continental army. Following a discouraging defeat at Charleston in 1780, Esther DeBerdt Reed, the wife of the governor of Pennsylvania, and Sarah Franklin Bache, the daughter of Benjamin Franklin, organized the Ladies Association of Philadelphia to raise the considerable sum of $300,000 for the troops. In a powerfully worded broadside, Reed announced that "the Women of America manifested a firm resolution to contribute as much as could depend on them, to the deliverance of their country." The broadside urged prosperous women to go without luxuries to aid the cause and asked poorer women to offer what they could. After outlining the rationale for the fund-raising, Reed challenged anyone who would doubt the group's patriotic purpose: "[H]e cannot be a good citizen who will not applaud our efforts for the relief of the armies which defend our lives, our possessions, our liberty."[23]

The Pennsylvania women publicized their efforts and sent letters to women in other states, urging them to raise funds as well. In Virginia, the scattered nature of settlement made an exact duplication of Pennsylvania's door-to-door effort impossible, but Martha Wayles Jefferson, wife of Governor Thomas Jefferson, did encourage other Virginia women to raise funds (Martha herself was not in good health), describing it as an "opportunity of proving that they also participate on those virtuous feelings."[24] In most cases, the sums raised were modest. In New Jersey, women collected $15,488 in paper dollars, but because of high inflation, the money purchased only 380 pairs of stockings for the state's soldiers.

The distribution of donations that the Philadelphia women collected offers a revealing insight into perceptions of women's supporting role. Writing to Washington, Reed explained that the women did not want the money to go into a general fund that would provide soldiers "an article to which they are entitled from the public." Rather, the women hoped that their money — approximately $2 per soldier in hard currency — might be given directly to the soldiers. Washington demurred: the men might waste it on liquor, and having hard currency, when they were generally paid in paper money, might create discontent and exacerbate inflation. He declared that their "benevolent donation" should be used to provide men with shirts and requested further that the women make the shirts themselves. In the midst of the exchange, Reed died of dysentery, but Bache followed through with the project, eventually sending Washington 2,200 shirts. A French visitor to Bache's home reported that "on each shirt was the name of the married or unmarried lady who made it."[25]

Thus, however novel the Philadelphia women's plan may have been, Washington's response placed their efforts firmly in the realm of woman's more traditional sphere — of sewing for her family. The Philadelphia women's efforts may have been more overtly political than the service of poor women following the army, but in both cases women's contributions were constrained by traditional notions of women's roles. The link between women's patriotism and the domestic sphere was to be one of the principal ideological legacies of the Revolution.

◆ REVOLUTIONARY ERA LEGACIES

The patriots emerged victorious in 1781 when the British surrendered at York-town, Virginia. In that same year, the colonies, now states, ratified the Articles of Confederation, their first attempt at national governance. Weaknesses in that body led eventually to adoption of the U.S. Constitution in 1788 and the inauguration of George Washington as the new nation's first president in 1789. As a national government was being framed, the various states also wrote constitutions. The period was rich with debates about the nature of government and the rights of citizens, as Americans pondered the implications of their Revolution. What were the legacies of the Revolution for women? For many, war and revolution translated into hardship and poverty; for others, new opportunities emerged, but these were always constrained by prevailing assumptions about women's marginal role in public life.

A Changing World for Native American Women

The American victory realigned European settler claims on the continent and brought changes to many Native women's lives as their people encountered a new republic intent on western expansion. Indian groups that sided with Britain, in particular, suffered devastating losses in the war. American forces in New York invaded Iroquois territory in 1779, burning forty towns and destroying crops. The Cherokees in the Appalachian region to the south suffered a similar destruction. Native American men's preoccupation with warfare and their role in diplomacy may have heightened their power within their own communities, but it also increased women's responsibilities in maintaining their communities in the men's prolonged absences, and in the face of destruction, disease, and starvation.

   In the postwar period, as the weakened Native Americans started to come under the power of the new federal government, challenges to traditional gender roles arose. Men acted as primary mediators between their nations and the newly created American government. As men's roles took on magnified importance, women may have correspondingly lost influence in their communities. The example of Cherokee leader Nancy Ward, however, diverges from this general trend. Since her participation in a battle against the Creek in the 1750s, Ward had been recognized as a "War Woman," a position that garnered high esteem and broader authority over the fates of war captives. Along with Cherokee male leaders, Ward spoke to U.S. commissioners in treaty negotiations during and after the Revolutionary War. At the 1781 meeting at the Holston River in present-day Tennessee, Ward used a language of kinship and her symbolic maternal authority to call for peace between the United States and the Cherokee: "Let your women's sons be ours; our sons be yours. Let your women hear our words."[26] Almost forty years later, at the age of eighty, Ward would still be invoking her authority as an elder "Beloved Woman" to protect her people's land and sovereignty. (See Reading into the Past: "Beloved Children: Cherokee Women Petition the National Council," pp. 178–79.) By that time, however, Cherokee women's pathways to political authority had narrowed considerably.

◆ **Redefining Gender Roles among the Creeks**
This early nineteenth-century painting features Creek Indians as U.S. agent Benjamin Hawkins introduces them to plows as a first step in "Americanizing" them. Hawkins focuses his attention on the men, placing his back to a woman who stands amid the foodstuffs she has produced. This stance represents white officials' and missionaries' goal of redefining gender roles among the Creek so that men would abandon hunting in exchange for farming, while women would give up their traditional role of raising crops to undertake domestic roles in the home. *The Granger Collection, New York.*

The government's efforts to encourage Native Americans to assimilate to white norms also disturbed traditional patterns of gender. American leaders insisted that men give up hunting to become farmers and that Native American women become farmers' wives. In a letter to the Cherokees in 1796, President Washington was explicit about his expectations. "You will easily add flax and cotton which you may dispose of to the White people; or have it made up by your own women into clothing for yourselves. Your wives and daughters can soon learn to spin and weave."[27] But if white Americans envisioned a family order in which women were subordinate, Cherokee women adapted to the new expectations in ways that maintained their traditional roles in the community. They continued their customary farming work, tended livestock, and took on the responsibilities of spinning and weaving. In contrast, men found it far more difficult to adjust to their changed circumstances. Loss of land and depletion of fur-bearing animals deprived men of hunting, an important masculine activity with both economic and spiritual significance. Native Americans' overuse of alcohol also contributed to their exploitation and to unhappy domestic situations in which women were abused.

After the Revolution, Native Americans with the most proximity to the expanding white population became the objects of Protestant missionary activity. Although white missionaries sought to convert the Natives, calls for change also came from within Indian nations. Handsome Lake, a Seneca religious prophet who had been influenced by the Quakers, called for major reforms for his people. He promoted a return to some of the old ways, especially in regard to religion. He condemned the abuse of alcohol and criticized men's physical mistreatment of their wives. At the same time, however, Handsome Lake also urged that the Iroquois follow the family patterns of whites: men should take up farming and women should limit themselves to spinning and weaving. Privileging the nuclear family and the husband-wife relationship, he downplayed the older emphasis on kinship relations and was especially critical of Iroquois matrons. In the long run, assimilative pressures and a changed economic and political order undermined women's position among many Native American peoples, especially where men took on economic roles of increased importance to the community and their families. But that process was neither immediate nor universal.

For Indian women farther to the west, however, the American Revolution paled in importance to other changes in economy, culture, and health. In 1776, for example, the Lakota Sioux expanded into the Black Hills and incorporated this mountainous region as a sacred site for their expanding horse- and bison-based society. California Indians attacked a San Diego mission in 1775, responding in part to the abuse of Native women by Spanish soldiers. Northwest Coast Indians found their economy and gendered labor transformed by the late eighteenth-century international rush for sea otter pelts. Similar to the earlier fur trade of the northeast, the otter skin trade introduced new textiles and metal goods into indigenous culture. In some cases, Northwest Coast groups offered Native women captives as sex workers to European, American, and Russian traders who appeared on their coast. Finally, between 1779 and 1784, a terrible smallpox pandemic decimated indigenous western communities — hitting pregnant women and children especially hard — as it spread along continental trade routes. Some Plains Indian bands lost up to 80 percent of their members, causing further migration and regrouping for survival.[28]

These were some of the transformed Indian societies that the young Shoshone woman Sacagawea observed as she joined Meriwether Lewis and William Clark on a transcontinental journey to the Pacific Ocean, in 1804–1806. Sacagawea first met Lewis and Clark in the Mandan-Hidatsu village in what is now North Dakota. As a young girl, she had been taken from her homeland in the Rocky Mountains and eventually sold to the man who would become her husband, a French Canadian trader named Toussaint Charbonneau. Sacagawea accompanied Charbonneau when he was hired by Lewis and Clark's exploratory expedition of the newly acquired Louisiana Purchase. Pregnant when she began this journey, Sacagawea gave birth to her son as the party traveled westward. Other Shoshone women also

◆ **Sacagawea Monument, Portland, Oregon**

The Shoshone woman known as Sacagawea left a powerful legacy, although differing versions of her biography, and even her name continue, to be debated. This statue of Sacagawea was commissioned in 1905 by the white women's clubs of Portland, Oregon, in recognition of the Shoshone guide and translator to the Lewis and Clark expedition a hundred years before. The statue, by Denver sculptor Alice Cooper, was one of the first monuments to depict an actual historical woman in the United States. From this point on, Sacagawea's role as national symbol, both of the contribution of Native people to American history and their tragic fate at the hands of white settlers, began to grow. She is almost always represented as she is here: with her baby on her back and her hand pointing the way west. *MPI/Getty Images.*

helped Lewis and Clark cross the Continental Divide, driving pack horses and carrying burdens, as women, especially captives, were expected to do in both Mandan and Shoshone society. Sacagawea proved invaluable to the expedition as someone who knew the Rocky Mountain terrain and Shoshone language. Although Lewis's diary entries on Shoshone people emphasized the "drudgery" of the women, he also inadvertently recorded female skills of horse care, transportation, and gathering of "wild fruits and roots" necessary to cross-country travel.[29] By focusing on Sacagawea, we can understand that Lewis and Clark's much celebrated journey utilized the everyday knowledge, labor, and mobility of Native American women.

African American Women: Freedom and Slavery

For African American women, the Revolution also left a complex, but completely different, legacy. At the end of the war, many slaves, known as "Black Loyalists," who had fled to the British to achieve their freedom, were evacuated by ship from New York, Charleston, and Savannah. Of those who left from New York and whose sex is known, 42.3 percent were women, and apparently many had their children with them. Some of these African Americans were sold again into slavery in the West Indies; others were shipped to Nova Scotia, where they eked out an existence in harsh conditions; and some ended up in another marginal environment, a new colony in Sierra Leone, West Africa. Mary Perth, born into slavery in Virginia, joined this migration along with her children and her husband, Caesar. The Perth family traveled in company with other devout black Methodists who had established a new meetinghouse in Sierra Leone. Perth supported her children by running a boardinghouse and restaurant near the Freetown wharves, where she had to interact with sailors from the British slave ships working close to the small West African colony of free migrants.[30] For Mary Perth and other black loyalist women, the revolutionary conflict resulted in global migration and great risks taken to establish new lives in another part of the British Empire.

For some African Americans who had not joined the British, the most important legacy of the Revolution was freedom. Even before the conflict, a small movement had supported manumission (owners granting slaves their freedom), primarily the result of the Quakers' growing revulsion against slavery. The ideological issues at the center of the Revolution, especially those concerning natural rights and liberty, encouraged some white Americans to examine the institution of slavery. Even for those with little humanitarian interest in slaves themselves, the incongruity of building a nation based on notions of liberty while maintaining chattel slavery was troublesome. More mundane concerns also promoted antislavery sentiment — white immigrant workers who were increasingly available and who were easily hired and fired became more attractive in the urban commercial culture of the North. Anxieties about slave insurrections during the war raised further questions about the slave system.

African Americans were active participants in the emancipation process, especially in Massachusetts. Mum Bett, later known as Elizabeth Freeman, was the slave of Colonel John Ashley in Sheffield, Massachusetts. In 1781, she petitioned a Massachusetts county court for her freedom. Freeman's suit, *Brom and Bett v. Ashley*, combined with several others, led to the state court's 1783 decision that "there can be no such thing as perpetual servitude of a rational creature."[31] In other northern states, manumission came through legislation. Only Vermont, in 1777, provided for immediate emancipation. Elsewhere, the process was protracted. In Pennsylvania, unborn children of slaves would be apprenticed until they were twenty-eight years old. Although each year more slaves became free in the North, one-fourth of northern blacks were still enslaved as late as 1810. This gradualism meant that slave women would continue to bear children who would not be fully free until they were adults, but they could take some comfort in their grandchildren's future freedom.

The emancipation laws, as well as individual manumissions in the North and the Upper South and the migration of southern free blacks, created growing free black populations in the last years of the eighteenth century, especially in cities such as Philadelphia, Boston, and New York. Although a small number of these African Americans were able to carve out a modest success, constrained education and pervasive discrimination limited their opportunities. Most women worked at jobs similar to those that had occupied them when they were slaves — domestic work, washing, cooking, and child care. Some black women were proprietors, especially of boardinghouses, where they would have been important resources for the

◆ **Susan Anne Livingston Ridley Sedgwick,** *Elizabeth Freeman ("Mum Bett")* **(1811)**
After her successful freedom suit that led to the end of slavery in Massachusetts, Mum Bett adopted the name Elizabeth Freeman. She lived the remainder of her life as a paid servant in the family of Theodor Sedgwick, who had served as her lawyer. Theodor's daughter Catherine Sedgwick later wrote an account of her freedom suit and Catherine's sister-in-law Susan Sedgwick painted the watercolor shown here. In the original portrait, Freeman's dress is vivid blue, and she wears what is apparently a gold necklace around her neck. Why do you suppose the Sedgwick family members made the effort to document Freeman's life in words and portrait? What is the artist hoping to convey about Freeman in this image? *The Granger Collection, New York.*

READING INTO THE PAST

Ona Judge's Escape

Ona Maria Judge, listed as "Oney" in this runaway ad, was born in 1773 on the Mount Vernon estate of George and Martha Washington to her enslaved mother, Betty. At the age of sixteen, Judge traveled north to serve as the First Lady's domestic slave in New York. When the U.S. capitol moved to Philadelphia in 1790, Judge was again moved with other enslaved men and women to work in the new Executive Mansion. But Philadelphia had passed a law that required all incoming slaveowners to free any enslaved adults who stayed in the state longer than six months. George Washington and his legal advisors worked out a plan to get around the manumission requirement by circulating the Washingtons' slaves back and forth between Philadelphia and Mount Vernon every six months. These periodic visits between 1791 and 1796 to Mount Vernon allowed Judge to stay connected to friends and family she had left behind, but they also kept her in bondage. When Judge learned that she was to be sent back to Virginia permanently as a wedding present for Martha's granddaughter, Elizabeth Parke Custis, the twenty-two-year-old Judge gathered her courage and escaped from Philadelphia to Portsmouth, New Hampshire. Although the Washingtons tried repeatedly to recapture her and her life in New England was often hard, Ona Judge lived the rest of her days as a free woman until her death at age fifty-two.

The document below is a copy of the ad placed in several newspapers by Frederick Kitt, Executive Mansion steward. Runaway ads like this appeared frequently in the newspapers of the early republic.

Ten Dollars Reward.

ABSCONDED from the household of the President of the United States, on Saturday afternoon, ONEY JUDGE, a light Mulatto girl, much

freed blacks migrating to the cities during this period. Others opened shops and restaurants that built upon their domestic skills. In Portsmouth, New Hampshire, Dinah Gibson, locally well known for her baking, established "Dinah's Cottage."

A handful of women were prominent enough to make a mark in the historical record. Lydia York, for example, petitioned the Philadelphia Abolition Society to assist her in indenturing her niece Hetty. Jane Coggeshall, who gained her freedom during the war when she and two other slaves gave information about British troops to Rhode Island patriots, later petitioned the state to confirm her freedom, lest her former owners attempt to reenslave her. Catherine Ferguson, an ex-slave freckled, with very black eyes, and bushy black hair — She is of middle stature, but slender and delicately made, about 20 years of age. She has many changes of very good clothes of all sorts, but they are not sufficiently recollected to describe.

As there was no suspicion of her going off, and it happened without the least provocation, it is not easy to conjecture whither she is gone — or fully, what her design is; but as she may attempt to escape by water, all masters of vessels and others are cautioned against receiving her on board, altho' she may, and probably will endeavour to pass for a free woman, and it is said has, wherewithal to pay her passage.

Ten dollars will be paid to any person, (white or black) who will bring her home, if taken in the city, or on board any vessel in the harbor; and a further reasonable sum if apprehended and brought home, from a greater distance, and in proportion to the distance.

May 24   FRED. KITT, Steward

SOURCE: *Claypoole's American Daily Advertiser*, May 25, 1796, in Erica Armstrong Dunbar, *Never Caught: The Washingtons' Relentless Pursuit of Their Runaway Slave, Ona Judge* (New York: 37Ink/Atria, 2017), 99.

QUESTIONS FOR ANALYSIS

1. What language does the ad use to speculate about Judge's motives for running away, and what assumptions does this wording reveal?
2. What evidence can such ads offer about the history of enslaved women during the postrevolutionary period? What silences do they contain?

who had purchased her own freedom, established a school for poor black and white children in New York in 1793. Another former slave, Eleanor Harris, became the first black teacher in Philadelphia. Ona Judge gained notoriety as the fugitive slave of Martha Washington who escaped the Executive Mansion in Philadelphia for a free home in New Hampshire. (See Reading into the Past: "Ona Judge's Escape.")

As they worked at their jobs and cared for their families, many free black women participated in building the network of black institutions, including churches and benevolent societies devoted to self-help efforts that had emerged by the turn of the century. Their role in these organizations, however, has remained largely obscured in the historical record. These free black institutions were a source of strength and pride for the community, but they also exemplified the segregated lives that African Americans lived in the North. Emancipation brought freedom for some black women and men, but within the constraints of a racial and economic hierarchy. The egalitarian promises implicit in revolutionary ideology were closed to African Americans.

In the South, these promises were even less in evidence. In the Upper South, there was a spate of individual manumissions, especially through the wills of slaveholders, and the free black population did expand significantly. But there was no widespread sentiment for dispensing with the institution altogether. Most slaveowners were not unduly troubled by the implications of a rhetoric of individual freedom and natural rights for their system of chattel labor. Indeed, slaveowners became more deeply entrenched in the institution after the war, especially in the Deep South, where the 1793 invention of the cotton gin, which mechanically removed the seed and hull from the cotton fiber, made the crop more productive and thus more profitable. This gave new impetus to the slave system, which was also reinforced by increased importation of African slaves, a trade explicitly permitted by the U.S. Constitution until 1808. The regional differences in patterns of slavery grew after the Revolution, with slaves in the Deep South more likely to maintain a more distinct African-based culture and to live in more isolation from whites.

In the Chesapeake region, tobacco declined in importance and the region's economy diversified, creating more varied jobs for slave populations. While some women had developed textile skills during the revolutionary period, for the most part the skilled slaves in the Upper South were men, trained as wagon makers, mill workers, or builders. As some male slaves became artisans, women inherited more of the disagreeable labor such as breaking new ground and collecting manure. Slaves also became extremely important to the growing urban areas of the region, and women in particular were used in the tobacco factories of Petersburg and Richmond, Virginia. Women also served as domestic workers and participated in city markets, selling wares such as cakes, oysters, and garden produce, an occupation that gave them an unusual amount of liberty to move about the city.

Most slaves, however, enjoyed little personal freedom. This was particularly evident in the way in which slaveholders in the Upper South increasingly sought to reproduce the slave population, forcing some black women into sexual relations with men not of their own choosing. Others encouraged slaves to form families. Thomas Jefferson provided gifts for at least one couple on his Virginia plantation and explicitly commented on the value of a fertile female slave: "I consider a woman who brings a child every two years as more profitable than the best man on the farm."[32]

Despite their appreciation of female slaves as breeders, slaveowners throughout the South expected pregnant women to work well into their pregnancy and to return to their labors almost immediately after delivery. The hardships of being a mother under these conditions were magnified by the constant threat of separation. A white observer in Wilmington, North Carolina, in 1778 described the

◆ **Women Slaves in the Tobacco Fields**

In 1798, architect Benjamin Henry Latrobe produced this image labeled "An overseer doing his duty. Sketched from life near Fredericksburg." Latrobe apparently recognized the irony presented by the overseer, a white male in the employ of the plantation owner, standing idly on a tree stump, his duty merely to watch the two women slaves hard at work hoeing in a tobacco field. *The Granger Collection, New York.*

trauma he witnessed: "A wench clung to a little daughter, and implored, with the most agonizing supplication, that they might not be separated."[33] Children could be sold from their parents, and husbands from their wives, even in the households of paternalistic owners. The effects of financial reversals or the death of the master often rippled through the slave quarters, undercutting slaves' efforts to create a stable family life.

White Women: An Ambiguous Legacy

Just as the Revolution had mixed results for black women, its meaning for white women eludes easy generalizations. Petitions from widows and soldiers' wives provide eloquent evidence for the personal tragedies that came with war. Sarah Welsh's husband had died in 1780, but "being a destress widow not knowing how to or whom aplication was to be made . . . untill it was too late," she waited until 1791 to ask the government for his back pay.[34] Many wives of Tory men, too, found themselves in dire straits. After the war, they waged lengthy, and only rarely successful, legal battles to regain property seized when their husbands left to fight with the British. Many impoverished women worked in the few avenues of employment offered to women, such as shopkeepers, teachers, innkeepers, servants, seam-stresses, or milliners. By 1800, as the nation moved toward the first stages of industrialization and the "putting-out" industries (those industries focused on producing goods such as textiles, shoes, and straw bonnets) expanded, poorer women increasingly turned to doing piecework in their homes (see pp. 167–68). For more privileged educated women, war and revolution contributed to a changed conception of self, as many expanded their horizons beyond the narrow sphere of the hearth. Women whose husbands served in the army or in the new state or fed-eral governments were left alone for extended periods. As women had been doing since the early colonial period, they became "deputy husbands," managing farms and businesses and often rising impressively to the new challenges.[35]

In the extant correspondence and diaries from this period, primarily from the wives of officers and politicians, a distinct pattern concerning women's roles as deputy husbands emerges. Men originally left detailed instructions, urging their wives to consult male kin or neighbors. Through time, many men began to trust their wives' judgment; New Yorker James Clinton, for example, commented to his wife, Mary, "I Can't give any Other Directions About Home more than what I have done but must Leave all to your good Management."[36] Women themselves often made pointed reference to their own competence, and some even asserted a new language of companionate marriage. When Lucy Flucker Knox in New York wrote to her husband, Henry Knox, she commented that she was "quite a woman of business," adding, "[I hope that in the future] you will not consider yourself as commander in chief of your own house — but be convinced that there is such a thing as equal command."[37]

Although few women challenged their subordinate position as overtly as Lucy Knox, the postwar years did see a significant questioning of white women's status in the home and, to some extent, in politics. Early in the revolutionary crisis, women speaking about politics often made apologies, almost ritualistically accepting wom-en's inferiority. In a June 1776 letter to a female friend, Elizabeth Feilde followed her comments on contemporary politics with the following self-deprecating remark: "No; I assure you it's a subject for which I have not either Talents or Inclination to enter upon."[38] But in the turmoil of rebellion and war, the apologies became less evi-dent as astute women got caught up in the dramatic events unfolding before them. Eliza Wilkinson of South Carolina frankly resented men's claim that women had no business with politics, writing to a friend in 1782, "I won't have it thought that because we are the weaker sex as to bodily strength, my dear, we are capable of noth-ing more than minding the dairy, visiting the poultry-house, and all such domestic concerns. . . . They won't even allow us the liberty of thought, and that is all I want."[39]

As Wilkinson's term "liberty of thought" suggests, some women made overt connections between the ideology of the Revolution concerning natural rights, liberty, and equality and the position of women. Abigail Adams's admonition to her husband, John Adams, that the men drawing up the new government and its code of laws should "remember the ladies" is probably the most famous expression of the handful of elite women who hoped to see at least modest changes in women's status. The issue attracted a significant amount of attention in the decade after the Revolution. Following publication in the United States in 1792 of *A Vindication of the Rights of Woman* by the English activist Mary Wollstonecraft, American magazines debated women's rights and roles. Some articles referred to marriage as a form of slavery. Others blamed women's limited education for women's vanity and superficiality.

Limited Citizenship: White Women's Legal Status and Education

Did the flurry of attention to women's rights in the postrevolutionary era lead to an improvement in white women's status? The states in the new nation were now free of British legal statutes and could theoretically construct laws in keeping with the new emphasis on protecting individual rights. Divorce law was one area in which women did benefit. British common law did not allow divorce, but now all states except South Carolina permitted it. Still, the procedure was difficult. In most states, divorce petitions required action by the state assembly. Courts in Pennsylvania and the four New England states could decree divorce. Causes offered for divorce changed over time, hinting at a slight shift in marital expectations. During most of the colonial period, women were far more likely than men to seek a divorce, usually doing so on the grounds of desertion. After the Revolution, the grounds women used expanded to include adultery, and more men began to seek divorce, usually for desertion. The changes were subtle ones, as one historian concedes: "All one can say, and perhaps it is enough, is that after the war women were physically moving out of their unhappy households, an action that, judging from the divorce literature, had been relatively uncommon before the war."[40]

In other legal matters, white women gained little. In many states, widows' rights to their dower were, if anything, eroded in the years after the Revolution. In addition, states maintained the British system of coverture, a major impediment to married women's autonomy. Women continued to be excluded from juries and from legal training and thus were excluded from the male political culture that centered at the courthouse.

Most significantly, women were denied the vote. Despite the revolutionary rhetoric of equality, the majority of the founding fathers believed that in a democratic republic only independent people should be permitted to vote, and independent people, by definition, owned property. Thus propertyless men and all women were excluded. In the case of women, however, exclusion was less a matter of property than of sex. Married or not, women were assumed to be dependent creatures by nature. The fleeting exception to this assumption was New Jersey, whose 1776 state constitution did not explicitly define the qualifications for voters, declaring only that "all inhabitants" who met certain property and residence requirements "shall be entitled to vote," thus technically permitting both white women and blacks to vote. In the 1780s, some property-holding women seized the initiative and voted in local elections. A 1796 statute specifically excluded black people of both sexes but reaffirmed white women's right to vote.

By 1800, however, criticism of women as voters in New Jersey had mounted. Some concern was voiced about occasional voting by wives and daughters who lived at home (and were thus not independent) and by men without property. When an 1807 referendum election revealed extensive fraud, the legislature moved to tighten suffrage requirements. All women were excluded on the grounds that they were easily manipulated by men. But at the same time, the state expanded suffrage to include propertyless white men and sons living at home, further emphasizing the different political stature of men and women.

The results in New Jersey lend credence to the conclusion that, while men gained as a result of the Revolution, white women actually lost ground. After 1800, as states granted universal white male suffrage, women's exclusion from suffrage defined their political dependence and inequality more sharply than ever before. But to define women's experience solely in terms of their formal political and legal roles obscures other significant factors that shaped their lives. For many women, the revolutionary years sparked a political consciousness, one that encouraged women to move outside their preoccupations of home and family. At the same time, improvements in white women's education — the substantial number of revolutionary women's diaries and letters indicate that more women had become fully literate — helped to broaden women's vision and open some opportunities.

The move for improved education for both men and women accelerated after the war — for practical as well as ideological reasons. As the new nation began the long process of industrialization, its more complex economy required literacy and other skills. Formal education became more necessary as print replaced oral traditions. Americans also believed that the new republic required an educated, enlightened citizenry. For women, the interest in educational reform was linked to the civic good. Observers roundly criticized the type of education elite white women most often received. Beyond basic literacy, women were taught domestic skills and refinements meant to enhance their position in the marriage market. But what sort of wife and mother could such a poorly educated woman become? The image of flighty women concerned primarily with fashion and sentimental novels seemed especially out of step with the expectations of the new nation.

Critics who addressed the issue of women's education at length included Mercy Otis Warren, Judith Sargent Murray, and Dr. Benjamin Rush. Although they challenged conventional assumptions that more fully educating women would make them less feminine and more discontented with their lot, these critics continued to recommend that women be educated primarily to remain within the domestic sphere. Most of the proponents of improved education for women articulated an ideology that historians have called Republican Motherhood, the idea that women had vital roles in educating their children for their duties as citizens. One notable advocate, Abigail Adams, wrote, "If we mean to have heroes, statesmen, and philosophers, we should have learned women. If as much depends as it is allowed upon the early education of youth and the first principles which are instilled take the deepest root great benefit must arise from the literary accomplishments in women."[41] In addition to this emphasis on children, the ideology of the postrevolutionary years stressed that women's enlightened and

◆ **John Singleton Copley,** *Mercy Otis Warren* **(1763)**

The 1763 portrait by John Singleton Copley makes Mercy Otis Warren's high status quite clear. The picture also emphasizes her femininity. Contemporaries understood the nasturtiums entwined in her hands as symbols of fertility, and indeed she had given birth the year before she sat for this portrait and would have another child the following year. Through her prolific writing and elite social networks, Warren carried on an active political and intellectual life. She wrote plays and poetry and commented astutely on political questions of the day, such as the debate over ratification of the Constitution. Her 1805 *History of the Rise, Progress and Termination of the American Revolution,* a monumental three-volume work, reflected Warren's deep commitment to the cause of the Revolution and her hope for America's future as a repository of republican virtue. Consider Warren's bearing and pose in this portrait. What sort of personality is suggested? How does Copley reveal Warren as a woman of many accomplishments? *Museum of Fine Arts, Boston, Massachusetts, USA/ Bequest of Winslow Warren/Bridgeman Images.*

virtuous influence on their husbands could contribute mightily to civic culture and order. (See Primary Sources: "Education and Republican Motherhood," pp. 147–53.)

The new thinking about women's education bore some fruit. Not only did some states, like Massachusetts in 1789, institute free elementary public schooling for all children, but academies and boarding schools specifically designed for middle-class and elite women proliferated in the North and eventually appeared in the South. Parents and educators expected that this enhanced education would, according to one historian, "allow women to instruct their sons in the principles of patriotism, to make their homes well-run havens of efficiency, to converse knowledgeably with their husbands on a variety of subjects, and to understand family finance."[42] Rather than discouraging women from domestic pursuits, education was expected to improve their chances for a suitable and happy marriage. But many of the women educated at the new academies apparently were inspired to move beyond the household sphere. Some became writers, missionaries, or reformers, and a substantial number became teachers themselves, pursuing jobs that offered the earliest form of professional opportunity for American women. The ideology of Republican Motherhood and the educational reforms it inspired began a long process of expanded opportunities for women. Eventually women would demand opportunities to learn as much as, and even alongside, men.

Women and Religion

In addition to the impact of new educational opportunities, religious communities and the continued influence of evangelical revivals offered important venues of expression for black and white women living in the early republic. Two radical religious groups centered around charismatic women who broke dramatically with traditional female piety and gender conventions. After recovering from a serious illness in 1776, Jemima Wilkinson, a former Quaker, believed that she had been resurrected for the sole purpose of preaching repentance before the final days of judgment. Wilkinson traveled the northeast, primarily in Rhode Island and Connecticut, attracting a host of devoted followers. Mother Ann Lee, a founder of the "Shaking Quakers," or more simply "Shakers" (so named for the ecstatic dances that were part of their worship), styled herself as a preacher and prophet. In different ways, both of these remarkable women minimized their femaleness. Wilkinson dressed in male-style clothing and insisted on the gender-neutral title of Public Universal Friend. Followers consistently referred to the Friend with the pronouns "he" and "him." Mother Ann Lee required celibacy not only for herself but also for her followers. Lee's adamant denial of sexuality kept the issue of gender from undercutting her religious leadership.

In newer congregations, such as northern Baptist churches, white women, and some black women as well, could vote to elect deacons and even "exhort," or act as a lay preacher. One of the more radical groups, the Separates, or Strict Congregationalists, explicitly affirmed women in their "just Right . . . to speak openly

◆ *Jemima Wilkinson (The Public Universal Friend),* **1844**
This lithograph of the self-styled Public Universal Friend was based on a painting made by John L. D. Mathies in 1816 near the end of Wilkinson's life. The image conveys Wilkinson's lifelong adoption of men's clothing. After hearing the Friend preach in New Haven, Connecticut, one critical observer described Wilkinson in 1787 as wearing "a light cloth Cloke with a Cape like a Man's — Purple Gown, long sleeves to Wristbands — Mans shirt down to the Hands with neckband — purple handkerchief or Neckcloth tied around the neck like a man's — No Cap — Hair combed turned over & not long — wears a Watch — Man's Hat."[43] How does the artist present the preacher's gender in this portrait? Although Wilkinson's style of dress may have stemmed from the religious belief that it was possible to transcend sex, why else might Wilkinson have preferred male attire? *Library of Congress. From* Memoir of Jemima Wilkinson, *1844.*

in the Church."[44] In the South, only one group, the Separate Baptists, permitted women official roles, appointing them as deaconnesses and eldresses. A Baptist minister traveling in Virginia and the Carolinas in the early 1770s described the duties of the eldresses as "praying, and teaching at their [women's] separate assemblies; presiding there for maintenance of rules and government; consulting with sisters about matters of the church which concern them, and representing their sense thereof to the elders; attending at the unction of sick sisters; and at the baptism of women, that all may be done orderly."[45]

But none of the larger denominations accepted women as preachers equal to male ministers. In backcountry regions, some women may have been traveling preachers, but generally their roles, even in evangelical churches, were unofficial. Typically, they served as counselors. Women created informal religious groups, encouraging friends and families along the road to conversion. Sarah Osborn, a white woman of Newport, Rhode Island (not the same Sarah Osborn who participated in the Revolutionary War), organized a young women's religious society in 1737 that met more or less continuously for fifty years. In the 1760s, she expanded her focus and on Sunday evenings taught a group of African Americans in her home. Although Osborn was criticized for usurping the role of male ministers, throughout her life she continued to exert considerable influence within her congregation, an experience shared by many women in evangelical churches throughout the country.

By 1800, the ability of white women to be active in doctrinal disputes and matters of church discipline and procedures diminished. In northern Baptist churches, for example, women's public voices were increasingly silenced after the Revolution. As the Baptists matured as a religious denomination, a growing bureaucracy and a new emphasis on an educated ministry eroded women's position in favor of men. Establishing respectability for the church often meant controlling "disorderly" women. This shift in women's influence was accomplished despite the fact that women outnumbered men in the congregation almost two to one, yet another indication that the egalitarian spirit of the postrevolutionary era did not encompass white women.

This suppression of women's voices was not long-lived, however. Beginning around 1795, another series of revivals, loosely categorized as the Second Great Awakening, swept the nation in periodic waves, lasting through the 1830s. In the eighteenth century, women's role in evangelical religion paralleled their course in the public sphere, where the ideas formulated around Republican Motherhood articulated a civic role for patriotic women that was only partially realized. Yet both evangelical religion and Republican Motherhood formed an important rationale for women's expanding roles in a wide range of benevolent and reform associations, other areas of informal public space that white women claimed as their own in the nineteenth century.

The religious ferment that so powerfully affected white women also touched the lives of many African American women. A wide diversity of religious practices existed among the enslaved population of the early American republic. By the late eighteenth century, a minority of African-born elders lived alongside a younger American-born majority. In certain regions, such as the Lowcountry Sea Islands, some families continued to practice Islam, brought with them on the Middle Passage from West Africa. Although poorly documented, ritual practices of West African and Kongo-Angolan ancestors also persisted in areas with large slave populations. Women played significant roles in such religious expression, often serving as healers, mediums, or priestesses.

In addition, both free and enslaved African Americans continued to adopt Christianity by infusing their theology and worship practice with West African–influenced elements. Some scholars suggest that the evangelical emphasis on spontaneous conversion harmonized with West African beliefs that "the deity entered the body of the devotee and displaced his or her personality."[46] Southern slaves infused this new form of Protestantism with African religious elements to create a distinctive religious style. In turn, African influences — especially dances and shouts typical of West African religious rituals — influenced the shape of white evangelicalism. Black women were highly visible in their communities of worship. They consistently made up the majority of congregants in Baptist and Methodist churches of Virginia in the 1790s, for example. Barred from being ordained for-mally as preachers, black women made their voices heard in black and interracial evangelical meetings through personal testimony and a form of spiritual encour-agement known as "exhortation." In these ways, black women were able to create a sphere of influence and spiritual power for themselves, roles that would assume even greater importance in the nineteenth century, as independent black denom-inations emerged in the North and black Christianity spread in the slave quarters of the South.

◆ CONCLUSION: To the Margins of Political Action

Whatever their social or racial group, women living on the eastern part of the continent in the late eighteenth century were affected by the imperial conflicts that eventually resulted in the founding of a new nation. Most women's activities were filtered through traditional expectations about their female roles: slave women tried to protect their children; Native Americans maintained villages while men were at war; elite ladies sewed shirts for George Washington's army; poor women cooked for soldiers. Yet despite these traditional trajectories — and despite the fundamentally male character of eighteenth-century diplomacy, politics, and warfare — women did exercise some choice in the revolutionary era. They acted politically when they decided to escape slavery by fleeing to the British, when they participated in their Native councils' deliberations over alliances, or when they chose to be loyalists or patriots.

The revolutionary era's dramatic events affected women in widely varying ways. Slave women in the North benefited from gradual emancipation, while many in the South suffered from their owners' deepening commitment to the institution of slavery. Both free and enslaved black women confronted a deepening racial ideology that defined citizenship as a white inheritance of the Revolution. Many Native American women saw their traditional roles erode under the pressures of assimilation, yet most scholars marvel at their resilience and adaptability. White women's positions became more limited in some respects, as white men's political rights expanded.

But if the Revolution did not prompt a deep-seated questioning of women's rights and roles, it did embody harbingers of change, especially for white women. The economic expansion of the new nation would lead to industrial development and an expanded presence of women in the paid workforce. The U.S. territorial expansion would not only promote western migration of white women and their families but also significantly affect Native Americans and slaves. In addition, revolutionary ideology, educational advancements, and the egalitarianism of the Great Awakening sowed the seeds for greater participation of middle-class and elite women in public life, not in politics per se, but in informal spheres of public spaces — churches, benevolent societies, and reform movements — which were to be such an important part of nineteenth-century American culture.

CHAPTER 3 REVIEW

KEY TERMS AND PEOPLE

Terms
First Great Awakening
"Liberty's Daughters"
Ladies Association of
    Philadelphia
"deputy husbands"
Republican Motherhood
Second Great Awakening

People
Molly Brant
Deborah Sampson
Sacagawea
Mary Perth
Elizabeth Freeman
    ("Mum Bett")
Abigail Adams

Mary Wollstonecraft
Mercy Otis Warren
Judith Sargent Murray
Benjamin Rush
Jemima Wilkinson
Phillis Wheatley

REVIEW QUESTIONS

1. What were some of the factors leading to open conflict between Britain and its North American colonies? What forms of colonial resistance particularly depended on women's participation?

2. Discuss the various kinds of "profound disruptions and complex decisions" that the Revolutionary War brought to Anglo-American women colonists, enslaved and free black women, and Native American women. What did "taking sides" mean for each of these groups of women?

3. What changes in free women's status during the late eighteenth century, if any, can be attributed to the legacy of the American Revolution? How was the shift from colony to nation significant for enslaved black women? For Native American women? How did the impact of the Revolution on white, black, and Native American women vary depending on geographic region?

4. **Making Connections** Between the 1750s and 1800s, how did women's gendered labor and relationship to the family change? Was the American Revolution a "revolution" for America's women? How did free versus slave status and settler versus indigenous identity matter in answering these questions?

PRIMARY SOURCES

Gendering Images of the Revolution

Ⓘ N ADDITION TO THE REPRESENTATIONS OF American women contained in the portraits of the late eighteenth century are a variety of other images specifically connected to the American Revolution. Many of these—whether paintings or cartoons—had propagandistic purposes. Few portray actual women and instead render females as abstractions, often as icons of "Liberty."

Englishmen on both sides of the Atlantic often ridiculed women's interest in fashion and represented them as weak-minded and frivolous. These negative stereotypes about women took on propagandistic value in Figure 3.1, a British

◆ **Figure 3.1 "A Society of Patriotic Ladies" (1774)**
Library of Congress, LC-USZ62-12711.

cartoon, "A Society of Patriotic Ladies," created as a response to the fifty-one women of Edenton, North Carolina, who signed a pledge in 1774 to uphold the boycotts against British goods. By depicting fashionable women neglecting their children (note the child on the floor being licked by a dog) and acting in unfeminine ways (note the grotesque woman with the gavel), the cartoon devalues the boycott and American women at the same time.

Consider the choices of the cartoonist. Why do you think he decided to include a black servant in his drawing? Why did he depict the woman in the center being fondled by a man?

A number of images of women holding muskets circulated during the revolutionary era. Scholars think that the 1770 drawing in Figure 3.2 was modeled after a 1750 woodcut of Hannah Snell, an Englishwoman who had joined the British navy in 1745. Though *Miss Fanny's Maid* predates the outbreak of fighting, it coincides with the disruptive atmosphere of Boston in the 1770s. The American illustration was probably not intended to refer to a specific woman bearing arms; the story of cross-dressing Deborah Sampson (see pp. 112–13) was not made public until 1781, for example. What do you think might have been the purpose of this image for revolutionary propagandists?

◆ **Figure 3.2** *Miss Fanny's Maid* **(1770)**
American Antiquarian Society, Worcester, Massachusetts, USA/ Bridgeman Images.

The tendency to depict women as abstractions was most evident in the widespread popularity of images of "Liberty." The convention of using a stylized woman to represent political virtues such as liberty or justice was a long-standing one in Western European art, though, as one historian explains, "the female form [of liberty] does not refer to particular women, does not describe women as a group, and often does not even presume to evoke their natures."[47] Instead, this idealized image was intended to embody the principles for which men were fighting. During the 1770s, the American colonies were sometimes personified as a Native American woman, rather than as a classical European figure.

Figure 3.3, "The Female Combatants," portrayed the conflict between Britain and the North American colonies as a lively fistfight between women. This hand-colored engraving by an unknown artist appeared in January 1776, the same month in which Thomas Paine published *Common Sense*.

Decoding the image requires attention to both words and material objects. Begin with the speech bubbles. How does the artist use sexual insult and familial relations ("Rebellious Slut" and "Mother") to comment on political resistance to Britain? Next, move to the visual symbolism. What is the meaning of the white Mother Britain's aristocratic dress? Why is America portrayed as a bare-breasted Native American woman? Note the Phrygian liberty cap on America's tree (look for this ancient icon elsewhere in this document set). The combatants' shield and banner slogans also differ. The shield on the left holds a compass pointing north, while the one on the right depicts a Gallic rooster, symbol of France. The banners juxtapose British "Obedience" with American "Liberty." A historian who has analyzed the image asks, "Does the artist believe Britain holds the moral right; does the cartoon display America's winning ideology?"[48] How would you answer this question using specific evidence from the image?

◆ **Figure 3.3** "The Female Combatants" (1776)
Courtesy of The Lewis Walpole Library, Yale University.

An alternative rendering of a female version of Liberty appeared in the well-known painter Edward Savage's engraving "Liberty in the Form of the Goddess of Youth Giving Support to the Bald Eagle," created in 1796. In Figure 3.4, the youthful Liberty, clad in white with a garland of flowers, nourishes an eagle, who symbolizes the Republic. In the background is the flag of the union with a liberty cap. At the bottom right, lightning surrounds the British fleet in the Boston harbor. Crushed under Liberty's feet are symbols of the British monarchy: a key, a broken scepter, and the garter of a royal order. This version of Liberty was so popular that it was reproduced in many forms—including needlework—well into the nineteenth century. Why do you think Savage depicts Liberty as a "goddess of youth"? Why was the image so popular with Americans?

A somewhat unusual depiction of a female Liberty had more radical political meaning than most versions. Figure 3.5 suggests the way in which revolutionary ideology ignited questions about women's and slaves' freedom. *Liberty Displaying the Arts and Sciences,* by Samuel Jennings (1792), was initially suggested by the

◆ **Figure 3.4**   Edward Savage, *Liberty in the Form of the Goddess of Youth Giving Support to the Bald Eagle* (1796)
Library of Congress, 3a17616.

◆ **Figure 3.5** **Samuel Jennings, *Liberty Displaying the Arts and Sciences* (1792)**
The Granger Collection, New York.

artist himself to the Library Company of Philadelphia, an institution founded by Benjamin Franklin and others in 1731. The directors specifically asked Jennings to portray a tableau of "Liberty (with her Cap and proper Insignia) displaying the arts by some of the most striking Symbols of Painting, Architecture, Mechanics, Astronomy, &ca. whilst She appears in the attitude of placing on the top of a Pedestal, a pile of Books, lettered with, *Agriculture, Commerce, Philosophy & Catalogue of Philadelphia Library*."[49] The directors, many of whom were active antislavery advocates, also requested the inclusion of African Americans and the symbolic broken chains. In the image, Liberty is offering a book to the grateful African Americans.

Examine the images associated with Liberty. What do they suggest? What did the library directors hope to convey in combining a depiction of Liberty, books, and freed slaves?

QUESTIONS FOR ANALYSIS

1. How do these diverse images of women contribute to our understanding of how gender shaped the experience of the American Revolution?

2. The images presented here have propagandistic purposes. What do these images suggest about the role gender and sexuality play in conceptualizing both war aims and patriotic service?

3. How can historians analyze these propagandistic images in the effort to reconstruct the actual experiences of women in the revolutionary era?

PRIMARY SOURCES

Phillis Wheatley, Poet and Slave

Eighteenth-century American women left behind far more written material than those in the seventeenth century; we have diaries, letters, essays, and books to help us flesh out the lives of many women, especially educated white women. The experiences of individual black women are far more obscure in the historical record, with the important exception of poet Phillis Wheatley (c. 1753–1784). At age seven or eight, Wheatley made a terrifying passage from the Senegambia region of West Africa to Boston in the hold of her namesake, the slave ship *Phillis*; nearly a quarter of her fellow captives died along the way. Her owners, John and Susannah Wheatley, informed by their own expectations of African intellectual inferiority, were immediately impressed with her precociousness. "Without any Assistance from School Education, and by only what she was taught in the Family, she, in sixteen Months Times from her Arrival, attained the English Language, to which she was an utter Stranger before, to such a Degree, as to read any, the most difficult Parts of the Sacred Writings, to the great Astonishment of all who heard her."[50] The Wheatleys, especially Susannah and her daughter Mary, took pride in their slave's learning but also in her quick and deeply felt conversion to Protestantism. Their own evangelical beliefs, reflecting the First Great Awakening sweeping through the colonies, made them open to the notion of blacks' spiritual equality and led them to encourage Wheatley's religious and intellectual gifts.

Phillis Wheatley began writing poetry as early as 1765 and apparently published her first poem in 1767 at age fourteen. By 1772, she had attempted, with the help of Susannah Wheatley and other sponsors, to publish a book of collected works in Boston. When that venture failed, she found a publisher in London and had the opportunity to accompany the son of her owner to London, where she was able to complete the arrangements for *Poems on Various Subjects, Religious and Moral* (1773).

Figure 3.6, a portrait of Phillis Wheatley, was commissioned as the frontispiece for her book. John and Susannah had sent Phillis's poems to the London bookseller Archibald Bell. He in turn had taken them to an antislavery noblewoman, the Countess of Huntington, to receive permission for Wheatley to dedicate the book to her, a common practice designed to enhance a book's prestige. Huntington, enthusiastic about the poems, apparently asked for reassurance that the author was "*real,* without a deception." Perhaps to offer proof to future readers that Wheatley was indeed of African descent, the countess requested a picture of Wheatley for the frontispiece. The painting was executed by an enslaved artist, Scipio Moorhead, owned by a Boston minister, and sent to England for engraving.

Wheatley appreciated Moorhead's talents and wrote the following poem to "SM. a young *African* painter":

> To show the lab'ring bosom's deep intent,
> and thought in living characters to paint,
> When first thy pencil did those beauties give,
> And breathing figures learnt from thee to live,
> How did those prospects give my soul delight,
> A new creation rushing on my sight?
> Still, wond'rous youth! each noble path pursue,
> On deathless glories fix thine ardent view:
> Still may the painter's and the poet's fire
> To aid thy pencil, and thy verse conspire![51]

Why do you think Wheatley was so pleased by the portrait? What details in the image convey Wheatley's literacy and authorship? Why do you suppose the painting includes the information that Wheatley was "servant to Mr. John Wheatley"?

Shortly after Wheatley became a published author, her owners granted her freedom. Wheatley continued to write, undeterred by such life-changing events as the deaths of her former owners, Susannah Wheatley in 1774 and John Wheatley in 1778, and her own marriage in 1778 to a free black, John Peters. Her poems, such as one in honor of General George Washington, were published individually, but she failed to gain backing for her proposal, printed in the *Evening Post & General Advertiser* (1779), in which she described herself as a "female African" who sought subscriptions to print a second book of poems and letters to be dedicated to Benjamin Franklin. Other disappointments followed. Toward the end of her life, she worked as a scrubwoman in a boardinghouse. Two of her children died, and she and her third baby died of complications in childbirth on December 8, 1784.

Because of the profoundly religious content of much of her work, Wheatley's poetry was warmly received by evangelical Protestants, both in England and in America. Apparently some slaveowners read

◆ **Figure 3.6 Scipio Moorhead, *Phillis Wheatley* (1773)**
The Granger Collection, New York.

Wheatley's poems to their slaves to encourage their conversion. Opponents of slavery also welcomed the poet's work, viewing her as proof of the humanity and capabilities of Africans and therefore useful evidence in their campaigns against both slavery and the slave trade.

LETTERS

Twenty-two of Wheatley's letters have survived. The first one, printed below, is to a black friend, Arbour Tanner, a servant to James Tanner in Newport, Rhode Island, who shared Wheatley's religious ardor. The letter refers to a frequent theme in the poet's work: the conversion of her fellow Africans. What is the purpose of Wheatley's letter to Tanner? How might her abduction from Africa as a child have informed her views of her land of birth as a place of "darkness"?

To Arbour Tanner
Boston May 19th 1772

Dear Sister

I rec'd your favour of February 6th for which I give you my sincere thanks, I greatly rejoice with you in that realizing view, and I hope experience, of the Saving change which you So emphatically describe. Happy were it for us if we could arrive to that evangelical Repentance, and the true holiness of heart which you mention. Inexpressibly happy Should we be could we have a due Sense of the Beauties and excellence of the Crucified Saviour. In his Crucifixion may be seen marvellous displays of Grace and Love, Sufficient to draw and invite us to the rich and endless treasures of his mercy, let us rejoice in and adore the wonders of God's infinite Love in bringing us from a land Semblant of darkness itself, and where the divine light of revelation (being obscur'd) is as darkness. Here, the knowledge of the true God and eternal life are made manifest; But there, profound ignorance overshadows the Land, Your observation is true, namely that there was nothing in us to recommend us to God. Many of our fellow creatures are pass'd by, when the bowels of divine love expanded towards us. May this goodness & long Suffering of God lead us to unfeign'd repentance.

It gives me very great pleasure to hear of so many of my Nation, Seeking with eagerness the way to true felicity, O may we all meet at length in that happy mansion. I hope the correspondence between us will continue, (my being much indispos'd this winter past was the reason of my not answering yours before now) which correspondence I hope may have the happy effect of improving our mutual friendship. Till we meet in the regions of consummate blessedness, let us endeavor by the assistance of divine grace, to live the life, and we Shall die the death of the Righteous. May this be our happy case and of those who are travelling to the region of Felicity is the earnest request of your affectionate

Friend & hum. Sert. Phillis Wheatley

Source: Julian D. Mason Jr., ed., *The Poems of Phillis Wheatley* (Chapel Hill: University of North Carolina, 1989), 190.

THE FOLLOWING LETTER, to Rev. Samson Occom, a Mohegan Indian and Presbyterian minister, was published in the *Connecticut Gazette; and the Universal Intelligencer* on March 11, 1774, and widely reprinted. Written after Wheatley had gained freedom, it is her most critical statement about slavery. What is the essence of her criticism? To whom is she referring in the phrase "our modern Egyptians"?

To Rev. Samson Occom

Rev'd and honor'd Sir,

I have this Day received your obliging kind Epistle, and am greatly satisfied with your Reasons respecting the Negroes, and think highly reasonable what you offer in Vindication of their natural Rights: Those that invade them cannot be insensible that the divine Light is chasing away the thick Darkness which broods over the Land of Africa; and the Chaos which has reign'd long, is converting into beautiful Order, and [r]eveals more and more clearly the glorious Dispensation of civil and religious Liberty, which are so insep[a]rably united, that there is little or no Enjoyment of one without the other. Otherwise, perhaps, the Israelites had been less solicitous for their Freedom from Egyptian slavery; I do not say they would have been contented without it, by no means, for in every human Breast, God has implanted a Principle which we call Love of Freedom; it is impatient of Oppression and pants for Deliverance; and by the Leave of our modern Egyptians I will assert, that the same Principle lives in us. God grant Deliverance in his own Way and Time and get him honour upon all those whose Avarice impels them to countenance and help forward the Calamities of their fellow Creatures. This desire not for their Hurt, but to convince them of the strange Absurdity of their Conduct whose Words and Actions are so diametrically opposite. How well the Cry for Liberty, and the reverse Disposition for the exercise of oppressive Power over others agree, — I humbly think it does not require the Penetration of a Philosopher to determine.

SOURCE: Mason, *Poems of Phillis Wheatley*, 203–4.

POEMS

OVER FIFTY OF WHEATLEY'S POEMS have survived. They encompass a wide range of topics, from elegies to thoughts "On Virtue," from religious commentaries to a patriotic ode to George Washington. Her references to Africa, Africans, and slavery are particularly interesting for the ways in which her poetry insists on the humanity of Africans and makes criticisms — sometimes veiled — of slavery.

On the surface, this 1772 poem seems to adopt white Christians' condescension toward pagan Africans, but what does the final line suggest? Is it possible to read this troubling poem as Wheatley's challenge to biological theories of white superiority?

On Being Brought from Africa to America

'Twas mercy brought me from my *Pagan* land,
Taught my benighted soul to understand
That there's a God, that there's a *Saviour* too:

SOURCE: Mason, *Poems of Phillis Wheatley*, 53.

Once I redemption neither sought nor knew.
Some view our sable race with scornful eye,
"Their colour is a diabolic die."
Remember, *Christians*, Negroes, black as Cain,
May be refin'd, and join th' angelic train.

THE FOLLOWING POEM, addressed to the British secretary of state for North America, was written in a period when tensions had eased — temporarily — between the colonies and the mother country, hence Wheatley's statement in the second stanza about grievances being addressed. The poem reveals not only her sensitivity to the political turmoil of the period but also her understanding of the parallels between the colonists' desire to resist British "enslavement" and her own people's experience of slavery. What does she seem to be asking Lord Dartmouth for in the final stanza?

To the Right Honourable William, Earl of Dartmouth, His Majesty's Principal Secretary of State for North America

HAIL, happy day when, smiling like the morn,
Fair *Freedom* rose *New-England* to adorn:
The northern clime beneath her genial ray,
Dartmouth, congratulates thy blissful sway:
Elate with hope her race no longer mourns,
Each soul expands, each grateful bosom burns,
While in thine hand with pleasure we behold
The silken reins, and *Freedom's* charms unfold.
Long lost to realms beneath the northern skies
She shines supreme, while hated *faction* dies:
Soon as appear'd the *Goddess* long desir'd,
Sick at the view, she languish'd and expir'd;
Thus from the splendors of the morning light
The owl in sadness seeks the caves of night.
No more, *America*, in mournful strain
Of wrongs, and grievance unredress'd complain,

SOURCE: Mason, *Poems of Phillis Wheatley*, 82–83.

No longer shalt thou dread the iron chain,
Which wanton *Tyranny* with lawless hand
Had made, and with it meant t' enslave the land.
Should you, my lord, while you peruse my song,
Wonder from whence my love of Freedom sprung,
Whence flow these wishes for the common good,
By feeling hearts alone best understood,
I, young in life, by seeming cruel fate
Was snatch'd from *Afric's* fancy'd happy seat:
What pangs excruciating must molest,
What sorrows labour in my parent's breast?
Steel'd was that soul and by no misery mov'd
That from a father seiz'd his babe belov'd:
Such, such my case. And can I then but pray
Others may never feel tyrannic sway?
For favours past, great Sir, our thanks are due,
And thee we ask thy favours to renew,
Since in thy pow'r, as in thy will before,

To sooth the griefs, which thou did'st once deplore.
May heav'nly grace the sacred sanction give
To all thy works, and thou for ever live
Not only on the wings of fleeting *Fame*,
Though praise immortal crowns the patriot's name,

But to conduct to heav'ns refulgent fane,
May fiery coursers sweep th' ethereal plain,
And bear thee upwards to that blest abode,
Where, like the prophet, thou shalt find thy God.

QUESTIONS FOR ANALYSIS

1. What do these selections of Wheatley's poems and letters reveal about the importance and role of religion in her life?

2. What are the grounds for her criticism of slavery?

3. How might opponents of slavery have used her poetry to criticize the institution?

4. How did Wheatley use both her image and her writing to challenge prevailing ideas about racial difference and African intellect?

PRIMARY SOURCES

Education and Republican Motherhood

For much of the colonial period, women's opportunities for education were quite limited. A small number of slave women were instructed by benevolent owners, and some Native American women had access to missionary schools where the emphasis was on assimilation rather than education. White women had little formal schooling, and their training usually emphasized domestic skills with a smattering of reading and sums. By the time of the Revolution in New England, 90 percent of white men could write, while fewer than half of white women could.

The Revolution and its aftermath ushered in significant changes. Outside the South, where public schools were rare, primary public education for white women and men became more common. Women's opportunities for higher education—while not universally endorsed—also expanded. While some of the most famous schools, like Philadelphia's Young Ladies Academy, were in urban areas, educational entrepreneurs also established them in small towns such as Litchfield, Connecticut, where Sarah Pierce's school attracted young women from throughout the region, as well as from other states. The Bethlehem, Pennsylvania, Moravian Seminary had special appeal for parents eager to give their daughters a rigorous education; in addition to academic subjects, the school encouraged its students' industry and moral development. While the new schools still offered ornamental skills such as needlework and dancing, they emphasized academic subjects such as history, grammar, geography, logic, and philosophy.

The post-Revolution improvement in white women's education was in part a product of the efforts of reformers, who eagerly promoted the idea that in a republic, all citizens needed education to contribute to the general public good. In keeping with the ideas associated with Republican Motherhood (see pp. 125–27), supporters of women's education argued that mothers needed to be well educated to prepare their children, especially their sons, for their duties as citizens. Advocates also emphasized the importance of women's influence on their husbands. While a number of people participated in the call for expanded opportunities, including Mercy Otis Warren and Sarah Pierce, two of the most significant, whose writings are reproduced here, were Dr. Benjamin Rush and Judith Sargent Murray.

"A PECULIAR MODE OF EDUCATION"

BENJAMIN RUSH SIGNED the Declaration of Independence and was the preeminent physician and medical teacher of the revolutionary era. His essay *Thoughts upon Female Education* reflects both increased expectations as well as the limits to new ideas about women's education. The curriculum he promoted included geography, bookkeeping, reading, and arithmetic and omitted the traditional female accomplishment of needlework. But he did not recommend that women study advanced mathematics, natural philosophy, or Latin or Greek, subjects that remained hallmarks of educated men. Rush and most other reformers emphasized the utilitarian potential of an academic curriculum for women. Although Rush lectured to both men at the College of Philadelphia and women at the Young Ladies Academy on natural philosophy, his presentation for the latter — "Lectures, Containing the Application of the Principles of Natural Philosophy, and Chemistry to Domestic and Culinary Purposes" — was tailored to their perceived future roles. Still, Rush's views were progressive for his time, when many people felt that too much learning might "unsex" a woman and make her unfeminine.

The following selection is from an essay based on a speech Rush gave to the Board of Visitors of the Young Ladies Academy of Philadelphia in 1787. As you read, take note of Rush's major justifications for educating women.

BENJAMIN RUSH
Thoughts upon Female Education (1787)

There are several circumstances in the situation, employments and duties of women in America which require a peculiar mode of education.

I. The early marriages of our women, by contracting the time allowed for education, renders it necessary to contract its plan and to confine it chiefly to the more useful branches of literature.

II. The state of property in America renders it necessary for the greatest part of our citizens to employ themselves in different occupations for the advancement of their fortunes. This cannot be done without the assistance of the female members of the community. They must be the stewards and guardians of their husbands' property. That education, therefore, will be most proper for our women which teaches them to discharge the duties of those offices with the most success and reputation.

III. From the numerous avocations to which a professional life exposes gentlemen in America from their families, a principal share of the instruction of children naturally devolves upon the women. It becomes us therefore to prepare them, by a suitable education, for the discharge of this most important duty of mothers.

IV. The equal share that every citizen has in the liberty and the possible share he may have

SOURCE: Frederick Rudolph, ed., *Essays on Education in the Early Republic* (Cambridge, MA: Belknap Press of Harvard University Press, 1965), 27–40.

in the government of our country make it necessary that our ladies should be qualified to a certain degree, by a peculiar and suitable education, to concur in instructing their sons in the principles of liberty and government.

V. In Great Britain the business of servants is a regular occupation, but in America this humble station is the usual retreat of unexpected indigence; hence the servants in this country possess less knowledge and subordination than are required from them; and hence our ladies are obliged to attend more to the private affairs of their families than ladies generally do of the same rank in Great Britain. "They are good servants," said an American lady of distinguished merit . . . in a letter to a favorite daughter, "who will do well with good looking after." This circumstance should have great influence upon the nature and extent of female education in America.

[Rush proceeds to discuss the most important "branches of literature most essential for a young lady in this country," in which he emphasizes "a knowledge of the English language," "the writing of a fair and legible hand," "some knowledge of figures and bookkeeping," so that she "may assist her husband with this knowledge," "an acquaintance with geography and some instruction in chronology [history]," vocal music and dancing, "the reading of history, travels, poetry, and moral essays," and the "regular instruction in the Christian religion."]

A philosopher once said, "let me make all the ballads of a country and I care not who makes its laws." He might with more propriety have said, let the ladies of a country be educated properly, and they will not only make and administer its laws, but form its manners and character. It would require a lively imagination to describe, or even to comprehend the happiness of a country where knowledge and virtue were generally diffused among the female sex. . . .

The influence of female education would be still more extensive and useful in domestic life. The obligations of gentlemen to qualify themselves by knowledge and industry to discharge the duties of benevolence would be increased by marriage; and the patriot — the hero — and the legislator would find the sweetest reward of their toils in the approbation and applause of their wives. Children would discover the marks of maternal prudence and wisdom in every station of life, for it has been remarked that there have been few great or good men who have not been blessed with wife and prudent mothers.

"ALL THAT INDEPENDENCE WHICH IS PROPER TO HUMANITY"

ALTHOUGH JUDITH SARGENT MURRAY (1751–1820), the daughter of a distinguished and wealthy Gloucester, Massachusetts, family, also believed in the tenets of Republican Motherhood, she was far more radical than Rush in her approach to women's capabilities and needs. Murray's parents denied her the opportunity for the extensive education that they provided for her brother, but she was a voracious reader of both American and European writers. A contemporary of the English historian Catharine Macaulay and the English women's rights activist Mary Wollstonecraft, Murray was an early American proponent of women's rights and an accomplished writer. Intensely religious, she had left the Puritan fold for Universalism, a far more egalitarian faith that encouraged her to challenge traditional authority. Already influenced by her religion, as well as her frustration over her limited schooling, Murray was further energized by the ideas swirling around the American Revolution that led her to articulate her belief in men's and women's mental and spiritual equality. As she contemplated the themes of liberty, equality, and independence, she struggled with her own dependence.

After she was widowed in 1787, her second marriage in 1788, like her first, provided little financial security, and she was highly conscious of the legal and financial constraints on women. It is not surprising, then, that many of her essays call for an education that would help women to be self-reliant and even self-supporting. She pointed out that she would want her daughters to be taught "industry and order." They "should be enabled to procure for themselves the necessaries of life; independence should be placed within their grasp."[52] Unlike reformers such as Rush, who saw women's education primarily as a tool for promoting the family and the public good, Murray understood it as something contributing to women's independence, to a reverence of self. But she shared with more conventional reformers the assumption that most women would marry and have children and that women's improved education would make them better wives and virtuous Republican Mothers.

In 1782, Murray anonymously published her first work, a religious piece titled *Catechism.* By that time, however, she had already drafted a much more radical piece, "On the Equality of the Sexes," which appeared finally in the *Massachusetts Magazine* in 1790, under the pseudonym "Constantia." Although writing under pen names was a common eighteenth-century practice, Murray probably did so with a knowledge of how subversive it was for women to write publicly at all, let alone on political matters. In addition, her biographer suggests, she enjoyed the game of hiding her identity under multiple names and may have thought that the pseudonym helped readers to focus on the content of the piece rather than on the identity of the writer.[53] Murray began this essay with a poetic question for "the lordly sex." Why, she queried, do "[t]hey rob us of the power t' improve / And then declare we only trifles love"? She then went on to argue that if women's intellect was deficient, it was because of men's advantage in education, rather than birth. A good part of her essay, excerpted here, focuses on reason — a prominent theme in Enlightenment ideas about human intellectual abilities. What curriculum does Murray favor for girls' education? What consequences does she see for the inferior education women receive? In what sense is she arguing that women and men are equal? In what ways does this piece reflect Murray's upper-class identity?

JUDITH SARGENT MURRAY
On the Equality of the Sexes (1790)

Is it upon mature consideration we adopt the idea, that nature is thus partial in her distributions? Is it indeed a fact, that she hath yielded to one half of the human species so unquestionable a mental superiority? I know that to both sexes elevated understandings, and the reverse, are common. But, suffer me to ask, in what the minds of females are so notoriously deficient, or unequal. . . .

Are we [women] deficient in reason? we can only reason from what we know, and if an opportunity of acquiring knowledge hath been denied us, the inferiority of our sex, cannot fairly be deduced from thence. . . . Yet it may be questioned, from what doth this superiority in this determining faculty of the soul, proceed. May we not trace its source in the difference of education, and continued advantages? Will it be said that the judgment of a male of two years old, is more sage than that of a female's of the same age? I believe the reverse is generally observed to be true. But from that period what partiality! how is the one exalted, and the other depressed, by the contrary modes of education which are adopted! the one is taught to aspire, and the other is early confined and limitted. As their years increase, the sister must be wholly domesticated, while the brother is led by the hand through all the flowery paths of science. Grant that their minds are by nature equal, yet who shall wonder at the *apparent* superiority, if indeed custom becomes second nature; nay if it taketh place of nature, and that it doth the experience of each day will evince. At length arrived at womanhood, the uncultivated fair one feels a void, which the employments allotted her are by no means capable of filling. What can she do? to books she may not

apply; or if she doth, *to those only of the novel kind*, lest she merit the appellation of a *learned* lady; and what ideas have been affixed to this term, the observation of many can testify. Fashion, scandal, and sometimes what is still more reprehensible, are then called in to her relief; and who can say to what lengths the liberties she takes may proceed. Meantime she herself is most unhappy; she feels the want of a cultivated mind. Is she single, she in vain seeks to fill up time from sexual employments or amusements. Is she united to a person whose soul nature made equal to her own, education hath set him so far above her, that in those entertainments which are productive of such rational felicity, she is not qualified to accompany him. She experiences a mortifying consciousness of inferiority, which embitters every enjoyment. Doth the person to whom her adverse fate hath consigned her, possess a mind incapable of improvement, she is equally wretched, in being so closely connected with an individual whom she cannot but despise. Now, was she permitted the same instructors as her brother, (with an eye however to their particular departments) for the employment of a rational mind an ample field would be opened. In astronomy she might catch a glimpse of the immensity of the Deity, and thence she would form amazing conceptions of the august and supreme Intelligence. In geography she would admire Jehovah in the midst of his benevolence; thus adapting this globe to the various wants and amusements of its inhabitants. In natural philosophy she would adore the infinite majesty of heaven, clothed in condescension; and as she traversed the reptile world, she would hail the goodness of a creating God. A mind, thus filled, would have little room for the trifles with which our sex are, with too much justice, accused of amusing themselves, and they would thus be rendered fit companions for those, who should one day wear them as their crown. Fashions, in their variety, would then give place to conjectures, which

SOURCE: Constantia [Judith Sargent Murray], "On the Equality of the Sexes," *Massachusetts Magazine; or Monthly Museum Containing the Literature, History, Politics, Arts, Manners and Amusements of the Age 2* (March 1790): 132–35 and (April 1790): 223–24.

might perhaps conduce to the improvement of the literary world; and there would be no leisure for slander or detraction. Reputation would not then be blasted, but serious speculations would occupy the lively imaginations of the sex. Unnecessary visits would be precluded, and that custom would only be indulged by way of relaxation, or to answer the demands of consanguinity and friendship. Females would become discreet, their judgments would be invigorated, and their partners for life being circumspectly chosen, an unhappy Hymen would then be as rare, as is now the reverse.°

Will it be urged that those acquirements would supersede our domestick duties. I answer that every requisite in female economy is easily attained; and, with truth I can add, that when once attained, they require no further *mental attention*. Nay, while we are pursuing the needle, or the superintendency of the family, I repeat, that our minds are at full liberty for reflection; that imagination may exert itself in full vigor; and that if a just foundation is early laid, our ideas will then be worthy of rational beings. If we were industrious we might easily find time to arrange them upon paper, or should avocations press too hard for such an indulgence, the hours allotted for conversation would at least become more refined and rational. Should it still be vociferated, "Your domestick employments are sufficient"—I would calmly ask, is it reasonable, that a candidate for immortality, for the joys of heaven, an intelligent being, who is to spend an eternity in contemplating the works of Deity, should at present be so degraded, as to be allowed no other ideas, than those which are suggested by the mechanism of a pudding, or the sewing the seams of a garment? Pity that all such censurers of female improvement do not go one step further, and deny their future existence; to be consistent they surely ought.

Yes, ye lordly, ye haughty sex, our souls are by nature *equal* to yours; the same breath of God animates, enlivens, and invigorates us; and that we are not fallen lower than yourselves, let those witness who have greatly towered above the various discouragements by which they have been so heavily oppressed; and though I am unacquainted with the list of celebrated characters on either side, yet from the observations I have made in the contracted circle in which I have moved, I dare confidently believe, that from the commencement of time to the present day, there hath been as many females, as males, who, by the *mere force of natural powers*, have merited the crown of applause; who, thus unassisted, have seized the wreath of fame. I know there are who assert, that as the animal powers of the one sex are superiour, of course their mental faculties also must be stronger; thus attributing strength of mind to the transient organization of this earth born tenement. But if this reasoning is just, man must be content to yield the palm to many of the brute creation, since by not a few of his brethren of the field, he is far surpassed in bodily strength. Moreover, was this argument admitted, it would prove too much, for occular demonstration evinceth, that there are many robust masculine ladies, and effeminate gentlemen. Yet I fancy that Mr. Pope,°° though clogged with an enervated body, and distinguished by a diminutive stature, could nevertheless lay claim to greatness of soul; and perhaps there are many other instances which might be adduced to combat *so unphilosophical an opinion*. Do we not often see, that when the clay built tabernacle is well nigh dissolved, when it is just ready to mingle with the parent soil, the immortal inhabitant aspires to, and even attaineth heights the most sublime, and which were before wholly unexplored. Besides, were we to grant that animal strength proved any thing, taking into consideration the accustomed impartiality of nature, we should be induced to imagine, that she had invested the female mind with superiour strength as an equivalent for the bodily powers of man. But waving this however palpable advantage, for *equality only*, we wish to contend.

°° "Mr. Pope" refers to Alexander Pope, an English poet and writer famous for such pieces as "An Essay on Man" (1733–1734) and "The Rape of the Lock" (1712).

° Hymen was the Greek god of marriage.

QUESTIONS FOR ANALYSIS

1. What do Rush and Murray see as the benefits of female education? How does the proper education of females differ from that of males? Are there any differences between Rush's and Murray's arguments?

2. What do Rush and Murray assume about the abilities of females?

3. How do Rush's and Murray's ideas accord with the ideas associated with Republican Motherhood?

NOTES

1. Mary Beth Norton and Ruth M. Alexander, eds., *Major Problems in American Women's History*, 2nd ed. (Lexington, MA: D. C. Heath, 1996), 81.

2. Mary Beth Norton, *Liberty's Daughters: The Revolutionary Experience of American Women, 1750–1800* (Boston: Little, Brown, 1980), 166.

3. Cynthia Kierner, *Beyond the Household: Women's Place in the Early South, 1700–1835* (Ithaca, NY: Cornell University Press, 1998), 75.

4. Norton, *Liberty's Daughters*, 164.

5. Ibid., 168.

6. "Penelope Barker," National Women's History Museum, http://www.nwhm.org/education-resources/biography/biographies/penelope-barker.

7. Norton, *Liberty's Daughters*, 159.

8. Ibid.

9. *Virginia Gazette*, September 15, 1774.

10. Marylynn Salmon, *The Limits of Independence: American Women, 1760–1800* (New York: Oxford University Press, 1994), 58.

11. Norton, *Liberty's Daughters*, 169.

12. Colin G. Calloway, *First Peoples: A Documentary Survey of American Indian History* (Boston: Bedford/St. Martin's, 2016), 163.

13. Benjamin Quarles, *The Negro in the American Revolution* (Chapel Hill: University of North Carolina Press, 1961), 135.

14. Ibid., 142.

15. Linda K. Kerber, *Women of the Republic: Intellect and Ideology in Revolutionary America* (Chapel Hill: University of North Carolina Press, 1980), 52.

16. Ibid., 54.

17. Holly A. Mayer, *Belonging to the Army: Camp Followers and Community during the American Revolution* (Columbia: University of South Carolina Press, 1996), 20.

18. Julie Wheelwright, *Amazons and Military Maids: Women Who Dressed as Men in Pursuit of Life, Liberty, and Happiness* (London: Pandora, 1989), 133.

19. Kerber, *Women of the Republic*, 59.

20. Mayer, *Belonging to the Army*, 124.

21. Kerber, *Women of the Republic*, 64.

22. Catherine Van Cortlandt, "Secret Correspondence of a Loyalist Wife," in Robert Marcus and David Burner, eds., *America Firsthand*, 4th ed. (Boston: Bedford, 1997), 2:109–11.

23. Norton, *Liberty's Daughters*, 80.

24. Ibid., 184.

25. Ibid., 187.

26. Theda Perdue, *Cherokee Women: Gender and Culture Change, 1700–1835* (Lincoln: University of Nebraska Press, 1998), 87, 101.

27. Ibid., 111.

28. Calloway, *First Peoples*, 226–32.

29. Virginia Scharff, *Twenty Thousand Roads: Women, Movement, and the West* (Berkeley: University of California Press, 2002), 19.

30. Cassandra Pybus, "'One Militant Saint': The Much Traveled Life of Mary Perth," *Journal of Colonialism & Colonial History* 9.3 (Winter 2008).

31. Peter Kolchin, *American Slavery, 1619–1877* (New York: Hill and Wang, 1993), 78.

32. Salmon, *Limits of Independence*, 111.

33. Jeffrey J. Crow, *The Black Experience in Revolutionary North Carolina* (Raleigh: North Carolina Department of Cultural Resources, 1977), 17.

34. Kierner, *Beyond the Household*, 99.

35. Barbara E. Lacey, "Women in the Era of the American Revolution: The Case of Norwich, Connecticut," *New England Quarterly* 53 (December 1980): 539.

36. Norton, *Liberty's Daughters*, 216.

37. Ibid., 223–24.

38. Ibid., 171.

39. Kerber, *Women of the Republic*, 226.

40. Ibid., 163–64.

41. Linda Grant De Pauw, *Founding Mothers: Women in America in the Revolutionary Era* (Boston: Houghton Mifflin, 1975), 211.

42. Norton, *Liberty's Daughters*, 287.

43. Catherine A. Brekus, *Strangers and Pilgrims: Female Preaching in America, 1740–1845* (Chapel Hill: University of North Carolina Press, 1998), 87.

44. Ibid, 49.

45. Ibid., 63–64.

46. Sylvia R. Frey and Betty Wood, *Come Shouting to Zion: African-American Protestantism in the American South and British Caribbean to 1830* (Chapel Hill: University of North Carolina Press, 1998), 13.

47. Marina Warner, *Monuments and Maidens: The Allegory of the Female Form* (New York: Atheneum, 1985), 12.

48. Stephanie McKellop, "America, the 'Rebellious Slut': Gender & Political Cartoons in the American Revolution," *Common-Place* 17, no. 3 (Spring 2017), http://common-place.org/book/vol-17-no-3-mckellop.

49. Edwin Wolf II and Marie Elena Korey, *Quarter of a Millennium: The Library Company of Philadelphia 1731–1981* (Philadelphia: The Company, 1981), 79.

50. Daniel C. Littlefield, *Revolutionary Citizens: African Americans, 1776–1804* (New York: Oxford University Press, 1997), 14.

51. Phillis Wheatley, *Poems on Various Subjects, Religious and Moral* (1773).

52. Kerber, *Women of the Republic*, 205.

53. Sheila L. Skemp, *First Lady of Letters: Judith Sargent Murray and the Struggle for Female Independence* (Philadelphia: University of Pennsylvania Press, 2009), 227–28.

SUGGESTED REFERENCES

General Works

Carol Berkin, *Revolutionary Mothers: Women in the Struggle for American Independence* (2005).

Edward Countryman, *Enjoy the Same Liberty: Black Americans and the Revolutionary Era* (2012).

Linda K. Kerber, *Women of the Republic: Intellect and Ideology in Revolutionary America* (1980).

Susan E. Klepp, *Revolutionary Conceptions: Women, Fertility, and Family Limitation in America, 1760–1820* (2010).

Mary Beth Norton, *Separated by Their Sex: Women in Public and Private in the Colonial Atlantic World* (2011).

Marylynn Salmon, *The Limits of Independence: American Women, 1760–1800* (1994).

Women and the American Revolution

Catherine Adams and Elizabeth H. Pleck, *Love of Freedom: Black Women in Colonial and Revolutionary New England* (2010).

Vincent Carretta, *Phillis Wheatley: Biography of a Genius in Bondage* (2014).

Patricia Cleary, *Elizabeth Murray: A Woman's Pursuit of Independence in Eighteenth-Century America* (2000).

Linda Grant De Pauw, *Four Traditions: Women of New York during the American Revolution* (1974).

Joan R. Gunderson, *To Be Useful to the World: Women in Revolutionary America, 1740–1790*, revised edition (2006).

Kate Haulman, *The Politics of Fashion in Eighteenth-Century America* (2011).

Cynthia Kierner, *Beyond the Household: Women's Place in the Early South, 1700–1835* (1998).

Mary Beth Norton, *Liberty's Daughters: The Revolutionary Experience of American Women, 1750–1800* (1980).

Alfred F. Young, *Masquerade: The Life and Times of Deborah Sampson, Continental Soldier* (2004).

Revolutionary Legacies for Women

Norma Basch, *Framing American Divorce: From the Revolutionary Generation to the Victorians* (1999).

Catherine A. Brekus, *Strangers and Pilgrims: Female Preaching in America, 1740–1845* (1998).

Erica Armstrong Dunbar, *Never Caught: The Washingtons' Relentless Pursuit of Their Runaway Slave, Ona Judge* (2017).

Kathleen DuVal, *Independence Lost: Lives on the Edge of the American Revolution* (2016).

Sylvia R. Frey and Betty Wood, *Come Shouting to Zion: African-American Protestantism in the American South and British Caribbean to 1830* (1998).

Susan Juster, *Disorderly Women: Sexual Politics and Evangelicalism in Revolutionary New England* (1994).

Linda K. Kerber, *No Constitutional Right to Be Ladies: Women and the Obligation of Citizenship* (1998).

Lucia McMahon, *Mere Equals: The Paradox of Educated Women in the Early American Republic* (2012).

Jessica Millward, *Finding Charity's Folks: Enslaved and Free Black Women in Maryland* (2015).

Paul B. Moyer, *The Public Universal Friend: Jemima Wilkinson and Religious Enthusiasm in Revolutionary America* (2015).

Theda Perdue, *Cherokee Women: Gender and Culture Change, 1700–1835* (1998).

4

Pedestal, Loom, and Auction Block

1800–1860

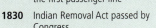

1790s Second Great Awakening begins

1800 Thomas Jefferson elected president

1807 Robert Fulton launches the *Clermont*, the first American steamboat

1808 Congress ends the African slave trade

1810s– States abolish property requirements
1820s among white men for voting and officeholding

1812– War of 1812 against England
1814 interrupts transatlantic trade

1816 African Methodist Episcopal Church established in Philadelphia

1819 Panic causes economic collapse and hardships for debtors

1819– Conflict over admission of Missouri
1820 as a slave state ends with the Missouri Compromise

1823 First textile mill opens in new city of Lowell, Massachusetts

1824 Erie Canal completed, accelerating commerce

1828 Andrew Jackson elected president, initiating era known as Jacksonian democracy

1830 *Godey's Lady's Book* begins publication

1830 Baltimore and Ohio Railroad opens the first passenger line

1830 Indian Removal Act passed by Congress

1830s Growth of first commercial cities

1830s Labor movement gains strength

1830s Temperance movement expands

1833– Lucy Larcom works in Lowell
1842 textile mills

1834 Female operatives at Lowell first go on strike

1834 First Female Moral Reform Society formed

1835– Runaway slave Harriet Jacobs
1842 hides in her grandmother's attic

LUCY LARCOM SPENT HER TEENAGE YEARS AS A MILL worker in the new factory town of Lowell, Massachusetts, on the Merrimack River. In 1835, at the age of eleven, she had moved to Lowell with her widowed mother, who had taken a job as manager of one of the company-owned boardinghouses to support herself and her children. For Lucy, working in the textile factory, a "rather select industrial school for young people," was the formative experience of her life, and she carried the memory into her future career as a poet and writer.[1] She loved doing work that was significant to the larger society and wrote of "the pleasure we found in making new acquaintances among our workmates." But in later years, she became uneasy with the condescension toward her humble past as a factory girl. "It is the first duty of every woman to recognize the mutual bond of universal womanhood," Larcom wrote in her memoirs. "Let her ask herself whether she would like to hear herself or her sister spoken of as a shopgirl or a factory-girl or a servant-girl, if necessity had compelled her for a time to be employed."[2]

Larcom's experiences embodied two of the three crucial elements shaping the lives of women in the United States during the first half of the nineteenth century. First, she subscribed to the influential ideology of womanhood, home life, and gender relations that treated women as fundamentally different from men; this ideology placed women on a pedestal, simultaneously elevated and isolated by their special domestic role. Second, Larcom was participating

photos: top, The Granger Collection, New York; middle, The New York Public Library/Art Resource, NY; bottom, Cornell University Library, ATHM Textile Photographs Collection in the first wave of American industrialization, a process that dramatically redirected the young nation's economy and created new dimensions of wealth and poverty, new levels of production and consumption, and new ways of life. Historians tend to identify these two elements with two different and emerging classes — domestic ideology with the middle class, industrialization with the working class — but through the eyes of women like Lucy Larcom, it is possible to see that they were mutually influential.

The very cotton fibers that mill girls like Larcom spun and wove symbolize the third major element considered in this chapter: slavery. By the nineteenth century, slavery was a southern social and economic system but one with profound national implications. Slavery was of incomparable importance to American women in the antebellum (pre–Civil War) years, not only to slaves and those who lived by or profited from unfree labor but also to those who dedicated themselves to ending slavery and, ultimately, to all who would endure the devastating conflict fought over it.

◆ **THE IDEOLOGY OF TRUE WOMANHOOD**

Lucy Larcom's concern with the implications of her factory years for her character as a woman reflects a powerful ideology of gender roles that historians have variously labeled "the cult of true womanhood," "the ideology of separate spheres," or simply "domesticity." This system of ideas, which took hold in the early years of the nineteenth century just as the United States was coming into its own as an independent nation, treated men and women as complete and absolute opposites, with almost no common human traits that transcended the differences of gender. The ideology of true womanhood also saw the larger society as carved into complementary but mutually exclusive "spheres" of public and private concerns, work and home life, politics and family. "In no country has such constant care been taken as in America to trace two clearly distinct lines of action for the two sexes," declared Alexis de Tocqueville, the French observer of American culture in the 1830s. "American women never manage the outward concerns of the family, or conduct a business, or take a part in political life; nor are they, on the other hand, ever compelled

photos: top, The Irish Collection, John J. Burns Library, Boston College; bottom, Library of Congress, LC-B8171-152-A

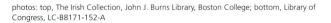

to perform the rough labor of the fields, or to make any of those laborious exertions, which demand the exertion of physical strength. No families are so poor, as to form an exception to this rule."[3]

The experience of innumerable women in antebellum America—the slave women of the South, the mill girls of the North, the impoverished widows of the new cities, the rising number of female immigrants, even the hardworking farm wives—contradicted these assertions. Yet no aspect of this complex reality seemed to interfere with the widespread conviction that this gender ideology was "true." The challenge of understanding American women's history in the first half of the nineteenth century is to reconcile the extraordinary hegemony—that is, breadth and power—of the ideology of separate spheres with the wide variety of American women's lives in these years, many of which tell a very different story.

Christian Motherhood

An ideology as culturally widespread as that of true womanhood is difficult to reduce to a set of beliefs, but several basic concepts do stand out. First and foremost, proponents situated true women in an exclusively domestic realm of home, family, and childrearing. They considered housewifery and childrearing

◆ **Teaching the Scriptures,** ***The Religious Souvenir*** **(1839)** Edited by Lydia H. Sigourney, *The Religious Souvenir* collected devotional poems and stories for Christian readers. This engraving of a mother and daughter studying the Bible vividly conveys the ideals of domesticity and piety at the heart of white women's true womanhood. Fine furniture, clothing, and decorative objects also reflect the increased consumer activity of the middle-class home. A Romantic landscape fills the background, while abundant foliage inside and out suggests the woman's fertility and the child's growth under her tutelage. *Harvard University Libraries.*

not as work but as an effortless expression of women's feminine natures. Action and leadership were reserved for man; inspiration and assistance were woman's province. The home over which women presided was not merely a residence or a collection of people but, to use a popular phrase, "a haven in a heartless world," where men could find solace from a grueling public existence. "The perfection of womanhood . . . is the wife and mother, the center of the family, that magnet that draws man to the domestic altar, that makes him a civilized being, a social Christian," proclaimed the popular women's magazine *Godey's Lady's Book* in 1860. "The wife is truly the light of the home."[4]

At the core of the idea of woman's sphere was motherhood. This basic contention was present in late eighteenth-century rhetoric about the importance of Republican Motherhood to the success of the American democratic experiment (see pp. 127–30). In stark contrast to the self-serving individualism expected of men and rewarded by economic advancement in the larger world, proponents of true womanhood described motherhood as a wholly selfless activity built around service to others. Oddly enough, given the importance that American political culture placed on independence of character, maternal selflessness was seen as the very source of national well-being, training citizens of the new nation to be virtuous, concerned with the larger good, and yet industrious and self-disciplined. Even women without children could bestow their motherly instincts on society's unloved and ignored unfortunates. "Woman's great mission is to train immature, weak and ignorant creatures, to obey the laws of God," preached author and domestic ideologue Catharine Beecher in one of her many treatises on true womanhood, "first in the family, then in the school, then in the neighborhood, then in the nation, then in the world."[5] Beecher herself was unmarried and childless (see Reading into the Past: "The Peculiar Responsibilities of the American Woman").

Women's expansive maternity was thought to make them natural teachers and underlay the feminization of this profession in the early nineteenth century. Whereas in the eighteenth century, teaching was seen as a fundamentally male vocation, by the nineteenth century women were increasingly regarded as best suited to instruct the young, and primary school teaching became an overwhelmingly female occupation. Especially in New England, public education was becoming widespread, and classrooms were staffed by young Yankee women, literate but less expensive to hire than men. By one estimate, one-quarter of all women born in New England between 1825 and 1860 were schoolteachers at some point in their lives.[6]

Women's motherly vocation had a deeply religious dimension. True womanhood was a fervently Protestant notion, which gave a redemptive power to female devotion and selfless sacrifice. The true woman functioned as Christ's representative in daily life, and the domestic environment over which she presided served as a sort of sacred territory, where evil and worldly influences could be cleansed away. Beecher insisted that "the preparation of young ministers for the duties of the church does not surpass in importance the training of the minister of the nursery and school-room."[7]

The special identification of women with Christian piety was firmly established by a new wave of religious revivals that swept through American society in the late

READING INTO THE PAST

CATHARINE BEECHER
The Peculiar Responsibilities of the American Woman

In the first chapter of A Treatise on Domestic Economy *(1841), a book devoted to the details of childrearing and homemaking, author and domestic ideologue Catharine Beecher (1800–1878) elaborates her theory of American democracy and women's place in it. She insists that women's inclusion in the American promise of equality is completely compatible with the subordination that she believed was divinely ordained in wives' relations to their husbands.*

In this Country, it is established, both by opinion and by practice, that woman has an equal interest in all social and civil concerns; and that no domestic, civil, or political, institution, is right, which sacrifices her interest to promote that of the other sex. But in order to secure her the more firmly in all these privileges, it is decided, that, in the domestic relation, she take a subordinate station, and that, in civil and political concerns, her interests be intrusted to the other sex, without her taking any part in voting, or in making and administering laws. . . . In matters pertaining to the education of their children, in the selection and support of a clergy-man, in all benevolent enterprises, and in all questions relating to morals or manners, [women] have a superior influence. In such concerns, it would be impossible to carry a point, contrary to their judgement and feelings; while an enterprise, sustained by them, will seldom fail of success.

If those who are bewailing themselves over the fancied wrongs and injuries of women in this Nation, could only see things as they are, they

eighteenth and early nineteenth centuries. Beginning in the frontier communities of Ohio, Kentucky, and Indiana, the Second Great Awakening moved east by the 1810s and 1820s. Western New York was known as the "burned-over district" because of the zealous religiosity that swept through it in these years. Conveyed by preachers inspired by personal spiritual conviction rather than theological training, religious fervor especially thrived outside large cities. In the South, blacks and whites were drawn together in similar extended revivals. A cultural phenomenon with many different sources, the Second Great Awakening was a reaction both to the political preoccupations of the revolutionary period and to swift changes in the American economic system. This religious revivalism also had a populist element, would know, that . . . there is nothing reasonable, which American women would unite in asking, that would not readily be bestowed. . . . To us [Americans] is committed the grand, the responsible privilege, of exhibiting to the world, the beneficent influences of Christianity. . . . But the part to be enacted by American women, in this great moral enterprise, is the point to which special attention should here be directed. . . . The proper education of a man decides the welfare of an individual; but educate a woman, and the interests of the whole family are secured. . . .

The woman, who is rearing a family of children; the woman, who labors in the schoolroom; the woman, who, in her retired chamber, earns, with her needle, the mite, which contributes to the intellectual and moral elevation of her Country; even the humble domestic, whose example and influence may be moulding and forming young minds, while her faithful services sustain a prosperous domestic state; — each and all may be animated by the consciousness, that they are agents in accomplishing the greatest work that ever was committed to human responsibility.

SOURCE: Catharine Beecher, *A Treatise on Domestic Economy* (New York: Marsh, Capen, Lyon, and Webb, 1841), ch. 1.

QUESTIONS FOR ANALYSIS

1. What does this passage, written more than a half century after the American Revolution, indicate about Beecher's vision of the grand political purposes served by women's special domestic role, for both the United States and the rest of the world?

2. How do Beecher's ideas compare to the Republican Motherhood concept of the earlier revolutionary years?

as it bypassed established clerical authority in favor of more direct spiritual experience among the broad mass of the American people. New evangelical forms of Protestant worship, especially in Baptist and Methodist congregations, stressed personal conversion and commitment to rooting out sin in this world.

Religious enthusiasm and activism gave women, who were the majority of converts in these revivals, an arena for individual expression and social recognition that they were denied in secular politics. To establish their reputations as effective religious leaders, popular evangelical preachers relied on their female followers. Catharine Beecher's father, Lyman, and her brother, Henry Ward, were two such evangelical ministers. As for Catharine herself, she was never able to experience a full personal conversion and always doubted the depth of her religious conviction. Nonetheless, the career she was able to build for herself as an authority on proper Christian womanhood was much assisted by the association of the Beecher name with evangelical piety.

Women's reputation for deeper religious sentiment was closely related to the assumption that the true woman was inherently uninterested in sexual expression, that she was "pure." The notion of woman's natural sexual innocence was a relatively modern concept. In traditional European Christian culture, women had been considered more dangerously sexual than men. The belief in women's basic "passionlessness," as one historian has named it, was a new idea that, in the context of the time, served to raise women's stature.[8] In the hierarchical nineteenth-century Protestant worldview, woman was less tied to humanity's animal nature than man was, and this lifted her closer to the divine. Sexual appetite in the white, middle-class female was virtually unimaginable.[9] However, poor women, and especially women of African and Native American descent, continued to be viewed by white Americans as excessively sexual beings. These class- and race-based assumptions about female sexuality made the presence of prostitutes profoundly disturbing to nineteenth-century moralists. If women were as lustful as men, there would be no one to control and contain sexual desire. As Dr. William Sanger wrote in his path-breaking 1858 study of prostitution in New York City, "Were it otherwise, and the

THE GREAT SOCIAL EVIL.

TIME:—Midnight. A Sketch not a Hundred Miles from the Haymarket.

Bella. "AH! FANNY! HOW LONG HAVE YOU BEEN GAY?"

◆ **New York City Prostitutes**
Whether the number of prostitutes rose dramatically in the mid-nineteenth century, as many observers charged, in large cities they were certainly more visible and thus more disturbing to the middle-class public. Prostitutes and their clients commonly frequented the "third tier" of theaters, which was informally reserved for them. As this contemporary cartoon indicates, they could even be found at the most elegant theaters. The joke in this cartoon refers to the difficulty of distinguishing between prostitutes and reputable women of fashion. The term "gay" referred to prostitution, not homosexuality, in the nineteenth century. © *Look and Learn/Peter Jackson Collection/Bridgeman Images.*

passions in both sexes equal, illegitimacy and prostitution would be far more rife in our midst than at present."[10] (See Primary Sources: "Prostitution in New York City, 1858," pp. 191–95.)

Starting in the 1820s, pious women expanded their religious expression beyond churchgoing to participation in a wide variety of voluntary organizations that promoted the spiritual and moral uplift of the poor and unsaved. Some of these female benevolent associations sponsored missionary efforts to bring the blessings of Christianity to unbelievers at home and abroad. By the 1830s, an extensive network of Protestant women's organizations was sending money to church missions throughout Asia and Africa. A handful of adventuresome women went to preach the gospel abroad, mostly as wives of male missionaries. Ann Hasseltine Judson, who served with her husband in the 1820s in Rangoon, Burma, was the first American woman missionary in Asia. Closer to home, female missionaries brought Christian solace to the American urban poor. Pious middle-class women joined their ministers in "friendly visiting" to preach the word of Christ to society's downtrodden and outcast.

Many free black women in the northern states embraced the culture of middle-class female Christian piety, yet entrenched racial and economic inequality created tensions between the ideals of true womanhood and the realities of free

LIFE IN PHILADELPHIA.

◆ **Edward Clay, "Is Miss Dina at home?"** *Life in Philadelphia* **series (1828)**
Edward Clay, a white engraver and printmaker of Philadelphia, created a series of popular prints mocking antebellum social pretensions. Reflecting the racial animosity of many northern whites, Clay often caricatured free black life in his series *Life in Philadelphia*. The caption in this print mocks a black man's use of a calling card, common to nineteenth-century middle-class social etiquette, in his visit to "Dina." ("Dina" was a common generic name used for black domestic workers in nineteenth-century racist humor.) The exchange between the woman and man reads: "Is Miss Dina at home? Yes Sir but she potickly engaged in washing de dishes. Ah! I am sorry I cant have the honour to pay my devours to her. Give her my card." How does Clay combine speech and image to ridicule free African American claims to citizenship and equality? *Library of Congress, LC-DIG-pga-11034.*

black life. By 1840, almost 171,000 free African Americans resided in the northern states, especially in the cities of New York, Philadelphia, and Boston. Hundreds of mutual aid societies, churches, and schools sprung up in these black communities. The first independent black Protestant denomination, the African Methodist Episcopal (A.M.E.) Church, founded in Philadelphia in 1816, had a large membership of free black women. Most free black women worked as domestics or laundresses, and others became accomplished seamstresses and milliners. Even when economic reality did not match the domestic ideal, free black women asserted their dignity and personhood through a culture of respectability based on moral conduct and self-improvement.

A Middle-Class Ideology

Despite the wide range of those who subscribed to its tenets, the ideology of true womanhood was a thoroughly middle-class social ethic. Certainly, the assumption that a woman should be insulated from economic demands to concentrate on creating a stable and peaceful home environment presumed she was married to a man able to support her as a dependent wife. The middle-class wife in turn was responsible for what Beecher characterized as "the regular and correct apportionment of expenses that makes a family truly comfortable."[11] The idealized true woman, presiding over a virtuous family life, was a crucial staple of the way Americans contrasted themselves with European aristocratic society. Adherence to the ideology of true womanhood also helped people of the middle classes to distinguish themselves from those they regarded as their social and economic inferiors. In their charitable activities among the poor, true women preached the gospel of separate sexual spheres and female domesticity, convinced that the absence of these family values, rather than economic forces, was what made poor people poor.

These ideas reflected changing conditions in middle-class American women's lives. The birthrate for the average American-born white woman fell from 6 in 1800 to 4.9 in 1850, in part because economic modernization meant that children were less important as extra hands to help support the family and more likely to be a financial drain. Also, technological developments — for example, the new cast-iron stove, which was easier and safer than open-hearth cooking — were just beginning to ease women's household burdens. As the industrial production of cloth accelerated, women no longer had to spin and weave at home, although they still cut and sewed their family's clothes. Depending on their husbands' incomes, middle-class women might be able to hire servants to help with their labors. Even so, the middle-class housewife did plenty of work herself. Despite technological developments, leisure time was a privilege for only the very richest women. Laundry, the most burdensome of domestic obligations, remained a difficult weekly chore.

The doctrine of domesticity was elaborated by ministers in sermons and physicians in popular health books. But women themselves did much of the work of spreading these ideas. The half century in which this rigid ideology of gender first flourished was also the period in which writing by women first found a mass audience among middle-class women. Lydia Sigourney, a beloved woman's poet; Mrs. E. D. E. N. Southworth, popular author of numerous sentimental novels; and Sarah Josepha Hale, editor of the influential women's magazine *Godey's Lady's Book* (with 150,000 subscribers in 1860), all built successful careers elaborating the ideology of true womanhood. (See Primary Sources: "*Godey's Lady's Book*," pp. 204–10.) In her influential and much reprinted *Treatise on Domestic Economy* (1841), Catharine Beecher taught that woman's sphere was a noble "profession," equal in importance and challenge to any of the tasks assigned to men. Her younger half sister, Harriet Beecher Stowe, relied heavily on the ideas of woman's sphere in her book *Uncle Tom's Cabin* (1851), which became the most widely read American novel ever written.

In the judgment of such women, the tremendous respect paid to woman's lofty state was one of the distinguishing glories of nineteenth-century America. While proponents of true womanhood insisted that woman's sphere differed from man's, they regarded it as of equal importance to society and worthy of respect. Lucy Larcom put it this way: "God made no mistake in her [woman's] creation. He sent her into the world full of power and will to be a *helper*. . . . She is here to make this great house of humanity a habitable and a beautiful place, without and within, a true home for every one of his children."[12]

The many women of the nineteenth century who energetically subscribed to the ideas of true womanhood were not brainwashed victims of a male ideological conspiracy. Private writings of middle-class women from this period, letters and diaries notably, show women embracing these ideas and using them to give purpose to their lives. Not only could the true woman claim authority over the household and childrearing, but the widespread belief in her special moral vocation legitimated certain kinds of activity outside the domestic sphere. Despite its middle-class character, the doctrine of true womanhood was strikingly widespread throughout antebellum American society. Almost the only women during this period who openly challenged its tenets were the women's rights radicals (see pp. 243–48).

Domesticity in a Market Age

By fervently insisting that women had to be insulated from the striving and bustle of the outside world, the advocates of true womanhood were implicitly responding to the impact of larger economic pressures on women's lives. The ideology of separate spheres and women's sheltered domesticity notwithstanding, women's history during this period can be understood only in the context of the burgeoning market economy. The development and growth of a cash-based market-oriented economy — as opposed to one in which people mostly produced goods for their own immediate use — reaches back to the very beginnings of American history and forward into the twentieth century. But early nineteenth-century America is rightly seen as the time in which the fundamental shift toward market-oriented production took place.

The spread of market relations had particular implications for women. In preindustrial society, men's work as well as women's was considered fundamentally domestic. Both sexes worked within and for the household, not for trade on the open market. By the eighteenth century, this was already changing as commercial transactions were growing in significance. Especially within urban areas, various household goods — soap and candles, for example, or processed foods like flour and spices — were available for purchase. By the early nineteenth century, households needed to acquire more and more cash to buy consumer goods to fill the needs of daily life. Acquiring this money became men's obligation.

With the rise of the market economy, much of men's work moved outside the home, and women alone did work in the domestic realm for direct use. Because work was increasingly regarded as what happened outside the home, done by men and compensated for by money, what women did in the home was becoming invisible as productive labor. From this perspective, the lavish attention the proponents of true womanhood paid to the moral significance of woman's domestic sphere might be seen as ideological compensation for the decline in its economic value.

Industrial depressions, which affected the entire society and not just the lower rungs of wage earners, were becoming a regular, seemingly inescapable characteristic of industrial society, the bust that inevitably followed the boom. In 1837, the U.S. economy, which had been growing by leaps and bounds, violently contracted, and prices dropped precipitously, banks collapsed, and wages fell by as much as a third. The Panic of 1837, as it was called for the response of investor and wage earner alike, was an early and formative experience in the lives of many women, among them the future women's rights leader Susan B. Anthony, whose father lost his grain mill business in that year.

Despite waning recognition of women's role in economic production, popular nineteenth-century ideology assumed that in the household, women could counteract some of the more disturbing aspects of economic expansion. A woman's household management skills and emotional steadiness were supposed to be crucial in helping her family weather the shifting financial winds that were such an unnerving aspect of the new economy. "When we observe the frequent revolutions from poverty to affluence and then from extravagance to ruin, that are continually taking place around us," wrote Mrs. A. J. Graves in her popular handbook *Woman in America* (1841), "and their calamitous effects upon families brought up in luxury and idleness, have we not reason to fear that our 'homes of order and peace' are rapidly disappearing?"[13] Seen this way, the proper conduct of woman's sphere virtually became a matter of economic survival.

◆ WOMEN AND WAGE EARNING

As Mrs. Graves's admonition indicates, the depiction of woman's sphere as unconnected to the striving and bustle of the outside world is misleading. Indeed, women felt the pressures of a consumer-based (or cash-based) market economy in many ways. Some women found ways to make money from within their households — for instance, by selling extra butter or eggs. Barely visible to a society focused on its own capacity for productive prosperity, impoverished urban women, widowed or deserted by men, scrounged or begged for pennies to buy shelter, food, and warmth.

Of all women's intersections with the cash economy and the forces of the market revolution, none was more important for women's history than the employment of young New England women like Lucy Larcom as factory operatives at the power-driven spindles and looms of the newly established American textile industry. Though their numbers were small, these young women constituted the first emergence of the female wage labor force (see the Appendix, p. A-18).

From Market Revolution to Industrial Revolution

To understand the experiences of early nineteenth-century women factory workers, we must place them in the setting of the era's industrial transformations. The growth of a market economy encouraged the centralization and acceleration of the production of goods. This industrializing process was gradual and uneven, a fact that becomes especially clear when we focus on the distinct contribution of women workers. For a long time after industrialization began, people continued to produce goods at home, even as their control over what they made and their share of its value were seriously eroded. In this transitional form of manufacture for sale, male entrepreneurs, or "factors," purchased the raw materials for production and distributed them to workers in their homes, then paid for the finished goods and sold them to customers. Workers no longer received the full cash value of what they had produced since the factor also made money from the process. In essence, the workers were receiving a wage for their labor instead of being paid for their products, which were no longer theirs to sell. Their labor was increasingly considered only a part, not the entirety, of the production process.

Shoemaking is a particularly interesting example, both because its transition to full industrialization was prolonged and because women and men underwent this transition at different rates. Making shoes for sale was already an established activity by the early nineteenth century, especially in cities north of Boston, notably Lynn, Massachusetts. At first, shoes were manufactured in home-based workshops in which the male head of the household was the master artisan and his wife, children, and apprentices worked under his direction. Starting in the 1820s and 1830s, a new class of shoemaking entrepreneurs brought male shoemakers, who specialized in cutting and sewing soles, to a centralized site, while women continued to sew the shoes' uppers and linings at home. By the 1840s and 1850s, women's labor was being directed and paid for by the entrepreneurs. It was not until later in the nineteenth century, after the Civil War, that women's part in shoe production moved into factories.

Clothing manufacture remained in a similar "outwork" phase for a long time. Women working at home produced most of the clothing manufactured for sale in the antebellum period. By 1860, there were sixteen thousand seamstresses in New York City alone.[14] Industrialization ravaged many of these mid-nineteenth-century poor women and their families. Other than for slaves, manufacture of clothing did not begin to shift into factories until after the Civil War — and well into the twentieth century the workshop form of production continued to thrive, in sweatshops. Other industries that relied on women out-workers included straw-hat making and bookbinding. Limited to their homes by childrearing responsibilities, married women remained home-based industrial outworkers much longer than did men or unmarried women. The more exclusively female that outwork was, the more poorly it paid.

Manufacturing could be said to be fully industrialized only when it shifted to a separate, centralized location, the factory, at which point home and work were fully separated. In factories, entrepreneurs could introduce more expensive machinery and supervise labor more closely, both intended to maximize their profits. Factories and the machines within them were the manufacturers' contribution to the process, the "capital" that gave them control and ownership over the product of the workers.

Male artisans, no longer the masters of their family workshops, experienced the shift to the factory as absolute decline; for women the shift of manufacturing to outside the home offered a more mixed experience. Factory ownership was entirely in the hands of men, and women, whose secondary status had already been established in home manufacturing, earned a much lower wage than men for tasks that were inevitably considered less skilled. Yet women's turn to factory labor also gave them the chance to earn wages as individuals, and at times to experience a taste of personal freedom. As Lucy Larcom explained, young women like herself "were clearing away a few weeds from the overgrown track of independent labor for other women."[15]

The Mill Girls of Lowell

By the 1820s, textile production, one of the most important of America's early industries — and certainly the most female dominated — was decisively shifting in the direction of factory labor. If the impoverished "tailoresses" working out of their dark urban garrets stood for the depredation of women by industrial capitalists, the factory girls of the textile industry came to represent the better possibilities that wage labor might offer women. And "girls" they were — unmarried, many in their teens. (See Primary Sources: "Early Photographs of Factory Operatives and Slave Women," pp. 211–18.) Though they were only a tiny percentage of women — as of 1840, only 2.25 percent[16] — these first female factory workers understood themselves, and were understood by others in their society, as opening up new vistas of personal independence and economic contribution for their sex.

The story of the first women factory workers began in the American textile industry during and immediately after the War of 1812. At the beginning of the nineteenth century, Americans bought wool, linen, and cotton cloth manufactured in the textile factories of Great Britain. The war with England interrupted the transatlantic trade in factory-made cloth, creating an irresistible opportunity for wealthy New England merchants, who had heretofore made their money by importing British textiles, to invest in American-based industry. In 1814 in Waltham, Massachusetts, a group of local merchants opened the first American factory to house all aspects of textile production under one roof. In an early and daring example of industrial espionage, they had spirited out of England designs for water-driven machinery for both spinning and weaving. The investors enjoyed quick and substantial profits, and in 1823 the same group of venture capitalists opened a much larger operation twenty-three miles away, on Merrimack River farmland north of Boston. The new factory town, named after the leading figure in the merchant capital group, Francis Cabot Lowell, soon became synonymous with the energetic American textile industry and with the young women who provided its labor force.

Previously, in England and in earlier, unsuccessful efforts at factory textile production in the United States, whole families who would otherwise be destitute were the workers: children worked the spinning machines and looms. This impoverished working population gave factory production a bad name, best captured by British poet William Blake's terrifying 1804 image of the "dark satanic mills" soiling "England's green and pleasant land."[17] Textile factories were regarded as poorhouses designed for keeping indigent people from disrupting society. Given the availability of land for farms in the United States, this type of labor force was not as obtainable for aspiring American textile industrialists. But an alternative had been identified as early as the 1790s by President George Washington's secretary of the treasury, Alexander Hamilton, an early promoter of American industrial production. Hamilton advocated hiring the unmarried daughters of farming families, who could move in and out of industrial production without becoming a permanent and impoverished wage labor force like that which haunted England. By laboring for wages in textile factories, these young women could for a time help provide their families with the cash that they increasingly required. The fact that the spinning of fiber for cloth had been the traditional work of women in the preindustrial household (especially unmarried women, hence the term "spinster") provided an additional argument for turning to a female labor force.

To the delight of New England textile capitalists, girls from Yankee farm families took to factory labor in the 1820s and early 1830s with great enthusiasm. Earning an individual wage offered them a degree of personal independence that was very attractive to these young women. Many were eager to work in the factories, despite thirteen-hour days, six-day workweeks, and wages of $1 to $2 per week.[18] "I regard it as one of the privileges of my youth that I was permitted to grow up among these active, interesting girls," Lucy Larcom wrote in her memoirs, "whose lives were not mere echoes of other lives, but had principles and purposes distinctly their own."[19] Even though they saved their wages and sent as much as possible to their families, the mill girls occasionally spent some of their earnings on themselves; for this they were regarded by contemporaries as spoiled and self-indulgent. And although their workdays were extraordinarily long and the labor much more unrelenting than that to which they were accustomed, they reveled in the small amounts of time they had for themselves in the evenings. Larcom's reminiscences detail the classes she and her sister attended, the writing they did, and the

◆ The *Lowell Offering*

The *Lowell Offering* was the mill owner–sponsored publication of original writings by women workers known as "factory girls." Conditions in the mills had already begun to deteriorate by 1845, the date of this publication. Nonetheless, the image's foreground shows a confident, literate, individual woman stepping out into the larger world. In the background are the mills and boardinghouses in which the working girls lived and worked. Note the idealized pastoral frame, so different from the actual reality of the industrial process and its impact on the city, factories, and workers of Lowell. © *Everett Collection Historical/Alamy.*

friendships they made. Factory girls at Lowell and elsewhere even formed female benevolent societies, as did their more middle-class counterparts.

One problem, however, stood in the way of the success of this solution to the problem of factory labor: Where were the young women workers to live? Given the scale of the labor force required by the large new factories and the decentralized character of the New England population, young women would have to be brought from their homes to distant factories. Parents were reluctant to allow their daughters to be so far from home and away from family supervision. Factory work for women, probably because it had been so dreadfully underpaid in England, was suspected of being an avenue to prostitution. The manufacturers' solution to both the housing and moral supervision dilemmas was to build boardinghouses for their young workers and to link work and living arrangements in a paternalistic approach to industrial production. Four to six young women shared each bedroom, and their behavior was closely supervised. The boardinghouses, and the camaraderie among young women that flourished there, added to the allure of factory labor. To the farm girls of New England, this was greater cosmopolitanism than they had ever known.

For about a decade, the city of Lowell and the Lowell system (as the employment of young farm girls as factory workers was called) were among the glories of the new American nation. Visitors came from Europe to see and sing the praises of the moral rectitude and industry of the women workers in this new type of factory production, free of the corruptions of the old world. "They were healthy in appearance, many of them remarkably so," Charles Dickens wrote after a visit in 1842, "and had the manners and deportment of young women; not of degraded brutes of burden."[20] The dignity and probity of the Lowell girls were crucial elements in the optimism that temporarily thrived regarding the possibilities of a genuinely democratic American version of industrial factory production, in which all could profit from the new levels of wealth. "The experiment at Lowell had shown that independent and intelligent workers invariably give their own character to their occupation," Larcom proudly wrote.[21] Young women workers wrote stories, essays, and poems about their experience at the factories for their own literary journal, the *Lowell Offering*, to put their uprightness and their intelligence on display. Larcom began a long career as a writer this way. Factory owners, not insensitive to the propaganda value of such efforts, underwrote the magazine, paid the editor's salary, and distributed issues widely.

The End of the Lowell Idyll

Eventually, however, economic pressures took their toll on Lowell's great promise, at least for the workers. Declining prices for cotton and wool and investors' expectations of high returns led factory owners to slash wages. Within the first decade, wages were cut twice. The factory owners counted on the womanly demeanor of their employees to get them to accept the cuts. But they were wrong. In 1834 and 1836, in response to lower wages, Lowell girls "turned out" — conducted spontaneous strikes — and in the process began to question notions of womanhood that forbade such demonstrations of individual and group assertion. They repudiated the deference and subordination expected of them on the grounds of their sex and championed, instead, their dignity and independence as proud "daughters of freemen." One young striker, Harriet Hanson, who went on to become a leader in the woman suffrage movement, remembered that the strike "was the first time a woman had spoken in public in Lowell, and the event caused surprise and consternation among her audience."[22] But the Panic of 1837, which triggered contraction of the entire industrial economy, doomed the efforts of the women operatives to act collectively, defend their jobs, and preserve the level of their wages. Workers were laid off and mills shut down. Young girls went back to their farm families to wait out the economic downturn.

When the economy revived and the mills resumed full production, workers were expected to increase their pace, tend more machines, and produce more cloth. Production levels rose, but wages did not. Moral concerns were giving way to the bottom line. In 1845, Lowell's women workers formed the Lowell Female Labor Reform Association and joined with male workers in other Massachusetts factories in petitioning the state legislature to establish a ten-hour legal limit to their workdays as a way to resist work pressure and keep up levels of employment. This turn to the political system to redress group grievance was part of the larger democratic spirit of the period. It is especially striking to find women engaged in these methods at a time when politics was regarded as thoroughly outside of woman's sphere. Indeed, the legislative petitions of the women textile workers of the 1840s are an important indicator that women were beginning to imagine themselves as part of the political process. But for precisely this reason, because women still lacked whatever voting power male workers could muster, they were unable to secure any gains by their legislative petitions.

Conditions of factory labor were changing in other ways as well, most notably in the composition of the labor force. The Lowell system had been devised in the context of a shortage of workers willing to take factory jobs. By the 1840s, however, immigrants were providing an ever-growing labor pool for industrial employment. Coming to the United States in large numbers, they poured into the wage labor force. The Irish were both the largest and the most economically desperate of all the new arrivals. Starting in 1845, a terrible blight on the potato crop that was the staple of the Irish diet, exacerbated by the harsh policies of England toward its oldest colony, threw the population into starvation conditions and compelled well over a million Irish men and women to emigrate to the United States. The textile capitalists, no longer pressured by labor shortages to make factory employment seem morally uplifting, paid low wages to and enforced harsh working conditions on these new immigrant workers, who soon constituted the majority of mill laborers.

Part of the initial attraction that native-born farm girls had for capitalists was the knowledge that they would eventually marry and return to their families and farms, and therefore their factory labor would be only a brief episode in their lives. The dreaded old world fate of becoming a permanently degraded and dependent wage labor class went instead to the Irish Catholic immigrants, who by 1860 were well over half of the workers in the industry. Immigrant men now worked the

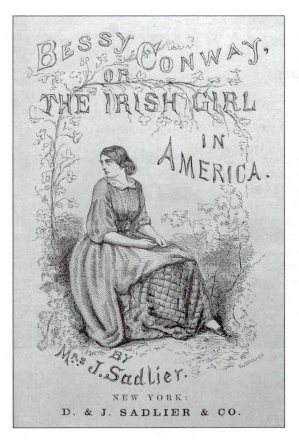

looms and immigrant women the spindles. Public celebrations of the high moral character of the factory operatives — the womanly demeanor and hunger for self-improvement that were once the boast of the industry — disappeared. Wage earning was increasingly seen as undermining respectable femininity. Working women and true women were going their separate ways.

At the Bottom of the Wage Economy

Tremendous prejudice was directed at the Irish in the early years of industrialization, in no small part because they were becoming so thoroughly identified with wage labor. The Irish were one of the very few immigrant groups in nineteenth-century American history in which the number of women roughly equaled that of men. Those who did not work in factories labored as domestic servants. In preindustrial America, the housewife had turned to young neighbors or relatives as "helps" in her domestic obligations. Lucy Larcom worked for her sister in this traditional capacity whenever the downturns in factory conditions were too much for her. But in industrializing America, especially as the numbers of Irish immigrants grew, mistress and maid were becoming separated by a much greater cultural and economic gap and losing their sense of common task and purpose. In 1852, Elizabeth Cady Stanton, founding mother of the American women's rights movement (see pp. 243–48), complained of the "two undeveloped Hibernians in my kitchen" whose ignorance of modern household procedures she felt powerless to remedy.[23] The industrious, Protestant, Yankee middle-class housewife saw the Catholic Irish "girls" she hired to cook and clean and do laundry as dirty, ignorant, and immoral.

The divide between native-born middle-class mistress and immigrant wage-earning maid could almost be said to define class distinctions among free women. Complaints about the difficulty of finding or keeping "good help" were a staple of middle-class female culture (see Figure 4.6, p. 208). Some women organized societies to place needy girls as workers in suitable homes. However, the objects of their charity rarely regarded domestic service as a privilege. Domestic servants' habits of working erratically, changing employers often, and presenting a sullen demeanor were means of protesting a form of employment they did not like and that was not respected in democratic America, where the deference expected in personal service already had given it a bad name. Their female employers could never understand why, even when wages were competitive, their domestic servants did their best to switch to factory employment. There, though the workday was long and the labor hard, a factory job ended with the dismissal bell after which a young woman's time became her own.

At the very bottom of the economic ladder, beneath even the lower rungs of domestic service, were the urban poor. America had always had its poor people, but this destitute class was new, as it included able-bodied people willing to work but unable to find jobs that would support themselves and their families. The most desperate of the urban poor were the women with children but without men (or, more precisely, without access to the higher wages a man could earn). These poor urban women were the absolute antithesis of true womanhood. The rooms in which they lived could hardly be called homes: they were not furnished, clean, or private. Unschooled and unsupervised, their children went into the streets or worked for a pittance to help support their families. Housework was especially difficult for poor urban women: they carried water for laundry or coal for warmth or small amounts of food for dinner up steps into tiny tenement apartments or down into cellar spaces (where twenty-nine thousand lived in New York City as of 1850).[24] After each downturn of the industrial economy, the numbers of urban poor swelled.

The Society for the Relief of Poor Widows, formed in New York City in 1799, was the first American charity organized by women for women.[25] The charitable ladies did not provide outright cash or employment, instead dispensing spiritual and moral ministrations along with occasional food, coal, and clothing. In such exchanges, just as in the relationship between mistress and maid, middle-class and poor women met each other across the class divide, probably struck more with what separated them than with what they allegedly shared by virtue of their common gender.

◆ **William Henry Burr, *The Intelligence Office***
This 1849 painting of an employment office dramatically portrays the harsh reality of poor
working women in search of employment, as two young women are displayed before a
potential employer by the male proprietor. The sign at the back reads "Agents for Domestics.
Warranted Honest." © *Collection of the New-York Historical Society, USA/Bridgeman Images.*

◆ WOMEN, SLAVERY, AND THE SOUTH

Perhaps the greatest irony embedded in the dynamic beginnings of industrial capitalism is the degree to which it rested on a very different social and economic system
that also thrived in early nineteenth-century America: chattel slavery. As northern
states gradually abolished slavery, the institution became identified exclusively with
the South. At the same time, the North and the South were linked in important
ways. Both regions added new states to the west that displaced Native Americans
through various wars and treaties. In the South, the gigantic cotton crop grown
by slave labor was the raw material of New England's textile industry. Among the
greatest advocates of American democracy were numerous southern slaveholders,

including four of this country's first five presidents. And at many levels, the North and South shared a national culture. Their citizens read the same books and magazines, worshipped in the same Protestant denominations, voted for the same political parties, and embraced a doctrine of manifest destiny. Southern white women followed many essentials of the cult of domesticity. But underlying these similarities were fundamental differences, signifying a conflict that eventually led to civil war.

The absence in the South of the wage relationship between producer and capitalist lay at the heart of these sectional differences. Property owners accumulated great profits in the South, and much of what was produced there was intended for sale. But the workers of the system were not paid any wages for their labor. They were *chattel* slaves, human property, the value of whose current and future labor, along with the land they worked, constituted the wealth of their owners. Like the factory buildings and machines that produced wealth in the Northeast, they were capital; but they were also human beings. While the southern states expanded their system of human property, white southern politicians also set their sights on the extensive territory of southeastern Native Americans. Paired with aggressive state legislation, a new U.S. Indian removal law remade the map of Indian America.

Southern Native Americans and U.S. Removal Policy

While planters owned their growing captive labor force, Native American societies still claimed much of the land in the trans-Appalachian South. In the early nineteenth century, slavery and cotton began to expand into what was called the "new" or "lower" South (western Georgia, Florida, Alabama, Arkansas, Mississippi, Louisiana, and Texas). This move was greatly facilitated by a sustained, concerted effort of land-hungry whites, aided by the state governments of Georgia and the Carolinas and legal manipulation by the U.S. government under President Andrew Jackson. Together, white settler violence backed by new state and federal laws as well as military force worked to push the Indian peoples of the Southeast — the Creeks, Chickasaws, Choctaws, and Cherokees — off their extensive lands. The Cherokees in particular had tried to adapt to American society and resist land sales (see Reading into the Past: "Cherokee Women Petition the National Council"), and Cherokee women had learned the domestic tasks of housewifery. The Cherokee leader Sequoyah had devised a written language, enabling the translation of the Christian Bible and the drafting of a political constitution. Some Cherokee families — as well as those in other southeastern Indian tribes — grew wealthy as owners of large cotton plantations and enslaved African-descended workers. Although Native American societies already had long-standing practices of captivity and servitude, this new market-oriented form of chattel slavery supplanted the tradition of Indian women's agricultural labor and introduced racialized notions of black inferiority.

All of these efforts to maintain sovereign Indian lands through assimilation proved ineffective, however, once Andrew Jackson was elected president. Jackson pushed the Indian Removal Act of 1830 through Congress and then, ignoring Supreme Court decisions partially favoring Cherokee sovereignty, sent federal troops to Georgia to enforce a treaty that had been signed by only a small faction of the Cherokee nation. In 1838, the Cherokees were forcibly driven into the newly established Indian Territory west of the Mississippi, across what the Cherokees called the "Trail of Tears." The lands taken from them became the center of slave-grown cotton and tobacco productivity. Meanwhile, in the older southern states of Virginia, Maryland, and the Carolinas, where soil had become exhausted and productivity slumped, slaves themselves became a kind of crop, a surplus to be sold.

Plantation Patriarchy

Over the first half of the nineteenth century, slaveownership became increasingly concentrated in the hands of fewer and fewer whites. By 1860 only an estimated 25 percent of southern white families owned any slaves; of these, only a small minority owned enough to qualify for elite status and significant political and economic power. Planters owning anywhere from twenty to over one thousand slaves controlled the large concentrations of land and labor that formed the power basis of southern slave society (see Map 4.1). On large market-oriented agricultural

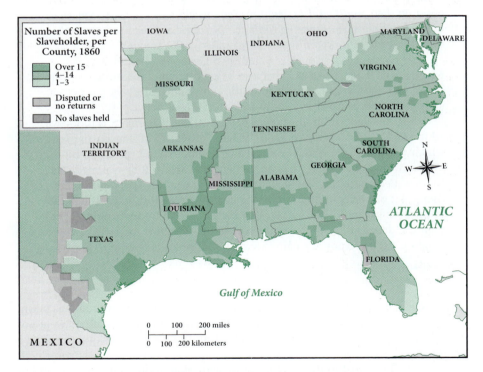

◆ **Map 4.1 Number of Slaves per Slaveholder, per County, 1860**
The cotton boom shifted enslaved African Americans to the lower and western South. In 1790, most slaves lived and worked on the tobacco plantations of the Chesapeake and in the rice and indigo areas of South Carolina. By 1860, the centers of slavery lay along the Mississippi River and in an arc of fertile cotton land sweeping from Mississippi through Georgia.

READING INTO THE PAST

Beloved Children: Cherokee Women Petition the National Council

The expansion of chattel slavery and plantation agriculture into the lower South required the United States to assist its property-hungry citizens to take over the lands of the Native peoples living there. In the early nineteenth century, the federal government negotiated a number of land cessions in treaties with southern tribes, including the Cherokee. In 1817, thirteen Cherokee women sent this petition to their own National Council to warn against the transfer of any more lands to white ownership. Among the signers was eighty-year-old Nancy Ward (see p. 116), whose high standing among her people harked back to an earlier age in which women shared political and social authority with men. The signers spoke for those women who had given up their traditional agricultural responsibilities in favor of American domestic tasks, such as making clothing. Nonetheless, their words indicate a continuing identification through their gender with the land.

May 2, 1817: The Cherokee ladys now being present at the meeting of the chiefs and warriors in council have thought it their duty as mothers to address their beloved chiefs and warriors now assembled.

Our beloved children and head men of the Cherokee Nation, we address you warriors in council. We have raised all of you on the land which we now have, which God gave us to inhabit and raise provisions. We know that our country has once been extensive, but by repeated sales [it] has become circumscribed to a small track, and [we] never have thought it our duty to interfere in the disposition of it till now. If a father or mother was to sell all their lands which they had to depend on, which their children had to raise their living on, [it] would be indeed bad & [so would it to] be removed to another country. We do not wish to go to an

estates slaves were organized into large work gangs in which they raised the cotton, rice, sugar, and tobacco that made the South wealthy. These plantations were not only the economic core but the social, political, and cultural centers of slave society. In general, the nineteenth-century slave South did not develop the dynamic civil society that flourished in the North. The growth of an industrial economy and of a wage labor class was limited in the South to a few urban centers, such as Richmond and Atlanta. With the sole exception of party politics, which wealthy men dominated, public life did not thrive. As a result, plantation women's lives varied significantly from those of northern women.

unknown country to which we have understood some of our children wish to go over the Mississippi, but this act of our children would be like destroying your mothers.

Your mothers, your sisters ask and beg of you not to part with any more of our land. We say ours. You are our descendants; take pity on our request. But keep it for our growing children, for it was the good will of our creator to place us here, and you know our father, the great president, will not allow his white children to take our country away. Only keep your hands off of paper talks for it's our own country. For [if] it was not, they would not ask you to put your hands to paper, for it would be impossible to remove us all. For as soon as one child is raised, we have others in our arms, for such is our situation & [they] will consider our circumstance.

Therefore, children, don't part with any more of our lands but continue on it & enlarge your farms. Cultivate and raise corn & cotton and your mothers and sisters will make clothing for you which our father the president has recommended to us all. . . . Nancy Ward to her children: Warriors to take pity and listen to the talks of your sisters. Although I am very old yet [I] cannot but pity the situation in which you will here [sic] of their minds. I have great many grand children which [I] wish them to do well on our land.

SOURCE: Presidential Papers Microfilm: Andrew Jackson (Washington, D.C., 1961, series 1, reel 22).

QUESTIONS FOR ANALYSIS

1. How is Cherokee women's identification with the land reflected in their petition?
2. What sources of authority do Cherokee women invoke to validate their petition to "their beloved chiefs and warriors"?

To begin with, family life was different. The ideological distinction between public and private, work and family—much touted in the North—did not really exist on the great southern plantations. The plantation was residence and workplace simultaneously, and the white male head of household presided over both. Instead of the mutually exclusive but allegedly equal gender roles dictated by the northern culture of domesticity, slave society was proudly patriarchal, with men's social and political power derived from their leadership in the home. Wealthy white southern men were fiercely jealous of the honor of their women and their families, and they were notorious for their willingness to resort to violence to avenge any perceived slights against them. Female deference to male authority was considered a virtue, and any moral superiority granted to women gave them no social or political authority. Inasmuch as wealthy women left the daily tasks of childrearing to their slaves, maternity was neither revered nor sentimentalized.

Owners regarded slave men and women not just as workers but as permanently childlike dependents — at best amusing, guileless, but lacking in judgment and authority. By this obfuscating ideology, the plantation community was treated as a single large family, with master-parents and slave-children, bound by devotion and reciprocal obligations of service and protection. One white woman, writing about her father's plantation, truly believed that "the family servants, inherited for generations, had come to be regarded with great affection. . . . The bond between master and servant was, in many cases, felt to be as sacred and close as the tie of blood."[26] When slavery was abolished, masters and mistresses were often astounded to discover the degree of hostility their former slaves felt toward them.

Plantation patriarchy was a gender and family system, but one organized around racial difference and inequality. The structures and inequalities of race, much like those of gender, were so omnipresent as to seem natural and God-given. "Black" equaled "slave" and was understood as the opposite not only of "white" but of "free." In contrast to this belief, it is important to recognize that by 1830 there were a third of a million black people in the United States who were not slaves, half of them living in the South. The lives of these people and their claims to free status were deeply compromised by the power of slavery and racial inequality. In the South, they were kept out of certain occupations, forbidden to carry firearms, denied the right to assembly, made to carry passes when traveling, and often legally required to register in court with a white guardian. Free black women in the South shared many of the same occupations with their counterparts in the North. In Augusta County, Virginia, for example, the 1860 census revealed sixty-seven females of color, ranging from age fourteen to seventy-two, who listed their occupations. Domestic work was most common, followed by laundering, whereas only five of these women listed themselves as seamstresses.[27]

Despite slave society's insistence that the racial divide was absolute, the line that separated "black" from "white" was constantly being breached. Masters could — and certainly did — compel slave women to have sexual relations with them. When a slave woman gave birth to her master's child, how was the racial divide on which slave patriarchy was premised to be maintained? The legal answer was that the child followed the status of the mother: the child was a slave because her female parent was a slave. This simple legal answer to a complex set of social relations hidden within slave society had enormous implications for the lives of southern women, black and white. While slavery is usually considered a system for organizing labor and producing profit, it was also a way of organizing and restraining sexual and reproductive relations, of controlling which sexual encounters produced legitimate children. In other words, managing race necessitated managing gender and sexuality.

Plantation Mistresses

The link between racial inequality and gender ideals is evident in the effusive liter-ary and rhetorical praise devoted to the southern white feminine ideal. Elite white women in plantation society were elevated to a lofty pedestal that was the ideolog-ical inverse of the auction block on which enslaved women's fate was sealed. As in the North, white women were supposed to be selfless, pure, pious, and possessed of great, if subtle, influence over husbands and sons. But the difference in the South was that white women's purity was defined in contrast not to the condition of men but to the condition of black slave women.

As slavery came under more and more open criticism from northern oppo-nents during the nineteenth century, rhetorical devotion to elite white women's leisure and culture, to the preservation of their beauty and their sexual innocence, and to their protection from all distress and labor intensified. The message seemed to be that the purity of elite white womanhood, rather than the enslavement of black people, was the core value of southern society. "We behold," proclaimed southern writer Thomas Dew, "the marked efficiency of slavery on the conditions of woman — we find her at once elevated, clothed with all her charms, mingling with and directing the society to which she belongs, no longer the slave, but the equal and the idol of man."[28] For the most part, women of the slaveholding class also held to the opinion that a lady's life on a southern plantation was a great priv-ilege. Any greater political and economic rights for white women were "but a piece of negro emancipation," declared Louisa McCord, daughter of an important South Carolina slaveholder and politician, in 1852.[29] She was sure that women like herself wanted no part of such a movement.

Whereas in the North, womanly virtues were meant to be universal, in the South, they were proudly exclusionary, applicable only to the few, a mark of the natural superiority of the elite and their right to own and command the labor of others. While the northern true woman was praised for her industrious domes-ticity, in the South a real lady was not allowed to sully herself or risk her charms with any actual labor, which was the mark of the slave. Leisure was especially the privilege of the unmarried young woman of the slaveholding class, who was not only spared any household obligations but also relieved of even the most intimate of responsibilities — dressing herself, for instance — by the presence of personal slaves. "Surrounded with them from infancy, they form a part of the landscape of a Southern woman's life," one woman recalled of her servants long after slavery had ended. "They watch our cradles; they are the companions of our sports; it is they who aid our bridal decorations; and they wrap us in our shrouds."[30]

Once a woman married, however, she took on managerial responsibility for the household. Unlike their husbands, who hired overseers to manage slaves in the fields, plantation mistresses themselves oversaw the labor of the household slaves and the feeding, clothing, and doctoring of the entire labor force. One admittedly unusual plantation mistress, who insisted that she was more put upon than privileged by the ownership of slaves, recalled that when she heard the news of the Emancipation Proclamation, she exclaimed, "Thank heaven! I too shall be free at last!"[31]

Because slavery was a labor system in which there were no positive incentives for hard work, the management of workers relied almost entirely on threats and punishments, including beatings. Within the household, the discipline of slaves was the responsibility of the mistress. The association of allegedly delicate womanhood with brutal violence was a disturbing aspect of the slave system, even to its most passionate adherents. Opponents of slavery played endlessly on this theme to indicate the fundamental corruption of the system, which reached even to the women of slaveholding families. "There are *female tyrants* too, who are prompt to lay their complaints of misconduct before their husbands, brothers, and sons, and to urge them to commit acts of violence against their helpless slaves," wrote Angelina Grimké, daughter of a powerful southern slaveowner, who left the South in 1829 to fight against the system (see p. 242).[32] Fannie Moore, who came of age on a North Carolina plantation, agreed with Grimké. Speaking of her former mistress, Moore said, "She shore was a rip-jack." This particular woman viewed slaves as animals, who were "not like other folks." Moore recalled, "She whip me, many time wif a cow hide, til I was black and blue."[33] (See Primary Sources: "Mothering under Slavery" pp. 196–203.)

In the South, as in the North, marriage for free women legally prohibited them from the privileges of property ownership. Changing this practice was one

◆ **How Slavery Improves the Condition of Women**
This illustration was published in *The Anti-Slavery Almanac* in 1838, just as women in abolitionism were becoming more assertive. The title ironically juxtaposes the evils of slavery and the ideology of female purity and protection. Not only does it show slave women being whipped and beaten, but it suggests that the white mistress herself has become brutalized by joining in the violence. *Private Collection/The Stapleton Collection/Bridgeman Images.*

of the initial goals of the American women's rights movement (see pp. 243–48), within which southern white women, committed to the plantation patriarchy, were notoriously absent. Thus it is ironic that the first states to liberalize property laws for married women were southern — Mississippi (in 1839) and Arkansas (in 1840). They did so in order to protect the inheritance of slaveownership. Far more than middle-class northern women, elite southern women were expected to bring dowries — wealth packages — into their marriages, and it was not uncommon for a young woman to bring into her new home slaves from her parents' plantation. This was one of the many ways in which slaves were separated from their own families. To protect their daughters — and the family property that had been transferred with them — against spendthrift husbands, southern patriarchs modified married women's property laws to allow wives to retain title to inherited property. By contrast, the first married women's property law to be reformed in the North in response to pressure from women's rights activists was not until 1848 in New York State.

In all other ways, however, the slave system made for more severe constraints on free women than in the North. The rhetorical weight that rested on elite white women's purity meant that women's public activities were extremely limited. Unlike northern women, respectable southern white women had no means of earning money. Women who remained unmarried faced futures as marginal members in the households of their married kin. Whatever education existed for young women was oriented to the ornamental graces rather than more serious subjects. The sorts of charitable societies that northern middle-class women formed to care for the indigent and poor did not exist in the South, although plantation mistresses, defensive about whether they were sufficiently benevolent, frequently claimed that the care and feeding of their own slaves constituted an equivalent moral responsibility.

For the most part, slaveholding women and men did not regard themselves as heading up a brutal and inhumane system. On the contrary, they were convinced that the society over which they presided, which elevated them to lives of such enviable grace and culture, was the best of all possible worlds, certainly better than the lives led by money-grubbing capitalists and degraded wage workers in the North. They regarded their slaves as well treated compared to the northern wage earners, whom they believed were ignored and eventually abandoned, their welfare of no concern to bosses who wanted only to exploit their labor and then dispose of them. "How enviable were our solidarity as a people, our prosperity and the moral qualities that are characteristic of the South," one southern matron mourned many years after the Civil War. Even in retrospect, she believed that white southerners' "love of home, their chivalrous respect for women, their courage, their delicate sense of honour, their constancy . . . [all] are things by which the more mercurial people of the North may take a lesson."[34]

Non-elite White Women

While the power of southern society lay in the hands of the plantation elite, the majority of whites were not large slaveholders. Indeed, close to three-quarters of all white families owned no slaves and relied on their own labor, occasionally hiring a slave or two from a neighbor. Even the great majority of those who did own slaves were working farmers themselves, living and laboring alongside the few slaves they owned. These small farmers are often called yeomen, a British term signifying the non-noble agricultural classes. The slave system would not have worked without the active support of the many white people who did not profit personally from it. Non-elite white men patrolled the roads for runaway slaves, voted in favor of aggressively proslavery state governments, and served as overseers and skilled craftsmen on the great plantations.

Women on the small farms and modest households of the South had much less interaction with planter culture than did their husbands. There was no common women's culture that linked them to plantation mistresses — another difference with the North. Indeed, the class gap between elite and non-elite whites was clearest when it came to women's roles. While elite women lived lives of leisure in their grand plantation houses, women of the yeoman class worked very hard both outside and inside their small homes. They continued to produce goods mainly for their own family's consumption, for instance, spinning and wearing homespun long after northern farm women were purchasing factory-made cloth. They sold a smaller portion of their produce for cash than those in the North. About the only thing that took such non-elite southern women away from their homes and farms was church. And even there, they lacked the numerous voluntary activities and associations that Protestant women formed in the North in pursuit of moral uplift.

Although southern yeomen had few or no slaves over whom to establish their patriarchal authority, they did have wives. Thus female subordination was prized in this sector of southern society. If the difference between the lives of non-elite and elite women was one of the most pronounced distinctions among southern whites, the ethic of male headship bonded white men across class boundaries. "As masters of dependents, even if only, or perhaps if especially, of wives and children," one historian observes, "every freeman was bound to defend his household, his property, against invasion."[35]

Enslaved Women

Far more than even the most impoverished, degraded wage worker in the North, bondmen and bondwomen enslaved to southern masters were forbidden the basic elements of personal freedom — to live with their own families, to move about, to be educated, to marry and raise children — not to mention the loftier rights of citizenship. The legal definition of enslaved people as property was recognized by the laws of all the southern states and protected by the careful wording of the U.S. Constitution. Indeed, the Constitution, in permitting legislation ending the transatlantic slave trade after 1808 and relegating control over the institution of slavery entirely to the states, laid the foundation for an enormous commerce in slaves within the United States that depended on enslaved women's reproduction. The profitable, vigorous internal market in slaves touched the lives of virtually all African Americans, for each man, woman, and child experienced either the horror of being sold, the fear of being sold, or the heartrending knowledge of a loved one being sold. The auction block loomed over all.

When we recall Tocqueville's confident assertion in 1830 that American women were so privileged and honored that they "never labor in the fields," we begin to see the degree to which the slave women of the South were not only ignored in all the sweeping generalizations of true womanhood but also excluded from the category of "woman" altogether. Ninety percent of the slave women of the South labored in the cotton, sugar, tobacco, and rice fields that generated the expanding region's wealth. Plantation patriarchy extolled an image of slaves who provided personal and domestic service in planter households (see Figures 4.11 and 4.12, pp. 215 and 216), but these were a small minority. It was the giant mass of agricultural slaves on whom the power of the planter class rested.

Nowhere in early nineteenth-century America was labor less divided by gender than in the fields of the plantation South. To be clear, some farming tasks, such as enslaved women's sowing of rice fields, still relied on gendered divisions of labor. On many plantations, enslaved women spent some of their days in all-female work gangs. However, a great deal of agricultural labor was assigned according to skill and strength, rather than gender. Enslaved women and men hoed and planted and

Hale's Dag⁴⁰   J. Andrews for S.A.Schoff Sc.

ELLEN CRAFT,
The fugitive Slave.

♦ Ellen Craft, The Fugitive Slave (1860)

This engraving of Ellen Craft (1826–1891) serves as the frontispiece for her husband William Craft's slave narrative, *Running a Thousand Miles for Freedom*, published in London in 1860. As the daughter of an enslaved woman and her white owner, Ellen was able to use her light skin to masquerade as a young invalid white man traveling North with his enslaved valet (William). William stealthily procured an extra man's hat, shirt, and coat, while Ellen sewed a set of men's trousers for her escape. During their long journey, Ellen pretended to be deaf to avoid having to speak to fellow travelers. Her race- and gender-crossing ruse successfully fooled even a white acquaintance they encountered along the route from Georgia to Boston. William's dramatic narrative, self-authored after he learned to read and write, conveyed the perils braved by both Ellen and William Craft to reach a free community where their future children would not be born into slavery. © *Mary Evans Picture Library/The Image Works.*

reaped alongside each other in gangs that worked from sunup to sundown under the threat of the overseer's whip. In coastal plantations in Georgia and South Carolina, in fact, enslaved women frequently made up the majority of field workers. African American oral histories are full of stories of individual women famous for their strength and ability to work as hard as any man. Cornelia, enslaved on a small Tennessee farm, proudly remembered her mother's speed and strength: "She cooked, washed, ironed, spun, nursed, and labored in the field. She made as good a field hand as she did a cook. . . I tell you, she was a captain."[36] Even among household slaves, estimated at about 10 percent of the labor force of the South, men served as personal valets, as butlers, and occasionally even as nursemaids for their owners' young sons.

In addition to their skilled agricultural work, enslaved women supplied knowledge and labor that sustained enslaved communities and supported the privileges of the slaveholding class. On the larger plantations, where some specialization of labor was possible, slave men had more access to trades such as blacksmithing and carpentering while individual women might gain reputations as expert midwives, seamstresses, and cooks. Large slaveholding estates often relied on enslaved women's knowledge of medicine and long hours of caregiving in plantation "hospitals" as well as white households. One Georgia planter in 1832 directed his overseer never to call a white doctor unless Elsey, "the Doctress of the Plantation" — also the neighborhood midwife — had first tried her hand at a cure.[37]

Although often made to "work like a man," bondwomen also became targets of gendered violence. The particular vulnerabilities of their sex were exploited when they were beaten. Numerous stories record that enslaved women's skirts were raised over their heads before whippings, to humiliate them and perhaps to make their physical sufferings greater. Only a woman in the late stages of pregnancy might be spared the worst whippings, and only then to protect her baby, who, when born, would be worth a great deal to the slaveowner. Similarly, after giving birth, women were suspended from field labor just briefly. Northern visitors commented frequently on the sight of an old slave woman bringing infants to the fields so that their young mothers could nurse them quickly and return to work. When beatings failed to discipline female slaves who resisted their masters' control, sale was an even greater threat, especially if it meant separating a woman from her child. A runaway slave named Mrs. James Seward told the story of her sister in Maryland who was punished for resisting her master in all these ways: after beating her, the master controlled her by "taking away her clothes and locking them up. . . . He kept her at work with only what she could pick up to tie on her for decency. He took away her child which had just begun to walk." Fearing the woman's physical strength, this slaveholder waited to whip her until she had just given birth. "Now I can handle you," he exclaimed, "now you are weak."[38]

As chattels rather than persons with rights, slaves were not permitted legally binding marriage contracts, which might interfere with the master's right to buy and sell them away from their husbands or wives. Nonetheless, men and women under slavery went to great lengths to sustain conjugal and parental relationships. Slaves had their own ritual for solemnizing their marriages, by together "jumping the broom." Frequently, such unions linked women and men who belonged to different masters. In these "abroad marriages," it usually fell to the man to visit his wife and children. Often traveling at night to visit his family, without his master's knowledge or permission, the abroad husband risked being whipped or even sold away. To some extent, what enslaved husbands and wives expected of each other bore similarities to the gender roles of free couples. Yet, as one historian who studies the institution of slave marriage argues, "The daily realities of the slave system, bent on maximizing profits, meant that neither women nor men could strictly adhere to the gender assignments of the dominant society."[39] The daily aspirations of both enslaved wives and their husbands continually ran up against slaveholder attempts to control their time, labor, and mobility.

Motherhood also distinguished the lives of slave women from those of slave men. For slave women, childbearing was simultaneously the source of their greatest personal satisfaction and their greatest misery, because their children ultimately belonged to the master. (See Primary Sources: "Mothering under Slavery," pp. 196–203.) Slave mothers had the immensely difficult task of teaching their children to survive their owners' power and at the same time to know their own worth as human beings. The woman Cornelia, quoted above, remembered her spirited mother's lessons in self-defense: "I'll kill you, gal, if you don't stand up for yourself. . . . Fight, and if you can't fight, kick; if you can't kick, then bite."[40] Not all bondwomen chose the dangerous route of open resistance. Many worked collectively with other enslaved women to impart lessons of survival and care for each other's children in the face of sale and high mortality.

Sexual relations between masters and enslaved women were an open secret in the South, heartily denied by slaveowners and yet virtually endemic to the society. The light complexions and white features of numerous nineteenth-century slaves were eloquent testimony to this intimate connection between slave and master. Mary Boykin Chesnut, a member of South Carolina's slaveholding aristocracy, knew of this hidden reality. Her diaries are much quoted by historians for what they reveal about slave society's contradictions (see Reading into the Past: "Slavery a Curse to Any Land").

While running afoul of Christian morality, masters' sexual exploitation of enslaved women was encouraged by everything else about the slave system, from the master's control of bondwomen's bodies to their legal ownership of any resulting children. Slaveholders certainly did not limit their sexual abuse to females, but black women and girls in the South bore the brunt of sexual coercion, ranging from gang-rape to concubinage that extended over many decades. Southern rape laws specifically named only white women as capable of being raped, so free black women also experienced considerable sexual violence. In one of the best-known accounts of a master's sexual aggression toward a female slave, Harriet Jacobs described how, when she was only fifteen, her master began to insist that she have sex with him. Some slave mothers attempted to prepare their daughters for the dangers ahead. Later in her life, Minnie Folkes recalled how her mother told her, "Don't let nobody bother yo' principle; cause dat wuz all yo' had."[41] Many who were unable to avoid abuse lived with deep trauma. Others erupted in rage. In 1856,

READING INTO THE PAST

MARY BOYKIN CHESNUT
Slavery a Curse to Any Land

The diary kept by the South Carolina slave mistress Mary Boykin Chesnut (1823–1886) has long been regarded as a major source for insights into the minds of southern slaveholders. More recently, historians have explored Chesnut's views on the position of the women of this class.

March 14, 1861: I wonder if it be a sin to think slavery a curse to any land. . . . [W]e live surrounded by prostitutes. An abandoned woman is sent out of any decent house elsewhere. Who thinks any worse of a Negro or Mulatto woman for being a thing we can't name. God forgive us, but ours is a monstrous system & wrong & iniquity. Perhaps the rest of the world is as bad. This is only what I see: like the patriarchs of old, our men live all in one house with their wives & their concubines, & the Mulattos one sees in every family exactly resemble the white children — & every lady tells you who is the father of all the Mulatto children in everybody's household, but those in her own, she seems to think drop from the clouds or pretends so to think — . . . . My disgust sometimes is boiling over — . . . . Thank God for my countrywomen — alas for the men! No worse than men everywhere, but the lower their mistresses, the more degraded they must be.

SOURCE: Mary Boykin Chesnut, *A Diary from Dixie* (1905; repr., Boston: Houghton Mifflin, 1949), 21.

QUESTIONS FOR ANALYSIS

1. In her writings about the hidden but extensive sexual relations between slaveholding men and their female slaves, why does she seem so resentful of rather than sympathetic to slave women?

2. What assumptions is Chesnut making when she calls enslaved women who have had sexual relations with white slaveholding men "prostitutes"?

nineteen-year-old Celia was executed by the state of Missouri for killing her master Robert Newsome after five years of enduring his repeated sexual assaults. As Celia's case reminds us, the sexual exploitation of enslaved women cannot be understood solely in property terms but must also be seen as reflecting dynamics of social and psychological domination under the racialized system of southern slavery.

The issue of deliberate breeding was an explosive one in the slave South. Opponents of slavery accused owners of encouraging and arranging pregnancies among their female slaves to produce more slaves to sell on the lucrative internal slave market. Evidence suggests that they were right. "Marsa used to sometimes pick our wives fo' us," former slave Charles Grandy recalled. "Marsa would stop de old niggertrader and buy you a woman. . . . All he wanted was a young healthy one who looked like she could have children, whether she was purty or ugly as sin."[42] Women of childbearing age who were described as "good breeders" brought a higher price on the auction block. The painful imprint of these practices stayed with black women for decades. Faced with the threat of being sold away from her family, for example, the sixteen-year-old Rose Williams "yielded" to forced breeding. Yet, as she told Federal Writers' Project (FWP) interviewers in the 1930s, the scarring experience left her unable or unwilling to have anything more to do with marriage or childbearing.[43]

Any hope that the solidarities of gender might have crossed the boundaries of race and class was crushed by the tensions that the unacknowledged sexual exploitation of enslaved women spread throughout southern society. Jealous or suspicious mistresses vented on their slaves the anger and rage they dared not express to their husbands. Harriet Jacobs feared her mistress every bit as much as she did her master. Female slaves who worked in the plantation house were at greatest risk, exposed day in and day out to the mistress's moods. Slave narratives frequently describe an impatient or intolerant mistress striking out at a cook or a nursemaid or even a slave child unable to handle an assigned task. In their diaries and letters, slaveowning white women recorded their secret fears of violent retribution from slaves. As Civil War was breaking out, Mary Boykin Chesnut wrote anxiously about the death of a cousin who, it was suspected, had been "murdered by her own people."[44] Although both black and white women suffered in the slave system, only white women also benefited from it. Slave women knew they could expect no sympathy from their mistresses. The luxury and culture of the white southern woman were premised on the forced labor and sexual oppression of her slaves. Violence against and violations of slave women mocked southern deference to womanhood and female sexual purity. With only the rarest of exceptions, slavery turned black and white women against each other and set their interests and their perspectives in direct opposition.

◆ CONCLUSION: True Womanhood and the Reality of Women's Lives

Perhaps at no other time in American history were the prescriptions for a proper domestic role for women more precise and widely agreed on than in antebellum America. Much of the young country's hope for stability and prosperity rested on the belief in a universally achievable middle-class family order, with the devoted, selfless wife and mother at the center.

As we shall see in the next chapter, some women were able to use the ideology of true womanhood to expand their sphere in subtle ways, but even so, this ideology was exceedingly rigid and limiting, ignoring the reality of women who led very different sorts of lives. Factory operatives were outside the boundaries of acceptable womanhood because they lived and worked in what *Godey's Lady's Book* editor Sarah Josepha Hale called "the accursed bank note world" that only men were supposed to occupy.[45] And slave women were deprived — absolutely — of the protection and privileges that were meant to compensate true women for their limited sphere. While the rhetoric of true womanhood seemed to place domestic women at the heart of American society, in reality the giant processes in which these other women were caught up — industrialization and slavery — were the dynamic forces shaping the young American nation and foreshadowing the trends and crises of its future.

CHAPTER 4 REVIEW

KEY TERMS AND PEOPLE

Terms
"true womanhood"
Godey's Lady's Book
Second Great Awakening
Lowell Offering
Lowell Female Labor Reform
    Association

African Methodist Episcopal
    Church
Indian Removal Act

People
Lucy Larcom
Catharine Beecher

Sarah Josepha Hale
Fannie Moore
Mary Boykin Chesnut
Harriet Jacobs

REVIEW QUESTIONS

1. How did the "hegemonic" ideology of true womanhood shape northern women's lives, even when their economic and social realities didn't match the ideal? How does the answer to this question change when discussing working-class women as opposed to middle-class women?

2. What made Lowell millwork so liberating for young white women from New England? When and why did millwork become more exploitive of its laborers?

3. The text notes that "slavery turned black and white women against each other and set their interests and their perspectives in direct opposition." Explain this statement by explaining how the system of slavery both connected and divided black and white women. Be sure to include nonslaveholding white women in this discussion.

4. **Making Connections** One of the most important developments of the first half of the nineteenth century was the emergence of commercial capitalism and a market economy. How was women's labor (black and white, slave and free, northern and southern) central to this development? Consider both domestic and public labor in your answer.

Prostitution in New York City, 1858

As chief physician in the 1850s for the New York City "lock hospital" (where prostitutes suspected of venereal diseases were both incarcerated and treated), Dr. William Sanger had both knowledge of and compassion for the women he attended. Hopeful that more accurate information would help to eradicate prostitution, he interviewed two thousand prostitutes, using a carefully drawn-up set of questions. He was determined to bring the facts of prostitution to light and to convey the prostitutes' experiences and thoughts more realistically. The originals of Sanger's interviews were destroyed in a fire the year after he gathered them, so his published report to the trustees of the New York Alms House brings us as close as we can get to the prostitutes themselves. Interestingly, Sanger did no research into the men who were the prostitutes' clientele.

Sanger's sample, although not randomly selected, was large enough to allow for useful generalizations: most prostitutes were from fifteen to twenty years old; three-fifths were native-born; among the immigrants, 60 percent were Irish; one-fifth were married; half had children; half were or had been domestic servants; half were afflicted with syphilis; the average length of life after entering prostitution was four years.

Sanger estimated that six thousand women were engaged in commercial sex in New York City, a number based on his careful survey of police records, lock hospitals, and known brothels. Others estimated much higher numbers. Even so, Sanger's estimates were distressing. As Sanger repeatedly insisted, they reflected not the inherent lack of virtue of the prostitutes but rather the relentless financial pressure on poor urban women. The effects of a sharp economic depression in 1857 are detected everywhere in the prostitutes' descriptions of their situations.

Sanger believed that women were too often blamed for prostitution; he wanted to show that they were the victims, both of men's callousness and their own lack of economic opportunity. Despite these reformist sentiments, however, Sanger held conventional notions of femininity. Indeed, he championed prostitutes because he was certain that most women would never of their own accord undertake a life of casual sex. Rather, he believed, they must have been deserted, seduced, driven by destitution, or forced into prostitution by some other extraordinary event over which they had no control. Underlying his compassion for those who were remorseful, the traces of a harsher set of judgments can be found. Thus Sanger's report can be read as evidence of middle-class attitudes toward female sexuality, as well as of prostitutes' own experience.

What follows is Sanger's summary and analysis of the two thousand answers given to one of his most revealing questions: "What are the causes of your becoming a prostitute?" As you read, think about how the personal stories that Sanger relates allow us to imagine a more complicated set of explanations for individual women's entry into prostitution than the categories he uses.

WILLIAM W. SANGER
The History of Prostitution: Its Extent, Causes, and Effects throughout the World (1858)

[Question:] *What are the causes of your becoming a prostitute? . . .*

Causes	Numbers
Inclination	513
Destitution	525
Seduced and abandoned	258
Drink, and the desire to drink	181
Ill-treatment of parents, relatives, or husbands	164
As an easy life	124
Bad company	84
Persuaded by prostitutes	71
Too idle to work	29
Violated	27
Seduced on board emigrant ships	16
Seduced in emigrant boarding houses	8
Total	2000

This question is probably the most important of the series, as the replies lay open to a considerable extent those hidden springs of evil which have hitherto been known only from their results. First in order stands the reply [which 513 respondents chose], "Inclination," which can only be understood as meaning a voluntary resort to prostitution in order to gratify the sexual passions. . . .

SOURCE: William W. Sanger, *The History of Prostitution: Its Extent, Causes, and Effects throughout the World* (New York: Harper & Brothers 1858, 1921), 488–522.

The force of desire can neither be denied nor disputed, but still in the bosoms of most females that force exists in a slumbering state until aroused by some outside influences. . . . In the male sex nature has provided a more susceptible organization than in females, apparently with the beneficent design of repressing those evils which must result from mutual appetite equally felt by both. In other words, man is the *aggressive* animal, so far as sexual desire is involved. Were it otherwise, and the passions in both sexes equal, illegitimacy and prostitution would be far more rife in our midst than at present.

Some few of the cases in which the reply "Inclination" was given are herewith submitted, with the explanation which accompanied each return. C. M.: while virtuous, this girl had visited dancehouses, where she became acquainted with prostitutes, who persuaded her that they led an easy, merry life; her inclination was the result of female persuasion. E. C. left her husband, and became a prostitute willingly, in order to obtain intoxicating liquors which had been refused her at home. E. R. was deserted by her husband because she drank to excess and became a prostitute in order to obtain liquor. . . . Enough has been quoted to prove that, in many of the cases, what is called willing prostitution is the sequel of some communication or circumstances which undermine the principles of virtue and arouse the latent passions.

Destitution is assigned as a reason in five hundred and twenty-five cases. In many of these it is unquestionably true that positive, actual want, the apparent and dreaded approach of starvation, was the real cause of degradation. . . .

During the progress of this investigation in one of the lower wards of the city, attention was drawn to a pale but interesting-looking girl, about seventeen years of age, from whose replies the following narrative is condensed, retaining her own words as nearly as possible.

"I have been leading this life from about the middle of last January (1856). It was absolute want that drove me to it. My sister, who was about three years older than I am, lived with me. She was deformed and crippled from a fall she had while a child, and could not do any hard work. . . . One very cold morning, just after I had been to the store, the landlord's agent called for some rent we owed, and told us that, if we could not pay it, we should have to move. The agent was a kind man, and gave us a little money to buy some coals. We did not know what we were to do, and were both crying about it, when the woman who keeps this house (where she was then living) came in and brought some sewing for us to do that day. She said that she had been recommended to us by a woman who lived in the same house, but I found out since that she had watched me, and only said this for an excuse. When the work was done I brought it home here. I had heard of such places before, but had never been inside one. I was very cold, and she made me sit down by the fire, and began to talk to me, saying how much better off I should be if I would come and live with her. . . . When I got home and saw my sister so sick as she was and wanting many little things that we had no money to buy, and no friends to help us to, my heart almost broke. However, I said nothing to her then. I laid awake all night thinking, and in the morning I made up my mind to come here. . . . I thought that, if I had been alone, I would sooner have starved, but I could not bear to see her suffering. She only lived a few weeks after I came here. I broke her heart. I do not like the life. I would do almost any thing to get out of it; but, now that I have *once done wrong*, I can not get any

one to give me work, and I must stop here unless I wish to be starved to death."

These details give some insight into the undercurrent of city life. The most prominent fact is that a large number of females, both operatives and domestics, earn so small wages that a temporary cessation of their business, or being a short time out of a situation, is sufficient to reduce them to absolute distress. Provident habits are useless in their cases; for, much as they may feel the necessity, *they have nothing to save,* and the very day that they encounter a reverse sees them penniless. The struggle a virtuous girl will wage against fate in such circumstances may be conceived: it is a literal battle for life, and in the result life is too often preserved only by the sacrifice of virtue. . . .

Moralists say that all human passions should be held in check by reason and virtue, and none can deny the truthfulness of the assertion. But while they apply the sentiment to the weaker party, who is the sufferer, would it not be advisable to recommend the same restraining influences to him who is the inflictor? No woman possessed of the smallest share of decency or the slightest appreciation of virtue would voluntarily surrender herself without some powerful motive, not preexistent in herself, but imparted by her destroyer. Well aware of the world's opinion, she would not recklessly defy it, and precipitate herself into an abyss of degradation and shame unless some overruling influence had urged her forward. This motive and this influence, it is believed, may be uniformly traced to her weak but truly feminine dependence upon another's vows. . . . Thus there can be little doubt that, in most cases of seduction, female virtue is trustingly surrendered to the specious arguments and false promises of dishonorable men.

Men who, in the ordinary relations of life, would scruple to defraud their neighbors of a dollar, do not hesitate to rob a confiding woman of her chastity. They who, in a business point of view, would regard obtaining goods under false pretenses as an act to be visited with all the severity of the law, hesitate not to obtain by even viler fraud the surrender of woman's virtue to their fiendish lust. Is there no inconsistency in the social laws which condemn a swindler to the state prison *for his offenses,* and condemn a woman to perpetual infamy *for her wrongs*? Undoubtedly there are cases where the woman is the seducer, but these are so rare as to be hardly worth mentioning.

Seduction is a social wrong. Its entire consequences are not comprised in the injury inflicted on the woman, or the sense of perfidy oppressing the conscience of the man. Beyond the fact that she is, in the ordinary language of the day, ruined, the victim has endured an attack upon her principles which must materially affect her future life. The world may not know of her transgression, and, in consequence, public obloquy may not be added to her burden; but she is too painfully conscious of her fall, and every thought of her lacerated and bleeding heart is embittered with a sense of man's wrong and outrage. . . . It can not be a matter of surprise that, with this feeling of injustice and insult burning at her heart, her career should be one in which she becomes the aggressor, and man the victim; for it is certain that in this desire of revenge upon the sex for the falsehood of one will be found a cause of the increase of prostitution. . . .

In one of the most aristocratic houses of prostitution in New York was found the daughter of a merchant, a man of large property, residing in one of the Southern states. She was a beautiful girl, had received a superior education, spoke several languages fluently, and seemed keenly sensible of her degradation. Two years before this time she had been on a visit to some relations in Europe, and on her return voyage in one of her father's vessels, she was seduced by the captain, and became pregnant. He solemnly asserted that he would marry her as soon as they reached their port, but the ship had no sooner arrived than he left her. The poor girl's parents would not receive her back into their family, and she came to New York and prostituted herself for support. . . .

"Ill-treatment of parents, husbands, or relatives" is a prolific cause of prostitution, one

hundred and sixty-four women assigning it as a reason for their fall. . . .

J. C.: "My father accused me of being a Prostitute when I was innocent. He would give me no clothes to wear. My mother was a confirmed drunkard and used to be away from home most of the time." Here we have a combination of horrors scarcely equaled in the field of romance. The unjust accusations of the father, and his conduct in not supplying his child with the actual necessaries of life, joined with the drunkenness of the mother, present such an accumulation of cruelty and vice that it would have been a miracle had the girl remained virtuous. It is to be presumed that no one will claim for this couple the performance of any one of the duties enjoined by their position. . . .

Great as are the duties and responsibilities of a father, they are equaled by those devolving upon a husband. He has to provide for the welfare of his wife besides caring for the interests of his children. . . . All married prostitutes can not be exonerated from the charge of guilt, yet the facts which will be hereafter quoted prove that many were driven to a life of shame by those who had solemnly sworn to protect and cherish them. . . .

C. H.: "I was married when I was seventeen years old, and have had three children. The two boys are living now; the girl is dead. My oldest boy is nearly five years old, and the other one is eighteen months. My husband is a sailor. We lived very comfortably till my last child was born, and then he began to drink very hard, and did not support me and I have not seen him or heard any thing about him for six months. After he left me I tried to keep my children by washing or going out to day's work, but I could not earn enough. I never could earn more than two or three dollars a week when I had work, which was not always. My father and mother died when I was a child. I had nobody to help me, and could not support my children, so I came to this place. My boys are now living in the city, and I support them with what I earn by prostitution. It was only to keep them that I came here." . . . In order to feed her helpless offspring she was forced to yield her honor; to prevent them suffering from the pains of hunger, she voluntarily chose to endure the pangs of a guilty conscience; to prolong their lives she periled her own. And at the time when this alternative was forced upon her, the husband was lavishing his money for intoxicating liquor. If she sinned — and this fact can not be denied, however charity may view it — it was the non-performance of his duty that urged, nay, positively forced her to sin. She must endure the punishment of her offenses, but, after reading her simple, heart-rending statement, let casuists° decide what amount of condemnation will rest upon the man whose desertion compelled her to violate the law of chastity in order to support his children. . . .

Seventy-one women were persuaded by prostitutes to embrace a life of depravity. One of the most common modes by which this end is accomplished is to inveigle a girl into some house of prostitution as a servant, and this is frequently done through the medium of an intelligence office. . . . [At such establishments] servants who wish to obtain situations register their wants and pay a fee. . . .

Keepers of houses sometimes visit these offices themselves, but generally some unknown agent is employed, or, at times, one of the prostitutes is plainly dressed, and sent to register her name as wishing a situation, so as to be able to obtain admission into the waiting-room. There she enters into conversation with the other women, whom she uses all the art she possesses to induce to visit her employer. . . .

Some of the sources of prostitution have been thus examined. To expose them all would require a volume; but it is hoped that sufficient has been developed to induce observation and inquiry, and prompt action in the premises.

QUESTIONS FOR ANALYSIS

1. Why does Sanger think it highly unlikely that women ever are responsible for their entry into prostitution? Do you agree with him on this?

2. How does Sanger distinguish his approach to and opinions about prostitution from the views of those he calls "moralists"?

3. Where do economic conditions show up in Sanger's account of the causes of prostitution?

° Those who are logical yet unfeeling.

Mothering under Slavery

Motherhood, so elevated in the ideology of true womanhood, presented enslaved women with dilemmas that free women simply did not have to face. Nineteenth-century slave states still followed the principle of *partus sequitur ventrem*, instituted during the colonial period, which imposed a property claim on each and every slave woman's child (see pp. 56–59). Once the United States outlawed the transatlantic slave in 1808, slaveowners and their physicians placed greater emphasis on enslaved women's fertility to ensure the future of the plantation economy. Southern doctors like the well-known J. Marion Sims even targeted some bondwomen for experimental surgeries that contributed to the emergence of obstetrics and gynecology as a medical specialty. The public and derogatory way in which whites discussed black women's sexuality and childbearing led an older woman in the 1930s to describe slavery as a time when "women wasn't nothing but cattle."[46] Added to their reproductive labor of childbearing and child care, bondwomen also shouldered the burden of agricultural labor in the fields. Motherhood thus pulled enslaved women in conflicting directions while the wider society denied them any of the respect or status accorded to free white middle-class mothers.

One way to think about the multiple meanings of motherhood for enslaved women is through the history of black women's bodies. In theory, suggests one historian, enslaved women "possessed at least three bodies."[47] The first body was the body dominated by slaveowners and subjected to commodification, coerced labor, and sexual violence. Motherhood from this perspective was strictly an exploitive institution, reinforced by both the law and the customs of white society. The second body was the site of sorrow and pain that resulted from this process of domination. Viewed through the second body, enslaved motherhood primarily entailed suffering, as women mourned the sale, mistreatment, and neglected deaths of their sons and daughters. Yet enslaved people were never defined solely by slaveholders' domination or by their own suffering. For this reason, an exploration of slave motherhood would not be complete without the inclusion of a third body: "a thing to be claimed and enjoyed, a site of pleasure and resistance." For slave mothers, the third body could be expressed in moments of stolen enjoyment, acts of fierce protection, and even in the rejection of motherhood under the master's terms.

The many facets of mothering under slavery can best be grasped by reading several different types of sources. Due to the emphasis on oral culture within enslaved communities and white society's devaluation of enslaved people's history, much first-person testimony from enslaved women has been lost. Yet the historical record is still plentiful. Antebellum narratives, retrospective oral histories, plantation records, newspaper ads, and photographs, just to name a few of the extant sources, all carry important evidence of enslaved women's mothering histories. As you examine these sources, carefully consider the perspective, audience, assumptions, and insights of each document or image.

A SOUTH CAROLINA DOMESTIC MEDICINE MANUAL

DURING A PERIOD WHEN MOST MEDICAL CARE still occurred at home, antebellum domestic medicine manuals dispensed advice about treating common ailments. Physician J. Hume Simons's guide, aimed at the households of southern planters, included a section titled "General Directions for Raising Negroes." At the time of this manual's publication, deepening racial ideology painted black mothers as inept and uncaring. Georgia lawyer Thomas R. R. Cobb, for example, wrote that African Americans' "natural affections are not strong, and consequently he is cruel to his offspring, and suffers little by separation from them."[48] Where do you see racialized ideas about black mothering and inept child care reflected in the passage below? What consequences for enslaved mothers might have resulted from the author's assumption that white planters should be the provider and protector of slave health?

The Planter's Guide and Family Book of Medicine (1848)

On every plantation . . . there should be a capable and trusty nurse, to attend the sick and to report all new cases. A faithful and trusty woman (not as is commonly the case, a decrepit old woman), but a strong, able, and healthy woman to attend the negro children; for mothers who have infants at the breast will frequently obtain leave of absence from the field to nurse their infants and employ the time given them in sleeping [instead].

Source: J. Hume Simons, M.D., *The Planter's Guide and Family Book of Medicine* (Charleston, SC, 1848), 208.

The person selected for the little negroes should also be made to cook for them, and to see that they are fed regularly with victuals well cooked. For it is a common practice among negroes to eat victuals half raw, and of course to give the same to their children. Some do it from laziness, others from ignorance of cooking, and some leave the feeding of their children entirely to their little nurses. I have several times been called to attend little children on plantations, who were poor and emaciated, and as the planter or overseer termed it, not thriving, but who were evidently suffering actually from starvation and want of water, owing to the negligence of their parents and little nurses.

FWP INTERVIEW

IN THE 1930S, AS PART OF THE NEW DEAL works project administration (see pp. 498–508), federally funded interviewers from the Federal Writers' Project (FWP) were sent throughout the South to record the memories of the last generation of black people to have lived under slavery, all of whom had been children or young adults at the time and were now almost eighty or older. Preserved only as typescripts (and in a few cases, as primitive tape recordings), the FWP oral histories were finally made available in published form in the 1960s. Despite their valuable content, these twentieth-century sources also have many limitations. Most of the interviewers were white and many of the interviewees were probably deferential to or intimidated by them. In most cases, interviewers wrote down the words of their informants after the interview was concluded, a process that introduced many errors and omissions. Furthermore, interviewers were expected to render the testimony in dialect. Readers today need to be aware that the appearance of the printed interviews reflects FWP editors' assumptions about black southerners as poor and uneducated as much as it reflects the actual speech of the narrators.

Nevertheless, Fannie Moore provided an unvarnished portrait of her girlhood in bondage on a South Carolina plantation. What does Moore remember most about her mother and grandmother? Many FWP interviewees spoke of their mothers' and grandmothers' knowledge of herbal medicines. A Texas woman named Harriet Collins, for example, began her lengthy account of plant-based remedies with this assertion: "My mammy larned me a lots of doctorin', what she larnt from old folkses from Africy, and some de Indians larnt her."[49] In Fannie Moore's account below, who was responsible for the care of sick children? How might memory and the conditions of the FWP interviews have shaped the way that Moore told her life story?

Fannie Moore Remembers Her Mother and Grandmother (1937)

My granny she cook for us chillens while our mammy away in de fiel. Dey wasn't much cookin to do. Jes make co'n pone and bring in de milk. She hab a big wooden bowl wif enough wooden spoons to go 'roun'. She put de milk in de bowl and break it up. Den she put de bowl in de middle of de flo' an' all de chillum grab a spoon.

My mammy she work in de fiel' all day and piece and quilt all night. Den she hab to spin enough thread to make four cuts for de white folks ebber night. Why sometime I nebber go to bed. Hab to hold de light for her to see by. She hab to piece quilts for de white folks too. . . .

I never see how my mammy stan' sech ha'd work. She stand' up fo' her chillum tho'. De ol' overseeah he hate my mammy, case she fight him for beatin' her chillun. Why she git more whuppins for dat den anythin' else. She hab twelve chillun. . . . My mammy she trouble in her heart 'bout de way they treated. Ever night she pray for de Lawd to git her an' her chillum out ob de place. . . .

My mammy grieve lots over brothah George, who die wif de fever. Granny she doctah him as bes'

SOURCE: *Federal Writers' Project: Slave Narrative Project, Vol. 11, North Carolina, Part 2, Jackson-Yellerday*, 1936. 128–135. Manuscript/Mixed Material. Retrieved from the Library of Congress, https://www.loc.gov/item/mesn112.

she could, evah time she git way from de white folks kitchen. My mammy nevah git chance to see him, 'cept when she git home in de evenin'. George he jes lie. One day I look at him an' he had sech a peaceful look on his face, I think he sleep and jes let him lone. Long in de evenin I think I try to wake him. I touch him on de face, but he was dead. Mammy nebber know til she come at night. Pore mammy she kneel by de bed an' cry her heart out'. Ol' uncle Allen, he make pine box for him an' carry him to de graveyard over on de hill. My mammy jes plow and cry as she watch em' put George in de groun'. . . .

Folks back den never heah tell of all de ailments de folks hab now. Dey war no doctahs. Jes use roots and bark for teas of all kinds. My ole granny uster make tea out o' dogwood bark an' give it to us chillum when we have a cold, else she make a tea outen wild cherry bark, pennyroil, or hoarhound. My goodness but dey was bitter. We do mos' enythin' to git out a takin' de tea, but twarnt no use granny jes git you by de collar hol' yo' nose and you jes swallow it or get strangled. When de baby hab de colic she git rats vein [a local medicinal plant] and make a syrup an' put a little sugar in it an' boil it. Den soon as it cold she give it to de baby. For stomach ache she give us snake root. Sometime she make tea, other time she jes cut it up in little pieces an' make you eat one or two ob dem. When you hab fever she wrap you up in cabbage leaves or ginseng leaves, dis made de fever go."

PHOTOGRAPHS

WHILE SLAVEHOLDERS OCCASIONALLY posed white family members with enslaved women as tokens of status, few photographers took portraits of enslaved (or previously enslaved) women as the primary subjects of interest. (See Primary Sources: "Early Photographs of Factory Operatives and Slave Women," pp. 211–18.) The two photographs on page 200 are exceptions to this rule, although they too have complicated backstories laden with postemancipation racial politics.

In addition to the collection of life stories, the Federal Writers' Project also photographed almost two hundred African American elders who had been born during slavery, emancipated under the Thirteenth Amendment, and grown into old age in the segregated South. What overall impression does Figure 4.1 of Fannie Moore make? Based on your reading of Moore's interview above, how do you think she might have wanted to be represented in this image? What clues can you gather from her clothing, facial expression, and direction of her gaze?

The unusual photograph in Figure 4.2 depicts an intimate moment in which an older woman peacefully works on a young girl's hair. However, the image is part of a Jim Crow–era photo album titled "Rosemary: A Plantation Home," most likely assembled by a white planter family in Alabama as a gift for Tennessee statesman Edward Ward Carmack around the turn of the twentieth century. The album and its racially derogatory captions convey a nostalgic portrait of harmonious relations between white paternalistic plantation owners and their black laborers. How is black women's maternal care depicted in this photo? White southern memoirists of the period often romanticized the figure of the slave "Mammy." Does the rise of the Mammy stereotype lend insight into the photo's caption — "The Givers"? Despite the intentions of the album maker, is it possible to read this photograph as a reminder of moments enslaved women and girls may have shared while finding temporary respite from plantation labor demands (historians call this "reading against the grain")? Try to argue both sides of this question.

◆ **Figure 4.1** Fannie Moore, Age 88 (c. 1937)
Library of Congress.

◆ **Figure 4.2** "Rosemary"
**Plantation Photo Album
(c. 1890s–1910s)**
*From the Edward Ward
Carmack Papers, #01414,
Southern Historical Collection,
The Wilson Library, University
of North Carolina at Chapel Hill.*

ADVERTISEMENTS FOR WET NURSES

EVEN INTIMATE MOMENTS OF NURTURE could be given a price in the market economy of chattel slavery. Evidence from newspaper ads and white women's diaries and letters suggest an "informal market in enslaved wet nurses, in which white women were the primary arbiters and beneficiaries."[50] Enslaved mothers were both hired and sold in the American South for the primary purpose of breastfeeding white infants. What words do advertisers use to promote enslaved wet nurses? What is the significance of the first advertisement's use of the phrase "without a child" as an attractive feature of this particular wet nurse? What other kinds of labor might wet nurses also be expected to do? How do these ads hint at white expectations for black women's relationships to their own children?

City Gazette and Daily Advertiser, Charleston, South Carolina (October 28, 1795)

> TO BE HIRED,
> A Healthy Black WET NURSE, without a child, with a good breast of milk. Enquire of Mrs. Dawson, at Mr. Patrick Hind's, in Beausain-Street. October 24

The Southern Patriot, Charleston, South Carolina (May 10, 1842)

> WET NURSE, SEAMSTRESS, WASHER, IRONER, AND HOUSE SERVANT TO HIRE — A young healthy Woman with her child about 6 weeks old, and a Boy to attend to it. She will be hired either as a Wet Nurse, or either of the above capacities. She is a complete Seamstress, Washer and Ironer, and House Servant; to be seen at my house until hired. Apply to

> THEODORE A. WHITENEY,
> Broke and Auctioneer,
> 24 Holrlbeck's Alley, next to King St., May 10

The Charleston Mercury (June 7, 1856)

> Private Sales.
> *Healthy Young Wet Nurse.*
> *Capers & Heyward*
> Offer at private sale, a young and healthy WET NURSE. For further particulars, apply at our office, SOUTH SIDE ADGERS' WHARF, June 7

SOURCE: Stephanie Jones-Rogers, "'[S]he Could . . . Spare One Ample Breast for the Profit of Her Owner': White Mothers and Enslaved Wet Nurses' Invisible Labor in American Slave Markets," *Slavery & Abolition* 38, no. 2 (2017): 337–55.

ANTEBELLUM SLAVE NARRATIVE

SLAVE NARRATIVES PUBLISHED by women who managed to escape to the North in the antebellum period provide valuable first-person accounts. Harriet Jacobs's (1813–1897) narrative, *Incidents in the Life of a Slave Girl*, is the most well-known of the female-authored accounts. Jacobs was born into bondage in Edenton, North Carolina. From the age of fifteen, she was sexually harassed and abused by her master, the white physician James Norcom (whose young daughter was Jacobs's legal owner). To escape the constant predation of her master, Jacobs sought the protection of another white man by whom she had two children. In the midst of fear and sexual abuse, Jacobs described each of her beloved children as a "tie to life" that motivated her survival. After a decade, she escaped from Norcom, but because of her attachment to her children, she stayed nearby, hidden in the cramped attic room of her free grandmother. There she remained for seven years until she and her two children finally escaped the South.

In the excerpt below, Jacobs describes the atmosphere of violence and tension surrounding the birth of her second child, a daughter. Note that Jacobs uses pseudonyms in her narrative — Linda Brent for herself and Dr. Flint for Norcom. With a northern audience in mind, Jacobs was well aware of her readers' assumptions about Christian women's piety and sexual purity. What does she mean when she says that there was "no chance for me to be respectable"? How does Jacobs's grandmother attempt to provide maternal protection, and what are the limits to her efforts? What are Jacobs's feelings about giving birth to a daughter?

HARRIET JACOBS
Incidents in the Life of a Slave Girl (1861)

CHAPTER 14: ANOTHER LINK TO LIFE

I had not returned to my master's house since the birth of my child. The old man raved to have me thus removed from his immediate power; but his wife vowed, by all that was good and great, she would kill me if I came back; and he did not doubt her word. Sometimes he would stay away for a season. Then he would come and renew the old threadbare discourse about his forbearance and my ingratitude. He labored, most unnecessarily, to convince me that I had lowered myself. The venomous old reprobate had no need of descanting on that theme. I felt humiliated enough. My unconscious babe was the ever-present witness of my shame. I listened with silent contempt when he talked about my having forfeited his good opinion; but I shed bitter tears that I was no longer worthy of being respected by the good and pure. Alas! slavery still held me in its poisonous grasp. There was no chance for me to be respectable. There was no prospect of being able to lead a better life.

Sometimes, when my master found that I still refused to accept what he called his kind offers, he would threaten to sell my child. "Perhaps that will humble you," said he.

Humble me! Was I not already in the dust? But his threat lacerated my heart. I knew the law gave him power to fulfil it; for slaveholders have been cunning enough to enact that "the child shall follow the condition of the mother," not of the father; thus taking care that licentiousness shall not interfere with avarice. This reflection made me clasp my innocent babe all the more firmly to my heart. Horrid visions passed through my mind when I thought of his liability to fall into the slave trader's hands. I wept over him, and said, "O my child! perhaps they will leave you in some cold cabin to die, and then throw you into a hole, as if you were a dog."

When Dr. Flint learned that I was again to be a mother, he was exasperated beyond measure. He rushed from the house, and returned with a pair of shears. I had a fine head of hair; and he often railed about my pride of arranging it nicely. He cut every hair close to my head, storming and swearing all the time. I replied to some of his abuse, and he struck me. Some months before, he had pitched me down stairs in a fit of passion; and the injury I received was so serious that I was unable to turn myself in bed for many days. He then said,

"Linda, I swear by God I will never raise my hand against you again"; but I knew that he would forget his promise.

After he discovered my situation, he was like a restless spirit from the pit. He came every day; and I was subjected to such insults as no pen can describe. I would not describe them if I could; they were too low, too revolting. I tried to keep them from my grandmother's knowledge as much as I could. I knew she had enough to sadden her life, without having my troubles to bear. When she saw the doctor treat me with violence, and heard him utter oaths terrible enough to palsy a man's tongue, she could not always hold her peace. It was natural and motherlike that she should try to defend me; but it only made matters worse.

When they told me my new-born babe was a girl, my heart was heavier than it had ever been before. Slavery is terrible for men; but it is far more terrible for women. Superadded to the burden common to all, they have wrongs, and sufferings, and mortifications peculiarly their own.

QUESTIONS FOR ANALYSIS

1. What claims about slave mothering does each primary source make, and what contradictions can you see between various sources?

2. What ideals of motherhood did enslaved women develop out of their daily experiences? How did these ideals compare to those of various groups of free women?

3. Interpret the sources here using the model of the three different "bodies" discussed in the introduction. Which sources best reveal the agency of enslaved mothers' "third body"?

Godey's Lady's Book

By 1850 *Godey's Lady's Book*, with forty thousand subscribers, was the most widely circulated "ladies' magazine" in the United States. For $3 a year, readers from all over the country enjoyed a rich monthly collection of fiction, history (specializing in heroes and heroines of the American Revolution), poetry, and illustrations. Contributors to the magazine included well-known writers such as Nathaniel Hawthorne, who elsewhere bitterly castigated women writers as "that damned mob of scribbling women."[51] Lavish pictorial "embellishments," printed from full-page, specially commissioned steel engravings and hand-colored by the magazine's special staff of 150 female colorists (wage laborers, unlike most of the magazine's readers), lifted *Godey's* above the run-of-the-mill periodicals published for the literate female public. Subscribers treasured their issues, circulated them among friends, and preserved them in leather bindings. The magazine's large readership was testimony to the degree to which *Godey's* both reflected and affected the sympathies and values of its subscribers.

Godey's Lady's Book was edited by a woman and published by a man. Sarah Josepha Hale, a schoolteacher, mother, and widow from Boston, had turned to magazine editing to support herself and her children after the death of her husband in 1828. Like Catharine Beecher, she had pronounced views on the dignity and power of woman's distinct domestic sphere. In the aftermath of the Panic of 1837, she joined forces with a commercially minded publisher, Louis Godey, to become the editor of *Godey's Lady's Book*, which he had founded in 1830. Her concerns for feminine values were now combined with his eye for women's possibilities as consumers. The magazine's illustrations thus combined advertisements for the latest fashions (which readers took to their seamstresses to duplicate) with illustrations promoting the feminine ideal of selflessness, purity, and subtle maternal influence. Although as the editor Hale was consistent in preaching this notion of women's redemptive, domestic influence throughout her career, her position became more defensive in the 1840s in reaction to the rising tide of the women's rights movement, which she thought dangerous both to women and to the nation (see pp. 243–48): "The elevation of the [female] sex will not consist in becoming like man, in doing man's work, or striving for the dominion of the world. The true woman . . . has a higher and holier vocation. She works in the elements of human nature."[52]

Through stories and images, *Godey's Lady's Book* preached a compelling if conservative doctrine of women's importance to the nation. In a society rapidly being transformed by economic growth and political upheaval, domestic women were expected to provide emotional and spiritual stability. They were to function,

◆ **Figure 4.3** *The Constant, or the Anniversary Present* **(1851)**
P 201.2 (v.42, Jan. 1851), Houghton Library, Harvard University.

as Figure 4.3 advocates, as "the constant" to middle-class American family life. This drawing illustrated a story of a young wife whose quiet, steady love wordlessly convinced her wandering husband to join with her in embracing the healing "close communion of home life."[53] Note the woman's pose, at once submissive to her husband and protective of her child. This image was juxtaposed against another illustration warning women against being a flirtatious "coquette."

The ideology of true womanhood imbued motherhood with both secular and spiritual roles. *Godey's Lady's Book* considered mothers as crucial to preserving the memory of the American Revolution and to securing its legacy within a stable, peaceful, and permanent American nation. Mothers accomplished this task by raising the next generation of citizens. The citizen-child was usually figured as male. "How Can an American Woman Serve Her Country?" *Godey's* asked. The answer: "By early teaching her sons to consider a republic as the best form of government in the world."[54]

While preaching the virtues of motherhood and domesticity, female ideologues of middle-class femininity portrayed teaching as a natural profession for

◆ **Figure 4.4** *The Teacher* (1844)
The Granger Collection, New York.

women, drawing as it did on maternal virtues and emotions. Hale wrote that "the reports of common school education show that women are the *best* teachers," in response to which she sponsored a petition to Congress urging public support for women's teacher training.[55] Teaching had previously been the province of men and began changing into a woman's occupation only during the 1820s and 1830s. Outside of the South, public education, considered essential to a virtuous citizenry, was expanding at a rapid rate. Inasmuch as female teachers were usually paid a third or less of what men were paid, the reasons for the shift were economic as well as ideological. How does the image in Figure 4.4 reconcile a woman working for wages with the ideology of true womanhood?

◆ **Figure 4.5** *Purity* (1850)
The New York Public Library/Art Resource, NY.

Barbara Welter, the first modern historian to examine the ideology of true womanhood, identified its four basic elements as domesticity, piety, submission, and purity.[56] Purity of course referred to sexuality (not just experience but also desire), of which the true woman was expected to be innocent. In Figure 4.5, the feminine virtue of purity is illustrated at the same time as it is used to advertise designs for fashionable wedding dresses. How do ideological and economic concerns come together in this image?

The middle-class character of the doctrine of domesticity was revealed in the frequent illustrations of the difficulties that the true woman had in hiring

◆ **Figure 4.6** *Cooks* **(1852)**
The New York Public Library/Art Resource, NY.

and supervising household servants. Although — or because — the relation between mistress and maid was one of the more distressing of the middle-class housewife's domestic obligations, the stories and drawings about this dilemma were invariably humorous, with the incompetent and stupid housemaid or cook as the butt of the joke. The very face and figure of the cook in Figure 4.6 indicate a female quite different from the mistress. How is the mistress designated as a true woman while the cook is not? What does the illustration suggest about the relationship of husband and wife, as well as that of mistress and maid?

◆ **Figure 4.7** *Shoe Shopping* (1848)
The New York Public Library/Art Resource, NY.

Although *Godey's Lady's Book* insisted on the distinction between woman's domestic sphere and man's worldly obligations, it hinted at the ways that economic realities and the larger society impinged on middle-class women's efforts to practice their home-based ideals. Hale preached women's special virtues as an antidote to the distressingly materialistic world outside the home, but *Godey's* itself purveyed those same worldly values. The true woman was a frequent shopper, and in 1852 the magazine instituted a shopping service to assist its readers in the purchase of accessories and jewelry. Figure 4.7 portrays middle-class women leaving their cloistered homes for the pleasures and luxury of an elegant shoe emporium, presided over by a male clerk. Looking at this mid-nineteenth-century illustration, keep in mind the women workers who manufactured these shoes. Note also how shopping is portrayed as a recreational activity already at this early stage in market society.

QUESTIONS FOR ANALYSIS

1. Examine the expressions, demeanor, and dress of the women from the *Godey's* illustrations shown here. What do they have in common? Why do they show so little variety? How might women readers have regarded these images and tried to imitate them?

2. Look at the profiles of the true women from *Godey's*. Notice their tiny waists, the composure of their hands, the elegance of their bearing. How do these and other details reinforce the message that women are unfit for the public sphere?

3. Consider *Godey's* in light of fashion magazines you are familiar with today. What is the appeal of fashion magazines for women? How seriously do you take the lifestyle and the profiles modeled in the magazines you read? How can such sources be read critically to reveal something about contemporary times?

Early Photographs of Factory Operatives and Slave Women

P HOTOGRAPHY, INVENTED IN FRANCE in the 1830s, came to the United States in the 1840s. By 1850, commercial photographers were working in all the major cities. Compared to portrait painting, photography was quick and relatively inexpensive, exactly the modern form of artistic representation appropriate to a young, democratic nation. Perhaps also because so many Americans were on the move, they wanted these small, portable pictures of themselves to send to loved ones. In Massachusetts alone, there were four hundred photographic studios by 1855.[57] Nationwide the estimate is three thousand by 1860.[58] Pocket-size portraits could be had for a few dollars, and common folks, not just the well-to-do, were eager to purchase their likenesses. In 1853, the *New York Tribune* estimated that 3 million photographs were being made annually. Unfortunately, only a very few have survived.[59]

The earliest of these photographs are known as daguerreotypes, named for Louis Jacques Daguerre, the Frenchman who invented the technology in 1837. The daguerreotypist created a positive image on a metal plate treated with mercury and exposed to light. The finished product was enclosed in a case to protect it from light over time. In the United States, the technology gave way in the mid-1850s to simpler and less expensive processes: the tintype (which shortened the sitting time and reduced the cost) and the ambrotype (which used glass instead of metal for the photographic plate and produced a negative rather than a positive image).[60] By the early 1860s, photographers were learning how to make multiple positive prints on paper from negative glass plates. In the early studio photographs, sitters had to remain still for minutes, sometimes with their heads in braces to keep them still; not surprisingly, few smiled. The images that resulted were extremely fragile but also often stunning in their intimacy and delicacy. The sitters seem to look out at us across time, inviting us to study them and detect their sentiments.

For modern students of history, who rely on images for a great deal of information, photographs are particularly satisfying as a source of historical documentation. In our eagerness to see precise, seemingly objective images of the past, however, it is important to realize that the objects of these early historical photographs are selective: some things — and people — were photographed relatively frequently and others not at all. To put it another way, we cannot see photos of everything about which we are curious, only of what previous generations wanted to be seen. Thus, in addition to the obvious visible information that these early photographs convey about the American past, they also document what versions and aspects of themselves nineteenth-century Americans wanted to preserve.

The images that follow — of female factory workers and of slaves — represent women living and working outside the dominant, middle-class ethic of mid-nineteenth-century true womanhood. Their existence prompts us to ask: who took care to purchase and preserve these images and why?

FACTORY OPERATIVES

Female textile factory operatives arranged to have their own photographs taken. They posed in their work clothes and held shuttles as symbols of their work as spinners and weavers of cloth. The tools signified that the sitter was a skilled worker, with valuable knowledge, experience, and ability. As these images indicate, the women were proud of their presence in and contribution to the burgeoning industrial economy of those years.

Workers often posed for these portraits in groups, which suggests that they thought of their labor as collective and of their coworkers as friends. For women, coworkers were often relatives as well; sisters and cousins followed their kin into the mills, took jobs that had been secured for them, and worked in the same room at the same task. Factory work was a new experience for most of these young women, and the presence of familiar faces may have eased their transition into a strange environment. Family relations were still crucial elements of their lives, even in the impersonal environment of the textile factory.

By 1860, textile factories and the women who worked in them were found throughout much of New England. The four young women shown in Figure 4.8

◆ **Figure 4.8 Four Women Mill Workers (1860)**
Cornell University Library, ATHM Textile Photographs Collection.

were photographed near Winthrop, Maine. The two Lowell weavers pictured in Figure 4.9 look enough alike to be sisters. By 1860, when both of these tintypes were taken, Irish newcomers were beginning to take over from Yankee workers in the textile industry, and these women may have been Irish-born. As you study the photographs presented in Figures 4.8 and 4.9 examine the poses, settings, and props. What do they suggest about these women's identities and perhaps even their thoughts? What do the photographs capture about these women's relationships?

The unusual collection of ambrotypes in Figure 4.10 was taken in 1854 in Manchester, New Hampshire, by a group of male and female employees of the Amoskeag Manufacturing Company and presented to the foreman who oversaw their labor. Although the men and women worked together in the carding room, preparing the raw cotton for the spinning process, they did different work. The men worked the carding machines, which began the process, while the women tended the drawing frames and double-speeders, which turned the raw fibers into crude strands in preparation for spinning. Despite earning lower wages than the men, women who worked in the carding room were among the best paid of their sex. These subjects posed themselves as dignified, upstanding

◆ **Figure 4.9 Two Women Mill Workers (1860)**
Cornell University Library, ATHM Textile Photographs Collection.

individuals, dressed in their best clothes for the camera's eye. What does the fact that men and women allowed themselves to be photographed together suggest about gender relations in factories? How do Figures 4.8, 4.9, and 4.10 represent the pride that early factory workers took in their position?

◆ **Figure 4.10 Amoskeag Manufacturing Company Workers (1854)**
Courtesy of the Manchester (N.H.) Historic Association.

ENSLAVED WOMEN

◆ **Figure 4.11** **The Hayward Family's Slave Louisa with Her Legal Owner (c. 1858)**
The Granger Collection, New York.

Unlike factory operatives, slaves did not choose to have their photographs taken. The following photographs of slave women come from two different sources. The first group is that of slave baby nurses, portrayed with their white charges or as part of a larger family group. The white slaveholders who arranged for these photographs meant to convey that these black women, the "mammies" of southern nostalgic memory, were beloved, trusted servants to their families. Dissenting from opponents' portrayal of slaveholders as a violent, inhumane class, many regarded themselves as benevolent masters and mistresses who lived in harmony and intimacy with the slaves entrusted to their care.

From the perspective of the twenty-first century, nearly 150 years after the abolition of slavery, such photographs can tell a different story. These nineteenth-century black women look out at us with a humanity and individuality that slavery denied they had. Their expressions and poses suggest the complex, if controlled, meanings that their responsibilities to care for white children may have had for them. What appeared to be maternal love was actually unpaid labor. These photographs belonged not to them but to their masters. Where were their own children as they attended to those of their owners?

Of the numerous photographs of enslaved "mammies," we know more about the individuals in Figure 4.11 than we do about most. At a slave auction in New Orleans in 1858, the Hayward family bought the slave woman Louisa, age twenty-two, to serve as nursemaid. The tiny child in the photograph was her legal owner. Many decades later, after he had grown up, he gave the ambrotype to the Missouri Historical Society.[61] What does the fact that he so treasured this photograph tell you about the relations between slaves and masters? As you look into Louisa's eyes, try to recover what she was feeling when the photograph was taken.

By contrast, nothing is known about the family portrayed in Figure 4.12, although the photographer, Thomas Easterly of St. Louis, was well known. What is most striking about this 1850 family photograph is the absence of a white woman. We have to wonder what happened to her and what her absence means for the

◆ **Figure 4.12 Thomas Easterly, Family with Their Slave Nurse (c. 1850)**
Thomas Martin Easterly (American, 1809–1882). Father, Daughters, and Nurse, about 1850,
Daguerreotype, hand-colored. The J. Paul Getty Museum, Los Angeles. Digital image courtesy of the Getty's
Open Content Program.

black woman who is included. The slave mistress may have died, leaving the black
woman to take over her domestic and childrearing duties. Could the man, like
so many slave masters, have had his own sort of intimate relationship with the
unnamed black woman whom he includes in his family portrait? Consider the
affectionate grouping of the father and daughters and the physical isolation of
the black woman. What does this composition suggest about this family? Again,
what do you see in the face of the slave nurse?

In a different category from the photographs of domestic slaves are the images
of freed slave women that northern photographers made in the context of the Civil
War. Like the famous photographs that Mathew Brady took of battlefields and
male soldiers, these images were meant to document the North's purposes in the

◆ **Figure 4.13** **Timothy O'Sullivan,** *Plantation in Beaufort, South Carolina* **(1862)**
Library of Congress, LC-B8171-152-A.

war and the Union army's military conduct. Figure 4.13 shows a photograph taken in 1862 by Timothy O'Sullivan, a colleague of Brady, on a plantation in Beaufort, South Carolina.

O'Sullivan was traveling with the Union army, which had seized and occupied the coastal Sea Islands of eastern Georgia and South Carolina early in the war.

Their masters and overseers having fled, these black people continued to work the plantations where they lived but now under the supervision of northern officers, in anticipation of the relationship later formalized within the U.S. Army's Freedmen's Bureau (p. 297). O'Sullivan posed this picture of an entirely black, multigenerational family just freed from slavery. Contrast this image with Figures 4.11 and 4.12, the photographs taken by slaveholders to document their notions of the sentiments that bound slaves to white families. How does O'Sullivan's photograph give evidence to the bonds of love and kinship among black people that the cruelties of the plantation system ignored and threatened? Do you see anything different in the faces and postures of these people?

QUESTIONS FOR ANALYSIS

1. Compare the attitudes and expressions of the factory operatives and the slave women, especially the slave "mammies." How does the fact that one group chose to photograph themselves while the others were photographed by their masters change the meaning of the photographs?

2. All of these early photographs show women defined by their labor. Does work, in any way, offer common ground between factory operatives and slaves? How are the women in these photographs different from the images in *Godey's Lady's Book* (Primary Sources, pp. 204–10) of middle-class "true women"? What do you think of the fact that the former were more likely to come down to us in photographs, while the images of the latter were preserved in illustrations and paintings?

3. Consider what photographs add to historical documentation. What can photographs, even at this early stage, tell us about women's history that other sorts of images cannot? Conversely, how should we analyze photographs to avoid the temptation of regarding them simply as mirrors of a lost historical reality?

NOTES

1. Lucy Larcom, *A New England Girlhood: Outlined from Memory* (Boston: Houghton Mifflin, 1889), 222.
2. Ibid., 200.
3. Alexis de Tocqueville, *Democracy in America* (1841; repr., New York: Schocken Books, 1977), 6.
4. Harvey Green, *The Light of the Home: An Intimate View of the Lives of Women in Victorian America* (New York: Pantheon, 1983), 56.
5. Catharine Beecher, *Woman Suffrage and Woman's Profession* (Hartford: Brown & Gross, 1871), 175.
6. Nancy Cott, *The Bonds of Womanhood: "Woman's Sphere" in New England, 1780–1835*, 2nd ed. (New Haven: Yale University Press, 1997), 28.
7. Beecher, *Woman Suffrage and Woman's Profession*, 28.
8. Nancy Cott, "Passionlessness: An Interpretation of Victorian Sexual Ideology, 1790–1850," *Signs* 4 (1978): 219–36.
9. Ibid.
10. William W. Sanger, M.D., *The History of Prostitution: Its Extent, Causes, and Effects throughout the World* (New York: Harper & Brothers, 1858, 1921), 489.
11. Catharine Beecher, *A Treatise on Domestic Economy* (1841; repr., New York: Schocken Books, 1978), 178.
12. Larcom, *New England Girlhood*, 198.
13. Mrs. A. J. Graves, *Woman in America: Being an Examination into the Moral and Intellectual Condition of American Female Society* (New York: Harper and Brothers, 1841), 58.
14. American Social History Project, *Who Built America? Working People and the Nation's Economy, Politics, Culture and Society* (New York: Pantheon Books, 1989), 1:249.
15. Larcom, *New England Girlhood*, 196.
16. Alice Kessler-Harris, *Out to Work: A History of Wage-Earning Women in the United States* (New York: Oxford University Press, 1982), 47.
17. "Jerusalem," in *William Blake: Selected Poems* (1804; repr., London: Bloomsbury Publishing Ltd., 2004), 114.
18. Cott, *Bonds of Womanhood*, 38.
19. Larcom, *New England Girlhood*, 196.
20. Charles Dickens, *American Notes* (London: Chapman and Hall, 1842), ch. 4.
21. Larcom, *New England Girlhood*, 146.
22. Harriet Hanson Robinson, *Loom and Spindle: Or Life among the Early Mill Girls* (New York: T. Y. Crowell, 1889), 83.
23. Elizabeth Cady Stanton to Paulina Wright Davis, December 6, 1852, in Ann D. Gordon, ed., *The Selected Papers of Elizabeth Cady Stanton and Susan B. Anthony: In the School of Anti-Slavery, 1840 to 1866* (New Brunswick, NJ: Rutgers University Press, 1997), 214.
24. Christine Stansell, *City of Women: Sex and Class in New York, 1789–1860* (New York: Alfred A. Knopf, 1986), 47.
25. Ibid., 14.
26. Susan Smedes, *Memorials of a Southern Planter* (Baltimore: Cushings and Bailey, 1887), 48.
27. Augusta County, Virginia, 1860 Population Census, *Valley of the Shadow: Two Communities in the American Civil War*, Virginia Center for Digital History, University of Virginia Library, http://valley.vcdh.virginia.edu/govdoc/popcensus.html.
28. Brenda E. Stevenson, *Life in Black and White: Family and Community in the Slave South* (New York: Oxford University Press, 1996), 42.
29. Stephanie McCurry, *Masters of Small Worlds: Yeoman Households, Gender Relations, and the Political Culture of the Antebellum South Carolina Low Country* (New York: Oxford University Press, 1995), 223.
30. Caroline Howard Gilman, *Recollections of a Southern Matron* (New York: Harper and Brothers, 1838), 94.
31. Caroline Elizabeth Merrick, *Old Times in Dixie Land: A Southern Matron's Memories* (New York: Grafton Press, 1901), 18.
32. Angelina Grimké, *An Appeal to the Women of the Nominally Free States* (1838), in Nancy Cott, ed., *Root of Bitterness: Documents of the Social History of American Women* (Boston: Northeastern University Press, 1986), 197.
33. Fannie Moore, *Federal Writers' Project: Slave Narrative Project, Vol. 11, North Carolina, Part 2, Jackson-Yellerday*, 1936, p. 128. Manuscript/Mixed Material. Retrieved from the Library of Congress, https://www.loc.gov/item/mesn112.
34. Virginia Clay-Clopton, *A Belle of the Fifties: Memories of Mrs. Clay of Alabama: Covering Social and Political Life in Washington and the South* (New York: Doubleday, 1905), 212.
35. McCurry, *Masters of Small Worlds*, 260.
36. Gerda Lerner, ed., *Black Women in White America: A Documentary History* (New York: Vintage Books, 1992), 34–35.
37. Sharla M. Fett, *Working Cures: Healing, Health, and Power on Southern Slave Plantations* (Chapel Hill: University of North Carolina Press, 2002), 111.
38. Benjamin Drew, ed., *A North-Side View of Slavery: The Refugee; or, The Narratives of Fugitive Slaves in Canada Related by Themselves* (Boston: J. P. Jewett and Co., 1856), 187.
39. Tera W. Hunter, *Bound in Wedlock: Slave and Free Black Marriage in the Nineteenth Century* (Cambridge, MA: Harvard University Press, 2017), 14.
40. Lerner, *Black Women in White America*, 38.
41. Stevenson, *Life in Black and White*, 236.
42. Ibid., 232.
43. Deborah Gray White, *Ar'n't I a Woman? Female Slaves in the Plantation South*, rev. ed. (New York: Norton, 1999), 102–3.
44. Mary Boykin Chesnut, *A Diary from Dixie* (1905; repr., Boston: Houghton Mifflin, 1949), 212.

45. Cott, *Bonds of Womanhood*, 68.

46. White, *Ar'n't I a Woman?*, 31.

47. Stephanie M. H. Camp, *Closer to Freedom: Enslaved Women and Everyday Resistance in the Plantation South* (Chapel Hill: University of North Carolina Press, 2004), 66–68.

48. Thomas R. R. Cobb, *An Inquiry into the Law of Negro Slavery in the United States of America. To Which Is Prefixed, an Historical Sketch of Slavery* (Philadelphia: T. & J.W. Johnson/Savannah/W.T. Williams), 39.

49. *Federal Writers' Project: Slave Narrative Project, Vol. 16, Texas, Part 1, Adams-Duhon.* 1936. Manuscript/Mixed Material. Retrieved from the Library of Congress, https://www.loc.gov/item/mesn161/ (accessed July 25, 2017).

50. Stephanie Jones-Rogers, "'[S]he Could . . . Spare One Ample Breast for the Profit of Her Owner': White Mothers and Enslaved Wet Nurses' Invisible Labor in American Slave Markets," *Slavery & Abolition* 38, no. 2 (2017): 348.

51. Susan Conrad, *Perish the Thought: Intellectual Women in Romantic America, 1830–1860* (Secaucus, NJ: Citadel Press, 1978), 20. See Nathaniel Hawthorne, "Witches: A Scene from Main Street," *Godey's Lady's Book* 42 (1851): 192.

52. Sarah Josepha Hale, "Editors' Table," *Godey's Lady's Book* 42 (1851): 65.

53. Alice B. Neal, "The Constant, or the Anniversary Present," *Godey's Lady's Book* 42 (1851): 5.

54. Kate Berry, "How Can an American Woman Serve Her Country?" *Godey's Lady's Book* 43 (1851): 362.

55. Sarah Josepha Hale, "Editor's Table," *Godey's Lady's Book* 47 (1853): 554.

56. Barbara Welter, "The Cult of True Womanhood, 1820–1860," *American Quarterly* 18 (1966): 151–74.

57. John Wood, ed., *America and the Daguerreotype* (Iowa City: University of Iowa Press, 1991), 95.

58. Oliver Jensen et al., *An American Album* (New York: American Heritage Publishers, 1968), 21.

59. Ibid.

60. Kenneth E. Nelson, "A Thumbnail History of the Daguerreotype," Daguerreian Society, http://daguerre.org/resource/history/history.html (accessed February 15, 2015).

61. Information from Duane Sneddeker, photographic curator, Missouri Historical Society.

SUGGESTED REFERENCES

True Womanhood

Nancy Cott, *The Bonds of Womanhood: "Woman's Sphere" in New England, 1780–1835*, 2nd ed. (1997).

Barbara Cutter, *Domestic Devils, Battlefield Angels: The Radicalism of American Womanhood, 1830–1865* (2003).

Cathy N. Davidson and Jessamyn Hatcher, eds., *No More Separate Spheres! A Next Wave American Studies Reader* (2002).

Amy S. Greenberg, *Manifest Manhood and the Antebellum American Empire* (2005).

Shawn Johansen, *Family Men: Middle-Class Fatherhood in Industrializing America* (2001).

Mary Ryan, *Cradle of the Middle Class: The Family in Oneida County, 1780–1835* (1983).

Kathryn Kish Sklar, *Catharine Beecher: A Study in American Domesticity* (1976).

Barbara Welter, *Dimity Convictions: The American Woman in the Nineteenth Century* (1976).

Early Industrial Women Workers

Mary Blewett, *Men, Women, and Work: Class, Gender, and Protest in the New England Shoe Industry, 1780–1910* (1988).

———, *We Will Rise in Our Might: Workingwomen's Voices from Nineteenth-Century New England* (1991).

Jeanne Boydston, *Home and Work: Housework, Wages, and the Ideology of Labor in the Early Republic* (1990).

Susanna Delfino and Michele Gillespie, eds., *Neither Lady nor Slave: Working Women of the Old South* (2002).

Thomas Dublin, ed., *Farm to Factory: Women's Letters, 1830–1860*, 2nd ed. (1993).

———, *Women at Work: The Transformation of Work and Community in Lowell, Massachusetts, 1826–1860* (1981).

Martha Hodes, *The Sea Captain's Wife: A True Story of Love, Race and War in the Nineteenth Century* (2006).

Bernice Selden, *The Mill Girls: Lucy Larcom, Harriet Hansen Robinson, Sarah G. Bagley* (1983).

Christine Stansell, *City of Women: Sex and Class in New York, 1789–1860* (1986).

Carole Turbin, *Working Women of Collar City: Gender, Class, and Community in Troy, New York, 1864–1886* (1992).

Prostitution

Patricia Cline Cohen, Timothy J. Gilfoyle, and Helen Lefkowitz Horowitz, eds., *The Flash Press: Sporting Male Weeklies in 1840s New York* (2008).

Barbara Meil Hobson, *Uneasy Virtue: The Politics of Prostitution and the American Reform Tradition* (1987).

Women in Slave Society

Daina Ramey Berry, *"Swing the Sickle for the Harvest Is Ripe": Gender and Slavery in Antebellum Georgia* (2007).

———, *The Price for Their Pound of Flesh: The Value of the Enslaved from Womb to Grave in the Building of a Nation* (2017).

Stephanie M. H. Camp, *Closer to Freedom: Enslaved Women and Everyday Resistance in the Plantation South* (2004).

Christie Anne Farnham, ed., *Women of the American South: A Multicultural Reader* (1997).

Elizabeth Fox-Genovese, *Within the Plantation Household: Black and White Women of the Old South* (1998).

Sharla M. Fett, *Working Cures: Healing, Health, and Power on Southern Slave Plantations* (2002).

Thavolia Glymph, *Out of the House of Bondage: The Transformation of the Plantation Household* (2008).

Tera W. Hunter, *Bound in Wedlock: Slave and Free Black Marriage in the Nineteenth Century* (2017).

Jacqueline Jones, *Labor of Love, Labor of Sorrow: Black Women, Work, and the Family from Slavery to the Present* (1985).

Barbara Krauthamer, *Black Slaves, Indian Masters: Slavery, Emancipation, and Citizenship in the Native American South* (2013).

Suzanne Lebsock, *The Free Women of Petersburg: Status and Culture in a Southern Town, 1784–1860* (1984).

Stephanie McCurry, *Masters of Small Worlds: Yeoman Households, Gender Relations, and the Political Culture of the Antebellum South Carolina Low Country* (1995).

Melton A. McLaurin, *Celia, A Slave: A True Story* (1999).

Tiya Miles, *The House on Diamond Hill: A Cherokee Plantation Story* (2010).

Deirdre Cooper Owens, *Medical Bondage: Race, Gender, and the Origins of American Gynecology* (2017).

Marie Jenkins Schwartz, *Birthing a Slave: Motherhood and Medicine in the Antebellum South* (2006).

Brenda E. Stevenson, *Life in Black and White: Family and Community in the Slave South* (1996).

Deborah Gray White, *Ar'n't I a Woman? Female Slaves in the Plantation South,* rev. ed. (1999).

5

Shifting Boundaries

EXPANSION, REFORM, AND CIVIL WAR 1840–1865

THE YEAR 1848 WAS A DECISIVE ONE IN THE HISTORY of the nation and its women. Mexico, on the losing side of a grueling war with the United States, had just signed the Treaty of Guadalupe Hidalgo and transferred 1.5 million square miles of land and thousands of human beings to U.S. sovereignty. The term "Manifest Destiny," coined a few years before, described the young nation's ambition to wrest much of the continent from its resident peoples, who, U.S. expansionists claimed, could not be trusted to exploit its potential riches. Responding to this crusade, tens of thousands of land-hungry American women and men crossed the central plains to settle on the Pacific Coast. Less than a year after the end of the Mexican War, the discovery of gold in California dramatically accelerated this migration.

The beginning of the American women's rights movement also dates from 1848. Female reformers had been engaged for several decades in efforts to reshape and perfect American society. As proponents of temperance and opponents of slavery, women had pushed at the boundaries of the so-called woman's sphere and moved into more public roles in these years. With the inauguration of the women's rights movement at the Seneca Falls Convention of 1848, they openly breached these boundaries, directing their utopian hopes and activist energies toward the freedom of women themselves.

Finally in 1848, the issue of slavery began to move into American party politics. Although Congress had been evading the issue of slavery for decades, in that year the first political party to oppose the expansion of slavery, the Free Soil Party, was established, followed by the formation of the Republican Party six years later. On the basis of its antislavery platform, the Republican Party captured the presidency in 1860, prompting eleven southern slave states to secede and fracturing the nation. The resulting Civil War threw the lives of all women, Union and Confederate, white, black, and Native American, into upheaval for four deadly years.

In different ways, each of these historical processes was a kind of "movement." In this dynamic period in American history, when traditional social arrangements were being challenged and reformulated, when politics were confronting fundamental questions about the nature of American democracy and the future of the American nation, when the physical nation itself was breaking and remaking its borders, and when these vital sources of growth gave way to war and destruction and death, American women were on the move as well. Despite cultural conventions about their rootedness at home, American women struck out in all sorts of directions, playing a distinctive part in the nation's history and transforming themselves in the process.

◆ AN EXPANDING NATION, 1843–1861

For a century before and a half century after 1848, continental expansion was a defining aspect of the American experience. Starting in the 1840s, however, the westward movement of American settlers entered a distinctive phase. The Oregon Trail was mapped in 1843 — the first of the overland routes across the Rocky Mountains — and over the next two decades approximately 350,000 Americans crossed the continent, moving through the Indian lands of mid-America to reach the Pacific Coast. The migrants were mostly young American families: men charged with economic obligation and women with childbearing and childrearing responsibilities. Except for slaves brought by southerners, they were for the most part white and, given the costs of the trek, from the middle ranks of society. When gold was discovered in California in 1848,

photos: top, Mary Evans Picture Library; middle, Library of Congress, 3b31109; bottom, The Granger Collection, New York

1848	**First New York State Married Women's Property Act passed**
1848	**Seneca Falls Convention initiates women's rights movement**
1848	Free Soil Party founded
1850	Compromise of 1850, including Fugitive Slave Law, passed
1850	California becomes a state
1850	**First National Women's Rights Convention held in Worcester, Massachusetts**
1851	**Susan B. Anthony and Elizabeth Cady Stanton's partnership begins**
1852	**New York Women's Temperance Society formed**
1852	**Harriet Beecher Stowe's *Uncle Tom's Cabin* published**
1854	Republican Party formed
1854	**Elizabeth Cady Stanton addresses New York legislature on women's rights**
1856	**Margaret Garner tried in Cincinnati**
1857	Supreme Court decides *Dred Scott v. Sandford*, rejecting possibility of black citizenship
1860	**Second New York State Married Women's Property Act passed**
1860	Republican candidate Abraham Lincoln elected president
1860–1861	Southern states secede
1861	Civil War begins
1863	Emancipation Proclamation declares slaves in rebel territory free
1863	**Women's National Loyal League established**
1863	Battle of Gettysburg proves turning point in war
1863	Food riots in Richmond, Virginia, and draft riots in New York City erupt
1865	Robert E. Lee surrenders
1865	Lincoln assassinated
1865	Thirteenth Amendment ratified

223

the character and purposes of American migration changed. Hordes of eager, ambitious men — and a few intrepid women — rushed to California to realize their dreams of quick wealth rather than permanent settlement. The outbreak of the Civil War effectively curtailed the overland migration, and when expansion resumed, it took a different form, following the nation's new railroad system to concentrate on the great expanse of the trans-Mississippi plains (see pp. 363–66 and the map at the end of the book).

Throughout the period of migration along the overland trails, women from the diverse cultures that met in the West came into conflict. Mexican women who lived in the Southwest were pushed aside as American women moved into their lands. Self-identified "respectable" women shunned prostitutes and female adventurers. Through it all, Indian women and girls were hired or captured by newcomers for domestic labor, and by the outbreak of the Civil War, Mexican women were beginning to labor for American women in the same capacity. The conflicts between different groups of women were sometimes overt, sometimes implicit, but always more significant than the commonalities that the ideology of true womanhood claimed they shared.

Overland by Trail

Historians and American popular culture have long celebrated the selfless wives and pioneer mothers for their role on the overland crossing, and it is undoubtedly true that men alone could not have made the new claims of continental nationhood a reality. But what of the actual experience of the individual women who pulled up stakes, cooked and laundered out of their primitive wagons for half a year or longer, gave birth and tended children across more than two thousand miles? Men usually made the decision to move. In 1852, Martha Read wrote to her sister of her reluctance to emigrate from New York with her husband: "It looks like a great undertaking to me but Clifton was bound to go and I thought I would go rather than stay here alone with the children."[1] Other women undertook the crossing with the same eagerness as did their men. Looking west from the banks of the Missouri River that same year, Lydia Rudd wrote in her diary, "With good courage and not one sign of regret . . . [I] mounted my pony."[2] Individual families joined together in long lines ("trains") of thirty to two hundred covered wagons to share the effort and the danger of the trip. Many single men made the overland crossing, but few unmarried women did. Enslaved women had no choice in the matter when southern slaveholders decided to take their households westward.

Occasionally, documents left by the migrants provide glimpses into the domestic tension that accompanied the difficult decision to uproot and migrate. A month into her 1848 trip to Oregon Territory, Keturah Belknap recorded a quarrel she overheard in a nearby wagon between a husband and wife: "She wants to turn back and he won't, so she says she will go and leave him . . . with that crying baby." Then Belknap heard a "muffled cry and a heavy thud as if something was thrown against the wagon box." She heard the wife say, "Oh you've killed it," to which the husband responded that "he would give her more of the same."[3] In another of these rarely

◆ **Madonna of the Trail Monument**
Twelve exact replicas of this 10-foot-tall statue, located from Maryland to California, trace the westward, transcontinental movement of nineteenth-century American settlers. The Daughters of the American Revolution initiated and funded the project in the late 1920s, after the organization had become radically conservative and fervently nationalistic. The statue commemorates the era of Manifest Destiny as the backbone of American nationalism and honors motherhood as women's highest form of patriotic service. However, the monumentality of the figure also evokes masculine characteristics. © *Jim West/The Image Works.*

recorded incidents of desperate female resistance, one woman on the trail was so determined to turn back that she set the family's wagon on fire.[4]

Throughout the crossing, men and women had distinctive responsibilities. Men drove the wagons and tended the animals. Women fed their families, cared for their children, and did their best to "keep house" in a cramped wagon bumping its way across the country. As the months wore on and the horses and oxen weakened, women walked more often than they rode. Men's tasks were concentrated during the day; after the wagons stopped and the animals were tended, they could snatch a bit of time to relax. If decisions about direction or pace had to be made, the men met alone and made them. The women's workdays were effectively the reverse. They woke up earlier to prepare breakfast, cared for children as the train moved forward, and worked for many hours after the wagons stopped to prepare for the next day. On an overland trail, everyone worked to the full limit of her or his capacities. Even so, the average woman's workday was several hours longer than that of a man.

Overlanders took care to bring with them some of the few household improvements American women had gained in settled areas by the mid-nineteenth century, such as industrially spun cloth, prepared flour, and soap. Other modern inventions—iron stoves, for example—could not be carried easily, returning women to the domestic conditions of their mothers' and grandmothers' generations. On the rare days when the wagon train stopped, many women did laundry, pounding the dirt out of clothes in cold running streams. Often women convinced men to stop the train to observe the Sabbath, but instead of resting, women caught up on their work.

In certain situations, women had to help the men drive the wagons or tend the stock. Rather than seize the chance to show that they could do a man's job, white women were frequently reluctant to undertake new and difficult obligations on top of their regular work, clinging to the ideas of true womanhood as a way to preserve dignity on the trail. As Catherine Haun's party crossed the Rockies, she described how she joined in to keep the wagons from plunging uncontrollably back and forth. She complained bitterly, not so much that the work was difficult as that it was "unladylike."[5] Enslaved women were even more exposed than free women to hard labor in these westward caravans. Bridgette "Biddy" Mason, for example, made the overland journey in 1848 with her Mormon owners. Although a nursing mother with three daughters, Mason was charged with the dusty job of tending the cattle trailing the wagon trains.

Women had exclusive responsibility for children on the trip. Since the average period between births for white women in 1850 was twenty-nine months, it is reasonable to assume that many, perhaps most, women of childbearing age were either pregnant or nursing and caring for infants in the wagons. Pregnancy was not discussed publicly, although "confinement" was not possible on a wagon train. Often the only way that a historian reading a woman's letters or diary can detect a pregnancy is through the woman's references to "getting sick," followed soon afterward by mention of a new child. "Still in camp, washing and overhauling the wagons," Amelia Stewart Knight wrote in her 1853 trail diary. "Got my washing and cooking done and started on again . . . (here I was sick all night, caused by my washing and working too hard)." Within two weeks, just as their trip ended, she gave birth to her eighth child. She had been pregnant but had not referred directly to it for the entire six-month trip west.[6]

In contrast to the infrequent references to birth, deaths, especially of children but also adults, were amply described. On her way to Oregon, Jane Gould Tortillott wrote about overtaking a particularly ill-fated wagon train. "There was a woman died in this train yesterday," she wrote. "She left six children, one of them only two day's [sic] old."[7] As the number of overlanders rose, more and more graves marked the trail. Lydia Rudd, who had begun her trip west so optimistically, within weeks was counting the graves she passed. Many migrants died of cholera, a swift-moving infectious disease that killed by severe dehydration. The disease had come with European immigrants in the mid-nineteenth century, and the overland migrants brought it with them as they traveled west. Sarah Royce wrote in her diary about the death of a man in her group: "Soon terrible spasms convulsed him. . . . Medicine was administered which afforded some relief . . . but nothing availed and in two or three hours the man expired." After the body was buried and the wagons were cleansed, Royce could only wait. "Who would go next?"[8]

Women's relief at having arrived at their destination in Oregon or Washington or California was quickly replaced by the realization that they still had to build homes and establish communities. Long after they had moved west, many continued to miss the lives and families they had left behind. Yet, while individual women suffered during the crossing, their way of life and standards for womanhood eventually triumphed, and for most, their willingness to move west was vindicated. In contrast, Native women and the resident Mexican citizens experienced the United States's growing continental reach as conquest and displacement. The process of American expansion set women against each other on the grounds of culture, race, and ethnicity.

The Underside of Expansion: Native Women and Californianas

In the Far West, three groups of people — emigrants from the East, Indians, and Californios (Mexican citizens who lived in California prior to American statehood) — came upon each other with various combinations of curiosity, hospitality, alliance, exploitation, and violence. Starting in the late eighteenth century, Californios thinly populated the Pacific Coast up to the San Francisco Bay. Coastal Natives became their laborers and servants. Inland and to the north, larger numbers of Indians still lived the lives of their ancestors. The arrival of emigrants beginning in the mid-1840s brought rapid change. Within a few years, the Californios had lost control of the coastal lands, the lives of the Natives had been profoundly disrupted by epidemics, warfare, and death, and California had become the thirty-first state of the United States. As migrating overlanders crossed through Indian Territory in large numbers, they imagined that they were constantly at risk from the "red man." Over and over, trail accounts speak of Indian "attacks" that turn out to be something quite different. Hunger and epidemics were spreading among the Plains Indians, a consequence of encroaching American settlement. To alleviate their poverty, Indians begged for or demanded food and money from the emigrants as they passed through their lands. In 1849, Sarah Royce's wagon train was stopped outside of Council Bluffs, Iowa, by Sioux who wanted payment of a toll. A tense encounter ensued, but the Americans refused to pay and declared that "the country we were traveling over belonged to the United States and that these red men had no right to stop us." Royce recorded "the expression of sullen disappointment, mingled with a half-defiant scowl" on the Indians' faces as the emigrants moved on.[9]

In and around the U.S. Army forts and trading posts that dotted the trail were Native women who had left their own people to live with white men in informal sexual and domestic unions but who had been abandoned when the men married white women. In some cases their Native communities did not allow them to return, so these women ended up on the edges of white culture, as domestic servants to women settlers or prostitutes to men, and were met with scorn as "black dirty squaws."[10] "Squaw" had originally been used by white people simply to mean "Indian woman," but the word had come to hold exclusively negative connotations of sexual degradation and unrelenting, unrewarded, and unskilled female labor.

Compared to the numerous accounts from white women who feared Indians, few Native women left records of how they felt about white people. In her autobiography, Sarah Winnemucca, a Paiute from the eastern side of the Sierra Nevada, related her encounter with American emigrants who crossed into her people's lands when she was a small child: "They came like a lion, yes, like a roaring lion, and have continued so ever since, and I have never forgotten their first coming." The Paiutes had their own rumors that the white people "were killing everybody and eating them." The men of her father's band were away from camp and the women and children were gathering seeds when they realized that whites were approaching. The terrified women buried their children up to their necks in mud and then hid their faces with bushes. "Can any one imagine my feelings buried alive . . . ?" Winnemucca recalled. "With my heart throbbing and not daring to breathe, we lay there all day." Her parents rescued her later that night. Soon after, the band's winter supplies were burned by a party of white men, and their impoverishment began.[11]

Native peoples on the Pacific Coast suffered severe losses as Americans poured into their lands. California Indians were particularly devastated. Their traditional sources of food were destroyed by American mining and agriculture. Sarah Winnemucca's mother feared that her "young and very good-looking" sister was unsafe among white men, even those whom her family considered friends. These assaults, along with the sexually transmitted diseases that American men brought with them, dramatically reduced Native women's fertility. The Indian population of California, which had already been cut in half by disease and poverty in the years of Mexican rule, declined even more precipitously — from 150,000 to 30,000 — between 1850 and 1860.

Californios, descendants of the original Mexican colonists, also experienced loss of land as well as status under American rule. Most of the first Mexican women who had come to California (Californianas) were the wives of soldiers and banished convicts. However, both Mexican and American legend romanticized the women of the small class of grand Mexican landholders. Starting in the 1830s, American men who went to California made their way into Mexican society by marrying the women of these elite families. In 1841, Abel Stearns, an ambitious merchant from Massachusetts, married Arcadia Bandini, daughter of one of the

AN INDIAN WOMAN GATHERING ACORNS.

◆ **An Indian Woman Gathering Acorns, 1859**

Collecting acorns was part of California indigenous women's traditional gathering work. Women dried and ground the acorns as a staple of their diets. However, by the time the *Hutchings' California Magazine* published this image, California Indians had already undergone a horrific decade of intentional decimation and forced removal to reservations carried out by American colonists. The accompanying article stated that Indians were "the lowest in morality and intellectual ability on this continent." Like European colonists of earlier eras, the unnamed author pointed to the subsistence labor of indigenous women as a sign of Indian backwardness. The scene of acorn gathering therefore both romanticized and racialized the work of Indian women.

largest landholders in California. Arcadia, who was fourteen when she married the forty-year-old Abel, outlived her husband; when she died in 1912, she was the richest woman in southern California.

Arcadia Bandini Stearns was unusual. While Mexican law gave married women more control over their property than did U.S. law, this did not protect them from the loss of wealth and standing that they, along with their men, suffered once California was absorbed into the United States. (See Reading into the Past: "Narrative of Mrs. Rosalía Vallejo Leese," pp. 230–31.) This was the experience of Maria Amparo Ruiz de Burton, a Mexican woman who married an American army officer when she was seventeen and he was thirty. She became the first person to chronicle her people's experience for an English-speaking audience. In her 1885 historical romance, *The Squatter and the Don*, she gave a powerful fictional account of the long legal process by which the U.S. government's guarantees to the citizens of Mexican California were abrogated and their lands gradually taken from them. Despite Ruiz de Burton's high literary and political standing, she died landless and impoverished in 1895. Instead of Ruiz de Burton's work, which was based on personal experience, the more enduring fictional account of the Californio experience has become the 1880 novel *Ramona: A Romance of the Old Southwest*, written by the Massachusetts writer Helen Hunt Jackson.

READING INTO THE PAST

Narrative of Mrs. Rosalía Vallejo Leese, Who Witnessed the Hoisting of the Bear Flag in Sonoma on the 14th of June, 1846

Rosalía Vallejo was born in Monterey in 1811 to a prominent military family who helped to colonize Alta California for Spain. In the late 1830s, after Mexican independence, she married a naturalized citizen named Jacob Leese. After residing several years in Yerba Buena (now San Francisco), Rosalía and Jacob built a family ranch on a land grant in Sonoma that had been secured by Rosalía's brother Mariano Vallejo. In Sonoma, Rosalía Vallejo de Leese encountered the small group of American settlers who had invaded Sonoma and declared an independent "republic" in June of 1846. Almost thirty years later, she shared her testimonio in Spanish with Henry Cerruti, one of the interviewers hired by Hubert Howe Bancroft to gather materials for a comprehensive history of California. The interview focused on the event known in American history as the "Bear Flag Revolt," but which Vallejo de Leese described as the "all-out robbery of California." Cerruti, a European immigrant whose first language was neither Spanish nor English, wrote down Vallejo de Leese's words in English. In this version of her testimonio, bilingual scholars have revised Cerruti's awkward translation for clearer expression.

As soon as the Bear Flag was raised, I was told by the thieves' interpreter that I was now a prisoner. This interpreter's name was Solís. He was a former servant of my husband's. Solís pointed to four ragged desperados who were standing close to me with their pistols drawn. I surrendered because it would have been useless to resist. They demanded the key to my husband's storehouse and I gave it to them. No sooner had I given them the key than they called their friends over and began ransacking the storehouse. There were enough provisions and liquor there to feed two hundred men for two years. A few days after my husband was taken away, John C. Frémont arrived in Sonoma. He said that his sole purpose for coming was to arrange matters to everyone's satisfaction and protect everyone from extortion or oppression. Many paid writers have characterized Frémont with a great number of endearing epithets, but he was a tremendous coward. Listen to me! I have good reason to say this. On June 20, we received news that Captain Padilla was on his way to Sonoma with a squad of one hundred men to rescue us. As soon as Frémont heard about this, he sent for me. He ordered me to write Padilla a letter and tell him to return to San José and not come near Sonoma. I flatly refused to do that, but Frémont was bent on having his own way. He told me that if I refused to tell Padilla exactly what he told me to say, and if Padilla approached Sonoma, he would order his men to burn down our houses with us inside. I agreed to his demands, not because I wanted to save my own life, but because I was pregnant and did not have the right to endanger the life of my unborn child. Moreover, I judged that a man who had already gone this far would stop at nothing to attain his goals. I also wanted to spare the Californio women from more trouble, so I wrote that ominous letter which forced Captain Padilla to retrace his steps. While on alert for Padilla's possible attack, Frémont changed out of his fancy uniform into a blue shirt. He put away his hat and wrapped an ordinary handkerchief around his head. He decided to dress like this so he would not be recognized. Is this the way a brave man behaves?

During the whole time that Frémont and his ring of thieves were in Sonoma, robberies were very common. The women did not dare go out for a walk unless they were escorted by their husband or their brothers. One of my servants was a young Indian girl who was about seventeen years old. I swear that John C. Frémont ordered me to send that girl to the officers' barracks many times. However, by resorting to tricks, I was able to save that poor girl from falling into the hands of that lawless band of thugs who had imprisoned my husband. . . .

I could tell you about the many crimes committed by the Bear Flag mob, but since I do not wish to detain you any longer, I will end this conversation with this: those hateful men instilled so much hate in me for the people of their race that, even though twenty-eight years have gone by since then, I still cannot forget the insults they heaped upon me. Since I have not wanted to have anything to do with them, I have refused to learn their language.

Source: Rose Marie Beebe and Robert M. Senkewicz, translators and editors, *Testimonios: Early California through the Eyes of Women, 1815–1848* (Berkeley: Heyday Books, Bancroft Library, University of California, Berkeley), 28–29.

QUESTIONS FOR ANALYSIS

1. What parts of Vallejo's testimonio emphasize her experiences as a woman and a mother?

2. How did Vallejo de Leese draw on ideals of manhood to challenge the prevailing heroic narratives about Frémont and the Bear Flag "revolt"?

◆ **Rosalía Vallejo de Leese, with spouse and children, c. 1850**
Rosalía Vallejo came from an extended family of colonial Mexican military officers. Against
the wishes of her brother, she married Jacob Reese, who had converted to Catholicism, and
became a Mexican citizen. Through dress and posture, this landowning Californio family
conveyed their dignity and privilege, which at the time of the photograph had been upset by
American occupation. By the end of the Civil War, Jacob Reese returned to New York, leaving
Rosalía and her children in California. *Courtesy of San Mateo County History Museum.*

Once California became a state in 1850, legislators sought to preserve some of
the advantages that Mexican law provided married women, but gradually state courts
and legislatures began to rewrite and reinterpret the laws of marital property to
conform to the American standard, which favored husbands over wives. These legal
shifts may have helped to accelerate the transfer of California lands from Mexican to
American ownership in the 1850s and 1860s. As this happened, many Californianas
followed the path of Native women into landlessness, domestic service, and poverty.

The Gold Rush

The combination of the discovery of gold in 1848 with the end of the Mexican War
and the achievement of statehood in 1850 greatly accelerated the Americanization
of California. The year before the discovery of gold, there were four thousand

overland migrants; the year after, there were thirty thousand. Overlanders were joined by other gold-seekers who sailed around the southern tip of South America or crossed the Panamanian isthmus. International migrants flocked to the gold-fields from Chile, Sonora Province in Mexico, and even China. At the end of the war with Mexico, California had been populated by one hundred thousand Indians, perhaps a tenth as many Mexicans, and only a few thousand Americans. After the discovery of gold, it became one of the most cosmopolitan places on earth. Based on almost unlimited hopes for the quick achievement of fortune, California society was thoroughly cash-dependent; anything could be bought, and everything cost dearly.

Most of the gold-seekers were men. For every one hundred men who came to gold country, there were only three women.[12] Some of these women came with their husbands, either to share in the adventure or to fulfill a sense of conjugal duty. But some women longed to go west to pursue their own adventurous dreams. In a letter to her mother soon after news broke of the discovery of gold, Susan B. Anthony, later one of the founders of the women's rights movement, wrote, "I wish I had about $100,000 of the precious dust. I would no longer be [a] School marm."[13] Anthony did not go, but there were women who did join the rush, some to work close to the mines and others to set up businesses in San Francisco or Sacramento and make their fortunes at a distance. (See Primary Sources: "Female Labor in the Gold-Rush Economy," pp. 257–65.) One of the few African American women in gold-rush San Francisco was Mary Ellen Pleasant, who ran a boarding-house and a restaurant from 1849 through 1855. "A smart woman can do very well in this country," one woman wrote to a friend back east. "It is the only country that I ever was in where a woman recev'd anything like a just compensation for work."[14]

Despite the economic unpredictability of gold-rush California, women continued to maintain class differences among themselves. Only rarely did middle class women live at the goldfields. Most white women at the diggings lived more hardscrabble lives. While their husbands sought their fortunes at the mines, they supported their families by feeding, housing, sewing, and laundering for the hordes of unmarried men who were willing to pay well for such services. Mary Ballou, who ran a supper table for miners, was astounded at the money she could make in California compared to how little women's labor was worth in the East. Even so, she concluded, "I would not advise any Lady to come out here and suffer the toil and fatigue that I have suffered for the sake of a little gold."[15]

Of all the women in gold-rush California, prostitutes have drawn the most attention from historians, much of it either romantic or salacious. "The first females to come were the vicious and unchaste," wrote Hubert Howe Bancroft, the state's first historian. "Flaunting in their gay attire, they were civilly treated by the men, few of whom, even of the most respectable and sedate, disdained to visit their houses."[16] This image of the gold-rush prostitute who was accorded the respectability in California denied to her elsewhere in American society is inaccurate. So, too, is the claim that sexual labor provided these women with wealth and independence. The glamorous whores of California legend were few and limited to San Francisco. Closer to the goldfields, the majority of prostitutes worked in seedy

FIG. 95. — Croquis californien par Cham.
* Allusion aux Agences matrimoniales.

◆ "Entreprise de Mariages," *Charivari*, 1849

This French satirical cartoon demonstrates the immense international interest in the California gold rush and the notable scarcity of women in the gold fields. In the wake of the 1848 French Revolution which encouraged republican freedom of the press, Parisian humor magazines poked fun at the absurdities of gold-rush life. Here, *Charivari* lampoons writer and reformer Eliza Farnham's plan to send brides to California miners. The sign behind the merchant indicates a wedding business that promises an "assortment of widows" to repair California bachelor households and the caption indicates that this commercial item is in "high demand." *The New York Public Library/Art Resource, NY.*

"crib hotels," where they had sex with many men for $1 or $2 per customer. All were at great risk for venereal disease, violence, and early death.

The hierarchy of sex service in midcentury California reflected sharp racial and national distinctions, with white American and French women in the highest strata, and Mexicans, South Americans, and African Americans much lower. At the very bottom were the Chinese. By the late 1850s, approximately thirty-five thousand Chinese men had come as miners but had been forced by discriminatory laws into low-paid, unskilled labor. The much smaller numbers of immigrant Chinese women were found almost exclusively in prostitution, a situation that did not change until federal measures restricted Chinese immigration in 1882 (see p. 372). By 1860, approximately two thousand women had been kidnapped or purchased in China and sent to the United States, where they were resold for tremendous profits.

Chinese prostitutes were held in virtual slave conditions. Their terms of indenture were repeatedly extended for all sorts of spurious reasons, and many did not outlive their terms. Should they somehow elude their captors and the Chinese syndicates that organized the trade, they had no place to turn. U.S. courts ruled that prostitutes who had run away were guilty of the crime of property theft (of themselves) and brought them back to their masters. A few Chinese prostitutes were able to marry Chinese laborers, but American law prohibited marriage to white American men.

◆ ANTEBELLUM REFORM

The physical expansion of the United States, along with the economic transformation of early industrialization, generated a thriving spirit of moral and social activism from 1840 to the Civil War. Antebellum reformers pushed beyond established social and cultural norms in their attempts to improve, even perfect, both the individual and the society. The centers of this reform ferment were in New York and New England, as if the era's impatience with established boundaries took a metaphoric rather than physical form in that region. Initially rooted in deeply religious conviction, the antebellum reform movement eventually followed the lodestar of moral virtue to arrive at the deeply political issues of abolition and women's rights. Accordingly, reform activism was virtually nonexistent in the slave South.

Women played a notable role in antebellum reform. By one estimate, at any given time as many as 10 percent of adult women in the Northeast were active in benevolent and reforming societies in these years.[17] The influential ideology of true womanhood credited women with the selflessness necessary to counterbalance male individualism. Women's modest efforts on behalf of the community's welfare were thus compatible with domesticity and female respectability. But over time, women's dedication to moral and social causes led them beyond their homebound roles and to the edges of woman's allotted sphere. In the case of women's rights, some women crossed over into new gender territory altogether.

Expanding Woman's Sphere: Maternal, Moral, and Temperance Reform

Following the intense wave of revivals in the late 1820s known as the Second Great Awakening (see pp. 160–62), women from an ever-wider swath of American society became involved in efforts to deepen and broaden the Protestant faith. Initially their role was to support male missionaries in bringing Christianity to the unconverted at home and abroad. For the most part, they deferred to male clergy and kept to their place, but the fervor of their faith inspired some to venture into new territory, figuratively and literally. In 1836, for instance, Narcissa Whitman and Eliza Spaulding traveled with their minister husbands to Oregon Territory by wagon, probably the first American women to do so, to convert the Nez Perce and Cayuse Indians.

Even in these supportive roles, however, pious women began to form their own organizations dedicated to aspects of their religious duty. They formed mothers' societies to protect the virtue of their children from the rampant immorality they perceived in a society in social and economic flux. These organizations published magazines to advise mothers and established and administered orphanages and Sunday religious schools. By emphasizing the Christian exercise of maternal responsibility, their members wielded their maternal role to expand social authority for their sex. Pious women also formed moral reform societies to combat the upsurge of drink, prostitution, and other forms of what they called "vice." By the early 1840s, there were four hundred female moral reform societies in New England and New York. Moral reform enthusiasm was expansive enough to cross boundaries of race and class. Women of the tiny African American middle class formed their own societies to encourage standards of sexual decorum and family respectability in the free black community. The Lynn, Massachusetts, branch brought together artisans' wives and unmarried seamstresses to guard against the prostitution that they feared would take root in factory towns.

Moral reform societies were particularly concerned with the increase in casual sexuality among young women impoverished by the economic forces of rapid industrialization. Female moral reformers raised money to send ministers to save the souls of those women who had already "fallen" and campaigned to exclude from upstanding society "persons of either sex known to be licentious."[18] Eventually they became bolder and reached out directly to prostitutes, despite the threat that such actions posed to their own womanly respectability. Because they considered sexual excess as fundamentally male and regarded all women, even prostitutes, as its victims, they felt that sexual immorality represented sin in its most distinctly male form. To be sure, if prostitutes were not sufficiently penitent, they lost their claim to Christian women's sympathy. Nonetheless, women's moral reform activism deepened many middle-class women's gender consciousness and expanded their sense of common womanhood, thus helping to lay the foundations for the women's rights movement.

Women's religiously motivated social activism in the mid-nineteenth century reached its height in the temperance movement. Americans were heavy drinkers in these years, but the temperance fervor focused on more than alcohol abuse. In an era of rapid and disorienting economic growth, the lack of self-restraint expressed through drunkenness provided a convenient explanation for why so many people suffered dramatic downward social mobility. The gospel of temperance promised that if a man could just control his impulses, subdue his appetites, and redirect his energies, his family might survive and even prosper through economic shifts. No reform movement was more widely supported in the 1840s and 1850s.

Although drunkenness was considered an exclusively male vice, images of its female victims — the suffering wives and children of irresponsible drunkards — figured prominently in anti-alcohol propaganda. Not content to remain mere symbols for the tragedies that "King Alcohol" wreaked, women became active proponents of temperate living. They began to form their own Daughters of Temperance societies to challenge both the morality and the legality of commerce in alcohol. When New York women activists created a women's temperance society in 1852, five hundred women attended the convention.

◆ *The Fruits of Temperance,* **1848**
Created by the famous lithographer Nathaniel Currier, this hand-colored engraving was published in New York by J. B. Allen. Available at an affordable price for middle-class families, it illustrated the domestic harmony that flowed from a temperate father and husband. Furthermore, in an era of numerous financial "panics," the prosperous factories in the background also tied temperance to commercial growth and upward mobility. The fine-print caption reads: "Behold the son of Temperance, with buoyant heart and step, returning to his home, the partner of his bosom looks up and smiles his welcome; his children fly to meet him, their little arms embrace him, and with lip and heart they bless him." How might this image have appealed to men and women for different reasons? *Library of Congress, LC-DIG-pga-08736.*

Like the moral reform associations, women's temperance organizations incubated the expression of female discontent with middle-class family life and marital practices. Temperance activism allowed women to criticize men for their failure to live up to the marital bargain, by which wives would subordinate themselves to their husbands so long as the men were reliable breadwinners and evenhanded patriarchs. Numerous female activists began their reform careers within the temperance movement, among them Susan B. Anthony, the women's rights pioneer, and Frances Ellen Watkins Harper, the most prominent midcentury African American woman writer and speaker. After the Civil War, women's temperance activism continued to grow until it led to the most important women's organization of the Gilded Age, the Woman's Christian Temperance Union (see pp. 319–20).

Exploring New Territory: Radical Reform in Family and Sexual Life

As women's enthusiasm for moral reform and temperance suggests, family and sexual life were important concerns of antebellum female reformers. The private nuclear family that was so central to the middle-class cult of domesticity was also a locale for domestic violence, sexual abuse, and female disempowerment. Some antebellum reformers called for more radical changes in women's sexual and reproductive lives and for the establishment of alternative social systems not based on the private family.

Women's menstrual, reproductive, and sexual complaints made them eager advocates and consumers of health reform. Unwilling to rely on the questionable diagnoses of regular physicians, health activists developed alternative therapeutic regimes to increase bodily vitality. They made use of natural, non-invasive methods and urged against too much sensual stimulation, believing it unhealthy. The "water cure," a system that emphasized cold-water baths and loose clothing, offered comfort to women worn out from too many and too frequent pregnancies. A program developed by reformer Sylvester Graham stressed the benefits of cold, unspiced foods (from which we inherited the Graham cracker) and promised to remedy sexual as well as digestive complaints.

Mary Gove Nichols, an outspoken critic of the sexual abuses hidden within marital life, advocated both the Graham and water-cure systems. Through the 1840s, she spoke forcefully and wrote explicitly about women's physical frustrations and sufferings in marriage. Insistent that "a healthy and loving woman is impelled to material union"—that is, sexual intercourse—"as surely, often as strongly as man," she declared that "the apathy of the sexual instinct in woman is caused by the enslaved and unhealthy condition in which she lives."[19] The Ladies Physiological Society of Boston, active between 1837 and 1841, enthusiastically sponsored Nichols's direct speech about female sexuality. In addition to hosting lectures on physiology and anatomy, Society members gathered in each other's home, cultivating an "intimate, confessional peer education model," where white women activists could support each other in achieving sexual virtue.[20] Black abolitionist Sarah Mapps Douglass also embraced the cause of women's health education in the 1850s, giving public lectures in Philadelphia on female physiology with the aid of a "French manikin."

Radical reformers of sexuality and the family could be found as residents of the many communitarian experiments that sprang up in the 1830s and 1840s. These intentional communities posed a range of challenges to conventional notions of marriage and the family. The Shakers occupied one end of the continuum, prohibiting all sexual relations, even within marriage. Men and women lived and worshipped in separate but conjoined communities, coming together to dance and sing their religious ecstasies. Obviously unable to enlarge their numbers by biological reproduction, Shakers took in orphans, apprentices, and individuals in flight from unhappy families, including destitute widows. In the 1830s, an estimated six thousand Shakers lived in nineteen communities throughout the country.

Their celibate way of life and the alternative they offered to the private, patriarchal family strongly appealed to women, particularly inasmuch as their founder and chief saint was a woman. Mother Ann Lee (see p. 130) had emigrated in the 1770s from England, where she had suffered marital rape and domestic abuse. She taught that God was both male and female, and that marriage was based on the subjugation of women and thus violated divine law.

On the other end of the continuum, the Oneida community sanctified extramarital sexuality. Moved by deep dissatisfaction with his own marriage, John Humphrey Noyes founded a community in 1848 in Oneida, near Syracuse, New York. Its members owned property collectively and raised children communally, but the collectivization of sexual relations was the source of the community's greatest notoriety. Both men and women were sexually active but foreswore monogamy, lest they substitute attachment to an individual for the exclusive love of God. They also practiced a strict contraceptive regime that required men to withhold ejaculation through prolonged sexual intercourse. Despite the Oneidans' sexual radicalism, they were deeply Christian and justified all their practices in biblical terms. The collectivization of housework, the availability of different sexual partners, male responsibility for contraception, and what might fairly be called the institutionalization of foreplay offered women at Oneida alternatives available nowhere else. Yet Noyes's insistence on retaining authority over all community life (including assigning sexual partners) also gave Oneida a deeply patriarchal air. Nonetheless, the Oneida community survived into the 1880s.

The Church of Jesus Christ of Latter-day Saints, commonly known as the Mormons, was the most historically significant of these intentional antebellum communities. It is also difficult to assess through the eyes of women, because the estimations of insiders and outsiders were so different with respect to women's status in it. Founded in 1830 in Palmyra, New York, the Mormons numbered fifteen thousand nine years later. The group migrated several times, eventually forming a cooperative community in Nauvoo, Illinois. Responding to rumors that Mormon leaders had multiple wives, non-Mormons drove them out, and starting in 1847, the community trekked farther west to Utah. There, polygamy became an open practice, a sign of special divinity. In 1870, in response to federal pressure against polygamy, the Utah Territory enfranchised its women to indicate their power and stature. When Elizabeth Cady Stanton, the great philosopher of nineteenth-century women's rights, brought her own critique of marriage to Salt Lake City in 1871, she reported that "the Mormon women, like all others, stoutly defended their religion, yet they are no more satisfied [with their marriage practices] than any other sect."[21] The Mormons held to the practice of polygamy until 1896, when they formally rejected it in order for Utah to be admitted as a state.

While the Shakers, the Oneidans, and the Mormons were inspired by radical Christian notions of human perfectibility, there were other communal experiments based on more secular, indeed socialist, ideas. The most famous was Brook Farm, founded in Roxbury, Massachusetts, in 1841 by members of the Boston-based intellectual circle known as the Transcendentalists. For its brief existence, Brook Farm combined high culture and cooperative labor. Although young Georgiana Bruce, recently arrived from England, was not one of the luminaries of the experiment, she enthused, "[T]he very air seemed to hold more exhilarating qualities than any I had breathed before."[22] Margaret Fuller was the most prominent woman associated with Brook Farm, which she visited frequently as she was writing the first full-length feminist treatise in American history, *Woman in the Nineteenth Century.* "What woman needs is not as a woman to act or rule," she wrote, "but as nature to grow, as an intellect to discern, as a soul to live freely and unimpeded."[23]

Crossing Political Boundaries: Abolitionism

Of all the forms of antebellum social activism, the movement to abolish chattel slavery had the most profound impact on American history, contributing significantly to the social and political tensions leading to the Civil War. Like temperance and moral reform, abolitionism arose out of a deep religious conviction that truly God-fearing Christians had the obligation to eliminate sin — in this case slaveholding. "Let but each woman in the land do a Christian woman's duty," implored the Boston Female Anti-Slavery Society in 1836, "and the result cannot fail to be [the slave's] instant, peaceful, unconditional deliverance."[24] But unlike other reform movements, abolitionism brought its proponents, women along with men, into open conflict with America's basic political and religious institutions.

The call for immediate, uncompensated abolition of slavery and full civil rights for black people first came from the free black community, which by 1820 numbered over a quarter of a million. Many free blacks were kin to enslaved people, whom they struggled to purchase or smuggle into freedom through the Underground Railroad, the elaborate system of escape routes developed to aid fleeing slaves. African American women sustained black abolitionist work through fund-raising, writing, and public speaking. In 1831, Maria Stewart, a black domestic servant from Connecticut, became the first American woman known to have

◆ **Am I Not a Woman and a Sister?**
This image, widely used in antislavery literature, expresses the complex sentiments that underlay women's abolitionist activism. The rhetorical question "Am I Not a Woman and a Sister?" challenges the fundamental premise of chattel slavery that the slave woman was mere property. This version appeared in the special pages for women in William Lloyd Garrison's abolitionist newspaper, the *Liberator. The Granger Collection, New York.*

spoken publicly before mixed audiences of women and men. Stewart championed the intellectual contributions of African American women to the cause of racial equality. In one of her speeches, published by the abolitionist newspaper the *Liberator*, Stewart demanded: "How long shall the fair daughters of Africa be compelled to bury their minds and talents beneath a load of iron pots and kettles?"[25]

Black men and women who had experienced slavery directly also challenged the institution. Frederick Douglass escaped slavery in Maryland in 1838 to become an internationally renowned advocate of freedom for his people. Sojourner Truth was born in New York in 1797 as Isabella Baumfree, a slave before the institution was abolished in that state. After her emancipation, she spent several years in a religious community in New York City, dropped her slave name, and rechristened herself Sojourner Truth to signify her self-chosen vocation as an itinerant preacher and prophet. Starting in 1846, she also became an abolitionist lecturer, traveling as far west as Kansas. Unlike most other black abolitionists, Truth did not present a respectable, middle-class face to the world. She spoke and acted like the woman she was — unlettered, emotionally intense, opinionated, and forthright. In her dialect and style, she made a tremendous impact, especially on white audiences. Author Harriet Beecher Stowe praised "her wonderful physical vigor, her great heaving sea of emotion, her power of spiritual conception, her quick penetration, and her boundless energy."[26]

Knowing that their numbers and influence were insufficient to uproot slavery, African American abolitionists sought sympathetic white allies, beginning with William Lloyd Garrison. From 1831 until 1865, Garrison edited the *Liberator*. Women were always a substantial proportion of Garrison's followers. His radical principles, universalist notions of human dignity, and personal appreciation for women's discontent with their sphere made him a trusted leader. Elizabeth Cady Stanton — not one to bestow praise on men lightly — wrote of him: "I have always regarded Garrison as the great missionary of the gospel of Jesus to this guilty nation, for he has waged uncompromising warfare with the deadly sins of both Church and State. My own experience is, no doubt, that of many others. . . . [A] few bold strokes from the hammer of his truth and I was free!"[27]

In 1833, Garrison founded the American Anti-Slavery Society, which was committed to the immediate, uncompensated abolition of slavery. Its membership was racially integrated, although the majority of its members were white. At first, men led the organization and women took supporting roles. Lucretia Mott, an influential Quaker who went on to become the leader of female abolitionists, attended the founding meeting of the American Anti-Slavery Society, but neither she nor any other women were listed as members. "I do not think it occurred to any one of us at the time, that there should be propriety in our signing the [founding] document," she later wrote.[28]

Accordingly, women abolitionists, white and black, organized separate auxiliary female societies. In the Philadelphia Female Anti-Slavery Society, formed also in 1833, black women were 10 percent of its members and an even higher proportion of its officers.[29] Among the most prominent were Charlotte Forten (grandmother of the better-known Charlotte Forten Grimké); Forten's daughters,

Margaretta, Sarah Louise, and Harriet; and Grace Bustill and Sarah Mapps Douglass (not related to Frederick). Despite having greater wealth and education than the overwhelming majority of African Americans, these women were no strangers to racial prejudice. In 1838, when a nationwide meeting of women abolitionists was held in Philadelphia, a mob, infuriated by witnessing black and white women meeting together, attacked them and burned down Pennsylvania Hall, the building they had just dedicated to the abolitionist movement.

Female abolitionists' willingness to go beyond the limits of female propriety to defeat slavery, combined with their increasing realization that free women, white as well as black, experienced barriers to full personhood like those faced by slaves, pushed many of them in the direction of women's rights. Sarah and Angelina Grimké led the way. Born into a wealthy and politically prominent slaveholding family in South Carolina, in 1829 the sisters fled to Philadelphia, where they became Quakers and abolitionists. Driven by their deep conviction of slavery's profound sinfulness, they followed Maria Stewart's lead in 1836 and preached against slavery to "promiscuous" (mixed) audiences of men and women, providing shockingly detailed descriptions of the sexual corruptions of slavery. The Massachusetts General Association of Congregationalist clergy publicly reprimanded them: "We appreciate the unostentatious prayers and efforts of woman in advancing the cause of religion at home and abroad . . . but when she assumes the place and tone of man as a public reformer, . . . her character becomes unnatural. . . . We especially deplore the intimate acquaintance and promiscuous conversation of females with regard to things 'which ought not to be named.'"[30] The sisters neither admitted error nor retreated. Instead, they insisted that it was not man's place but God's to assign woman's sphere. Combining religious conviction and American democratic ideals, Sarah wrote: "Men and women were CREATED EQUAL; they are both moral and accountable beings; and whatever is *right* for man to do, is *right* for woman."[31]

The Grimkés' courageous defense of their equal rights as moral beings and social activists produced a split in the abolitionist movement over the role of women. One wing, led by Garrison, moved to include women as full and equal participants in the work of converting white Americans to realize the moral necessity of abolishing slavery. After 1840, women served as officers and paid organizers of the American Anti-Slavery Society. A second wing, which included among its leaders Frederick Douglass, insisted that the issue of women's equality needed to be kept separate from that of abolition. The non-Garrisonians moved in the direction of more pragmatic, political methods, including the formation of political parties against slavery. These two issues — separating abolition from women's rights and moving beyond moral to political methods — were connected. Women, who were identified with moral purity and who lacked political rights, had little to offer a more political approach to abolitionism, at least until they began to make claims for suffrage.

The surfacing of political methods within abolitionism reflected the dramatic democratization of electoral politics in this period. By 1840, virtually all adult white men, regardless of wealth, had the right to vote. White men of all ranks followed elections closely, boasted proudly of their partisan inclinations, and contended openly for the candidates of their choice. Historians have labeled this expansion of political involvement "Jacksonianism" because the Democratic Party, formed in 1828 to nominate Andrew Jackson for the presidency, was its first institutional embodiment, followed in 1834 by the formation of the Whig Party. While in 1824 only 30 percent of adult white men went to the polls, 80 percent did so in 1840. However, many free black men lost political rights in these years and, by 1860, they were enfranchised in only four states — Maine, Massachusetts, New Hampshire, and Vermont.

Nor were women included in the Jacksonian expansion of the franchise. On the contrary, the right to vote was becoming the distinguishing characteristic of white American manhood. Yet, as the reformist spirit of the age began to spill over into politics, women were drawn into the excitement of electoral contests. They participated in political discussions and championed candidates and parties. When they felt compelled to formally register their political opinion on an issue, they turned to the only mechanism allowed to them: petitioning their legislators. As early as 1830, non-Indian women petitioned the U.S. government to halt the violent removal of the Cherokees from their own lands. Women also petitioned their state legislatures to ban the sale of alcohol and to make men's seduction of women punishable by law.

Women abolitionists conducted the most controversial of these petition campaigns. Starting in the 1830s, they began to gather thousands of signatures on petitions to Congress to ban slavery in the territories and in Washington, D.C., and to end the slave trade from state to state. "Let us know no rest til we have done our utmost to . . . obtain the testimony of every woman . . . against the horrible Slave-traffic," they declared.[32] In 1836, Congress passed a "gag rule" to table all petitions on slavery without discussion, but abolitionist women only intensified their efforts. Their congressional champion, John Quincy Adams (who had become a Massachusetts congressman after a single term as president), defended the movement of women beyond the boundaries of woman's sphere into the male world of politics. "Every thing which relates to peace and relates to war, or to any other of the great interests of society, is a political subject," he declared. "Are women to have no opinions or actions on subjects relating to the general welfare?"[33]

Entering New Territory: Women's Rights

Starting in the 1840s, all of these developments — moral reform and temperance, circulating petitions against slavery, the Grimkés' defense of their equal right to champion slaves — led many women reformers into women's rights. But unlike other activists, advocates of women's rights openly challenged the basic premise of true womanhood — that women were fundamentally selfless — and insisted that women had the same claim on individual rights to life, liberty, property, and happiness as men.

First articulated in 1792 by the English radical Mary Wollstonecraft, the doctrine of women's rights was brought to the United States in the 1820s by Frances Wright, a Scotswoman who gained great notoriety by her radical pronouncements on democracy, education, marriage, and labor. The threat that Wright's ideas represented to notions of respectable Christian womanhood can be appreciated by Catharine Beecher's horrified description of her: "There she stands, with brazen front and brawny arms, attacking the safeguards of all that is venerable and sacred in religion, all that is safe and wise in law, all that is pure and lovely in domestic virtue."[34] For several years, any woman who publicly advocated radical ideas was derisively called a "Fanny Wright woman."

For women's rights to grow from a set of ideas associated with one maligned individual into a reform movement took several decades. Changing state laws that deprived married women of all independent property rights was an early goal. These laws treated wives as nonpersons before the law, on the grounds that they were dependent on and subordinate to their husbands' authority. This pervasive Anglo-American legal principle was called "coverture," a term signifying the notion that marriage buried (or "covered") the wife's selfhood in that of the husband (see p. 53). A law to undo coverture by granting married women the same rights to earnings and property as single women and all men was introduced into the New York State legislature in 1836 by Elisha Hertell. Hertell was assisted by Ernestine Rose, a Jewish immigrant who had fled from an arranged marriage in Poland to England. There she married a man of her own choosing and later settled with him in New York City, where she became a leader in the "free — thinking" (atheistic) community. Despite great effort, however, Rose was able to gather only a handful of women's names on a petition supporting Hertell's bill.

By the 1840s, two other women joined Rose to work on behalf of married women's economic rights. One was Paulina Wright (later Davis), an activist who had started her career as a women's health educator. The other was Elizabeth Cady Stanton, destined to become the greatest women's rights thinker of the nineteenth century. (See Primary Sources: "Women's Rights Partnership: Elizabeth Cady Stanton and Susan B. Anthony in the 1850s," pp. 266–72.) Born into a wealthy and politically conservative New York family, Elizabeth Cady possessed great intelligence and high spirits that consistently led her afoul of the boundaries of woman's sphere. Her father, Daniel Cady, was a prominent lawyer and a judge, and although she could never hope to follow in his footsteps, she studied law informally in his office. As a young woman, she was deeply influenced by her cousin, the abolitionist Gerrit Smith. In his home, a stop on the Underground Railroad, she met fugitive slaves. She also met her future husband, the charismatic abolitionist orator Henry Stanton. In 1840, despite her father's opposition, Elizabeth and Henry married. When Henry introduced his new bride to Sarah and Angelina Grimké, they noted that they "were very much pleased" with Elizabeth but wished "that Henry was better calculated to help mould such a mind."[35]

Elizabeth Cady Stanton soon found her mentor in Quaker and abolitionist leader Lucretia Mott. On her honeymoon in London in 1840, she met Mott at an international antislavery convention at which female delegates were confined behind an opaque curtain and barred from participating in formal discussions. Both women were incensed, but the thrill of meeting each other outweighed the insult. "The acquaintance of Mrs. Mott, who was a broad, liberal thinker on politics, religion, and all questions of reform, opened to me a new world of thought,"

BLOOMERISM—AN AMERICAN CUSTOM.

◆ Bloomer Costumes

The heavy skirts worn by middle-class women in the mid-nineteenth century were awkward and confining. In 1851, women's rights advocates began to adopt a "reform dress" that featured loose trousers under a shortened skirt. The fashion was named after Amelia Bloomer, a Seneca Falls neighbor of Elizabeth Cady Stanton. Bloomer championed the outfit in her reform magazine, the *Lily*, and "bloomerism" traveled widely. This image was published in 1851 in the British satirical magazine *Punch*. That year, London hosted the first World's Fair, where bloomer-outfitted women were frequently sighted. The cartoonist, John Leech, published over two dozen such cartoons, linking "bloomerism" with women engaged in unpleasant male activities such as smoking and drinking in pubs. The cartoonist visually exaggerates the bloomered women and their outfits and contrasts them with the respectable, modest women who shy away from them. In the image, street urchins also publicly ridicule them. Elizabeth Cady Stanton later observed that this ridicule is what eventually convinced her to abandon the outfit, much as she liked it. *Mary Evans Picture Library.*

Cady Stanton later recalled.[36] For the next several years, Mott instructed her young protégée in the principles of women's rights. Cady Stanton lobbied in the New York legislature for reform of married women's economic rights. In April 1848, the legislature passed the first New York State Married Women's Property Act that gave wives control over inherited (but not earned) wealth.

By this time, Cady Stanton was the mother of four boys and living in the small industrial town of Seneca Falls, New York. Her husband was often away working for the abolitionist cause. With Lucretia Mott as her teacher and Henry Stanton as her husband, Elizabeth Cady Stanton was perfectly situated to bridge the gap between the moral activist tradition of women reformers and the increasingly political focus within abolitionism. She was also eager for a dramatic change in her own life. "The general discontent I felt with woman's portion as wife, mother, housekeeper, physician, and spiritual guide," she wrote, "the wearied, anxious look of the majority of women impressed me with a strong feeling that some active measures should be taken to right the wrongs of society in general, and of women in particular."[37] In July 1848, Cady Stanton, Lucretia Mott, Mott's sister Martha Coffin Wright, and two other local female abolitionists called a public meeting in a local church to discuss "the social, civil and religious condition of Woman." Of the approximately three hundred women and men who attended, one-third, including a large contingent of Quakers, endorsed a manifesto titled "Declaration of Sentiments and Resolutions," which, in part, rewrote the Declaration of Independence to declare that "all men *and women* are created equal" (emphasis added).[38]

The Seneca Falls manifesto went on to list eighteen instances of "repeated injuries and usurpations on the part of man toward woman." (See the Appendix, p. A-1, for the complete text.) Women were unjustly denied access to professions, trades, and education; their rights in marriage and motherhood; their self-confidence; and their moral equality before God. The most controversial resolution asserted women's equal right to vote. To abolitionist purists, however, resort to the ballot represented participation in a fundamentally corrupt system. Yet more and more issues about which women cared — including temperance and abolition — were being debated and resolved within the electoral arena. And, as Cady Stanton repeatedly insisted, all the other changes needed in women's condition would ultimately require women's ability to affect the law. Frederick Douglass, living nearby in Rochester, was the only man in the room who could not vote, and he supported the suffrage resolution eloquently. After debate, the delegates passed it.

In the years after the Seneca Falls Convention, the women's rights movement grew energetically but haphazardly. Lucy Stone, the first U.S. woman college graduate and a traveling lecturer on abolition and women's rights, inspired many women to join the ranks. Women learned about the new movement from friends and relatives. In 1851, Susan B. Anthony, living in nearby Rochester, heard about it from her mother and sister, traveled the short distance to Seneca Falls, and there met Cady Stanton. The two women immediately formed a working friendship that lasted sixty years. Women brought women's rights ideas with them as they migrated west. In 1850, California emigrants Eliza Farnham and Georgiana Bruce (later Kirby) debated women's rights as side by side they plowed their Santa Cruz farm. Beginning with a national women's rights meeting in Worcester, Massachusetts, in 1850, women's rights advocates met in conventions to share ideas, recruit new adherents, and fortify themselves for future efforts. At one such meeting, in 1851 in Akron, Ohio, abolitionist and former slave Sojourner Truth delivered a women's rights speech that has come down through the years as a forceful case for a new standard of womanhood expansive enough to include women like herself (see Reading into the Past: "I Am as Strong as Any Man").

READING INTO THE PAST

SOJOURNER TRUTH
I Am as Strong as Any Man

The most oft-cited version of Sojourner Truth's eloquent 1851 women's rights speech was published by a white activist, Frances D. Gage, twelve years after it was delivered. Recently, historian Nell Painter has drawn attention to a version of the speech published in the Anti-Slavery Bugle *at the time Truth made her remarks. In this presumably more accurate version, Truth makes her important argument for women's rights on the basis of her own experience of black womanhood but without the southern dialect, the "Ain't I a woman" refrain, or the lament for her children lost to slavery, all of which Gage attributed to her.*

I am a woman's rights [woman]. I have as much muscle as any man, and can do as much work as any man. I have plowed and reaped and husked and chopped and mowed, and can any man do more than that? I have heard much about the sexes being equal; I can carry as much as any man, and can eat as much too, if I can get it. I am as strong as any man that is now. . . .

   I can't read, but I can hear. I have heard the Bible and have learned that Eve caused man to sin. Well, if woman upset the world, do give her a chance to set it right side up again. The Lady has spoken about Jesus, how he never spurned woman from him, and she was right. When Lazarus died, Mary and Martha came to him with faith and love and besought him to raise their brother. And Jesus wept and Lazarus came forth. And how came Jesus into the world? Through God who created him and the woman who bore him. Man, where was your part?

SOURCE: Marius Robinson, *The Anti-Slavery Bugle*, June 21, 1851, reprinted in Nell Irvin Painter, *Sojourner Truth: A Life, a Symbol* (New York: Norton, 1996).

QUESTIONS FOR ANALYSIS

1. How is Truth using her own experience to expand the definition of womanhood?
2. How does Truth interpret the Bible through a women's rights lens?

Gradually, these pioneering activists began to reform the laws that denied women, especially wives, their rights, particularly their economic rights. Cady Stanton and Anthony conducted the most successful of these early campaigns in New York State. Cady Stanton, confined by her growing brood of children, wrote the speeches and petitions from her Seneca Falls home. In these years, she spoke in public only once, in 1854, before the members of the New York legislature. Anthony, freer as an unmarried woman, traveled through the state to collect signed petitions on behalf of women's civil and political rights. Women's rights reformers also confronted cultural practices such as fashion that, along with laws, constrained women.

In 1860, the New York State legislature finally passed a more comprehensive Married Women's Property Act that gave wives the rights to own and sell their own property, to control their own wages, and to claim rights over their children upon separation or divorce. Cady Stanton was ready to move on to a campaign to liberalize divorce laws, but this was too much even for women's rights radicals. Moreover, by this point, political conflicts over slavery between North and South had reached such a level of intensity that, like other Americans, women's rights activists were thoroughly preoccupied with the fate of the Union.

◆ CIVIL WAR, 1861–1865

Ever since the northern states had ended slavery early in the nineteenth century, national political leaders had tried to ignore the practice as an exclusively southern problem. In 1820, Congress had crafted the Missouri Compromise, which drew a line across the territories of the Louisiana Purchase at the southern border of the new slave state of Missouri and declared that no further slave states (with the exception of Missouri itself) could be established north of it. The goal was to keep the number of slave and nonslave states equal so as to give neither side an advantage in the Senate. Despite the petitions of abolitionist women, the two major parties, the Democrats and the Whigs, cooperated in keeping debate over slavery out of national politics. But continuing western expansion, especially the 1848 acquisition of lands from Mexico that lay outside the Louisiana Territory, eroded this fragile political balance.

In 1850, congressional leaders crafted a second compromise. California would enter the Union as a nonslave state, in exchange for which special federal commissioners would be appointed with the power to return people charged with being runaway slaves to those who claimed to be their masters. Although slave-catching of fugitive slaves was already protected by the Constitution and existing federal legislation, the 1850 Fugitive Slave Act strengthened the law in favor of slaveholders and increased the threat of kidnapping for free people of color in the North. What southerners regarded as proper federal protection of their property rights, northerners regarded as evidence that an expansive slave power was taking over the country. From this point forward, the expansion of slavery became an increasingly explosive national political issue, culminating in

♦ **Margaret Garner**

Six years after the Fugitive Slave Act was passed, Kentucky slave Margaret Garner and her family fled across the Ohio River to freedom. When slave-catchers caught up with them, Garner killed her daughter Priscilla rather than see her returned to slavery. The ensuing fugitive slave trial, the longest in American history, defended Margaret from return to Kentucky on the grounds that she must be tried for murder under Ohio law. The strategy failed and she was reenslaved, sold further south, and died of typhoid two years later. Both abolitionists and proslavery forces made her trial a cause célèbre. Which position does this 1867 painting of the episode support? *Library of Congress, 3b31109.*

the secession of South Carolina in December 1860 and the beginning of the Civil War in April 1861.

Just as the Civil War pitted brother against brother, women, too, were intensely divided in their loyalties, with the difference, of course, that women were barred from both the ballot box and the battlefield. But as in all civil wars, the home front was impossible to separate from the battle front. Women on both sides actively supported their causes and their armies. A small but surprising number participated directly, either on the battlefield or in the politics that shaped the changing purposes for which the war was fought. All women were affected by the war — its passions, victories, devastations, and deaths.

Women and the Impending Crisis

As the political conflict over slavery intensified, women were drawn into the growing crisis. Most famously, Harriet Beecher Stowe wrote *Uncle Tom's Cabin* to dramatize the dangers facing the escaping slave under the new federal law. By far the most popular American novel ever written, the story of the slave Eliza fleeing slave-catchers to save her child was avidly read when it first appeared in installments in an antislavery newspaper in 1851 and 1852. Inspired by Stowe's book, Harriet Jacobs, who had actually escaped from slavery twelve years before, determined to write her own story. *Incidents in the Life of a Slave Girl: Written by Herself* was published in 1861, with the help of white abolitionist Lydia Maria Child. (See Chapter 4.)

Throughout the political events of the 1850s, women's involvement was everywhere. In 1854, the Republican Party was founded to oppose the expansion (though not the existence) of slavery, and it succeeded in bringing the issue squarely into the center of national politics. The party's 1856 presidential nominee was U.S. senator John Frémont of California, one of the men who had originally surveyed the Oregon Trail. His wife, Jessie Benton Frémont, was the first wife of a presidential candidate to figure significantly in a national campaign. Daughter of U.S. senator Thomas Hart Benton of Missouri, the young, attractive, and vivacious woman was considered a liberal influence on her husband. Campaign paraphernalia advertised Jessie as much as her husband. Although John Frémont was defeated by the Democratic candidate, James Buchanan, the Republicans succeeded in displacing the Whigs to become one of the two major national parties.

Then, in 1857, the Supreme Court ruled in favor of slavery in the momentous case *Dred Scott v. Sandford*. The case might more appropriately be called the Dred and Harriet Scott case since it involved not only Missouri slave Dred Scott but also his wife, Harriet. Together they sued their owner for their freedom and that of their two daughters. By being brought in 1834 into federal territory where slavery was not lawful, the Scotts argued, they had become free persons. A majority of the Supreme Court ruled against the Scotts. In addition, Chief Justice Roger B. Taney wrote an opinion that the entire legal framework dating back to the Missouri Compromise was unconstitutional because it violated slaveowners' property rights. The sons of the Scotts' original owner eventually bought them their freedom, but the larger battle between pro- and antislavery forces for control of the federal government had been profoundly intensified by the decision.

The election of 1860 took place against the background of abolitionist John Brown's abortive guerrilla raid on the federal armory in Harpers Ferry, Virginia, which was intended (but failed) to start a general slave uprising. To southerners, the handful of black and white antislavery warriors under Brown's command constituted exactly the violent threat that they long had feared from abolitionists. Many northerners regarded Brown quite differently, as a martyr. "I thank you that you have been brave enough to reach out your hands to the crushed and blighted of my race," Frances Ellen Watkins Harper wrote to Brown as he awaited execution

◆ **Harriet Beecher Stowe**
This is likely the earliest photograph of author Harriet Beecher Stowe. Although the exact date is unknown, it was probably taken between the birth of her fifth child in 1843 and the publication, in 1852, of the novel that made her world-famous. *Private Collection/Bridgeman Images.*

after his capture by federal forces. "I hope from your sad fate great good may arise to the cause of freedom."[39]

For president, the Republicans nominated former Illinois congressman Abraham Lincoln, a moderate critic of slavery, hardly an abolitionist. Nonetheless, his election was intolerable to the South because he was a Republican. But to many northerners, Lincoln's election was cause to celebrate. Twenty-one-year-old

Frances Willard, who would go on to head the Woman's Christian Temperance Union in the 1870s, observed events from her Illinois home: "Under the present system I am not allowed to vote for [Lincoln], but I am as glad on account of this Republican triumph as any man who has exercised the elective franchise can be."[40]

By April 1861, eleven southern slave states had seceded from the Union to form the Confederate States of America. On April 13, South Carolina slaveholder Mary Chesnut watched as southern gunboats fired on U.S. ships that Lincoln had sent to provision federal Fort Sumter in Charleston harbor. She recorded her reaction upon learning that federal forces had surrendered to the Confederates: "[I] sprang out of bed and on my knees—prostrate—I prayed as I never prayed before."[41]

Chesnut understood that war had begun in earnest. North and South, men and boys rushed to enroll in their local regiments, and wives and mothers prepared to say good-bye. "Love for the old flag became a passion," wrote Mary Livermore from Illinois, "and women crocheted it prettily in silk, and wore it as a decoration on their bonnets and in their bosoms."[42] Both sides hoped for a brief war and a glorious victory but got instead a four-year conflict, the deadliest war in American history.

Women's Involvement in the War

Although formally excluded from enlistment and armed service, both Union and Confederate women were deeply involved in the war. Eager and patriotic, a minority found their way to the battlefields, as nurses, spies, and strategists; a few, disguised as men, even served as soldiers. (See Primary Sources: "Women on the Civil War Battlefields," pp. 273–86.) Far more women participated at a distance. Because both armies were decentralized and almost entirely unprovisioned—except for munitions—by their respective governments, women volunteers were responsible for much of the clothing, feeding, and nursing of the soldiers. In the South, this was done at a local level. Within a few months after the conflict had begun, Mary Ann Cobb, wife of a Confederate officer in Georgia, found herself charged with rounding up provisions for a company of eighty men, largely by going door-to-door among her neighbors.

In the North, where women had greater experience in running their own voluntary associations, soldiers' relief was better organized. Local societies were drawn together in a national organization known as the United States Sanitary Commission. Mary Livermore spent the war directing the Chicago branch. Her duties were manifold: "I . . . delivered public addresses to stimulate supplies and donations of money; . . . wrote letters by the thousand . . . ; made trips to the front with sanitary stores . . . ; brought back large numbers of invalid soldiers . . . ; assisted to plan, organize, and conduct colossal [fund-raising] fairs . . . ; detailed women nurses . . . and accompanied them to their posts."[43] The experience turned Livermore and others like her into skilled, confident organization women, and after the war they used these experiences to build even more ambitious women's federations. On the basis of her experience organizing relief supplies for northern soldiers, Clara Barton went on to found the American division of the International Red Cross.

The labors of such women earned them elaborate praise. But for the average woman on either side of the conflict, these were not so much years of uplifting service or patriotic heroism as years of prolonged suffering. Women struggled to support their families without the aid of husbands, sons, and brothers. Anna Howard Shaw, who later became one of America's leading suffragists, was a young woman living in rural Michigan in 1861: "I remember seeing a man ride up on horseback, shouting out Lincoln's demand for troops. . . . Before he had finished speaking the men on the [threshing] machine had leaped to the ground and rushed off to enlist, my brother Jack . . . among them. . . . The work in our community, if it was done at all, was done by despairing women whose hearts were with their men."[44]

Since the North lost much of its labor force to the fighting, the South, which relied on slave workers, initially had the advantage. Even so, most white southerners were small-scale subsistence farmers who relied almost entirely on their own labor rather than on that of slaves. Numerous women from these families demanded that the Confederate government excuse their husbands from service or provide them with the wherewithal to support their families. For a group of women who had long served only as symbols of southern patriotism and objects of husbandly protection, this signaled the beginning of direct political engagement. With or without official leaves, numerous southern soldiers responded to the entreaties of their wives to leave their posts, come home, and bring in the harvest. "Since your connection with the Confederate army, I have been prouder of you than ever before . . . ," one such woman wrote to her husband, "but before God, Edward, unless you come home we must die."[45] By the middle of the war, such seasonal desertions, conservatively estimated at more than one hundred thousand, as much as 10 percent of the Confederate forces, were a major strain on the South's capacity to fight.

As the conflict wore on, patriotism and optimism gave way to discontent on both sides. In the South, the situation was exacerbated by a Union naval blockade that led to food shortages and triple-digit inflation. In the spring of 1863, the women of Richmond rampaged through the streets protesting the high cost of food and demanding that they be able to buy bread and meat at the same prices as the Confederate armies. Three months later, New York City was paralyzed by mobs protesting passage of a federal Conscription Act that allowed wealthy men to buy themselves out of the draft for $300. Elizabeth Cady Stanton, who had just moved to the city with her three youngest children, found herself in the middle of the upheaval. She watched with horror as one of her older sons was recognized by the rioters as "one of those three-hundred-dollar fellows." "You may imagine what I suffered in seeing him dragged off," she wrote to her cousin. Alone with her children, Cady Stanton prepared a speech to deliver, if necessary, which aimed to "appeal to them as Americans and citizens of the Republic."[46] As the mob redirected their violence toward the city's African Americans, Adelaide Butler, the free black matron of the Colored Orphan Asylum also sprang into action to shepherd over two hundred children to safety while the orphanage burned to the ground behind them.

Emancipation

While the South was fighting to preserve slavery and defend its sovereignty, the war aims of the North remained muddled. For more than a year, Lincoln insisted that his only goal was to end secession and restore the Union. The president was unwilling to declare opposition to slavery for fear that the border states of Kentucky, Missouri, Maryland, and Delaware, where slavery was legal, would leave the Union and join the Confederacy. The abolition of slavery became the Union's goal only after slaves themselves took action through a massive, prolonged process of what has been characterized as "self-emancipation." Like the slaves who for decades had run away, men and women in large numbers began to flee into the arms of the Union army, buoyed by news of northern victories and hoping that they would be freed. One woman described her escape onto a Union gunboat sailing down the Mississippi River. "We all give three times three cheers for the gunboat boys and three times three cheers for big Yankee sojers an three times three cheers for gov'ment," she recalled; "an I tell you every one of us, big and little, cheered loud and long and strong, an' made the old river just ring ag'in."[47] Union officers disagreed on how to respond to the masses of refugees. Those unsympathetic to the antislavery cause wanted to return them to their owners, but the army eventually decided on a policy of accepting them under the category of confiscated enemy property. Thousands of these human "contraband" provided crucial aid to the Union army as laborers, cooks, and servants. As many as forty thousand gathered in Washington, D.C., where Sojourner Truth, Harriet Jacobs, and others organized a freedmen's village.

As their numbers increased, Lincoln realized that the steady flight of the southern slave labor force offered an irresistible military advantage to the Union. Accordingly, he issued the Emancipation Proclamation, to take effect on January 1, 1863, which declared all slaves in rebel territory "forever free" and instructed the Union army and navy to "recognize and maintain the freedom of such persons." The status of slaves living in the Union border states and areas of the Confederacy already under Union control, however, was left untouched. Since the Union could not actually emancipate slaves in lands it did not control, the proclamation was meant only to encourage slaves in the renegade regions to abandon their masters and free themselves. Despite its limits, however, the Emancipation Proclamation finally made the Civil War a war against slavery.

Women's rights leaders Elizabeth Cady Stanton and Susan B. Anthony were determined to push Lincoln to enact a more comprehensive abolition policy. "If it be true that at this hour, the women of the South are more devoted to their cause than we to ours, the fact lies here," wrote Cady Stanton. "The women of the South know what their sons are fighting for. The women of the North do not."[48] (See Primary Sources: "Women's Rights Partnership: Elizabeth Cady Stanton and Susan B. Anthony in the 1850s and 1860s," pp. 266–72.) Along with Lucy Stone and other women's rights activists, they formed the Women's National Loyal League to force Lincoln to adopt a broader emancipation policy. As abolitionist women had done thirty years before, they gathered signatures on petitions to Congress to "pass at the earliest practicable day an act emancipating all persons of African descent."[49] The league collected and submitted to Congress 260,000 signatures, two-thirds of them from women. The first popular campaign ever conducted on behalf of a constitutional amendment, these efforts contributed significantly to the 1865 passage and ratification of the Thirteenth Amendment, which permanently abolished slavery throughout the United States.

In 1863, after two years of grueling warfare, the military tide began to turn in the Union's favor. An important factor was the Union army's decision to permit African American men to fight. Close to two hundred thousand enlisted, providing a final burst of military energy as well as a manly model of black freedom. Black women such as Susie King Taylor and Harriet Tubman lived and traveled with these troops, serving as nurses, spies, and military laborers. (See Primary Sources: "Women on the Civil War Battlefields," pp. 273–86.) On July 4, 1863, the Union won a decisive battle at Vicksburg, Mississippi, just one day after its equally decisive victory at Gettysburg, Pennsylvania. Still, the war lasted two more years. In the autumn of 1864, General William Tecumseh Sherman marched the western division of the Union army across Georgia and South Carolina, determined to break the spirit of the rebellion by destroying everything of value as he went. At her plantation, Mary Chesnut found "every window was broken, every bell torn down, every piece of furniture destroyed, every door smashed in."[50]

Finally, on April 9, 1865, almost four years to the day after the attack on Fort Sumter, General Robert E. Lee, head of the Confederate army, surrendered. An ex-slave woman from South Carolina remembered, "[On] de fust day of freedom we was all sittin' roun' restin' an' tryin' to think what freedom meant an ev'ybody was quiet an' peaceful."[51] "The people poured into the streets, frenzied with gladness," wrote Mary Livermore, "until there seemed to be no men and women in Chicago, — only crazy, grown-up boys and girls." Then, five days later, Lincoln was assassinated. "From the height of this exultation," Livermore wrote, "the nation was swiftly precipitated to the very depths of despair." She continued, "Never was a month so crowded, with the conflicting emotions of exultation and despair, as was the month of April 1865."[52] Not all women saw it the same way. "Thank God, the wretch has gotten his just deserts," exulted a Confederate woman.[53]

◆ CONCLUSION: Reshaping Boundaries, Redefining Womanhood

In the years from 1840 to 1865, the women of the United States had traveled a tremendous distance. They had taken a country across a continent. They had joined in a series of social movements to remake and reform American society. They had challenged slavery and undertaken systematic reform in their own status as women. They had begun to demand their inclusion in the democratization of American politics. And, along with men but in their own ways, they had joined in the fight over the character and existence of the Union, participating in the Civil War both on and off the battlefield.

Their experiences through these changes had by no means been the same. Some women had taken possession of new land, in the process displacing others from their homes of long standing. Some had challenged crucial elements of American society and culture and ended up challenging conventional notions of womanhood itself. And while some had defended and lost their right to own slaves, those who had been slaves became free women. Through all of this, however, American women had been deeply involved in these years of momentous national change and had been changed in the process. In the decades after the Civil War, in the victorious North and the defeated South, they began to enter more fully into public life, as workers and socially engaged citizens, in civic organizations and in colleges. Like 1848, 1865 was a decisive year in the history of the nation and of its women.

CHAPTER 5 REVIEW

KEY TERMS AND PEOPLE

Terms
moral reform societies
Daughters of Temperance
    societies
Ladies Physiological Society of
    Boston
Philadelphia Female Anti-
    Slavery Society
New York State Married
    Women's Property Act
Seneca Falls Convention
Uncle Tom's Cabin

People
Sarah Winnemucca
Arcadia Bandini Stearns
Susan B. Anthony
Mary Gove Nichols
Sarah Mapps Douglass
Elizabeth Cady Stanton
Harriet Beecher Stowe
Lucretia Mott
Sarah and Angelina Grimké
Frances Wright
Ernestine Rose

Lucy Stone
Margaret Garner
Susie King Taylor
Harriet Tubman
Mary Ann Bickerdyke

REVIEW QUESTIONS

1. What was the significance of U.S. territorial expansion for American women? How did expansion bring different groups of women into conflict with each other across lines of race, ethnicity, region, and class?

2. How did women's reform movements either strengthen or challenge the tenets of true womanhood? Analyze the underlying connections *between* various women's reform movements — for instance, the relationship between abolition and health reforms.

3. Although war is often viewed through a male frame, how would you describe women's involvement in the Civil War, both on the home front and on the battlefield?

4. **Making Connections** How did America's diverse women engage with the overarching idea of Manifest Destiny and the increasingly controversial institution of slavery in these decades of national expansion? When considering various women's labor and family roles, what changes and continuities can you identify in the antebellum period?

Female Labor in the Gold-Rush Economy

THE GOLD RUSH PRESENTED CALIFORNIA'S working women with both unusual entrepreneurial opportunities and greater vulnerability to exploitation. The 1850 census showed that women and girls made up only 8 percent of California's nonnative population. By 1860, the proportion of females increased to 28 percent. Within communities of new migrants, the scarcity of females put a premium on the domestic and sexual labor traditionally provided by women. With access to capital and a bit of luck, some women were able to take advantage of their circumstances and even accumulate family property. Many working-class women and women of color living near mining camps pursued the same promise of upward mobility but frequently encountered isolation, poverty, and violence. Indigenous women, who had long been hired as domestic workers on Californio ranchos, now encountered new and lethal forms of coercive labor under U.S. occupation. While individual stories offer examples of remarkable resourcefulness and initiative, the overall economic prospects of California's women in the gold-rush era divided along lines of race, class, and indigeneity.

The new technology of photography produced many images of diverse communities of men at work panning gold. Figure 5.1 offers a rare photograph of a woman at a mining site. Judging from her clothing and the basket in her hand, what economic contributions is she likely to be making to this group of miners?

FAMILY ECONOMIES AND WOMEN'S DOMESTIC WORK

AS THE FOLLOWING DOCUMENTS ON WHITE, African American, and Native American women and girls reveal, women's working lives during the gold rush varied as much as their ethnic and class backgrounds. Although some women spent time prospecting for gold, they were more likely to do cooking, laundering, boarding, and sewing for miners willing to pay high prices. In many migrant households, married women's domestic work brought much-needed cash to the family economy, especially when prospecting proved fruitless. The sources that follow reflect a range of women's experiences with economic success and failure in the gold fields northeast of Sacramento. Compare and contrast the documents by or about white "49er" Luzena Wilson, former slave Nancy Gooch, and Cherokee migrant Barbara Longknife. How did the gender segregation of labor shape the earning abilities of gold-rush women? How might each of these women have viewed their work for money in relation to their unpaid labor for their families?

◆ **Figure 5.1 Panning for Gold in Auburn Ravine (c. 1852)**
The Granger Collection, New York.

LUZENA STANLEY WILSON '49ER

LUZENA STANLEY HUNT WAS BORN TO A QUAKER FAMILY in North Carolina, but later moved to Missouri and married Mason Wilson. Luzena and Mason Wilson traveled overland to California in 1849 with their two small boys. In 1881 she recounted her days as a "Forty-niner" to her daughter Correnah Wilson Wright, who typed up her narrative. Mills College, Correnah's alma mater, published the memoir in 1937. After a grueling continental crossing and six months of residence in Sacramento, the Wilsons moved out to the mining camp of Nevada City, where Luzena looked for an opportunity to contribute to the family income. From Wilson's vantage point, women's scarcity elevated their position and opened the door to economic opportunity. How does Wilson use her domestic skills to her family's advantage? In doing so, does she adhere to the conventions of true womanhood or transgress them? What do you make of Wilson's statement that "I shortly after took my husband into partnership"? Who might she have hired for her cook and waiters? How might this account have been different if Wilson had been keeping a diary instead of retelling the family history to her daughter thirty years later?

Memories Recalled Years Later for Her Daughter (1937)

Chapter Six

From the brow of a steep mountain we caught the first glimpse of a mining camp. Nevada City, a row of canvas tents lining each of the two ravines, which, joining, emptied into Deer Creek, lay at our feet, flooded with the glory of the spring sunshine. The gulches seemed alive with moving men. Great, brawny miners wielded the pick, and shovel, while others stood knee deep in the icy water, and washed the soil from the gold. Every one seemed impelled by the frenzy of fever as men hurried here and there, so intent upon their work they had scarcely time to breathe. Our entrance into the busy camp could not be called a triumphal one, and had there been a "back way" we should certainly have selected it. Our wagon wheels looked like solid blocks; the color of the oxen was indistinguishable, and we were mud from head to foot. I remember filling my wash-basin three times with fresh water before I had made the slightest change apparent in the color of my face; and I am sure I scrubbed till my arms ached, before I got the children back to their natural hue. We were not rich enough to indulge in the luxury of a canvas home; so a few pine boughs and branches of the undergrowth were cut and thrown into a rude shelter for the present, and my husband hurried away up the mountain to begin to split out "shakes" for a house. Since our experience of rain in Sacramento, we were inclined to think that rain was one of the daily or at least weekly occurrences of a California spring, and the first precaution was to secure a water-tight shelter. Our bedding was placed inside the little brush house, my cook stove set up near it under the shade of a great pine tree, and I was

established, without further preparation, in my new home. When I was left alone in the afternoon — it was noon when we arrived — I cast my thoughts about me for some plan to assist in the recuperation of the family finances. As always occurs to the mind of a woman, I thought of taking boarders. There was already a thriving establishment of the kind just down the road, under the shelter of a canvas roof, as was set forth by its sign in lamp-black on a piece of cloth: "Wamac's Hotel. Meals $1.00."

I determined to set up a rival hotel. So I bought two boards from a precious pile belonging to a man who was building the second wooden house in town. With my own hands I chopped stakes, drove them into the ground, and set up my table. I bought provisions at a neighboring store, and when my husband came back at night he found, mid the weird light of the pine torches, twenty miners eating at my table. Each man as he rose put a dollar in my hand and said I might count him as a permanent customer. I called my hotel "El Dorado."

From the first day it was well patronized, and I shortly after took my husband into partnership. The miners were glad to get something to eat, and were always willing to pay for it. As in Sacramento, goods of all kinds sold at enormous figures, but, as no one ever hesitated to buy on that account, dealers made huge profits. The most rare and costly articles of luxury were fruits and vegetables. One day that summer an enterprising pioneer of agricultural tastes brought in a wagon load of watermelons and sold them all for an ounce (sixteen dollars) each. I bought one for the children and thought no more of the price than one does now of buying a dish of ice-cream. Peaches sold at from one to two dollars each and were miserable apologies for fruit at that. Potatoes were a dollar a pound and for a time even higher. As the days progressed we prospered. In six weeks we had saved money enough to pay the man who brought us up from Sacramento the seven hundred dollars we owed him. In a little time, the frame of a house grew up around me, and presently my cook stove and brush house were enclosed under a roof. This house was gradually enlarged room by room, to afford accommodation for our increasing business. . . . We had then from seventy-five to two hundred boarders at twenty-five dollars a week. I became luxurious and hired a cook and waiters. Maintaining only my position as managing housekeeper, I retired from active business in the kitchen.

SOURCE: *Luzena Stanley Wilson, '49er: Memories Recalled Years Later for Her Daughter Correnah Wilson Wright* (Oakland, CA: The Eucalyptus Press, 1937).

NANCY GOOCH REUNITES HER FAMILY IN CALIFORNIA

LIKE LUZENA WILSON, NANCY GOOCH TRAVELED from Missouri to California but her overland journey was a forced one. Slaveholder William Gooch took Nancy and Peter with him when he struck out for the goldfields, leaving behind the enslaved couple's three-year-old son Andrew. In 1850, when California passed a constitution outlawing chattel slavery, Nancy and Peter began to work for themselves. Nancy Gooch did domestic work and took in laundry. The Gooches bought farmland in Coloma by 1858 and eventually even acquired the original gold discovery site of Sutter's Mill. They did so in a hostile legal environment in which state laws prevented African Americans from voting or testifying against whites in court. The state even passed its own Fugitive Slave Law in 1852 to allow former slaveholders to claim enslaved people who arrived with them in California before the 1850 state constitution was ratified. After Peter passed away in 1861, Nancy Gooch continued her domestic work, carefully accumulating the $700 needed to send for her son Andrew and his family.[54] Postwar emancipation opened the door Gooch had been waiting for and by 1870, she used her savings to bring her son to California. She lived until 1901 in Coloma, surrounded by her extended family.

Domestic portraiture for both white and black Americans in the mid-nineteenth century served as a sign of respectability and middle-class aspiration. The photo shown in Figure 5.2 was taken in 1857, when Nancy and Peter Gooch were still struggling to acquire land and save enough money to reunite their family. At this point, their son remained enslaved and beyond their reach. Figure 5.3 portrays the Gooch/Monroe family around 1870, when Nancy had finally managed to bring together her son, Andrew (seated with a child on his lap), along with his wife and other sons. Considered together, what do these photographs convey to you about the importance of marriage and extended family for black Californians? What is the possible significance of the book Nancy Gooch is holding in Figure 5.3? What comparisons can you make between Nancy Gooch's status as a domestic worker and laundrywoman and her self-presentation in these family portraits? Note the photographers' backgrounds, clothing, facial expression, and posture.

◆ **Figure 5.2** **Peter and Nancy Gooch Portrait, San Francisco (1858)**
Courtesy of California State Parks.

◆ **Figure 5.3** **Nancy Gooch and the Monroe Family (c. 1870)**
El Dorado County Historical Museum.

BARBARA LONGKNIFE WRITES HOME TO INDIAN COUNTRY FROM THE GOLDFIELDS

L IVING IN COLOMA DURING THE 1850S, the Cherokee woman Barbara Longknife could easily have known Nancy Gooch. The migration to California wasn't her first overland journey, for as a ten-year-old girl, Barbara had been forcibly removed with her family from Cherokee traditional lands in the East to Indian Territory (see pp. 176–77). In 1850, pregnant with her first child, Barbara and her husband, William Longknife, journeyed with a larger group of Cherokees to California. Barbara's letters to Stand Watie, head of a prominent family in the Cherokee Nation, offer a "counter narrative of the gold rush" that speaks mainly of a working woman's economic struggle and home-sickness.[55] Responsibilities for her family—in particular for her sick daughter—com-pounded the burden of Longknife's domestic work. The letters preserve Longknife's original spelling. What insight do these letters give you into Longknife's contributions to her family's survival? What are the main sources of her dissatisfaction? How did Longknife use her letters to maintain her ties with family in the Cherokee Nation?

Barbara Longknife to Stand Watie, Coloma, June 8, 1854

Dear Sir,

I gladly embrace the present opertunity of addressing you by the way of this letter. we are in moderate health at the present time and hope these lines may find you and your family emjoying the same blessing. we have made nothing in this country as yet more than barely supported the family. William has been trying his luck in the mines, did not make it pay over board, we have had a great deal of sickness in our family since we came to this Country and our doctor bills has cost us a great many dollars together with other expenses connected with Dr. Bills. we are still living in Coloma and I think it is very probable we will remain here as long as we stay in this Country. I would like very much to see all my old friends in the nation. California is not what it was represented to be, if I was back again I would let California be the last place that I would go to. I am engage in washing at present and have been for a considerable length of time it pays better than anything else that I can do. give my best respects to Mr. Huss and all enquiring friends & receive for your self and family the same. You will please write when this comes to hand and give me all the news of importance. William & myself are the only ones of the mess that I know anything about. R. Tuff died on the plains. Welch died after we got here, the last I heard of your Brother Charles he was going north in 52, have'nt heard from him since. John Candy is in this country somewhere, was in this place a few days since, he has not made his pile yet. when you write you will direct your letter to Coloma Eldorado Co California

Very respectfully your friend
Barbary Longknife

Barbara Longknife to Stand Watie, Coloma, October 11, 1857

Dear Cir
I take this opertunity of wrighting you a few lines to let you no we are yet in the land of the living. Charles E. Watie was hear to day, he is working at 3 dolars per day, that is good wages for this time. we are all well except my little girl, she has had the bilious fevor and it has left her all most blind of boarth eays. I live in hopes that her site will come back a gain. if I had money I would take her to some other Doctor but as it is I have the best Doctor thir is in this place. we have made a living in this Country and that is all. to rase money enough to take us home we could not if it was to save us all. we could not do that mush and we have not had that mush at one time cince we have bin in the country and Charles says he dont know wether he ever will make that mush or not;

that he feels old now that he has worked so hard. not only him that has worked I have worked hard as the next one in the Country and all I have is a living. if I did not work as I do we would be so mush behind that we never would get strate again and if I had never come to this Country I would have now what I have not and that is good health. We have dun the best we could cince hire we have been. Every thing has been hy and is yet. baken is 28c per pound pork 25c per pound and beef 25c per pound . . . no the times is gon when Labor was from 5 to 8 a day for some people. It was good for some but not all. . . . now I say to Mr. Longkife if we doe not have moeny enought in two years to take us home I will then Baige min and my childs way home. to stay hear and work as I do any longer than that time I will not put up with it if I can help it. I am willing to help all I can but I an tyeard of this Country. . . .

Mrs. Barbra Longknife

SOURCE: Edward Everett Dale and Gaston Litton, eds., *Cherokee Cavaliers* (Norman: University of Oklahoma Press, 1939).

ENSLAVEMENT AND APPRENTICESHIP OF CALIFORNIA INDIAN WOMEN AND GIRLS

THE RAPID GROWTH OF CALIFORNIA'S POPULATION that brought economic opportunity to some migrant women proved disastrous for Native American women. Tens of thousands of Indian women and girls living in California on the eve of the gold rush suffered extreme violence and terror, including wars of extermination, rape, and de facto slavery in the ensuing years of white expansion.

Figure 5.4 is a hand-colored engraving of a young Native American woman created in the 1850s during peak years of anti-Indian violence. The sobering French caption reads, "Sixteen-year-old Southern California Indian female at the price of a pound of gunpowder and a bottle of brandy."[56] Everything else, from the girl's own story to the artist's name and the purpose of the image, is unknown. What details do you notice in the portrait of the young woman? What further questions would you want to ask about her image and its context?

Apart from de facto trafficking, California Indian children also became subject to an institutionalized system of child labor. State laws governing Native American apprenticeship posed one of the primary contradictions to California's status as a "free" state. The ironically named 1850 Act for the Government and Protection of Indians regulated relations between whites and Native Americans in matters dealing with labor, land and court procedures. It established an Indian convict leasing system, institutionalized whipping as a legal penalty for Indians convicted of stealing, and denied Indian testimony in court against a white person. Section 3, excerpted on the following page, claimed to guard against the "compulsory" detention of Indian minors but, in reality, it opened the door to numerous child kidnappings and even the murder of Indian parents. One historian argues that these laws made Indian children's bonded labor "culturally invisible" because they placed Indian children alongside other family dependents under the patriarchal oversight of white male household heads.[57]

◆ **Figure 5.4 "Indienne Californienne du Sud" (c. 1850s)**

Robert B. Honeyman, Jr. collection of early Californian and Western American pictorial material [graphic], BANC PIC 1963.002:1305:F—ALB. Courtesy of The Bancroft Library, University of California, Berkeley.

California Statutes, Chapter 133
"An Act for the Government and Protection of Indians," 1850, Section 3

Any person having or hereafter obtaining a minor Indian, male or female, from the parents or relations of such Indian minor, and wishing to keep it . . . shall go before Justice of the Peace in his Township, with the parents or friends of the child, and if the Justice of the Peace becomes satisfied that

SOURCE: Kimberly Johnson-Dodds, *Early California Laws and Policies Related to California Indians* (Sacramento: California Research Bureau, September 2002), 28.

no compulsory means have been used to obtain the child from its parents or friends, shall enter on record, in a book kept for that purpose, the sex and probable age of the child, and shall give to such person a certificate, authorizing him or her to have the care, custody, control and earnings of such minor, until he or she obtain the age of majority. Every male Indian shall be deemed to have attained his majority at eighteen, and the female at fifteen years.

A YUKI GIRL'S CONTESTED APPRENTICESHIP

THE CASE OF THE YUKI GIRL "Shasta" (so named for her Shasta mountain origins) demonstrates how guardianship laws worked to give white families legal control over Indian minors. In 1857, San Francisco courts heard white physician Oliver Wozencraft's plea for the return of a young Indian girl he claimed as his ward. Wozencraft charged that a "negro woman" named Charlotte Sophie Gomez had abducted the child from him three years earlier. The details of the case are not fully clear but some additional background is known. Wozencraft had served as a delegate to the California state constitutional convention, where he unsuccessfully proposed a ban on admitting free blacks into the state. Around the time Wozencraft first took Shasta into his household, he had served as a federal Indian Commissioner who attempted to negotiate treaties with northern California Indian tribes. Charlotte Gomez lived in a small community of black San Franciscans who were involved in aiding free blacks whose former owners attempted to have them sent illegally back into southern slave states. Thus, it is possible that Gomez had attempted to shelter Shasta because she believed Wozencraft was holding her captive. Yet, under California law, Gomez could not have testified against Wozencraft in court and, in fact, she found herself facing perjury charges for denying any role in Shasta's removal from Wozencraft's household. In July 1857, a San Francisco probate court, following the law allowing apprenticeship of Indian minors, determined that Wozencraft was a "suitable person to be appointed guardian." Shasta returned to the Wozencraft household, where she resided until at least the 1880s.

Nineteenth-century newspapers can be read for both surface facts and underlying biases. For example, the *Sacramento Daily Union* article on the following page related Wozencraft's version of Shasta's story from her "adoption" to her "abduction." Under what circumstances did Shasta first come into Wozencraft's family? Was she actually an orphan? How does the newspaper describe the actions of Charlotte Gomez and other free African Americans involved in the case? How do they discuss Shasta's Yuki family of birth? It isn't clear whether or not Shasta, like so many other Indian minors, was being held as a domestic laborer. Is it possible that Shasta was truly considered a member of Wozencraft's family?

"Story of 'Shasta,' an Indian Orphan Child" (1856)

An application was made, yesterday, to the Judge of the 4th District Court, for a *habeas corpus* to bring up the person of a little Indian girl, aged about 8 years, and named "Shasta." The application was made by Dr. Oliver M. Wozencraft, and it is from him that we learn the following romantic story:

In the year 1851, Dr. Wozencraft was Indian Commissioner and Agent, and was engaged in making treaties with the various aboriginal tribes living in the remoter portions of the State. In the month of August, of that year, he made arrangements to go among the Uka [Yuki] tribe, who inhabited the Shasta mountains. . . . His object was to chastise the Ukas, for having a short time before surprised a train of packers, whom they murdered and despoiled of all their pack animals and merchandise. They had also endeavored to burn the town of Shasta. . . . Accordingly, the Commissioner, with twenty mounted dragoons and thirty Ylackas [a different group of California Indians] proceeded against the Ukas, and chased them for several days along the stream on which they were located, but the Indians continually escaped up the mountains. . . . [After more than a day's pursuit, the soldiers managed to chase the Yuki men into the remote mountains, but captured a group of "squaws and children secreted in the bushes."]

SOURCE: "Story of 'Shasta,' an Indian Orphan Child," *Sacramento Daily Union*, December 15, 1856.

The following morning, Wozencraft learned that the "captives" had silently escaped from the area under cover of night] . . . but left a little orphan girl about three years old, whom they had during the march treated with great neglect. Dr. Wozencraft took charge of the little unfortunate, and sent her to Mrs. Wozencraft, in San Francisco. That lady adopted, as it were, the orphan, and raised her; becoming more and more attached to her, until some time in September, 1853, "Shasta," for that was the appropriate name bestowed upon the girl, disappeared. Nothing more was heard of her until only a few days ago, when the Doctor and his lady as they were returning from church, met their former ward in the streets. On investigation it was discovered that she was living with certain colored persons, name Collyer and Charlotte Sophie Gomez. The Doctor immediately took measures to regain the custody and care of "Shasta," and procured the issuance of the writ of *habeas corpus*, to which we have referred above.

It may not be uninteresting to state, in connection with the story of Shasta, that the stream upon which the Commissioner encamped has since been named "Squaw Creek," in commemoration of the capture of the Uka women, which took place there. Many miners are located in its region, and the town of Natches is built upon its banks. We also learn that the Uka Indians afterwards accepted the alternative of peace, and became friendly.

QUESTIONS FOR ANALYSIS

1. What role did class, race, and family networks of support play in shaping the kind of gendered labor done by each of the women represented here?

2. How might discriminatory legislation like the testimony laws or the Native American apprenticeship law have curtailed the ability of some groups of women to make a living and acquire property?

3. What opportunities and vulnerabilities to exploitation did women encounter during the California gold rush? How were some women's opportunities related to other women's vulnerabilities?

Women's Rights Partnership: Elizabeth Cady Stanton and Susan B. Anthony in the 1850s and 1860s

Tracing the early nineteenth-century women's rights movement through the half-century-long relationship between Elizabeth Cady Stanton and Susan B. Anthony reminds us that many aspects of that history are best understood in terms of the bonds between women. This particular relationship, though always oriented toward important political events, also illustrates the degree to which domestic demands constrained and informed female reformers, not just wives and mothers like Cady Stanton but also single, self-supporting women like Anthony.

The documents excerpted here allow us to follow the first decade of their relationship through their rich correspondence, augmented by autobiographical and biographical reminiscences, excerpts from the speeches they worked together to produce, and occasional newspaper reports of their activities.

The following account from Cady Stanton's autobiographical reminiscences recalls the friends' first meeting in Seneca Falls, sometime in 1850 or 1851, in connection with an antislavery meeting. The two lived in booming industrial towns only a few hours from each other in upstate New York. Cady Stanton wrote her account thirty years after the fact. How might the intervening years have affected her memories of the event?

Elizabeth Cady Stanton Recalls Meeting Susan B. Anthony (1881)

It was in the month of May, of 1851, that I first met Miss Anthony. . . . There she stood with her good earnest face and genial smile, dressed in gray silk, hat and all the same color, relieved with pale blue ribbons, the perfection of neatness and sobriety.

It is often said by those who know Miss Anthony best, that she has been my good angel, always pushing and guiding me to work. . . . Perhaps all this is in a measure true. With the cares of a large family, I might in time, like too many

women, have become wholly absorbed in a narrow family selfishness, had not my friend been continually exploring new fields for missionary labors. Her description of a body of men on any platform, complacently deciding questions in which women had an equal interest, without an equal voice, readily roused me to a determination to throw a firebrand in the midst of their assembly. . . .

[From 1848 through 1860], Susan B. Anthony circulated petitions both for the civil and political rights of woman throughout the State [New York], traveling in stage coaches and open wagons and sleighs in all seasons, and on foot from door to door through towns and cities, doing her uttermost to rouse women to some sense of their natural rights as human beings, to their civil and political rights as citizens of a republic; . . . they would gruffly tell her they had all the rights they wanted, or rudely shut the door in her face, leaving her to stand outside, petition in hand, with as much contempt as if she were asking alms for herself. None but those who did that petition work in the early days for the slaves and the women, can ever know the hardships and humiliations that were endured.

SOURCE: Elizabeth Cady Stanton, Susan B. Anthony, and Matilda J. Gage, eds., *History of Woman Suffrage* (Rochester, NY: Susan B. Anthony, 1881), 1:56–62.

A PARTICULARLY RICH EXCHANGE OF LETTERS between the two coworkers in 1856 concerns Anthony's involvement in the educational reform movement of the time. Two-thirds of the teachers in the state of New York were women — including, for a while, Anthony herself. Yet only men were allowed to speak at the annual state teachers' conventions. Since 1853, Anthony had challenged that exclusion, and now that she had succeeded, she was getting ready to address the meeting on behalf of an issue of great meaning to her: coeducation. While she was struggling to prepare for one of her first public speeches, her friend was herself preparing for the birth of her sixth child. (For the historic contributions that this daughter grew up to make, see page 418 on Harriot Stanton Blatch's own career as a feminist reformer.) What do these letters tell us about the psychological challenges that women like these faced in undertaking careers as public reformers? How do the personal obstacles that the two women faced differ?

Anthony to Cady Stanton, Rochester
(May 26, 1856)

I hear the [women's rights] movement much talked of & earnest hopes for its spread expressed. But these women dare not speak out their sympathy. . . . Don't you think it would be a good plan to first state what we mean by educating the sexes together, then go on to show how the few institutions that profess to give equal education fail . . . and lastly that it is folly to talk of giving to the sexes equal advantages, while you withhold from them equal motive to improve those advantages. . . . When will you come to Rochester to spend those days, I shall be most happy to see whenever it shall be . . . [you may bring your servant] Amelia and the two babies of course and as many more as convenient. With love.[58]

SOURCE: Ellen Carol DuBois, ed., *The Elizabeth Cady Stanton–Susan B. Anthony Reader: Correspondence, Writings, Speeches* (Boston: Northeastern University Press, 1992), 60–61.

Anthony to Cady Stanton, Home-Getting, along towards 12 O'Clock (June 5, 1856)

And Mrs. Stanton, *not* a *word written* on that Address for *Teachers Convention. This* week was to be *leisure* to me and lo, our [servant] *girl, a wife,* had a *miscarriage* . . . and the Mercy only knows when I can get a moment; and what is *worse*, as the *Lord knows full well,* is, that if I *get all the time* the *world has,* I *can't get up a decent document.* So for the love of me, and for the saving of the

reputation of *womanhood,* I beg you, with one baby on your knee and another at your feet, and four boys whistling, buzzing, hallooing *Ma, Ma,* set your self about the work. . . .

. . . [N]o man can write from *my stand point,* nor no woman but *you,* for all, all would base their *strongest* argument on the *unlikeness* of the *sexes.* . . . Those of you who have the *talent* to do honor to poor — oh! how poor — womanhood, have all given yourselves over to baby-making; and left poor brainless me to battle alone.[59]

SOURCE: DuBois, *Cady Stanton–Anthony Reader,* 61–62.

Cady Stanton to Anthony, Seneca Falls (June 10, 1856)

Dear Susan, Your servant is not dead, but liveth. Imagine me, day in and day out, watching, bathing, nursing, and promenading the precious contents of a little crib in the corner of my room. I pace up and down these two chambers of mine like a caged lioness, longing to bring nursing and house keeping cares to a close. Is your speech to be exclusively

on the point of educating the sexes together, or as to the best manner of educating women? . . . Come here and I will do what I can to help you with your address, if you will hold the baby and make the puddings. . . . It is not well to be in the excitement of public life all the time. . . . You, too, need rest Susan; let the world alone awhile. We cannot bring about a moral revolution in a day or two. Now that I have two daughters, I feel fresh strength to work for women. . . . It is not in vain that in myself I feel all the wearisome cares to which woman even in her best estate is subject. Good night.

SOURCE: Ann D. Gordon, ed., *The Selected Papers of Elizabeth Cady Stanton and Susan B. Anthony,* vol. 1, *In the School of Anti-Slavery, 1840–1866* (New Brunswick, NJ: Rutgers University Press, 1997), 325.

THE FOLLOWING ARE THE FRAGMENTARY NOTES that Anthony left on the speech on coeducation she was struggling to compose in the winter of 1856–57. Her notes are supplemented [in brackets] by quotations of her speech from a contemporary newspaper report. From the bullet point–like notes, can you imagine Anthony delivering her ideas to an audience of not particularly sympathetic men? How does Anthony's approach focus on education as a route to equality for the sexes? What connections did she make between equal education and economic independence for women, an issue to which she was especially attuned?

SUSAN B. ANTHONY
Why the Sexes Should Be Educated Together (1856)

Because their life work is so nearly identical . . . [To earn their bread and live is the work of both sexes. Every woman is born into the world alone and goes out of the world alone. . . . All women do not have husbands, and, besides, fathers and husbands die sometimes, and their wives and daughters may be obliged to earn a livelihood. Every father should educate his sons and daughters alike for upon each may devolve the task of earning their own bread.] The grand thing that is needed is to give the sexes like motives for acquirement — very rarely a person studies closely without hope of making that knowledge useful — as means of support or house or something to them.

That man may learn from his boyhood that woman is his intellectual equal and thus no longer look upon her as his inferior — Oh, dear dear there is so much to say & I am so without constructive power to put in symmetrical order —

Because separation and restraint stimulates the desires and passions . . . [Is it possible that boys and girls who have always associated together cannot go to college together? . . . The sexes behave better and learn better together.]

SOURCE: Enclosure in June 5, 1856, letter, in Gordon, *Selected Papers*, 323–24; and "Address by SBA on Educating the Sexes Together," *Rochester Daily Democrat*, February 4, 1857, ibid., 334–38.

By the end of the 1850s, the two friends were immersed in the national crisis over slavery. Not only were North and South at odds, but so were radical and moderate opponents of slavery. Both Cady Stanton and Anthony, who were strong partisans of the abolitionist movement to end slavery immediately, absolutely, and without compensation to slaveowners, were among the former.

The following are two abolitionist speeches, one given by Anthony in 1859 and the other by Cady Stanton in 1860. While the nation was poised on the brink of civil war, neither the newly arisen Republican Party nor the Lincoln administration it had elected was ready to commit to the abolition of slavery. How do you think Anthony and Cady Stanton sought to increase popular support in the North for the more radical policy of making emancipation of the slaves the purpose of the impending war? How do you think each connects her own condition as a free woman to the suffering of male and female slaves?

SUSAN B. ANTHONY
Make the Slave's Case Our Own (1859)

Let us, my friends, for the passing hour, make the slave's case our own. . . . Let us feel that it is our own children, that are ruthlessly torn from our yearning mother hearts, and driven into the "coffle gang," . . . That it is our own loved sister and daughter, who are shamelessly exposed to the public market, and whose beauty of face, delicacy of complexion, symmetry of form, and grace of motion, do but enhance their monied value, and the more surely victimize them to the unbridled passions and lusts of their proud purchasers.

. . . If, by some magic power, the color of our skins could be instantly changed and the slave's fate made really our own, then would there be no farther need of argument or persuasion, or rhetoric or eloquence. But we . . . look upon the slave, as a being all unlike ourselves. . . . [T]he fact that he has for so many generations been the victim of the white man, seem conclusive evidence to the masses, that a condition that would be torture worse than death to us, is quite endurable, nay, congenial to him. Again, it is argued that we of the North are not responsible for the crime of slave holding, that the guilty ones dwell in the South. . . . Thus, do we put the slave's case far away from us.

SOURCE: Susan B. Anthony, "Make the Slave's Case Our Own," c. 1859, original in Susan B. Anthony Papers, Library of Congress, Washington, DC.

ELIZABETH CADY STANTON
To the American Anti-Slavery Society
(May 8, 1860)

Eloquently and earnestly as noble men have denounced slavery on this platform, they have been able to take only an objective view. . . . [B]ut a privileged class can never conceive the feelings of those who are born to contempt, to inferiority, to degradation. Herein is woman more fully identified with the slave than man can possibly be, for she can take the subjective view. She early learns the misfortune of being born an heir to the crown of thorns, to martyrdom, to womanhood. For while the man is born to do whatever he can, for the woman and the negro there is no such privilege. . . . [A]ll mankind stand on the alert to restrain their impulses, check their aspirations, fetter their limbs, lest, in their freedom and strength, in their full development, they should take an even platform with proud man himself. To you, white man, the world throws wide her gates; the way is clear to wealth, to fame, to glory, to renown, the high places of independence and honor and trust are yours; all your efforts are praised and encouraged; . . . all your successes are welcomed with loud hurrahs and cheers; but the black man and the woman are born to shame. The badge of degradation is the skin and sex.

SOURCE: DuBois, *Cady Stanton–Anthony Reader*, 82–83. The original transcript appeared in the *Liberator*, May 18, 1860, p. 78.

THE FOLLOWING TWO LETTERS SPEAK to the more personal impact on Cady Stanton and Anthony of the grand historic events surrounding the Civil War. The first, written by Cady Stanton in 1859, concerns John Brown's failed raid on the federal armory in Harpers Ferry, Virginia. While white southerners were terrified by Brown's actions, which were intended to spark a nationwide slave revolt, Cady Stanton revered him as a martyr to the cause of abolition. Her more personal connection came through the cousin she mentions, the wealthy abolitionist Gerrit Smith, who covertly supported Brown and suffered a mental breakdown when the plot failed and was exposed.

Five and a half years later, Anthony wrote to Cady Stanton days after the assassination of Abraham Lincoln, just after his second inauguration and the surrender of the Confederacy. Anthony begins by quoting a letter that she wrote to their male ally, Wendell Phillips. None of these abolitionists had supported Lincoln's reelection, because they found his plans for postwar reconstruction too easy on the South. Still, the murder of Lincoln and the prospect of his untried successor, Andrew Johnson, taking over the presidency clearly unnerved Anthony. What do these two letters suggest about the impact of great historic events on individual women's lives? How do Cady Stanton and Anthony express women's frustration over the thwarting of their intense desire to take an active part in the historic conflicts swirling around them?

Cady Stanton to Anthony, Seneca Falls
(December 15, 1859)

The death of my father, the worse than death of my dear cousin Gerrit, the martyrdom of that great and glorious John Brown — all this conspires to make me regret more than ever my dwarfed and perverted womanhood. In times like these, every soul should do the work of a fullgrown man. When I pass the gate of the celestial city and good Peter asks me where I wish to sit, I will say: "Anywhere so that I am neither a negro nor a woman. Confer on me, great angel, the glory of white manhood, . . . so that henceforth I may enjoy the most unlimited freedom."

SOURCE: Ida Husted Harper, *The Life and Work of Susan B. Anthony*, vol. 1 (Indianapolis: Bowen-Merrill, 1899), 181–82.

Anthony to Cady Stanton, Leavenworth, Kansas
(April 19, 1865)

I have this second finished a note to ever glorious [Wendell] Phillips. . . . Told Phillips "if the people had been assembled to consult as to the ability of the Vice President to take forward the Government, the vast majority would have shaken their heads in doubt — but the terrible blow came — the office was vacant — Johnson takes it — and the people already feel him the chosen of God to end the war.["] . . . Was there ever a more terrific command to a nation to "Stand still and know that I am God" since the world began — The Old Book's terrible exhibitions of God's wrath sinks into nothingness — And this blow fell just at the very hour he was declaring his willingness to consign those five millions faithful brave, only loving loyal people of the South to the tender mercies of the ex-slave lords of the lash.

SOURCE: Gordon, *Selected Papers*, 543–44. The original is in the Elizabeth Cady Stanton Papers, Library of Congress, Washington, DC.

THE FINAL DOCUMENT IS A PUBLIC CALL, issued by Cady Stanton and Anthony in mid-1863, to create an organization of "loyal women" of the North. Women on both sides of the war had organized to support their troops (see Primary Sources: "Women on the Civil War Battlefields," pp. 273–86), but women's rights leaders in the North wanted something more. They wanted women to gather together and act politically to make emancipation official nationally; they also wanted women, in Anthony's words, "to give support to the government in so far as it makes a war for freedom."[60] The organization they formed, the Women's National Loyal League, circulated petitions and collected signatures to urge Congress to pass the Thirteenth Amendment to abolish slavery in the United States (see p. 255). How did Cady Stanton and Anthony seek to use the crisis of the Civil War to advance women's consciousness of their political obligations and capacities? What do you think they meant by "loyal"?

ELIZABETH CADY STANTON AND SUSAN B. ANTHONY
Call for a Meeting of the Loyal Women of the Nation (1863)

In this crisis it is the duty of every citizen to consider the peculiar blessings of a republican form of government, and decide what sacrifices of wealth and life are demanded for its defense and preservation. . . . A grand idea of freedom or justice is needful to kindle and sustain the fires of a high enthusiasm. . . . Woman is equally interested and responsible with man in the final settlement of this problem of self-government; therefore let none stand idle spectators now. When every hour is big with destiny and each delay but complicates our difficulties, it is high time for the daughters of the Revolution in solemn council to unseal the last will and testament of the fathers, lay hold of their birthright of freedom and keep it a sacred trust for all coming generations. . . . On behalf of the Woman's Central Committee, ELIZABETH CADY STANTON, SUSAN B. ANTHONY.

SOURCE: Harper, *Susan B. Anthony*, 226–27.

QUESTIONS FOR ANALYSIS

1. What tensions did Cady Stanton and Anthony each experience as they moved into public life?

2. How were Cady Stanton and Anthony able to support each other in their reform work?

3. How did the reforms and political developments of the 1850s affect Cady Stanton and Anthony's beliefs and arguments relating to women's rights?

PRIMARY SOURCES

Women on the Civil War Battlefields

T HE BATTLEFIELD has not always been an exclusively male space. Wives and mothers of common soldiers came to cook, launder, and nurse the men of their families, while officers' wives were permitted social visits with their husbands. But women went to the scene of fighting for other reasons too. Political passions are no respecter of gender, and patriotism, dedication to cause, eagerness to be a part of historic events, and the simple desire for adventure brought women to the bloody heart of the Civil War.

The most common battlefield role of women was nurse — the "angel" of the battlefield who comforted wounded and dying soldiers, representing domestic tranquility in the midst of armed conflict. Despite the desperate need for medical personnel to care for the enormous number of casualties, female nurses had to fight their own kinds of battles with male medical officers for the opportunity to serve. A much smaller number of women also served the Union and Confederate armies in less conventionally womanly ways, as spies, strategists, and even soldiers.

While the Civil War had a tremendous impact on women overall, generating aspirations for greater public responsibilities and more rights, those who had had direct battlefield experience found it difficult to have their particular contributions fully appreciated. Northern male veterans could count on an old-age army pension in recognition of their services. Finally, in 1890, the U.S. government granted pensions to twenty thousand women who served as paid nurses. Approximately one-tenth of these were African American women. Southern white women, of course, had no government to whom they could turn.

Many of the images in this essay are taken from memoirs written by women who served on and around battlefields, who wrote to make sure that the historical record included their stories. They succeeded in permitting us to see the Civil War through women's eyes.

THE NURSES

An estimated ten thousand women served as nurses during the Civil War.[61] Nursing was not yet a profession requiring special training and would not become so until the turn of the twentieth century (see p. 421). At first, both military hospitals and battlefield infirmaries were run by male surgeons who had little to offer the wounded beyond the removal of a limb and whiskey to blunt the pain. Their assistants were also men, themselves often recuperating from battlefield injuries.

Nursing under wartime conditions seemed too brutal for women, an unacceptable offense against their modesty.

Nonetheless, care of the sick and injured was traditionally a female skill, and women began to offer their services as soon as the first call for troops was issued. In the North, Dorothea Dix, already well known for her work to improve the treatment of the insane, persuaded Edwin Stanton, U.S. secretary of war, to appoint her as superintendent of nursing for the Union army. "All nurses are required to be plain looking women," Dix declared. "Their dresses must be brown or black with no bows, no curls, no jewelry and no hoop skirts."[62] Clothing had to be not only respectable but also functional in the gory environment of the military hospitals. Louisa May Alcott, unmarried and struggling to become a writer, was one of those Dix recruited. "I love nursing and *must* let out my pent-up energy in some new way," she wrote in the journal that became her first published book, *Hospital Sketches*. "I want new experiences and am sure to get 'em if I go."[63] In 1861 Congress authorized pay of $12 a month for the female nurses under Dix's supervision, about a third of what male nurses received.

In the regimental hospitals away from Washington, D.C., women whose relatives had been wounded or who felt moved to care for the troops convinced local medical staff to allow them to serve without army commission or pay. Mary Ann Bickerdyke of Illinois became a legend for her battlefield stamina and disregard for military hierarchy. Bickerdyke was a mother and widow in her midforties. She was a dedicated caregiver, moving from battlefield to battlefield, cooking and laundering as well as tending to the Union army wounded. Eventually, she was appointed field agent for the United States Sanitary Commission, which, despite its name, was not part of the government but rather a massive, largely female, volunteer organization that provided clothing and medical supplies to the Union army.

Like other nineteenth-century women with commanding personalities, Bickerdyke assumed the powerful female appellation of "Mother." In an environment that reserved official control for men, the title of "Mother" could be translated into informal public authority. Bickerdyke insisted that she had the right to be near the action and to tend to the troops as she saw fit, on the basis of selfless concern for "her" boys. Indeed, Mother Bickerdyke seems to have treated most of the military men with whom she came into contact, including surgeons and generals, as overgrown boys for whom she knew best. Like other such female figures with unusual public standing who called themselves Mother—such as the late nineteenth-century labor organizer Mother Jones—Bickerdyke used this reworked maternal ideal as a framework for venturing beyond the genteel middle-class role of true womanhood.

Bickerdyke saw much military action. She arrived in Vicksburg, Mississippi, in time for the city's surrender to General Ulysses S. Grant and escorted home Union soldiers released from the notoriously brutal Confederate prison at Andersonville, Georgia. In 1864, she joined General William Tecumseh Sherman, with whom she claimed a special bond, for his devastating march across the heart of the South. At the end of the war, when Sherman and his troops paraded through Washington, D.C.,

◆ **Figure 5.5** F. O. C. Darley, *Midnight on the Battlefield* (1890)
The New York Public Library/Art Resource, NY.

to celebrate victory, Mother Bickerdyke rode in a place of honor. Then she slipped back into private life. In 1886, the army awarded her a pension of $25 a month.

Figure 5.5 depicts the initial episode of the Bickerdyke story, her role at the battle of Fort Donelson, Tennessee, site of an early Union victory. Bickerdyke achieved renown for her courage in remaining at the killing fields late at night, until she was absolutely sure that she had found all survivors. The illustration, a steel engraving, was commissioned for *My Story of the War*, an account of the wartime contribution of the women of the Sanitary Commission, written in 1889 by Mary Livermore. It pictures Bickerdyke as a female savior, alone in her attempt to sustain life in a field of death. How did the artist choose to idealize her? How does the use of light (and dark) suggest women's role on the battlefield?

Although the gender conventions of southern society were more restrictive and less encouraging of the kind of public presence and demonstration of organizational talent that characterized women's nursing involvement with the Union cause, southern white women provided hospital care for Confederate soldiers as well. They could be found in the mammoth military hospitals in the capital of Richmond and at temporary medical facilities close to the battlefields and near their own homes and communities. Because records of the Confederacy, including lists and numbers of women who served as nurses, were destroyed in the Union seizure and burning of Richmond, it is impossible even to estimate their numbers.

White women showed their patriotic dedication to the Confederate cause by attending wounded soldiers' bedsides, talking them through their suffering and dying, reading to them, and writing letters to their families. The dirtier jobs — bathing wounds, cleaning up the bloody sites of surgery, preparing corpses — were often done by slave women brought along by their mistresses. Relatively early, in 1862, the Confederate Congress began paying women for their nursing services. Their wages ranged from $30 to $40 a month, figures that seem quite high until the wildly inflated currency of the Confederacy is taken into account. Wages were allotted even for slave women, although the money was no doubt paid to their masters and mistresses.

The painting depicted in Figure 5.6 is one of the few images we have of southern women acting as nurses for Confederate soldiers. The painting is not a portrait of a particular woman, but a generalized image of southern white womanhood devoted to the Confederate cause. The artist, William Ludwell Sheppard, served in the Army of Northern Virginia and began his career as an illustrator and watercolorist of the war from a romanticized, southern perspective. *In the Hospital* was painted in the first year of the war. What audience did Sheppard have in mind? If we could compare it with an image from 1863 or 1864, what might be different? What are the similarities and differences between this and the prior image, of Mother Bickerdyke ministering to a Union soldier? How did this image help to build what later became, as one historian puts it, "the legend of female sacrifice, . . . of Confederate women's unflinching loyalty"?[64]

Catholic religious women were the only group of women on the battlefield with any prior experience in caring for the wounded. Their selflessness and virtue were unassailable. For these reasons, they were more welcomed than other Civil War nurses by the male military establishment, an attitude that is particularly remarkable given the rampant anti-Catholic prejudice of the era. Civil War chronicler Mary Livermore, no admirer of "the monastic institutions of that [Catholic] church," nonetheless praised the Catholic nurses: "They gave themselves no airs of superiority or holiness, shirked no duty, sought no easy place, bred no mischief."[65] Livermore thought the sisters represented a model of organized public service that Protestant women would do well to follow. Dorothea Dix, on the other hand, resented the Catholic women, who were not under her supervision.

Dedicated to the service of God and humanity rather than the victory of North or South, the sisters attended both Confederate and Union wounded. During the long Union siege of Vicksburg, the Daughters of Charity cared for Confederate

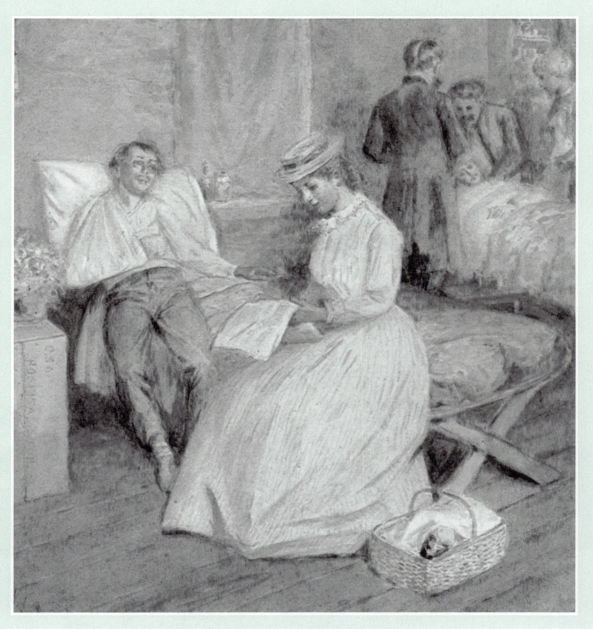

◆ **Figure 5.6 William Ludwell Sheppard,** *In the Hospital* **(1861)**
The Granger Collection, New York.

soldiers and civilians alike. A similar community provided nurses for the giant Satterlee Hospital in Philadelphia, which received many of the Union wounded from the war's deadliest battle, Gettysburg. Figure 5.7 shows most of the forty sisters who served at Satterlee. How did the sisters' religious habits solve the problems of uniform and functional clothing for nurses? While other Civil War nurses were portrayed individually, why and with what effect did these women appear as a group?

Most of the women valorized for their contributions to the war effort were white. Yet African American women, for whom the outcome was of the greatest importance, found their own way to the battlefields. Some were free black women from the North who went south to attend to the welfare of freed slaves living in areas occupied by the Union army. But others were themselves fugitives from slavery, who provided an important source of support labor for the northern

◆ **Figure 5.7 Daughters of Charity with Doctors and Soldiers, Satterlee Hospital, Philadelphia (c. 1863)**
Courtesy, Daughters of Charity, Province of St. Louise, St. Louis, MO.

war effort. These women served as cooks and laundresses for the Union troops and as servants for the officers. Although much of their labor was subservient, they were participating in an enterprise that would bring their people freedom, and this gave their labor new meaning.

Susie King Taylor, depicted in the photograph in Figure 5.8, is the rare example of a refugee from slavery whose name and wartime story we know. She was born near Savannah, Georgia, in 1848 to a fourteen-year-old slave mother. Her grandmother, who lived nearby, was free and taught Susie to read and write. In the spring of 1863, she fled with relatives to a South Carolina coastal island that was Union occupied, where she secured her own freedom. There the Union army encouraged the refugees to undertake formal marriages, and Susie, fourteen at the time, wed Edward King.

Like other eager freed slaves, her husband enlisted in one of the special "colored" divisions of the Union army, and King went to the battlefield with him. She worked as a laundress but was also entrusted with cleaning and caring for the musketry. The privilege of holding and handling guns was one of the markers of freedom for freed male slaves and for Susie King as well. "I learned to handle a musket

◆ **Figure 5.8 Susie King Taylor**
Library of Congress, 3a03575.

very well while in the regiment," she wrote, "and could shoot straight and often hit the target."[66] Primarily, however, she was a nurse and served in a segregated military hospital for black soldiers. She and the other black nurses received $10 a month, $2 less than white women.

After the war, King worked as a teacher and a domestic servant in Georgia until she was widowed. She then moved to Boston, where, in 1879, she married Russell Taylor. In 1902, she published A *Black Woman's Civil War Memoirs*. Of the more than one hundred extant Civil War reminiscences by women, hers is the only account by a former slave woman. Part of the impulse to publish her story may have been to clarify that her wartime service — and perhaps that of other freedwomen as well — went beyond that of a laundress. Figure 5.8 is the image she chose as the frontispiece for her book. Compare it to the Sisters of Charity photograph shown in Figure 5.7. How does King convey her sense of dignity and historic contribution to the war effort?

THE SPIES

By far, the most well-known African American woman on the battlefield was Harriet Tubman, renowned for her role as conductor on the Underground Railroad. Born a slave in Maryland about 1821, she ran away from her master in 1849 and returned numerous times, often disguised as a man, to rescue as many as seventy enslaved relatives and friends. When the war began, she came back from Canada, where she had gone to evade the Fugitive Slave Law, and made her way to the Union-occupied South Carolina coastal islands to offer her services. There, she functioned in virtually every role available to women in and around the fighting. She was a nurse, a liaison between the Union army and the many refugees from slavery, a spy, and a military strategist for Union coastal invasions into Georgia and South Carolina.

Tubman began her military service in the way that most women did, as a nurse, first to the former slaves and then to black troops along the Carolina coast. There is some indication that cures she learned as a slave made her especially valuable in this role. But it soon became clear that, as a black woman who could appear to be a common slave, she could move easily about the South, gathering information for the Union army. Union officers asked her to organize a corps from among the black male refugees to serve with her as military spies and scouts.

In 1863, on the basis of Tubman's reports, a regiment of 150 black Union soldiers sailed up South Carolina's Combahee River to cut the enemy's supply lines, seize or destroy foodstuffs, and encourage the desertion of the slave labor force of the plantations along the banks. Eight hundred black men and women — "thousands of dollars worth of property," according to a contemporary newspaper account — fled to the Union gunboats and were transferred to the freedmen's encampments on the occupied Sea Islands.[67] The raid was commemorated more than a century later when a group of black feminists from Massachusetts took as their name the Combahee River Collective (see p. 643).

Despite influential supporters, after the war Tubman was never able to secure the back pay or army pension that white women such as Mother Bickerdyke received. In 1867, her husband, John Tubman, was murdered by a white man, who was acquitted of the crime. She spent the rest of her life in Auburn, New York, struggling to raise money to support herself and an old-age home for ex-slaves that she established. Proceeds from her memoir, *Scenes in the Life of Harriet Tubman*, were her major source of income. Tubman was not literate, and so her oral reminiscences were recorded in book form by a neighbor and friend, Sarah H. Bradford. Figure 5.9, the book's frontispiece, is described as a woodcut likeness of Tubman in her "costume as scout." Like other women on the battlefield (see Figure 5.11), Tubman wore a combination of men's and women's clothing. The jacket may have been military issue. What about this outfit reconciles her femaleness with the largely male nature of the battlefield? What might have been the impact on her readers of showing this former slave woman posed in front of a military camp, carrying an ammunition pouch and a gun?

◆ **Figure 5.9 Harriet Tubman**
Hulton Archive/Getty Images.

If Tubman's race allowed her to spy for the North, white southerner Rose O'Neal Greenhow's sex allowed her to spy for the South. In the Union capital of Washington, D.C., nearby southern sympathizers were able to conduct a brisk trade in military information. Some of these spies were women who made use of their sexual attractiveness to serve their cause. Greenhow, one of the best known, was described by a contemporary as possessed of "almost irresistible seductive powers."[68]

When the war broke out, Greenhow was a widow and mother in her mid-thirties. She was prominent in Washington, D.C., social circles and had connections to important congressmen, including her nephew, Senator Stephen A. Douglas of Illinois. Committed to the Confederate cause and opposed to freedom for black people, she gathered political and military information helpful to the South from her numerous admirers and lovers, allegedly including information that helped the Confederates win the first battle of Bull Run. Although constantly under suspicion, she avoided arrest by appealing to principles of gentlemanly chivalry shared by North and South alike.

Eventually, however, Greenhow was arrested and sent to a special Washington prison reserved for enemy agents, many of them women. She was subsequently released to Virginia. The circumstances of her death, soon after, were as extraordinary as those of her life. In 1864, she was a passenger on a British boat running the Union naval blockade off the Carolina coast. Northern gunships fired, and Greenhow's lifeboat capsized. She was close to shore and would have made it to land except that she held on to her purse, which was heavy with gold, and therefore drowned.

The photograph in Figure 5.10 was taken by a member of the studio of renowned Civil War photographer Mathew Brady, when Greenhow was imprisoned. One historian writes that her gender was her disguise.[69] What comment does the photographer's artful posing make on Greenhow's career as a Confederate spy? What do Greenhow's dress, pose, and the presence of her daughter suggest about her imprisonment at Union hands?

THE SOLDIERS

Although we will never know their numbers, hundreds of women, possibly more, fought on the battlefields of the Civil War. These women warriors fall into two categories: those who were known to be women at the time and those who passed themselves off as men. In the first category were the so-called daughters of the regiment. Often arriving in camp with their newly enlisted husbands, a few may have also been as motivated by the desire to see military action as by marital sentiment. After performing such womanly tasks as nursing, cooking, and laundering, occasionally these women took on the all-important job of carrying the regiment's flag (or standard) into battle. Soldiers, who were recruited at the local and state level, fought as much out of loyalty to their regiment as out of allegiance to the army or the nation, and the way their regimental colors were displayed represented their comradeship and military fervor. The standard bearer's job was to lead and encourage the troops, and women who undertook this role inspired tremendous devotion from their comrades.

Bridget Divers, known as "Michigan Bridget," was one of these regimental daughters. An Irish immigrant, she came to the First Michigan Calvary with her husband. Early in the war, her regiment was the object of a surprise attack, and the troops panicked. One of Divers's comrades remembered how she leaped to her

◆ **Figure 5.10** **Rose O'Neal Greenhow in the Old Capitol Prison with Her Daughter (1862)**
Library of Congress, LC-DIG-cwpbh-04849.

feet, grabbed the flag, and yelled, "Go in Boys and bate [beat] Hell out of them."[70] Divers found army life so much to her liking that, after the war, she continued to serve with her husband in the western Indian conflicts.

As with other such women, the legends that accrued around Michigan Bridget emphasized her combination of manly bravery and female sympathy. Figure 5.11, a steel engraving commissioned, like that of Mary Ann Bickerdyke (Figure 5.5), by Mary Livermore for *My Story of the War*, portrays Divers bearing the U.S. flag in the midst of battle. Divers knew how to shoot, and Livermore approvingly wrote of her, "When a soldier fell she took his place, fighting in his stead with unquailing courage."[71] How and with what purpose does the artist position Divers with respect to the battle? Why might she have been pictured with a flag instead of the gun that

◆ **Figure 5.11** F. O. C. Darley, *A Woman in Battle—"Michigan Bridget" Carrying the Flag* **(1888)**

The New York Public Library/Art Resource, NY.

she allegedly knew how to use? And why might the artist have chosen to show her carrying not the regimental colors but the U.S. flag?

"Of the three hundred and twenty-eight thousand Union soldiers who lie buried in national cemeteries," the editors of the *History of Woman Suffrage* (1881) wrote, ". . . hundreds are . . . women obliged by army regulation to fight in disguise."[72] "Passing women," as historians have come to label such women, fought in many wars, but they seem to have been particularly numerous in the U.S. Civil War. The Union army discovered and dismissed many women among its recruits, and the sex of others was not discovered until they were wounded or killed. During the war, authorities' greatest fear was that women who had sneaked into the ranks would engage in immoral sexual activities with male soldiers. Stories of women who disguised themselves as men in order to fight continued to surface for many decades. In 1910, an Illinois Civil War pensioner who had gone by the name Albert Cashier was discovered to be a woman, declared insane, sentenced to an asylum, where he dressed as a woman.[73] For a long time after the war, some passing women, like Cashier, lived as men. They worked in men's occupations and even married women, who invariably claimed to have believed their husbands to be men, which is hard to believe but impossible to dismiss.

With one exception, all of the well-known passing women of the Civil War era were Union soldiers. Loreta Velazquez, a Cuban immigrant, began her career in the Confederate army with her husband's support but maintained her masquerade even after he was killed. Using the name Harry T. Buford, Velazquez fought as an officer with several regiments and participated in the Confederate victory at the first battle of Bull Run. Although she was wounded, she escaped detection and continued to live a life of high adventure after the war.

In 1876, Velazquez wrote a popular and controversial memoir, *The Woman in Battle*, in which she described her lifelong habit of wearing men's clothes and the attraction that being able to make money like a man held for her. Her book included the illustrations shown in Figure 5.12 of her female and male personae.

◆ **Figure 5.12 Madam Velazquez in Female Attire (*left*) and Harry T. Buford, 1st Lieutenant, Independent Scouts, Confederate States Army (*right*)**
The Granger Collection, New York.

How did she depict herself as a woman, and what designated her visually as a man? Above all, what point might she have been seeking to make by demonstrating through illustrations that she could shift from role to role? How does her story begin to suggest what today is called the social construction of gender?

QUESTIONS FOR ANALYSIS

1. What are the similarities in the images of women who served as Civil War nurses? What attitudes toward women help explain these similarities?

2. Male soldiers are issued official uniforms to designate their rank and military affiliation. What similarities do you notice in Divers's and Tubman's outfits? How might this clothing have constituted a kind of informal uniform for women on the battlefield?

3. The Civil War was fought between two cultures as much as between two economic and racial systems. Do you detect patterns in the images of northern versus southern women? What do these differences tell you about the gender dimensions of the North–South divide?

4. Taken as a group, do these images indicate that the women who participated directly in the war did more to maintain or to undermine standard gender roles?

NOTES

1. Martha S. Read to Lorinda Shelton, April 6, 1852, Norwich, NY, http://xroads.virginia.edu/~HYPER/HNS/domwest/read.html (accessed June 16, 2004).

2. Lillian Schlissel, ed., *Women's Diaries of the Westward Journey* (New York: Schocken Books, 1982), 188.

3. Cathy Luchetti, ed., *Women of the West* (St. George, UT: Antelope Island Press, 1982), 145.

4. John Mack Faragher, *Women and Men on the Overland Trail* (New Haven: Yale University Press, 1979), 172.

5. Schlissel, *Women's Diaries of the Westward Journey*, 179–80.

6. Ibid., 214.

7. Ibid., 223.

8. Sarah Royce, *A Frontier Lady*, excerpted in Ida Rae Egli, ed., *No Rooms of Their Own: Women Writers of Early California* (Berkeley: Heyday Books, 1992), 15.

9. Ibid., 13.

10. Glenda Riley, *A Place to Grow: Women in the American West* (Arlington Heights, IL: Harlan Davidson, 1982), 127.

11. Sarah Winnemucca Hopkins, *Life among the Piutes: Their Wrongs and Claims* (1883; repr., Bishop, CA: Sierra Media, 1969), 5, 11.

12. J. S. Holliday, *The World Rushed In: The California Gold Rush Experience* (New York: Simon and Schuster, 1981), 164.

13. Susan B. Anthony to Mary Anthony, February 7, 1848, in Ann D. Gordon, ed., *The Selected Papers of Elizabeth Cady Stanton and Susan B. Anthony*, vol. 1, *In the School of Anti-Slavery, 1840–1866* (New Brunswick, NJ: Rutgers University Press, 1996), 134.

14. Anonymous to Catherine D. Oliver, 1850, in Edith Sparks, *Capital Instincts: Female Proprietors in San Francisco, 1850–1920* (Chapel Hill: University of North Carolina Press, 2006), 58.

15. Christiane Fischer, ed., *Let Them Speak for Themselves: Women in the American West* (New York: E. P. Dutton, 1978), 43–45.

16. Holliday, *The World Rushed In*, 165.

17. Nancy Hewitt, *Women's Activism and Social Change: Rochester, New York, 1822–1872* (Ithaca, NY: Cornell University Press, 1984), 40.

18. Constitution of the New York Female Moral Reform Society, 1836, reprinted in Dawn Keetley and John Pettegrew, eds., *Public Women, Public Words: A Documentary History of American Feminism*, vol. 1, *Beginnings to 1900* (Madison, WI: Madison House, 1997), 129.

19. T. L. Nichols, M.D., and Mrs. Mary S. Gove Nichols, *Marriage: Its History, Character and Results; Its Sanctities and Its Profanities; Its Science and Its Facts* (New York: T. L. Nichols, 1854), 202.

20. April Haynes, *Riotous Flesh: Women, Physiology, and the Solitary Vice in Nineteenth-Century America* (Chicago: University of Chicago Press, 2015), 85.

21. Elizabeth Cady Stanton, *Eighty Years and More: Reminiscences, 1815–1897* (1898; repr., Boston: Northeastern University Press, 1993), 284.

22. Georgiana Bruce Kirby, *Years of Experience: An Autobiographical Narrative* (New York: G. P. Putnam's Sons, 1887), 99.

23. Bell Gale Chevigny, *The Woman and the Myth: Margaret Fuller's Life and Writings*, rev. ed. (Boston: Northeastern University Press, 1997), 248.

24. Boston Female Anti-Slavery Address, July 13, 1836, reprinted in *Our Mothers before Us: Women and Democracy, 1789–1920* (Washington, DC: Foundation for the National Archives, 1998), 11–23.

25. Maria Stewart, "Religion and the Pure Principles of Morality," *Liberator*, October 1831.

26. Harriet Beecher Stowe, "Sojourner Truth: The Libyan Sibyl," *Atlantic Monthly*, April 1863, 473–81.

27. Elizabeth Cady Stanton, "Speech to the Anniversary of the American Anti-Slavery Society," *Liberator*, May 18, 1860, 78.

28. Carolyn Williams, "The Female Antislavery Movement: Fighting against Racial Prejudice and Promoting Women's Rights in Antebellum America," in Jean Fagan Yellin and John C. Van Horne, eds., *The Abolitionist Sisterhood: Women's Political Culture in Antebellum America* (Ithaca, NY: Cornell University Press, 1994), 162.

29. Jean R. Soderlund, "Priorities and Power: The Philadelphia Female Anti-Slavery Society," in *The Abolitionist Sisterhood*, 73.

30. "Pastoral Letter of the Massachusetts Congregationalist Clergy," 1837, in Aileen Kraditor, ed., *Up from the Pedestal: Selected Writings in the History of American Feminism* (Chicago: Quadrangle Books, 1968), 51.

31. Elizabeth Ann Bartlett et al., eds., *Sarah Grimké: Letters on the Equality of the Sexes and Other Essays* (New Haven: Yale University Press, 1988), 38.

32. Boston Female Anti-Slavery Address, July 13, 1836, 11–23.

33. Quoted in Lori D. Ginzberg, *Women and the Work of Benevolence: Morality, Politics, and Class in the Nineteenth-Century United States* (New Haven: Yale University Press, 1990), 93.

34. Ibid., 26.

35. Angelina Grimké Weld to Gerrit and Anne Smith, June 18, 1840, in Gilbert Barnes and Dwight Dumond, eds., *Letters of Theodore Dwight Weld, Angelina Grimké Weld, and Sarah Grimké, 1822–1844* (New York: Appleton-Century, 1934), 2:842.

36. Cady Stanton, *Eighty Years and More*, 83.

37. Ibid., 147–48.

38. "Declaration of Sentiments and Resolutions, Seneca Falls Convention," 1848, reprinted in Kraditor, *Up from the Pedestal*, 183–89.

39. Frances Ellen Watkins Harper, letter to John Brown, November 25, 1859, reprinted in James Redpath, *Echoes of Harpers Ferry* (Boston: Thayer and Eldridge, 1860), 418–19.

40. Frances Willard, *Glimpses of Fifty Years: The Autobiography of an American Woman* (Chicago: H. J. Smith, 1889), 155.

41. Mary Chesnut, April 12, 1861, in C. Vann Woodward, ed., *Mary Chesnut's Civil War* (New Haven: Yale University Press, 1981), 46.

42. Mary Livermore, *My Story of the War* (Hartford: A. D. Worthington, 1898), 465.

43. Ibid., 472.

44. Anna Howard Shaw, with the collaboration of Elizabeth Jordan, *The Story of a Pioneer* (New York: Harpers Bros., 1915), 51.

45. Bell Irvin Wiley, *Confederate Women* (Westport, CT: Greenwood Press, 1975), 177.

46. Elizabeth Cady Stanton to Nancy Smith, July 20, 1863, in Theodore Stanton and Harriot Stanton Blatch, eds., *Elizabeth Cady Stanton as Revealed in Her Letters, Diary, and Reminiscences* (New York: Harper & Brothers, 1922), 95.

47. Dorothy Sterling, ed., *We Are Your Sisters: Black Women in the Nineteenth Century* (New York: W. W. Norton, 1984), 239.

48. Elizabeth Cady Stanton, "To the Women of the Republic," April 24, 1863, reprinted in Gordon, *Selected Papers*, 483.

49. Elizabeth Cady Stanton, Susan B. Anthony, and Matilda J. Gage, eds., *History of Woman Suffrage* (Rochester, NY: Susan B. Anthony, 1881), 1:79.

50. Mary Chesnut, May 7, 1865, in *Mary Chesnut's Civil War*, 802.

51. Sterling, *We Are Your Sisters*, 244.

52. Livermore, *My Story of the War*, 469.

53. Cited in Marilyn Mayer Culpepper, *All Things Altered: Women in the Wake of Civil War and Reconstruction* (Jefferson, NC: McFarland, 2002), 23.

54. Shirley Ann Wilson Moore, *Sweet Freedom's Plains: African Americans on the Overland Trail* (Norman: University of Oklahoma Press, 2016), 160–62.

55. Rose Stremlau, "Witnessing the West: Barbara Longknife and the California Gold Rush," in Tim Alan Garrison and Greg O'Brien, eds. *The Native South* (Lincoln: University of Nebraska Press, 2017), 163.

56. Benjamin Madley, *American Genocide: The United States and the California Indian Catastrophe* (New Haven: Yale University Press, 2016), 54–56.

57. Stacey L. Smith, *Freedom's Frontier: California and the Struggle over Unfree Labor, Emancipation, and Reconstruction* (Chapel Hill: University of North Carolina Press, 2013), 11.

58. The original is in the Elizabeth Cady Stanton Papers, Vassar College, Poughkeepsie, New York. A slightly different transcription can be found in Gordon, *Selected Papers*, 319–21.

59. The original is in the Elizabeth Cady Stanton Papers, Library of Congress, Washington, DC. The version in Gordon, *Selected Papers*, 321–23, is closer to the original in small details of underlining and punctuation.

60. Ida Husted Harper, *The Life and Work of Susan B. Anthony*, vol. 1 (Indianapolis: Bowen-Merrill, 1899), 229.

61. Mary Denis Maher, *To Bind Up the Wounds: Catholic Sister Nurses in the U.S. Civil War* (New York: Greenwood Press, 1989), 51.

62. Ibid., 53.

63. Louisa May Alcott, *The Journals of Louisa May Alcott*, ed. Joel Myerson, Daniel Sheahy, and Madeleine B. Stern (Boston: Little, Brown, 1989), 110.

64. Drew Gilpin Faust, "Altars of Sacrifice: Confederate Women and the Narratives of War," *Journal of American History* 76 (1990): 1203.

65. Maher, *To Bind Up the Wounds*, 39.

66. Susie King Taylor, *A Black Woman's Civil War Memoirs: Reminiscences of My Life in Camp with the 33rd U.S. Colored Troops, Late 1st South Carolina Volunteers*, excerpted in Eve Merriam, ed., *Growing Up Female in America: Ten Lives* (New York: Dell, 1971), 195.

67. *Commonwealth*, July 10, 1863, cited in Earl Conrad, *Harriet Tubman* (Washington, DC: Associated Publishers, 1943), 169.

68. Elizabeth Leonard, *All the Daring of the Soldier: Women of the Civil War Armies* (New York: W. W. Norton, 1999), 94.

69. Stephanie McCurry, *Confederate Reckoning: Power and Politics in the Civil War South* (Cambridge, MA: Harvard University Press, 2010), 103.

70. Ibid., 123.

71. Livermore, *My Story of the War*, 116.

72. Stanton, Anthony, and Gage, *History of Woman Suffrage*, 2:23.

73. Leonard, *All the Daring of the Soldier*, 188–89.

SUGGESTED REFERENCES

Women and the Antebellum West

Gae Whitney Canfield, *Sarah Winnemucca of the Northern Paiutes* (1983).

María Raquél Casas, *Married to a Daughter of the Land: Spanish-Mexican Women and Interethnic Marriage in California, 1820–1880* (2009).

John Mack Faragher, *Women and Men on the Overland Trail* (1979).

Ramón A. Gutiérrez and Richard J. Orsi, eds., *Contested Eden: California before the Gold Rush* (1997).

Lisbeth Haas, *Saints and Citizens: Indigenous Histories of Colonial Missions and Mexican California* (2013).

Albert L. Hurtado, *Intimate Frontiers: Sex, Gender, and Culture in Old California* (1999).

Anne F. Hyde, *Empires, Nations, and Families: A New History of the North American West, 1800–1860* (2011).

Susan Lee Johnson, *Roaring Camp: The Social World of the California Gold Rush* (2000).

JoAnn Levy, *They Saw the Elephant: Women in the California Gold Rush* (1990).

Shirley Ann Wilson Moore, *Sweet Freedom's Plains: African Americans on the Overland Trail* (2016).

Women and Reform Movements

Bonnie S. Anderson, *Joyous Greetings: The First International Women's Movement, 1830–1860* (2000).

Erica L. Ball, *To Live an Antislavery Life: Personal Politics in the Antebellum Black Middle Class* (2012).

Charles Capper, *Margaret Fuller: An American Romantic Life*, vols. 1 and 2 (1994 and 2010).

Ellen Carol DuBois, *Feminism and Suffrage: The Emergence of an Independent Women's Movement in America, 1848–1869*, 2nd ed. (2003).

Carol Faulkner, *Lucretia Mott's Heresy: Abolition and Women's Rights in Nineteenth-Century America* (2011).

Lori D. Ginzberg, *Women in Antebellum Reform* (2000).

April R. Haynes, *Riotous Flesh: Women, Physiology, and the Solitary Vice in Nineteenth-Century America* (2015).

Nancy A. Hewitt, *Women's Activism and Social Change, Rochester, New York, 1822–1872* (1984).

Julie Roy Jeffrey, *The Great Silent Army of Abolitionism: Ordinary Women in the Antislavery Movement* (1998).

Andrea Moore Kerr, *Lucy Stone: Speaking Out for Equality* (1992).

Bonnie Laughlin-Schultz, *The Tie That Bound Us: The Women of John Brown's Family and the Legacy of Radical Abolitionism* (2013).

Gerda Lerner, *The Grimké Sisters from South Carolina* (1967).

Scott C. Martin, *Devil of the Domestic Sphere: Temperance, Gender, and Middle-Class Ideology, 1800–1860* (2008).

Jean L. Silver-Isenstadt, *Shameless: The Visionary Life of Mary Gove Nichols* (2002).

Kathryn Kish Sklar and James Brewer Stewart, *Women's Rights and Transatlantic Antislavery in the Era of Emancipation* (2007).

Lisa Tetrault, *The Myth of Seneca Falls: Memory and the Women's Suffrage Movement, 1848–1898* (2014).

Margaret Washington, *Sojourner Truth's America* (2009).

Shirley J. Yee, *Black Women Abolitionists: A Study in Activism, 1828–1860* (1992).

Women and the Civil War

Karen Abbott, *Liar, Temptress, Soldier, Spy: Four Women Undercover in the Civil War* (2014).

Jean H. Baker, *Mary Todd Lincoln: A Biography* (1987).

Mary Farmer-Kaiser, *Freedwomen and the Freedmen's Bureau: Race, Gender, and Public Policy in the Age of Emancipation* (2010).

Drew Gilpin Faust, *This Republic of Suffering: Death and the American Civil War* (2008).

_____, *Mothers of Invention: Women of the Slaveholding South in the American Civil War* (1996).

Libra R. Hilde, *Worth a Dozen Men: Women and Nursing in the Civil War South* (2012).

Stephanie McCurry, *Confederate Reckoning: Power and Politics in the Civil War South* (2012).

Victoria E. Ott, *Confederate Daughters: Coming of Age during the Civil War* (2008).

Barbara A. White, *The Beecher Sisters* (2003).

1865	U.S. Civil War ends
1865	Abraham Lincoln assassinated
1865	Thirteenth Amendment, ending slavery, ratified
1865	Freedmen's Bureau established to aid former slaves
1865	Repressive "black codes" are passed in former Confederate states
1865	**Vassar College founded**
1866	**American Equal Rights Association formed**
1866	Ku Klux Klan first appears
1868	Fourteenth Amendment, defining national citizenship, ratified
1868	**Sorosis and the New England Women's Club formed**

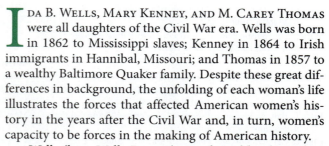

1868– 1870	**Susan B. Anthony publishes the *Revolution***
1869	**American Woman Suffrage Association and National Woman Suffrage Association formed**
1869	Knights of Labor founded
1869– 1870	Women enfranchised in Wyoming and Utah Territories
1870	Fifteenth Amendment, forbidding disfranchisement by "race, color or previous condition of servitude," ratified
1870	***The Woman's Journal* begins publication**
1872	**Victoria Woodhull arrested under the Comstock Law**
1873	**Susan B. Anthony tried for voting in the 1872 presidential election**

1873	**Remington Arms Company begins manufacturing typewriters**
1873	National economy collapses in severe industrial depression
1874	**Woman's Christian Temperance Union (WCTU) formed**
1875	**Supreme Court rules in *Minor v. Happersett* that voting is not a right of citizenship**

6

Reconstructing Women's Lives North and South

1865–1900

I DA B. WELLS, MARY KENNEY, AND M. CAREY THOMAS were all daughters of the Civil War era. Wells was born in 1862 to Mississippi slaves; Kenney in 1864 to Irish immigrants in Hannibal, Missouri; and Thomas in 1857 to a wealthy Baltimore Quaker family. Despite these great differences in background, the unfolding of each woman's life illustrates the forces that affected American women's history in the years after the Civil War and, in turn, women's capacity to be forces in the making of American history.

Wells (later Wells-Barnett) was shaped by the violent struggles between former slaves seeking to realize their emancipation and white southerners seeking to retain their racial dominance. As a journalist, Wells exposed new, brutal methods of white supremacy, and her work sparked an organized women's movement among African Americans. Kenney (later O'Sullivan) was a lifelong wage earner who recognized that workers needed to act collectively rather than individually to improve their lives. A pathbreaking female labor organizer, she helped form the Women's Trade Union League (WTUL) in 1903 (see pp. 422–24). Thomas, a self-proclaimed tomboy as a child, never married and became a pioneer of higher education for women. She was one of the first women to graduate from Cornell University and to receive a doctorate (in Switzerland), and she was the founding dean of Bryn Mawr College. In the post–Civil

War (or postbellum) years, such individuals laid the basis for an era of extraordinary achievement by American women.

"Reconstruction" is the term used to describe the period of American history immediately after the Civil War, the revision of the U.S. Constitution to deal with the consequences of emancipation, the rebuilding of the South after the devastations of war, and the reconstitution of national unity after the trauma of sectional division. The formal period of Reconstruction lasted twelve years. It ended in 1877 when U.S. troops withdrew from the former Confederacy, leaving the South to work out its own troubled racial destiny without federal oversight and the North to concentrate on industrial development and economic growth.

The word "reconstruction" can also be used to cover a longer period, during which the U.S. economy was reconstituted entirely around industrial capitalism. The free-labor ethic on which the Republican Party was founded evolved into a commitment to unbridled industrialization. The resulting wealth, optimism, and productivity were not shared equally. On the contrary, the gap between rich and poor grew enormously during the postbellum years, producing great tension and violence between owners and workers. With chattel slavery eliminated, industrial society could no longer ignore its internal class divisions, and by the end of the century, conflict between labor and capital overtook the inequalities of race as the most overt challenge to national unity.

Women were reconstructing their lives in these years as well. In the defeated South, women emancipated from slavery grappled with the challenges and dangers of their tentative freedom, while their former mistresses sought to maintain the privileges of white supremacy under new conditions. In the North, a determined group of women sought equal political rights, and the woman suffrage movement came into its own. Industrial capitalism generated both a rapidly expanding female labor force and new leisure and wealth for middle- and upper-class women. Between 1865 and 1900, women's wage labor, the terms of appropriate womanhood within which women lived, and their scope for public action all expanded. By the end of the nineteenth century, the basis had been laid for an epoch of female assertion and accomplishment unparalleled in American history.

photos top: © Atlas Archive/The Image Works; bottom, Klau Library, Cincinnati, Hebrew Union College–Jewish Institute of Religion

◆ GENDER AND THE POSTWAR CONSTITUTIONAL AMENDMENTS

American history's first presidential assassination (Abraham Lincoln), followed quickly by its first presidential impeachment (Andrew Johnson), left the executive branch in shambles and the legislative branch in charge of national Reconstruction. Republicans controlled Congress, and former abolitionists, known as Radicals, controlled the Republican Party. To protect the North's victory and their party's control over Congress, the Radicals were determined to enfranchise the only population on whom the Republicans could depend in the defeated Confederacy — former slaves. In 1866, Radicals proposed an amendment to the U.S. Constitution to establish the citizenship of ex-slaves. The Fourteenth Amendment began with a simple, inclusive sentence: "All persons born or naturalized in the United States, and subject to the jurisdiction thereof, are citizens of the United States and of the State wherein they reside."

Leaders of the women's rights movement hoped to further revise the Constitution and reconstruct democracy without distinction of either race *or* gender. Despite their best efforts, however, the ratification of the Fourteenth Amendment in 1868, followed by that of the Fifteenth Amendment in 1870, established black suffrage without reference to woman suffrage. Thwarted in Congress, these women turned to the U.S. Supreme Court to argue that women's political right to the franchise was included within the new constitutional definitions of national citizenship and political rights.

Their efforts failed. The only actual enfranchisement of women in the Reconstruction era occurred in the territories of Wyoming (1869) and Utah (1870), where a handful of legislators accorded women the vote in territorial and local elections. Even so, the movement for women's enfranchisement changed and expanded, drawing new adherents from the Midwest and the Pacific Coast. The old alliance with abolitionists was shattered, and most white women's efforts for women's equality were no longer linked to those for racial equality. The advocates of woman suffrage undertook a campaign that would require an additional half century and another constitutional amendment — the Nineteenth, ratified in 1920 — to complete (see pp. 450–52).

Constitutionalizing Women's Rights

In 1865 and 1866, as Congress was considering how to word the Fourteenth Amendment, women's rights activists called for woman suffrage to be joined with black suffrage in a single constitutional act. Many northern women had fought for the end of slavery, so, in the memorable words of Elizabeth Cady Stanton, "Would it not be advisable, when the constitutional door is open, for [women] to avail ourselves of the strong arm and blue uniform of the black soldier to walk in by his side?"[1] To pursue this goal, Cady Stanton, Anthony, and others formed the American Equal Rights Association, dedicated to both black and woman suffrage. "We resolved to make common cause with the colored class — the only other disfranchised class," observed Lucy Stone, "and strike for equal rights for all."[2]

But Radicals in Congress contended that pursuing woman suffrage and black suffrage simultaneously would doom the latter, which was their priority. Accordingly, they wrote the second section of the Fourteenth Amendment, meant to encourage states to grant voting rights to former slaves, to apply only to "male inhabitants . . . twenty-one years of age and citizens of the United States." This was the first reference to gender in the U.S. Constitution. Woman suffragists petitioned Congress to get the wording changed, but abolitionist Wendell Phillips told them, "This hour belongs to the Negro," leaving Cady Stanton to wonder impatiently if "the African race is composed entirely of males."[3]

Two years after the 1868 ratification of the Fourteenth Amendment, congressional Radicals wrote the Fifteenth Amendment to advance black suffrage more forcefully, explicitly forbidding states from disfranchisements on the grounds of "race, color or previous condition of servitude." Again gender was not included, leading Cady Stanton to charge that "all mankind will vote not because of intelligence, patriotism, property or white skin but because it is male, not female."[4]

◆ **Susan B. Anthony and Elizabeth Cady Stanton**
Taken in 1891, this is a photographic portrait of a political and personal partnership lasting over four decades. Together Anthony (*left*), the organizer, and Cady Stanton (*right*), the writer, speaker, and orator, provided leadership to the U.S. woman suffrage movement as it grew from a radical offshoot of antislavery into a mature, mass-based women's movement. By the 1890s, Anthony was widely admired as the personification of dedication to the cause of women while Cady Stanton continued to push at the edges of acceptable opinion. Nonetheless, their bond remained firm until Cady Stanton's death, a decade later. *Universal History Archive/Getty Images.*

The American Equal Rights Association collapsed, and in its wake, woman suffragists divided over whether to endorse the Fifteenth Amendment. Elizabeth Cady Stanton and Susan B. Anthony broke with their former Radical Republican allies and formed the rival National Woman Suffrage Association (NWSA). To reconcile woman suffrage advocacy with the Radical Republican agenda, Lucy Stone and her husband, Henry Ward Blackwell, took a different route. In 1869, they organized the American Woman Suffrage Association. They focused on campaigns for suffrage at the state level and in 1870 inaugurated the *Woman's Journal*, a weekly newspaper published for the next fifty years.

Of the two societies, NWSA pursued the more aggressive, independent path. The organization's newspaper, defiantly named the *Revolution*, lasted only two years. It proclaimed on its masthead: "Women their rights and nothing less; men their rights and nothing more." NWSA gained political autonomy for the suffrage movement but at the cost of an important part of the women's rights legacy: attention to the interrelation of the hierarchies of race and gender. As the larger society left behind the concerns of the ex-slaves and of Radical Reconstruction, much of the woman suffrage movement did, too, envisioning women's emancipation largely in terms of white women.

A New Departure for Woman Suffrage

Once the new constitutional amendments had been ratified, NWSA proposed an inventive, bold interpretation of them. The argument was both simple and profound: first, women were "persons" whose rights as national citizens were established by the first sentence of the Fourteenth Amendment; second, the right to vote was central to and inherent in national citizenship. Third, and most important, women's right to vote was thus already established and did not require any additional constitutional change.

This argument, which was called the New Departure, brought to prominence one of the most unusual advocates in the history of woman suffrage, Victoria Claflin Woodhull. Born into poverty, Woodhull made her way into the highest ranks of New York society, in large part by cultivating powerful men. Aided by a congressman friend and without the knowledge of other suffragists, in 1871 she presented the case for the New Departure before the Judiciary Committee of the U.S. House of Representatives. Within a year, however, Woodhull, who had boldly criticized sexual hypocrisy within middle-class marriages, had become involved in the most notorious sexual scandal of the age. She went public with her knowledge that Henry Ward Beecher, powerful Brooklyn minister and brother of Catharine Beecher and Harriet Beecher Stowe (see pp. 160–61, 250–51), had had an adulterous affair with one of his parishioners. Under a new federal anti-obscenity law, the Comstock Act (named for Anthony Comstock, the "social purity" crusader who drafted the legislation), Woodhull was jailed for using the federal mail system to distribute her newspaper, which included accounts of the scandal. Cady Stanton, one of the few suffragists who steadfastly defended Woodhull, insisted, "We have already women enough sacrificed to this sentimental, hypocritical prating about purity. If this present woman be crucified, let men drive the spikes."[5] Woodhull avoided jail but dropped out of public life; she eventually moved to England, where she married a wealthy man, remade her reputation, and lived until 1927.

Independent of Woodhull, suffragists around the country pursued their voting rights on the basis of the New Departure theory that they needed only to take hold of the right to vote, which was already theirs. During the elections of 1871 and 1872, groups of women went to their local polling places, put forth their constitutional understanding to stunned election officials, and stepped forward to submit their votes. In Washington, D.C., the African American journalist Mary Ann

Shadd Cary was able to register but not to vote. Susan B. Anthony convinced polling officials in her hometown of Rochester, New York, to let her vote. "Well I have been & gone & done it!!" she wrote exuberantly. "Positively voted the Republican ticket."[6] Two weeks later, she was arrested for the crime of illegal voting, based on a federal law meant to disfranchise former Confederates. Her trial was a spectacle from start to finish. The judge ordered the jury to find Anthony guilty, which it did, and the judge's final insult was to refuse to jail Anthony so as to keep her from appealing her verdict.

The U.S. Supreme Court finally considered the suffragists' argument in 1875, in the case of Virginia Minor, of St. Louis, Missouri, who sued the official who had not allowed her to vote. In *Minor v. Happersett*, one of the most important rulings in the history of women's rights (see the Appendix, p. A-6), the Supreme Court ruled unanimously that, while Minor was indeed a citizen, voting was not a right but a privilege bestowed by the federal government as it saw fit. Not only did this decision strike the New Departure theory dead, but it also indicated that the Court was bent on narrowing the meaning of the Fourteenth and Fifteenth Amendments in general. Subsequently, the Court permitted more and more ways to deprive black men of their franchise and constitutional civil rights.

After the *Minor* decision, NWSA began to advocate a separate constitutional amendment, modeled on the Fifteenth, to bar states from disfranchising "on the grounds of sex." This was the wording that would eventually go into the Nineteenth Amendment (1920), but for the time being, the proposed amendment made little headway. In 1876, NWSA leaders, uninvited, forced their way into the national celebration in Philadelphia of the hundredth anniversary of the Declaration of Independence. "Our faith is firm and unwavering in the broad principles of human rights proclaimed in 1776, not only as abstract truths, but as the corner stones of a republic," they declared. "Yet we cannot forget, even in this glad hour, that while all men of every race, and clime, and condition, have been invested with the full rights of citizenship under our hospitable flag, all women still suffer the degradation of disfranchisement."[7]

◆ WOMEN'S LIVES IN SOUTHERN RECONSTRUCTION AND REDEMPTION

Meanwhile, life in the defeated South was being reconstructed as well. No element of freedom came easily or automatically for the former slaves, and southern whites changed their lives and expectations reluctantly. Black women fought for control over their labor, their children, and their bodies. Elite white women sought new capacities and strengths to accommodate the loss of the labor and wealth that slaveowning had given them. White women from the middle and lower ranks remained poised between loyalties of race and the resentments of class.

By 1870, all the southern states had met the terms Congress mandated for readmission to the Union. After the removal of federal troops in 1877, white southerners, in a process known as Redemption, moved to reclaim political control and to reassert white supremacy. As they did so, new laws institutionalized segregation and a race-based system of convict labor. The region's economy, still largely agricultural, slowly began to industrialize. The complex result of these post-Reconstruction social, political, and economic changes was known as the New South.

Black Women in the New South

After the defeat of the Confederacy, many freedwomen and freedmen stayed on with their masters for months because they did not know they had been freed or had nowhere to go. Others took to the road to find long-lost spouses and family members. Those who could not travel posted advertisements, such as this one in the *Anglo-African Magazine:* "Martha Ward Wishes information concerning her sister, Rosetta McQuillan, who was sold from Norfolk, Va. About thirty years ago to a Frenchman in Mobile, Ala."[8]

The hard-won family reunions of the freed slaves did not always end happily. Some spouses had formed new unions. Laura Spicer, sold away from a Virginia plantation, was contacted by her husband three years after the war ended. He had since become attached to another woman and was deeply conflicted. "I do not

◆ **The Right to Marry**
As abolitionists considered disregard of slave marriage one of the fundamental immoralities of slavery, immediately after the Civil War the Freedmen's Bureau rushed to legalize marriages among freedpeople, who were eager to have their unions recognized. To indicate that slaves had been married in fact if not in law, bureau officials "solemnized" rather than authorized these marriages. In this engraving, an African American chaplain presides at a ceremony for two former slaves; the husband was serving in the U.S. Army. *Library of Congress, 3c38383.*

know which I love best, you or Anna," he wrote to Spicer. "[T]ry and marry some good, smart man . . . and do it because you love me, and not because I think more of the wife I have got than I do of you."[9] Nor were parents always recognized by the children they had been forced to leave behind. "At firs' I was scared of her, 'cause I didn't know who she was," one child remembered of her mother. "She put me in her lap an' she most' nigh cried when she seen de back o' my head . . . where de lice had been an' I had scratched em."[10]

In 1865, the U.S. Army, charged with occupying and governing the defeated Confederacy, organized a special division to deal with the former slaves. The Freedmen's Bureau provided temporary aid, oversaw their labor, and adjudicated disputes with former masters. It was the first government agency established by the United States to address the needs of an oppressed racial minority. One of its tasks was to ensure that freedpeople had rights to their own children. On returning to the Union, southern states had passed laws, known as black codes, to limit the freedoms of newly emancipated slaves. Apprenticeship laws provided for the indenture of black children into servitude regardless of the wishes of their parents. Black mothers and grandmothers fought especially hard against the black codes. "We were delighted when we heard that the Constitution set us free," Lucy Lee of Baltimore explained, "but God help us, our condition is bettered but little; free ourselves, [but] deprived of our children. . . . Give us our children and don't let them be raised in the ignorance we have [been]."[11]

The deepest desire of the freedpeople was to have their own family farms. However, Congress was unwilling to reapportion the southern lands that might have established genuine black self-sufficiency. A few former slaves became homesteaders on public lands in Florida, Kansas, Texas, and Alabama, and a handful were able to buy their own property. But the overwhelming majority found that they had to continue to work for others as agricultural labor. The fundamental dilemma of Reconstruction for most ex-slaves centered on their returning to work for white people: On what terms? With what degree of personal freedom? And for what compensation?

One of the most subtle and complex aspects of this dilemma concerned the disposition of black women's labor. During slavery, women worked alongside men in the fields (see p. 184–89). Black women began to leave field work immediately after emancipation, much to the dismay of white landowners, who knew women's importance to the agricultural labor force. Some observers reported that black men, eager to assert the rights of manhood over their families, were especially determined that their wives not work for whites. Black women, who discovered that any assertion of autonomy toward white employers might be punished as unacceptable "cheekiness," had their own reasons for withdrawing their labor.

To achieve even a small degree of independence from direct white oversight, three out of four black families ended up accepting an arrangement known as sharecropping. Working on small farms carved out of the holdings of white landowners, sharecropping families kept only a portion of the crops they grew. There were no foremen to drive and beat them, and they could work together as families. But in bad times, the value of their yield did not equal the credit that white landowners had extended them to cover their expenses, and most ended up in permanent indebtedness.

The ex-slaves were more successful in realizing their desire for education. Even before the war ended, black and white women from the North had gone south to areas occupied by the Union army to begin teaching the black population. Throughout Reconstruction, freedpeople built their own schools, funded by the Freedmen's Bureau and northern missionary societies, to gain the basics of literacy. Charlotte Forten (later Forten Grimké), born into a prominent free black activist family in Philadelphia, brought her idealism and hopes of racial uplift to her post in coastal South Carolina. "I shall gather my scholars about me, and see smiles of greeting break over their dusky faces," she wrote. "My heart sings a song of thanksgiving, at the thought that even I am permitted to do something for a long-abused race, and aid in promoting a higher, holier, and happier life on the Sea Islands."[12]

Many of the colleges and universities that are now referred to as "historically black" began during the era of Reconstruction. Unlike long-standing prestigious white institutions, many of these institutions — for instance Howard University, established in 1867 in Washington, D.C. — were open to women as well as to men. In 1881, white multimillionaire John D. Rockefeller founded the Atlanta Baptist Female Seminary, an all-female school that later became Spelman College. While most of these institutions provided little more than a high school education throughout the nineteenth century, they nonetheless played a major role in educating black leaders. They educated women who went on to become teachers throughout the South. This fragile educational infrastructure helped to create a small southern black middle class in cities like Atlanta, Richmond, and New Orleans.

The right to vote awarded to ex-slave men by the Fourteenth and Fifteenth Amendments lay at the very core of ex-slaves' hopes for the future. During Reconstruction, freedmen's exercise of the ballot, protected by federal troops, helped to elect approximately two thousand black men to local, state, and national political office. Despite their own disfranchisement, black women understood the political franchise as a community rather than an individual right. They regularly attended political meetings and told men who had the vote how to use it. Southern white women, by contrast, regarded the enfranchisement of black men as yet another insult to their sex and their race.

White Women in the New South

At the end of the war, white women in the South faced loss and defeat. Food shortages were compounded by the collapse of the economy. More than a quarter million southern white men died on Civil War battlefields, leaving one generation of widows and another that would never marry. Occupation by federal troops after the war deepened white southerners' feelings of humiliation. One historian argues that southern white women, who did not share men's sheer relief at getting off the battlefield, harbored greater resentment than southern white men toward the North.[13]

Elite white women felt the loss of their slaves acutely. If they wanted black men in their fields and black women in their kitchens, they had to concede to some of the freedpeople's new expectations for wages, personal autonomy, and respect. Elite white women began for the first time to cook and launder for themselves and their families. "We have most of the housework to do all the time," complained Amanda Worthington of Mississippi, "and . . . it does not make me like the Yankees any better."[14]

Non-elite white southerners were less affected by the withdrawal of slave labor, but because they lived much closer to the edge of subsistence, they suffered far more from the collapse of the economy and the physical devastation of the South. Economic pressures drove many into the same sharecropping arrangement and permanent indebtedness as ex-slaves. Poor southern white women and their children also provided the labor force for the textile mills that northerners and a new class of southern industrialists began building in the 1880s. Inasmuch as black people were not allowed to work in the mills, white women experienced textile work as a kind of racial privilege. Many poor white women believed as fervently as former plantation mistresses in the inviolability of racial hierarchies.

Even so, the collapse of the patriarchal slave system provided new opportunities for public life for those white women who chose to take them. Elite women became involved in the memorialization of the Confederacy. They raised funds, built monuments, and lionized the men who had fought for southern independence, all the while creating an expanded civic role for their sex. Poor farm women found their opportunities in the Grange, a social and educational movement that later fed into the rise of Populism (see pp. 376–79). With a very few exceptions, however, southern white women kept their distance from woman suffrage efforts, which reminded them all too much of the federal intervention to enfranchise their former slaves.

Racial Conflict in Slavery's Aftermath

Changes in gender and racial relations together generated considerable violence in the postwar South. Whites experienced African American autonomy as a profound threat. The Ku Klux Klan, founded in 1866 in Pulaski, Tennessee, terrorized freedpeople for asserting their new freedoms. Klan members sexually humiliated, raped, and murdered many freedwomen. In Henry County, Georgia, two Klansmen pinned down Rhoda Ann Childs; she told a congressional investigation in 1871, "[They] stretched my limbs as far apart as they could . . . [and] applied the Strap to my Private parts until fatigued into stopping, and I was more dead than alive." She was then raped with the barrel of a gun.[15] Through such actions, white men meant both to punish black men and reassert their slave-era control over black women's bodies.

Having had no legal recourse under slavery, however, African American women determined to use their newly won rights to defend themselves. According to one historian, "black women articulated a radical vision of sexual citizenship" that sought to include bodily sovereignty as part of their equal protection under the law.[16]

After the deadly 1866 Memphis race riots, for example, five African American women who had been raped by rampaging white men came forward to give testimony before a congressional committee. Among them, sixteen-year-old Lucy Smith told how a group of men assaulted her in her own home. The women's courageous stand led the Republican committee report to acknowledge and condemn sexual violence against black women.

Eventually, the region's hidden history of cross-racial sex took an even more deadly form. Whites charged that black men were sexual predators seeking access to white women. The irony, of course, was that under slavery, it was white men who had unrestricted sexual access to black women. Southern white women of all classes supported these charges against black men, and most white northerners assumed

◆ Women Exodusters (Late 1800s)

This late nineteenth-century photograph shows LeAnna Samuels and her daughters (from left to right) Harriet, Margaret, and Mary in the yard of their Nicodemus, Kansas, home. Nicodemus was founded by "Exodusters," a group of about six thousand African Americans who set out in 1879 for Kansas to escape white violence and economic oppression in Mississippi and Louisiana. As the image shows, black women and men were able to acquire homesteads in Kansas and live in relative safety compared to the Deep South. *The Nicodemus Historical Society Collection, Bogue, Kansas and the Kenneth Spencer Research Library, University of Kansas Libraries.*

that they were true. At the slightest suspicion of the merest disrespect to a white woman, black men could be accused of sexual aggression and lynched—killed (usually hanged) by mobs who ignored legal process to execute their own form of crude justice. Lynchings, often involving gruesome mutilation as well as murder, were popular events in the post-Reconstruction South, with white women and children attending amid a carnival-like atmosphere. In 1892, the high point of this practice, 160 African Americans, some women included, were lynched.[17]

Ida B. Wells, an African American journalist from Memphis, Tennessee, inaugurated a campaign, eventually international in scope, to investigate and expose the false charges behind the epidemic of lynchings and to get leading white figures to condemn it. In her publication *Southern Horrors: Lynch Law in All Its Phases*, Wells recognized that false allegations of black men's lewd behavior toward white women were closely related to assumptions of black women's sexual disreputability and that black women had a major role to play in challenging the system that led to lynchings. Her efforts helped to catalyze the organization of an African American women's reform movement. (See Primary Sources: "Ida B. Wells, 'Race Woman,'" pp. 325–29.)

Southern blacks' efforts to claim their rights suffered many major setbacks in the late nineteenth century. One by one, all-white Democratic parties "redeemed"

◆ **Mary Tape and Her Family (c. 1884–1885)**

Pictured from left to right are Joseph, Emily, Mamie, Frank, and Mary Tape, Chinese American residents of San Francisco in the 1880s. Mary Tape emigrated from China in the 1860s and married Chinese immigrant Joseph Tape in 1875. The family became well-known for a legal challenge to school segregation that culminated in a landmark 1885 California Supreme Court decision, *Tape v. Hurley*. (See Reading into the Past: "What Right Have You?") Mary Tape took her Anglicized maiden name from Mary McGladery, the matron of the San Francisco Ladies Protection and Relief Society where Mary lived when she first arrived from China as a young orphan. *Smith Collection/Gado/Getty Images.*

READING INTO THE PAST

MARY TAPE
"What Right Have You?"

De jure (stated by law) racial segregation was not limited only to the South. Chinese immigrants Mary and Joseph Tate established their home in San Francisco in the expectation that their children could attend public schools. When the principal of their local primary school refused to enroll their daughter Mamie, Mary Tape sued the school. In the 1885 Tape v. Hurley *case, the California Superior Court decided that Mamie Tape had a right to attend the school on the basis of both California law and the U.S. Constitution. Although the state Supreme Court upheld the decision, the school board lobbied the state legislature to quickly pass a provision that legalized the segregation of students of "Mongolian or Chinese descent." In response, Mary Tape wrote a fiery letter of protest to the San Francisco School Board, excerpted here with original spelling and punctuation. Though visionary, Tape's objections proved unsuccessful and her children ultimately attended the segregated Chinese primary school.*

Mary Tape, 8 April 1885

    To the Board of Education—Dear Sirs: I see that you are going to make all sorts of excuses to keep my child out off the Public schools. Dear sirs, Will you please to tell me! Is it a disgrace to be Born a Chinese? Didn't God make us all!!! What right! have you to bar my children out of

state governments from Republicanism and ended what they called "black rule," instituting legal devices to disfranchise black men, such as requiring voters to demonstrate literacy, to pay exorbitant poll taxes, or to prove that their grandfathers had been voters. By the beginning of the twentieth century, black voting had been virtually obliterated throughout the South.

    In addition to repudiating civil rights legislation, southern states also instituted new penal codes that shunted black women and men into involuntary labor as leased convicts and prison farmworkers. In Georgia, for instance, the state rented black women, alongside black and white men, to railroad, mining, and brickmaking companies as well as plantations. By the 1890s, reform efforts resulted in a sex-segregated system that assigned black women to hard labor on all-female prison plantations where deprivation and sexualized violence were the norm. Moreover, Georgia's penal system reinforced elevated notions of white southern womanhood by granting clemency and medical care to white female convicts while denying the school because she is a chinese Decend. . . . It seems no matter how a Chinese may live and dress so long as you know they Chinese. Then they are hated as one. There is not any right or justice for them. . . . It seems to me Mr. Moulder [school superintendent] has a grudge against this Eight-year-old Mamie Tape. I know they is no other child I mean Chinese child! care to go to your public Chinese school. May you Mr. Moulder, never be persecuted like the way you have persecuted little Mamie Tape. Mamie Tape will never attend any of the Chinese schools of your making! Never!!! I will let the world see sir What justice there is When it is govern by the Race prejudice men! just because she is of the Chinese decend, not because she don't dress like you because she does. Just because she is decended of Chinese parents I guess she is more of a American then a good many of you that is going to prewent her being Educated. Mrs. M. Tape.

SOURCE: "Chinese Mother's Letter," *Daily Alta California*, April 16, 1885.

QUESTIONS FOR ANALYSIS

1. What appeals to equality and American identity does Mary Tape use to make her case?
2. Why does Tape focus on the question of her daughter's dress versus her ethnicity in the letter?

black women all forms of gendered concessions. Many African American club women used their organizational clout to protest convict leasing, and Ida B. Wells decried convict leasing and lynching as the "twin infamies" of southern society.

Meanwhile, a new legal system of rigid racial separation in social relations was being put in place. Called Jim Crow, after a foolish minstrel character played by whites in black makeup, these laws and practices were a way to humiliate and intimidate black people. Under slavery, when black people had no rights, racial segregation operated as a customary practice, but now its codification became a way to reassert white domination. Recalling what enforced segregation felt like, a southern black woman wrote, "I never get used to it; it is new each time and stings and hurts more and more. It does not matter how good or wise my children may be; they are colored. . . . Everything is forgiven in the South but color."[18]

Segregation affected many things, including education, public services, and public accommodations, but black women particularly resented Jim Crow regulations in public transportation. Wells began her career as a defender of her race in 1884 by suing the Tennessee railroad company that ejected her from a special "ladies" car and sent her instead to the "colored" car. Twelve years later, the Supreme Court considered a similar suit by Homer Plessy against a Louisiana railroad for its segregation policy. In *Plessy v. Ferguson* (1896), the Court characterized the entire Jim Crow regime as "separate but equal" and thus compatible with the Fourteenth Amendment's requirement of equality before the law. This constitutional defense of segregation survived for nearly sixty years. (See Appendix, p. A-7.) (For a case of legal segregation outside of the South, see Reading into the Past: "What Right Have You?")

◆ FEMALE WAGE LABOR AND THE TRIUMPH OF INDUSTRIAL CAPITALISM

Industrial growth accelerated tremendously after the defeat of the slave system and the northern victory in the Civil War. Intense competition between industrialists and financial magnates gradually gave way to economic consolidation. By 1890, industries such as steel, railroads, coal mining, and meat production were dominated by a handful of large, powerful corporate entities. The mirror reflection of the growth of capital, the American working class, also came into its own and organized to find ways to offset the power of its employers.

The growth of the female labor force was an important part of this development, although it flew in the face of the still-strong presumption that women belonged exclusively in their homes. Domestic service was the largest sector, but manufacturing labor by women, especially the industrial production of garments, with its distinctive and highly exploitative form of production — the sweatshop — was growing faster.

The dynamic growth of industrial society produced a level of class conflict in the last quarter of the nineteenth century as intense as any in American history. Starting in 1877, as the federal army retreated from the South and the first postwar depression receded, waves of protests by disgruntled workers shook the economy and drew a powerful and violent response from big business and government. Coming so soon after the Civil War, escalating class antagonism seemed to threaten national unity again, this time along economic rather than sectional lines. Women played a major role in these upheavals and, in doing so, laid the groundwork for a female labor movement in the early twentieth century (see pp. 422–24).

Women's Occupations after the Civil War

Between 1860 and 1890, the percentage of the nonagricultural wage labor force that was female increased from 10.2 to 17 percent (see Chart 6.1). Since the population in these years increased enormously, the change in absolute numbers was even more dramatic: by 1890, 3.6 million women were working for pay in nonagricultural labor, more than twice the number in 1870. The average pay for women remained a third to a half of the pay for men. The great majority of white working women were young and unmarried. The outlines of black women's labor were somewhat

◆ **Chart 6.1 Women and the Labor Force, 1800–1900**

Year	Percentage of All Women in the Labor Force	Percentage of the Labor Force That Is Female
1800	4.6	4.6
1810	7.9	9.4
1820	6.2	7.3
1830	6.4	7.4
1840	8.4	9.6
1850	10.1	10.8
1860	9.7	10.2
1870	13.7	14.8
1880	14.7	15.2
1890	18.2	17.0
1900	21.2	18.1

SOURCE: W. Elliot Brownlee and Mary M. Brownlee, *Women in the American Economy: A Documentary History* (New Haven: Yale University Press, 1976). *Historical Statistics of the United States: Colonial Times to 1970*, part 1, Bicentennial Edition, Bureau of the Census, U.S. Department of Commerce, 1975. "Marital and Family Characteristics of Workers," March 1983, U.S. Department of Labor. *Statistical Abstract of the United States*, Bureau of the Census, U.S. Department of Commerce, 1983 and 1992; Daphne Spain and Suzanne Bianchi, *Balancing Act* (New York: Russell Sage, 1996).

different, remaining largely agricultural until well into the twentieth century. Black women also were much more likely to work outside the home after marriage.

Much of what historians have written about working women of the nineteenth century, especially the numbers and statistics, is guesswork. Although women had been working for wages since the 1830s, it was not until 1890 that the U.S. census began to identify or count working women with any precision. After the Civil War, some states investigated female wage labor, framing their inquiries in moralistic terms. State labor bureaus paid a great deal of attention, for instance, to disproving the assertion that working women were inclined to prostitution. These statistical portraits were fleshed out by investigative reporting, usually by middle- or upper-class women who went among the working classes to report on their conditions. (See Primary Sources: "The Woman Who Toils," pp. 330–35.)

Nonetheless, it is clear that for white women, paid domestic work was on the decline. Domestic servants, who before the war were the majority of the white female labor force, constituted less than 30 percent by the end of the century. Working women had long been impatient with domestic service and left it whenever they could, usually for factory labor. After the Civil War, the end of slavery tainted personal service even more. Investigator Helen Campbell took testimony in the mid-1880s in New York City from women who had abandoned domestic service. "I hate the very words 'service' and 'servant,'" an Irish immigrant renegade from domestic labor explained. "We came to this country to better ourselves, and it's not bettering to have anybody ordering you around."[19]

As white women workers shifted out of domestic service, their percentage in manufacturing increased to 25 percent as of 1900. Women continued to work in the textile industry, and in the shoe industry women organized their own trade union, the Daughters of St. Crispin (named after the patron saint of their trade), but it survived only a few years. The biggest change in women's manufacturing labor was the rise of the garment industry, as the antebellum outwork system began to give way to more fully industrialized processes (see pp. 167–68).

The industrial manufacture of clothing depended on the invention of the sewing machine, one of the most consequential technological developments in U.S. women's history. The introduction of the sewing machine accelerated the sub-division of clothing production into discrete tasks. Thus a single worker no longer made an entire piece of clothing but instead spent her long days sewing sleeves or

◆ **Stripping Tobacco Leaves in a Tobacco Factory (c. 1890)**
The filthy and exhausting work of processing tobacco leaves was one of the few industrial jobs open to African American women. In this Richmond, Virginia, factory
during the 1890s, both women and children worked in close quarters to strip the leaves
from tobacco plants. White southern photographer Huestis Cook made the photograph
as part of a series on tobacco production from field to factory. What does the image
tell you about the physical conditions of black women and children's industrial labor?
*© Cook Collection/The Valentine Richmond History Center. Courtesy of the Virginia
Commonwealth University Libraries. https://thevalentine.org.*

seams, incurring the physical and spiritual toll of endless, repetitive motion. Unlike the power looms and spindles of the textile mills, sewing machines did not need to be housed in massive factories but could be placed in numerous small shops. As sewing machines were also comparatively inexpensive, the cost of buying and maintaining them could be shifted to the workers themselves, who were charged rent or made to pay in installments for them.

Profits in the garment industry came primarily from pushing the women workers to produce more for less pay. This system became designated as the "sweating" system, meaning that it required women workers to drive (or sweat) themselves to work ever harder. Women workers were usually paid for each piece completed, whereas men tended to be paid for time worked. Employers set a low piece rate, lowering it even further as women produced more. Often workers were charged for thread and fined for sewing errors. The work was highly seasonal, and periods of twelve-hour workdays alternated with bouts of unemployment. At the beginning of the Civil War, the average earnings of sewing women were $10 per week; by 1865, they were $5 per week.

Regardless of their ability or speed, women in the garment, textile, and shoe industries were generally considered unskilled workers, in part because they worked in a female-dominated industry, in part because they were easily replaced by other women, and in part because they learned their work on the job rather than through a formal apprenticeship. The higher pay associated with so-called skilled labor was reserved for trades that men dominated. A few women gained entrance to male-dominated trades, such as typesetting, where they earned up to $15 per week. Initially, women made their way into print shops by replacing male workers who were out on strike, but they were let go when the men came back to work. Eventually, the printers' union voted to admit women as equal members, only the second male trade union to do so.

In the 1870s, a new field began to open up for female wage earners: office work. Before 1860, the office environment had been totally male, filled by young men aspiring to careers in business or law. During the Civil War, young women began to replace men as government copyists and stenographers. The shift to female labor was accelerated by another crucial technological development, the typewriter. Women, with their smaller hands, were thought to be especially suited to typing. Office work required education and a command of the English language, adding to its prestige as an occupation for women. It also paid more than textile mills or garment sweatshops. Yet from the employers' perspective, hiring women rather than men to meet the growing demand for clerical labor constituted a considerable savings. By 1900, office work was still only 9 percent of the female labor force, but it was the fastest-growing sector, a harbinger of things to come in the twentieth-century female labor force (see the Appendix, p. A-20).

Who Were the Women Wage Earners?

Age and marital status were crucial elements in the structure of the female labor force. In 1890, three-quarters of white working women were unmarried. As a leading historian of working women puts it, "In the history of women's labor market experience in the United States the half century from about 1870 to 1920 was the era of single women."[20] Unlike working men, whose wages were supposed to provide for an entire family, these young women allegedly had no one but themselves to support. "Working girls" were expected to work for pay for only a few years, then marry and become dependent on the earnings of their husbands. This was the principle of the so-called family wage, which justified men's greater wages as much as it did women's lesser. Wage labor for women was meant to be an interlude between childhood and domestic dependence, while men expected to work throughout their adult lives.

The reality of working women's lives was considerably more complex. Approximately 10 to 15 percent of urban families were headed by single mothers and were acutely disadvantaged by the family wage system.[21] A working woman who was a wife and/or mother was considered at best an anomaly and at worst an indicator of family and social crisis. African American women wage earners were three times as likely as white women to be married, partly because their husbands' pay was so low and partly because many chose to work themselves rather than send their daughters into work situations where they would be vulnerable to sexual harassment from white men. In historical hindsight, African American women were pioneering the modern working women's pattern of combining wage labor

◆ **Advertising Women and Typewriters**

A practical machine for mechanical writing was devised just after the Civil War. It was first manufactured for the mass market by the Remington Company, which adapted the production process it had developed for rifles. The machine retained the name Remington even after production shifted to the Wyckoff, Seamans, and Benedict Company. This 1897 advertisement explicitly links the modernity of its product to its skilled women operators. The elegantly dressed, self-composed typist suggests a quite different image from that of the overworked, underpaid woman factory worker, a contrast that is made explicit by the claim that technology means "less labor" for her and yet more output for her boss. *Jay Paull/Getty Images.*

and domestic responsibilities, but at the time, the high number of black working mothers was the object of much disparagement.

Most unmarried wage-earning women lived in their parents' homes, where, contrary to the ideal of the single male breadwinner, their earnings were crucial supplements to family support. However, perhaps as many as a third of single women wage earners lived outside of families. Carroll Wright, a pioneering labor statistician, reported in *The Working Girls of Boston* (1889), a Massachusetts Bureau of Statistics of Labor report, that in Massachusetts many young women workers were "obliged to leave their homes on account of bad treatment or conduct of [a] dissipated father or because they felt the need of work and not finding it at home, have come to [a large city]."[22] Philanthropists established charity boarding-houses to protect these "women adrift," who seemed vulnerable without parents or husbands to protect them. One of the major purposes of the Young Women's Christian Association (YWCA), formed soon after the Civil War, was to provide supervised housing for single, urban working women.

Responses to Working Women

Contemporaries' attempts to grapple with the growing female labor force contained a revealing contradiction. On the one hand, social observers contended that only women driven by sheer desperation should work outside the home. Less desperate working women were taking work away from truly needy women and — even more disturbing — from male breadwinners. If young working women used any part of their pay to buy attractive clothing or go out with men, they were castigated for frivolity. "[Working girls] who want pin-money do work at a price impossible for the self-supporting worker, many married women coming under this head," observed journalist Helen Campbell.[23]

On the other hand, those women who were driven into wage labor by absolute necessity were so ill-paid, so unrelentingly exploited, as to constitute a major social tragedy. "All alike are starved, half clothed, overworked to a frightful degree," wrote the same Helen Campbell, "with neither time to learn some better method of earning a living, nor hope enough to spur them in any new path."[24] Sympathetic observers concluded that the only humane response was to remove young women from the labor force altogether. Wage-earning women were therefore criticized if they worked out of choice or pitied if they worked out of need. In either case, they seemed to be trespassing where they did not belong: in the wage labor force.

Set against middle-class social observers' steady chorus of criticism or lament, the lives and choices of working women hint at a different picture. Working girls objected to the constant supervision at philanthropic working girls' homes, stubbornly spent their wages as they pleased, engaged in recreational activities that were considered vulgar, occasionally continued to work even after they got married, and preferred their morally questionable factory jobs to the presumed safety of domestic service. Though they were criticized for taking jobs away from the truly deserving, many regarded themselves simply as women who liked to earn money, preferred the sociability of sharing work with others, chose the experience of manufacturing over endless domestic routine, and enjoyed their occasional moments of hard-earned personal freedom.

Class Conflict and Labor Organization

Women participated in all the dramatic strikes and labor conflicts of the late nineteenth century. During the nationwide rail strikes in 1877, in which workers protested layoffs and wage cuts, women joined the mobs that burned roundhouses and destroyed railroad cars. Women's involvement in such violent acts underlined the full fury of working-class resentment at the inequalities of wealth in postbellum America. "Women who are the wives and mothers of the [railroad] firemen," reported a Baltimore newspaper, "look famished and wild and declare for starvation rather than have their people work for the reduced wages."[25] President Rutherford B. Hayes sent federal forces, recently withdrawn from occupying the South, to suppress the riots. More than a hundred strikers were killed nationwide.

In the late 1870s, many angry workers joined the Knights of Labor, originally a secret society that became the largest labor organization of the nineteenth century. The Knights aimed to unite and elevate working people and to protect the country's democratic heritage from unrestrained capitalist growth. In 1881, the Knights, unlike most unions, admitted women (housewives as well as wage earners). At its peak, the Knights of Labor had 750,000 members, of whom some 10 percent were women. Its goal was to unite "the producing classes," regardless of industry or occupation or gender. Race was more complicated. In the South, the Knights admitted black workers in segregated local chapters, but in the West, the organization excluded Chinese men, whom it regarded as unfair economic competitors rather than as fellow workers.

The Knights played a major role in the nationwide campaign to shorten the workday for wage earners to eight hours, a movement of obvious interest to women. On May 1, 1886, hundreds of thousands of workers from all over the country struck on behalf of the eight-hour day. At a related rally a few days later in Chicago's Haymarket Square, a bomb exploded, killing seven policemen. Although the bomb thrower was never identified, eight male labor leaders were charged with conspiracy to murder.

◆ **Lucy Parsons**

Lucy Gonzalez Parsons was born in Texas of black, Mexican, and Native heritage. She crossed the color line to marry and moved with her husband to Chicago, where they were both labor activists. Albert Parsons was one of the eight men arrested for the alleged conspiracy behind the Haymarket Riot of 1886. Lucy fought and failed to prevent his conviction and execution. An avowed anarchist, she continued to lead protests and give speeches against social, racial, and gender inequality for another thirty years. © *Atlas Archive/The Image Works.*

READING INTO THE PAST

LEONORA BARRY
Women in the Knights of Labor

Leonora Barry (1849–1930) was one of the first female labor organizers. Her first report after being appointed head of the Women's Department of the Knights of Labor revealed a wide variety of industries with often unhealthy, low-paid, and dangerous labor performed by women. Barry, a widow when she began her assignment, resigned in 1890 when she remarried. She frequently expressed her frustration with the difficulties of organizing female labor. This report began by calling for more education of working women by the Knights of Labor. Barry decried the "selfishness of their brothers in toil" who had "sworn to demand equal pay for equal work" but failed to invest energy in female laborers. She then went on to review her many factory inspections and meetings with women wage earners.

December 6th I went to Trenton, N.J., in compliance with the request of L.A. 4925 [the L.A., or local assembly, was the basic organizing unit of the Knights of Labor]. While there made an investigation in three woolen mills, and found the condition of the female operatives to be in every respect above the average. Also visited the potteries, where many women are employed. Those people stand greatly in need of having their condition bettered, as they receive poor wages for laborious and unhealthy employment. Also visited the State Prison, and noticed, with regret, the vast amount of work of various kinds the inmates were turning out to be put on the market in competition with honest labor. While in the city, I addressed five local assemblies and held one public meeting of working women. . . .

On January 6, 1887, took up the work again in Trenton, N.J., per instruction. Held several meetings, both public and private, of working-women for the purpose of getting them into the order, as the women of this city are not well organized. Went to Bordentown to a shirt factory there, but the unjust prejudice which they have always held towards organized labor cropped out on this occasion and they refused me admission.

SOURCE: Leonora Barry, Report to the Knights of Labor, October 1886–1887, reprinted in *Tenth Annual Report of the Bureau of Statistics of Labor and Industries of New Jersey* (Somerville: Unionist-Gazette Printing House, 1888), 202–3.

QUESTION FOR ANALYSIS

1. How did Leonora Barry use her position to attempt to both improve women's working conditions and heighten the political consciousness of working-class women?

Lucy Parsons, the wife of one of the accused, helped conduct their defense. A mixed-race woman, Lucy had met her husband in Texas, where he had gone after the war to organize black voters for the Republican Party. Defense efforts eventually won gubernatorial pardons for three of the accused men, although not in time to save Albert Parsons. The violence and repression unleashed by the Haymarket incident devastated the Knights of Labor. By 1890, it had ceased to play a significant role in American labor relations. The eight-hour workday would not be won for many decades.

After the collapse of the Knights, the future of organized labor was left to male-dominated trade unions and their umbrella organization, the American Federation of Labor (AFL), founded in 1886 by Samuel Gompers, a cigar maker from New York City. While the goal of the Knights was inclusive, to unify the producing classes, the purpose of AFL unions was exclusive, to protect the jobs of skilled and relatively well-paid labor from less-skilled, lower-paid workers. Most members of AFL unions regarded women workers as exactly this sort of threat: unskilled, underpaid workers who took men's jobs during strikes. Adapting the domestic ideal of true womanhood from the middle class, the AFL subscribed to the notion that women belonged in the home and that a male worker deserved a wage sufficient to keep his wife out of the labor force.

Nonetheless, the late nineteenth-century labor movement did provide a few exceptional working women with the chance to begin speaking and acting on behalf of female wage earners. Leonora Barry and Mary Kenney were among the first women appointed by unions to organize other women workers. In 1886, the Knights of Labor designated Barry, a widowed Irish-born garment worker, to head its Woman's Department (see Reading into the Past: "Women in the Knights of Labor"). Although meeting with her might mean being fired, women workers around the country shared with Barry their complaints about wages and working conditions. Barry was their devoted advocate, but after two years, frustrated with the timidity of many working women and perhaps also with the limits of her support from the male leadership of the organization, she resigned her position.

Mary Kenney's trade was bookbinding. She joined an AFL union in Chicago and in 1891 was appointed the federation's first paid organizer for working women. She believed that working women should organize themselves but that they also needed the moral and financial support of middle- and upper-class women. The AFL was less committed to working women than the Knights, and Kenney was dismissed from her post after only six months. In the decades to come, many more female labor activists followed Barry and Kenney to play important roles in shaping women's history.

◆ WOMEN OF THE LEISURED CLASSES

Paralleling the expansion of the American working class was the dramatic growth, both in numbers and wealth, of the middle and upper classes. For this reason, one of several terms used for the post-Reconstruction years is the Gilded Age.

The phrase, first used by Mark Twain in a novel about economic and political corruption after the Civil War, captured both the riches and superficiality of the wealthier classes in the late nineteenth century. In the United States, with its proud middle-class ethic, the distinction between upper and middle class has always been hard to draw with precision, but in these years what was more important was the enormous and growing gap between those who lived comfortable, leisured lives and those who struggled with poverty. While the poor labored unceasingly, the upper class enjoyed unprecedented new wealth and influence, and the middle class imitated their values of material accumulation and display. For women of the middle and upper class, the Gilded Age meant both new affluence but also growing discontent with an exclusively domestic sphere.

New Sources of Wealth and Leisure

The tremendous economic growth of the post–Civil War era emanated from the railroads that wove together the nation and carried raw materials to factories and finished goods to customers. The great fortunes of the age were made especially in iron mining, steel manufacturing, and railroad building—and in financing these endeavors. New technologies, government subsidies, cutthroat competition, and the pressure on workers to work faster and more productively contributed to this development. Dominated by a few corporate giants, this wealth was distributed very unevenly; in 1890 an estimated 1 percent of the population controlled fully 25 percent of the country's wealth.[26] In New York City alone, the number of millionaires went from a few dozen in 1860 to several hundred in 1865. Indeed, many of the great American family fortunes were begun in the Gilded Age: John D. Rockefeller in oil, Cornelius Vanderbilt in railroads, J. P. Morgan in finance, and Andrew Carnegie in steel. One of the very few women to amass spectacular wealth on her own was Hetty Robinson Green. She began her financial career with a $10 million inheritance, which she multiplied tenfold through shrewd investment. Because she operated in the man's world of high finance, her womanliness was suspect. The popular press played up her eccentricities, dubbing her "the witch of Wall Street" rather than one of the brilliant financiers of the epoch.

Wives of wealthy men faced no such criticism. On the contrary, they were regarded as the ultimate in womanly beauty and grace. In the world of the extremely wealthy, men's obligation was to amass money while women's was to display and spend it. Wealthy women were also responsible for the conduct of "society," a word that came to mean the comings and goings of the tiny upper class, as if the rest of the population faded into insignificance by contrast. In *The Theory of the Leisure Class* (1899), sociologist Thorstein Veblen astutely observed that upper-class women not only purchased expensive commodities but were themselves their husbands' most lavish and enviable possessions.

Shopping was a new and important role for leisure-class women in the postbellum years. Middle-class women, who no longer had responsibility for a great deal of productive household labor, became active consumers. With the dramatic increase in the country's manufacturing capacity, their obligation was now to purchase rather than to produce, to spend rather than to economize. They flocked to the many department stores established in this period, grand palaces of commodities such as Marshall Field's in Chicago (founded in 1865), Macy's in New York (1866), Strawbridge and Clothier in Philadelphia (1868), Hudson's in Detroit (1887), and May's in Denver (1888). They filled the elaborate interiors of their homes with furniture and decorative items. Even at a distance from the proliferating retail possibilities of the cities, rural women had mail order catalogs to look at, long for, and occasionally purchase the many commodities of the age.

Rising incomes lifted the burden of housekeeping off urban middle- and upper-class women in other ways. Cities laid water and sewer lines, but only in wealthy neighborhoods in which households could afford the fees; indoor plumbing and running water made housework easier for prosperous women. But the most important factor in easing the load of housekeeping for leisure-class women was undoubtedly the cheap labor of domestic servants. Despite constant complaints about the shortage of domestic help, middle-class families regarded having at least one or two paid domestic servants as a virtual necessity. The wealthy had small armies of them. Laundry, which required enormous energy and much time when done in an individual household, was sent out to commercial establishments, where poor and immigrant women pressed and folded sheets and linens in overheated steam rooms.

Another important factor in freeing middle- and upper-class women from domestic demands was the declining birthrate (see the Appendix, p. A-17). Between 1850 and 1890, the average number of live births for white, native-born women fell from 5.42 to 3.87. African American birthrates were not recorded in the federal census until several decades later, but by all impressionistic evidence, they declined even more dramatically, as freedwomen took control of their lives at the most intimate level. Ironically, birthrates declined in inverse proportion to class status: the wealthiest, with money to spare, had proportionately fewer children than the very poor, whose earnings were stretched to the limit but who relied on their children for income.

In understanding the many individual decisions that went into the declining birthrate among leisure-class women, the explanation is not obvious. There were no dramatic improvements in contraceptive technology or knowledge in these years. On the contrary, traditional means of controlling pregnancy — early versions of condoms and diaphragms — were banned by new laws that defined them as obscene devices; even discussions aimed at limiting reproduction were forbidden. Following the Comstock Act of 1873, which outlawed the use of the U.S. mails for distributing information on controlling reproduction, twenty-four states criminalized the dissemination of contraceptive devices.

Rather, declining birthrates seem to have been both a cause and an effect of the expanding sphere of leisure-class women. Women's decisions to limit their pregnancies reflected a growing desire for personal satisfaction and social contribution beyond motherhood. Even though maternity remained the assumed destiny of womanhood, many women were coming to believe that they could choose when and how often to become pregnant. In advocating "voluntary motherhood,"

◆ **Rike-Kumler Co. Department Store, Dayton, Ohio**
Department store counters were one place where working- and leisure-class women met. Neat dress, good English, and middle-class manners were job requirements, even though pay was no better than for factory work. Customers like the woman being fitted for gloves in this 1893 photograph sat, but clerks stood all day, one of the conditions of their work to which they most objected. *Bettmann/Getty Images.*

Harriot Stanton Blatch, Elizabeth Cady Stanton's daughter, encouraged women to choose for themselves when to have sexual intercourse. Her speeches brilliantly exploited the nineteenth-century belief that motherhood was woman's highest vocation, in order to argue for women's rights to control whether and when they had children. Reformers like Blatch did not yet envision the separation of women's sexual activity from the possibility of pregnancy, but they did believe that women should have control over both. The very term "birth control" and the movement to advance it came later in the twentieth century (see pp. 441–44), but basic changes in female reproductive behavior were already under way.

As women's reproductive lives changed, so did their understanding of their sexuality. To be sure, many restrictive sexual assumptions remained in place.

Some physicians still regarded strong sexual desire in women as a disease, which they treated by methods ranging from a diet of bland foods to surgical removal of the clitoris. But the heterosexual double standard — that men's sexual desire was uncontrollable and that women's was nonexistent — was beginning to come under fire. By the end of the century, even the conservative physician Elizabeth Blackwell was writing in carefully chosen language that "in healthy, loving women, uninjured by the too frequent lesions which result from childbirth, increasing physical satisfaction attaches to the ultimate physical expression of love."[27]

Lesbianism, in the modern sense of women openly and consistently expressing sexual desire for other women, had not yet been named, but in these years many leisure-class women formed intense attachments with each other. These "homosocial" relationships, as modern historians have designated them, ranged from intense, lifelong friendships to relationships that were as emotionally charged, as beset by jealousy and possessiveness, and quite possibly as physically intimate, as any heterosexual love affair. Mary (Molly) Hallock and Helena De Kay were two such friends. They met in 1868 as art students in New York and wrote frequently and passionately to each other. When Helena announced that she was marrying New York publisher Richard Gilder, Molly angrily wrote to him: "Until you came along, sir, I believe she loved me almost as girls love their lovers."[28]

Most of what we know about such homosocial relations comes from leisure-class women, perhaps because they wrote more letters that were preserved and handed down to families and archivists than working-class women did. But surely some working-class women experienced similar passions. A set of letters between two African American women living in Connecticut during the 1860s offers the rare example of a cross-class homosocial relationship, moreover one that was strongly suggestive of physical intimacy. Rebecca Primus, a schoolteacher, and Addie Brown, a seamstress, domestic worker, and laundress, conducted what the historian of their bond calls "a self-consciously sexual relationship" focused on fondling breasts.[29]

By the late nineteenth century, such intense bonds were coming under scrutiny from physicians. Recognizing the obvious erotic qualities of these intense same-sex relationships, neurologists sought to give them the dignity of scientific recognition, even as they characterized them as "unnatural" or "abnormal." Women-loving women who, in an earlier decade, would have believed unquestioningly in the asexual purity and innocence of their attachments, were beginning to read scientific writings about homosexuality and to wonder about the meaning and nature of their own feelings.

The "Woman's Era"

Before the Civil War, women had formed charitable and religious societies and had worked together on behalf of temperance, abolition, and women's rights (see pp. 235–48). After the war, associational fervor among women was more diverse, secular, and independent of male oversight. Participation in Gilded Age women's societies provided numerous women with new opportunities for collective

◆ **Alice Austen and Friends Dress Up as Men (1891)**

This photograph is by and of Alice Austen, a brilliant amateur photographer who left a visual record of Gilded Age leisure-class female lives. Here, Austen (on the left) posed in drag with two of her female friends. "Maybe we were better looking men than women," she quipped when, as an old woman, she looked once again at the photo. In the context of Austen's decision not to marry but to live her life with another woman, this photo made her a historical icon for modern lesbians. *Alice Austen Collection, Staten Island Historical Society.*

activity, intellectual growth, and public life. By the end of the nineteenth century, leisure-class women had almost totally commandeered nongovernmental civic life from men. Thus, another apt label for the post-Reconstruction years is the Woman's Era.

The women's club movement began in the Northeast just after the Civil War among white middle-class women. In 1868, New York City women writers formed a group they named Sorosis (a botanical term that suggested sisterhood) to protest their exclusion from an event held by male writers. Simultaneously, a group of Boston reformers led by Julia Ward Howe (author of "The Battle Hymn of the Republic") organized the New England Women's Club, dedicated to the cultivation of intellectual discussion and public authority for leisure-class women.

Despite their impeccable reputations, both groups were publicly lambasted for their unladylike behavior. "Woman is straying from her sphere," warned the *Boston Transcript*.[30]

Despite such criticisms, women's clubs thrived among those middle-aged married women whose childrearing years were behind them. The concerns of the women's club movement evolved from literary and cultural matters in the 1870s to local social service projects in the 1880s to regional and national federations for political influence in the 1890s. Many public institutions established in the Gilded Age — hospitals and orphanages as well as libraries and museums — were originally established by women's clubs. From the Northeast, the club movement spread to the West and then the South.

Clubs by their nature are exclusive institutions, and the sororal bonds of women's clubs reflected their tendency to draw together women of like background. In the larger cities, class differences distinguished elite women's clubs from those formed by wives of clerks and shopkeepers. Working women's clubs were rarely initiated by wage-earning women themselves but were likely to be uplift projects of middle- and upper-class clubwomen. Race and religion were especially important principles of association. German Jewish women and African American women organized separately from the mainstream women's club movement, which was largely white and Protestant. Generally, middle-class Jewish or African American women formed their own clubs both to assist poorer women and to cultivate their own skills and self-confidence.

The ethic of women's clubs was particularly compelling to African American women. They formed organizations not just to enlarge their horizons as women but to play their part in the enormous project of post-emancipation racial progress. "If we compare the present condition of the colored people of the South with their condition twenty-eight years ago," explained African American clubwoman Sarah J. Early in 1893, "we shall see how the organized efforts of their women have contributed to the elevation of the race and their marvelous achievement in so short a time."[31] By her estimate, there were five thousand "colored women's societies" with half a million members. Black women organized separately from white women because they were serving a different population with distinctive needs but also because they were usually refused admission into white women's clubs. Racism was alive and well in the women's club movement.

The relation of the Gilded Age women's club phenomenon to woman suffrage is complex. At first, white women who formed and joined clubs took care to distinguish themselves from the radicalism and notoriety associated with woman suffragists. Yet women's rights and woman suffrage were standard subjects for club discussion, and over time members came to accept the idea that women should have political tools to accomplish their public goals. Black clubwomen were less hesitant to embrace woman suffrage in light of their concerns over the disfranchisement of black men. Over time women's clubs incubated support for woman suffrage within a wide swath of the female middle class and prepared the way for the tremendous growth in the suffrage movement in the early twentieth century (see pp. 434–39).

The Woman's Christian Temperance Union

The largest women's organization of the Woman's Era was the Woman's Christian Temperance Union (WCTU). Following on women's temperance activities in the 1850s (see pp. 236–37), the WCTU was formed in 1874 after a series of women's "crusades" in Ohio and New York that convinced local saloon owners to abandon the liquor trade. Initially focused on changing drinking behavior at the individual level, the organization soon challenged the liquor industry politically and undertook a wide range of public welfare projects such as prison reform, recreation and vocational training for young people, establishment of kindergartens, labor reform, and international peace. These projects and the ability of the WCTU to cultivate both organizational loyalty and individual growth among its members were characteristics it shared with women's clubs, but the WCTU was different in crucial ways.

◆ Frances Willard Learns to Ride a Bicycle

Frances Willard, president of the WCTU, combined sympathy with conventional Protestant middle-class women and an advanced understanding of women's untapped capacities. In 1895, "sighing for new worlds to conquer," she learned to ride a bicycle, one of the signature New Woman activities of the period. "Reducing the problem to actual figures," she methodically reported, "it took me about three months, with an average of fifteen minutes' practice daily, to learn, first, to pedal; second, to turn; third, to dismount; and fourth, to mount."[32] Willard, not yet sixty, died in 1898, after which the WCTU never regained its prominence or progressive vision. *Courtesy of the Frances E. Willard Memorial Library and Archives.*

On the one hand, it defined itself explicitly as Christian; on the other, it was racially more inclusive than the club movement. The writer Frances Ellen Watkins Harper was one of several African American WCTU spokeswomen, and black women were welcomed into the organization, though in segregated divisions. The WCTU's centers of strength were less urban and more western and midwestern than those of women's clubs.

Finally, unlike the women's club movement, the WCTU was to a large degree the product of a single and highly effective leader, Frances Willard. Willard was born in 1839 and raised on a farm in Ohio. She never married. Determined to serve "the class that I have always loved and that has loved me always — the girls of my native land and my times,"[33] she became the first Dean of Women at Northwestern University at age thirty-four. In 1879, she was elected president of the WCTU, rapidly increasing its membership, diversifying its purposes, and making it the most powerful women's organization in the country. Disciplined and diplomatic, she was able to take the WCTU to levels of political action and reform that the unwieldy mass of clubwomen could never reach. Notably, this included active advocacy of woman suffrage, which the WCTU formally and enthusiastically endorsed in 1884. "If we are ever to save the State," Willard declared, "we must enfranchise the sex . . . which is much more acclimatized to self-sacrifice for others. . . . Give us the vote, in order that we may help in purifying politics."[34]

Consolidating the Gilded Age Women's Movement

The endorsement of woman suffrage by the WCTU convinced Susan B. Anthony to encourage and draw together the pro-suffrage leanings developing within so many women's organizations. "Those active in great philanthropic enterprises," she insisted, "[will] sooner or later realize that so long as women are not acknowledged to be the political equals of men, their judgment on public questions will have but little weight."[35] Accordingly, in 1888, in honor of the fortieth anniversary of the Seneca Falls Convention, the National Woman Suffrage Association sponsored an International Congress of Women, attended by representatives of several European countries and many U.S. women's organizations. Out of this congress came an International Council of Women and a U.S. National Council of Women, both formed in 1893. Both organizations were so broadly inclusive of women's public and civic activities as to admit anti-suffrage groups, and much to Anthony's disappointment, neither served as the vehicle for advancing the prospects of woman suffrage.

Other overarching organizational structures were formed. In 1890, NWSA and the American Woman Suffrage Association reconciled, forming the National American Woman Suffrage Association (NAWSA), which led the suffrage movement for the next thirty years. On the international level, U.S. suffragists joined with European colleagues to initiate the formation of an International Woman Suffrage Association in 1902. The associative impulse was constantly tending to greater and greater combination, amalgamating women in clubs, clubs in state federations, and state federations in national organizations. The vision shared by these federative efforts was of a unity of women so broad and ecumenical as to obliterate all differences between women. But the vision of all-inclusivity was a fantasy. For as women's social activism and public involvement grew, so did their ambitions and rivalries. Even as the National Council of Women was formed, the leaders of the venerable Sorosis club, who felt they should have been chosen to head this endeavor, set up a rival in the General Federation of Women's Clubs. Nor were federations any more racially inclusive than individual clubs. The General Federation of Women's Clubs refused to admit black women's clubs. In 1895, African American women's clubs federated separately as the National Association of Colored Women, and the next year the National Council of Jewish Women was formed.

The ambitious scope and unresolved divisions of "organized womanhood" were equally on display in Chicago in 1893 at the World's Columbian Exposition, America's first world's fair. The Board of Lady Managers received public funds to build and furnish a special Woman's Building. Eighty sessions held at the Congress of Representative Women addressed "all lines of thought connected with the progress of women." But African American women were excluded from the planning and management, and women from indigenous cultures, including the American Eskimo, were "on display" on the fair's midway as exotics.

Looking to the Future

By 1890, a new, more modern culture was slowly gathering force under the complacent surface of late nineteenth-century America. The Gilded Age was

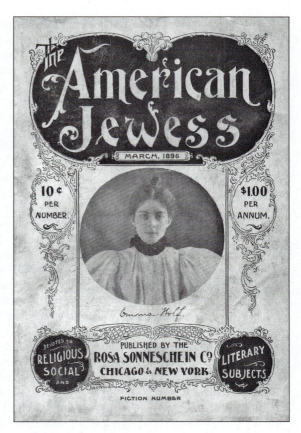

◆ The American Jewess
In the 1890s, many Jewish American women became active in promoting social reform and Americanization programs through the National Council of Jewish Women (founded in 1896), which was part of the broader movement toward women's clubs. Printed from 1895 to 1896, *The American Jewess* was the first English-language magazine for Jewish women. It was published by Rosa Sonneschein, a progressive who challenged the discrimination women experienced within the synagogue and sought to promote an Americanized Jewish identity for women. As she put it, *The American Jewess* was intended "to connect the sisters dwelling throughout . . . this blessed country, concentrate the work of scattered charitable institutions, and bring them to the notice of the various communities as an imposing and powerful unit." *Klau Library, Cincinnati, Hebrew Union College–Jewish Institute of Religion.*

organized around grand and opposing categories: home and work, black and white, capital and labor, virtue and vice, masculine and feminine. While nineteenth-century society subscribed to a rigid hierarchy of values and a firm belief in absolute truth, modernist convictions allowed for greater contingency and relativism in assessing people and ideas. The concept of morality, so crucial to nineteenth-century cultural judgment, was losing some of its coercive force, giving way to a greater emphasis on individuality, inner life, the free development of personality, and psychological variety.

An important sign of this cultural shift was the growing displacement of the ideal of the "true woman" by the image of the "New Woman," both in women's rights circles and in popular representations of femininity. For modern women of the late nineteenth century, true womanhood no longer seemed virtuous and industrious but idle and purposeless. New Women pushed against the boundaries of woman's sphere to participate in public life. (See Primary Sources: "The New Woman," pp. 345–52.) Their ethic emphasized "woman's work," a term that sometimes meant paid labor, sometimes public service, but always an alternative to exclusive domesticity.

Clubwoman and author Charlotte Perkins Gilman was the first great spokeswoman for the New Woman. Gilman went so far as to criticize the single family household and the exclusive dedication of women to motherhood. "With the larger socialization of the woman of today, the fitness for and accompanying desire for wider combination, more general interest, . . . more organized methods of work for larger ends," she wrote in her widely read *Women and Economics* (1898), "she feels more and more heavily the intensely personal limits of the more primitive home duties, interests, methods."[36] Gilman's writings emphasized a second element of the New Woman ethic, the importance of female individuation, of each woman realizing her distinctive talents, capacities, and personality. Individualism was a long-standing American value, but it had been traditionally reserved for men. Men were individuals with different abilities; women were members of a category with common characteristics. New Womanhood challenged this vision of contrasting masculinity and femininity and claimed the legacy of individualism for women.

At age seventy-seven, Elizabeth Cady Stanton stressed this individualist dimension in her 1892 speech "The Solitude of Self," presented to a committee of the U.S. Congress and then to the National American Woman Suffrage Association. "The point I wish plainly to bring before you on this occasion," she began, "is the individuality of each human soul. . . . In discussing the rights of woman, we are to consider, first, what belongs to her as an individual, in a world of her own, the arbiter of her own destiny."[37] The speech was Cady Stanton's swan song from suffrage leadership. Anthony's vision of a moderate, broad-based suffrage movement contrasted with Cady Stanton's inclination to challenge relentlessly women's conventional values. A few years later, Cady Stanton went so far as to lambaste the Bible for its misogyny. The greatest expression of her lifelong passion for individual women's freedom, "The Solitude of Self" looked forward to a future of women's efforts for emancipation that would be so different from the approach of the Woman's Era, so modern in its emphasis on the self and on psychological change, as to require a new name: feminism.

◆ CONCLUSION: Toward a New Womanhood

The end of the Civil War ushered in a period of great conflict. Reconstruction sought to restore the Union and to replace sectionalism with a unified sense of nationhood, but at its end in 1877 unity remained elusive for all Americans. Various terms for the post-Reconstruction era indicate its different aspects. In the New South during Redemption, black and white women regarded each other over an embattled racial gulf, altered and intensified by emancipation. Meanwhile, in the America of the Gilded Age, a new divide had opened up between labor and capital. As the American economy became increasingly industrialized, the numbers and visibility of women wage earners grew, along with their determination to join in efforts to bring democracy to American class relations. For their part, middle- and upper-class women created what is called the Woman's Era as they pursued new opportunities in education, civic organization, and public authority. (See Primary Sources: "The Higher Education of Women in the Postbellum Years," pp. 336–44.)

Two other aspects of the changing face of America in the late nineteenth century are considered in Chapter 7: the massive immigration that underlay the growth, and much of the assertiveness, of the American working class; and the physical expansion and consolidation of the nation through the further incorporation of western lands. Women were important actors in the multifaceted political crisis in the 1890s, which brought together all of these phenomena — racial and class conflict, woman's expanding sphere, massive ethnic change, and the nation's physical expansion up to and beyond its borders. By 1900, women were poised on the brink of one of the most active and important eras in American history through women's eyes, the Progressive years.

CHAPTER 6 REVIEW

KEY TERMS AND PEOPLE

Terms
Thirteenth, Fourteenth, and
　　Fifteenth Amendments
Comstock Act
Minor v. Happersett
Knights of Labor
"voluntary motherhood"
Women's Christian
　　Temperance Union
National American Woman
　　Suffrage Association

General Federation of Women's
　　Clubs
National Association of
　　Colored Women
National Council of Jewish
　　Women
"New Woman"

People
Victoria Woodhull
Mary Ann Shadd Cary
Charlotte Forten Grimké
Ida B. Wells
Lucy Parsons
Leonora Barry
Mary Kenney
Frances Willard
Frances Ellen Watkins Harper
Charlotte Perkins Gilman

REVIEW QUESTIONS

1. What was the impact of the Fourteenth and Fifteenth Amendments on the women's rights movement, and what new strategies did suffragists develop after their ratification?
2. Analyze the different meanings of emancipation for black and white women of the South. How did race, class, and gender politics in the "New South" compare to those in the Old South?
3. What were the most significant changes in women's labor between 1865 and 1900? How, if at all, did labor organizations in this period attempt to address women worker's issues?
4. What new organizations did American middle-class and leisure-class women create to address the conditions resulting from industrialization?
5. **Making Connections** How did women shape American society in the post–Civil War decades as workers, social and political reformers, and intellectuals?

PRIMARY SOURCES

Ida B. Wells, "Race Woman"

I N THE YEARS AFTER 1877, when the federal protections of Reconstruction ended and the freed black population of the South was left on its own to resist resurgent white supremacy, a generation of exceptional female African American leaders emerged. Of these, none was more extraordinary than Ida B. Wells. Born in 1862 in Mississippi, she was orphaned at the age of sixteen by a yellow fever epidemic. Determined to assume responsibility for her siblings and to keep her family together, she found work first as a teacher and then as a journalist. In 1889 in Memphis, she purchased part ownership of an African American newspaper, *Free Speech and Headlight*. Her goal was to expose and publicize the mistreatment of her people. In an age notable for its florid and euphemistic writing, Wells's style was straightforward and explicit. She was not afraid to use the word "rape" to describe the accusations against black men and the experiences of black women.

Wells was catapulted into the role that changed her life when her friend Thomas Moss, a prosperous grocer and mail carrier, was lynched by a Memphis mob in 1892. Taken in the months following the lynching, Figure 6.1 shows Ida B. Wells posing with widow Betty Moss and the Moss children. Wells spent time with the Moss family as they mourned the loss of a father and husband. She recalled how "the baby daughter of Tom Moss, too young to express how she misses her father, toddles to the wardrobe, seizes the legs of his letter-carrier uniform, hugs and kisses them with evident delight and stretches her little hands to be taken up into arms that will never more clasp his daughter's form."[38] What details in the photograph provide clues to the close emotional bond between Ida Wells and Betty Moss?

◆ **Figure 6.1 Ida B. Wells with the Family of Thomas Moss (1893)**
Special Collections Research Center, University of Chicago Library.

Although the practice of lynching had a long history elsewhere, in the South during this period, the accused were black and the mobs white. Wells concluded that Moss's "crime" had been the competition that his successful grocery business posed to whites. Over a hundred years later, we take for granted the connections that she was the first to make: between the postwar political and economic gains made by freedpeople and the brutal violence unleashed on them by resentful whites; and between the long history of sexual exploitation of black women during slavery and the inflammatory charges made after emancipation to justify lynching—that black men were sexual predators.

Perhaps the most remarkable element of Wells's analysis was her insistence that black and white people sometimes voluntarily chose to be each other's sexual partners. She was not particularly in favor of the practice. She was what was called in this period a "race woman," meaning that her concerns were less for integration than for the happiness and progress of African Americans. "A proper self-respect is expected of races as individuals," she later wrote. "We need more race love; the tie of racehood should bind us [through] . . . a more hearty appreciation of each other."[39] Nonetheless, she appreciated the difference between willing and coerced sex and defended the former while criticizing the latter. She understood that so long as interracial sex was concealed as a fact of southern life, black people would pay the deadly price.

Her investigations into the practice of lynching got her driven out of Memphis in 1892. This autobiographical account details the impact that her harrowing experience had on African American women in the North, who went on to form the National Association of Colored Women and to join in the work of exposing the true nature, extent, and causes of southern lynchings. Exiled from the South, she moved to Chicago, where in 1895 she married Frederick Barnett, also a journalist and activist, and continued to battle for justice for her race by working for greater political power for black people. She played an early role in organizing African American women to secure and use the right to vote. Her autobiography remained unfinished and unpublished until brought into print by her youngest child, Alfreda Duster, more than a century after her mother's birth.

As you read, consider what led Wells to undertake an exposé of lynching and how doing so challenged the expectations of race and gender that she faced. What does Wells's analysis of the causes of and attitudes toward the lynching of African Americans reveal about the dynamics between whites and blacks several decades after the end of slavery?

IDA B. WELLS
Crusade for Justice: The Autobiography of Ida B. Wells (1970)

While I was thus carrying on the work of my newspaper, . . . there came the lynching in Memphis which changed the whole course of my life. . . .

Thomas Moss, Calvin McDowell, and Henry Stewart owned and operated a grocery store in a thickly populated suburb. . . . There was already a grocery owned and operated by a white man who hitherto had had a monopoly on the trade of this thickly populated colored suburb. Thomas's grocery changed all that, and he and his associates were made to feel that they were not welcome by the white grocer. . . .

One day some colored and white boys quarreled over a game of marbles and the colored boys got the better of the fight which followed. . . . Then the challenge was issued that the vanquished whites were coming on Saturday night to clean out [Thomas's] Colored People's Grocery Company. . . . Accordingly the grocery company armed several men and stationed them in the rear of the store on that fatal Saturday night, not to attack but to repel a threatened attack. . . . The men stationed there had seen several white men stealing through the rear door and fired on them without a moment's pause. Three of these men were wounded, and others fled and gave the alarm. . . . Over a hundred colored men were dragged from their homes and put in jail on suspicion.

All day long on that fateful Sunday white men were permitted in the jail to look over the imprisoned black men. . . . The mob took out of their cells Thomas Moss, Calvin McDowell, and Henry Stewart, the three officials of the People's Grocery Company. They were loaded on a switch engine of the railroad which ran back of the jail, carried a mile north of the city limits, and horribly shot to death. One of the morning papers held back its edition in order to supply its readers with the details of that lynching. . . . The mob took possession of the People's Grocery Company, helping themselves to food and drink, and destroyed what they could not eat or steal. The creditors had the place closed and a few days later what remained of the stock was sold at auction. Thus, with the aid of city and county authorities and the daily papers, that white grocer had indeed put an end to his rival Negro grocer as well as to his business. . . .

SOURCE: Alfreda M. Duster, ed., *Crusade for Justice: The Autobiography of Ida B. Wells* (Chicago: University of Chicago Press, 1970), 47–82.

Like many another person who had read of lynchings in the South, I had accepted the idea meant to be conveyed—that although lynching was irregular and contrary to law and order, unreasoning anger over the terrible crime of rape led to the lynching; that perhaps the brute deserved death anyhow and the mob was justified in taking his life.

But Thomas Moss, Calvin McDowell and Henry Stewart had been lynched in Memphis, one of the leading cities of the South, in which no lynching had taken place before, with just as much brutality as other victims of the mob; and they had committed no crime against white women. This is what opened my eyes to what lynching really was. An excuse to get rid of Negroes who were acquiring wealth and property and thus keep the race terrorized and "keep the nigger down." I then began an investigation of every lynching I read about. I stumbled on the amazing record that every case of rape reported . . . became such only when it became public.

Many cases were like that of the lynching which happened in Tunica County, Mississippi. The Associated Press reporter said, "The big burly brute was lynched because he had raped the seven-year-old daughter of the sheriff." I visited the place afterward and saw the girl, who was a grown woman more than seventeen years old. She had been found in the lynched Negro's cabin by her father, who had led the mob against him in order to save his daughter's reputation. That Negro was a helper on the farm. . . .

It was with these and other stories in mind in that last week in May 1892 that I wrote the following editorial:

Eight Negroes lynched since last issue of the *Free Speech*. They were charged with killing white men and five with raping white women. Nobody in this section believes the old thread-bare lie that Negro men assault white women. If Southern white men are not careful they will overreach themselves and a conclusion will be drawn which will be very damaging to the moral reputation of their women.

This editorial furnished at last the excuse for doing what the white leaders of Memphis had long been wanting to do: put an end to the *Free Speech.* . . .

Having lost my paper, had a price put on my life, and been made an exile from home for hinting at the truth, I felt that I owed it to myself and to my race to tell the whole truth now that I was where I could do so freely. Accordingly, the fourth week in June, the *New York Age* had a seven-column article on the front page giving names, dates and places of many lynchings for alleged rape. This article showed conclusively that my editorial in the *Free Speech* was based on facts of illicit association between black men and white women.

Such relationships between white men and colored women were notorious, and had been as long as the two races had lived together in the South. . . . Many stories of the antebellum South were based upon such relationships. It has been frequently charged in narratives of slave times that these white fathers often sold their mulatto children into slavery. It was also well known that many other such white fathers and masters brought their mulatto and quadroon children to the North and gave them freedom and established homes for them, thus making them independent.

All my life I had known that such conditions were accepted as a matter of course. I found that this rape of helpless Negro girls and women, which began in slavery days, still continued without . . . hindrance, check or reproof from church, state, or press until there had been created this race within a race — and all designated by the inclusive term of "colored."

I also found that what the white man of the South practiced as all right for himself, he assumed to be unthinkable in white women. They could and did fall in love with the pretty mulatto and quadroon girls as well as black ones, but they professed an inability to imagine white women

doing the same thing with Negro and mulatto men. Whenever they did so and were found out, the cry of rape was raised, and the lowest element of the white South was turned loose to wreak its fiendish cruelty on those too weak to help themselves. . . .

The more I studied the situation, the more I was convinced that the Southerner had never gotten over his resentment that the Negro was no longer his plaything, his servant, and his source of income. The federal laws for Negro protection passed during Reconstruction had been made a mockery by the white South where it had not secured their repeal. This same white South had secured political control of its several states, and as soon as white southerners came into power they began to make playthings of Negro lives and property. This still seemed not enough "to keep the nigger down."

Here came lynch law to stifle Negro manhood which defended itself, and the burning alive of Negroes who were weak enough to accept favors from white women. The many unspeakable and unprintable tortures to which Negro rapists (?) [here Wells inserted a parenthetical question mark to indicate her skepticism of these charges] of white women were subjected were for the purpose of striking terror into the hearts of other Negroes who might be thinking of consorting with willing white women.

I found that in order to justify these horrible atrocities to the world, the Negro was branded as a race of rapists, who were especially after white women. I found that white men who had created a race of mulattoes by raping and consorting with Negro women were still doing so wherever they could; these same white men lynched, burned and tortured Negro men for doing the same thing with white women; even when the white women were willing victims.

That the entire race should be branded as moral monsters and despoilers of white womanhood and childhood was bound to rob us of all the friends we had and silence any protests that they might make for us. For all these reasons it seemed a stern duty to give the facts I had collected to the world. . . .

About two months after my appearance in the columns in the *New York Age*, two colored women remarked on my revelations during a visit with each other and said they thought that the women of New York and Brooklyn should do something to show appreciation of my work and to protest the treatment which I had received. . . . A committee of two hundred and fifty women was appointed, and they stirred up sentiment throughout the two cities which culminated in a testimonial at Lyric Hall on 5 October 1892.

This testimonial was conceded by the oldest inhabitants to be the greatest demonstration ever attempted by race women for one of their number. . . . The leading colored women of Boston and Philadelphia had been invited to join in this demonstration, and they came, a brilliant array . . . behind a lonely, homesick girl who was an exile because she had tried to defend the manhood of her race. . . .

So many things came out of that wonderful testimonial.

First it was the beginning of the club movement among the colored women in this country. The women of New York and Brooklyn decided to continue that organization, which they called the Women's Loyal Union. These were the first strictly women's clubs organized in those cities. Mrs. Ruffin of Boston, who came over to that testimonial . . . called a meeting of the women at her home to meet me, and they organized themselves into the Woman's Era Club of that city. Mrs. Ruffin had been a member of the foremost clubs among white women in Boston for years, but this was her first effort to form one among colored women. . . .

Second, that testimonial was the beginning of public speaking for me. I have already said that I had not before made speeches, but invitations came from Philadelphia, Wilmington, Delaware, Chester, Pennsylvania, and Washington, D.C. . . .

In Philadelphia . . . Miss Catherine Impey of Street Somerset, England, was visiting Quaker relatives of hers in the city and at the same time was trying to learn what she could about the color question in this country. She was the editor of *Anti-Caste*, a magazine published in England in behalf of the natives of India, and she was therefore interested in the treatment of darker races everywhere. . . . [Thus happened] the third great result of that wonderful testimonial in New York the previous month. Although we did not know it at the time, the interview between Miss Impey and myself resulted in an invitation to England and the beginning of the worldwide campaign against lynching.

QUESTIONS FOR ANALYSIS

1. What were the underlying tensions and larger conflicts that led to the lynching of Thomas Moss?

2. What was the prevailing opinion about lynching that Wells was determined to challenge?

3. What did Wells see as the relationship between the long history of white men raping black women and the charges raised against black men of raping white women?

4. How did Wells's campaign contribute to the consolidation of the organized African American women's movement?

The Woman Who Toils

THE LIVES AND LABORS of white wage-earning women and leisure-class women intersected in numerous ways in the late nineteenth century. Maids, cooks, nannies, and laundresses provided the labor that made possible the elaborate homes and active social lives of leisure-class women. Working women and their children were the objects of the charitable and philanthropic projects that middle- and upper-class women, aiming for a larger role in community affairs, organized in these years. Above all, working women provided the labor to manufacture the food, clothing, and luxuries that distinguished the rich from the poor. As the authors of *The Woman Who Toils* explained to wealthy women, working women provided "the labour that must be done to satisfy your material demands."[40]

By the end of the century, working-class women were also the subject of professional women's journalistic and sociological investigations, of which *The Woman Who Toils: Being the Experiences of Two Ladies as Factory Girls* (1903) is a notable example. The authors, Bessie and Marie Van Vorst, were upper-class women. Marie was born a Van Vorst, and Bessie married into the family. Neither went to college. Both were educated instead in the manner preferred by the upper classes for their daughters, by private tutors and at female academies. After Bessie's husband (Marie's brother) died, the two women, both still in their thirties, decided together to establish greater economic independence for themselves. They moved to Paris and cowrote a novel about an upper-class American woman abroad. Their next collaborative effort was *The Woman Who Toils*, a journalistic account of the lives of wage-earning women. As upper-class New Women aspiring to independence, they were motivated by both their growing awareness of the lives of working-class women and their own authorial ambitions.

To research the book, they returned to the United States, assumed fictional identities, and took a series of working-class jobs. Marie worked in a New England shoe factory and a southern textile mill. Bessie became the Irishwoman "Esther Kelly" and took a job in a pickling factory in Pittsburgh, where she went from eagerness to exhaustion in a few short days. Moving from job to job in the factory, Bessie explored how different it felt to work for a preset daily wage and to work for payment by the piece — an arrangement that led workers to drive themselves to work faster. A day in the male workers' dining room allowed her to compare manufacturing to domestic service labor.

Throughout Bessie's account, the distance she maintained from the women she wrote about is evident. She and her sister-in-law chose a subtitle to clarify that they were still "ladies" despite their brief stint as factory girls. The young men with whom their coworkers associated, the recreation they sought, and the clothes they wore seemed to them "vulgar." Like most reformers, they did not endorse wage labor for women with children, a point emphasized by President Theodore Roosevelt in his introduction to their book. Nonetheless, Bessie came to appreciate the generosity of her coworkers, the pleasures of collective work, and the "practical, progressive" democracy of working-class life. Above all, it was the sheer physical demands of doing the job, descriptions of which are among the best parts of the Pittsburgh pickling section of *The Woman Who Toils*, that seem to have broken through her shield of gentility and brought her a measure of closeness to the women workers about whom she wrote.

As you read this account of working in the pickle factory, identify what Bessie Van Vorst finds attractive about the jobs she does and the women who do them, and what she finds repellent. Consider the points at which her class prejudices emerge, and the points at which she gets beyond them.

Mrs. John (Bessie) Van Vorst and Marie Van Vorst
The Woman Who Toils: Being the Experiences of Two Ladies as Factory Girls (1903)

"What will you do about your name?" "What will you do with your hair and your hands?" "How can you deceive people?" These are some of the questions I had been asked by my friends.

Before any one had cared or needed to know my name it was morning of the second day, and my assumed name seemed by that time the only one I had ever had. As to hair and hands, a half-day's work suffices for their undoing. And my disguise is so successful I have deceived not only others but myself. I have become with desperate reality a factory girl, alone, inexperienced, friendless. I am making $4.20 a week and spending $3 of this for board alone, and I dread not being strong enough to keep my job. I climb endless stairs, am given a white cap and an apron, and my life as a factory girl begins. I become part of the ceaseless, unrelenting mechanism kept in motion by the poor. . . .

My first task is an easy one; anybody could do it. On the stroke of seven my fingers fly. I place a lid of paper in a tin jar-top, over it a cork; this I press down with both hands, tossing the cover, when done, into a pan. In spite of myself I hurry; I cannot work fast enough — I outdo my companions. How can they be so slow? Every nerve, every muscle is offering some of its energy. Over in one corner the machinery for sealing the jars groans and roars; the mingled sounds of filling, washing, wiping, packing, comes to my eager ears as an accompaniment for the simple work assigned to me. One hour passes, two, three hours; I fit ten, twenty, fifty dozen caps, and still my energy keeps up. . . .

When I have fitted 110 dozen tin caps the forewoman comes and changes my job. She tells me to haul and load up some heavy crates with pickle jars. I am wheeling these back and forth when the twelve o'clock whistle blows. Up to that time the room has been one big dynamo, each girl a part of it. With the first moan of the noon signal the dynamo comes to life. It is hungry; it has friends and favourites — news to tell.

SOURCE: Mrs. John Van Vorst and Marie Van Vorst, *The Woman Who Toils: Being the Experiences of Two Ladies as Factory Girls* (New York: Doubleday, Page & Co, 1903), 21–58.

We herd down to a big dining room and take our places, five hundred of us in all. The newspaper bundles are unfolded. The menu varies little: bread and jam, cake and pickles, occasionally a sausage, a bit of cheese or a piece of stringy cold meat. In ten minutes the repast is over. The dynamo has been fed; there are twenty minutes of leisure spent in dancing, singing, resting, and conversing chiefly about young men and "sociables."

At 12:30 sharp the whistle draws back the life it has given. I return to my job. My shoulders are beginning to ache. My hands are stiff, my thumbs almost blistered. The enthusiasm I had felt is giving way to numbing weariness. I look at my companions now in amazement. How can they keep on so steadily, so swiftly? . . . New girls like myself who had worked briskly in the morning are beginning to loiter. Out of the washing-tins hands come up red and swollen, only to be plunged again into hot dirty water. Would the whistle never blow? . . . At last the whistle blows! In a swarm we report: we put on our things and get away into the cool night air. I have stood ten hours; I have fitted 1,300 corks; I have hauled and loaded 4,000 jars of pickles. My pay is seventy cents. . . .

For the two days following my first experience I am unable to resume work. Fatigue has swept through my body like a fever. Every bone and joint has a clamouring ache. . . .

The next day is Saturday. I feel a fresh excitement at going back to my job; the factory draws me toward it magnetically. I long to be in the hum and whir of the busy workroom. Two days of leisure without resources or amusement make clear to me how the sociability of factory life, the freedom from personal demands, the escape from self can prove a distraction to those who have no mental occupation, no money to spend on diversion. It is easier to submit to factory government which commands five hundred girls with one law valid for all, than to undergo the arbitrary discipline of parental authority. I speed across the snow-covered courtyard. In a moment my cap and apron are on and I am sent to report to the head forewoman. . . .

She wears her cap close against her head. Her front hair is rolled up in crimping-pins. She has false teeth and is a widow. Her pale, parched face shows what a great share of life has been taken by daily over-effort repeated during years. As she talks she touches my arm in a kindly fashion and looks at me with blue eyes that float about under weary lids. "You are only at the beginning," they seem to say. "Your youth and vigour are at full tide, but drop by drop they will be sapped from you, to swell the great flood of human effort that supplies the world's material needs. You will gain in experience," the weary lids flutter at me, "but you will pay *with your life* the living you make."

There is no variety in my morning's work. Next to me is a bright, pretty girl jamming chopped pickles into bottles.

"How long have you been here?" I ask, attracted by her capable appearance. She does her work easily and well.

"About five months."

"How much do you make?"

"From 90 cents to $1.05. I'm doing piecework," she explains. "I get seven-eighths of a cent for every dozen bottles I fill. I have to fill eight dozen to make seven cents. . . ."

"Do you live at home?" I ask.

"Yes; I don't have to work. I don't pay no board. My father and my brothers supports me and my mother. But," and her eyes twinkle, "I couldn't have the clothes I do if I didn't work."

"Do you spend your money all on yourself?"

"Yes."

I am amazed at the cheerfulness of my companions. They complain of fatigue, of cold, but never at any time is there a suggestion of ill-humour. The suppressed animal spirits reassert themselves when the forewoman's back is turned. Companionship is the great stimulus. I am confident that without the . . . encouragement of example, it would be impossible to obtain as much from each individual girl as is obtained from them in groups of tens, fifties, hundreds working together.

When lunch is over we are set to scrubbing. Every table and stand, every inch of the factory floor must be scrubbed in the next four hours. . . .

The grumbling is general. There is but one opinion among the girls: it is not right that they should be made to do this work. They all echo the same resentment, but their complaints are made in whispers; not one has the courage to openly rebel. What, I wonder to myself, do the men do on scrubbing day. I try to picture one of them on his hands and knees in a sea of brown mud. It is impossible. The next time I go for a supply of soft soap in a department where the men are working I take a look at the masculine interpretation of house cleaning. One man is playing a hose on the floor and the rest are scrubbing the boards down with long-handled brooms and rubber mops.

"You take it easy," I say to the boss.

"I won't have no scrubbing in my place," he answers emphatically. "The first scrubbing day they says to me 'Get down on your hands and knees,' and I says — 'Just pay me my money, will you; I'm goin' home. What scrubbing can't be done with mops ain't going to be done by me.' The women wouldn't have to scrub, either, if they had enough spirit all of 'em to say so."

I determined to find out if possible, during my stay in the factory, what it is that clogs this mainspring of "spirit" in the women. . . .

After a Sunday of rest I arrive somewhat ahead of time on Monday morning, which leaves me a few moments for conversation with a piece-worker who is pasting labels on mustard jars. . . .

"I bet you can't guess how old I am."

I look at her. Her face and throat are wrinkled, her hands broad and scrawny; she is tall and has short skirts. What shall be my clue? If I judge by pleasure, "unborn" would be my answer; if by effort, then "a thousand years."

"Twenty," I hazard as a safe medium.

"Fourteen," she laughs. "I don't like it at home, the kids bother me so. Mamma's people are well-to-do. I'm working for my own pleasure."

"Indeed, I wish I was," says a new girl with a red waist. "We three girls supports mamma and runs the house. We have $13 rent to pay and a load of coal every month and groceries. It's no joke, I can tell you." . . .

Monday is a hard day. There is more complaining, more shirking, more gossip than in the middle of the week. Most of the girls have been to dances on Saturday night, to church on Sunday evening with some young man. Their conversation is vulgar and prosaic; there is nothing in the language they use that suggests an ideal or any conception of the abstract. . . . Here in the land of freedom, where no class line is rigid, the precious chance is not to serve but to live for oneself; not to watch a superior, but to find out by experience. The ideal plays no part, stern realities alone count, and thus we have a progressive, practical, independent people, the expression of whose personality is interesting not through their words but by their deeds.

When the Monday noon whistle blows I follow the hundreds down into the dining-room. . . . I am beginning to understand why the meager lunches of preserve-sandwiches and pickles more than satisfy the girls whom I was prepared to accuse of spending their money on gewgaws rather than on nourishment. It is fatigue that steals the appetite. I can hardly taste what I put in my mouth; the food sticks in my throat. . . . I did not want wholesome food, exhausted as I was. I craved sours and sweets, pickles, cakes, anything to excite my numbed taste. . . .

Accumulated weariness forces me to take a day off. When I return I am sent for in the corking-room. The forewoman lends me a blue gingham dress and tells me I am to do "piece"-work. There are three who work together at every corking-table. My two companions are a woman with goggles and a one-eyed boy. We are not a brilliant trio. The job consists in evening the vinegar in the bottles, driving the cork in, first with a machine, then with a hammer, letting out the air with a knife stuck under the cork, capping the corks, sealing the caps, counting and distributing the bottles. These operations are paid for at the rate of one-half a cent for the dozen bottles, which sum is divided among us. My two companions are earning a living, so I must work in dead earnest or take bread out of their mouths. . . .

There is a stimulus unsuspected in working to get a job done. Before this I had worked to make the time pass. Then no one took account of how much I did; the factory clock had a weighted pendulum; now ambition outdoes physical strength. The hours and my purpose are running a race together. But, hurry as I may, as we do, when twelve blows its signal we have corked only 210 dozen bottles! This is no more than day-work at seventy cents. With an ache in every muscle, I redouble my energy after lunch. The girl with the goggles looks at me blindly and says: "Ain't it just awful hard work? You can make good money, but you've got to hustle."

She is a forlorn specimen of humanity, ugly, old, dirty, condemned to the slow death of the over-worked. I am a green hand. I make mistakes; I have no experience in the fierce sustained effort of the bread-winners. Over and over I turn to her, over and over she is obliged to correct me. During the ten hours we work side by side not one murmur of impatience escapes her. When she sees that I am getting discouraged she calls out across the deafening din, "That's all right; you can't expect to learn in a day; just keep on steady." . . .

The oppressive monotony is one day varied by a summons to the men's dining-room. I go eagerly, glad of any change. . . . The dinner under preparation is for the men of the factory. There are two hundred of them. They are paid from $1.35 to $3 a day. Their wages begin upon the highest limit given to women. The dinner costs each man ten cents. The $20 paid in daily cover the expenses of the cook, two kitchen maids, and the dinner, which consists of meat, bread and butter, vegetables and coffee, sometimes soup, sometimes dessert. If this can pay for two hundred there is no reason why for five cents a hot meal of some kind could not be given to the women. They don't demand it, so they are left to make themselves ill on pickles and preserves. . . .

[In the dining room] I had ample opportunity to compare domestic service with factory work. We set the table for two hundred, and do a thousand miserable slavish tasks that must be begun again the following day. At twelve the two hundred troop in, toil-worn and begrimed. They pass like locusts, leaving us sixteen hundred dirty dishes to wash up and wipe. This takes us four hours, and when we have finished the work stands ready to be done over the next morning with peculiar monotony. In the factory there is stimulus in feeling that the material which passes through one's hands will never be seen or heard of again. . . .

My first experience is drawing to a close. I have surmounted the discomforts of insufficient food, of dirt, a bed without sheets, the strain of hard manual labor. . . . In the factory where I worked men and women were employed for ten-hour days. The women's highest wages were lower than the men's lowest. Both were working as hard as they possibly could. The women were doing menial work, such as scrubbing, which the men refused to do. The men were properly fed at noon; the women satisfied themselves with cake and pickles. Why was this? It is of course impossible to generalize on a single factory. I can only relate the conclusions I drew from what I saw myself. The wages paid by employers, economists tell us, are fixed at the level of bare subsistence. This level and its accompanying conditions are determined by competition, by the nature and number of labourers taking part in the competition. In the masculine category I met but one class of competitor: the bread-winner. In the feminine category I found a variety of classes: the bread-winner, the semi-bread-winner, the woman who works for luxuries. This inevitably drags the wage level. The self-supporting girl is in competition with the child, with the girl who lives at home and makes a small contribution to the household expenses, and with the girl who is supported and who spends all her money on her clothes. It is this division of purpose which takes the "spirit" out of them as a class. There will be no strikes among them so long as the question of wages is not equally vital to them all. . . .

On the evening when I left the factory for the last time, I heard in the streets the usual cry of murders, accidents and suicides; the mental food of the overworked. It is Saturday night. I mingle with a crowd of labourers homeward bound, and with women and girls returning from a Saturday sale in the big shops. They hurry along delighted at the cheapness of a bargain, little dreaming of the human effort that has produced it, the cost of life and energy it represents. As they pass, they draw their skirts aside from us, the cooperators who enable them to have the luxuries they do; from us, the multitude who stand between them and the monster Toil that must be fed with human lives. Think of us, as we herd in the winter dawn; think of us as we bend over our task all the daylight without rest; think of us at the end of the day as we resume suffering and anxiety in homes of squalour and ugliness; think of us as we make our wretched try for merriment; think of us as we stand protectors between you and the labour that must be done to satisfy your material demands; think of us — be merciful.

QUESTIONS FOR ANALYSIS

1. What different sorts of women does Bessie Van Vorst meet in the factory, and how and why do their responses to their work vary?

2. Why does Van Vorst conclude that working women are passive in accepting their working conditions and unwilling to stand up for themselves in the way of working men? Do you think she is right?

3. How might the working women described in *The Woman Who Toils* have responded on reading the book?

4. In light of Van Vorst's final comments, how do you think her life and attitudes were changed by her experience as a factory girl?

The Higher Education of Women in the Postbellum Years

Wherever women have begun to improve their lives, almost invariably they have started by aspiring to better education. "The neglected education of my fellow-creatures is the grand source of the misery I deplore," wrote British feminist Mary Wollstonecraft in 1792.[41] In the era of the American Revolution, grateful political leaders praised educated women for their role in mothering an enlightened (male) citizenry (see pp. 128, 130). Within fifty years, women were teachers in America's burgeoning system of public education. Even so, women continued to have far less access to education than men. Before the Civil War, women could rise no further than the high school level at all-female seminaries. Only Ohio's Oberlin College, an evangelical Protestant institution founded in 1833, admitted a few women to its regular baccalaureate course, most famously women's rights advocate Lucy Stone, who graduated in 1847. Even at Oberlin, however, most women students were educated in a special "ladies' program," with easier language and mathematics requirements than those for men.

Two developments in the 1860s made higher education much more available to women. In 1862, the Morrill Land Grant Act provided federal lands to states and territories for the support of public institutions of higher education. While the act did not explicitly mention women, as one historian has explained, "taxpayers demanded that their daughters, as well as their sons, be admitted."[42] As coeducation spread, long-standing concerns that such easy association between the sexes would coarsen women students and distract men began to give way. Not only were many new land-grant institutions of higher education established throughout the West and Midwest in the 1860s and early 1870s, but public universities founded earlier changed their policies to admit women. Private institutions such as Northwestern and the University of Chicago in Illinois, Stanford in California, Tulane in Louisiana, and Grinnell in Iowa also followed the trend. By the end of the century, coeducational institutions granted college degrees to approximately four thousand women each year.

The University of California was one of the first of the newly established public universities to enroll women. Founded in 1868, "Cal" graduated its first woman, Rosa L. Scrivener, in 1874. By 1878, women's rights to equal education, including in the university's law school, were enshrined in the state constitution. By 1882, women constituted over 30 percent of the student body. Being a college student meant access not only to the serious matter of higher education, but also to a tradition of high-spirited and sometimes transgressive carousing. This part of the

◆ **Figure 6.2 Women Students Modeling Senior Plugs, University of California (c. 1900)**
Roland Letts Oliver photograph collection [graphic], BANC PIC 1960.010 ser. 1 :0556—NEG. Courtesy of the Bancroft Library, University of California, Berkeley.

college experience was more difficult for women, with their obligations to maintain a ladylike demeanor, but by the end of the century at Cal they had broken through this barrier as well. In Figure 6.2, Berkeley women students are happily sporting the headgear that college juniors and seniors of the era prized — "plug" hats that had been battered and generally made to look as disgusting as possible. What do you imagine joining in these carefree practices meant to these young women?

After the Civil War, the establishment of all-women's colleges were the other source of increased women's opportunities for higher education. The first of these, Vassar College, opened in 1865, funded by a wealthy brewer from Poughkeepsie, New York, who wanted to create an educational institution "for young women which shall be to them, what Yale and Harvard are to young men."[43] Philanthropists endowed other all-female institutions, and by 1891 Smith and Wellesley Colleges in Massachusetts, Bryn Mawr College outside Philadelphia, and Goucher College near Baltimore were graduating women with bachelor's degrees. (Mount Holyoke in Massachusetts, begun many years before as a female seminary, upgraded to college level in 1890.) These all-women institutions produced about sixteen hundred college graduates each year. According to statistics combining all-female and coeducational institutions, both public and private, by 1890 women were approximately 40 percent of the total of college graduates — an extraordinary development in less than four decades.

There was much debate about whether women students received a better education and had a better collegiate experience at an all-women's college or at a coeducational institution. To strengthen their claims to intellectual superiority, the top women's colleges were dedicated to providing a first-class education in the sciences, which were becoming increasingly important in modern higher education. The Wellesley College class pictured in Figure 6.3 is studying zoology. The students are examining a fish skeleton and a piece of coral to learn about animal physiology. This photograph, like so many photos of late nineteenth-century college women, is carefully posed. How does the deliberate positioning of the students convey the intellectual seriousness, intensity, and engagement of the scientific learning going on in this all-female classroom? Consider the simple and functional character of

◆ **Figure 6.3** **Class in Zoology, Wellesley College (1883–1884)**
Courtesy of Wellesley College Archives, photo by Seaver.

the students' clothes, especially compared to the elaborate and costly appearance of elite women engaged in less serious pursuits (see photo on p. 315).

Figure 6.3 also underscores the opportunities that all-female colleges in this period provided for the employment of educated women. Here, unlike in most coeducational schools, women could be professors and administrators. The zoology professor, the young woman seated at the center, is Mary Alice Wilcox, a graduate of Newnham College, the women's college of Britain's Cambridge University. Standing behind her and slightly to the right is Alice Freeman, the twenty-eight-year-old Wellesley College president. Freeman, an early graduate of the University of Michigan, was the first woman to head an institution of higher education in the United States. In 1886, she married Harvard professor George Herbert Palmer and resigned her position as college president. Why might women professors have been employed only at all-women's colleges? What difference do you think they made to women's experience of higher education? How might the youth of professors such as Wilcox and administrators such as Freeman have influenced the learning of these women students?

Concerns went beyond the intellectual. Did coeducation provide too many opportunities for undue familiarity between young unmarried men and women? Were women's colleges hotbeds for passionate female friendships? Anxiety that higher education would have a negative impact on women's health, in particular on their reproductive capacities, haunted the early years of women's higher education. In 1873, Dr. Edward Clarke published a controversial book, *Sex in Education*, in which he argued that higher education for women drained vital physical energy—literally blood—from the reproductive organs to the brain.

Defenders of women's education rushed to challenge Clarke's argument that higher education endangered women's reproductive and maternal capacities. They undertook scientific studies of women college students to demonstrate that physical health and intellectual growth were not incompatible. Proponents of women's education were particularly anxious to prove that the menstruation of college girls was not disrupted by too much study.

To further counter the charge that higher education weakened women physically, but also to strengthen women's bodies as well as their minds, colleges added women's athletics and physical education to their curricula. Competition, however, was prohibited as unladylike, certainly between the sexes in coeducational institutions, but even among the women themselves. Nonetheless, in the 1890s, soon after basketball was introduced among young men, a modified version of the game became the rage among college women. Figure 6.4 is a photograph of the team of the class of 1904 from Wells College, an all-women's college in Aurora, New York. In addition to their white-tie blouses, the players are wearing loose, divided "bloomer" skirts. What in the photograph gives evidence of the physical freedom that sports brought to women's college experience? Why might the photographer have posed the team members with their hands folded, rather than in a more forceful representation of young women in action?

Black women faced extraordinary educational challenges. In the first years of emancipation, the overwhelming goal for ex-slaves was basic literacy. During Reconstruction, black educational institutions were founded, virtually all of them opened to women as well as men, but these schools provided secondary and vocational rather than baccalaureate education. Even the nation's premiere all-black

◆ **Figure 6.4 Basketball Team, Wells College (1904)**
Wells College Archives, Louis Jefferson Long Library, Aurora, New York.

college, Howard University, founded in Washington, D.C., in 1867, did not open its collegiate program until 1897 and did not graduate its first woman BA until 1901. In the same year, Atlanta's all-female Spelman College also granted its first BA degree.

By 1900, an estimated 252 African American women held bachelor's degrees, but almost all had been granted by predominantly white institutions, one-quarter from Oberlin College alone. Committed to equal education by both race and gender, Oberlin had produced the very first black woman college graduate — Mary Jane Patterson — in 1862. Many of its black female graduates, including Mary Church Terrell and Anna Julia Cooper, went on to become leading spokeswomen for their race and their sex.

In southern black educational institutions, the dramatic downturn in race relations in the 1880s and 1890s had a discouraging impact on higher education for African Americans. Instead of striving for academic equality with white colleges, they concentrated on preparing their students for skilled trades and manual vocations. This approach to higher education was preached by Booker T. Washington, the era's premiere African American educator. Figure 6.5 is a photograph of a history class at Virginia's Hampton Institute, where Washington began his career. A school for ex-slaves founded in 1868, Hampton was a model for many similar institutions throughout the South. In a controversial experiment in interracial education, Hampton also began enrolling Native American students in 1878.

Freedpeople regarded the educational opportunities that Hampton and other such schools provided them as immense privileges. Speaking at the 1873 graduation, Alice P. Davis, born a slave in North Carolina in 1852, praised Hampton Institute as her alma mater: "[A] mother indeed she has been to us, for she has given us more instruction in these three years than our dear but illiterate mothers ever could."[44] Nonetheless, such institutions, which were often overseen by white benefactors, maintained strict controls over their black students and trained them in the virtues of industriousness and self-discipline. The young women were prepared for jobs as teachers, but also as domestic servants and industrial workers.

In 1899, Hampton's white trustees hired America's first important female documentary photographer, Frances Benjamin Johnston, who was white, to portray the students' educational progress. Her photographs were displayed at the Paris Exposition of 1900, where they were much praised for both their artistic achievement and their depiction of racial harmony. Figure 6.5, titled "Class in American History," is an exceptionally rich image for the diversity of its subjects and the complexity of its content. A white female teacher stands among her female and male, African American and Native American, students. All are contemplating a Native American man in ceremonial dress. He can be likened in some way to the scientific specimens in Figure 6.3. Consider what the man himself might have been thinking as he was exhibited to the gaze of both the photographer and the history class. Historian Laura Wexler has unearthed the name of one of the students, the young Indian woman standing at the far right: she is Adele Quinney, a member of the Stockbridge tribe.[45] What lessons were she and the other students being taught about American history by the living exhibit of traditional Indian ways placed

◆ **Figure 6.5** **Class in American History, Hampton Institute (1899–1900)**
Library of Congress, 3a38505.

before them? What do their precise posing and uniform dress suggest about the discipline expected of Hampton students?

During the post–Civil War years, many "normal colleges" were established to concentrate exclusively on the training of teachers. Such schools provided a briefer, less demanding program of study than baccalaureate courses. With less competitive standards for admission and lower costs, they educated a much larger number of women students. The first teacher training institution supported with public funds was founded in 1839 in Framingham, Massachusetts. Normal colleges also benefited from the 1862 Morrill Act and were an important avenue of upward mobility for the working class, immigrants, African Americans, and other people of color.

Many of these institutions survived into the twentieth century and became full-fledged colleges and universities. Figure 6.6 is a photo of a class at Washington, D.C.'s

◆ **Figure 6.6** Science Class, Washington, D.C., Normal College (1899)
Library of Congress, 3a16945.

Normal College, established twenty-six years before in 1873. Because Washington was a southern town, public education there was racially segregated, and the Normal College enrolled only white students. Washington's Myrtilla Miner Normal School, founded in 1851 and named after a heroic white woman educator of African American girls, enrolled only African American students. The two schools remained separate and segregated until 1955, one year after the Supreme Court found segregated education unconstitutional in the case of *Brown v. Board of Education* (see p. 573). Then they were merged into the District of Columbia Teachers College, now named the University of the District of Columbia.

As in Figure 6.3, the students in Figure 6.6 are studying science, once again illustrating the importance of this subject in meeting the ambitions of the leaders of women's higher education to offer young women a modern and intellectually challenging education. And yet the kinds of teaching and learning that went on in an elite college such as Wellesley and a teacher training institution such as the Normal College were very different. The former had a far more educated faculty and resources of equipment and specimens that the latter lacked. Consider what other differences can be detected by comparing this photograph with Figure 6.3. Figure 6.6 also invites comparison with Figure 6.5 because both photographs were taken by Frances Johnston. How has Johnston positioned her subjects in this picture, compared to those at Hampton Institute? What educational message is this different staging meant to communicate?

Like teachers, doctors were trained in specialized medical colleges. For most of the nineteenth century, a bachelor's degree was not a prerequisite to study medicine in the United States. Instead, students studied medicine at special medical schools and in undergraduate medical departments of large universities. The first major obstacle that women faced was gaining admission into these all-male programs of medical education. Anxieties about coeducation were particularly intense over the prospect of women sitting beside men at lectures about the human body. But women's desire for medical education was strong. Medicine, unlike other professions such as law or the ministry, fit comfortably with women's traditional role as healers. In 1849, after applying to a dozen major medical schools, Elizabeth Blackwell broke this educational barrier by graduating from Geneva Medical College in upstate New York.

One remedy was the establishment of all-female medical colleges. The Boston Female Medical College was established in 1849 by Dr. Samuel Gregory, who wanted to train women to attend their own sex in childbirth. Dr. Elizabeth Blackwell founded the Women's Medical College of New York in 1868 to help other women follow her into the profession. Such all-female schools played a major role in educating women physicians, but as they lacked adequate clinical resources and opportunities, women continued to demand admission to men's medical colleges, where they were eventually accepted.

By 1890, women represented between 15 and 20 percent of all medical students. After 1890, the number of medical colleges shrank, even as their standards rose. Educationally, the crucial change came in 1893 when the Johns Hopkins University in Baltimore established the first postgraduate medical course in the United States. A group of women, led by Mary Garrett, close friend of Bryn Mawr College dean M. Carey Thomas, donated $500,000 to the new postgraduate medical college on the condition that women be admitted along with men. Overall, however, women began to lose access to medical education after 1890, and the percentage of women in most medical schools dropped by half or more by the turn of the century.

Figure 6.7 is a photograph of the 1876 class of the Medical College of Syracuse University, which in 1872 absorbed the resources of Geneva Medical College, Elizabeth Blackwell's alma mater. This medical class was impressively diverse, not only because four of the students were women but because one of them was African American. Sarah Loguen (after marriage, Fraser) was the daughter of a fugitive slave who became an abolitionist. After graduation, she practiced medicine in Washington, D.C. Notice that the men look much more directly at the photographer than the women, several of whom look down or away. Does this photograph provide any hints about how the male students regarded their female colleagues or how the women felt about their presence in the medical classroom?

◆ **Figure 6.7 Graduating Class, Medical College of Syracuse University (1876)**
Moorland-Spingarn Research Center, Howard University.

QUESTIONS FOR ANALYSIS

1. Nineteenth-century women's higher education proceeded along two parallel lines: the struggle for coeducation and the establishment of all-women's institutions. What were the advantages and disadvantages of each approach?

2. In what way did the motivations for and rewards of higher education differ for white and African American women?

3. How did the growth of higher education for women relate to other major postbellum developments in women's history discussed in this chapter?

PRIMARY SOURCES

The New Woman

Beginning in the 1880s and continuing into the 1920s, a new form of femininity evoked the ways in which women were beginning to break down barriers in both the public and private realms. Americans watched as the "New Woman" agitated for suffrage and reform, pursued higher education, and made modest gains in the professional world. She also demonstrated new patterns of private life, from shopping in the new urban department stores to riding bicycles and playing golf, hinting at changes in what was considered appropriate behavior. African American women, especially those associated with reform organizations, envisioned a New African American Woman, much in the mode of Ida B. Wells (pp. 325–29). But in the popular imagination, the New Woman was white and of the leisure class.

The concept of the New Woman set off an immense controversy in the late nineteenth century. Critics insisted that voting, higher education, and athletic endeavors would damage women's health and undermine their femininity and that professional women's work and increased personal freedoms would harm the middle-class family ideal. Defenders praised the New Woman as an icon of progress and modernity. The many versions of this new phenomenon emerged particularly clearly in visual representations.

Critics of the New Woman in the 1890s often satirized her in cartoons and drawings that featured men and women swapping roles. Usually, men are shown in emasculating situations, doing housework or tending a baby, while women appear in mannish clothing and are depicted variously as attorneys, suffragists, and businesswomen. Figure 6.8, from the humor magazine *Puck*, is typical of this representation. How does the image convey the sense that "What We Are Coming To" is an alarming state of affairs? How are both man and woman made to appear ludicrous?

Contrast Figure 6.8 with Figure 6.9, an 1895 *Life* illustration titled "In a Twentieth Century Club," which features women at leisure, enjoying an atmosphere that replicated a men's drinking and eating club. Here, although role reversal still provides the humor, the women waitresses and patrons are physically attractive. While the women's unladylike posture and clothing would have been viewed as shocking, equally significant is the cross-dressing entertainer: a man dressed in an abbreviated female costume typical of the burlesque shows designed for male audiences. What is the artist suggesting about the New Woman's sexuality by the inclusion of the male dancer? What other features in the drawing hint at the possibility of new sexual patterns in the twentieth century?

In contrast to these negative or ambiguous portrayals of women's demands for political and economic advancement, the New Woman's physical vitality was attractive to some illustrators, most famously Charles Dana Gibson. Starting in

WHAT WE ARE COMING TO.

THE TYPEWRITER.— Beg pardon! Did you say "My learned *sister* is mistaken —?"
THE LAWYER.— Yes; Miss Bigfee is the opposing counsel in this case.

◆ **Figure 6.8 What We Are Coming To (1898)**
Collection of the New-York Historical Society, USA/Bridgeman Images.

the mid-1890s, his creation of the beautiful and statuesque "Gibson Girl" became a pervasive icon of American femininity. She appeared not only in print media, but on jewelry and calendars, and her clothing and hairstyle were imitated across class and race lines. The Gibson Girl was independent, athletic, educated, and confident. Yet this self-assurance was oriented not toward careers, social reform, or politics, but toward attracting, and generally manipulating, men through her beauty. As one historian has noted, in many ways Gibson appropriated the New Woman and adjusted her attributes to more conservative ends.[46] Although the Gibson Girl often appeared engaged in genteel athleticism, such as bicycling or golfing, the beauties in Figure 6.10 sit somewhat languorously on the beach. As in Figure 6.9, the contours of women's legs are shown. How do these two depictions of the modern New Woman compare? Note that these hourglass figures are accomplished through corsets. What does that suggest about the extent of the New Woman's physical freedom?

Conservative critics argued that bicycling for women might damage their reproductive health and certainly undermined their femininity. Authors in medical journals even worried that a bicycle saddle might stimulate the rider sexually. Women's rights activists like Frances Willard, however, viewed the bicycle as a means of female independence (p. 319). As Susan B. Anthony put it in 1896, the bicycle "has done more to emancipate women than anything else in this world. It gives her a feeling of self-reliance and independence the moment she takes her seat; and away she goes,

IN A TWENTIETH CENTURY CLUB.

"WHY DON'T YOU FETCH YOUR BROTHER HERE SOME NIGHT?"
"OH, I THINK IT'S A BAD ATMOSPHERE FOR A YOUNG MAN WHO HAS BEEN CAREFULLY BROUGHT UP."

◆ **Figure 6.9 In a Twentieth Century Club (1895)**
Beinecke Rare Book and Manuscript Library, Yale University.

the picture of untrammeled womanhood."[47] Although working-class women apparently used the bicycle to travel to and from work, its most common use was recreational. By 1895, the sight of women astride bicycles, dressed in a variety of costumes, including bloomers, had become commonplace. Certainly, the images of women bicyclists were everywhere in print media and advertising. Figure 6.11 is a coversheet for a dance tune, "The Scorcher." The title referred to a fast, speeding bicyclist. Why might the illustrator have chosen to feature the young woman in the foreground? What aspects of her demeanor and dress convey the qualities of the New Woman?

An actual embodiment of the career-driven New Woman was Elizabeth Jane Cochran, a journalist who went by the pen name of Nellie Bly. Bly was one of the

◆ **Figure 6.10** **Picturesque America (1900)**
The Granger Collection, New York.

most famous of the many women "stunt" reporters who blended "hard" news, usually associated with male writers, with "soft" news, or emotional, personal interest stories. These reporters often engaged in gimmicks such as impersonation to get their stories, which moved them from the society page to the front page. Bly worked for *the New York World* and first came to fame when she pretended to be a madwoman in order to gain entrance to New York's Women's Lunatic Asylum. The serialized report established her as a crack investigative reporter whose sensational stories sold newspapers. Bly's most famous exploit was a replication of the fictional journey of Phineas Fogg, Jules Verne's hero of *Around the World in 80 Days*. She set forth on November 24, 1889, alone and carrying only a small traveling bag and $250. As she sent back reports, the *World*'s circulation climbed. Close to a million readers sent in coupons for a contest to guess the exact length of time her journey would take. On her triumphant return to New York seventy-two days later, Bly commented, "It's not so very much for a woman to do who has the pluck, energy

◆ **Figure 6.11 The Scorcher (1897)**
Courtesy, Lilly Library, Indiana University, Bloomington, Indiana.

◆ **Figure 6.12 Nellie Bly, on the Fly (1890)**
Old Paper Studios/Alamy Stock Photo.

and independence which characterize many women in this day of push and get-there."[48] Bly's celebrity led to a successful board game and a thriving advertising, or "trade" card, market for a wide range of products. Figure 6.12 depicts "Nellie Bly, on the Fly." She wears her trademark plaid traveling coat and neat hat and carries her single bag. How does her clothing and bearing suggest Bly's New Womanhood? How does the surrounding imagery convey her adventurous spirit?

A Roof-top Study.

◆ **Figure 6.13** **Women Bachelors in New York (1896)**
Yale Collection of American Literature, Beinecke Rare Book and Manuscript Library.

As a successful working woman, Bly represented the independent New Woman of the city. Single women professionals, such as doctors and lawyers, were part of this phenomenon, but so too were artists, illustrators, writers, and actresses. New Woman Mary Heaton Vorse, in reflecting on her own move to New York City, wrote of "the strange army of all the girls who in my mother's time would have stayed at home and I wonder what necessity sent us all out . . . more and more of us coming all the time, . . . and as we change the world, the world is going to change us."[49]

Mary Guy Humphreys's 1896 article, "Women Bachelors in New York," described the army Vorse identified. Although Humphreys argued that these women worked primarily to finance consumer goods and pleasures, she also stressed their pleasure in independence, in earning one's own income, and in living alone or with female flatmates. The article's illustrations show women reporters at work at night, commenting that "Mr. Edison's" electric lights offered women more freedom of the streets. Other images depict the women's small but cozy quarters. In commenting on the attention given to comfortable surroundings, Humphreys noted, "In the measure that women are determining their own lives, they want their own homes. . . . The woman who is occupied with daily work needs greater freedom of movement, more isolation, more personal comforts, and the exemption, moreover, from being agreeable at all times and places."[50] Figure 6.13 features the woman "bachelor" reading in her "roof-top study." In what ways does the artist convey a different kind of home life for women as part of their newfound freedom? What is the significance of the city skyline in the distance?

QUESTIONS FOR ANALYSIS

1. What qualities of the New Woman do these popular culture images convey?

2. How does the Gibson Girl (Figure 6.10) compare with other positive renditions of the New Woman (Figures 6.11, 6.12, and 6.13)?

3. Why do you suppose the New Woman, portrayed in either a positive or a negative light, was such a pervasive image in the popular culture of the era?

NOTES

1. Elizabeth Cady Stanton, "This Is the Negro's Hour," *National Anti-Slavery Standard*, November 26, 1865, reprinted in Elizabeth Cady Stanton, Susan B. Anthony, and Matilda J. Gage, eds., *History of Woman Suffrage* (Rochester, NY: Susan B. Anthony, 1881), 2:94.

2. Ellen Carol DuBois, *Feminism and Suffrage: The Emergence of an Independent Women's Movement in America, 1848–1869* (Ithaca, NY: Cornell University Press, 1999), 63.

3. Ibid., 60.

4. Ibid., 175.

5. Elizabeth Cady Stanton to Lucretia Mott, April 1, 1872, in Theodore Stanton and Harriot Stanton Blatch, eds., *Elizabeth Cady Stanton as Revealed in Her Letters, Diary and Reminiscences* (New York: Harper and Brothers, 1922), 137.

6. Susan B. Anthony to Elizabeth Cady Stanton, November 5, 1872, Ida H. Harper Collection, Huntington Library, San Marino, CA.

7. Stanton, Anthony, and Gage, *History of Woman Suffrage*, 3:31.

8. Dorothy Sterling, ed., *We Are Your Sisters: Black Women in the Nineteenth Century* (New York: Norton, 1984), 313.

9. Story told by Lucy Chase of the Freedmen's Aid Society, in a letter to unnamed correspondent, 1868, American Antiquarian Society, Worcester, Massachusetts, excerpted in Nancy Woloch, ed., *Early American Women: A Documentary History, 1600–1900* (Belmont, CA: Wadsworth, 1992), 401.

10. Sterling, *We Are Your Sisters*, 311.

11. Ibid., 314.

12. Charlotte Forten, "Life in the Sea Islands," *Atlantic Monthly*, June 1864, 676.

13. Marilyn Mayer Culpepper, *All Things Altered: Women in the Wake of Civil War and Reconstruction* (Jefferson, NC: McFarland, 2002), 135.

14. Ibid., 123.

15. Tera W. Hunter, *To 'Joy My Freedom: Southern Black Women's Lives and Labors after the Civil War* (Cambridge, MA: Harvard University Press, 1997), 33.

16. Crystal Feimster, "'What If I Am a Woman?' Black Women's Campaigns for Sexual Justice and Citizenship," in Gregory Downs and Kate Masur, eds. *The World the Civil War Made* (Chapel Hill: University of North Carolina Press, 2015), 250.

17. Arthur F. Raper, *The Tragedy of Lynching* (Chapel Hill: University of North Carolina Press, 1933), 13–14.

18. "The Race Problem," 586–89.

19. Nancy Cott et al., eds., *Root of Bitterness: Documents of the Social History of American Women*, 2nd ed. (Boston: Northeastern University Press, 1996), 360.

20. Claudia Goldin, "The Work and Wages of Single Women: 1870 to 1920," National Bureau of Economic Research Working Paper, no. WO375, 1979, 1.

21. Linda Gordon, *The Great Arizona Orphan Abduction* (Cambridge, MA: Harvard University Press, 1999), 8.

22. Nancy Cott, ed., *Root of Bitterness: Documents of the Social History of American Women* (Boston: Northeastern University Press, 1986), 319.

23. Helen Campbell, *Women Wage-Earners: Their Past, Their Present, and Their Future* (Boston: Roberts Brothers, 1893), 190.

24. Ibid., 191.

25. Quoted in Barbara Wertheimer, *We Were There: The Story of Working Women in America* (New York: Pantheon Books, 1977), 178.

26. Gary B. Nash et al., *The American People: Creating a Nation and a Society*, brief 5th ed. (New York: Addison Wesley Longman, 2000), 481.

27. Elizabeth Blackwell, "On Sexual Passion in Men and Women," 1894, reprinted in Cott, *Root of Bitterness* (1986), 302.

28. Women's historians first encountered the De Kay/Hallock romance in Carroll Smith-Rosenberg's pathbreaking essay, "The Female World of Love and Ritual: Relations between Women in Nineteenth Century America," which can be found in her collection of essays, *Disorderly Conduct: Visions of Gender in Victorian America* (New York: Oxford University Press, 1985), 53–76. Their relationship also formed the basis of Wallace Stegner's Pulitzer Prize–winning 1971 novel, *Angle of Repose*. Winslow Homer is thought to have been infatuated with De Kay, and painted a lovely, haunting portrait of her "in repose." Hallock became an important writer and illustrator of the West. The quote is from Smith-Rosenberg, 57.

29. Karen V. Hansen, "'No Kisses Is Like Yours': An Erotic Friendship between Two African-American Women during the Mid-Nineteenth Century," *Gender History* 7 (1995): 153.

30. Karen Blair, *The Clubwoman as Feminist: True Womanhood Redefined, 1868–1914* (New York: Holmes and Meier, 1980), 34.

31. Sarah J. Early, "The Organized Efforts of the Colored Women of the South to Improve Their Condition," 1893, reprinted in Dawn Keetley and John Pettegrew, eds., *Public Women, Public Words*, vol. 1 (Madison, WI: Madison House, 1997), 316.

32. Frances E. Willard, *How I Learned to Ride the Bicycle: Reflections of an Influential 19th Century Woman*, ed. Carol O'Hare (1895; repr., Sunnyvale, CA: Fair Oaks, 1991), 17, 75.

33. Mary Earhart, *Frances Willard: From Prayers to Politics* (Chicago: University of Chicago Press, 1944), 93.

34. Suzanne Marilley, *Woman Suffrage and the Origins of Liberal Feminism in the United States, 1820–1920* (Cambridge, MA: Harvard University Press, 1996), 128–29.

35. Ellen Carol DuBois, ed., *The Elizabeth Cady Stanton–Susan B. Anthony Reader: Correspondence, Writings, Speeches*, rev. ed. (Boston: Northeastern University Press, 1992), 176.

36. Charlotte Perkins Gilman, *Women and Economics: A Study of the Economic Relation between Men and Women as a Factor in Social Evolution* (Boston: Small, Maynard & Company, 1898), 156.

37. Elizabeth Cady Stanton, "The Solitude of Self," 1892, http://historymatters.gmu.edu/d/5315 (accessed July 1, 2015).

38. Mia Bay, *To Tell the Truth Freely: The Life of Ida B. Wells* (New York: Macmillan, 2011), 117–18.

39. Patricia Schechter, *Ida B. Wells-Barnett and American Reform, 1880–1930* (Chapel Hill: University of North Carolina Press, 2001), 62–63.

40. Mrs. John Van Vorst and Marie Van Vorst, *The Woman Who Toils: Being the Experiences of Two Ladies as Factory Girls* (New York: Doubleday, Page & Co., 1903), 58.

41. Alice Rossi, ed., *The Feminist Papers from Adams to de Beauvoir* (Boston: Northeastern University Press, 1988), 40.

42. Rosalind Rosenberg, "The Limits of Access," in John Mack Faragher and Florence Howe, eds., *Women and Higher Education: Essays from the Mount Holyoke College Sesquicentennial Symposia* (New York: Norton, 1988), 110.

43. Helen Lefkowitz Horowitz, *Alma Mater: Design and Experience in Women's Colleges from Their Nineteenth-Century Beginnings to the 1930s* (New York: Knopf, 1984), 29.

44. M. F. [Mary Frances] Armstrong and Helen W. Ludlow, *Hampton and Its Students, by Two of Its Teachers, Mrs. M. F. Armstrong and Helen W. Ludlow* (New York: G. P. Putnam, 1874), 89–90.

45. Laura Wexler, *Tender Violence: Domestic Visions in an Age of U.S. Imperialism* (Chapel Hill: University of North Carolina Press, 2000), 168.

46. Martha Patterson, " 'Survival of the Best Fitted': Selling the American New Woman as Gibson Girl, 1896–1910," *ATQ: A Journal of American 19th Century Literature and Culture* (June 1995): 73–87.

47. Ida Husted Harper, *The Life and Work of Susan B. Anthony*, vol. 3 (Indianapolis: The Hollenbeck Press, 1908), 1293.

48. Brooke Kroeger, *Nellie Bly: Daredevil, Reporter, Feminist* (New York: Three Rivers Press, 1994), 167.

49. Dee Garrison, *Mary Heaton Vorse: The Life of an American Insurgent* (Philadelphia: Temple University Press, 1989), 21.

50. Mary Guy Humphreys, "Women Bachelors in New York," *Scribner's Magazine* 20 (November 1896): 633.

SUGGESTED REFERENCES

Woman Suffrage

Faye Dudden, *Fighting Chance: The Fight Over Woman Suffrage and Black Suffrage in Reconstruction America* (2011).

Eleanor Flexner and Ellen Fitzpatrick, *Century of Struggle: The Woman's Rights Movement in the United States*, enlarged ed. (1996).

Laura E. Free, *Suffrage Reconstructed: Gender, Race, and Voting Rights in the Civil War Era* (2015).

Christine L. Ridarsky and Mary M. Huth, eds., *Susan B. Anthony and the Struggle for Equal Rights* (2012).

Allison L. Sneider, *Suffragists in an Imperial Age: U.S. Expansionism and the Woman Question, 1870–1929* (2008).

Marjorie Spruill Wheeler, *New Women of the New South: The Leaders of the Woman Suffrage Movement in the Southern States* (1993).

Black and White Women in the New South

Mia Bay, *To Tell the Truth Freely: The Life of Ida B. Wells* (2010).

Laura F. Edwards, *Gendered Strife and Confusion: The Political Culture of Reconstruction* (1997).

Crystal N. Feimster, *Southern Horrors: Women and the Politics of Rape and Lynching* (2009).

Paula Giddings, *When and Where I Enter: The Impact of Black Women on Race and Sex in America* (1996).

Glenda Elizabeth Gilmore, *Gender and Jim Crow: Women and the Politics of White Supremacy in North Carolina, 1896–1920* (1996).

Sarah Haley, *No Mercy Here: Gender, Punishment, and the Making of Jim Crow Modernity* (2016).

Evelyn Brooks Higginbotham, *Righteous Discontent: The Women's Movement in the Black Baptist Church, 1880–1920* (1994).

Tera W. Hunter, *To 'Joy My Freedom: Southern Black Women's Lives and Labors after the Civil War* (1997).

Dolores Janiewski, *Sisterhood Denied: Race, Gender, and Class in a New South Community* (1986).

Talitha L. LeFlouria, *Chained in Silence: Black Women and Convict Labor in the New South* (2015).

Anne Firor Scott, *The Southern Lady: From Pedestal to Politics, 1830–1930* (1970).

Working Women in the North

Marjorie W. Davies, *Woman's Place Is at the Typewriter: Office Work and Office Workers, 1870–1930* (1982).

Alice Kessler-Harris, *Out to Work: A History of Wage-Earning Women in the United States* (1982).

Joanne J. Meyerowitz, *Women Adrift: Independent Wage Earners in Chicago, 1880–1930* (1988).

Kathy Peiss, *Cheap Amusements: Working Women and Leisure in Turn-of-the-Century New York* (1986).

Lara Vapnek, *Breadwinners: Working Women and Economic Independence, 1865–1920* (2009).

Leisure-Class Women in the North

Elaine S. Abelson, *When Ladies Go A-Thieving: Middle-Class Shoplifters in the Victorian Department Store* (1989).

Maureen A. Flanagan, *Seeing with Their Hearts: Chicago Women and the Vision of the Good City, 1871–1933* (2002).

Helen Lefkowitz Horowitz, *Alma Mater: Design and Experience in the Women's Colleges from Their Nineteenth-Century Beginnings to the 1930s* (1984).

Anne Firor Scott, *Natural Allies: Women's Associations in American History* (1991).

Ian Tyrrell, *Woman's World/Woman's Empire: The Woman's Christian Temperance Union in International Perspective, 1880–1930* (1991).

Martha Vicinus, *Intimate Friends: Women Who Loved Women, 1778–1928* (2004).

7

Women in an Expanding Nation

CONSOLIDATION OF THE WEST, MASS IMMIGRATION, AND THE CRISIS OF THE 1890s

Twenty-three-year-old Shige Kushida arrived in San Francisco in 1892. American influences had already reached her in her native Japan. She was Protestant, Western-oriented, and one of the few women who dared to speak in Japan before a mixed audience of men and women. She intended to get an education in the United States and return to her home country, but her experience, like that of so many other immigrants, did not go according to plan. Instead of studying, she married another Japanese Christian and settled in Oakland. There she raised her children and became a leader of the Issei (first-generation Japanese American) community. She saw to it that her daughters got the education she did not.[1]

The life of Shige Kushida Togasaki illustrates two grand historical processes that were reshaping American society at the end of the nineteenth century. First, the United States was beginning an unprecedented wave of immigration, which brought with it tremendous social challenges and national transformations. Second, the western part of the continent was being consolidated into the American nation. The frontier — in the sense of a westward-moving line of American settlement — was entering its final stages

photos: top, Detail, courtesy of the Peabody Museum of Archaeology and Ethnology, Harvard University; middle, Lac qui Parle County Historical Society/Museum; bottom, The Granger Collection, New York and, according to the 1890 census, coming to a close. Western settlement, which seems like a quintessentially American phenomenon, and mass immigration, which brought the nation into greater interaction with the rest of the world, shared important links. Both involved enormous movements of people across oceans and continents, bringing different cultures into contact and sometimes into conflict. Both involved efforts to "Americanize," sometimes violently, different cultures into the national mainstream. Both developments were motivated at the individual level by hopes for better lives, greater prosperity, and more personal freedom. And yet both processes dashed hopes as much as they realized them, among the immigrant poor and especially among the Native Americans pushed aside by continuing westward expansion.

Mass immigration and the consolidation of the West together helped to set the stage for a major economic and political crisis in the 1890s, as discontented immigrants, farmers, and wage workers found ways to challenge what they saw as a failure of America's democratic promise, notably the unequal distribution of America's new wealth and the unwillingness of the two established political parties to offer any vision of a better social and political path. The resolution of the crisis in favor of corporate power and the established political parties prepared the way for America's first forays abroad as an imperial power.

In all these developments — western consolidation, mass immigration, the political and economic crises of the 1890s, and the beginnings of American imperialism — women were involved, active, influential, and, as a result, changed. In these two great movements of people into and through American society in the late nineteenth century, men initially predominated, but women soon followed. When they did, families were formed and temporary population shifts became permanent new communities. By the early twentieth century, American women's participation in the radical challenges of the 1890s, along with their support for or criticism of their country's ventures abroad, had made them a significant new force in U.S. political life.

1892	Immigrant receiving station established at Ellis Island in New York Harbor
1892	People's Party formed in St. Louis
1893	Illinois Factory and Workshop Inspection Act passed
1893	Chicago hosts World's Columbian Exposition
1893	Frederick Jackson Turner delivers paper, "The Significance of the Frontier in American History"
1893	**Colorado women win equal voting rights with men**
1893–1897	National economic depression
1894	Pullman strike and national railroad disruption
1895	**Illinois Supreme Court invalidates state limits on women workers' hours**
1896	**Idaho women enfranchised**
1896	Populist Party collapses as William McKinley defeats William Jennings Bryan for president
1896	**Mary Harris ("Mother") Jones's fame as labor agitator begins**
1898	United States goes to war against Spain in Cuba
1898	United States annexes Hawaii
1899–1902	United States fights Filipino independence movement
1900	**Zitkala-Ša's autobiographical writings begin to appear in the *Atlantic Monthly***
1903	**President Theodore Roosevelt speaks out against "race suicide"**
1907	U.S. and Japanese governments issue "Gentlemen's Agreement" to limit Japanese immigration
1910	Mexican Revolution spurs immigration to the United States
1910	Angel Island immigrant receiving station established in San Francisco Bay

photos: top, Jacob A. Riis/Museum of the City of New York/Getty Images; bottom, Denver Public Library, Western History Collection/Bridgeman Images

◆ CONSOLIDATING THE WEST

American settlement reached the Pacific Coast before the Civil War, but the continent's broad heartland remained largely Indian territory. This changed in the last decades of the nineteenth century as white settlement and expansion overtook the Great Plains. The tremendous postbellum growth in industrial capitalism traced in Chapter 6 had as one of its major consequences the steady integration of the entire continent into the national economy. The growth of the transcontinental railroad system constituted the infrastructure for a booming national market that could provide eager consumers throughout the country with the beef, wheat, and lumber produced in abundance in the broad expanse of the trans-Mississippi West.

These western lands were consolidated as part of the American nation through two main processes, which were distinguished as much by their gender practices as by anything else. Large numbers of single men and a few women went west to realize quick profits or find jobs in the region's mines and on its cattle ranges. This form of American expansion has long been celebrated as the "Wild West" in national legend and popular culture. But there was also a "Settler West" in which primarily white migrants colonized the prairies of America's heartland. Women and women's labor were as fundamental to this Settler West as men and men's labor were to the other.

Native Women in the West

Despite their differences, both kinds of westerners shared a basic premise: Indians would have to be removed to make way for the new settlers, for their economic ambitions, and for what they regarded as their superior civilization. Here, the U.S. Army, fresh from its victory over the Confederacy, was crucial. After 1865, federal forces moved with full strength against the western tribes to wrest control of the Great Plains and open these huge interior expanses to white settlement. Native American raids against encroaching white settlers provoked military retaliation in an escalating series of wars that wore away at Native unity and resources. There were occasional Indian victories, most famously the 1876 Battle of the Little Big Horn in Montana, in which Lakota Sioux warriors annihilated the U.S. Seventh Cavalry commanded by George A. Custer. The army was able to keep Native peoples in a state of constant defense, wearing away at their ability to resist.

Bands of Native Americans who resisted pacification were regarded as "hostiles" who could be killed with impunity by Americans. Made up not only of male warriors but also of women and children, they moved constantly to elude pursuing troops. One of the last such groups was Geronimo's band of Warm Springs Apache. His female lieutenant, Lozen, exemplified the Native American practice of allowing exceptional individuals to cross the gender divide. Lozen never married, was skilled in tracking the enemy, and performed the spiritual and military duties of a true warrior. Her brother called her "strong as a man, braver than most, and cunning in strategy."[2] For almost a decade, she helped her people evade and attack the U.S. Army, until the Apaches finally surrendered in southern New Mexico in 1886.

The massacre at Wounded Knee Creek in South Dakota in the winter of 1890 is often cited as the tragic end to the Indian Wars. Following their defeat at the Little Big Horn, U.S. Army troops had relentlessly pursued the Lakota Sioux. Deeply dispirited, the Lakotas began a new religious practice, the Ghost Dance, which promised restoration of their traditional lands and lives. Male and female dancers alike wore special robes, said to be designed by a woman, that they believed would protect them against bullets fired by white people. Believing that the Ghost Dance signaled a new organized insurgency, skittish soldiers fired on a camp of mostly unarmed Native people, killing many hundred. "Women with little children on their backs" were gunned down, one white witness to the Wounded Knee massacre recalled, and in blizzard conditions it was many days before their frozen bodies could be retrieved and buried in a mass grave.[3]

Assaults against the Plains Indians took forms other than outright military conflict. By the 1880s, hunters and soldiers with new high-powered rifles had decimated the buffalo herds that were the material basis of Plains Indians' traditional way of life. Hunger made the Plains peoples vulnerable to forced relocations on government reservations of the sort that had been pioneered in the 1850s among Pacific Coast tribes (see Map 7.1). Allegedly designed to protect Indians from aggressive white settlers, these reservations instead became what one historian calls "virtual prisons."[4] Unable to support themselves by either farming or hunting, reservation Indians were dependent on food and clothing doled out by federal agents, who often embezzled as much as they dispensed. Instead of their traditional role in gathering and preparing food, Indian women were relegated to standing in long lines, waiting for rations that frequently did not come.

On the reservations, Native Americans were subjected to intense pressures to assimilate. White women became central to this effort when the federal United States Indian Service began hiring women as superintendents and teachers and in a wide range of other jobs. Believing that the route to "civilizing" the Indian was through the restructuring of the family, or what scholars call "intimate colonialism" of a conquered people, policy makers thought that white women of exemplary character could teach through moral example. As Helen Hunt Jackson, a noted advocate for reforming federal Indian policy and author of the influential 1881 exposé of government mistreatment of Native peoples, *A Century of Dishonor*, explained, "[W]omen have more courage and self-denying missionary spirit, sufficient to undertake such a life, and have an invaluable influence outside their school rooms. They go familiarly into the homes, and are really educating the parents as well as the children in a way that is not within the power of any man."[5] In the late nineteenth century, thousands of women, mostly single ones, served in this growing federal bureaucracy. By 1898, they made up 42 percent of the agency's employees. Many came with a missionary impulse, undoubtedly influenced by the efforts of the religiously based Women's National Indian Association, a white women's reform organization founded in 1879 to publicize the plight of Native Americans. Others sought better salaries or the freedom from the restrictive lives

◆ **Map 7.1 The Indian Frontier, to 1890**
As settlers pushed westward after the Civil War, Native Americans put up bitter resistance, which ultimately failed. Over a period of decades, they ceded most of their lands to the federal government. By 1890, they were confined to reservations where the most they could expect was an impoverished and alien way of life. *Map reproduced courtesy of Colin Calloway.*

many middle-class women led. Despite the emphasis on moral suasion, many felt that they needed to use coercion — such as a threat to send a father to the local jail or remove a child from the home — to receive much cooperation from their clients who resisted the efforts to suppress their culture.

In conjunction with this assimilative process on the reservations, U.S. policy coerced Native children into government-run boarding schools to be forcibly reeducated in the values and ways of dominant American culture. By the 1890s, several thousand children per year were removed from their parents' control and

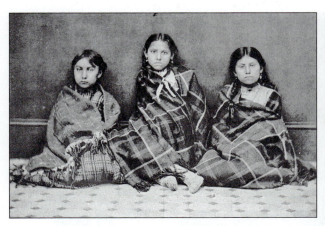

◆ **Before and after Americanization**
These "before-and-after" pictures of Indian children at government-run boarding schools were common in the late nineteenth century and were sometimes sent to philanthropic donors to illustrate the schools' success in Americanizing Indians. Within a little more than a year, these three girls sat on chairs, not the floor, and had lost their blankets and braids, but they retained their sad faces. The book on the lap of Sarah Walker, the girl on the right in the "after" photograph, was meant to indicate her ability to read English. *Courtesy of the Peabody Museum of Archaeology and Ethnology, Harvard University.*

sent to schools where they were made to stop dressing, speaking, thinking, and believing "like Indians." Half the students were girls, whose forcible reeducation was regarded as crucial to the cultural transformation of Native people. Too frequently, Native girls' assimilation into American culture consisted of training in menial occupations and in American standards of domesticity, which they learned as servants in the homes of nearby white families.

The goal of such programs was to save the child by "destroying the Indian," but the transformations sought were elusive. Evidence of repeated and harsh punishments testifies to the refusal of girls as well as boys to give up their Indian ways. One elderly Indian woman recalled later, "Two of our girls ran away . . . but they got caught. They tied their legs up, tied their hands behind their backs, put them in the middle of the hallway so that if they fell asleep or something, the matron would hear them and she'd get out there and whip them and make them stand up again."[6] Parents and tribal leaders protested the brutality of this coercive Americanization, but they could not stop it.

Despite boarding schools' coercive practices, many Native American women were able to acquire English literacy and other useful skills in the boarding school system. Their training gave them access to jobs in the Indian Service. In 1899, Native Americans made up 45 percent of those employed in the education division

◆ **Native American Nurses (1913)**
While many students at Native boarding schools received training for menial work, others were able to develop more professional skills. These Native women (Josie Cayou, Theresa Young, Myrtle Loughrey, Clara Jones, Emily Limon, and Annie Nason) were nurses at the Tulalip Indian Boarding School (1905–1932) in western Washington. *Museum of History & Industry, Seattle, 1988.11.63.*

of the agency, mostly in support services, but a significant number were teachers, clerks, or nurses. And while some may have adopted the assumptions of their employer, others used their position primarily to improve their charges' circumstances and even to oppose the government's harsh assimilation policy. Because the Indian Service preferred not to place employees with their own people, Native Americans who served outside their own communities may have even encouraged a fledgling sense of intertribal identity.

A few graduates of boarding schools who also worked for the federal government in some capacity, such as the Yankton Sioux writer Gertrude Simmons Bonnin (who wrote popular stories under her Native name, Zitkala-Ša) and the Omaha sisters Susan and Susette La Flesche, became public advocates for their people. Sponsored by the white women of the Woman's National Indian Association to attend the Women's Medical College of Pennsylvania, Susan La Flesche graduated in 1889 to become the first white-trained Native woman physician. She served her people for many years, both as a doctor and as a political leader. Susette La Flesche was a writer and speaker on behalf of Indian causes. She helped to convert several influential white women to the cause of Indian reform, including Helen Hunt Jackson. Bonnin became a well-known writer and activist for Native American causes. One renowned woman activist, Paiute Sarah Winnemucca, had little formal education and little use for the boarding school approach. In addition to her activities as translator, negotiator, and lecturer, she created a short-lived bilingual school to offer Paiute children an education that would respect their own cultures. (See Primary Sources: "Representing Native American Women in the Late Nineteenth Century," pp. 390–401.)

Protests against corruption in the reservation system led in 1887 to congressional passage of the Dawes Severalty Act, which divided reservation lands into allotments for individual Native families, the remaining acreage to be sold to non-Indians. Allotment was meant as a reform alternative to demeaning reservation existence, a proposal encouraged by reformers like Jackson, but the way the system played out actually exacerbated Native peoples' misery. Where land was not very fertile, Native American families could not support themselves on their allotments; and where the land could be productively farmed, whites managed to gain control of those lands. The allotment program also often deepened the dependency of Indian women on their men, following the pattern of white society. In contrast to communal landholding and farming practices, the allotment program meant that women who chose to divorce their husbands risked the loss of economic resources under the control of male heads of household. A group of Hopi women vainly protested to the Bureau of Indian Affairs in 1894. "The family, the dwelling house and the field are inseparable," they insisted, "because the woman is the heart of these, and they rest with her."[7] In some areas, however, Native women found other means of contributing to the household economy. As tourism flourished in the West toward the end of the century, the baskets and blankets women produced became desirable commodities. In the Pacific Northwest's Puget Sound area, for example, indigenous women from a number of tribes including the Snoqualmie became migrant farm laborers, providing crucial labor as hop-pickers on land that had once belonged to indigenous peoples. These same women further supplemented their income by selling local crafts, including baskets, to white women consumers and tourists or by posing for photographs.

Colonial Settler Families in the West

As Native American control over the West weakened, American colonial settlement across the vast continent continued apace. The passage of the Homestead Act in 1862 granted 160 acres to individuals willing to cultivate and "improve" the land. The railroads, themselves beneficiaries of federal largesse, also sold land to settlers to establish towns along their routes. Through this process, the broad central plains—from Minnesota to Montana to Oklahoma—were settled and Americanized. By the early twentieth century, one-quarter of the U.S. population lived west of the Mississippi.

This population was diverse. After Reconstruction, a small but steady stream of African American families was drawn west by the hope of independent farming. In all-black towns, such as Nicodemus, Kansas, and Langston, Oklahoma, African American women found ways to support their families that were less demeaning than working as domestic servants for white people. In Boley, Oklahoma, Lulu Smith started a dressmaking business; other women ran boardinghouses, catering services, and general stores.[8] European immigrants played a large role in western colonial settlement, especially in the northern territories. In the late nineteenth century, in the period of mass immigration, one out of every two western settlers was foreign-born. The Homestead Act allowed land grants to immigrants who intended to become citizens. They, too, formed their own communities where they could live and speak and farm as they had in their home countries.

For a while, in villages throughout New Mexico, Arizona, and southern California, Spanish-speaking women continued to live much as their mothers and grandmothers had. They maintained adobe homes and cultivated small plots, while the men in their families were increasingly drawn away to work in the mines, on the railroads, or on the commercial farms and ranches run by whites (known as Anglos). Ironically, while these Hispanic women were regarded by Anglo society as oppressed, they enjoyed considerable authority in their own communities. Local practices favored female property owning, and when widowed, women in these Hispanic enclaves preferred to head their own households rather than remarry. As the extension of the railroads brought national market pressures and a cash economy closer, however, the need for money became greater. Many of these women lost their distinctive advantages and followed their husbands into paid labor, as domestics in Anglo towns or agricultural wage laborers in Anglo fields.

Despite many differences, all these rural western communities relied on women's unpaid labor, in striking contrast to the emphasis on middle-class female leisure and working-class female wage labor in the more urbanized parts of American society. Western women cooked, did laundry, and made clothes without benefit of many of the technological improvements — such as running water — available in more industrialized areas. While their husbands cultivated specialized commercial crops, the wives cared for animals and grew food for the family table. One Arizona woman described her morning chores: "[G]et up, turn out my chickens, draw a pail of water, . . . make a fire, put potatoes to cook, then brush and sweep half inch of dust off floor, feed three litters of chickens, then mix biscuits, get breakfast, milk, besides work in the house, and this morning had to go half mile after calves." She also contributed to her family's unending need for cash by churning twenty-four pounds of butter in four days. "Quit with a headache," she wrote in her diary. "Done too much work."[9]

Some women were inspired to try homesteading on their own. Perhaps as many as 15 percent of late nineteenth-century American homesteads were at some point controlled by women. Unmarried women who controlled their own homesteads combined two resources irresistible to male settlers, land and female labor, and were besieged by marriage proposals. As one young Oklahoma woman wrote, as soon as she was awarded a claim, men started to court her: "The letters began pouring in — men wanting to marry me, men all the way from twenty-one to seventy-five."[10]

Western farm women did their homemaking in an environment where homes had to be built from scratch. On the plains, after spending the first few months living in temporary shelters, settler families would move into huts made of sod, the top layer of soil so dense with the roots of prairie grass that it could be cut into bricks. Women sprinkled their dirt walls and floors with water to keep down the dust, and decorated their unlikely homes as lavishly as they could, eager to banish the discomfort of being

◆ Immigrants in the Great Plains

As with the growth of American industry, the settling of the Great Plains required immigrant labor and determination. Scandinavians were particularly drawn to homesteading. This Norwegian immigrant to Minnesota, Beret Olesdater Hagebak, sits alone in front of a small house made of sod, the most common building material available on the treeless plains. Her picture captures the difficult experience of immigrant farm women, who suffered both the cultural disorientation of immigration and the isolation of Plains farm life. *Lac qui Parle County Historical Society/Museum.*

surrounded by dirt. Westering was an ongoing process; as families frequently moved and resettled on more promising land, it was left to the women to repeat the work of creating—both physically and emotionally—new home environments.

Of all the burdens for women settlers on the Great Plains, drudgery and loneliness seem to have been the worst, especially in the years when towns were still being established. Unlike their husbands, women rarely left the homestead—slaves, as some put it, to the cookstove and the washtub. Ignored when she complained that she "never got to go nowhere, or see anybody . . . or [do] anything but work," one Oklahoma woman packed up the children and fled. Overtaken by a wind and ice storm, she almost froze to death and ended up back at the homestead, disabled for life.[11]

In 1867, the organization of an agricultural communities' group, the National Grange (the full title was the Order of the Patrons of Husbandry), helped overcome women's isolation on the prairies. By the mid-1870s, three-quarters of the farmers of Kansas had joined.[12] Based on the premise that farm families had to cooperate to succeed against the corporate power of railroads and other monopolies, the Grange established farmer-run stores and grain elevators and promoted laws against unfair railroad rates. It also sponsored social and cultural events that enriched local community life and were of special importance to women, who played a prominent role in the Grange. Local chapters were required to have nine female members for every thirteen male members, and women served as officers and delegates to the national meetings. The sense of community that the Grange created prepared the way for more overtly political expressions of agricultural discontent, including the Farmers' Alliance in the late 1880s and the Populist movement of the 1890s (see pp. 376–79).

The "Wild West"

Alongside the families drawn by the promise of land and economic self-sufficiency were other westerners pursuing riskier schemes for getting rich. Both groups Americanized the West, but in different ways. While family settlement imported the American social and cultural values of industriousness and domesticity, these other westerners brought with them capitalism, wage labor, and subordination to growing corporate power. Despite their status as icons of individual freedom, the colorful cowboys of the cattle range and the grizzled miners of the gold and silver mines were wage laborers and suffered from wage dependence as much as industrial workers in New York and Chicago.

The contrasts between the Wild West and the Settler West are particularly clear in terms of the radically different gender practices on which they rested. In the mines and cattle ranges, women wage earners were rare. Annie Oakley's riding and roping skills made her a featured player in Buffalo Bill Cody's Wild West Show in the 1890s, but cowgirls were a staple only in the Wild West of popular culture. The rapidly expanding female labor force found elsewhere in America existed in the West only in the largest cities, such as Denver, San Francisco, and Seattle.

There were other sorts of women in the Wild West, however. At first, most were prostitutes. Like the miners and cowboys who were their customers, they were black and white, English- and Spanish-speaking, native- and foreign-born. Initially, many of these women worked for themselves, as what one historian calls "proprietor prostitutes."[13] A few were able to earn or marry their way into respectable society. Others bought or rented brothels, hired other women, and became successful, if disreputable, businesswomen. In 1890, in Helena, Montana, one of the most prosperous real estate entrepreneurs was an Irish-born former prostitute, "Chicago Joe." But for most, prostitution was a thoroughly losing proposition. Two-thirds of prostitutes died young of sexually transmitted diseases, botched abortions, alcohol or drug abuse, suicide, or homicide. As in other western businesses, the initial period of entrepreneurial exuberance was replaced by consolidated ownership. By the early twentieth century, men — pimps, landlords, and police — enjoyed most of the profits from western prostitution.

More women — some rich, most poor — gradually began to move to western centers of industry. The wives of western mine owners lived in expensive, elegant homes, hired servants, and imported luxuries. The determination of a few to use their husbands' fortunes on behalf of their own social and philanthropic ambitions was legendary. Phoebe Appleton Hearst, whose husband got rich in the mines of

California and Nevada, was a major benefactor of the University of California at Berkeley. Margaret (Molly) Tobin Brown, the daughter of Irish Catholic immigrants, married one of the rare individual prospectors to become wealthy off the mines. She bought and refurnished an elegant Denver mansion, hired tutors to teach her the ways of the upper class, and became a generous civic donor. In 1912, she survived the sinking of the ill-fated *Titanic*, earning herself the nickname of "Unsinkable Molly Brown."

At the other end of the class scale, wage-earning miners and cowboys also formed families. The immigrant copper miners of Anaconda, Montana, married the young Irish women who worked as domestic servants for their bosses or as waitresses in the local hotels. Mexican miners in Colorado brought their wives north to live with them and settle permanently in the United States. These working-class wives rarely took jobs outside the home, although they did earn money by feeding and housing single male miners, cowboys, and lumberjacks.

Western housewives lived with the constant fear of losing their husbands to violent death on the range or in the mines. Recognizing that unions would fight to raise wages and make working conditions safer, they were strong supporters of organized labor. They formed union auxiliaries that were very active during the militant strikes that rocked the region. In Cripple Creek, Colorado, miners' wives were involved in 1893 when the radical Western Federation of Miners won higher wages and in 1904 when the state militia drove union activists out of town. By far the most prominent female labor activist in the region was the legendary Irish-born Mary Harris ("Mother") Jones, who began her career as an organizer for miners' unions in the late 1890s. Mother Jones focused her attention on the miners — her "boys" — but she also understood the power of miners' wives and organized them into "mop and broom brigades" that effectively harassed strikebreakers. Referring to one of the family dynasties most identified with corporate greed, Jones declared: "God Almighty made women and the Rockefeller gang of thieves made the ladies."[14]

Jones's contempt for female gentility notwithstanding, western working-class wives were as careful as women of the leisure classes to maintain a distinction between their own status as respectable women and the status of the disreputable women who had preceded them. Family life was gradually displacing the world of the dance halls and brothels. Respectable women took care not to live in the same areas as "fast" women. "If the world of work was divided into laborers and employers," writes one historian of the western female experience, "the world of women was divided into good women and bad."[15]

◆ LATE NINETEENTH-CENTURY IMMIGRATION

While Americans were moving westward in the late nineteenth century, immigrants were pouring into the country, 27 million in the half century after 1880. These numbers dwarfed pre–Civil War immigration. Five million came from Italy and an equal number from Germany, as well as 2 million Eastern European Jews, 1 million Polish Catholics, and 1 million Scandinavians. A small but growing number of Asians and Mexicans also came to the United States in these years. By 1910, Asians constituted 2 percent of all arriving immigrants. Numbers of Mexican immigrants are harder to determine. Until 1924, when the U.S. Border Patrol was established, the Mexican-U.S. border was virtually unregulated, and those crossing back and forth melded into already existing Spanish-speaking communities. This massive immigration turned the United States into a much more ethnically and religiously diverse people, no longer preponderantly English and Protestant but now broadly European, with a growing minority of resident Asians and Mexicans.

The gender patterns of these immigrations were complex. Among Slavic, Greek, and Italian immigrants, more men than women came to the United States. However, many men came as temporary workers and returned eventually to their homelands. As they did, and as more women came to marry those who remained, sex ratios tended to even out. Some groups, notably Eastern European Jews and new Irish immigrants, initially came in more gender-balanced numbers. Eventually, women constituted between 30 and 40 percent of all immigrants (see the Appendix, p. A-21) in these years.

The Decision to Immigrate

Women decided to leave their homelands and come to the United States for many reasons, some of which they shared with men. Faced with poverty, limited opportunity, and rigid class structures at home, families dispatched members to work in the United States and send money back to those who remained. The booming U.S. economy had an insatiable need for workers in its factories, mines, and kitchens, and it lured men and women alike with its promises of high wages and easy prosperity. "This was the time . . . when America was known to foreigners as the land where you'd get rich," remembered Pauline Newman, who arrived from Lithuania in 1901. "There's gold on the sidewalk! All you have to do is pick it up."[16] Political persecution also pushed people out of their homelands. Jews began emigrating in large numbers in the 1880s to escape growing anti-Semitism in Eastern Europe, especially the violent, deadly riots called pogroms. Similarly, the upheavals that culminated in the Mexican Revolution of 1910 drove men and women north.

Women also had their own distinctive reasons for emigrating. Many were drawn by the reputation that the United States was developing as a society that welcomed independence for women. A common story for young women of all groups involved fleeing from an overbearing, patriarchal father and from the threat of an arranged marriage. That was why Emma Goldman fled Russia in 1885. Upon arriving in the United States, she began a life of political activism that eventually made her the most notorious radical in the United States (see Reading into the Past: "Living My Life").

READING INTO THE PAST

EMMA GOLDMAN
Living My Life

Emma Goldman (1869–1940) was raised in Russia by an overbearing father and an uninterested stepmother. She was already interested in radical politics before she left in 1885 to follow her sister Helena and to become a garment worker in Rochester, New York. Within a few years, she had become deeply involved with the anarchist movement. Her autobiography, Living My Life *(1931), is one of the most widely read life stories in American women's history.*

Helena also hated to leave me behind. She knew of the bitter friction that existed between Father and me. She offered to pay my fare, but Father would not consent to my going. I pleaded, begged, wept. Finally I threatened to jump into the Neva [River], whereupon he yielded. Equipped with twenty-five roubles — all that the old man would give me — I left without regrets. Since my earliest recollection, home had been stifling, my father's presence terrifying. . . . [Father] had tried desperately to marry me off at the age of fifteen. I had protested, begging to be permitted to continue my studies. In his frenzy he threw my French grammar into the fire, shouting: "Girls do not have to learn much! All a Jewish daughter needs to know is how to prepare gefüllte fish, cut noodles fine, and give the man plenty of children." I would not listen to his schemes; I wanted to study, to know life, to travel. Besides, I never would marry for anything but love, I stoutly maintained. It was really to escape my father's plans for me that I had insisted on going to America.

SOURCE: Emma Goldman, *Living My Life* (1931; repr., New York: Courier Dover Publications, 1970), 1:11.

QUESTION FOR ANALYSIS

1. As an anarchist, Goldman was very critical of U.S. politics and economic organization, yet in this passage she suggests the positive qualities America could represent to a young immigrant woman. What were they?

Other women came to the United States as wives or to become wives, to join husbands who had migrated before them or to complete arranged marriages. The Japanese government encouraged male immigrants to send back to Japan for women to marry. These women in turn sent letters and photographs to their potential husbands. This was a modern version of a traditional Japanese practice, but *shaskin kekkon* (literally, "photograph marriages") were regarded by Americans as akin to prostitution and still another indication of the allegedly low morals of Asians. Similar arrangements were common among European immigrants. Rachel Kahn came from Ukraine to North Dakota in 1894 to marry a Russian immigrant farmer with whom she had only exchanged pictures.[17]

Some women undoubtedly migrated for reasons so personal and painful that they were hidden from public view. Unmarried women who had become pregnant might flee or be sent away so that the scandal could be more easily hidden. The father of Lucja Krajulis's child would not marry her but sent her instead to the United States, where she was shuttled about among fellow Lithuanians.[18] During the 1910 Mexican Revolution, women in the countryside were raped by armed marauders, and crossing the border provided them escape from their shame.

The Immigrant's Journey

Having decided to move to the United States, immigrant women had many obstacles to negotiate. Passage in the steerage class of a transoceanic steamship in 1900 cost the modern equivalent of $400. It took ten to twenty days to cross from Italy to New York and twice as long from Japan to San Francisco, during which time passengers slept in cramped, unhealthy conditions below deck. One can only imagine the experience of pregnant women or mothers of infants. Photos of arriving immigrants show dazed women, with babies held tightly in their arms and older children clinging to their skirts.

In 1892, the first federal receiving station for immigrants was established on Ellis Island in New York Harbor. The majority of immigrants were passed through quickly, although individuals judged "unfit" for admission could be isolated, confined, and eventually deported. Asian women were more likely to be kept for long periods at Angel Island, the equivalent site established in San Francisco Bay in 1910. Assumed to be sexually immoral, they were detained until they could establish their respectability by answering endless questions about themselves and the men they planned to marry. "Had I known it was like this," a thirty-year-old Chinese mother recalled, "I never would have wanted to come."[19]

Young European women in transit were regarded as sexually vulnerable rather than sexually immoral. Stories circulated of unaccompanied and disoriented immigrant girls tricked or forced into prostitution. This phenomenon was known at the time as "white slavery," a term that invoked memories of chattel (black) slavery. Feared as an international conspiracy to waylay and prostitute young women, white slavery was a major focus for anxieties about women and immigration. The actual extent of the practice is difficult to determine.

Many immigrants kept on moving beyond their point of arrival in the United States, following friends or family or rumors of work. By the turn of the century, the populations of large midwestern cities such as Chicago and Milwaukee were preponderantly foreign-born. Numerous mining towns of the West were dense with immigrants as well. Many immigrants, wishing to retain something of their familiar homeland, preferred to live among people from their own village or region, but this could leave them ignorant of much about their new surroundings. Reformer Jane Addams told the poignant story of an Italian woman who had never seen roses in the few blocks of Chicago that she knew, thought they grew only in Italy, and feared that she would never enjoy their beauty again.[20]

Reception of the Immigrants

The United States's pride in its status as a nation of immigrants is embodied in New York Harbor's Statue of Liberty, a giant female figure presented to the United States by the people of France in 1885 to represent the two countries' common embrace of liberty. The poem inscribed on the statue's base was written by Emma Lazarus, a descendant of Sephardic Jews who had arrived in the mid-seventeenth century. The words she wrote welcome the world's oppressed, those "huddled masses yearning to breathe free, / The wretched refuse of your teeming shore." But Lazarus's sentiment was not the norm. In the late nineteenth century, many native-born Americans regarded the incoming masses as disturbingly different aliens who could never assimilate.

Anti-immigrant legislation initially targeted Asians. The Page Law of 1875, the very first federal legislation meant to discourage immigration, was directed at Chinese women, on the assumption that most were prostitutes. In 1882, Congress passed a more comprehensive law, the Chinese Exclusion Act, which banned further immigration of Chinese laborers and their families. The few women who could prove that they were the wives or daughters of Chinese merchants already living in the United States were exempted. Once Chinese immigration had virtually ceased, Japanese workers began to come to the United States, but by the 1890s, anti-Asian sentiment on the West Coast had surfaced against them as well. In 1907, in the so-called Gentlemen's Agreement, the U.S. and Japanese governments agreed to restrict further immigration.

Laws against European immigrants, who were far more central to the U.S. economy, were not passed until 1921 and 1924, when highly restrictive national quotas were established, remaining in place until 1965 (see pp. 722–23). Even before these laws, European immigrants were the targets of considerable prejudice and resentment. Degrading ethnic stereotypes were widely circulated as innocently amusing. Southern and Eastern European immigrants were seen as peoples whose strangeness and difference were fundamental, physical, and ineradicable. Religion was a major concern. The hundreds of thousands of Jews who arrived from Eastern Europe after 1880 were the first major group of non-Christians to settle in the United States. Even Catholics were regarded by American Protestants as so emotional and superstitious as barely to be fellow believers in Christ. Their devotion to

State of California,
CITY AND COUNTY OF SAN FRANCISCO.

Chin Lung, a resident of San Francisco, being duly
sworn according to law, deposes and says that he is a member
of the firm of Sing Kee & Company No. 808 Sacramento Street
in said City:

That his wife Leung Yee was a resident of this City
for 5o6 years, and that she left this City per Steamship
" Belgic " sailing for Hong Kong on the _____ day
of October 1889.

That his daughter, Ah Kum, was born in San Francisco
at No. 613 Dupont Street, in 1885, and left San Francisco
with her mother in October 1889.   Chin Lung

Subscribed and sworn to before me,
this 1st day of May A.D. 1892
F. B. Hoyt
NOTARY PUBLIC.

◆ A Document of Chinese Immigration

Through diligent research, historian Judy Yung uncovered this sworn testimony given by
her great-grandfather of her great-grandmother's immigration to the United States in 1892.
She found that there were several strategic lies embedded within the document. First, his
wife Leung Yee had not lived in the United States previously but was immigrating for the
first time in 1892. Second, the daughter that she claimed on this document was in fact
a young servant of the family. Such deceits were necessary — and common — to circumvent the prohibitions of the Chinese Exclusion Act of 1882. *File 12017/37232 for Leong
Lee, Chinese Departure Application Case Files, 1912–1943, San Francisco District Office,
Immigration and Naturalization Service, Record Group 85, National Archives and Records
Administration — Pacific Region, San Bruno, CA.*

a foreign pope was the source of much suspicion. Anti-Semitic and anti-Catholic attitudes abounded even among otherwise liberal-minded Americans. Susan B. Anthony could not understand by what logic "these Italians come over with the idea that they must be paid as much as intelligent white men."[21]

Americans were especially wary of immigrant gender relations, regarding their own attitudes as modern and those of the newcomers as Old World and patriarchal. They were particularly uneasy with the reproductive behavior of immigrant women. While the birthrates of native-born women had been falling for some time (see the Appendix, p. A-17), immigrant families were large. In 1903, President Theodore Roosevelt, concerned that immigrants' higher birthrates were overtaking those of native-born Americans, blamed middle-class women who were working or going to college instead of having babies for what he called "race suicide." "If the women do not recognize that the greatest thing for any woman is to be a good wife and mother," he declared in the introduction to *The Woman Who Toils* (see pp. 330–35), "why, that nation has cause to be alarmed about its future."[22] After some time in the United States, however, immigrant women started to want smaller families, too. Margaret Sanger, herself the daughter of Irish immigrants, founded the American birth control movement in the 1910s as a response to immigrant women's pleas for reliable ways to prevent unwanted pregnancy (see pp. 441–44).

Starting about 1910, settlement houses and other civic institutions initiated deliberate Americanization campaigns to assimilate immigrants into mainstream U.S. culture. While these programs did not regard immigrants as permanently alien to American society, they did look on their languages, religions, and cultural practices as foreign. Women's household routines were a particular object of reform, as were practices such as arranged marriages that seemed to violate American standards of family life. These Americanization programs became harsher during World War I, when nativism became much stronger and immigrants' patriotism was questioned.

Immigrant Daughters

Immigrant mothers and daughters confronted America very differently. Low wages made it difficult for immigrant men to meet the American standard of being the sole support of their families. Secondary wage earners were usually teenage children, not wives. Just as their families needed immigrant daughters' earnings, the expanding labor force needed their labor. Young girls were plunged immediately into the booming American economy, while their mothers remained largely homebound.

Young immigrant women predominated in the two largest categories of female wage labor, domestic labor and factory work. German, Polish, and Mexican girls met late nineteenth-century middle-class families' demand for servants. By contrast, Italian parents did not want their daughters to work as servants in strange households and preferred that they take jobs where other family members could oversee their activities, such as in seasonal fruit picking.

Young immigrant women were also drawn into factory work, making their greatest contribution to the garment industry. The mass production of clothes in the United States could not have occurred without their labor. By 1890, one out of three garment workers was a woman, and most of these women were immigrants. Some — Russian Jews, Japanese, Italians — had worked in clothing factories in their home countries. New York and Chicago were the centers of the ready-made clothing industry in the United States, but garment factories filled with immigrant women workers could be found throughout the country, from El Paso to San Francisco to Baltimore. Paid by the piece and pushed to work ever more quickly, young women earned low wages and risked occupational injuries. Sexual harassment was an additional problem for young immigrant women factory workers, as it was hard not to yield to the foremen who controlled their jobs.

Most of these young women workers lived with parents or other relatives, and intergenerational relations could be very tense. More than their brothers, girls were expected to turn over most of their wages to their parents. Mothers needed the money for household expenses, but daughters longed to spend some of their earnings on themselves. Disagreements did not end there. Daughters wanted to dress in the modern American style, while mothers wanted them to look and behave like respectable girls in the old country. Battles could be even more intense with fathers. No one resisted Old World patriarchy more intensely than its daughters. The Russian Jewish novelist Anzia Yezierska wrote often of this theme. "Should I let him crush me as he crushed [my sisters]?" a character in her 1925 novel, *Bread Givers*, said of her father. "No. This is America. Where children are people. . . . It's a new life now. In America, women don't need men to boss them."[23]

Immigrant Wives and Mothers

While unmarried immigrant women were more likely to be wage earners than native-born women, the opposite was true of their mothers — very few of whom worked outside their homes. This behavior was not simply a carryover of Old World standards; Eastern European Jewish wives, for instance, had traditionally been shopkeepers or market vendors. Given the family wage system in the United States, however, adult immigrant women had difficulty finding paid work. Immigrant wives were nonetheless expected to contribute to the family economy. Because of the numbers of single male immigrants and the preference of many groups for living among people from their own country, boarding was very common among immigrants. Middle-class observers, who regarded familial privacy as sacred, condemned the immigrant practice of boarders living within families. Immigrants recognized the tensions but regarded them more tolerantly, and stories of liaisons between amorous boarders and discontented housewives were a source of much amusement in immigrant culture.

Immigrant women's housekeeping and childrearing tasks were daunting, both because of poverty and the surrounding alien culture. In densely populated cities, apartments were crowded and residents still relied on backyard wells and outdoor privies, augmented by public baths. Children playing on busy city streets required additional supervision. Women hauled water up flights of stairs, as they did coal and wood purchased for fuel, and fought a constant battle against ash and soot. Photographer Jacob Riis did pioneering work documenting these conditions. (See Primary Sources: "Jacob Riis's Photographs of Immigrant Girls and Women," pp. 408–14.) Even so, American observers were frequently astonished at the levels of cleanliness immigrant women were able to maintain. While middle-class women dealt with their domestic obligations by hiring immigrant servants, immigrant women had no choice but to do their own scrubbing and ironing.

Immigrant mothers had the added responsibility of preserving customary ways against the tremendous forces working to Americanize them and their families. They continued to cook traditional foods and observe religious obligations, while their husbands and children entered into the American economic mainstream to make the family's living. As practices that were ancient and reflexive became deliberate and problematic, it fell to women to defend and perpetuate the old ways, thus laying the basis for what would eventually become American ethnic identity. Such practices constituted implicit resistance to the forces of Americanization and cultural homogenization. For the time being, however, such immigrant mothers were dismissed by their children as old-fashioned and quaint, their skills and knowledge irrelevant to the new world that their daughters mastered with such verve. Once again, Jane Addams subtly captured the emotional tenor of this role reversal in her description of the dilemma of immigrant women in search of runaway children in Chicago: "It is as if they did not know how to search for their children without the assistance of the children themselves."[24]

Despite these obstacles, adult immigrant women helped to construct lasting ethnic communities. In the mining town of Anaconda, Montana, Irish women, struggling to meet their family needs, nonetheless raised money to build St. Patrick's Catholic Church in 1888. This story was repeated in the immigrant neighborhoods within which the American Catholic church developed. Occasionally, immigrant wives' community activism took a political turn, as in 1902, when New York City Jewish women demonstrated against the rising cost of meat in the city's kosher markets. Like native-born middle-class women, late nineteenth-century immigrant women formed and joined associations, but for different reasons. They had been drawn to the United States by the promise of greater freedom, if not for themselves, then for their children. But they were learning that to realize that promise, they had to find ways to work together.

◆ CENTURY'S END: CHALLENGES, CONFLICT, AND IMPERIAL VENTURES

For many of the women who immigrated to the United States or who migrated across the continent, the American dream remained elusive. Their frustrated hopes helped to fuel a dramatic crisis at century's end. The national economy, which had gone through a series of boom and bust cycles since the beginnings of industrialization in the 1830s, experienced its greatest economic crisis yet in 1893, as overextension of the railroad system, decline in gold reserves, and international collapse in agricultural prices set off a long, deep economic contraction that kept layoffs high, wages low, and economic growth stalled for four years. In the cities, the newest immigrants bore the brunt of massive unemployment and deep family disruption. In the agricultural heartland, crops could not be sold at a profit, and family farms failed. Factory workers and farmers were not natural allies; they were not even particularly sympathetic to each other. Nonetheless, the two groups moved together to confront the wealthy strata that ruled a complacent nation. The turmoil of the 1890s unleashed an unprecedented wave of industrial strikes and raised the prospects for a political movement, Populism, that mounted the first systematic challenge to entrenched political power since the rise of the Republican Party in the 1850s.

In the hotly contested presidential contest of 1896, the probusiness Republican candidate William McKinley defeated the Democratic-Populist nominee William Jennings Bryan, ending for the time being these challenges to entrenched power. In the wake of their victory, corporate leaders and Republican politicians brought the United States to join European nations in the race to acquire overseas colonies.

Women were active everywhere in the crises of the 1890s. They were the victims of desperate economic conditions, ardent supporters of strikes, spokeswomen for political challenges, and supporters and opponents of the new imperial ventures. During this decade, American women reached a new level of political prominence through two distinct achievements — winning the first victories for woman suffrage in the West and establishing settlement houses to assist urban immigrants.

Rural Protest, Populism, and the Battle for Woman Suffrage

The years after Reconstruction were difficult for American farmers. With the dream of economic independence and self-sufficiency receding, farming families were driven into debt by the pressures of falling prices and rising costs. Culturally, rural Americans also felt that they were losing ground — and often their children — to the magnet of city life. The powerful railroad corporations that set rates for transporting their crops were a particular target of farmers' anger. "It is an undeniable fact that the condition of the farmer and their poor drudging wives is every year becoming more intolerable," Minnesotan Mary Travis complained in 1880. "We are robbed and crowded to the wall on every side, our crop [is] taken for whatever the middlemen are of a mind to give us, and we are obligated to give them whatever they have the force to ask for their goods or go without, and all this means so . . . much toil, and less help for the farmer's wife."[25]

The Grange gave way in the 1880s to farmers' alliances. While continuing to encourage community life, the alliances encouraged farmers to form buying and selling cooperatives to circumvent the powers of the banks and railroads. The Southern Alliance, which began in Texas in 1877, was particularly strong. In it, non-elite southern white women began to take a visible, public role. Southern black farmers organized a separate Colored Farmers' Alliance, approximately half of whose 750,000 members were women. African American sharecroppers, who were trapped in debt because they had to acquire their supplies from their landlords at exorbitant credit rates, were particularly attracted to cooperatives. The People's Grocery in Memphis, the lynching of whose owner in 1892 catapulted Ida B. Wells into her reform career (see pp. 325–29), was probably one such cooperative enterprise.

By 1892, farmers' alliances in the Midwest and South came together to form a new political party, ambitiously named the People's Party and commonly known as the Populists. Women were active in its meteoric life. Frances Willard, an important figure at the founding convention in St. Louis, brought the large and powerful Woman's Christian Temperance Union (WCTU) with her into the new effort. Several of the Populists' most successful organizers were also women. Kansan Mary Elizabeth Lease, daughter of Irish immigrants, was the fieriest of these radical female orators. "You wonder, perhaps, at the zeal and enthusiasm of the Western women in this reform movement," Lease proclaimed at the founding convention. "We endured hardships, dangers and privations, hours of loneliness, fear and sorrow; [w]e helped our loved ones to make the prairie blossom . . . yet after all our years of toil and privations, dangers and hardship upon the Western frontier, monopoly is taking our homes from us."[26]

The Populist insurgency lasted only four years, but it left an enduring mark on the history of women's rights. In the Reconstruction years, suffragists had fought for political rights via the U.S. Constitution (see pp. 292–94). During the 1890s, while national politics remained inhospitable to reform, the focus for woman suffrage, as for other democratic reforms, shifted to the state level. In several western states, the Populists endorsed woman suffrage, giving it new life. Voter referenda were held to amend state constitutions to include votes for women.

The most important of these campaigns occurred in 1893, when the women of Colorado's suffrage societies, labor union auxiliaries, WCTU chapters, and Knights of Labor locals joined together to convince male voters to enfranchise them. In contrast to the violent, widespread class conflict in the western mining industry, the advocates of woman suffrage were proud of their ability to "work unitedly and well" for a common goal.[27] Middle- and upper-class women contributed money to hold giant rallies. Their respectability offset the charge that prostitutes' votes would further corrupt the world of politics. Suffragists linked their cause to struggling farmers and wage earners and asked for the vote as a tool against the entrenched power of railroads and mining corporations. "The money question has power to reach into the most sheltered home and bring want and desolation," Lease proclaimed. "Women have not invaded politics; politics have invaded the home."[28] Although suffragists had appealed to all political parties, Populist support was crucial to victory. "There is less prejudice against and a stronger belief in equal rights in the newer communities," wrote suffrage journalist Ellis Meredith of this western victory. "The pressure of hard times, culminating in the panic of 1893, undoubtedly contributed to the success of the Populist Party and to its influence the suffrage cause owes much."[29] Three years later, Idaho women won a similar victory by an even greater margin.

Campaigns to get male voters to support woman suffrage amendments to state constitutions were also waged in Kansas and California, but they failed because of partisan conflict. In Kansas in 1894, two out of three male voters voted against woman suffrage and, according to Populist suffragist Annie Diggs, "the grief and

◆ **Early Women Voters in Colorado, 1907**
In 1893, the Populist-controlled legislature of Colorado called for a referendum to amend the state constitution to enfranchise women voters, the first time that the issue had been put before large numbers of male voters. Colorado was a booming state, the center of the mining industry, home both to the owners of great fortunes and a large, militant working class. The woman suffrage referendum won with a strong majority, passing in over three-quarters of the counties. Women followed up their victory by voting in substantial numbers for state and federal offices. The pride that they took in their new status as active, voting citizens is obvious in the faces and stances of these women, standing with male voters outside a Denver polling place. *Denver Public Library, Western History Collection/Bridgeman Images.*

the disappointment of the Kansas women were indescribable."[30] In 1896, the issue was put before the men of California. Seventy-six-year-old Susan B. Anthony went to the state to work for suffrage. At first, all three political parties endorsed the referendum, and labor, Socialist, Spanish-language, and immigrant newspapers also came out in its favor. But when national Populist leaders decided to campaign in the presidential election that year solely on the issue of currency reform ("free silver"), the political situation changed dramatically. The Democratic Party joined with the Populists in political unity, and the two parties "fused" behind the presidential candidacy of the charismatic Nebraskan orator William Jennings Bryan. Woman suffrage became a liability, and the Populists ceased to agitate on its behalf. Republicans turned against it, and the California referendum was defeated 45 percent to 55 percent. "We feel defeated, and it doesn't feel good," Anthony told a newspaper reporter. "But we must save ourselves for other States. 'Truth crushed to earth will rise again.'"[31]

In the South, woman suffrage, which had been held back by its association with black suffrage and with the Reconstruction-era effort to subordinate states' rights to federal authority, also got its first sustained support in the Populist era. In 1888, Texan Ann Other defended woman suffrage against its critics in the pages of the *Southern Mercury*, a Populist newspaper. "Those men who could think less of a woman because she took a judicious interest in the laws of her country would not be worth the while to mourn over," she wrote.[32]

Eventually, however, southern Populism was felled by the racial divisions inherited from slavery and deepening racial inequality at century's end. The threat of electoral cooperation between angry black and white farmers was countered by the new system of segregation and disfranchisement known as Jim Crow (see pp. 303–4). When southern suffrage campaigns resurfaced again in the twentieth century, they did so in the context of this aggressive racism, arguing for white women's votes as a means for countering black men's votes.

Nationally, the election of Republican William McKinley in 1896 signaled the defeat of the Populist movement. For women, however, the party's brief career had enormous consequences. The women of Colorado and Idaho now had full voting rights, in federal as well as state elections. Woman suffrage had become a live political issue, and its center had shifted from the Northeast, where the movement had begun, farther west, where male voters identified it with a more democratic political system. Having driven the People's Party from the electoral arena, the Republican Party absorbed some of its reform agenda. After 1896, the issue of woman suffrage passed into the hands of the reform-minded wing of the Republican Party, along with other Populist concerns, such as ameliorating the impact of economic growth on the poor and the need for government regulation of corporations. As with the Populists, women activists and reformers would prove to be numerous and influential among these newly designated "Progressives" (see pp. 427–29).

Class Conflict and the Pullman Strike of 1894

Just as Populism was reaching its high point in 1893, the national economy collapsed, thousands of businesses failed, and nearly a quarter of wage workers lost their jobs. The severe depression exposed critical problems and deep social rifts. Women suffered, both as out-of-work wage earners and as wives of unemployed men. Federal and state governments, following the laissez faire principle of nonintervention in the marketplace, offered no help. Private charities provided a few paying jobs — street cleaning for men and sewing for women — but their efforts were inadequate to meet the massive need. Across much of the country, the winter of 1893–94 was one of the coldest ever recorded. Rosa Cavalleri, a recent immigrant from Italy to Chicago, recalled waiting in a line for free food: "Us poor women were frozen to death."[33] The spread of disease under such conditions — smallpox and typhoid in Chicago, diphtheria in New York City—showed the middle and upper classes that, in a complex, modern society, misery and want could not be confined to one class. Poverty put entire communities at risk.

For a handful, the moment heralded a new American revolution. Amid rising working-class discontent, twenty-four-year-old Emma Goldman found her calling as a radical agitator and orator. She was already under suspicion for her role in the attempted assassination of the chairman of the Carnegie Steel Corporation during a violent strike at its Homestead, Pennsylvania, plant in 1892. The next year she led a phalanx of unemployed workers in New York City. An advocate of anarchism, the political philosophy that condemned all government as illegitimate authority, she challenged the crowd, "Do you not realize that the State is the worst enemy you have? . . . The State is the pillar of capitalism and it is ridiculous to expect any redress from it."[34] She was arrested, tried, and sentenced to a year in prison for "inciting to riot." In jail, Goldman learned the trade of midwifery and became an advocate of sexual and reproductive freedom for working-class women (see pp. 441–44).

The most dramatic of the strikes against falling wages and massive layoffs began in May 1894 at the Pullman Railroad Car Company just south of Chicago. Company founder George Pullman was proud of his paternalistic policy of providing for all his workers' needs; but now, determined to maintain profits, Pullman refused to lower rents in the company-owned housing, where employees were expected to live despite their diminished pay packets. Pullman's policy drew workers' wives as well as women workers into the conflict. "Holding their babies close for shields," the antistrike *Chicago Tribune* reported of a workers' demonstration, "the women still break past the patrol lines and go where no man dares to step."[35] As railroad workers nationwide shut down the railroad system rather than transport Pullman cars, pressure grew on the federal government to intervene. President Grover Cleveland sent six thousand federal troops to quell riots and occupy the rail yards in Chicago. By early July, the strike was broken.

The Settlement House Movement

The Pullman strike also affected the future of middle- and upper-class women by putting a new development in female social reform, the settlement house movement, on the historical map. Settlement houses were pioneered in England in the 1880s by male college graduates who chose to live among and serve the urban poor. By 1890, settlement houses were beginning to appear in the United States, with the important difference that most of their participants were middle- and upper-class women. The most influential settlement house was Hull House, established in Chicago in 1889 by Jane Addams. (See Primary Sources: "Jane Addams, *Twenty Years at Hull House*," pp. 402–7.)

Soon Hull House was serving several thousand people per week, helping immigrant mothers with child care and encouraging the spread of American values and culture. In contrast to later, more coercive forms of Americanization, however, Hull House valued immigrants for their home cultures, struggling with the gulf between immigrant mothers and their Americanized children. Rooms were made available for union meetings and political discussion clubs. Immigrants in the neighborhood attended concerts and enjoyed the use of a gymnasium. A separate residence, named the Jane Club in homage to Addams, provided an alternative to commercial boardinghouses for young wage-earning women away from their families. "Hull House is meant to be the centre for all the work needed around it," a sympathetic observer explained, "not committed to one line of work, but open to all that leads the way to a higher life for the people."[36]

◆ College Settlement House, Philadelphia, 1895

Settlement houses similar to Hull House spread rapidly in the late nineteenth century. Women college graduates were at the forefront of establishing these sites in poor urban neighborhoods, where they sought to meet the needs of the urban poor. The College Settlement Association was founded in 1889 and grew to include alumnae of eleven institutions, among them Swarthmore, Wellesley, Smith, Vassar, Bryn Mawr, and Radcliffe Colleges. This 1895 image, taken by the well-known reformer and photographer Jacob Riis (see Primary Sources: "Jacob Riis's Photographs of Immigrant Girls and Women," pp. 408–14), is of a cooking class at the Philadelphia College Settlement. Founded in 1889, it served a neighborhood composed primarily of African Americans, Russian Jews, and Italians. © *Museum of the City of New York, USA/Bridgeman Images.*

The Pullman strike gave new prominence and impetus to the women of Hull House, who suddenly found themselves in the midst of Chicago's violent class conflict. Jane Addams, who had a reputation as an effective conciliator, was appointed to a special citizens' arbitration committee, but its members were unable to find a way to resolve the strike. Meanwhile, Florence Kelley, another Hull House member, was developing a more direct, long-term response to the frustration and demands of working-class immigrant families. The daughter of a Republican congressman and herself a Cornell University graduate, Kelley shared Addams's privileged background but had moved further beyond the expectations of women of her class. While living in Germany, she had become a socialist and corresponded with Karl Marx's collaborator, Friedrich Engels, about the condition of the Chicago poor. In 1892, she wrote him, "The most visible work is [being done] at the present moment by a lot of women who are organizing trade unions of men and women."[37] Kelley had come to Hull House to escape her own abusive husband and so knew something of wives' dependency. She deserves much of the credit for moving Hull House, and with it the entire settlement movement, decisively in the direction of modern social welfare reform.

Kelley crafted a body of labor laws designed to shield working-class families from the worst impact of the wage labor system. In 1893, she and others submitted a bill to the Illinois state legislature to prohibit the employment of children, constrain home-based manufacturing, establish an eight-hour workday for adult women workers, and enable state officials to visit and monitor work sites for safety and health conditions. Offered as a legislative response to the growing social and economic crisis of the poor, the Illinois Factory and Workshop Inspection Act was passed about a year before the Pullman strike. Kelley was appointed chief factory inspector for the state and empowered to search out and prosecute violations of the new laws. She and her deputy inspectors, including the trade union activist Mary Kenney (see pp. 422–24), drew the attention of reformers, the state government, and labor unions to the extent and abuses of the sweating system in Illinois and helped to initiate a nationwide campaign to improve conditions in the garment industry. Many states began to pass similar factory and tenement inspection laws.

Other provisions of the law were not so successful. Illinois garment manufacturers united in opposition to the eight-hour workday for women workers. In the bitter aftermath of the Pullman strike, the Illinois Supreme Court ruled in 1895 that limitations on the working hours of women were a violation of their individual freedom of contract, enacted without "due process of law." Kelley's father had helped to write the Fourteenth Amendment, which had enshrined the principle of due process in the U.S. Constitution, and she railed against the 1895 decision as a perversion of this principle, making it into "an insuperable obstacle for the protection of women and children."[38] Ending child labor also proved extremely difficult, as immigrant parents resisted efforts to deprive their families of young wage earners. But Kelley had chosen her life's work — to find the political backing and constitutional basis for social welfare provisions that would aid working-class women and families.

Women-based settlement houses soon appeared in other immigrant-dense cities, among them the Henry Street Settlement in New York City, led by Lillian Wald; the Neighborhood House in Dallas; and the Telegraph Hill Neighborhood

Association in San Francisco. While many white settlement leaders personally believed in greater racial justice, they yielded to the prejudices of the era and practiced racial segregation in the institutions they established. In the South, middle-class African American women organized their own settlements, most notably Atlanta's Neighborhood Union, organized in 1908 by clubwoman Lugenia Burns Hope (see pp. 454–61). In the North, all-black settlement houses were also organized. Ida B. Wells-Barnett set up the Negro Fellowship Association in a rented house on Chicago's south side. Hull House, which had experimented with a few black residents in the 1890s, switched in the twentieth century to encouraging and supporting a separate black settlement house, the Wendell Phillips House. Similar black-oriented settlement houses were the Robert Gould Shaw House in Boston, Karamu House in Cleveland, and Lincoln House in New York City.

Epilogue to the Crisis: The Spanish-American War of 1898

In an atmosphere shaped by the crisis of the 1890s, the United States embarked on its first extracontinental imperialist efforts. Imperial advocates contended that the acquisition of overseas colonies could provide both new markets to revive the American economy and a military challenge to invigorate American manhood. In an influential paper titled "The Significance of the Frontier in American History," historian Frederick Jackson Turner considered the advantages of an imperial future for the United States. Mourning the end of an era in which the defining national purpose was to conquer the American continent, and concerned that immigrants could not be fully Americanized in the absence of the frontier experience, Turner suggested that overseas expansion might be a way for the United States to continue to pursue its Manifest Destiny and maintain its frontier spirit.

Turner made his remarks in 1893 at the World's Columbian Exposition in Chicago. The fair was notable for its impressive "Woman's Building," which showcased women's accomplishments in the various industries, arts, and professions. But the Woman's Building mostly celebrated white women and like the rest of the fair its racial exclusivity reinforced the theme of the onward march of white American civilization. In particular, the exposition displayed the nation's rising imperial aspirations. The spatial organization of the grounds reflected the country's new ambitions for world leadership. At the center was the Court of Honor, where the United States welcomed and joined the great nations of Europe. Meanwhile, on the riotous Midway Plaisance at the fair's periphery, belly-dancing Arabs, tribal Africans, and exotic Asians drew enormous crowds, fascinated and amused by the unprecedented spectacle of the world's strange variety of peoples. Much of the Midway traded on what scholars today term "Orientalism." Beginning in the late nineteenth century, white Americans and Europeans engaged in fantasies of the Middle East, North Africa, and East Asia as simultaneously primitive and exotic, which tell us more about those who fantasized than those of the East themselves. These fantasies reflected a longing for a sensuality and eroticism seemingly absent or repressed in more modern culture, embodied particularly by the women of these cultures. Significantly, industrial nations exoticized people of these countries just as industrial countries were also

◆ Cairo Street Waltz

At the World's Columbian Exposition Midway, "Orientalist" fantasies were acted out in the popular and sexually suggestive performance of dancing girls variously described as "oriental," Turkish, or Persian. Barkers at the fair enticed audiences with promises such as "When she dances, every fiber and every tissue in her entire anatomy shakes like a jar of jelly from your Grandmother's Thanksgiving dinner." This drawing features an idealized "hootchy-kootchy" dancer on a sheet music cover from the Exposition. The crowd image sets the dancer against the supposed hubbub of the Egyptian street. Why do you think the only women included by the illustrator were white women tourists, most interestingly the one with the parasol atop a camel? What does the figure of the dancer, who is contained on the cover of a tambourine, suggest about the eroticism and exoticism attributed to Middle Eastern women? *Chicago History Museum, USA/Bridgeman Images.*

colonizing them in imperial ventures. The implication was clear: the people on the Midway, albeit fascinating, were inferior, uncivilized, and backward, and needed the stewardship of the United States and other Christian nations to advance.

Some of the earliest manifestations of this crusading sense of American national superiority had come from Protestant missionaries, among whom women were prominent. Since the 1830s, women with a strong religious vocation had been bringing American values and culture along with the English language and Christian Bibles to the peoples of Asia and Africa. Women's overseas missionary efforts entered a new, more organized phase in 1883 when the Woman's Christian Temperance Union (WCTU) created a division to undertake international work. Mary Clement Leavitt, a former schoolteacher from New Hampshire, became the first of the WCTU's "round the world missionaries," traveling around the Pacific, from Hawaii to New Zealand and Australia to Burma, Madagascar, China, and India, to spread the ideas of temperance.

Some Asian women were able to use the resources and perspective of the WCTU missionaries to address their own problems as they understood them. In Japan, for instance, the WCTU's combined message of female purity and activism became the basis for an anticoncubinage movement, while the antiliquor arguments were initially ignored by women. Nonetheless, the assumption of American superiority and world leadership constituted a kind of "soft" imperialism. Frances Willard made the link explicit when she said, "Mrs. Leavitt has been to the women of Japan what U.S. naval and economic power has been to its commerce: an opening into the civilized world."[39]

Willard wrote those words in 1898, the year that the United States entered into its first explicitly imperial overseas war and acquired its first formal colonial possessions. The Spanish-American War began in Cuba, which had long drawn American attention as a possible territorial acquisition. Cuban nationalists were showing signs of winning a prolonged insurgency against Spanish colonial control. In May, the United States joined the war on the side of the Cuban forces, ostensibly to avenge the destruction of the U.S.S. *Maine*, an American battleship blown up under suspicious circumstances in Havana harbor. (It was later determined that powder on the deck exploded, probably by accident.) Spain was quickly routed, but instead of supporting Cuban independence, the United States enforced a new type of foreign oversight on the island. While not making Cuba a formal colony, the U.S. Congress passed the Platt Amendment, giving the United States a supervisory role over Cuban affairs, which it retained until 1934.

As Spanish imperial power collapsed further, the United States claimed as colonies other Spanish possessions, including Puerto Rico and Guam. United States forces found it most difficult to consolidate control over the rich prize of the Spanish Philippines, the gateway to trade across the Pacific and throughout Asia. An indigenous Filipino independence movement fought back against the Americans, who had come in 1898 to liberate and stayed to control. The Filipinos turned what at first appeared to be a quick U.S. victory into a long and deadly conflict, which U.S. forces brought to an end only in 1902 through considerable expenditure of life (see Reading into the Past: "Women of the Philippines"). Unlike Cuba, the Philippines became a formal U.S. colony and remained so until 1946.

READING INTO THE PAST

CLEMENCIA LOPEZ
Women of the Philippines

Clemencia Lopez and her brother, Sixto, were leading advocates to the American people of the cause of Philippine independence. She defended her people's dignity and sovereign rights in this 1902 address to the New England Woman Suffrage Association, many members of which were active in the Boston-based Anti-Imperialist League. Subsequently she became a student at Wellesley College, one of the first Filipinas to attend a U.S. college.

You will no doubt be surprised and pleased to learn that the condition of women in the Philippines is very different from that of the women of any country in the East, and that it differs very little from the general condition of the women of this country. Mentally, socially, and in almost all the relations of life, our women are regarded as the equals of our men. . . .

. . . [I]t would seem to me an excellent idea that American women should take part in any investigation that may be made in the Philippine Islands, and I believe they would attain better results than the men. Would it not also seem to you an excellent idea, since representation by our leading men has been refused us, that a number of representative women should come to this country, so that you might become better acquainted with us?

. . . You can do much to bring about the cessation of these horrors and cruelties which are today taking place in the Philippines, and to insist upon a more humane course. I do not believe that you can understand or imagine the miserable condition of the women of my country, or how real is their suffering. . . . [Y]ou ought to understand that we are only contending for the liberty of our country, just as you once fought for the same liberty for yours.

SOURCE: Clemencia Lopez, "Women of the Philippines," address to the New England Woman Suffrage Association, published in *Woman's Journal*, June 7, 1902.

QUESTION FOR ANALYSIS

1. How does Lopez appeal to the ideals of the New England suffragists?

Alongside the economic justification for imperial expansion in search of new markets, a restless, insecure, and aggressive masculinity played a significant role in America's decision to go to war. Rising New York politician Theodore Roosevelt thoroughly embodied this phenomenon. With the memory of Civil War death tolls receding, men like Roosevelt were eager to demonstrate a middle-class American manliness they felt was being challenged by immigrant men and threatened by activist women. Newspapers encouraged popular support for intervention. In political cartoons, Americans were portrayed as the manly protectors of the Cuban people, who were regularly depicted as suffering women. These eager imperialists "regarded the war as an opportunity," says one historian, "to return the nation to a political order in which strong men governed and homebound women proved their patriotism by raising heroic sons."[40]

Most American women joined the clamor and supported intervention on what they believed was the side of the Cubans. Remembering female service in the Civil War, they raised funds for military hospitals. But when it came to the unprecedented policy of taking overseas colonies, opinion was much more divided. By nature a pacifist, Jane Addams recognized the threat that rising militarism posed to a more general spirit of reform. On the streets around Hull House, she observed, children were "playing war": "[I]n the violence characteristic of the age, they were 'slaying Spaniards.' "[41] Susan B. Anthony also opposed the war, while her longtime friend and political partner, Elizabeth Cady Stanton, took the opposite position and believed that colonization would civilize the Filipino people.

The annexation of Hawaii during the war illustrates another aspect of the many roles women played in the U.S. move toward empire. In 1891, Queen Liliuokalani became the reigning monarch of the sovereign nation of Hawaii. She had been educated by American Protestant missionaries, was a devout Congregationalist, spoke English, and was married to a white American. Wealthy American planters already had enormous economic power in Hawaii, but U.S. tariff policies put them at a disadvantage in selling their fruit and sugar, and they pressed for a formal U.S. takeover of the islands. Now that its monarch was a woman, they redoubled their claims that only annexation could assure Hawaii's stability and progress. The U.S. entry into the war against Spain created a political environment favorable to their aspirations, and in 1898 Congress voted to acquire Hawaii. Unlike Texas in 1845 and California in 1848, however, Hawaii did not become a state but was designated as a colonial territory.

The response of U.S. suffragists was not to condemn acquiring Hawaii as a colony, even though the deposed head of state was a woman, or to object that Congress was imposing a government on the islands instead of allowing its residents to organize their own. Rather, they protested Congress's intention to write a territorial constitution for the Hawaiians that confined political rights to men only. As one historian writes, suffragists "substituted a critique of imperialism with a critique of patriarchy, and in the process lent their tacit approval to America's colonial project."[42] Even when they seemed to defend the rights of women in the colonies, late nineteenth-century suffragists did so within a framework that assumed the superiority of American culture and their right, as white Americans, to play a role in the nation's expansive "civilizing" mission.

◆ CONCLUSION: Nationhood and Womanhood on the Eve of a New Century

While the end of the Civil War resolved, for the time being at least, the regional and racial divisions that had endangered the United States, the post-Reconstruction years brought new conflicts and dangers to American unity and national tranquility. Even as the American economy revived and geographic expansion reopened, new rifts in the American social fabric occurred over the distribution of these riches and resources. Immigrants were drawn into the booming economy and the growing cities, only to face ethnic discrimination, daunting poverty, and nativist legislation. Western families and ambitious entrepreneurs alike sought the removal of Native peoples to open up new lands for their own purposes.

Women were part and parcel of these two great movements of people — immigration and the removal of Native peoples — that did so much to transform the United States in the post–Civil War years. Their labor fueled dynamic new industries and contributed to growing corporate wealth, and their devotion relocated and rebuilt family lives. Native American women found ways to resist, record, or protest the relentless encroachment on their lands and the attacks on their cultures.

These conflicts culminated at century's end in a decade of political challenge and social turmoil. By the end of the century, the wealth produced by the U.S. economy more than equaled that of England, Germany, and France combined. The settlement of the western half of the continental United States gave a sturdy new physicality to American claims of nationhood. Strong and confident, the United States, once a colony itself, ended the century by acquiring its own colonies. The country was on its way to becoming a world power.

As this new era of national development and prominence dawned, women's prospects looked especially promising. Many, though not all, American women in 1900 were living more active, more public, more individualized, and more expansive lives than women of prior generations did. These women were prepared to make a major contribution to solving the problems that accompanied America's new prosperity and place in the world. In the coming era, important groups of women would achieve as much influence as in any period of U.S. history. Already the beneficiaries of American progress, they were about to become the mainstays of the Progressive era, in which America undertook the challenging task of both reforming and modernizing itself.

CHAPTER 7 REVIEW

KEY TERMS AND PEOPLE

Terms
Wounded Knee massacre
Woman's National Indian
    Association
Dawes Severalty Act
Homestead Act
National Grange
Ellis Island
Angel Island
Page Law

Chinese Exclusion Act
Populism
settlement house movement
Woman's Christian
    Temperance Union

People
Helen Hunt Jackson
Gertrude Simmons Bonnin/
    Zitkala-Ša

Sarah Winnemucca
Emma Goldman
Jane Addams
Frances Willard
Mary Elizabeth Lease
Lugenia Burns Hope
Queen Liliuokalani
Angel De Cora

REVIEW QUESTIONS

1. "Consolidating the West" had vastly different meanings for white women settlers and Native American women. What generalizations can you make about the two disparate groups' experiences?

2. How were women's experiences of immigration and settlement in the United States distinct from those of men? How were they similar?

3. How would you characterize the differences among women involved in industrial protest, the Populist movement, and the settlement house movement? What similarities do you see in the methods or goals of these movements?

4. **Making Connections** The chapter's introduction (pp. 356–57) states: "In all these developments — western consolidation, mass immigration, the political and economic crises of the 1890s, and the beginnings of American imperialism — women were involved, active, influential, and, as a result, changed." How might you characterize women's activity and influence, and how might they have been changed by their participation in these developments?

PRIMARY SOURCES

Representing Native American Women in the Late Nineteenth Century

POPULAR CULTURE IMAGES

Sixteenth-century Europeans were fascinated by the images produced by such artists as Theodor de Bry (see pp. 37 and 40). Yet these renderings were just the start of centuries-long representations of Native peoples in American popular culture. With the exception of the perennial favorite, Pocahontas (see Figure 1.8, p. 43, and Figure 1.9, p. 44), whose appeal to whites stemmed from the belief that she was an example of the triumph of civilization over savagery,[43] images of Native American women were less common than those of men. Until the Indian wars of the late nineteenth century subsided, the popular press tended to emphasize male ferociousness and often featured specific leaders from the Plains who were identified by names such as Sitting Bull and Crazy Horse. Women were depicted more generically, often without even their tribe identified.

In popular magazines such as *Harpers Weekly*, one of the most pervasive images featured the Indian woman as "squaw," a hardworking drudge mistreated by her lazy husband. The stereotype had changed little since the eighteenth century (see p. 229). The engraving in Figure 7.1 used technology that had revolutionized print media, making it cheaper to produce richly illustrated magazines in the post–Civil War era. The text that accompanied this 1875 drawing, "Indian Sledge Journey," explained the message of the image in clear terms:

> The mode of winter travel practiced by the Indians of the Northwest is depicted in our illustration . . . , which represents an Indian family on a journey through a snow-covered forest. On the sledge are packed the lodge, all the belongings of the household, including child and young dogs, and the load is drawn by the squaw, while the husband, carrying only his rifle, brings up the rear. Among the noble red men, in the division of labor all the hard work falls upon the squaws; there is no question as to their mission in life. The frame-work of the sledge is generally made of some flexible, tough wood, over which dry hides are tightly stretched, forming a strong but very light vehicle, which slides easily over the surface of the snow.

Note that the description of the sledge is far more precise than that of the Indian family. Do you think this detail lent a sense of accurate reporting to the image? How do the image and caption reinforce the argument — popular since George Washington's administration and that would become so popular with white

◆ **Figure 7.1 "Indian Sledge Journey,"** *Harper's Weekly* **(1875)**
Universal History Archive/UIG via Getty Images.

reformers — that the key to "civilizing" Native Americans was through restructuring gender relations?

Another theme common in late nineteenth-century images focused on assimilation. Photographs such as the ones on p. 361 were used to document the ways in which Native Americans could become assimilated to the American mainstream. This type of representation appeared not just in magazines but also in venues such as the World's Columbian Exposition (p. 383). But even as white observers were touting the modernization of indigenous peoples, others presented a romantic vision of a dying race. A subset of this nostalgia was the attention given to Native women's skill at traditional handicrafts such as basket making, rug weaving, and pottery. The interest in women's preindustrial work may have indicated anxiety about how modern industrial innovations had robbed modern women of traditional skills. It reflected, too, the interest in the "primitive" and "authentic," evident in the "Orientalism" of the image on page 384. In this narrative of the past, the now pacified Native Americans had become exotic examples of simpler times. The World's Columbian Exposition featured hundreds of displays of Native women's crafts and even showcased an actual Navaho woman at her loom. Dioramas (three-dimensional lifelike models) of indigenous women at traditional tasks borrowed from the Smithsonian appeared in an ethnological exhibit titled "Woman's Work in Savagery," in which the figures were enclosed in glass cases like zoological exhibits.

Photographs were perhaps the most compelling demonstration of traditional crafts work, and there is a substantial archive of such images, part of an ambitious campaign of photographers to capture traditional cultures while they still existed. Figure 7.2 shows the Arizona Hopi Nampeyo, surrounded by her pottery in 1900.

◆ **Figure 7.2 Hopi Potter Nampeyo**
National Archives, Identifier 520084.

The photographer, A. C. Vroman, often arranged the pottery to suit his vision and in this case included some pots made by another woman. Most pictures of women with their crafts did not identify the women by name. Indeed photographs of weavers usually focused on the rugs or blankets on the loom with the anonymous weaver's back to the photographer. Nampeyo is unusual in that she was well-known in her lifetime as a superb artist in particular for incorporating prehistoric designs into her ceramics, a technique that drew the attention of American museums and collectors. For her designs, Nampeyo borrowed from the artifacts archeologists had recently uncovered of prehistoric Hopi people. Besides their artistic appeal, what other reasons might have prompted her to draw upon these ancient patterns?

One outlet for Nampeyo to sell her wares was a local trading post, and these emporiums became an important part of the developing tourist industry of the West, where visitors could buy souvenirs to document their visit and adorn their homes. Postcards, many of them featuring Indian "princesses" or craftswomen like Nampeyo, helped to publicize the new tourist destinations. They suggest that not only had their blankets, pots, and baskets become commodities for white consumption, but so, too, had the women themselves.

Figure 7.3 is a particularly striking example of this phenomenon. Dating from 1902, the brightly colored postcard shows Pueblo women at a railway station offering their pottery to tourists while railroad staff looks on. The postcard was part of a promotional campaign mounted by the Fred Harvey Company, which had a

◆ **Figure 7.3 Pueblo Women in a 1902 Postcard**
Library of Congress, LC-DIG-ds-10121.

chain of hotels and restaurants. Why might this image have appealed to prospective tourists? Harvey initially hired Pueblo women to stand at train stations but eventually built permanent tourist shops that included "living" exhibitions of Native peoples. Nampeyo worked at Harvey's Hopi House in 1905, and a promotional brochure included a photograph of the potter and her family, along with the caption "These quaintly-garbed Indians on the housetop hail from Tewa, the home of Nampeyo, the most noted pottery-maker in all Hopiland. Perhaps you [will be] so fortunate as to see Nampeyo herself." Inviting the tourist to step inside this re-creation of a Hopi dwelling and see the Hopi work at their crafts, it promised that "They are the most primitive Indians in American with ceremonies several centuries old."[44]

Although few images of Native American women identified them by name, notable exceptions were the photographs of a handful of women writers or activists such as the La Flesche sisters, Sarah Winnemucca, and Gertrude Simmons Bonnin, who wrote under the name Zitkala-Ša (see p. 362). Bonnin first gained fame as a writer of autobiographic stories, fiction, and poetry, based on her life among the Yankton Dakotas of South Dakota. Her autobiographical writings began to appear in such prestigious magazines as the *Atlantic Monthly* in 1900. By the 1910s she had become an outspoken activist for Indian rights. One of her most compelling stories detailed the trauma of the cultural shock she experienced when she first went to a Native American boarding school. That experience notwithstanding, she prized education and went on to study violin at the New England Conservatory of Music. Like many Native American intellectuals, Bonnin often struggled with the dilemma posed by valuing aspects of Euro-American culture, especially education, while hoping to sustain Native American cultures.[45]

Although Bonnin was often photographed wearing elaborate Indian clothing, other photos of the time offer a more subtle vision of her identity. Figure 7.4, an 1898 portrait by Joseph Keiley, shows Bonnin in a simple dress, probably made of buckskin, holding what seems to be a sheaf of papers. Her beads and the striped blanket signal her native American identity. Keiley was part of a photography movement that promoted photographs as fine art. How does this image of Bonnin reflect his agenda?

Like Bonnin, Angel De Cora, originally named Hinook-Mahiwi-Kilinaka,

◆ **Figure 7.4 Gertrude Simmons Bonnin, photographed by Joseph T. Keiley (1898)**
National Portrait Gallery, Smithsonian Institution/Art Resource, NY.

a Winnebago from Nevada, received her education at a boarding school, Hampton Institute, where she studied for three years beginning in 1883. Eventually she trained as an artist at Philadelphia's Drexel Institute and the Museum of Fine Arts in Boston. She achieved substantial success as a commercial illustrator, contributing illustrations for many works by and about Native Americans in the early twentieth century. In 1901 she illustrated Zitkala-Ša's *Old Indian Legends*. Even before Zitkala-Ša published her works, De Cora's writing and illustrations appeared in *Harpers' New Monthly Magazine*. In one of her two published stories, "Grey Wolf's Daughter," the protagonist reflected on the young women she knew, comparing "one who had been to school, to another who had staid at home and was a thorough Indian, comparing the life of the one with the life of the other."[46] She determined to go to boarding school to learn "the white man's ways." The night before her departure, she adorned herself with beads and jewelry and, with village girlfriends, underwent a purification ceremony. Then, she removed all of her items, leaving herself with a simple dress and one ornament. Her father was sad to see her go, but recognized that "she had always had her own way."

What is most striking about the story are the drawings that accompany it. Figure 7.5 is a stunning image that richly details the skilled beadwork on De Cora's dress and belt. The painted hides behind her further illuminate a dazzling display of traditional Plains women's work. While the narrative might suggest a sense of loss as the young woman puts aside her Native adornments, historian Jane Simonsen maintains that the pensive expression and the celebration of the design work emphasize Grey Wolf's daughter's choice to establish a new identity in a new environment. "In the same way," Simonsen argues, "De Cora's identity as an artist began to take shape as she moved Native designs into the mainstream literary media. She removed her beads, as it were, only to place them in the pages of *Harper's*."[47] What do you make of this interpretation?

◆ **Figure 7.5 Grey Wolf's Daughter by Angel De Cora (1899)**
Harvard Library.

THE WORDS OF SARAH WINNEMUCCA, PAIUTE° ACTIVIST

Sarah winnemucca (1844?–1891), a member of the Nevada Paiutes and daughter of one of the tribe's headman, led an extraordinary life in which she served as U.S. Army messenger and translator, lectured extensively in western and eastern cities, visited Washington, D.C., at the request of President Rutherford B. Hayes in 1880, and wrote *Life Among the Piutes: Their Wrongs and Claims* (1883), the first book written by a Native American woman. Winnemucca was a controversial figure. Her relentless condemnation of the reservation system and numerous Indian Service agents she viewed as corrupt and incompetent provoked white hostility. Some newspapers depicted her negatively, drawing upon the squaw stereotype to question her morality. And, in keeping with many white assumptions about Native women's unrestrained sexuality, one Indian agent sought to undermine her credibility when she went to Washington by claiming that she was a prostitute. And her own people

◆ **Figure 7.6 Sarah Winnemucca**
National Portrait Gallery, Smithsonian Institution/Art Resource, NY.

° Winnemucca spelled it *Piute*, but the common modern spelling is *Paiute*.

were often suspicious, especially when she failed in her efforts to secure improved conditions and also because she willingly worked with the U.S. Army as a translator. Yet the story that scholars have developed suggest that her most impressive legacy was her critique of white western expansion generally and U.S. Indian policy specifically. She did not look back to some romantic vision of her people returning to the old ways, but hoped for a path leading to Native Americans becoming educated, even "civilized," without surrendering their culture and their autonomy.

Winnemucca first began giving lectures to white audiences in San Francisco in 1879, primarily to draw attention to the government's removal of a group of Paiutes from their reservation in Nevada to one in Yakima, Washington, as punishment for their alleged attacks on whites, a claim they and Winnemucca roundly disputed. For her lectures Winnemucca appeared in Native American attire, which was described in detail by the *Daily Alta California*: "A head-dress of long feathers was fastened to her forehead by a bright red band, her long, jet-black hair falling below her waist. A bright buckskin shirt and cape were trimmed with beads and long buckskin string. A bead necklace shone around her throat and a blue bead bracelet was worn around the right wrist. Bright red hose showed below the short skirt, and it might have been the pair of gaily-embroidered moccasins worn on the feet that attracted the attention of the men in that way."[48] Figure 7.6 is a photograph that shows Winnemucca in similar clothing. Why might she have chosen traditional garb instead of the western dresses she was also accustomed to wearing?

In 1883, encouraged by the patronage of two Boston sisters, Elizabeth Palmer Peabody and Mary Mann, Winnemucca (who published under her married name, Sarah Winnemucca Hopkins) turned her lectures into a book that told her own story while also explaining Paiute cultural traditions and describing the devastating impact of white conquest of the West and its Native people. In these two extracts from *Life Among the Piutes*, Winnemucca explains Paiute courtship and marriage. How might we read these passages as a response to white conventional representations of Indian families?

Life Among the Piutes

My people have been so unhappy for a long time they wish now to *disincrease*, instead of multiply. The mothers are afraid to have more children, for fear they shall have daughters, who are not safe even in their mother's presence.

SOURCE: Sarah Winnemucca Hopkins, *Life Among the Piutes: Their Wrongs and Claims,* (New York: G. P. Putnam's Sons, 1883), 36–37, 39–40, 64, 147–49.

Winnemucca then describes the courtship process that begins after a twenty-five day ritual that marks her having "come to womanhood."

It is thus publicly known that there is another marriageable woman, and any young man interested in her, or wishing to form an alliance, comes forward. But the courting is very different from the courting of the white people. He never speaks to her, or visits the family, but endeavors to attract her attention by showing his horsemanship, etc. As he knows that she sleeps next to her grandmother in the lodge, he enters in full dress after the family has retired for the night, and seats himself at her feet. If she is not awake, the grandmother wakes her. He does not speak to either young woman or grandmother, but when the young woman wishes him to go away, she rises and goes and lies down by the side of her mother. He then leaves as silently as he came in. This goes on sometimes for a year or longer, if the young woman has not made up her mind. She is never forced by her parents to marry against her wishes. When she knows her mind, she makes a confidant of her grandmother, and then the young man is summoned by the father of the girl, who asks him in her presence if he really loves his daughter, and reminds him, if he does, of all the duties of a husband. He then asks the daughter the same question, and sets before her minutely all her duties. And these duties are not slight. She is to dress the game, prepare the food, clean the buckskins, make his moccasins, dress his hair, bring all the wood, — in short, do all the household work. She promises to "be himself," and she fulfills her promise. Then he is invited to a feast and all his relatives with him. . . .

In an earlier passage Winnemucca expands upon women's duties and the nature of marriage in a description of tribal decision making.

We have a republic as well as you. The council-tent is our Congress, and anybody can speak who has anything to say, women and all. They are always interested in what their husbands are doing and thinking about. And they take some part even in the wars. They are always near at hand when fighting is going on, ready to snatch their husbands up and carry them off if wounded or killed. One splendid woman that my brother Lee married after his first wife died, went out into the battle-field after her uncle was killed, and went into the front ranks and cheered the men on. Her uncle's horse was dressed in a splendid robe made of eagles' feathers and she snatched it off and swung it in the face of the enemy, who always carry off everything they find, as much as to say, "You can't have that — I have it safe"; and she stayed and took her uncle's place, as brave as any of the men. It means something when the women promise their fathers to make their husbands *themselves*. They faithfully keep with them in all the dangers they can share. They not only take care of their children together, but they do everything together; and when they grow blind, which I am sorry to say is very common, for the smoke they live in destroys their eyes at last, they take sweet care of one another. Marriage is a sweet thing when people love each other. If women could go into your Congress I think justice would soon be done to the Indians. I can't tell about all Indians; but I know my own people are kind to everybody that does not do them harm; but they will not be imposed upon, and when people are too bad they rise up and resist them. This seems to me all right. It is different from being revengeful. There is nothing cruel about our people. They never scalped a human being.

As the beginning passage in the last excerpt suggests, in contrast to the respect Paiute men and women show each other, Winnemucca frequently comments on the sexual violence Indian women repeatedly experience at the hands of white men. In one passage she explains that a three-month war was started when white men raped and imprisoned two Paiute girls who had been out foraging for food. She also detailed her own experience with threatened assault, suggesting the ways in which Paiute women sought to protect themselves from the sexual violence that was a constant threat. She and a woman she described as her sister, although she may have been a cousin or other kin, were traveling alone, heading to Yakima after Winnemucca had been in Washington, D.C. They met up with a cousin who planned to go with them to their next stopping place.

He said there were very bad men there. Sometimes they would throw a rope over our women, and do fearful things to them.

"Oh, my poor cousins," he said, "my heart aches for you, for I am afraid they will do something fearful to you. They do not care for anything. They do most terrible outrageous things to our women."

I thought within myself, "If such an outrageous thing is to happen to me, it will not be done by one man or two, while there are two women with knives, for I know what an Indian woman can do. She can never be outraged by one man; but she may by two."

Although their fears were not realized, later on the journey, after the cousin had left them, they were being chased by three men and again Winnemucca described her plan to resist.

Away we went, and they after us like wild men. We rode on till our horses seemed to drop from under us. At last we stopped, and I told sister what to do if the whole three of them undertook us. We could not do very much, but we must die fighting. If there were only two we were all right, — we would kill them; if only one we would see what he would do. If he lassoed me she was to jump off her horse and cut the rope, and if he lassoed her I was to do the same. If he got off his horse and came at me she was to cut him, and I would do the same for her. Now we were ready for our work. They were a long back yet. We kept looking back to see how far off they were. Every time we would get out of sight, we would rest our horses, and at last, to our great joy, we only saw one coming. He would not dare to do us any harm.

Nothing happened and yet Winnemucca details yet another incident on the same trip when she was accosted at night in her bed by a white cowboy at the home of a white family. She rose up and "gave him a blow right in the face. I said, 'Go away, or I will cut you to pieces, you mean man!'" Here and elsewhere, Winnemucca made it clear that she understood that white male sexual violence "was intertwined with racial and economic oppression."[49]

While Winnemucca's book is a rich resource for uncovering the experiences of Paiute women of her era and particularly revealing about the sexual dimension of the imperialist march across the continent, much of Life Among the Piutes *focuses on the grave injustice*

of federal Indian policy. In the following excerpts, how does she characterize the white conquest of the West? What is the basis of her criticism of Indian agents? How does she attempt to appeal to white readers through a shared language of Christian ideals?

Dear reader, I must tell a little more about my poor people, and what we suffer at the hands of our white brothers. Since the war of 1860 there have been one hundred and three of my people murdered, and our reservations taken from us; and yet we, who are called blood-seeking savages, are keeping our promises to the government. Oh, my dear good Christian people, how long are you going to stand by and see us suffer at your hands? Oh, dear friend, you are wrong when you say it will take two or three generations to civilize my people. No! I say it will not take that long if you will only take interest in teaching us; and, on the other hand, we shall never be civilized in the way you wish us to be if you keep on sending us such agents as have been sent to us year after year, who do nothing but fill their pockets, and the pockets of their wives and sisters, who are always put in as teachers, and paid from fifty to sixty dollars per month, and yet they do not teach.

In another passage, Winnemucca details her outrage at the forced removal of a group of Paiutes from Nevada to Yakima, Washington.

Oh, for shame! You who are educated by a Christian government in the art of war; the practice of whose progression makes you natural enemies of the savages, so called by you. Yes, you, who call yourselves the great civilization; you who have knelt upon Plymouth Rock, covenanted with God to make this land the home of the free and brave. Ah, then you rise from your bended knees and seizing the welcoming hands of those who are the owners of this land, which you are not, your carbines rise upon the bleak shore, and your so-called civilization sweeps inland from the ocean wave; but, oh, my God! leaving its pathway marked by crimson lines of blood; and strewed by the bones of two races, the inheritor and the invader; and I am crying out to you for justice, — yes, pleading for the far-off plains of the West, for the dusky mourner, whose tears of love are pleading for her husband, or for their children, who are sent far away from them.

Once they arrived in Yakima, Winnemucca detailed their reception.

At the end of ten days we were turned over to Father [James H.] Wilbur [an agent who was also a minister] and his civilized Indians, as he called them. Well, as I was saying, we were turned over to him as if we were so many horses or cattle. After he received us he had some of his civilized Indians come with their wagons to take us up to Fort Simcoe. They did not come because they loved us, or because they were Christians. No; they were just like all civilized people; they came to take us up there because they were to be paid for it. They had a kind of shed made to put us in. You know what kind of shed you make for your stock in winter time. It was of that kind. Oh, how we did suffer with cold. There was no wood, and the snow was waist-deep, and many died off just as cattle or horses do after travelling so long in the cold.

Although some of the Paiutes found ways to escape from Yakima, aided by Winnemucca, they were not released until 1884, when a new agent replaced James Wilbur.

Beyond critiquing Indian policy, Winnemucca also challenged the assimilationist vision that shaped it by establishing a short-lived bilingual school at Lovelock, Nevada, in 1885. Although she promoted learning English and other aspects of western culture, in the words of her supporter Elizabeth Peabody, Winnemucca's school rejected the idea of "passive reception of civilizing influences proffered by white men who look down upon the Indian as a spiritual, moral, and intellectual inferior," and instead promoted "a spontaneous movement, made by the Indian himself, from himself, in full consciousness of free agency, for the education that is to civilize him."[50] *How do these two passages from newspaper articles convey Winnemucca's educational goals?*

From Silver Slate (July 9, 1886)

Education is my "hobby" although I have little myself. It seems strange to me that the Government has not found out years ago that education is the key to the Indian problem. Much money and many precious lives would have been saved if the American people had fought my people with Books instead of Powder and lead. Education civilized your race and there is no reason why it cannot civilize mine. Indian schools are failures at many Agencies, but it is not the fault of the children, but of the teacher and interpreter. . . . The most necessary thing for the success of an Indian school is a good interpreter, a perfect interpreter, a true interpreter, one that can and will do. Many Indians wars would be avoided if interpreters were only true instead of being the tool of the agents.

The same month, the Daily Alta California *(July 24, 1886) printed a message from Winnemucca, which was a copy of a letter she sent to Paiute school trustees in Inyo, California.*

Brothers and Sisters: Hearing you are about to start a school to educate your children, I want to say a word about it. You all know me; many of you are my aunts or cousins. We are of one race — your blood is my blood, so I speak to you for your good. I can speak five tongues — three Indian tongues, English and Spanish. I can read and write, and am a school teacher. Now I do not

SOURCE: *The Newspaper Warrior; Sarah Winnemucca Hopkins's Campaign for American Indian Rights, 1864–1891,* edited by Cari M. Carpenter and Carolyn Sorisio (Lincoln: University of Nebraska Press, 2015), 261–62.

say this to boast, but simply to show you what can be done. When I was a little girl there were no Indian schools; I learned under great difficulty. Your children can learn much more than I know, and much easier, and it is your duty to see that they go to school. . . . You are not asked to give money or horses — only to send your children to school. The teacher will do the rest. He or she will fit your little ones for the battle of life, so that they can attend to their own affairs instead of having to call in a white man. A few years ago you owned this great country; today the white man owns it all, and you own nothing. Do you know what did it? Education. You see the miles and miles of railroad, the locomotive, the Mint in Carson, where they make money. Education has done it all. Now what it has done for one many it will do for another. You have brains same as the whites, your children have brains, and it will be your fault if they grow up as you have. I entreat you take hold of this school, and give your support by sending your children, old and young, to it, and when they grow up to manhood and womanhood they will bless you.

QUESTIONS FOR ANALYSIS

1. It is unlikely that Sarah Winnemucca saw the etching in Figure 7.1, but she was undoubtedly familiar with the squaw stereotype. How might she have responded to *Harpers Weekly*'s conception of a Native woman?

2. Taking into account the images and Winnemucca's writing, what conclusions can you draw about the variety of Native women's experiences in the West? What common themes, if any, do you see?

3. What were the greatest challenges for Native American women in their interactions with white Americans?

Jane Addams, *Twenty Years at Hull House*

JANE ADDAMS (1860–1935) was the leader of the American settlement house movement. After graduating in 1882 from Rockford Seminary in Illinois, she went to Europe in search of a larger purpose for her life. Like other daughters of wealthy families, she was looking for an alternative to the leisured, home-bound life for which her class and gender destined her. Addams and women like her did not require paid labor, but they did need work of large social purpose and a place and community in which to live.

Visiting London, Addams learned of a "settlement" project of male college graduates who lived among and served the urban poor. She returned to Chicago, determined to establish a similar community of female college graduates dedicated to social service. In 1889, Addams persuaded a wealthy member of the Hull family to donate a mansion, now in the center of a crowded immigrant district, to be the site of her project. Soon many similar "settlement houses" would dot the American urban landscape. Published by Addams in 1910, *Twenty Years at Hull House* is a dual autobiography, focusing on Addams's path to social service and on Hull House as an institution.

The leisure-class women who joined Addams as "residents" of Hull House combined a palpable sympathy with the urban poor and a determination to find a nonrevolutionary solution to the era's class and ethnic conflicts. Their "neighbors" were working-class and poorer immigrant families living around them. Both the leisure-class residents and the working-class neighbors showed considerable organizational ability and political savvy in addressing the difficult daily conditions of these immigrant neighborhoods. *Twenty Years at Hull House* demonstrates that the

Jane Addams
The Granger Collection, New York.

public activism of the "Woman's Era" was not limited to native-born leisure-class women but characterized the immigrant working class as well.

There are many tensions at work in Addams's efforts to understand her neighbors and assist in their adjustment to American society. Her account of the development of the Labor Museum demonstrates her belief in steady economic progress alongside her realization that the loss of traditional culture — in this case the artisan skills of the older immigrant women — has gone unappreciated. She describes the ignorance that fuels ethnic clashes between different immigrant groups even as she recognizes that America's own "color problem" may be worse.

Addams's vignettes follow immigrant women through the many phases and challenges of their lives: Americanizing daughters and Old World mothers; wage earners and prostitutes (whom she euphemistically connects with "professional" or "disreputable" houses); mothers struggling to provide for their children and aged women left without means of support. To one degree or another, all suffer a common economic insecurity, based both on their class status and female dependence. Living among the immigrant poor, Addams recognized that financial security was probably the biggest difference between the classes in turn-of-the-century urban America.

Twenty Years at Hull House (1910)

There was in the earliest undertakings at Hull-House a touch of the artist's enthusiasm when he translates his inner vision through his chosen material into outward form. Keenly conscious of the social confusion all about us and the hard economic struggle, we at times believed that the very struggle itself might become a source of strength. The devotion of the mothers to their children, the dread of the men lest they fail to provide for the family dependent upon their daily exertions, at moments seemed to us the secret stores of strength from which society is fed, the invisible array of passion and feeling which are the surest protectors of the world. We fatuously hoped that we might pluck from the human tragedy itself a consciousness of a common destiny which should bring its own healing, that we might extract from life's very misfortunes

a power of cooperation which should be effective against them.

Of course there was always present the harrowing consciousness of the difference in economic condition between ourselves and our neighbors. Even if we had gone to live in the most wretched tenement, there would have always been an essential difference between them and ourselves, for we should have had a sense of security in regard to illness and old age and the lack of these two securities are the specters which most persistently haunt the poor. Could we, in spite of this, make their individual efforts more effective through organization and possibly complement them by small efforts of our own? . . .

At a meeting of working girls held at Hull-House during a strike in a large shoe factory, the discussions made it clear that the strikers who had been most easily frightened, and therefore first to capitulate, were naturally those girls who were paying board and were afraid of being put out if they

SOURCE: Jane Addams, *Twenty Years at Hull-House* (New York: Macmillan, 1910), excerpts from chaps. 7, 8, 11, and 13.

fell too far behind. After a recital of a case of peculiar hardship one of them exclaimed: "Wouldn't it be fine if we had a boarding club of our own, and then we could stand by each other in a time like this?" After that events moved quickly. . . . [O]n the first of May, 1891, two comfortable apartments near Hull-House were rented and furnished. The Settlement was responsible for the furniture and paid the first month's rent, but beyond that the members managed the club themselves. . . . At the end of the third year the club occupied all of the six apartments which the original building contained, and numbered fifty members. . . .

I recall our perplexity over the first girls who had "gone astray" — the poor, little, forlorn objects, fifteen and sixteen years old, with their moral natures apparently untouched and unawakened; one of them whom the police had found in a professional house and asked us to shelter for a few days until she could be used as a witness, was clutching a battered doll which she had kept with

her during her six months of an "evil life." Two of these prematurely aged children came to us one day directly from the maternity ward of the Cook County hospital, each with a baby in her arms, asking for protection, because they did not want to go home for fear of "being licked." . . . I well remember our perplexity when we attempted to help two girls straight from a Virginia tobacco factory, who had been decoyed into a disreputable house when innocently seeking a lodging on the late evening of their arrival. Although they had been rescued promptly, the stigma remained, and we found it impossible to permit them to join any of the social clubs connected with Hull-House, not so much because there was danger of contamination, as because the parents of the club members would have resented their presence most hotly. . . .

. . . .

That neglected and forlorn old age is daily brought to the attention of a Settlement which

Alley Tenements near Hull House; Illustration by Norah Hamilton, Hull House Resident and Artist

undertakes to bear its share of the neighborhood burden imposed by poverty, was pathetically clear to us during our first months of residence at Hull-House. . . .

Some frightened women had bidden me come quickly to the house of an old German woman, whom two men from the country agent's office were attempting to remove to the County Infirmary. The poor old creature had thrown herself bodily upon a small and battered chest of drawers and clung there, clutching it so firmly that it would have been impossible to remove her without also taking the piece of furniture. She did not weep nor moan nor indeed make any human sound, but between her broken gasps for breath she squealed shrilly like a frightened animal caught in a trap. The little group of women and children gathered at her door stood aghast at this realization of the black dread which always clouds the lives of the very poor when work is slack, but which constantly grows more imminent and threatening as old age approaches. . . . To take away from an old woman whose life has been spent in household cares all the foolish little belongings to which her affections cling and to which her very fingers have become accustomed, is to take away her last incentive to activity, almost to life itself. To give an old woman only a chair and a bed, to leave her no cupboard in which her treasures may be stowed, not only that she may take them out when she desires occupation, but that their mind may dwell upon them in moments of revery, is to reduce living almost beyond the limit of human endurance. . . .

We early learned to know the children of hard-driven mothers who went out to work all day, sometimes leaving the little things in the casual care of a neighbor, but often locking them into their tenement rooms. The first three crippled children we encountered in the neighborhood had all been injured while their mothers were at work: one had fallen out of a third-story window, another had been burned, and the third had a curved spine due to the fact that for three years he had been tied all day long to the leg of the kitchen table, only released at noon by his older brother who hastily ran in from a neighboring factory to share his lunch with him. . . . During our first summer an increasing number of these poor little mites would wander into the cool hallway of Hull-House. We kept them there and fed them at noon, in return for which we were sometimes offered a hot penny which had been held in a tight little fist "ever since mother left this morning, to buy something to eat with." Out of kindergarten hours our little guests noisily enjoyed the hospitality of our bedrooms under the so-called care of any resident who volunteered to keep an eye on them, but later they were moved into a neighboring apartment under more systematic supervision.

Hull-House was thus committed to a day nursery which we sustained for sixteen years first in a little cottage on a side street and then in a building designed for its use called the Children's House. . . .

While one was filled with admiration for these heroic women, something was also to be said for some of the husbands, for the sorry men who, for one reason or another, had failed in the struggle of life. . . . I could but wonder in which particular we are most stupid — to judge a man's worth so solely by his wage-earning capacity that a good wife feels justified in leaving him, or in holding fast to that wretched delusion that a woman can both support and nurture her children.

With all of the efforts made by modern society to nurture and educate the young, how stupid it is to permit the mothers of young children to spend themselves in the coarser work of the world! It is curiously inconsistent that with the emphasis which this generation has placed upon the mother and upon the prolongation of infancy, we constantly allow the waste of this most precious material. I cannot recall without indignation a recent experience. I was detained late one evening in an office building by a prolonged committee meeting of the Board of Education. As I came out at eleven o'clock, I met in the corridor of the fourteenth floor a woman whom I knew, on her knees scrubbing the marble tiling. As she straightened up to greet me, she seemed so wet from her feet up to her chin, that I hastily inquired the cause. Her reply was that she left home at five o'clock every night and had no opportunity for six hours to nurse her baby. Her mother's milk mingled with the very water with which she scrubbed the floors until she should return at midnight, heated and exhausted, to feed her screaming child with what remained within her breasts.

. . .

An overmastering desire to reveal the humbler immigrant parents to their own children lay at the base of what has come to be called the Hull-House Labor Museum. This was first suggested to my mind one early spring day when I saw an old Italian woman, her distaff against her homesick face, patiently spinning a thread by the simple stick spindle so reminiscent of all southern Europe. . . . It seemed to me that Hull-House ought to be able to devise some educational enterprise which should build a bridge between European and American experiences in such wise as to give them both more meaning and a sense of relation. . . . Could we not interest the young people working in the neighborhood factories in these older forms of industry, so that, through their own parents and grandparents, they would find a dramatic representation of the inherited resources of their daily occupation. If these young people could actually see that the complicated machinery of the factory had been evolved from simple tools, they might at least make a beginning toward that education which Dr. Dewey defines as "a continuing reconstruction of experience." . . .

We found in the immediate neighborhood at least four varieties of these most primitive methods of spinning and three distinct variations of the same spindle in connection with wheels. It was possible to put these seven into historic sequence and order and to connect the whole with the present method of factory spinning. The same thing was done for weaving, and on every Saturday evening a little exhibit was made of these various

forms of labor in the textile industry. Within one room a Syrian woman, a Greek, an Italian, a Russian, and an Irishwoman enabled even the most casual observer to see that there is no break in orderly evolution if we look at history from the industrial standpoint; that industry develops similarly and peacefully year by year among the workers of each nation, heedless of differences in language, religion, and political experiences. . . .

In some such ways as these have the Labor Museum and the shops pointed out the possibilities which Hull-House has scarcely begun to develop, of demonstrating that culture is an understanding of the long-established occupations and thoughts of men, of the arts with which they have solaced their toil. A yearning to recover for the household arts something of their early sanctity and meaning arose strongly within me one evening when I was attending a Passover Feast to which I had been invited by a Jewish family in the neighborhood, where the traditional and religious significance of the woman's daily activity was still retained. The kosher food the Jewish mother spread before her family had been prepared according to traditional knowledge and with constant care in the use of utensils; upon her had fallen the responsibility to make all ready according to Mosaic instructions. . . .

I recall a certain Italian girl who came every Saturday evening to a cooking class in the same building in which her mother spun in the Labor Museum exhibit; and yet Angelina always left her mother at the front door while she herself went around to a side door because she did not wish to be too closely identified in the eyes of the rest of the cooking class with an Italian woman who wore a kerchief over her head, uncouth boots, and short petticoats. . . . It was easy to see that the thought of her mother with any other background than that of the tenement was new to Angelina, and at least two things resulted; she allowed her mother to pull out of the big box under the bed the beautiful homespun garments which had been previously hidden away as uncouth; and she openly came into the Labor Museum by the same door as did her mother, proud at least of the mastery of the craft which had been so much admired. . . .

It is difficult to write of the relation of the older and most foreign-looking immigrants to the children of other people — the Italians whose fruit-carts are upset simply because they are "dagoes," or the Russian peddlers who are stoned and sometimes badly injured because it has become a code of honor in a gang of boys to thus express their derision. . . . Doubtless these difficulties would be much minimized in America, if we faced our own race problem with courage and intelligence, and these very Mediterranean immigrants might give us valuable help. Certainly they are less conscious than the Anglo-Saxon of color distinctions. . . .

. . . .

It is easy for even the most conscientious citizen of Chicago to forget the foul smells of the stockyards and the garbage dumps, when he is living so far from them that he is only occasionally made conscious of their existence but the residents of a Settlement are perforce constantly surrounded by them. . . . The Hull-House Woman's Club had been organized the year before by the resident kindergartner who had first inaugurated a mother's meeting. The new members came together, however, in quite a new way that summer when we discussed with them the high death rate so persistent in our ward. After several club meetings devoted to the subject, despite the fact that the death rate rose highest in the congested foreign colonies and not in the streets in which most of the Irish American club women lived, twelve of their number undertook in connection with the residents, to carefully investigate the conditions of the alleys. During August and September the substantiated reports of violations of the law sent in from Hull-House to the health department were one thousand and thirty-seven. For the club woman who had finished a long day's work of washing or ironing followed by the cooking of a hot supper, it would have been much easier to sit on her doorstep during a summer evening than to go up and down ill-kept alleys and get into trouble with her neighbors over the condition of their garbage boxes. . . . Nevertheless, a certain number of women persisted, as did the residents, and three city inspectors in succession were transferred from the ward because of unsatisfactory services. . . .

Many of the foreign-born women of the ward were much shocked by this abrupt departure into the ways of men, and it took a great deal of explanation to convey the idea even remotely that if it were a womanly task to go about in tenement houses in order to nurse the sick, it might be quite as womanly to go through the same district in order to prevent the breeding of so-called "filth diseases."

QUESTIONS FOR ANALYSIS

1. What does Addams mean about her initial naïve attitude (she uses the word "fatuous") about the "common destiny" she hoped to experience by living in an immigrant neighborhood? What led her to shed this assumption?

2. In what ways was the assistance that Hull House provided to poor immigrant women and children helpful, and in what ways was it not helpful?

3. To what degree can you rely on the personal stories Addams provides to understand the actual experiences of the immigrant poor?

PRIMARY SOURCES

Jacob Riis's Photographs of Immigrant Girls and Women

In the decade 1880–1890, more than 5 million immigrants came through the port of New York, and many remained in the city, swelling its population by 25 percent. By 1890, nearly half of the city's dwellings were classified as "tenements," overcrowded urban slums where vulnerable and desperately poor people were overcharged for filthy, cramped, and unsanitary lodgings.

This rise in immigration coincided with new forms of social documentation. Pioneering social scientists provided statistics on the growing industrial labor force, including the women who were entering the workplace in unprecedented numbers. Local and state health bureaus collected information on the epidemic diseases such as diphtheria, cholera, and tuberculosis that threatened family life in the burgeoning cities. And photographers created searing images of the horrible living and working conditions of newly arrived immigrants. These new methods of documentation, informed by a rising sense of public responsibility for improving social conditions and alleviating poverty, allow us to look back through the perspectives of those who did the documenting, into the lives of late nineteenth-century immigrant girls and women.

One of the first series of photographs of immigrant women and children in the United States was produced in the 1880s and 1890s by a man who was himself an immigrant. Jacob A. Riis arrived in New York City from Denmark in 1870. After more than a decade struggling to earn a living, he found regular work as a newspaperman. He began as a police reporter, writing in a male-oriented, journalistic genre that sensationalized the seamy side of "downtown" life. Riis's own impulses, however, were more humanitarian and allied him with urban reformers, many of whom were women. He worked closely with Josephine Shaw Lowell, who founded the Charity Organization Society of New York State in 1882. His particular focus was "the slum," by which he meant not only the dilapidated tenement homes of the poor but the larger urban environment in which they lived and worked. He was especially concerned with children, and through them the mothers of immigrant families.

Convinced that only photographs could convey the shocking reality of urban poverty, Riis included them in *How the Other Half Lives: Studies among the Tenements of New York* (1890), a pioneering work of sociology that is still mined by historians and scholars for the insights it provides into urban immigrant life, nineteenth-century attitudes toward poverty and ethnicity, and the visual conventions of early documentary photography. Though the majority of the photographs deal with male subjects — homeless street boys, male vagrants, and gang members — Riis also took pictures of women and girls that give us glimpses of their lives. In its frequent resort to sensational and melodramatic conventions, *How the Other Half Lives* reflects its author's roots in mass commercial journalism, but it also skillfully adopts strategies from literary realism and the emerging field of social science to convey a probing portrait of poverty and its consequences.

Consistent with the late nineteenth century's preoccupation with ethnic and racial characteristics, *How the Other Half Lives* is organized like a guided tour for the middle-class reader through the ethnic geography of lower New York City. Not surprisingly, it invokes both positive and negative stereotypes in its descriptions and illustrations. Riis, as a northwestern European immigrant, had clear ethnic biases, but his prejudices were tempered by empathy and the recognition that "we are all creatures of the conditions that surround us."[51] His goal was to call attention to the plight of the poor, not to castigate them for their poverty.

Chapter 5 of Riis's book, "The Italian in New York," focuses on those who, as recent arrivals, were "at the bottom" of the economic and social hierarchy.[52] The frequently reproduced photograph shown in Figure 7.7 depicts the wife and infant child of a "ragpicker" — one who barely made a living by picking through public rubbish cans and dumps for rags to sell — in their subterranean home. Riis developed the innovative technology used to make this photograph, a new chemical process that produced a "flash" bright enough to light up dark and windowless areas.

◆ **Figure 7.7 In the Home of an Italian Ragpicker: Jersey Street**
Jacob A. Riis/Museum of the City of New York/Getty Images.

The pose of the Italian mother and her tightly swaddled child, as well as her mournful, upturned gaze, is reminiscent of religious paintings of the Madonna and Child in which the Virgin Mary's sad expression foreshadows the suffering that awaits her infant son. In the chapter that includes this photograph, Riis offers an extended report, complete with comparative statistics, on the high mortality rates of infants and children in this Italian neighborhood. What other explanations can be offered for her upward look?

Italian families, no matter how poor, frowned on wives and mothers working outside the home. While the room in Figure 7.7 is sparsely furnished, what do the few items we see and their arrangement tell us about this woman and her daily life? In the text accompanying this photograph, Riis describes the Italian immigrant as "picturesque, if not very tidy."[53] Does his photograph support this characterization? What overall impression does it convey about Italian immigrant mothers? Also in the text relating to this image is Riis's description of Italian men as "hotheaded . . . and lighthearted" and of Italian women as "faithful wives and devoted mothers."[54] Note the man's straw hat hanging high on the wall. What are the possible explanations for the man's absence?

In Figure 7.8, Riis continues his progression through New York City's ethnic neighborhoods to "Jewtown," an area settled by large numbers of Eastern European

◆ **Figure 7.8 Knee Pants at Forty-Five Cents a Dozen—A Ludlow Street Sweater's Shop**
Bettmann/Getty Images.

Jews and marked by exceptional population density and industrial activity. As Riis notes, "Life here means the hardest kind of work almost from the cradle."[55] The "sweater" mentioned in the title of the photograph was a subcontractor who supplied garments to a larger manufacturer and hired other immigrants to do the work, often in his own tenement apartment. The ruthless competition to deliver finished goods at the lowest possible price pressured the sweater to offer impossibly low wages and push (or "sweat") workers to their physical limits during a working day that "lengthened at both ends far into the night."[56] While Riis criticizes the "sweater's . . . merciless severity"[57] in exploiting his fellow Jews, he concedes "he is no worse than the conditions that created him."[58]

Unlike the photograph shown in Figure 7.7, this photo was not posed and has no carefully arranged central figure. It catches its subjects off guard, and the blurring of some of their features suggests frantic activity and movement. The sweater is the moving figure with his back to the camera. The teenage girls in this picture are "greenhorns," newly arrived immigrant workers. One man looks up briefly from his work, but the other seems unwilling to lose a minute's time despite the photographer's presence. Piles of boys' short pants waiting to be finished are heaped on the floor and furniture. What visual clues tell us that this workshop is also a residence? What else goes on in this room? In what ways is it different from the living space of the Italian mother in Figure 7.7?

In contrast to the serious detachment of the adults, the young girl turns to smile directly into the lens and casually touches to her lips the long-bladed scissors she is using to cut the garments. Does this suggest she has not yet been disciplined to keep up with the brutal pace of piecework? Maybe Riis regarded her direct gaze as somewhat immodest, a consequence of work conditions that placed unsupervised young girls amid grown men. Or did she simply find pleasure in having her picture taken? In his second book, *The Children of the Poor* (1892), Riis noted that in contrast to adults, who resisted and feared being photographed, children loved posing for the camera and had a "determination to be 'took' . . . in the most striking pose they could hastily devise."[59] What other possible meanings can be suggested for this unusual and striking image of a young working woman?

Employers justified the low wages paid to female workers, which were inadequate for self-support, as supplements to a family income anchored by an adult male wage. Riis was sharply aware of the special hardships facing the unmarried, poor working women who had to live on their own. In his chapter "The Working Girls of New York," he describes the exploitation and harsh conditions they endured, sprinkling his narrative with tragic stories of underpaid and exhausted women workers driven to suicide, prostitution, and premature death. Like so many other late nineteenth-century reformers, Riis thought the best solution to working women's suffering was to get them out of the labor force. If they remained in it, their lives were bound to be intolerable.

When wages were too low or unemployment too high, such poor urban workers found themselves destitute and without shelter. Those who lacked even the pennies charged by commercial lodging houses ended up in overnight shelters in police stations. Of the half-million people seeking shelter in New York City in

1889, almost one-third sought refuge in makeshift facilities in police stations, and half of those were women. Riis knew firsthand about the filthy and dangerous conditions in the police station shelters. Recalling his own experience years before as a homeless vagrant in New York City, he observed that "never was parody upon Christian charity more corrupting to human mind and soul than the frightful abomination of the police lodging-house."[60] He was particularly concerned when homeless women slept in the same room as men.

The photograph in Figure 7.9 was an illustration for an article Riis wrote for the *New York Tribune* in 1892, condemning the police station shelters. The West Forty-Seventh Street police station was located in the aptly named Hell's Kitchen area of New York City, and there is no doubt that Riis intended to shock readers with a graphic, unstaged photograph of women expelled from the domestic sphere, stripped of their dignity and privacy, eating and sleeping on filthy bare floors like animals. The extent of homelessness among women pointed to the collapse

◆ **Figure 7.9 Police Station Lodgers: Women's Lodging Room in the West 47th Street Station**
The Granger Collection, New York.

of working-class family life and indicated how deeply the combination of mass immigration, rapid urbanization, and economic collapse had torn the social fabric. Notice the details that reveal how women manage to cooperate and care for their personal needs even under the harshest of circumstances. What do these details, and the facial expressions and postures of the women, reveal about social relations in this police station lodging room?

In *The Children of the Poor*, published originally as a series of articles in *Scribner's Magazine* in 1892, Riis turned his full attention to the group with whom he was most concerned, the children whose futures were being jeopardized by life in the tenements. Figure 7.10 is a rare individual portrait of an orphan, nine-year-old Katie, who attended the Fifty-Second Street Industrial School, a charitable institution for indigent children. Although Katie did not earn wages, she was not spared hard work, for she cooked and cleaned for her three older working siblings. "In her person and work, she answered the question . . . why we hear so much about the boys and so little about the girls," wrote Riis, "because the home claims their

◆ **Figure 7.10** **"I Scrubs": Katie Who Keeps House on West 49th Street**
The Granger Collection, New York.

work earlier and to a much greater extent."[61] Consider Katie's clothing, posture, and expression. What do they suggest about her character and her prospects? In acknowledgment of Katie's contribution to her family's survival, Riis called Katie by the nickname often given to immigrant children who cared for younger siblings, "little mother." What does this tribute say about the economic role that mothers and other adult women played in the lives of poor families?

QUESTIONS FOR ANALYSIS

1. Riis clearly intended to shock comfortable Americans with his images of the slums. What might contemporaries have found most disturbing about his representations of immigrant women and girls?

2. Using Riis as an example, how would you evaluate the impact of documentary photography on middle-class America's reaction to poverty in the late nineteenth century?

3. Drawing on both Riis and Bessie Van Vorst (see Primary Sources: "The Woman Who Toils," pp. 330–35) as sources, in what ways did women's experiences of poverty and underpaid labor in this period differ from those of men?

NOTES

1. Shige Kushida is mentioned in Mei Nakano, *Japanese American Women: Three Generations, 1890–1990* (Berkeley, CA: Mina Press, 1990). Our version of her life differs on the basis of information provided by Rumi Yasutake, Kobe University, author of *Transnational Women's Activism: The United States, Japan, and Japanese Immigrant Communities in California, 1859–1920* (New York: New York University Press, 2004).

2. Laura Jane Moore, "Lozen," in Theda Perdue, ed., *Sifters: Native American Women's Lives* (New York: Oxford University Press, 2001), 93.

3. Nelson Miles to George Baird, November 20, 1891, Baird Collection, Western Americana Collection, Beinecke Library, Yale University.

4. The term is from Alvin M. Josephy, *500 Nations: An Illustrated History of North American Indians* (New York: Knopf, 1994), 430.

5. Cathleen D. Cahill, *Federal Fathers and Mothers: A Social History of the United States Indian Service, 1869–1933* (Chapel Hill: University of North Carolina Press, 2013), 67.

6. Carolyn J. Marr, "Assimilation through Education: Indian Boarding Schools in the Pacific Northwest," http://content.lib.washington.edu/aipnw/marr.html (accessed June 28, 2004).

7. "A Man Plants the Fields of His Wife," in Ruth Barnes Moynihan, Cynthia Russett, and Laurie Crumpacker, eds., *Second to None: A Documentary History of American Women* (Lincoln: University of Nebraska Press, 1993), 2:82–83.

8. Linda Williams Reese, *Women of Oklahoma, 1890–1920* (Norman: University of Oklahoma Press, 1997), 152–53.

9. Diary of Lucy Hannah White Flake, excerpted in Joan M. Jensen, ed., *With These Hands: Women Working on the Land* (Old Westbury, NY: Feminist Press, 1981), 137–38.

10. Glenda Riley, *A Place to Grow: Women in the American West* (Arlington Heights, IL: Harlan Davidson, 1992), 239.

11. Reese, *Women of Oklahoma*, 38.

12. Michael Lewis Goldberg, *An Army of Women: Gender and Politics in Gilded Age Kansas* (Baltimore: Johns Hopkins University Press, 1997), 40.

13. The term comes from Paula Petrik, *No Step Backward: Women and Family on the Rocky Mountain Mining Frontier, Helena, Montana, 1865–1900* (Helena: Montana Historical Society Press, 1987), 28.

14. Mother Mary Jones, *Autobiography of Mother Jones* (1925; repr., Chicago: C. H. Kerr, 1990), 204.

15. Elizabeth Jameson, "Imperfect Unions: Class and Gender in Cripple Creek, 1894–1904," in Milton Cantor and Bruce Laurie, eds., *Class, Sex, and the Woman Worker* (Westport, CT: Greenwood Press, 1977), 171.

16. Joan Morrison and Charlotte Fox Zabusky, *American Mosaic: The Immigrant Experience in the Words of Those Who Lived It* (New York: E. P. Dutton, 1980), 9.

17. Linda Mack Schloff, *"And Prairie Dogs Weren't Kosher": Jewish Women in the Upper Midwest since 1855* (St. Paul: Minnesota Historical Society Press, 1996), 28.

18. Edith Abbott, *Immigration: Select Documents and Case Records* (Chicago: University of Chicago Press, 1924), 719.

19. Him Mark Lai, Genny Lim, and Judy Yung, *Island: Poetry and History of Chinese Immigrants on Angel Island, 1910–1940* (San Francisco: San Francisco Study Center, 1980), 74.

20. Jane Addams, *Twenty Years at Hull-House*, edited with an introduction by Victoria Bissell Brown (1910; repr., Boston: Bedford/St. Martin's, 1999), 72.

21. Aileen Kraditor, *Ideas of the Woman Suffrage Movement, 1890–1920* (New York: Columbia University Press, 1965), 128.

22. Theodore Roosevelt, introduction to Mrs. John Van Vorst and Marie Van Vorst, *The Woman Who Toils: Being the Experiences of Two Ladies as Factory Girls* (New York: Doubleday, Page & Co., 1903), vii.

23. Anzia Yezierska, *Bread Givers* (1925; repr., New York: George Braziller, 1975), 135.

24. Addams, *Twenty Years at Hull-House*, 166.

25. Ellen Carol DuBois, *The Elizabeth Cady Stanton–Susan B. Anthony Reader: Correspondence, Writings, Speeches,* rev. ed. (Boston: Northeastern University Press, 1992), 205.

26. Jensen, *With These Hands*, 157–58.

27. Susan B. Anthony and Ida H. Harper, eds., *History of Woman Suffrage* (Rochester, NY: Susan B. Anthony, 1902), 4:519.

28. Jensen, *With These Hands*, 147.

29. Ida H. Harper, ed., *History of Woman Suffrage* (New York: National American Woman Suffrage Association, 1922), 5:518.

30. Anthony and Harper, eds., *History of Woman Suffrage*, 4:647.

31. "Women Keep Up Courage," *San Francisco Chronicle*, November 5, 1896. Thanks to Ann Gordon for the citation.

32. Marion K. Barthelme, ed., *Women in the Texas Populist Movement: Letters to the* Southern Mercury (College Station: Texas A&M Press, 1997), 111.

33. Moynihan, Russett, and Crumpacker, *Second to None*, 2:81.

34. Emma Goldman, *Living My Life*, ed. Richard and Anna Maria Drinnon (New York: New American Library, 1977), 122.

35. Kathryn Kish Sklar, *Florence Kelley and the Nation's Work* (New Haven: Yale University Press, 1995), 272.

36. Alice Miller, "Hull House," *The Charities* (February 1892): 167–73.

37. Sklar, *Florence Kelley*, 215.

38. Ibid., 283.

39. Frances Willard, *The Autobiography of an American Woman, Glimpses of Fifty Years* (Chicago: Woman's Temperance Publishing Association, 1892), 431.

40. Kristin Hoganson, *Fighting for American Manhood: How Gender Politics Provoked the Spanish-American and Philippine-American Wars* (New Haven: Yale University Press, 1998), 11.

41. Allen Davis, *An American Heroine: The Life and Legend of Jane Addams* (New York: Oxford University Press, 1973), 140.

42. Allison L. Sneider, *Suffragists in an Imperial Age* (New York: Oxford University Press, 2008), 91.

43. John M. Coward, *Indians Illustrated: The Image of Native Americans in the Pictorial Press* (Urbana: University of Illinois Press, 2012), chap. 3.

44. Leah Dilworth, *Imagining Indians in the Southwest: Persistent Visions of a Primitive Past* (Washington, D.C.: Smithsonian, 1996), 89–90.

45. Francis Washburn, "Zitkala-Ša: A Bridge between Two Worlds," in *Their Own Frontier: Women Intellectuals Revisioning the American West*, ed. Shirley A. Leckie and Nancy J. Parezo (Lincoln: University of Nebraska Press, 2008), 273.

46. *Harper's New Monthly Magazine*, 99 (November 1899), 860.

47. Jane Simonsen, *Making Home Work: Domesticity and Native American Assimilation in the American West, 1860–1919* (Chapel Hill: University of North Carolina Press, 2006), 192.

48. Cited in *The Newspaper Warrior: Sarah Winnemucca Hopkins's Campaign for American Indian Rights, 1864–1891*, ed. Cari M. Carpenter and Carolyn Sorisio (Lincoln: University of Nebraska Press, 2015), 90.

49. Rose Stremlau, "Rape Narratives on the Northern Paiute Frontier: Sarah Winnemucca, Sexual Sovereignty, and Economic Autonomy," in *Portraits of Women in the American West*, ed. Dee Garceau-Hagen (New York: Routledge, 2005), 53

50. Sally Zanjani, *Sarah Winnemucca* (Lincoln: University of Nebraska Press, 2001), 266–67.

51. Jacob A. Riis, *How the Other Half Lives: Studies among the Tenements of New York*, ed. David Leviatin (1890; repr., Boston: Bedford/St. Martin's, 1996), 61.

52. Ibid., 92.

53. Ibid., 91.

54. Ibid., 95.

55. Ibid., 129.

56. Ibid., 141.

57. Ibid., 140.

58. Ibid., 139.

59. Jacob A. Riis, *The Children of the Poor* (New York: Scribner's Sons, 1892), 82.

60. Jacob A. Riis, *The Making of an American* (New York: Macmillan, 1929), 150.

61. Riis, *Children of the Poor*, 80.

SUGGESTED REFERENCES

Women and Western Settlement and Conquest

Susan Armitage and Elizabeth Jameson, eds., *The Women's West* (1987).

Cathleen D. Cahill, *Federal Fathers and Mothers: A Social History of the United States Indian Service, 1869–1933* (2013).

Sarah Deutsch, *No Separate Refuge: Culture, Class, and Gender on an Anglo-Hispanic Frontier in the American Southwest, 1880–1940* (1987).

Lisbeth Haas, *Conquests and Historical Identities in California, 1769–1936* (1995).

Margaret D. Jacobs, *White Mother to a Dark Race: Settler Colonialism, Maternalism, and the Removal of Indigenous Children in the American West and Australia, 1880–1940* (2009).

Elizabeth Jameson and Susan Armitage, eds., *Writing the Range: Race, Class, and Culture in the Women's West* (1997).

Valerie Sherer Mathes, *Helen Hunt Jackson and Her Indian Reform Legacy* (1997).

Theda Perdue, ed., *Sifters: Native American Women's Lives* (2001).

Nancy Shoemaker, ed., *Negotiators of Change: Historical Perspectives on Native American Women* (1995).

Jane E. Simonsen, *Making Home Work: Domesticity and Native American Assimilation in the American West, 1860–1919* (2006).

Immigrant Women

Elizabeth Ewen, *Immigrant Women in the Land of Dollars: Life and Culture on the Lower East Side, 1890–1925* (1985).

Donna Gabaccia, *From the Other Side: Women, Gender, and Immigrant Life in the U.S., 1820–1990* (1994).

Katrina Irving, *Immigrant Mothers: Narratives of Race and Maternity, 1890–1925* (2000).

Mei Nakano, *Japanese American Women: Three Generations, 1890–1990* (1990).

Vicki L. Ruiz, *From Out of the Shadows: Mexican Women in Twentieth-Century America* (1998).

Rumi Yasutake, *Transnational Women's Activism: The United States, Japan, and Japanese Immigrant Communities in California, 1859–1920* (2004).

Judy Yung, *Unbound Feet: A Social History of Chinese Women in San Francisco* (1995).

Women Reformers

Mina Carson, *Settlement Folk: Social Thought and the American Settlement Movement, 1885–1930* (1990).

Rebecca Edwards, *Angels in the Machinery: Gender in American Party Politics from the Civil War to the Progressive Era* (1997).

Elisabeth Lasch-Quinn, *Black Neighbors: Race and the Limits of Reform in the American Settlement House Movement, 1890–1945* (1993).

Rebecca J. Mead, *How the Vote Was Won: Woman Suffrage in the Western United States, 1868–1914* (2004).

Kathryn Kish Sklar, *Florence Kelley and the Nation's Work* (1995).

Allison L. Sneider, *Suffragists in an Imperial Age: U.S. Expansion and the Woman Question, 1870–1929* (2008).

Ian Tyrrell, *Woman's World/Woman's Empire: The Woman's Christian Temperance Union in International Perspective, 1880–1930* (1991).

1903	**National Women's Trade Union League founded in Boston**
1905	Supreme Court finds all laws restricting working hours unconstitutional in *Lochner v. New York*
1907	**Harriot Stanton Blatch organizes the Equality League of Self Supporting Women in New York City**
1908	***Muller v. Oregon* upholds regulation of working hours for women**
1908	**National College Equal Suffrage League formed**
1908	**Wage Earners Suffrage League organized in San Francisco**
1909	National Association for the Advancement of Colored People formed
1909	**New York City shirtwaist workers declare general strike**
1910	**Washington State enacts woman suffrage**
1911	**Triangle Shirtwaist fire in New York City kills 146 workers**
1911	**First mothers' pension program established in Illinois**
1911	**California enacts woman suffrage**
1912	**Textile strike in Lawrence, Massachusetts**
1912	**Federal Children's Bureau established, headed by Julia Lathrop**
1912	**Jane Addams seconds the nomination of Theodore Roosevelt for president on the Progressive Party's ticket**
1912	Eugene Debs gets 6 percent of presidential votes; Socialist Party at its height
1912	**Strike of women garment workers in Rochester, New York**
1912	Woodrow Wilson elected president
1912	**Kansas, Oregon, and Arizona enact woman suffrage**

8

Power and Politics

WOMEN IN THE PROGRESSIVE ERA, 1900–1920

THE DAY AFTER NEW YEAR'S DAY 1907, women met in New York City determined to find a new way to get the drive for woman suffrage onto a winning path. Their leader, Harriot Stanton Blatch, was the daughter of the nineteenth-century leader of the demand for political equality, Elizabeth Cady Stanton. She was also a veteran of numerous reform campaigns organized by civic-minded and politically savvy women, with goals ranging from cleaning up municipal political corruption to improving the wages and working conditions of female workers. Woman suffrage had historically been a middle-class movement, but at this meeting wage-earning women, most of them trade union activists, were joining with leisure-class college graduates, professionals, and social reformers. Still, no woman of color was invited to attend.

A modernized cross-class movement for votes for women was one aspect of Progressivism, a period of intense reform activism from the late 1890s to the years just after the conclusion of the First World War in 1918. The Progressive era profoundly altered the role of government in American life. During these years, American liberalism, which had traditionally regarded government as a threat to citizens' rights, now came to embrace government as the ultimate guarantor of public welfare. Catalyzed by the devastating social consequences of industrial capitalism, the activists of this period battled for new labor laws and social welfare policies, arguing that the fate of society's most

photos: top, © akg-images/The Image Works; middle, Courtesy of the Bancroft Library, University of California, Berkeley, Selina Solomons Papers, BANC MSS C-B 773:7 box 1; bottom, From the Albert R. Stone Negative Collection, Rochester Museum & Science Center, Rochester, New York impoverished sector was linked to the general national welfare. Many socially conscious Americans, jolted by the crises of the 1890s, were ready to join in this new spirit of public stewardship.

Women played a leading role during the Progressive period. As one historian writes, "[W]omen filled the progressive landscape."[1] There is considerable irony in the public influence and power women wielded in these years, because most women would not become fully enfranchised until 1920, in the aftermath of World War I. But they were widely mobilized, organized, and ambitious. Indeed, the victory of votes for women was as much a result as a cause of women's political mobilization in the Progressive era. Earlier Gilded Age developments such as the steady increase of the female labor force, the growth of college education among women, and the spread of women's organizations laid the basis for women's dramatic rush into the public arena in the Progressive era.

Around the edges of the broad-based mass mobilization of Progressive-era suffragism was a smaller, more daring, and more modern approach to women's emancipation for which a new name was invented — feminism. While the achievement of the larger movement was to complete the campaign for equal political rights begun before the Civil War, early twentieth-century feminism foreshadowed the women's liberation movement of the 1960s.

◆ THE FEMALE LABOR FORCE

A good way to start examining the dramatic changes in women's public lives in the Progressive era is to present a portrait of women workers. While the more obvious developments for women in this period were political, the underlying changes were economic, as the female labor force changed significantly.

The presence of large numbers of women in the workforce signaled the beginning of true modernity in female roles. Long a symbol of women's victimhood, the working woman came to stand for women's active presence in the larger world. The visibility and forcefulness of women workers were particularly manifest through a series

photos: top, Detroit Urban League records, Box 87, Bentley Historical Library, University of Michigan; bottom, Seaver Center for Western History Research, Los Angeles County Museum of Natural History

1913	**Alice Paul and Lucy Burns form the Congressional Union**
1913	**Ida B. Wells-Barnett organizes Illinois's first all-black suffrage club, in Chicago**
1914	World War I begins in Europe

1914–1919	Height of African American "Great Migration"
1915	**Woman's Peace Party formed**
1915	**Campaigns for woman suffrage fail in Massachusetts, New York, New Jersey, and Pennsylvania**
1915	**Jane Addams chairs International Council of Women peace meeting in The Hague**
1915	**Women's International League for Peace and Freedom founded**
1916	**Congressional Union becomes National Woman's Party (NWP)**
1916	**Margaret Sanger opens birth control clinic in Brooklyn**
1917	**Second New York referendum enfranchises women**
1917	**United States enters World War I; Montana congresswoman Jeannette Rankin votes against declaration of war**
1917	Bolshevik Revolution ends Russian participation in war

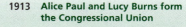

1917	**Women's Committee of the Council for National Defense established**
1917	**NWP members begin to picket the White House**
1917–1919	Urban race riots from St. Louis to Chicago
1918	Supreme Court overturns Keating-Owen Act limiting child labor
1918	Armistice ends World War I
1920	**Federal Woman's Bureau established**
1920	**Nineteenth Amendment (woman suffrage) ratified**

of spectacular strikes in the garment and textile industries. Middle- and upper-class reformers made the concerns of working women central to their activities.

Continuity and Change for Women Wage Earners

In 1900, 18.3 percent of the labor force was female, but this figure was rising and would reach 21.4 percent in 1920.[2] More than half of the female working population was foreign-born and/or nonwhite. The wage rate for women workers was very low: in 1900, the average woman worker made about half of what the average male worker earned.[3] This disparity reflected the fact that men and women largely worked in different occupations and distinct industries, a highly structured sexual division of labor that limited working women's options even as it shaped the American labor force. Domestic service was still the largest category of female employment, but manufacturing was steadily gaining. The average working woman was young and unmarried. Mothers and wives who worked outside the home for wages were few; only among African Americans did they constitute a significant portion of women workers.

Against this general portrait, new areas of women's paid work were beginning to emerge in the early twentieth century. Clerical work, once entirely male and a form of apprenticeship in the business world, was a rapidly growing and desirable field for women. The work was clean and safe, and the wages regular. The demand for clerical workers to coordinate the movement of resources, finished goods, and finances through an increasingly complex national economy was expanding. Yet just as clerical work was being feminized, it was becoming mechanized and routinized, and thus losing its capacity to offer upward mobility. In the offices of mail order houses, banks, insurance companies, and large corporations, the labor of secretaries and typists was beginning to look like factory labor, at times even including the use of piece-rate payment.

Women were also gaining greater entry into some professional fields. The gradual opening up of professional opportunities for women constituted a partial solution to the vocational dilemma that Jane Addams's generation of college graduates had confronted. Overall, the professional sector comprised just 12 percent of the female labor force in 1920, but it played a major role in changing society's view of paid labor for women.[4] Women professional workers expected personal independence and upward mobility from their jobs, and they worked more out of choice than out of need. As such, they paved the way for a new, more positive attitude toward paid labor for women.

The one male-dominated professional field in which women had made any gains by the end of the nineteenth century was medicine; women were between 5 and 6 percent of the profession by 1900. The legal profession was far more hostile to women (compare Figures 6.7, p. 344, and 6.8, p. 346). In 1900, fewer than six hundred women were practicing law in the United States. But as women moved energetically into other aspects of public life, the number of women lawyers began to climb; by 1920, this number had tripled. Inez Milholland, one of the most glamorous figures in the American suffrage movement, applied to

Harvard Law School after she graduated from Vassar in 1909 but was rejected. (Harvard Law did not admit its first woman until 1953.) Instead, she attended New York University Law School, where she specialized in labor, criminal, and divorce law.

In 1919, a group of New York City women lawyers were polled on their opinions about "the paradox of vocation and marriage" for women. The majority responded that women could continue professional life after marriage but should make family life a priority and put aside their profession while their children were small. A small minority believed that, with supportive husbands and enough paid household servants, it was possible to rear children and practice their professions simultaneously. Such a solution was available only to middle-class women who could hire maids and nannies. Even so, these professional women were beginning to grapple with the problem that would affect all working women later in the twentieth century.

More women found professional opportunities in the rise of new "female professions" where they did not have to break through a male monopoly. In these years, the profession of social work began to evolve out of the volunteer labor of women reformers in settlement houses. Practitioners were eager to upgrade traditional forms of benevolence by applying new social science methods. Sophonisba Breckinridge, a lawyer and the first American woman to receive a PhD in political science, convinced the University of Chicago to establish the Graduate School of Social Service Administration. By 1920, there were thirty thousand trained social workers, the majority of them women.

Nursing and teaching were the largest professions dominated by women. Since the Civil War, nursing had been shifting from a form of domestic service to a profession. Between 1900 and 1910, there was a tenfold increase in the number of professionally trained nurses. Many professional nurses worked as public health missionaries, going into immigrant homes to teach sanitation methods and to investigate epidemic disease. Teaching, a woman's occupation at the primary level since the 1830s, was also undergoing changes. In the Progressive era, teachers sought to upgrade their profession, ridding it both of intrusive moral constraints and political interference in hiring. Teacher training was moving from the two-year high-school-level institutions of the late nineteenth century to truly collegiate and university institutions (see Figure 6.6, p. 342). In Chicago, Mary Haley, a second-generation Irish American, organized a powerful teachers' union, which removed control of appointments from local politicians.

African American women were also part of this move to professionalization, although the growing practice of segregation meant that African Americans were excluded from the white-run training programs and occupational associations that structured professions. In the field of nursing, black women responded by establishing their own schools and a professional association, the National Association of Colored Graduate Nurses, formed in 1908. Ironically, Jim Crow provided opportunities for African American professional women in the separate institutions that served black communities, where they worked as librarians, physicians, and especially as teachers. Largely excluded from the National Educational Association, black women teachers formed their own teachers' organizations, through which they challenged racial discrimination in teachers' salaries.

Organizing Women Workers: The Women's Trade Union League

Despite the expansion of working opportunities for women in the clerical and professional strata, industrial workers, especially young immigrants, were considered the most typical working women of the Progressive era. Constituting 25 percent of the female labor force, they were a crucial factor in the tremendously productive power of the American economy and achieved an unprecedented level of public visibility. Many of the themes of the era—women's public prominence, their leadership of liberal causes, and their pursuit of independent lives—marked the women's labor movement of the Progressive period.

Working women received little assistance from the established trade union movement. The male-dominated American Federation of Labor (AFL), which provided the leadership of the trade union movement, regarded women wage earners not as potential union recruits but as either underpaid threats to their members' jobs or pitiful victims of capitalist greed. If women were to improve their wages and working conditions through labor organization, they were going to have to find assistance from allies of gender, not of class.

The Women's Trade Union League (WTUL) formed in 1903 to meet this need. Modeled after a British organization of the same name, the WTUL hoped to reconcile women workers and the organized labor movement. It did so with the reluctant permission of the AFL, the leaders of which were only too relieved to subcontract out the burden of organizing women workers. Membership was open to all committed to the labor organization of women, regardless of class or of union membership. The WTUL also aimed "to develop leadership among the women workers, inspiring them with a sense of personal responsibility for the conditions under which they work."[5]

The WTUL was a coalition of women trade union activists and leisure-class women (known as "allies"), primarily drawn from the settlement house movement. Mary Kenney O'Sullivan, who had begun her career in Chicago as a skilled bookbinder and had served as the AFL's first official female organizer, was one of the primary working-class founders (see pp. 310–12). She was aided by Leonora O'Reilly, a garment worker from New York City with connections to the Henry Street Settlement. O'Reilly recruited two wealthy sisters also from New York City, Mary Dreier and Margaret Dreier Robins, who provided most of the financial resources for the WTUL throughout the 1910s. Major chapters emerged in Boston, New York City, and Chicago; smaller groups formed in Milwaukee, St. Louis, Kansas City, Philadelphia, and San Francisco.

The WTUL's interclass collaboration struck a different note from the antagonistic class relations between leisured and wage-earning women in the Gilded Age. Nonetheless, Leonora O'Reilly was concerned that the WTUL would become a "charity" organization in which middle-class women approached workers with "the attitudes of a lady with something to give her sister."[6] Despite the organization's

◆ Women's Trade Union League

This photograph (c. 1910) of the headquarters of the Women's Trade Union League in New York City was probably taken in the midst of the 1910–1911 shirtwaist strike. The mixed-class nature of the WTUL is suggested by the two elegantly dressed women standing on the right, one of whom wears a fur coat. © *akg-images/The Image Works.*

commitment to developing working-class women's leadership abilities, formal control remained in the hands of leisure-class women until 1922, when Maud Swartz, a typesetter, took over as national president. Still, the WTUL was unique for its cross-class commitment to workers' empowerment.

While the WTUL worked hard on behalf of white and immigrant working-class women, its record was weak when it came to black women workers. Black workers, even more than white working women, faced hostility from the white men who led the American labor movement. They were not admitted into trade unions in this period, were hired at lower wages than white workers, and were employed as strikebreakers. The WTUL's association with the organized labor movement led it to go along with the AFL's racist antagonism to black workers throughout its early years.

After World War I, the organization shifted its emphasis from trade union organization to the passage of state maximum workday hours and minimum wage laws for working women. The first director of the Women's Bureau of the Department of Labor, established in 1920, was Chicago WTUL member and shoe worker Mary Anderson. Later, Rose Schneiderman, a garment worker who labored for the league throughout her career, helped to shape New Deal policy toward working women and working families (see pp. 498–508).

The Rising of the Women

A wave of early twentieth-century strikes put the modern wage-earning woman on the labor history map. The most famous of these took place over the winter of 1909–10 in New York City in the shirtwaist (blouse) industry. The strike began when Local 25 of the International Ladies' Garment Workers' Union (ILGWU), a small male-dominated organization, struck several manufacturers over low wages and bad working conditions. Day after day, the picketers, most of them young Jewish and Italian women, were harassed by thugs their bosses had hired, arrested by police, and fined and jailed by local magistrates. Then they turned to the WTUL. When leisure-class women joined the picket line, they were subjected to the same disrespectful treatment as the striking workers, which made the newspapers take notice. (See Primary Sources: "Parades, Picketing, and Power: Women in Public Space," pp. 462–69.)

The large clothing manufacturers were able to hold out against the workers by sending their unfinished garments to shops that the ILGWU was not targeting. Facing sure defeat, the union considered calling a general strike of the entire New York City shirtwaist industry. On November 22, 1909, more than fifteen thousand shirtwaist workers showed up at a mass meeting to discuss how to proceed against the manufacturers. As male labor leaders and leisure-class WTUL members on the stage hesitated to speak, seventeen-year-old shirtwaist maker Clara Lemlich spoke from the floor and galvanized the audience to walk off their jobs.

The next day, between twenty and thirty thousand workers, two-thirds of them Eastern European Jews, were on strike. The WTUL provided the strike pay, publicity, and legal support to keep the strike going. Some of the wealthiest women in New York City, including Anne Morgan, daughter of banking magnate J. P. Morgan, publicly endorsed the cause of the workers. The presence and commitment of young women on the picket line challenged the traditional image of women wage earners as passive victims.

After almost three months, the shirtwaist strike was settled. Many, but not all, of the manufacturers agreed to a fifty-two-hour workweek, no more fines for workers' mistakes, more worker involvement in setting wages, and even paid holidays. But they would not allow the ILGWU to represent the workers in future negotiations. Even so, the strike turned the ILGWU into a much more powerful labor organization. Individual working-class women, including Clara Lemlich and Rose Schneiderman, embarked on a lifetime of labor activism.

A tragic epilogue to the shirtwaist strike took place a little over a year later, highlighting why union recognition was so important to the workers. The Triangle Shirtwaist Company had begun locking the doors of its Manhattan factory after the workers arrived, to keep union organizers out and workers in. On March 25, 1911, a fire broke out on the tenth floor. Workers found that they were locked inside the building. Desperately they ran up to the roof. Some were able to escape, but 146 workers, more than a quarter of Triangle's employees, died. At a mass funeral held a few days later, Schneiderman delivered a bitter eulogy: "This is not the first time girls have been burned alive in this city. . . . Every year thousands of us are maimed. The life of men and women is so cheap and property is so sacred. There are so many of us for one job it matters little if [we] are burned to death."[7]

◆ **Triangle Shirtwaist Fire**

The actual number of dead was 146. This gruesome newspaper photograph shows the broken bodies of young women who jumped to escape the fire because the doors were locked from the outside and the fire escapes pulled away from the building. A policeman leans over to identify and tag the victims. To the right is the building that housed the Triangle Shirtwaist Company, site of both the 1909–1910 strike and the 1911 fire. As Rose Schneiderman predicted, it survived long after the workers died. Currently, it is owned by New York University. No one was ever convicted of liability for the tragedy. New York Herald, *March 26, 1911.*

In 1912, labor militancy broke out again in the textile factories of Lawrence, Massachusetts. As in the garment industry, textile workers were overwhelmingly immigrant, but the textile industry employed entire families, including children. Textile workers labored long hours for very low wages. Much of the industry was located in company towns, where employers exerted total control and workers could find no local allies. When a Massachusetts law established a maximum of fifty-four working hours per week, Lawrence manufacturers cut the wages of their workers proportionately, and the workers struck.

Because the AFL was not interested in their plight, the workers turned to the Industrial Workers of the World (IWW), a radical socialist labor organization. One of the organization's most famous leaders was twenty-two-year-old Elizabeth Gurley Flynn, a single mother and an accomplished organizer and public speaker. In Lawrence, Flynn encouraged greater involvement among Italian and other immigrant women, whose enthusiasm for the struggle gave the lie to their reputation as cloistered and conservative peasants. Besides going out on strike, immigrant women took to the streets in parades but also in informal groups, where they taunted and harassed local businessmen, police, and others they deemed unfriendly to their cause.

◆ **Elizabeth Gurley Flynn**
A socialist and feminist, Elizabeth Gurley Flynn was a charismatic organizer for the Industrial Workers of the World, a position that took her to the Midwest, West, and New England in the early twentieth century. In 1912, she was crucial in assisting immigrant workers in the Lawrence, Massachusetts, textile strike. Here she addresses a crowd of women during the Paterson, New Jersey, silk worker strike in 1913. *The Granger Collection, New York.*

The turning point in the strike involved the children of the town's workers. As police and militia attacks increased, Flynn decided it was time to relocate the younger children to the homes of out-of-town sympathizers. Children on their way to Philadelphia were beaten by Lawrence police, and their mothers were imprisoned for "neglect" by local courts. Nationwide outrage was so great that the employers were forced to agree to the strikers' demands for a fifty-four-hour week and wage increases as high as 25 percent (see Figure 8.1, p. 463). Ironically, the very magnitude of the Lawrence workers' victory contributed to the shift of much of the textile industry from New England to the South, in search of a more docile workforce.

The exceptional dedication and militancy of the women of the New York and Lawrence strikes — and other labor conflicts in Paterson, New Jersey; Chicago; and Atlanta — helped to transform the popular image of working women. No longer dependent on others to defend and protect them, they were now appreciated for the ability to fight their own battles. By the beginning of World War I, the number of women in trade unions had quadrupled. Even so, women remained a minority of the labor movement and had many obstacles — lack of male interest, middle-class condescension, and their own timidity — to overcome.

◆ THE FEMALE DOMINION

The WTUL was connected to what one historian has named the "female dominion," the women's wing of reform movements in the Progressive era. Middle- and upper-class white women created a network of reform organizations, became active in partisan politics, and lobbied for legislation to benefit poor women and children. Largely excluded from those groups, African American women created their own institutions that promoted social welfare and self-help in their communities. Although black women faced obstacles unknown to white reformers, both groups demonstrated a strong commitment to women's involvement in the dramatic political changes of the early twentieth century.

Public Housekeeping

Female social reformers frequently drew on the image of "public housekeeping" to describe women's activism in the Progressive era. "The very multifariousness and complexity of a city government demand the help of minds accustomed to . . . a sense of responsibility for the cleanliness and comfort of other people," explained Jane Addams in 1906 of the reform work that women were doing in Chicago.[8] What once could be accomplished from within the home, it was argued, now required that women become leaders in the public realm.

Women's public housekeeping took many forms. Despite their disfranchisement, women worked to drive out corrupt machine politics and install reform mayors in various cities. They worked to improve slum housing and to establish public amenities in Boston and New York. The Civic Club of Charleston, South

Carolina, established playgrounds and then convinced the city council to take them over. Many public libraries were founded by local women's clubs. Women were involved in the campaign to set health standards for food, especially for the notoriously impure milk supply, a particular threat to infants whose mothers did not breast-feed. Women played a major role in the establishment of special juvenile and family courts. Activist and budding historian Mary Beard chronicled the breadth and depth of this involvement in urban politics in her 1915 book, *Woman's Work in Municipalities*. Beard wrote that as women sought to address the problems of disease, "vice, crime, poverty and misery," they learned that "to 'swat the fly' . . . they must swat poor housing, evil labor conditions, ignorance, and vicious interests."[9] These public housekeepers worked through existing national organizations such as the Woman's Christian Temperance Union and the General Federation of Women's Clubs and its state affiliates. But they also formed new, more focused groups. Most important was the National Consumers' League (NCL), formed in 1899 in New York City by Florence Kelley, which brought together women's consumer organizations in various states. The NCL concentrated on working conditions for women and children.

Historians have developed the term "maternalism" to characterize the ideological core of women's reform concerns in the Progressive era.[10] Maternalist thinking

◆ **The Dirty Pool of Politics**
The image of civic-minded women sweeping out the dirt from the house of public life captures both the conventional and innovative nature of women's public activities in this period. The image was widely distributed by suffragists, suggesting that the link between politics and civic housewifery was an effective rhetorical tool with men and women alike. *Courtesy of the Bancroft Library, University of California, Berkeley, Selina Solomons Papers, BANC MSS C-B 773:7 box 1.*

had two parts. First, every sort of program advanced on women's behalf, even those having to do with women's wage labor, was justified on the grounds that society needed to protect maternal capacity. Second, the women who designed and advocated for these policies conceived of their own public involvement through the lens of motherhood. The dual meaning of "maternalism" obscured the different ways that standards of motherhood were applied to what were essentially two different classes of women, leisure-class policy makers and their working-class clients. The former legitimated themselves by expressing active maternal concern, wielded from within the public arena, while they viewed the beneficiaries of their policies as dependent and homebound mothers in need of protection. Thus, maternal power and maternal need were separated between two different classes rather than understood as linked and interdependent.

Maternalist Triumphs: Protective Labor Legislation and Mothers' Pensions

Maternalist presumptions underlay policies designed on behalf of working women and mothers alike. One of reformers' first goals was to establish a legal maximum workday for working women. However, in 1905, in the case *Lochner v. New York*, the U.S. Supreme Court ruled that *any* attempt to regulate wage labor relations for men or women was an unconstitutional infringement on individual freedom of contract. At this point, the NCL reasoned that the courts might allow special labor laws only for women workers on the grounds that their future maternal capacity needed to be protected.

An opportunity to test this theory came in 1908 when an Oregon maximum hours law only for women workers was challenged before the U.S. Supreme Court. Josephine Goldmark, NCL secretary, arranged for Louis Brandeis, her brother-in-law and later a member of the Supreme Court, to argue the case. The so-called Brandeis Brief proceeded on two grounds: (1) that "women are fundamentally weaker than men" in defending themselves against the assaults of wage labor and thus must rely on the state to safeguard them and (2) that protection of women's maternal capacity was necessary for the general welfare. In its 1908 decision *Muller v. Oregon*, the Supreme Court accepted the argument that while men's working hours could not be regulated by law, women's could (see the Appendix, p. A-7). Within a decade, all but nine states had passed maximum hours laws for working women.

These so-called protective labor laws were widely applauded by women activists and working women alike. But there were some limits to this victory. Women in domestic and agricultural labor were for the most part excluded, which meant that the great majority of African American and Mexican American women were not covered. More generally, in exchange for a desired improvement in their working conditions, working women had been formally labeled weaker than men, without the same claim on individual rights. From this perspective, the underlying principle of one of the era's great achievements for women, protective labor laws, conflicted with those of another great success, equal political rights.

Other protective labor legislation for working women was passed on the basis of maternal capacity. After 1908, many states passed laws prohibiting women from working at night. Female printers and other skilled women workers whose jobs required night work protested. Laws that set minimum wages for women workers, so that any decrease in women's working hours would not result in lower earnings, were also passed, provoking controversy from employers who objected to the higher labor costs that minimum wage laws would incur. In a 1923 case titled *Adkins v. Children's Hospital*, the U.S. Supreme Court reversed the logic of its earlier *Muller* decision and invalidated minimum wage laws for women, saying that women "are legally as capable of contracting for themselves as men."[11] The Court based this turnaround of perspective on the recently ratified Nineteenth Amendment to the Constitution giving women equal voting rights (see the Appendix, p. A-8).

The major forms of legislation directed at mothers were maternal pension programs, to shield mothers who were unsupported by male breadwinners from having to go out into the workplace to earn money, allowing them to stay at home with their children. Thus, the two different reforms—legislation focused on working women's hours and pensions for nonworking mothers—were closely linked by the maternalist ethic that it was the government's responsibility to protect motherhood from the incursions of the wage labor system and to conserve women's best energies for bearing and raising children.

The first mothers' pension program was established in 1911 in Illinois. A limited number of single mothers, whose neediness was determined by the Juvenile Court, received monthly grants of $50. Not surprisingly, African American mothers barely appeared on the mothers' pension rolls, kept off by institutional prejudice and their lack of knowledge that these programs existed. By 1920, thirty-eight other states had established mothers' pension programs with similar structures.

Maternalist Defeat: The Struggle to Ban Child Labor

Ironically, the least successful of the maternalist programs was the one that seems the most basic and obvious: ending child labor. In 1900, an estimated 2 million underage children were reported to be working for wages. While state legislatures passed maximum hours laws and mothers' pension programs, the campaign to outlaw child labor was one of the first social welfare efforts to focus on the federal government. In 1912, Congress established a Children's Bureau in the Department of Labor, which became headquarters for the campaign to stop child labor. With little federal funding for its work, the Children's Bureau used women's clubs, especially those associated with the General Federation of Women's Clubs, to conduct surveys and to lobby for state and federal legislation for children. One measure of their success came in 1916 when Congress passed the Keating-Owen Act, which prohibited paid labor for children under sixteen.

What seemed like an amazingly quick victory in a key Progressive reform soon turned into defeat. Crucial industries such as textile manufacturing and mining relied on child workers and opposed the law. In addition, immigrant families depended heavily on the labor of their children and stubbornly resisted the perspective of middle-class social workers to eliminate it. In 1918, the U.S. Supreme Court overturned the federal law as an unconstitutional violation of states' rights. Congress passed a constitutional amendment banning child labor in 1924, but its ratification failed, the victim of an energetic "anti"-campaign that labeled it as too "socialistic." It was not until 1938, with the anti-child-labor provision of the Fair Labor Standards Act, which the Supreme Court allowed to stand, that the practice of child labor in this country was outlawed.

Progressive Women and Political Parties

Despite the rhetoric of maternalism, many female reform activists were drawn to the traditionally male political arena. Even without the franchise, they involved themselves in the 1912 election in anticipation that their voting rights were just over the horizon.

Even though women tended to position themselves as nonpartisan, putting issues and candidates above party loyalty, they could be found in the ranks of all the major parties. Many politically active women reformers, such as the Dreier sisters of the WTUL, could be found in the reform wing of the Republican Party. In 1912, the reformers' candidate, former president Theodore Roosevelt, lost the Republican Party nomination to incumbent William Howard Taft. As a result, the reform forces bolted the party to create the independent Progressive Party. The Progressives supported woman suffrage and integrated women fully into all their activities. At the Progressive Party's national convention, the de facto leader of the women reformers, Jane Addams, was chosen to second Roosevelt's nomination as the party's presidential candidate. Most African American women, however, remained devoted to the regular Republicans, the party of Lincoln.

The 1912 presidential race also featured a strong Socialist candidate, Eugene V. Debs. While both the Progressive and Socialist Parties advocated woman suffrage and minimum wage laws for women, the Socialists' ultimate goal was working-class empowerment, whereas the Progressives sought interclass harmony. Socialist women came in different varieties. Kate Richards O'Hare, who had begun her reform career in Kansas as a temperance advocate, was a nationally prominent Socialist writer, journalist, and traveling lecturer. Rose Pastor Stokes, a Russian immigrant factory worker who made headlines when she married a wealthy New York reformer, was also prominent in the party.

In the 1912 election, Roosevelt received more popular votes than the regular Republican nominee, President William Howard Taft, but the winner of the election, profiting from the split in the Republican ranks, was the Democratic candidate, Woodrow Wilson. Wilson had a reputation as a reformer from his years as governor of New Jersey. Democrats did not have a record of cultivating female support, although this was beginning to change as full enfranchisement drew nearer. Debs won only 6 percent of the presidential vote, but Socialists were elected to local and state offices and even to Congress, marking the high point of electoral socialism in American history.

Outside the Dominion: Progressivism and Race

Race was a blind spot for white reformers in the Progressive era. Anti-Asian sentiment against Japanese immigration was strong and growing in the West. In the Southwest, the Mexican Revolution of 1910 swelled the numbers of Mexican immigrants — by 1920 they constituted 12 percent of the population of California — and nativist anxiety about these dark-skinned foreigners also grew stronger.

Inasmuch as the Progressive era coincided with the triumph of Jim Crow policies, however, the brunt of the era's racism fell on African Americans. In the South, white reformers advocated segregation and the disfranchisement of black men as a means to purge local political corruption. In the North, antiblack prejudice was reinforced by scientific theories of racial hierarchy that were current at the time. Even the most sympathetic whites saw the African American poor as less adaptable than European immigrants to urban industrial society. Given maternalist convictions about the importance of home-based childrearing, male breadwinning, and dedicated mothering, the tendency of black mothers to work outside the home seemed to white reformers to constitute an insurmountable barrier to their improvement.

Nonetheless, African American women shared the reform enthusiasms of the era. The small black middle class provided resources for the establishment of kindergartens for the children of working mothers and founded old-age homes for former slaves without families to care for them. By 1900, four hundred black women's clubs and societies were affiliated with the National Association of Colored Women (NACW). In addition to the antilynching work with which it had begun, the NACW had divisions for mothers' clubs, juvenile courts, domestic science, temperance, music, literature, and votes for women. Mary Church Terrell, an 1884 graduate of Oberlin College, was the association's first president. When the National Association for the Advancement of Colored People was founded in 1909, Terrell and Ida B. Wells-Barnett were the most prominent African American women admitted to the inner circle. (See Primary Sources: "Black Women and Progressive-Era Reform," pp. 454–61.)

Two other important black women of the era were business entrepreneurs, a category that had no real equivalent among white women of the period. Louisiana-born Sarah Breedlove Walker went from being a laundress to being the president of her own highly successful hair care business. As Madam C. J. Walker, she employed thousands of African American women who sold her products door-to-door. Virginia-born Maggie Lena Walker (no relation to Sarah) was the first woman president of a U.S. bank. Wealthy, philanthropic, and community-minded, both women deeply identified with the progress of the women of their race. Maggie Walker described her "great all absorbing interest" as "the love I bear . . . our Negro women . . . blocked and held down by the fears and prejudices of the whites, ridiculed and sneered at by intelligent blacks."[12]

During the Progressive era, Native Americans also began to serve as public advocates for their people. A generation educated in white institutions had gained familiarity with the dominant culture and acquired the political skills

◆ Madam C. J. Walker

During the Progressive era, many wealthy women were also reformers and philanthropists, but only one earned her own fortune and was African American. Madam C. J. Walker, born Sarah Breedlove, was the daughter of former slaves and worked in the cotton fields and as a laundress before she built her immensely successful hair care and cosmetics business. Walker was active in the National Association of Colored Women and was the single largest contributor to the National Association for the Advancement of Colored People's antilynching campaign, which picked up from the earlier efforts of black clubwomen. Walker died in 1919, and her daughter used the money her mother left her to become the most important black woman patron of the Harlem Renaissance. *Photo by Jim Mooney/NY Daily News Archive via Getty Images.*

needed to speak for themselves. Their goal was to undo the economic and political dependency that had resulted from late nineteenth-century Indian policy (see pp. 358–63). Gertrude Simmons Bonnin was the leading woman in this first generation of modern Indian activists. (See Primary Sources: "Representing Native American Women in the Late Nineteenth Century," pp. 390–401.) Writing under her Yankton Sioux name Zitkala-Ša, she advocated both preserving Native culture from destruction and securing full rights of citizenship for Native peoples. She became the secretary of the first secular national pan-Indian reform organization established by Native peoples, the Society of American Indians.[13]

◆ **First Annual Conference of the Society of American Indians**
This section of a 1911 photograph features attendants at the first annual conference of the Society of American Indians. The society valued assimilation for Native Americans, but also emphasized reforms on the reservations and lobbied for citizenship. Women were active in the organization. Pictured here from left to right are Nora McFarland, Sadie Wall, Ester M. Dagenett, Mary E. Finn, Emma D. Johnson, Marie L. B. Baldwin, Angel DeCora Deitz, and Jane M. Butler. *National Archives, no. 1105265.*

Other Native women also figured prominently in the Society of American Indians, but the society divided over numerous issues, including full citizenship rights for Native Americans, fearing that U.S. citizenship would weaken tribal communities. But in 1924, when Congress passed the Indian Citizenship Act, women were included, because by then the long battle for woman suffrage had come to a victorious end.

◆ VOTES FOR WOMEN

The labor militancy of women workers and the public involvement of Progressive women reformers together fueled a great and final drive for women's enfranchisement. Ever since the constitutional amendments of the Reconstruction years (see pp. 292–94), the woman suffrage movement had been accumulating advocates and reformulating its strategy. In 1890, the two rival suffrage societies, the National Woman Suffrage Association (founded by Elizabeth Cady Stanton and Susan B. Anthony) and the American Woman Suffrage Association (established by Lucy Stone and Henry Ward Blackwell), united as the National American Woman Suffrage Association (NAWSA). When Carrie Chapman Catt of Iowa took over the NAWSA presidency from Anthony in 1900, four states, all west of the Mississippi, had granted full voting rights to women.

A New Generation for Suffrage

A new generation of suffrage leaders was determined to expand the movement to the rest of the country and bring it into full conformity with the realities of urban, industrial, modern America. They rejected the outdated nineteenth-century term "woman suffrage" in favor of a more contemporary-sounding slogan, "votes for women." They were influenced by new developments in the British suffrage movement, which had adopted more public tactics that put pressure on political leaders, as well as increased involvement with working women in the British textile industry. American women were particularly inspired by Emmeline Pankhurst and her two daughters Christabel and Sylvia. They drew in previously uninvolved classes of women, from the wealthy to the working class, and learned to play legislative politics to their own benefit. They established small, flexible suffrage societies and turned to the most advanced cultural methods and artistic styles, anything to get over the old-fashioned image from which their cause suffered.

The revived movement of the Progressive era came back to life in a series of campaigns for equal political rights at the state level. But appeals to male voters in one state after another were exhausting, repetitive, and, east of the Mississippi River, impossible to win. At this point, suffrage activists shifted their focus back to a federal constitutional amendment, the movement's original goal in the 1860s. Large but slow to change, NAWSA was challenged by a small, more aggressive group of activists, known as "militants" and "suffragettes" (the latter a derogatory term that British suffrage activists had turned into a label of pride). By the mid-1910s, these two wings of the movement had generated the right combination of female energy, male support, and political will to effect a constitutional amendment for women's political rights.

Why, then, did it take so long to win votes for women? Organized opposition is part of the answer. Ever since the 1890s, a few mostly upper-class women actively opposed enfranchisement, either on the grounds that political rights would cost women their moral influence over men or that too many "unfit" women would vote. However, suffrage leaders were less concerned with the female anti-suffragists than with powerful male-led special interests — especially the liquor industry and manufacturers who exploited female and child labor — who worked against them from behind the legislative scenes.

But the really significant obstacles that had to be overcome were more elusive. Large numbers of women who otherwise had little in common had to unite in active pursuit of this single goal. Perhaps this was why, unlike the suffragists of Elizabeth Cady Stanton's day, the twentieth-century movement did not emphasize abstract justice but instead stressed the many concrete purposes to which organized political power could be put. With a large, diverse movement of women demanding the vote, male politicians and legislators were gradually compelled to act. That votes for women was a reform long past due did not make its final achievement any less a triumph; it was the most successful mass movement for the expansion of political democracy in American history.

Diversity in the Woman Suffrage Movement

In terms of diversity, the greatest achievement of the twentieth-century woman suffrage movement was its extremely broad class base. Reform collaboration between middle-class reformers and working-class trade unionists greatly facilitated outreach to women wage earners in the suffrage movement. By 1910, several new suffrage organizations were focused on recruiting working women. In San Francisco, Maud Younger, a wealthy woman who organized food servers, established a Wage Earners Suffrage League; similar organizations were founded in Los Angeles, New York City, and elsewhere. More and more suffrage parades featured large divisions of working women, often marching under the banners of their trade or union. Pro-suffrage literature was printed in the languages of immigrants — Yiddish, German, Italian, Portuguese, and Spanish — and explained how votes for women would raise women's wages and improve their working conditions. Wage-earning women brought with them the support of male family members and coworkers, who began to see in votes for women a tool for their own class interests.

Simultaneously, women from the very highest class of society became involved in the movement. Their wealth came from their husbands, but, aspiring to power of their own, they used their money to gain entrée into the world of women's politics. One of the richest was Alva Belmont, who had divorced one millionaire, William Vanderbilt, in order to marry another, August Belmont. Their money paid the salaries of organizers, rented offices, and supported the publication of newspapers and leaflets. Relations between the wealthy and the wage earning were superficially sisterly. But wealthy suffragists expected to lead the movement, and working-class suffragists were suspicious of their motives. "We want the ballot for very different reasons," explained Los Angeles working-class suffragist Minna O'Donnell in 1908. "Our idea is self protection; you want to use it [to help] some one else."[14] They approached the vote less in terms of individual rights than of group power.

The growth of suffragism among young college-educated women, whose numbers had been increasing since the 1860s, was also a new development. The College Equal Suffrage League, formed by students and young alumnae at Radcliffe College in 1898 because the administration would not permit pro-suffrage speakers on campus, became a national organization in 1908 under the leadership of Bryn Mawr president M. Carey Thomas. College graduates provided the energy of youth in many other organizations.

In contrast to such bridges across the class gap, the suffrage movement was almost completely racially segregated. NAWSA repeatedly refused to condemn discrimination against African American women and allowed southern white affiliates to refuse them membership. Moreover, southern suffrage leaders such as Kate Gordon of Louisiana and Laura Clay of Kentucky regarded the involvement of African American women as an outright threat to their plans to increase the political involvement of white women in their region. "The South will be compelled to look to its Anglo-Saxon women as the medium through which to retain the supremacy of the white race over the African," Belle Kearney of Mississippi hopefully predicted in 1903.[15]

Despite this discouragement, black suffragists continued to insist on their equal political rights. For black women, achieving suffrage was a way to counter the disfranchisement of the men of their race. Starting in the 1890s, African American women began to assert their political rights aggressively from within their own clubs and suffrage societies. "If white American women, with all their natural and acquired advantages, need the ballot," explained Adele Hunt Logan of Tuskegee, Alabama, "how much more do black Americans, male and female, need the strong defense of a vote to help secure their right to life, liberty and the pursuit of happiness?"[16]

Returning to the Constitution: The National Suffrage Movement

In the Reconstruction years, the suffrage movement had concentrated on getting woman suffrage recognized in the U.S. Constitution. Congress debated a woman suffrage amendment in 1878, but suffrage energies shifted to the state level soon after.

◆ **"The Awakening"**
Maps comparing states where women did and didn't have the right to vote became increasingly familiar in the movement's final years, to indicate that the drive for women's enfranchisement was growing, its final achievement irresistible. This powerful version, from the popular magazine *Puck*, refers to the 1915 New York campaign, which was unable to win an eastern state to the suffrage side. Here western women carrying the torch of enfranchisement, are coming to rescue the women of the east from their political purgatory. The poem at the bottom, by Alice Duer Miller, begins "Look forward, women, always; utterly cast away / The memory of hate and struggle and bitterness; / Bonds may endure for a night, but freedom comes with the day, / And the free must remember nothing less. . . ." How does this text help to explain the title, "The Awakening"? *Library of Congress, 3b49106.*

The modern revival of the American suffrage movement began in a series of campaigns focused on enfranchisement in particular states (see Map 8.1). In Washington State, where women had briefly voted in the 1880s only to have their suffrage revoked by the territorial legislature, they regained the vote in 1910. The next year, California women won suffrage by less than five thousand votes. In 1915, campaigns were mounted in Pennsylvania, New Jersey, Massachusetts, and, most important,

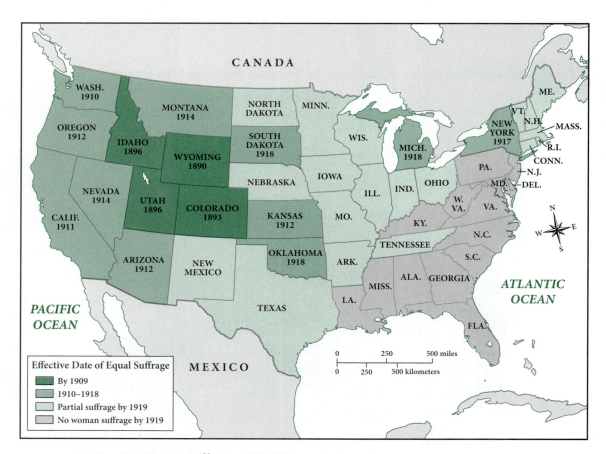

◆ **Map 8.1 Woman Suffrage, 1890–1919**
The woman suffrage movement in the United States was fought on both the state and federal levels. States traditionally defined their electorates, but starting with the Fifteenth Amendment in 1870, the Constitution prohibited particular forms of disfranchisement. In 1893, Colorado amended its state constitution to include women as voting citizens. By 1914, ten other states, all in the West, had followed suit, granting their women full voting rights, including for president and Congress. The voting power of women in these "suffrage states" became a potent political lever for moving the national parties to support what became the Nineteenth Amendment, which prohibits states from disfranchising their citizens on the basis of sex.

New York. Despite extraordinary efforts, the eastern campaigns of 1915 failed. Some suffrage leaders were beginning to conclude that the state-by-state approach was futile. Even if every state could be won this way—and many, certainly the entire South, could not—the time and money required were prohibitive. At this point, the momentum of the movement shifted back to an approach that would enfranchise all American women: a U.S. constitutional amendment.

NAWSA was slow to make the shift to focus on a federal amendment. Anna Howard Shaw, who had replaced Carrie Chapman Catt as NAWSA president in 1906, was unwilling to redirect organizational resources from the influential state chapters to a centralized national campaign. In 1913, two young women college graduates, Alice Paul and Lucy Burns, convinced NAWSA leaders to allow them to take over work on a federal amendment. In their very first act, they signaled their intention to energize a national effort with the same kind of spectacular methods that had worked in state campaigns. They organized a suffrage parade in Washington, D.C. (see Figure 8.4, p. 467), and chose March 3, the day before Woodrow Wilson's inauguration, because then the nation's attention would be on the city. When the president-to-be disembarked from the train, he was told that the crowds he had expected to greet him were down on Pennsylvania Avenue, watching the suffragists. Within a few weeks, the suffrage amendment was being debated in the House of Representatives for the first time in seventeen years.

Fresh off this victory, Paul and Burns formed a new, smaller, more activist, and more disciplined national organization. They named it the Congressional Union because its goal was to pressure Congress to pass a woman suffrage amendment. Paul and Burns understood that the votes of women who were already enfranchised by successful state campaigns in the West provided an important tool for putting political pressure on Congress to move. Accordingly, in 1916 they adjusted the name of their organization to the National Woman's Party (NWP) with a single plank, getting voting women to push for a constitutional amendment. That year, as President Wilson campaigned to be reelected, a corps of NWP activists fanned out through the West, urging women voters to withhold their votes from the Democrats until Wilson promised actively to back woman suffrage.

Although this tactic failed—Wilson won the election, including in states such as California where women voted—the NWP succeeded in redirecting suffrage energies to the national level. Even NAWSA loyalists who found the NWP's combative methods distasteful were compelled to develop an alternative way for their organization to push for federal-level enfranchisement. In 1915, NAWSA's most politically savvy leader, Carrie Chapman Catt, reassumed the national presidency. She mobilized NAWSA's enormous organizational structure in a concerted lobbying campaign for the federal amendment. Although the NWP and the NAWSA were hostile to each other, belying the notion of a loving sisterhood on behalf of suffrage, their two approaches were complementary, the former raising the political stakes by its radical efforts, the latter negotiating with congressmen to move the amendment forward. Nonetheless, it took another five years, and the upheaval of a world war, before the Constitution was amended to enfranchise women.

◆ THE EMERGENCE OF FEMINISM

As the votes-for-women movement grew, an avant-garde approach to modernizing womanhood that emphasized women's autonomy was surfacing. To distinguish themselves from the more conventional suffragists, the women who took this approach began to use the term "feminist," borrowed from the French *feminisme*. "All feminists are suffragists," they explained, "but not all suffragists are feminists."[17] Their agenda was a broad one, moving beyond political rights and economic advancement to embrace female individuality, sexual freedom, and birth control.

The Feminist Program

Feminism was a cultural development more than an organized movement. Most of its adherents were middle-class college graduates, aspiring professionals, and artists, but female labor activists and immigrants were also in its ranks. The definition of the word "feminism" was imprecise. On the one hand, feminists believed that women had all the capacities and talents of men; on the other, they believed that women's distinctive intelligence and powers had not yet been allowed to surface. Whether emphasizing similarities or differences with men, however, they agreed on feminism's power to disrupt the gender order. "Feminism was something with dynamite in it," Rheta Childe Dorr wrote. "It is the state of mind of women who realize that their whole position in the social order is antiquated . . . made of old materials, worn out laws, customs, conventions, fetishes, traditions and taboos."[18] Feminists were proud individualists, impatient with the female tradition of justifying all actions (including social reform) in terms of selfless, maternal service. (See Primary Sources: "Modernizing Womanhood," pp. 475–79.)

Unlike the votes-for-women movement, feminism placed the cutting edge of change in women's private lives, not in their public roles. Charlotte Perkins Gilman was a feminist favorite for her conviction that the family-oriented life of the middle class was narrow and inefficient, a point she explored in her pathbreaking books *Women and Economics* (1890) and *The Home* (1903). Gilman championed collectivizing housework, and New York City feminist Henrietta Rodman organized a communal apartment house for women to realize this vision.

Other feminists challenged the Gilded Age premise of female sexual restraint by insisting that women had sexual desires as well as maternal capacities. They were influenced by British psychologist Havelock Ellis, one of the most eminent among a growing circle of "sexologists." Although similar to Sigmund Freud, the founder of modern psychoanalysis, in emphasizing the erotic nature of all humans, Ellis and others, including Swedish feminist Ellen Key, tended to romanticize sexuality by investing it with mystical qualities and insisting that sexual gratification was necessary for emotional health. In contrast to Freud, they also paid special attention to women's sexuality.

In the spirit of the new feminism, younger women claimed that previous generations of female activists fostered too much "sex antagonism" toward men, and that it was possible for advanced women and men to live and love together in mutual passion. Clustering in inexpensive, often immigrant urban neighborhoods, most famously New York City's Greenwich Village, they innovated new lifestyles, living with men in "free unions." A handful of feminists lived openly as lesbians in partnerships with other women that clearly were sexual, in contrast to the ambiguous homosocial relationships of the past (see p. 316).

Feminists' rejection of Gilded Age middle-class notions of sexual restraint was reinforced by broader trends in the society, especially urban popular culture. The fledgling film industry often portrayed women in ways that emphasized their sexual attractiveness to men, but also their own sexual natures. In vaudeville — live entertainment that featured a variety of comedic skits, song-and-dance acts, and novelty performances — female performers, including Eva Tanguay and Gertrude Hoffmann, became immensely famous and were noted for being independent, unconventional, strong women who were paid top dollar. And like the movies, vaudeville portrayed female sexuality. The enormous popularity of the "Salome" persona, a revealingly clad woman who performed an erotically charged dance number, highlighted women who embraced their sexuality as a source of power and pleasure.

Young working-class women were eager to take advantage of new urban commercial entertainments like dance halls, skating rinks, and amusement parks. Working-class women living apart from their families congregated in "furnished-room" districts of the nation's cities, which were often associated with prostitution and vice. These areas had a freer sexual climate that allowed experimentation and extramarital cohabitation, both with men and other women. Constrained by their poor wages, many young working-class women inhabited a culture in which male suitors entertained them and bought them gifts in exchange for sexual favors. Elite urban women also began to frequent cabarets — the forerunners of today's nightclubs, where they learned syncopated dance steps in an atmosphere that suggested to some moral reformers "illicit sexuality."[19] The relative freedom of the urban environment and the attraction of popular amusements thus prompted early twentieth-century women to map out a new sexual terrain that coincided with feminists' articulation of sexuality as a crucial element of personal identity and fulfillment.

The Birth Control Movement

The most organized and politicized manifestation of cutting-edge feminism in the Progressive era was the campaign for birth control. Earlier women's rights champions had urged women to undertake pregnancy only voluntarily. Yet they regarded sexuality as fundamentally male, and they did not think it was important — or desirable — for women to have greater amounts of sexual intercourse freed of the threat of pregnancy. Emma Goldman was one of the first to speak widely on women's right to contraceptive information and methods, not only so that they could avoid unwanted pregnancy but also so that they could enjoy sexual intercourse.

In 1912, Margaret Sanger, a daughter of Irish immigrants, a trained nurse, and a Socialist, followed Goldman's lead to write and speak on behalf of women's right to control the frequency of their childbearing. She invented the term "birth control" to describe a practice that had long existed but had not been openly discussed or publicly advocated (see Reading into the Past: "Woman and Birth Control").

READING INTO THE PAST

MARGARET SANGER
Woman and Birth Control

*Margaret Sanger (1879–1966), Socialist, feminist, and birth control pio-
neer, attributed her determination to dismantle the legal and cultural
barriers keeping women from gaining access to contraceptive information
to her experience as a visiting nurse among the immigrant working class in
New York City. In this excerpt from the typescript of a draft for her speech
"Woman and Birth Control," which she gave during her 1916 American tour,
Sanger tells the story of a poor woman who died as a result of too many pregnancies and a self-induced abortion. Sanger did not blame individual men;
she understood that the doctor and the husband in her story were trapped
inside a system that regarded sexuality as a matter of morality rather than
health and disregarded women's perspectives and needs.*

This patient of mine was the wife of a struggling working man and the
mother of three children. She was suffering from the results of an attempted
abortion performed on her by herself. She lived on Grand St., the main
thoroughfare of New York['s] down-town Ghetto. I found her in a very serious condition and for three weeks both the attending physician and myself
labored night and day to bring her out of the valley of the shadow of death.
We finally succeeded in restoring her to her family circle. I remember the
day I was leaving. The doctor, too, was making his last call. As the doctor
put out his hand to say good-bye to her, I saw that she had something to
say to him, but was timid and shy about it. I started to leave the room to
leave them both alone, but she said, "No, don't go. How can both of you
leave me without telling me something that I can do to avoid a future illness
such as I have just passed through?" I was interested to hear the answer of

Indeed, by the time Sanger began her work, birthrates among native-born white
women had already fallen significantly. Sanger, like many feminists, viewed birth
control as a means to women's autonomy. As she put it, "It is none of society's business what a woman shall do with her body."[20]

Yet Sanger's socialism also led her to focus on the problems of poor women.
From her years of nursing, Sanger knew that immigrant women, without any access
to private physicians, suffered the most from the public ban on discussions of contraception. At first, Sanger did not have a reliable contraceptive technology to promote.
She concentrated instead on teaching young girls necessary reproductive and sexual
information through a series of articles titled "What Every Girl Should Know."

the physician, and came back and sat down beside her. To my amazement he answered her question lightly and jokingly, put her aside by telling her that there was nothing that she could do as long as there were laws upon the statute books, and he advised her to get her husband to change the laws.

Three months later I was aroused from my sleep at midnight. A telephone call from the husband of the same woman, requested me to come immediately, that she was dangerously ill. I arrived to find her beyond relief. Another conception had forced her into the hands of a cheap abortionist and she died at 4 o'clock the same morning, leaving behind her three little children and the frantic, helpless husband.

I arrived home as the sun was coming up from the roofs of that human beehive and I realized how futile my efforts and my work had been. I, too, like the philanthropist, the social worker and the quack had been dealing with the symptoms rather than the disease. I threw my nursing bag into the corner and announced to my family that I would never take it up again, that I would never take another case until I had made it possible for the working women in America to have the knowledge to control birth. I decided I had no moral right to respect a law, — a worn-out piece of parchment, — obsolete in every respect, I had no right to respect this above human life, and I decided to violate it wholesale.

Source: Margaret Sanger Papers, Library of Congress, LCM 129-12, reproduced online at the Margaret Sanger Papers Project, New York University, http://www.nyu.edu /projects/sanger/webedition/app/documents/show.php?sangerDoc=128002.xml.

QUESTIONS FOR ANALYSIS

1. Who do you think was the audience for Sanger's dramatic story?
2. What does she mean by the statement that she "had been dealing with the symptoms rather than the disease"?

In sending her writings through the U.S. mail, Sanger fell afoul of the Comstock anti-obscenity laws, which had been interfering with the spread of contraceptive information since the 1870s (see pp. 314–16). To avoid arrest, she fled to Europe, where a Dutch feminist doctor, Aletta Jacobs, taught her about the diaphragm (then known as a female pessary), an effective, female-controlled form of contraception. Sanger smuggled these devices into the United States and in 1916, in an immigrant neighborhood in Brooklyn, opened the first American birth control clinic. Days after the clinic opened, she was arrested for promoting birth control. After her 1917 trial and conviction, she served thirty days in jail. She remained dedicated to the cause of birth control for the next forty years, but she engineered a compromise with physicians by agreeing that diaphragms should be available only through prescription. Contraception became more respectable and more widely disseminated in the 1920s (see p. 493), but in the prewar years, like feminism itself, birth control was a radical idea that challenged conventional notions of women's sexuality and reproduction.

◆ THE GREAT WAR, 1914–1918

At the peak of the ferment of change prompted by Progressivism, suffragism, and feminism, international events dramatically altered the American political environment. In August 1914, war broke out in Europe, as a complex set of interlocking alliances pitted the Allied powers (Britain, France, and Russia) against the Central powers (Germany and Austria-Hungary). Even before the U.S. entered the war nearly three years later, the conflict had already had a significant impact on American women. Labor shortages benefited working women. African American men and women began a large-scale exodus out of the rural South into the industrial cities of the North. Most of these economic opportunities faded at war's end, but women's political achievements were more lasting. The war bolstered women's claims to enfranchisement and propelled passage and ratification of the Nineteenth Amendment.

Pacifist and Antiwar Women

In the two years that the United States watched the war from the sidelines, peace advocacy among American women was widespread. NAWSA president Carrie Chapman Catt expressed the common sentiment that "when war murders the husbands and sons of women, . . . it becomes the undeniable business of women."[21] In August 1914, women marched silently and solemnly down the streets of New York City to protest the violence of war. Five months later, suffragist and feminist Crystal Eastman organized the Woman's Peace Party (WPP). With over twenty thousand women members, the WPP was dedicated to resolving the conflict in Europe through peaceful, negotiated means.

In the spring of 1915, forty-seven WPP members joined a thousand women from twelve countries at an international peace conference of women in The Hague, Netherlands. Most were of the leisure class, but some working-class activists, such as Leonora O'Reilly, also attended. The organization they formed, the Women's International League for Peace and Freedom, still exists today. The participants vowed to meet again when the war ended. For her role in this movement, Jane Addams was awarded the Nobel Peace Prize in 1931, the first American woman so honored.

But peace was not in the offing and the United States inched closer to war. President Wilson's hopes for neutrality were literally sunk by German revival of unrestricted submarine warfare in the Atlantic, from which the United States was not spared. Wilson's position, as well as national sentiment, shifted toward entering the war. On April 6, 1917, Congress declared war on Germany and its allies.

Once the United States joined the war, women who opposed it were accused of political disloyalty, and the number and prominence of women speaking against militarism plummeted. Nonetheless, Jeannette Rankin, a suffragist from Montana and, in 1916, the first woman elected to the U.S. House of Representatives, voted against a formal declaration of war, for which she was turned out of office. Emily Balch was fired from her job as professor of economics at Wellesley College for challenging the government's right to draft young men to fight. Ida B. Wells-Barnett was threatened with jail for her efforts to defend black soldiers who had been convicted and executed for alleged insurrection in Texas. "I'd rather go down in history as one lone Negro who dared to tell the government that it had done a dastardly thing," she defiantly responded, "than to save my skin by taking back what I have said."[22]

After the 1917 Bolshevik Revolution, Russia negotiated a separate peace with Germany and left the war. This transformation of a former ally into a worker-run state intensified suspicion of American Socialists, who never recovered their prewar vitality. Kate Richards O'Hare was sentenced to five years in federal prison for voicing the same kind of sentiments against mothers' being forced to sacrifice their sons to war that had been common a few years before. Emma Goldman was imprisoned for her antidraft speeches; after the war, along with hundreds of other immigrant radicals, she was permanently deported from the United States and died in exile.

Within the suffrage movement, it was the militant wing that resisted the atmosphere of wartime jingoism. Prior to U.S. entry into the war, NWP members had begun picketing the White House — the first American activists ever to do so — to add to the pressure on President Wilson to support a federal suffrage amendment (see Figure 8.5, p. 468). Although the NWP did not formally oppose the war, it refused to halt its activities once war was declared. On the contrary, it upped the ante, carrying signs provocatively addressed to "Kaiser Wilson," declaring that "Democracy Should Begin at Home." Peaceful protest was now perceived as the act of traitors.

From 1917 through 1919, 168 suffrage picketers were arrested, and 97 served up to six months in federal prison. Considering themselves political prisoners, many went on hunger strikes and were forcibly fed through tubes pushed down their noses into their stomachs. NWP leader Alice Paul was repeatedly interrogated by a prison psychiatrist, who wanted to prove that she was mentally ill rather than deeply dedicated to the cause of woman suffrage. She defied her interrogators and insisted that her opinions were political, not paranoid.

Preparedness and Patriotism

While antiwar women and militant suffragists persisted in their protests, the majority of American women, including middle-of-the-road suffragists, threw themselves into the war effort. Wilson had described the United States' role in idealistic terms, claiming World War I as a war for democracy to spread American ideals throughout the world. Following his lead, the majority of Americans believed that their country was fighting for the ideals of peace and freedom and against autocracy. They hoped that war could be the fruition of many progressive hopes, and they were eager to help make it so. (See Primary Sources: "Uncle Sam Wants You: Women and World War I Posters," pp. 470–74.)

Activist women also viewed supporting the war as an opportunity to demonstrate not merely their patriotism but their claims to full citizenship. Carrie Chapman Catt set aside her long history of peace advocacy to lead NAWSA into active support for the war. "I am a pacifist, but not for peace without honor," she wrote in April 1917. "I'd be willing, if necessary, to die for my country."[23] Catt and others who supported the war pushed for the creation of the Women's Committee of the Council for National Defense (WCND) in 1917. Former NAWSA president Anna Howard Shaw became its head. Although the council was ostensibly advisory, the women appointed to the WCND made it a channel for delivering women's energies to the war effort.

The WCND set up state and local branches of the organization, which in turn used women's organizations such as the Young Women's Christian Association, the Woman's Christian Temperance Union, and the General Federation of Women's Clubs to mobilize women's voluntary war work. The WCND also had a subdivision for "colored women," with African American poet Alice Dunbar-Nelson as its field representative. Women labor activists served on another subcommittee, Women in Industry; this was transformed after the war into the U.S. Woman's Bureau, led by Mary Van Kleeck.

Women's prowar activities took many forms. Following the model of suffrage parades, women organized grand public marches to raise money for wartime "Liberty Bonds." They organized America's housewives to conserve meat, sugar, and wheat for the war effort. They raised relief funds for refugees in Europe.

◆ **Women's War Service and Suffrage**
Throughout World War I, NAWSA's journal, the *Woman Citizen*, published a steady stream of articles and illustrations linking American women's war service to the suffrage fight. How does this cover justify women's right to the vote? *Library of Congress.*

Several thousand women, organized by the American Red Cross, served as nurses and ambulance drivers on the battlefields of France.

Women were also active in what was called Americanization work. These were efforts to accelerate the assimilation of immigrants into American society, especially Germans, who were suspected of loyalty to America's opponents. In the Southwest, particular attention focused on Mexican immigrants, often regarded as potentially dangerous radicals because of the ongoing Mexican Revolution that began in 1910. Throughout the nation's cities, native-born women reformers taught English language, home, and health classes for immigrant women, while also instructing them in wartime food conservation measures.

The biggest contribution that women made to the war effort was through their labor. Although the United States did not enter the war until 1917, by 1915 the economy was already beginning to speed up to provision the Allies and prepare for possible American involvement. As European immigration was slowed to a halt by the naval war in the Atlantic, the accelerating needs of the labor force were met in part by white women workers. The female labor force increased to more than 10 million during the war years, and many women found new and better-paying

◆ **Japanese Women's Auxiliary to the Los Angeles Red Cross**
During World War I women actively supported mobilization by conserving food and raising funds for the Liberty Loan campaign, a major source of financing for the war. They also supported the American Red Cross, which not only sent nurses to the front but also provided warm garments and medical supplies for the troops. African Americans and immigrants, eager to express their patriotism, participated in these efforts. The women in this photograph were members of the Japanese Women's Auxiliary to the Los Angeles Red Cross, a group that took much pride in its work and its demonstration of loyalty to the United States. *Seaver Center for Western History Research, Los Angeles County Museum of Natural History.*

READING INTO THE PAST

African American Women Write about the Great Migration

Poor African Americans left behind few private papers for the historical record, so historians are fortunate to be able to turn to letters that southern migrants wrote to black newspapers like the Chicago Defender *and the* Atlanta Journal, *as well as to letters written to potential employers and friends and family back home. Women's letters reveal a variety of concerns. In the first example, a wife hopes to find out about work for her family. In the second, a woman working in Chicago in a meatpacking plant writes to her sister.*

Letter from McCoy, Louisiana, April 16, 1917

Dear Editor [of the *Chicago Defender*]: I have been takeing your wonderful paper and I have saved [each edition] from the first I have received and my heart is upset night and day. I am praying every day to see some one that I may get a pass [a free railway ticket] for me, my child and husband I have a daughter 17 who can work well and myself. please sir direct me to the place where I may be able to see the parties that I and my family whom have read the defender so much until they are anxious to come dear editor we are working people but we cant hardly live here I would say more but we are back in the jungles and we have to lie low but please sir answer and I pray you give me a homeward consolation as we haven't money enough to pay our fares.

Letter from Chicago, Illinois [undated]

My dear Sister: I was agreeably surprised to hear from you and to hear from home. I am well and thankful to say I am doing well. The weather and everything else was a surprise to me when I came. I got here in time to attend one of the greatest revivals in the history of my life — over 500 people joined the church. We had a Holy Ghost shower. You know I like

opportunities in the railroad, steel, and other heavy industries. Harriot Stanton Blatch characterized the situation with brutal honesty: "When men go awarring, women go to work. War compels women to work. That is one of its merits."[24]

The Great Migration

World War I was an especially monumental turning point for African Americans, women and men alike. Many seized the opportunity provided by the demand for wartime labor to flee southern segregation and exploitation and head north.

to have run wild. It was snowing some nights and if you didnt hurry you could not get standing room. Please remember me kindly to any who ask of me. The people are rushing here by the thousands and I know if you come and rent a big house you can get all the roomers you want. You write me exactly when you are coming. I am not keeping house yet I am living with my brother and his wife. My son is in California but will be home soon. He spends his winter in California. I can get a nice place for you to stop until you can look around and see what you want. I am quite busy. I work in Swifts packing Co. in the sausage department. My daughter and I work for the same company — We get $1.50 a day and we pack so many sausages we dont have much time to play but it is a matter of a dollar with me and I feel that God made the path and I am walking therein.

Tell your husband work is plentiful here and he wont have to loaf if he want to work. . . . Well goodbye from your sister in Christ.

P.S. My brother moved the week after I came. When you fully decide to come write me and let me know what day you expect to leave and over what road and if I dont meet you I will have some one ther to meet you and look after you. I will send you a paper as soon as one come along they send out extras two and three times a day.

SOURCE: *Journal of Negro History* 4 (October 1919): 426, 457–58.

QUESTIONS FOR ANALYSIS

1. In the first letter, why might the writer be unwilling to "say more" about conditions in the South? Would a franker letter refer to the sexual assault so many black women experienced?

2. Do you think the second letter would encourage the writer's sister to make the trip north? Why or why not?

Two to three times as many southern blacks, perhaps five hundred thousand, migrated in the decade after 1910 as in the decade before. Chicago's black population increased by 150 percent, Detroit's by 600 percent, and New York City's by 66 percent. This profound shift in population between 1914 and 1920, from the South to the North and from rural to urban life, is known as the Great Migration.

Unlike European and Asian migrations, in which men represented the vast majority, women constituted almost half the number of African American migrants. Their reasons for migrating were in part economic. For the first time, African American women, who had been almost exclusively employed in domestic and agricultural labor, entered factory work, although usually in the dirtiest and most dangerous jobs and only for the brief period of wartime mobilization. "I'll never work in nobody's kitchen but my own anymore," one black woman optimistically declared.[25] Even in domestic labor, a woman could earn more in a day up North than in a week in the South. Going north also meant escaping the constant threat of sexual harassment to which black women were exposed in the white homes in which black women worked, and with it the lynching that loomed for any black man who tried to protect his wife or daughters (see Reading into the Past: "African American Women Write about the Great Migration").

The new migrants needed aid in finding jobs and housing and adjusting to northern urban life. The NACW acted quickly to lift the burden, establishing a Women Wage Earners Association to assist migrating black women workers. The Young Women's Christian Association (YWCA) also responded by increasing the funding of its Division of Colored Work, designating $200,000 for work with young women in African American communities, and tripling the number of independent black branches. In 1919, the Women's Trade Union League, which had heretofore ignored the needs of African Americans, hired Irene Goins of Chicago as a special organizer for black women workers.

For the most part, however, black migrants met hostility in the North. In 1915, *Birth of a Nation*, one of the first great epics of the American film industry, presented a thoroughly racist account of the Civil War and Reconstruction, including a defense of lynching, to packed houses of white filmgoers across the United States. During and after the war, pent-up racial antagonism exploded in a series of race riots. In 1917, Ida B. Wells-Barnett risked her life to go to East St. Louis, Illinois, to investigate the 150 black people who were, in her words, "slaughtered" in a riot there (see pp. 455–57 and 468). In 1919, another deadly riot erupted in her hometown of Chicago, after a white mob killed an African American child who had wandered onto a whites-only beach. But despite the violence and disappointment African Americans faced in the North, migration offered black women and their families improved economic opportunities and an escape from the dead-end life of the South.

Winning Woman Suffrage

The United States entered World War I just as momentum for woman suffrage was peaking. Militant suffragists of the NWP demonstrated daily outside the White House, while the NAWSA, under Carrie Chapman Catt's leadership, steadily lobbied Congress. The victory of woman suffrage in a second New York referendum in 1917 boosted prospects for national victory. Catt had predicted that once New York women were enfranchised, the state's congressional delegation, the largest in the country, would swing over to woman suffrage and "the backbone of the opposition will be largely bent if not broken."[26] She was right. Two months after woman suffrage won in New York, the House of Representatives passed a constitutional amendment establishing full voting rights for all American women. The NWP named it the Susan B. Anthony Amendment to signify the long battle that had to be fought to win it.

◆ **African American Women at a Baby Clinic in Detroit**
When African Americans migrated to cities of the North, they often found the process of adjustment difficult. Few cities offered many social services to their black citizens, and black organizations like the National Association of Colored Women and the Urban League intervened to assist new migrants with housing, employment, and charity. While middle-class blacks were often condescending to the new migrants, whom they viewed as uncultivated, they offered vital services. In Detroit, the Urban League worked with other agencies to create a Baby Clinic, which offered advice on child care and child health and limited medical services. This 1919 photograph depicts the women clients and their children. *Detroit Urban League records, Box 87, Bentley Historical Library, University of Michigan.*

From the House, the Anthony Amendment went to the Senate, where it confronted the power and resistance of southern Democrats. With the Fourteenth and Fifteenth Amendments still rankling (see p. 292), southern Democrats were opposed to any further federal involvement in voting rights. President Wilson, who was himself a southern Democrat, finally yielded to pressure from suffragists, and went to the Senate to appeal for passage. "We have made partners of women in this war," he pleaded. "Shall we admit them only to a partnership of suffering and sacrifice and toil and not to a partnership of privilege and right?" Nonetheless, when the Senate voted in October 1918, the amendment fell two votes short of passage.

That same month, the war ended in victory for the Allies. Wilson left for Paris to negotiate the peace and fight for the establishment of a "league of nations," a multinational organization to achieve, in his words, "mutual guarantees of political independence and territorial integrity to great and small states alike."[27] A small army of American women activists went with him in hopes of influencing the outcome of the peace conference. Many of these American women then traveled to Zurich to fulfill the promise they had made in The Hague in 1915 to reconvene the international women's peace movement after the war. When Wilson returned to the United States with the Versailles Treaty, which included establishment of the League of Nations among its provisions, he was unable to convince a skeptical Congress to ratify it, a defeat that literally destroyed him. In October 1919, he suffered a disabling stroke, and for the last year of his presidency, First Lady Edith Bolling Galt Wilson took on many of the tasks of her husband's office (and was widely maligned for overstepping her bounds).

Through all this, suffragists still had to find the support they needed in Congress and the nation for the Susan B. Anthony Amendment. Finally, in June 1919, they secured exactly the necessary two-thirds of Congress members to vote for the amendment and the measure went on to the states for ratification. NAWSA's structure of strong state divisions was crucial in winning endorsement from the necessary thirty-six states. Of these, the only southern states were Texas, Kentucky, Arkansas, Missouri, and Tennessee. The final battle came down to Tennessee, one of the only southern states with a viable two-party system. The decisive vote came from a young Republican legislator named Harry Burn, in response to his mother's urging. "Don't forget to be a good boy," she wrote him, "and help Mrs. Catt put the 'Rat' in Ratification."[28]

On August 26, 1920, seventy-two years after the Seneca Falls Convention, the Nineteenth Amendment was added to the U.S. Constitution. Patterned after the Fifteenth Amendment, it reads, "The right of citizens of the United States to vote shall not be denied or abridged by the United States or by any State on account of sex." But American women's struggles for political equality were not yet complete. The courts ruled that the amendment did not affect the political status of women in the American colonies of Puerto Rico and the Philippines, which had to undertake their own campaigns — lasting eight and sixteen years, respectively — for voting rights. Most African American women in the South found that when they tried to register to vote, they were stopped by the same devices used against black men. And for all American women, the battle for parity and power within political parties had just begun. It would take another seven decades for voting women to become a force to be reckoned with in American politics.

◆ CONCLUSION: New Conditions, New Challenges

The gradual move of American women into public life that had begun in the middle of the nineteenth century reached its apex in the first decades of the twentieth. In few other periods of American history did women achieve greater public visibility and political influence. The inclusion of women's equal political rights in the

U.S. Constitution, after almost three-quarters of a century of effort, crowned a host of women's other achievements in the Progressive era.

By the same token, crucial changes were taking place just under the surface. Not only were the numbers of female workers continuing to rise but the place of paid labor in women's lives was shifting dramatically. Women had entered the Progressive era under the banner of motherhood; they were leaving it, unbeknownst to many of them, under the banner of worker. The sexual revolution and the birth control movement of these years also signified grand changes to come in women's lives. All of these developments would play out in the next decades as women faced different sorts of challenges and began to envision new collective goals.

CHAPTER 8 REVIEW

KEY TERMS AND PEOPLE

Terms
American Federation of Labor (AFL)
Women's Trade Union League
shirtwaist strike of 1909
Triangle Shirtwaist Company fire
National Consumers' League (NCL)
maternalism
Nineteenth Amendment
Muller v. Oregon
Children's Bureau
National Association of Colored Women (NACW)

National American Woman Suffrage Association (NAWSA)
Wage Earners Suffrage League
College Equal Suffrage League
National Woman's Party (NWP)
Woman's Peace Party (WPP)
Young Women's Christian Association (YWCA)
Great Migration

People
Inez Milholland
Rose Schneiderman
Elizabeth Gurley Flynn

Mary Beard
Jane Addams
Mary Church Terrell
Ida B. Wells-Barnett
Madam C. J. Walker
Carrie Chapman Catt
Anna Howard Shaw
Alice Paul
Lucy Burns
Charlotte Perkins Gilman
Margaret Sanger
Crystal Eastman
Nannie Burroughs

REVIEW QUESTIONS

1. What were the sources of working women's labor activism?
2. Page 419 states that "[W]omen filled the progressive landscape." How and why did women shape the Progressive movement? What is the significance of the terms "female dominion of reform" and "maternalism"? How do the two terms differ?
3. How do you explain the final success of the long drive to enfranchise women?

4. What were the main differences between the emerging feminist movement and the suffrage movement?
5. How would you characterize the impact of World War I on American women?
6. **Making Connections** Women's activism in this era embraced a wide range of issues and engaged a diverse group of women. What issues and experiences united women? What divided them?

PRIMARY SOURCES

Black Women and Progressive-Era Reform

Black women were largely excluded from the extensive female reform network of the white women reformers who shaped the social justice wing of the Progressive movement, but they, too, avidly supported reforms in their communities, working especially through the National Association of Colored Women (NACW), founded in 1895 (see Chapter 6). At the same time, many African American women leaders were increasingly outspoken about civil rights and racial violence in the early twentieth century and became ardent champions of woman suffrage. African American activism during and after World War I also played a part in encouraging black women to engage in international issues, including colonialism and the peace movement. All told, the early twentieth century witnessed a blossoming of black women's activism over a wide range of issues.

BLACK WOMEN'S CLUB LIFE

The NACW flourished in the early 1910s, and by 1914 there were more than a thousand clubs and membership totaled fifty thousand. These clubs focused on racial uplift by providing an array of social services for black communities. They created kindergartens and mothers' clubs, old-age homes and neighborhood clinics, job-training programs and black branches of the segregated YWCA. Among the most notable organizations was the Atlanta Neighborhood Union, a community agency that tackled a wide range of problems and created settlement houses. The driving force behind the Union, Lugenia Burns Hope, was a prominent black leader in Atlanta whose husband was president of Morehouse College. Hope had consulted with Jane Addams about settlement work in organizing the Atlanta agency, whose motto was "And Thy Neighbor as Thyself."[29] Hope wrote the document excerpted here, which included a summary of the Union's accomplishments. It is undated but probably dates close to the Union's founding in 1908. Why do you think the range of the Union's activities was so great? What concerns seemed to be the most important to the Atlanta women, and what tactics did they use to achieve their goals?

LUGENIA BURNS HOPE
The Neighborhood Union: Atlanta, Georgia (c. 1908)

An Organization for the Moral, Economic and Social Advancement of Negroes

The Neighborhood Union is an outgrowth of an organized effort of a number of Negro women to improve the social conditions of the city — particularly of their neighborhood.

. . . .

1. A playground has been provided for children.

2. Fourth of July Carnivals have been held for the amusement of the children, several hundred boys and girls being annually reached.

3. Clubs have been conducted for the physical and social improvement of children.

4. Domestic science classes have been conducted.

5. Many helpful lectures have been delivered to mothers of children.

6. The services of four trained nurses have been secured for those who are not able to pay for treatment.

7. Dives of immorality have been broken up.

8. Needy families have been given aid, some cases being turned over to the Associated Charities.

9. The people have been urged to keep their back yards and store premises sanitary.

10. Lights have been secured and holes and other defects in streets have been remedied through the effort of the organization.

11. Investigations have been made to aid other organizations in improving their work.

12. Children placed in homes, orphan asylums, and reformatories.

13. The use of the public school buildings has been obtained and recreation schools conducted in them during the vacation.

14. A settlement house has been purchased in Lee Street.

15. Five neighborhoods are now organized in Atlanta.

Immediate Purposes

The Neighborhood Union proposes to organize neighborhoods in each section of the city as speedily as possible. It is our desire to have a settlement house in each neighborhood where the people can gather for their meetings, clubs and classes and feel that it is their very own. Then the work outlined above can be done more systematically and effectively. You can help us to aid you by cooperating with us and calling our attention to the need of clubs and organizations in your particular community.

SOURCE: Gerder Lerner, ed., *Black Women in White America: A Documentary History* (Vintage Books: New York, 1973), 502–3.

PROTESTING RACIAL DISCRIMINATION AND VIOLENCE

IN THE EARLY TWENTIETH CENTURY, African American leaders, male and female, divided over promoting education and self-help versus challenging segregation and disfranchisement. Embodying the new approach, the National Association for the Advancement of Colored People was established in 1909 as a mixed-race organization committed to black civil rights. A number of black women were founding members, including Ida B. Wells-Barnett, Mary Talbert, Mary Church Terrell, and Maria Baldwin. Although black women and the NACW were divided over the wisdom of civil rights activism, leaders in the North and

Midwest were particularly active in organizing units of the NAACP. Although less militant, the NACW also paid attention to civil rights: in 1912 it passed resolutions against segregation in train travel and lynching.[30]

As the resolution against lynching suggests, African American women in the Progressive era also focused on racial violence, which was evident in both the rise in lynchings and the proliferation of race riots in the nation's cities (eighteen riots occurred between 1915 and 1919).

One of the worst of the riots took place in East St. Louis, Illinois, an industrial city home to a substantial number of African American migrants in this era. Convinced that blacks were economic competitors, a number of whites invaded the black section of town over several days in July 1917 and went on a rampage resulting in at least thirty-nine black and eight white deaths. African Americans throughout the nation were outraged, and women lent their voices to the protest. They shared in planning the silent protest march in New York City (see Figure 8.6, p. 469), as well as organizing prayer meetings in many cities and towns. Ida B. Wells-Barnett, in keeping with her long-standing campaign against racial violence, visited East St. Louis twice and led a delegation to Illinois governor Frank Orren Lowden to insist upon redress. She published a pamphlet, "The East St. Louis Massacre: The Greatest Outrage of the Century," which detailed the causes and nature of the riot and concluded with a call for action. An excerpt from this pamphlet appears below. What solutions does she suggest? Why does Wells-Barnett conclude that federal legislation is the only solution?

IDA B. WELLS-BARNETT
The East St. Louis Massacre: The Greatest Outrage of the Century (1917)

Gov. Lowden need not go far to find evidence of the utter failure of the major part of the forces of the Illinois National Guard to do their duty in stopping wholesale murder and arson in East St. Louis last Monday.

Carlos Hurd of the Post-Dispatch staff, who was an eyewitness of the atrocities on the East Side, told a plain circumstantial story of the outrages he witnessed. The assaults and murders were cold-blooded, deliberate and incredibly brutal. They were not the mob infuriated against particular offenders. They were the work of groups of men and women who sought out and burned out the Negroes and then shot, beat, kicked and hanged them. The work was done in a spirit of flippant, relentless barbarism. Mr. Hurd described it as a man-hunt.

Others who corroborated this testimony called it rabbit-hunting and rat-catching. Nothing like it in unmitigated cruelty has occurred before on American soil. It can be likened only to the fiendish atrocities of Turks in Armenia or the pogroms against the Jews incited by the Russian Black Hundred, in which helpless Jews were smoked or dragged from their homes to be beaten, outraged or murdered on the streets. The black skin, without regard to age, sex or innocence, was the mark for slaughter.

SOURCE: Ida B. Wells-Barnett, *The East St. Louis Massacre: The Greatest Outrage of the Century* (Chicago: The Negro Fellowship Herald Press, 1917).

All the impartial witnesses agree that the police were either indifferent or encouraged the barbarities, and that the major part of the National Guard was indifferent or inactive. No organized effort was made to protect the Negroes or disperse the murdering groups. The lack of frenzy and of a large infuriated mob made the task easy. Ten determined officers could have prevented most of the outrages. One hundred men acting with authority and vigor might have prevented any outrage.

The stain cannot be wiped from the record of Illinois, but the State may be vindicated by punishment of the officers responsible for the conduct of the guardsmen; and by the vigorous prosecution of the murder leaders. . . .

In the present state of our National development, the only remedy for the lynching and rioting evil of the American nation is to make it a federal crime. Public sentiment which has encouraged lynchings by silence or by sensational newspaper accounts must be aroused to see the evil to the whole American Nation. It is an awful commentary on our country's brand of Democracy — that aside from a few newspaper editorials — no persons in this country have spoken out against this black stain save Theodore Roosevelt and a minister of the gospel in a sermon preached in St. Louis, Mo., the Sunday following the massacre.

It rests then with the Negroes everywhere to stand their ground and sell their lives as dearly as possible when attacked; to work as a unit, demanding punishment for rioters; protection for workers, and liberty for all the citizens in our country. It is for the Negro to say whether they will unite their forces to make this country safe for the residence of any Negro anywhere he desires to live in it. It is for them to show whether we can bring sufficient influence to bear to see that the militia of Illinois, for whose wanton murder of hundreds of innocent men, women and children of our race, whom they failed to protect in that awful orgy of human butchery, which took place in East St. Louis, Illinois, on Monday, July 2nd, 1917.

NEGRO WOMEN HOLD HUMILIATION SERVICE

Sᴛᴀʀᴛɪɴɢ ᴡɪᴛʜ Wᴇʟʟs-Barnett's ᴇxᴘᴏsᴇ́ of lynching (see Primary Sources: "Ida B. Wells, 'Race Woman'," pp. 325–29), African American women had understood this ritualized form of murder as a way of keeping black men and women subordinated. Picking up on the spirit of black protest against discrimination and violence in the 1910s, a group of African American women in Savannah spoke out about a particularly brutal lynching of eleven African Americans, including Mary Turner. When Turner, eight months pregnant, protested the murder of her husband, who was accused of killing a white man, the mob seized her as well, brutally murdering her and her unborn child. Black women in Augusta, Georgia, called on women of their city and state "to unite in a service of humiliation and prayer as a protection against the awful lynchings that recently disgraced our state, especially that of Mary Turner." By drawing upon the Protestant tradition calling the nation to humble itself before God's judgment, the clubwomen seemed to be challenging the whites of the city to consider the morality and possible judgment of their actions by speaking a common Protestant language. Instead of meeting at a church, however, the women, who had just created a federation of City Colored Women's Clubs, chose to convene at the black branch of the American Red Cross, which in itself suggests their determination to frame themselves as loyal citizens serving the nation. After their prayer service, the women passed resolutions that they sent to President Woodrow Wilson, Governor Hugh Dorsey, and the presidents of the state and local white women's club federations. These resolutions were published in the *Savannah Tribune* under the title "Negro Women Hold Humiliation Service." On what basis do the Augusta women claim a special right to protest the killing of Mary Turner?

CITY COLORED WOMEN'S CLUBS OF AUGUSTA, GEORGIA
Resolution on Lynching (1918)

Whereas, the Negro Womanhood of Georgia has been shocked by the lynching of Mary Turner at Valdosta Sunday May 19, 1918, for an alleged unwise remark in reference to the lynching of her husband; and

Whereas, we the Negro women of the state are aroused by this unwarranted lawlessness and are discouraged and crushed by a spirit of humiliation and dread; and

Whereas, we deplore the migratory movement of the Negro from the South, yet we cannot counsel them to remain in the light of these conditions under which we live; and

Whereas, our labor is in these cotton and corn fields and rice swamps, and in this frightful hour of the great world war, our sons and husbands are giving their lives in defense of the country we all love so dearly; and

Whereas, in every forward movement in our national life the Negro has come to the front and shared in the advance and crimsoned every field of strife from Boston to "no man's land," for the principles held sacred by every true American; and

Whereas, we feel that our lives are unsafe as long as this iniquitous institution exists:

We therefore are asking that you use all the power of your great office to prevent similar occurrences and punish the perpetrators of this foul deed and urge that sure and swift justice be meted out to them.

SOURCE: "Negro Women Hold Humiliation Service," *Savannah Tribune*, June 8, 1918, Genealogy Bank, http://www.genealogybank.com/gbnk (accessed September 29, 2014).

BLACK WOMEN AND THE SUFFRAGE

WHILE LARGELY EXCLUDED FROM white women's suffrage groups, African American women reformers were ardent supporters of woman suffrage and created their own societies. Among the first was Chicago's Alpha Suffrage Club, led by Ida B. Wells-Barnett. Nannie Burroughs (1879–1961) was another outspoken supporter of enfranchising women. Burroughs, whose mother was an emancipated slave, was one of the founders of the Woman's Convention of the National Baptist Convention, an important reform locale for southern black women. Burroughs argued for woman suffrage in this article in *The Crisis*, the magazine of the recently formed National Association for the Advancement of Colored People. In what way were the arguments that Burroughs made different from those of white suffragists?

Nannie Burroughs
Black Women and the Suffrage (1915)

When the ballot is put in the hands of the American woman, the world is going to get a correct estimate of the Negro woman. It will find her a tower of strength of which poets have never sung, orators have never spoken, and scholars have never written.

Because the black man does not know the value of the ballot, and has bartered and sold his most valuable possession, it is no evidence that the Negro woman will do the same. The Negro woman therefore needs the ballot to get back, by the wise use of it, what the Negro man has lost by the misuse of it. She needs to ransom her race. . . . She carries the burdens of the Church and of the school and bears a great deal more than her economic share in the home.

Another striking fact is that the Negro woman carries the moral destiny of two races in her hand. Had she not been the woman of unusual moral stamina that she is, the black race would have been made a great deal whiter, and the white race a great deal blacker during the past fifty years. She has been left a prey for the men of every race, but in spite of this, she has held the enemies of Negro female chastity at bay. The Negro woman is the white woman's as well as the white race's most needed ally in preserving an unmixed race.

The ballot, wisely used, will bring to her the respect and protection she needs. It is her weapon of moral defense. Under present conditions, when she appears in court in defense of her virtue, she is looked upon with amused contempt. She needs the ballot to reckon with men who place no value upon her virtue, and to mould healthy public sentiment in favor of her own protection.

SOURCE: Nannie Helen Burroughs, "Black Women and Reform," *Crisis*, August 1915.

INTERNATIONAL PEACE MOVEMENT

Mary Church Terrell, an Oberlin College graduate, was a prominent African American activist who campaigned for woman suffrage and against racial discrimination. She was the first president of the NACW and a charter member of the NAACP. She was the only woman of color in the American delegation to the 1904 Berlin International Congress of Women. After World War I, a number of African American women, including Terrell, Burroughs, Margaret Murray Washington, and Addie Hunton, created the International Council of Women of the Darker Races of the World, to encourage "women in their local communities to learn more about international issues and hence see their day-to-day struggles in a larger global context," thus explicitly including European colonialism in her crusade.[31] Black women were also active in the peace movement. At the end of World War I, Terrell was invited to join the American delegates, including Jane Addams, at a women's international peace conference in Zurich. Here a new international organization, the Women's International League for Peace and Freedom, was formed.

In the following excerpt from her 1940 autobiography, A *Colored Woman in a White World*, Terrell recalls her satisfaction at being asked to speak before the conference, as well as her frustration with some of her sister delegates who criticized her proposal of a broad antiracist resolution. In what ways did her participation in this venue allow her to recast her understanding of racial injustice in a more international light?

MARY CHURCH TERRELL
A Colored Woman in a White World (1940)

Attending this Congress was as interesting, as illuminating and as gratifying an experience as it falls to the lot of the average woman to enjoy. In the first place, we were a group of women meeting to advocate peace after a war in which the major portion of the civilized world had engaged. I was about to say that women from all over the world were present. But on sober, second thought it is more truthful to say that women from all over the white world were present. There was not a single delegate from Japan, China, India or from any other country whose inhabitants were not white. For the second time in my life it was my privilege to represent, not only the colored women of the United States, but the whole continent of Africa as well, since I was the only one present at that meeting who had a drop of African blood in her veins. In fact, since I was the only delegate who gave any color to the occasion at all, it finally dawned upon me that I was representing the women of all the non-white countries in the world.

On the third day of the Congress Miss Addams called me to her and told me that the American delegates had voted unanimously to have me represent them the next night, Thursday.

[*In the meantime, Terrell learned that her resolution was to be presented at the meeting on Thursday morning, and she recalled the conflict within the delegation over its content.*]

I had written, rewritten and then done it all over again many times on the steamer [boat], before it was acceptable to the whole delegation. [I intended to protest] . . . against the discriminations, humiliations and injustices perpetrated, not only upon the colored people of the United States, but upon the dark races all over the world. Several members of the delegation objected to [my resolution] and thought they could improve upon it, but none of them expressed exactly the thought which I wished to convey. It was finally agreed to let me present the following resolution to the Congress: "We believe no human being should be deprived of an education, prevented from earning a living, debarred from any legitimate pursuit in which he wishes to engage or be subjected to humiliations of various kinds on account of race, color or creed."

It was a proud and gratifying moment in my life when I read that resolution in person in Zürich, Switzerland, to the Women's International Congress for Peace and Freedom. The only delegate who represented the dark races of the world had a chance to speak in their behalf.

I delivered my address that same night. . . . [I]n the first place, I thanked the broad-minded white women of the United States for inviting me to the Congress, making it possible for me to come and for giving me the opportunity to speak. In dealing with less favored groups, I said,

SOURCE: Mary Church Terrell, *A Colored Woman in a White World* (Washington, DC: Ransdell, 1940), 332–36, http:// 0-solomon.bltc.alexanderstreet.com.oasys.lib.oxy.edu /cgi-bin/asp/philo/bltc/getdoc.pl?S8294-D034.

if people everywhere had been imbued with the same breadth which they had displayed in this instance, race problems and a few others would long ago have disappeared from the world. It was my duty and my pleasure to state, I declared, that ever since slavery had been abolished in the United States, thousands of white people had helped with money and by personal efforts both to educate the emancipated slaves and their descendants and to lift them to a higher plane.

Then I reviewed the marvelous progress which the group [African Americans] had made along all lines of human endeavor in spite of the almost insurmountable obstacles in certain sections, referred to the fearful injustices of which we are often the victims and reminded my audience that the thousands of colored soldiers who had crossed the sea "to make the world safe for democracy" had fought in Europe for a freedom for others which in some sections of their own country they themselves did not enjoy.

I appealed for justice and fair play for all the dark races of the earth. "You may talk about permanent peace till doomsday," I predicted, "but the world will never have it till the dark races are given a square deal." I expressed regret also that at the Peace Conference in Paris "the two most highly civilized and the most Christian nations" in the world had denied racial equality to Japan which she had a right to demand. It was a great opportunity to enlighten the people of Europe on conditions confronting colored people in the United States and I tried to avail myself of it as best I could.

For once in my life I was satisfied with my effort.

QUESTIONS FOR ANALYSIS

1. What tactics did black women use to promote social reform and social justice?

2. Two of the documents, the pamphlet on the East St. Louis massacre and the resolution on lynching, are about racial violence. How are they different? How do you account for the difference?

3. Whether the topic was racial violence, community reform, suffrage, or the peace movement, many of the same national black women leaders' names emerge as advocates. Why might black activists have seen these issues as integral components of black rights as a whole?

PRIMARY SOURCES

Parades, Picketing, and Power:
Women in Public Space

Although American women were never as tightly restricted to the private sphere of the home as nineteenth-century cultural prescriptions suggested, by the turn of the century, women's presence in the public arena had notably expanded. Working-class women had jobs in factories, shops, and offices and filled crowded city streets. They frequented dance halls and amusement parks. Leisure-class women shopped in department stores, attended college, and participated in reform activities. In this essay, we analyze women's increased public visibility by examining the ways in which diverse groups of women took to the streets to march and picket, literally opening up new spaces for women in the society. Whether they were agitating for economic rights, the vote, or racial justice, their public visibility had political and cultural significance. The bold occupation of public space was an important demonstration of women's legitimacy as political actors.

THE STRIKERS

Women laborers had participated in strikes and public demonstrations as early as the 1830s, when the mill girls of Lowell, Massachusetts, "turned out" in response to lowered wages (see pp. 171–73). Nonetheless, when New York City women shirt-waist workers began picketing in front of their factories in 1909, many observers found their behavior shocking. These mostly young Jewish and Italian women were not only challenging their employers but transgressing against conventional notions of appropriate feminine behavior. When the demonstrations expanded to a general strike of the entire industry and the leisure-class women of the Women's Trade Union League (WTUL) became involved, the newspaper coverage became more sympathetic. From this point on, the events of the strike were widely reported in the popular press. The women made good copy, and their leaders eagerly sought publicity for the cause.

By 1909, newspapers had the technology to illustrate their stories with photographs. Given the limitations of that technology, these pictures were usually posed and static; the dramatic moments captured on film that would become the hallmark of modern photojournalism were a thing of the future. The hybrid illustration in Figure 8.1 appeared in the *New York Evening Journal* on November 10, 1909. The photograph shows, as the newspaper caption puts it, "Girl Strikers: each of

◆ Figure 8.1 "Girl Strikers," *New York Evening Journal* (November 10, 1909)

whom has been arrested five times for picketing." This somewhat formal picture is coupled with a drawing showing the action of police arresting the resisting women.

The photograph reveals something widely commented on in the newspaper reports. The women look fashionably dressed and, in particular, sport elaborate hats. People hostile to the strikers pointed to their clothing as evidence that the women were not suffering from dire poverty. Male union leaders and WTUL officials retorted that the clothes were cheap and bought through scrimping and going without food. Clara Lemlich was the only working woman to respond in the newspapers: "We're human, all of us girls, and we're young. We like new hats as well as any other young women. Why shouldn't we?"[32] Where critics of the strikers saw women dressed above their station, behaving in unladylike ways on the public streets, the strikers saw themselves as attractive, modern young women, willing to fight for their rights and a decent standard of living, dressed in their best to reflect the seriousness of their purpose and action.[33] Compare the photograph with the drawing. What response to the strikers did the newspaper editors seek to encourage by publishing this hybrid image?

The shirtwaist strike sparked dozens of garment industry strikes in other cities. Figure 8.2 portrays members of the Rochester, New York, branch of the Garment Workers Union as they picketed in the winter of 1912 for a cut in hours (but not pay), an end to subcontracting, and the union's right to represent the workers in negotiations with their employers. After four months—and the death of one seventeen-year-old striker shot by an excited employer—the workers won all their demands except union recognition. This image, in which the strikers are the only women in sight, suggests something of the transgressive meaning of women marching on picket lines. During the 1909 New York City shirtwaist strike, the

◆ **Figure 8.2 Members of the Rochester, New York, Branch of the Garment Workers Union (1913)**
From the Albert R. Stone Negative Collection, Rochester Museum & Science Center, Rochester, New York.

police conducted raids on brothels in the factory neighborhoods, pushing prostitutes into the street to mingle with the picketers. This effort to call into question the sexual respectability of union women proved a theme in many strikes. But note how the Rochester women posed themselves for this photograph. What attitude do they project about their right to take to the streets?

THE SUFFRAGISTS

For leisure-class suffragists to move into public space with their demonstrations was also difficult but for different reasons, as they were bound by standards of domestic propriety. The reputation for "respectability" that was key to their difference from the working class seemed endangered by such bold, forthright public activity. Precisely because public parades and demonstrations were such a radical move for leisure-class women, these events drew enormous crowds eager to see a mass violation of ladylike norms.

As the suffrage movement gathered steam in the early twentieth century, activists developed new promotional tactics and turned to the most advanced cultural methods and artistic styles, anything to get over the old-fashioned image from which their cause suffered. In their search to garner publicity and support, they appropriated public spaces and used novel techniques. They turned up on tugboats and in touring cars, appeared in department store windows and movie theaters, had bonfires and dramatic pageants. In Seattle, Lucy Burns even distributed leaflets from a hot-air balloon.

Perhaps the most dramatic innovation designed to provide entertainment and spectacle was the suffrage parade. New York City, home to one of the largest and most well-funded suffrage movements, also featured the most impressive parades. The 1910 and 1911 parades, held right after the settlement of the shirtwaist strike and the deadly Triangle Shirtwaist Company fire, respectively, were specifically inspired by the public demonstrations of working women, which leisure-class allies had supported. In the 1911 suffrage march, labor organizer Leonora O'Reilly was a featured speaker. Banners highlighted both political and economic rights, and working girls were prominent in the ranks of the paraders. Harriot Stanton Blatch, chief organizer of the marches, understood the symbolic and dramatic possibilities of suffrage parades: "What could be more stirring than hundreds of women, carrying banners, marching — marching — marching! The public would be aroused, the press would spread the story far and wide, and the interest of our own workers would be fired."[34]

In 1912 and 1913, the New York City parades were many times more spectacular, no longer foregrounding working women but instead emphasizing the participation of women of all classes (though not always of all races), cooperating for the common cause of woman suffrage. Male supporters also marched. A bill authorizing a referendum to grant full voting rights to the women of New York was before the state legislature, and the parade was intended to impress voters and legislators alike with suffragists' determination and power. As Figure 8.3 indicates, the crowds watching the 1913 parade on Fifth Avenue were ten and twelve deep. How do the dress and organization of the marchers emphasize their unanimity and discipline?

The most significant and highly publicized suffrage parade was held in Washington, D.C., in March 1913. This was not only the first suffrage parade to represent the movement on a national level but also one of the first such demonstrations held in the nation's capital on any issue. Extremely well organized by the young Alice Paul, just beginning her career as the leader of suffragism's militant wing (see pp. 437–39), the parade drew five thousand women from around the country. Banners identified some groups of marchers by their professions, from factory worker to lawyer. Other participants walked with women's clubs. Still others rode on floats that depicted women in roles of mother, worker, and citizen. Washington, D.C., was a southern city, and organizers required African American women to march at the back of the parade. The parade culminated at the steps of the U.S. Treasury building, where marchers enacted an allegorical pageant, with individual women performing the roles of America, Peace, Liberty, Hope, Justice, and Charity.[35] The *Washington Post* headline read: "Miles of Fluttering Femininity Present Entrancing Suffrage Appeal."[36] Although condescending, the newspaper's words vindicated the organizers' hopes that the attractiveness of the parade and its participants proved that suffrage and femininity were compatible.

◆ **Figure 8.3 Suffragists Marching down Fifth Avenue, New York City (1913)**
The New York Public Library/Art Resource, NY.

The photograph in Figure 8.4 captures women on a float at the parade, with the national capitol in the backdrop. Although Washington, D.C., officials tried to locate the march at a less central site, Paul was adamant that it take place on Pennsylvania Avenue, in the customary place for official parades, and on the day before the presidential inauguration of Woodrow Wilson. Despite the presence of mounted policemen, women marchers were physically attacked.

Ironically, the parade's greatest contribution to the suffrage cause may have been its disruption by enormous crowds of drunken men, the kind who always showed up for a presidential inauguration. The *Baltimore American* reported that the women "practically fought their way foot by foot up Pennsylvania Avenue through a surging throng."[37] Newspapers all over the country criticized not just the rowdy crowds but the police for failing to protect the marchers. The debacle led to a congressional hearing, which the suffragists skillfully exploited to generate favorable publicity for their cause. Anna Howard Shaw, former president of the National American Woman Suffrage Association, who generally disapproved of radical tactics, knew how to make the most of the episode: "Do you suppose that if we were voters the police would have allowed the hoodlums to possess the streets while we marched?"[38] In what ways does this photograph

◆ **Figure 8.4** **Suffrage Parade down Pennsylvania Avenue, Washington, D.C. (March 1913)**
Courtesy of the Sewall-Belmont House & Museum, Washington, DC.

indicate the contested quality of the suffragists' occupation of this political public space?

In Figure 8.5, taken in 1917, women's claim to public space for political ends comes full circle, back to picketing. It shows the suffrage militants of the National Woman's Party, spearheaded by Alice Paul, picketing the White House during World War I. College graduates, they identified themselves by their alma maters. Just as the working-class women illustrated in Figures 8.1 and 8.2 had hoped to attract publicity to their cause, these radical suffragists sought to embarrass President Wilson by graphically pointing out the hypocrisy of a war fought for democracy while women at home were not enfranchised. More moderate suffragists criticized the radicals' tactics, but how might images such as this one have played a role in bringing Wilson around to support of the suffrage amendment?

◆ **Figure 8.5** **National Woman's Party Picketers at the White House (1917)**
Library of Congress, 3a32338.

THE PROTESTERS

A very different kind of public protest took place in July 1917, when ten thousand African American men and women marched down New York's Fifth Avenue in a "silent" parade, with only muffled drums accompanying the sound of their feet. The parade, organized by the NAACP, was a response to a vicious riot in East St. Louis, Illinois. Black women activists were outspoken in their response. Nannie Burroughs (see pp. 458–59) organized a petition campaign demanding that Congress pass an antilynching law. Ida B. Wells-Barnett wrote an account in which she called the riot the "greatest outrage of the twentieth century," and many black women leaders called for public protests. The National Convention of the Mme. C. J. Walker Agents passed a resolution at their annual meeting that it sent to President Woodrow Wilson, and Walker herself was on the planning committee for the New York parade. The procession, while peaceful, reflected a rising militancy on the part of African Americans who resented the contradiction between American claims to fight a war for democracy and the lack of democracy they experienced at home. The parade featured men, women, and children. This image (Figure 8.6) shows a group of women, most of whom are dressed in white, as they marched together in neat rows. What is the significance of the women's choice to march separately from the men in this manner?

◆ **Figure 8.6 Protest against the East St. Louis Riots, New York City (1917)**
Library of Congress, LC-DIG-ds-00894.

QUESTIONS FOR ANALYSIS

1. Compare the photographs illustrating the strikers (Figures 8.1 and 8.2), the suffragists (Figures 8.3 to 8.5), and the protesters (Figure 8.6). How did these groups take to the streets, and what commonalities and differences do their uses of public space reveal?

2. A major motivation behind picketing and parading was to capture publicity. What other purposes could these activities serve? What possibilities and dangers did the courting of publicity pose for strikers? For suffragists? For African American women?

3. What does the popularity among women activists of these mass demonstrations suggest about the public involvement of women in the Progressive era?

Uncle Sam Wants You:
Women and World War I Posters

Prior to World War I, the federal government communicated with citizens primarily through press releases printed in newspapers. In April 1917, however, President Woodrow Wilson formed the Committee on Public Information (CPI) to promote public support for the war. The CPI established the Department of Pictorial Publicity, which drew on a well-established tradition of using posters for advertising as well as on the skills of well-known magazine illustrators. The federal government used other methods to build support for war needs such as conserving food, recruiting soldiers for the military and workers for war industries, and supporting Liberty Bond and Red Cross fund drives, but the posters were the most colorful and abundant device. Over 20 million copies of 2,500 different posters were produced during the war. State governments and civic associations such as the Red Cross also created these dramatic advertisements to "sell the war."

Wartime propaganda aimed at creating a strong sense of identification with the nation and an eagerness to support the military effort. Although building the army itself required the coercion of the draft, the government turned to persuasive measures when possible in keeping with the notion that the United States was going to "war for democracy." The posters reproduced here need to be understood as part of this massive drive to imbue Americans with intense loyalty and patriotism. There was a strong antiwar movement in the country, but dissent was repressed and many protesters were imprisoned and, if not citizens, deported (see pp. 444–45).

Women's efforts were central to the nation's call for patriotism. In the midst of the final stages of their drive for citizenship, many women saw themselves, if not quite as regular soldiers, as members of a volunteer army that blanketed the nation in support of various wartime mobilization drives. These activities required exceptional administrative skills, and for some leisure-class women this became full-time work.

Posters, of course, do not convey the complexity of these women's volunteer activity. The messages were simple. Women were urged to do their part as a demonstration of their citizenship, and their images were widely used to encourage all Americans to support the war. Given the eagerness with which women rushed into the public sphere to support the war, it is ironic that the majority of these images depicted traditional notions of womanhood.

Images of women have been used to represent the United States since the nation was founded. (See Primary Sources: "Gendering Images of the Revolution," pp. 135–40.)

Posters used female representations to give a feminine face to war aims. A beautiful woman flanked by the U.S. flag or dressed in the Stars and Stripes represented the patriotism of a nation at war. Figure 8.7 depicts a beseeching woman wearing a cap that clearly echoes the American flag. In the backdrop is a European city with its church towers in flames, a potent reminder to Americans safe at home of the devastating war across the Atlantic. The poster in Figure 8.8 features a female form to indicate that America's honor needed fighting men to protect it. What conventional ideas of femininity do these posters mobilize to bolster their messages?

Posters also traded on images of female sexuality. The saucy young woman dressed in a military uniform in Figure 8.9, an image created by well-known artist Howard Chandler Christy, provocatively exclaims, "Gee!! I Wish I Were a Man. I'd Join the Navy." What does this image suggest about modern notions of female sexuality emerging in the prewar years? How does the cross-dressed figure communicate the proper roles of men and women in wartime?

Even when posters encouraged women to participate in war activities by buying Liberty Bonds, supporting the Red Cross, knitting socks for soldiers, or conserving food, the images rarely challenged traditional ideas of women's proper place. Figure 8.10, for example, is a recruitment poster for the Land Army, a voluntary organization formed to mobilize women as temporary farmworkers. How does it link labor on the home front to the war? How are the women agricultural laborers represented?

◆ **Figure 8.7** **"Let's End It—Quick with Liberty Bonds"** *(top)*
Library of Congress, 3g09462.

◆ **Figure 8.8** **"It's Up to You. Protect the Nation's Honor. Enlist Now"** *(bottom)*
Library of Congress, 3g01960.

◆ **Figure 8.9** "Gee!! I Wish I Were a Man. I'd Join the Navy."
Library of Congress, 3a42473.

◆ **Figure 8.10** "The Woman's Land Army of America Training School"
Library of Congress, 3a42864.

Some posters depicted women supporting the war effort in the workforce. The government distributed one featuring a typist (typing was now almost wholly a female occupation) with the caption "The Kaiser is afraid of you!" On occasion, posters acknowledged women who crossed conventional gender barriers when they took jobs in war work. These images were usually issued by the Young Women's Christian Association (YWCA), which produced its own posters. During the war, the YWCA continued its prewar activism on behalf of young working women and distributed the poster depicted in Figure 8.11 as part of its fund-raising campaign. In keeping with YWCA literature that praised women factory workers' vital contribution to defense, this image emphasizes female strength and solidarity. Note too the graphic style of this image. How does it compare to government posters intended to convey more conventional ideas about women's war contribution?

◆ **Figure 8.11** "For Every Fighter a Woman Worker. Y.W.C.A."
Library of Congress, 3b52923.

World War I poster art is also revealing for what it did not picture, in particular the way in which it supported existing racial hierarchies. Government and voluntary agencies worked in black communities to encourage support for war programs. Alice Dunbar-Nelson's report "Negro Women in War Work," for example, detailed the fund-raising of the National Association of Colored Women, which raised close to $5 million in the third Liberty Loan drive. Yet despite the record of black women's participation, apparently no posters represented them or other women of color. Images of European immigrants appeared in a few World War I posters, but the diversity of American women was not reflected in this popular propaganda form.

War posters also failed to depict adequately the full range of ways in which women supported the war effort. The wartime growth in the wage labor force was rarely represented, and instead of images of women performing manual labor, most women depicted in posters were either icons for the nation or wartime volunteers. But if few posters challenged traditional expectations about women's domestic roles, women themselves did take advantage of wartime opportunities. Not only did working women temporarily break into traditionally male jobs, but suffragists used women's war service as a way of dramatically demonstrating their claim for full citizenship.

QUESTIONS FOR ANALYSIS

1. Figures 8.8 and 8.9 are both enlistment posters aimed at young men. What emotional responses do the artists seek to arouse in their intended audience? How are their methods alike, and how do they differ?

2. Until recently in the United States, only men officially served in combat, and it could be argued that by virtue of asking men to risk death, wartime gave them a heightened claim on citizenship. To what extent do these posters reinforce this notion? To what extent do they challenge it?

3. What are the similarities and differences between the way in which the World War I posters here use female images for propaganda purposes and the way in which images of women are used in Chapter 3 in Primary Sources: "Gendering Images of the Revolution" (pp. 135–40)?

Modernizing Womanhood

A S THE DRIVE FOR THE VOTE HEATED UP in the years before World War I, another less sharply defined movement emerged among more radical women, who called themselves feminists (see pp. 440–41). While women like Charlotte Perkins Gilman and Crystal Eastman supported the suffrage campaign, their ideas moved beyond women's political rights to include more modern themes of economic independence and more modern sexual relationships and marriages. Many feminists had socialist leanings and were associated with the struggles of working-class women; a few were union activists. Self-consciously rebellious, they viewed themselves as breaking from the suffocating conventions of respectable female behavior, demanding instead to be recognized, in the words of Edna Kenton, as "people of flesh and blood and brain, feeling, seeing, judging and directing equally with men, all the great social forces."[39]

In July 1914, Edna Kenton's commentary in *The Delineator* challenged critics who charged that feminism would undermine the family, marriage, and morality—or, in the words of one author she cited, "Underneath the whole argument [of feminism] lies the idea that woman can never be free and able to perform her earthly mission until she casts law, decency, and morality to the winds." How does Kenton redefine morality in the following passage?

Edna Kenton Says Feminism Will Give Men More Fun, Women Greater Scope, Children Better Parents, Life More Charm (1914)

The critic is right if he means by law, decency and morality, *his* law, *his* decency, *his* morality for her. This is what has been the matter with the world for so long, that women, bereft of any trade but marriage, or any means of livelihood but dependence upon their family or husbands, were forced, as complete dependents are forced, to take laws and decencies and moralities of others for their own, and to act, not according to their instincts of what was right for them, but according to what

others said was right for them. Which brings us to the heart of the Woman Question.

Feminism is not a concrete thing, to be touched with hands or seen of eyes; *it is any woman's spiritual and intellectual attitude toward herself and toward life. It is her conscious attempt to realize Personality;* to make her own decisions instead of having them made for her; to sink the old humbled or rebelling slave in the new creature who is mistress of herself.

To define this tremendous woman movement any more closely, for this generation, is to miss its spirituality entirely, for spirituality is an intensely personal thing, and every woman touched with this new flame must be filled with the larger charity that will grant to every other woman the right to seek her own personal goal by her own path.

Source: The Delineator, July 1914, 17.

It is a generation that is made up of experimentation with life; and women to-day, thanks to changed economic conditions, have the chance of sensing their souls through thought *plus* action as they have never had before.

Thinking one way and acting another is one of the most immoral things in life, and it was merely one of the countless personal immoralities to which women until recently had to bow, if they were to save their bodies alive.

I N 1913, ANOTHER MASS-CIRCULATION PERIODICAL, *McClure's Magazine,* noted that "no movement of this century is more significant or more deep-rooted than the movement to readjust the social position of women," and began a "department for women" to "represent the ideas of the more advanced thinkers of the feminist movement." High-profile suffrage activist and lawyer Inez Milholland wrote the articles. The following is an extract from her second essay.

INEZ MILHOLLAND
The Changing Home (1913)

PROPERTY RIGHTS IN WOMEN ARE DISAPPEARING

. . . The past fifty years, with their key discoveries in science, have unlocked the secrets of earth and air, have given us modern production and distribution, have brought the ends of the world together in an entirely new sort of neighborhood, with the beginnings of a new common understanding — have, in a word, expanded man's thought, feeling, and social power as the explorations of the sixteenth and seventeenth centuries expanded his geography.

Source: "The Changing Home," *McClure's Magazine,* March 1913, 206–19.

These discoveries and the resultant harnessing of newly discovered natural laws, have made possible the "social surplus" of which the Socialists say so much. For the first time in human history, the race can produce enough of the necessaries of life to go round. While we have not yet arrived at such a fair distribution, the tendency of modern social and political effort is distinctly taking that direction all over the world.

And, coincidentally with the struggles of workers everywhere for a share in the fruits of life under the new conditions, we see woman, with individual economic independence at last in sight, stirring and striving to free herself from property-subjection to man in industry, and in marriage itself.

THE HOME HAS BEEN REMOVED FROM THE WOMAN

It is still said, in some quarters, that "woman's place is the home"; but it is becoming increasingly difficult to understand the phrase. For the home, in the earlier sense of the term, has been pretty effectually removed from the woman. In the traditional idyllic home which apparently still exists in the fancy of many conservative thinkers (but which probably never existed as generally as these thinkers imagine), woman spun, wove, and made clothing, milked and churned, put up foods, and so on. Her duties were many, arduous, sometimes dignified and important. Her "sphere" was defined with some clearness. Within it she exercised a real authority. In addition, she bore and reared children. And she found time for all!

To-day, if woman is to "go back to the home" in the only sense that the phrase can possibly carry, she will have to follow it into the canning factory, the packing-house, the cotton and woolen mills, the clothing factory, the up-State dairy, the railroad that handles the dairy products, the candy factory, etc. As a matter of fact, she has already been forced in considerable numbers to follow these tasks into their new industrial environment. But, whereas in the home she had some authority and certain partnership rights, in industry she has no voice except as she can make herself heard through the medium of a trade union or (less directly) of the vote.

So the "home" has, in part, been removed, and the eight million women actually engaged in industry to-day indicate with some force that woman has had to go with it. To order her "back to the home" is, therefore, nonsense. It is like ordering the cab-driver, displaced by the taxicab chauffeur, back to the stage-coach to compete with the railroad.

MARRIAGE BY INTIMIDATION

No one, of course, — least of all the advanced feminist thinkers, — questions the imperative beauty and value of romantic love. Indeed, the hope is that marriage, far from being undermined or destroyed, can be made real and lasting. . . . What thoughtful women are distinctly beginning to object to is the time-honored belief that it is decent for a woman to bestow her sex, legally or illegally, in exchange for a guarantee of food, shelter, and clothing.

That millions of women have had to do precisely this in the past is too commonly known to be gainsaid. They have had to do it sometimes because there was no other way in which they could live according to reasonable standards of what living is, and sometimes, often, because the prevailing masculine ideal of the ornamental comparatively useless woman has withheld from them the training and equipment that would have enabled them to cope with life as it is.

But, now that the changing economic conditions have forced woman in some degree to meet life squarely and directly, and at the same time have begun to make some sort of economic independence seem possible for almost any individual, she is making the interesting discovery that she can in some measure subsist without throwing herself, legally or illicitly, on the mercy of the individual man. Accordingly, she is pressing and striving to increase her economic opportunity, even to gain some real economic authority; and at the same time she is getting a grip on the lever of political power. . . .

THE NEW POWER OF THE WAGE-EARNING WOMAN

. . . [T]hat this new condition carries with it a new social attitude toward divorce goes without saying. The promise of the new relationship between man and woman is that the deeply rooted, perennial mating instinct may begin to work more spontaneously and finely in conditions permitting freer choice. It is beginning to be recognized that real marriage can not be brought into existence through fear of want or through other social intimidation. . . .

A mere casual survey of current books and plays makes it evident that a calm, intelligent study of these elemental facts is rapidly taking the place of our traditional attitude of outward conformity tempered by inner panic. We are beginning to perceive that we can not successfully fit all of life into a preconceived mold; that our real task is to try, soberly and patiently, to learn what this strange substance we call life really is.

T HE THEME OF SEXUAL LIBERATION, evident in Milholland's *McClure's* article, appeared repeatedly in feminist writing and was often accompanied by a call for the legalization of birth control. In this article from the radical journal *Birth Control Review*, Crystal Eastman discusses the far-reaching implications of women's control over reproduction. Eastman's concern for economic as well as sexual liberation reflects both her socialist and feminist sensibilities.

CRYSTAL EASTMAN
Birth Control in the Feminism Program (1918)

Feminism means different things to different people, I suppose. To women with a taste for politics and reform it means the right to vote and hold office. To women physically strong and adventuresome it means freedom to enter all kinds of athletic contests and games, to compete with men in aviation, to drive racing cars, . . . to enter dangerous trades, etc. To many it means social and sex freedom, doing away with exclusively feminine virtues. To most of all it means economic freedom, — not the ideal economic freedom dreamed of by revolutionary socialism, but such economic freedom as it is possible for a human being to achieve under the existing system of competitive production and distribution, — in short such freedom to choose one's way of making a living as men now enjoy, and definite economic rewards for one's work when it happens to be "home-making." This is to me the central fact of feminism. Until women learn to want economic independence, i.e., the ability to earn their own living independently of husbands, fathers, brothers or lovers, — and until they work out a way to get this independence without denying themselves the joys of love and motherhood, it seems to me feminism has no roots. Its manifestations are often delightful and stimulating but they are sporadic, they effect no lasting change in the attitude of men to women, or of women to themselves.

Whether other feminists would agree with me that the economic is the fundamental aspect of feminism, I don't know. But on this side we are surely agreed, that Birth Control is an elementary essential in all aspects of feminism. Whether we are the special followers of Alice Paul, or Ruth Law, or Ellen Key, or Olive Schreiner, we must all be followers of Margaret Sanger. Feminists are not nuns. That should be established. We want to love and to be loved, and most of us want children, one or two at least. But we want our love to be joyous and free — not clouded with ignorance and fear. And we want our children to be deliberately, eagerly called into being, when we are at our best, not crowded upon us in times of poverty and weakness. We want this precious sex knowledge not just for ourselves, the conscious feminists;

SOURCE: Blanche Wiesen Cook, ed., *Crystal Eastman on Women and Revolution* (New York: Oxford University Press, 1978), 46–49.

we want it for all the millions of unconscious feminists that swarm the earth, — we want it for all women.

Life is a big battle for the complete feminist even when she can regulate the size of her family. Women who are creative, or who have administrative gifts, or business ability, and who are ambitious to achieve and fulfill themselves in these lines, if they also have the normal desire to be mothers, must make up their minds to be a sort of supermen, I think. They must develop greater powers of concentration, a stronger will to "keep at it," a more determined ambition than men of equal gifts, in order to make up for the time and energy and thought and devotion that child-bearing and rearing, even in the most "advanced" families, seems inexorably to demand of the mother. But if we add to this handicap complete uncertainty as to when children may come, how often they come or how many there shall be, the thing becomes impossible. I would almost say that the whole structure of the feminist's dream of society rests upon the rapid extension of scientific knowledge about birth control.

QUESTIONS FOR ANALYSIS

1. What role does women's economic independence play in feminist thought?
2. Why is birth control so crucial to the transformation in women's lives that feminists anticipated?
3. What changes in relationships and marriage did feminists promote?
4. Feminists were self-consciously "modern." What evidence do you see for this sensibility in these documents?

NOTES

1. Nancy S. Dye, "Introduction," in Nancy S. Dye and Noralee Frankel, eds., *Gender, Class, Race, and Reform in the Progressive Era* (Lexington: University Press of Kentucky, 1991), 1.

2. Lynn Wiener, *From Working Girl to Working Mother: The Female Labor Force in the United States, 1820–1980* (Chapel Hill: University of North Carolina Press, 1985), 4.

3. Estelle B. Freedman, *No Turning Back: The History of Feminism and the Future of Women* (New York: Ballantine Books, 2002), 162.

4. Nancy F. Cott, *The Grounding of Modern Feminism* (New Haven: Yale University Press, 1987), 350.

5. Barbara Mayer Wertheimer, *We Were There: The Story of Working Women in America* (New York: Pantheon, 1977), 271.

6. Elizabeth Anne Payne, *Reform Labor and Feminism: Margaret Dreier Robins and the Women's Trade Union League* (Urbana: University of Illinois Press, 1988), 48.

7. Meredith Tax, *The Rising of the Women: Feminist Solidarity and Class Conflict, 1880–1917* (New York: Monthly Review Press, 1980), 235.

8. Susan B. Anthony and Ida H. Harper, eds., *History of Woman Suffrage* (Rochester, NY: Susan B. Anthony, 1902), 4:178.

9. Mary Beard, *Woman's Work in Municipalities* (New York: National Municipal League, 1915), 221–22.

10. An early use of this term can be found in Seth Koven and Sonya Michel, eds., *Mothers of a New World: Maternalist Politics and the Origins of Welfare States* (New York: Routledge, 1993).

11. Alice Kessler-Harris, *Out to Work: A History of Wage-Earning Women in the United States* (New York: Oxford University Press, 1982), 198.

12. Darlene Clark Hine and Kathleen Thompson, *A Shining Thread of Hope: The History of Black Women in America* (New York: Broadway Books, 1998), 202.

13. Ruth Spack, "Dis/engagement: Zitkala-Ša's Letters to Carlos Montezuma, 1901–1902," Melus 26 (April 2001): 173.

14. Rebecca Mead, *How the Vote Was Won: Woman Suffrage in the Western United States, 1868–1914* (New York: New York University Press, 2004), 123–24.

15. Dawn Keetley and John Pettegrew, eds., *Public Women, Public Words: A Documentary History of American Feminism* (Madison, WI: Madison House, 1997–2002), 2:157.

16. Ibid., 2:164.

17. Christine Stansell, *American Moderns: Bohemian New York and the Creation of a New Century* (New York: Metropolitan Books, 2000), 228.

18. Rheta Childe Dorr, *A Woman of Fifty* (New York: Funk and Wagnalls, 1924), 286–69.

19. John D'Emilio and Estelle B. Freedman, *Intimate Matters: A History of Sexuality in America* (New York: Harper and Row, 1988), 213.

20. Ibid., p. 322.

21. Harriet Human Alonso, *Peace as a Women's Issue: History of the U.S. Movement for World Peace and Women's Rights* (Syracuse, NY: Syracuse University Press, 1993), 61.

22. Alfreda M. Duster, ed., *Crusade for Justice: The Autobiography of Ida B. Wells* (Chicago: University of Chicago Press, 1970), 370.

23. Carrie Chapman Catt, "Organized Womanhood," *Woman Voter*, April 1917, 9.

24. Harriot Stanton Blatch, *Mobilizing Woman Power* (New York: Woman's Press, 1918), 88–90.

25. Maurine Greenwald, *Women, War, and Work: The Impact of World War I on Women Workers in the United States* (Westport, CT: Greenwood Press, 1980), 24.

26. Quoted in Eleanor Flexner, *Century of Struggle: The Woman's Rights Movement in the United States* (Cambridge, MA: Belknap Press, 1959), 291.

27. Woodrow Wilson, Fourteen Points speech, in Arthur S. Link et al., eds., *The Papers of Woodrow Wilson* (Princeton, NJ: Princeton University Press, 1984), 45:536.

28. Flexner, *Century of Struggle*, 336.

29. Dorothy C. Salem, *To Better Our World: Black Women in Organized Reform, 1890–1920* (Brooklyn: Carlson, 1990), 97–100.

30. Deborah Gray White, *Too Heavy a Load: Black Women in Defense of Themselves, 1894–1994* (New York: W. W. Norton, 1999), 85.

31. Michelle Rief, "Thinking Locally, Acting Globally: the International Agenda of the African American Clubwomen, 1880–1941," *Journal of African American History* 89 (2004): 2162.

32. Susan Glenn, *Daughters of the Shtetl: Life and Labor in the Immigrant Generation* (Ithaca, NY: Cornell University Press, 1991), 165.

33. Nan Enstad, *Ladies of Labor, Girls of Adventure: Working Women, Popular Culture, and Labor Politics at the Turn of the Twentieth Century* (New York: Columbia University Press, 1999), 84–160.

34. Harriot Stanton Blatch and Alma Lutz, *Challenging Years: The Memoirs of Harriot Stanton Blatch* (New York: G. P. Putnam's Sons, 1940), 129.

35. Sarah J. Moore, "Making a Spectacle of Suffrage: The National Woman Suffrage Pageant, 1913," *Journal of American Culture* 20 (1997): 89–103.

36. Linda J. Lumsden, "Beauty and the Beasts: Significance of Press Coverage of the 1913 National Suffrage Parade," *Journalism and Mass Culture Quarterly* 77 (2000): 595.

37. Flexner, *Century of Struggle*, 269.

38. Lumsden, "Beauty and the Beasts," 595, 597.

39. Cott, *Grounding of Modern Feminism*, 36.

SUGGESTED REFERENCES

Women Workers and Social Housekeeping

Nancy Schrom Dye, *As Equals and as Sisters: Feminism, the Labor Movement, and the Women's Trade Union League of New York* (1980).

Alice Kessler-Harris, *Out to Work: A History of Wage-Earning Women in the United States*, 20th anniv. ed. (2003).

Lucy Maddox, *Citizen Indians: Native American Intellectuals, Race and Reform* (2005).

Robyn Muncy, *Creating a Female Dominion in American Reform, 1890–1935* (1991).

Cynthia Neverdon-Morton, *Afro-American Women of the South and the Advancement of the Race, 1895–1925* (1989).

Sharon Hartman Strom, *Beyond the Typewriter: Gender, Class, and the Origins of Modern American Office Work, 1900–1930* (1992).

Deborah Gray White, *Too Heavy a Load: Black Women in Defense of Themselves, 1894–1994* (1999).

Nancy Woloch, *A Class by Herself: Protective Laws for Women Workers, 1890s–1990s* (2015).

Woman Suffrage and Feminism

Nancy F. Cott, *The Grounding of Modern Feminism* (1987).

Ellen Carol DuBois, *Harriot Stanton Blatch and the Winning of Woman Suffrage* (1997).

Eleanor Flexner and Ellen Fitzpatrick, *Century of Struggle: The Woman's Rights Movement in the United States*, enlarged ed. (1996).

Linda Gordon, *The Moral Property of Women: A History of Birth Control Politics in America* (2002).

Susan E. Marshall, *Splintered Sisterhood: Gender and Class in the Campaign against Woman Suffrage* (1997).

Kathy Peiss, *Cheap Amusements: Working Women and Leisure in Turn-of-the-Century New York* (1986).

Christine Stansell, *American Moderns: Bohemian New York and the Creation of a New Century* (2000).

Rosalyn Terborg-Penn, *African American Women in the Struggle for the Vote, 1850–1920* (1998).

Mary Walton, *A Woman's Crusade: Alice Paul and the Battle for the Ballot* (2010).

World War I, the Peace Movement, and the Great Migration

Elizabeth Clark-Lewis, *Living In, Living Out: African American Domestics and the Great Migration* (1994).

Lynn Dumenil, *The Second Line of Defense: American Women and World War I* (2017).

Kimberly Jensen, *Mobilizing Minerva: American Women in the First World War* (2008).

David S. Patterson, *The Search for Negotiated Peace: Women's Activism and Citizen Diplomacy in World War I* (2008).

Victoria W. Wolcott, *Remaking Respectability: African American Women in Interwar Detroit* (2001).

9

Change and Continuity

WOMEN IN PROSPERITY, DEPRESSION, AND WAR, 1920–1945

FROM ONE PERSPECTIVE, WOMEN'S EXPERIENCES IN the period from 1920 to 1945 seem marked more by change than by continuity. Popular culture icons graphically capture the differences between the decades. The young, devil-may-care flapper with her short dress, rouged face, and rolled stockings symbolized the New Woman of the 1920s. Rebelling against the restraint of Victorian womanhood, the flapper eagerly embraced the growing consumer culture, with its emphasis on leisure and materialism, of this largely prosperous era. For the following decade, the most powerful icon is Dorothea Lange's widely reproduced photograph of a migrant mother (see p. 537), who symbolized Americans' dignified suffering as they weathered the devastating economic crisis of the 1930s. The migrant mother embodied, too, the popular assumption that woman's most important role during the Great Depression was an extension of her traditional responsibilities of maintaining the home and family. Images of women during World War II seemingly point in yet a third direction. "Rosie the Riveter"—the cheerful, robust woman in overalls working in the defense industry, taking on new and challenging work to serve her country in time of need—emphasized female independence and strength outside the home.

photos: top, Library of Congress, 8b21336; middle, Library of Congress, 8b29516; bottom, Bettmann/Getty Images

But although each decade had its distinctive qualities, overarching developments, especially in work and politics, link these seeming disparities into the larger trends in American women's history. In the immediate aftermath of the Nineteenth Amendment, women plunged into the responsibilities of active citizenship and struggled to carve out a base for political power and influence. Female participation in the paid labor market continued to grow, especially with respect to the growing numbers of working women who were also wives and mothers. Finally, cultural expectations for women shifted in two crucially related areas, consumerism and sexuality. Both of these shifts had implications for women's family lives as well. Yet despite these changes in women's lives, another theme also emerges, that of continuity with the past. Racial and ethnic prejudice continued to limit women's opportunities in the workforce and women's access to political influence. And for all women, traditional expectations about women's primary role in the home persisted, serving as the filter through which change would affect their lives.

◆ PROSPERITY DECADE: THE 1920S

On the surface, the 1920s appear to have been a decade of progress and prosperity. Industrial growth and international economic expansion created a society more affluent than ever before. An explosion of consumer goods, from mass-produced cars to gleaming bathroom fixtures and electrical kitchen appliances, helped to transform daily lives and gave women more power and pleasure as consumers. Underlying the bright prosperity of the decade, however, were darker currents. Many Americans continued to live below or near the poverty line. Farm families suffered from low prices and high indebtedness for most of the decade, and many rural women endured harsh, isolated lives. Cities provided more opportunities, but here, too, poor wages and living conditions, especially for Mexican Americans and African Americans, separated the haves from the have-nots.

Relatively few commentators in the 1920s delved beneath the surface image of prosperity to analyze the lives of those who did not participate in the boom times.

photos: top, Smithsonian American Art Museum, Washington, DC/Art Resource, NY; bottom, National Archives no. 537581

1935 National Youth Administration (NYA) created

1935 National Labor Relations (Wagner) Act passed

1935 Social Security Act passed

1935 Works Progress Administration (WPA) created

1935 Congress of Industrial Organizations (CIO) founded

1936 *United States v. One Package of Japanese Pessaries* **legalizes the dissemination of contraceptive information**

1936 **Mary McLeod Bethune appointed to head the National Youth Administration's Division of Negro Affairs**

1937 Japan invades China

1937 **Women create the Emergency Brigade in Flint, Michigan, strike**

1938 Fair Labor Standards Act passed

1939 World War II breaks out in Europe

1941 Fair Employment Practices Commission established

1941 United States enters World War II after Japan attacks Pearl Harbor

1942 **Women recruited into war industries**

1942 **Women's Army Corps given formal military status**

1942 Japanese immigrants and citizens of Japanese ancestry interned

1942– **Rationing increases women's**
1945 **domestic responsibilities**

1943 Congress extends the right of naturalization to Chinese immigrants

1945 Harry S. Truman becomes president after Roosevelt's death

1945 Japan surrenders, ending World War II

The same superficiality characterized the widely held image of the New Woman. In the popular mind, women had become liberated—by the freedom of wartime, by the exercise of the vote, by participation in the workforce, and by experiments with a new sexual morality. The image was an exaggerated generalization of the experience of young, urban, prosperous white women who were glamorized in the popular media. But contemporaries were correct in thinking that most women's lives had changed significantly since the nineteenth century, even though the goals of autonomy and equality remained elusive.

The New Woman in Politics

In 1920 women political activists were poised for a great adventure. With the energy they had brought to the suffrage campaign, women from all groups were now prepared to make women's votes count. African American women focused on using the new national amendment to extend suffrage in the South and on lobbying for a federal antilynching law. In 1920 white women formed the League of Women Voters (LWV), which emphasized lobbying, voter education, and get-out-the-vote drives in the overall mission to train women to be good citizens. An astute recognition of the growing importance of national organizations' lobbying efforts in Washington, D.C., led fourteen women's organizations to form the Women's Joint Congressional Committee, with the goal of promoting legislation backed by the member organizations. On the local and state levels, women also pursued their agendas, supporting child and women's labor laws, health and safety legislation, municipal reform, and a broad extension of women's legal rights. The lobbying efforts of these women's groups underline the importance of women activists in pioneering twentieth-century interest-group politics. (See Primary Sources: "Women's Lobbying in the 1920s," pp. 519–27.)

In addition to working through their organizations, activist women debated among themselves as to how, and whether, they should act within the Democratic and Republican Parties. The argument that women were unsullied by the corruption of political parties had been a common one in the suffrage battle, and many women had grave reservations about working within the established party system. Indeed, like its precursor, the National American Woman Suffrage Association, the LWV was established as a nonpartisan group that refrained from supporting political parties or their candidates. While some former suffragists attempted to exert influence within the Republican and Democratic Parties, others followed Alice Paul's lead and joined the National Woman's Party (NWP). Always a single-issue organization, the NWP focused exclusively on passage of an Equal Rights Amendment (ERA). First introduced in Congress in 1923, the ERA stated: "Men and women shall have equal rights throughout the United States and every place subject to its jurisdiction."

At first glance, the optimism of white women activists seems justified. In 1920 both Democrats and Republicans recognized women's issues in their platforms, presumably taking women at their word when they said that they planned to use their combined votes as a powerful political tool. And they opened up places within the organizational structure of their parties for female members, although the positions granted were rarely equal in terms of power or influence. As the *New York Times* magazine *Current History* summed it up, "Where there is dignity of office but little else, or where there is routine work, little glory, and low pay, men prove willing to admit women to an equal share in the spoils of office."[1] Women became officeholders, although only a handful were elected to the House of Representatives (a high of seven in 1928). Suffrage veteran and newspaper magnate Ruth Hanna McCormick's 1928 effort to become the first woman elected to the Senate was blocked by influential Republicans, including former California Progressive leader Hiram Johnson. But hundreds served at the state level in legislatures and executive positions earmarked as women's jobs, such as secretary of education and secretary of state. Women were more numerous in local governments, in part because many of these positions were nonpartisan and thus seemingly more in keeping with ideas that women should operate "above politics." Despite these inroads, female officeholders generally worked within the context of prevailing assumptions that women should relegate themselves to women's issues, or "municipal housekeeping," the same assumptions that limited their ability to wield much power within their political parties.

Women reformers also had mixed success in their lobbying activities. Many states passed laws urged by women activists, including those that expanded women's legal rights and those directed at maternalist social reform, such as child labor laws and wage and hour protective laws for women. At the federal level, the women's lobby saw an early success in the Sheppard-Towner Act of 1921, which gave matching funds for states to provide health care and other services for mothers and children. Sheppard-Towner funds brought midwife education classes to black, Mexican American, and immigrant practitioners, while also contributing to the eventual decline of lay midwives through the medicalization of childbirth. By the end of the decade, however, progress had slowed, especially on the national level. The Child Labor Amendment—passionately advocated after the Supreme Court invalidated a second national child labor law in 1921—failed to be ratified, and most national legislation supported by women lobbyists was unsuccessful. Congress cut the Sheppard-Towner Act's appropriations and ended its once-promising program in 1929. (See Primary Sources: "Women's Lobbying in the 1920s," pp. 519–27.)

Moreover, the women's rights movement itself was deeply divided as to tactics and goals. By decade's end, many women activists were disillusioned and embittered. Ironically, some of the problems hindering a sustained feminist movement grew out of the success of the suffrage battle. Before national suffrage was achieved, a great many women—equally excluded from this basic right of citizenship—came under the same umbrella of "votes for women." Once the Nineteenth Amendment was ratified, the lines that divided women—class, race, age, ideology—became more significant. By gaining the individual right they had so vigorously sought, they laid the groundwork for the fracturing of female communities. As one activist ruefully put it in 1923, "The American woman's movement, and her interest in great moral and social questions, is splintered into a hundred fragments under as many warring leaders."[2]

◆ The Sheppard-Towner Act in Action

Although the Sheppard-Towner Act was limited in how much assistance it offered mothers, the Children's Bureau nonetheless worked hard to educate women about "scientific" prenatal and child care designed to protect the health of mothers and children. It distributed 22 million pieces of advice literature and arranged for nursing visits to over 3 million homes in the seven years the Sheppard-Towner Act was in operation (1921–28). In the era the Act was in force, infant mortality rates dropped from 76 per 1,000 live births to 69. Despite efforts to connect with racial and ethnic minorities, the Children's Bureau was probably most successful in helping white rural women. This was in part because of the dire poverty of so many black and immigrant women, but also because the Bureau staff was suspicious of alternative forms of healing and of midwives, an attitude that may have limited their ability to reach racial and ethnic minorities. Beyond its outreach programs, the Bureau also conducted surveys and studies. This image from 1923 shows Anna Grosser of the Children's Bureau using a chart to demonstrate the Bureau's findings on infant mortality. The focus on income here reflects some of the Children's Bureau staffers' frustration, because without the ability to offer financial assistance to poor mothers, the Bureau was limited in what it could do to "save" babies. Note the emphasis in the chart on fathers' earnings. Today, a graph like this would use the term "family income." What does the term "fathers' earnings" suggest about Bureau staff assumptions? *Library of Congress, 3c27253.*

This was particularly evident in the ferocious debate over the Equal Rights Amendment. Under the leadership of Alice Paul, the NWP focused so exclusively on the ERA as a means of achieving political and economic equality with men that it appropriated the newly coined term "feminism" to refer to its specific agenda. Women interested in broader social reform were alarmed at this "blanket amendment," which they feared would undermine the protective labor laws that they had worked so hard to achieve in the states. Although not unsympathetic to the plight of working-class women, ERA supporters countered that such legislation treated women as invalids and could limit their economic opportunity. The controversy revealed differing attitudes about women's nature and the meaning of equality. Social reformers such as Julia Lathrop and Frances Perkins also cared about extending women's legal rights, but they nonetheless stressed the distinctiveness of their sex. They believed that biological attributes justified protective legislation. Moreover, their sense of women's moral superiority and special maternal qualities, rooted in the nineteenth-century ideology of separate spheres, shaped their commitment to social reform.

Other factors besides differences over the ERA would hamstring the development of a strong feminist movement. Young, middle-class white women often seemed more interested in the pleasures of consumption and leisure than in the social commitment involved in pursuing women's rights and social reform. If these women felt both ERA and anti-ERA supporters were quaintly old-fashioned, black women reformers found their white counterparts largely unresponsive to their concerns. This split emerged most concretely at a 1921 NWP meeting, where sixty black women representing the National Association of Colored Women were refused convention time to raise the subject of the failure of southern states to acknowledge the voting rights of black women. Alice Paul insisted that this was a "race issue," not a "woman's issue." The African American delegation, led by Addie Hunton, field secretary for the National Association for the Advancement of Colored People (NAACP), countered by reminding the convention that "five million women in the United States cannot be denied their rights without all the women of the United States feeling the effect of that denial. No women are free until all women are free."[3] Although this and other setbacks in the effort to secure the vote in the South led African American women to de-emphasize the voting issue, they persisted in their broad agenda of improving the lives of all African Americans; in particular, they continued their antilynching activities by working for federal legislation and even, in some cases, forging alliances with southern white women. (See Primary Sources: "Women's Lobbying in the 1920s," pp. 519–27.) Though some women could come together in interracial cooperation, the limited vision of white leaders such as Paul as to what constituted "women's issues" shut off possibilities for a broader, more inclusive conception of a feminist movement.

While the difficulties women reformers faced arose in part from women's disunity, a far more serious problem was the decade's conservative political climate. Citing declining overall voting participation in the 1920s (roughly half of those eligible voted), contemporary observers assumed that women's nonvoting accounted for the decline. With only sparse data of voting by sex available, many historians have echoed this assumption. More recent studies, however, maintain that women's participation in elections varied significantly by location and by election. Women in states that only recently had enfranchised them seem to have participated in fewer numbers than those living in states such as California, where women had longer experience with the electoral process. Notably, men's voting decreased in this period as well, following a long-standing trend of declining engagement in partisan politics. Jane Addams ruefully commented in 1924 that the question should not be "Is woman suffrage failing?" but rather, "Is suffrage failing?"[4] That both men and women were failing to vote in large numbers points to a political climate of disaffected or uninterested citizenry, and it is this broader context of American politics, not women's failures as voters, that offers the most compelling explanation for the difficulties women reformers faced.[5]

A related problem was a political climate hostile to reform that made it impossible to sustain the prewar enthusiasm for progressive measures. On the national scene, the Republicans dominated the White House and Congress, and, reflecting in part the party's ties to corporate business interests, resisted efforts to expand federal regulatory powers. Federal prohibition of alcohol, following ratification of the Eighteenth Amendment in 1919, further increased many Americans' wariness of intrusive social reforms. Prohibition met with vigorous opposition. Many Americans resented and circumvented the law, and others worried that the ineffectual effort to control alcohol consumption had fostered contempt for the legal system. That women reformers were so closely associated with the controversial amendment surely fueled hostility to the social reforms women activists promoted in the 1920s. Finally, the widening prosperity of the period may well have influenced many Americans to turn toward new consumer and leisure pleasures and away from political engagement and concern for the nation's poor.

Perhaps most damaging to reform and especially women's part in it was the "Red Scare" of 1919 to 1921. Prompted initially by the Russian Revolution of 1917 and the fear that the fledgling U.S. Communist Party was plotting a revolution to topple this nation's government, Americans succumbed to a hysteria in which wild-eyed Bolsheviks seemed to be lurking around every corner. The Red Scare led to the deportation of "suspicious" immigrants, the suppression of the labor movement, and massive violations of civil liberties. It also helped to fuel the growth of the second Ku Klux Klan, an organization opposed to immigrants, Catholics, Jews, and blacks that achieved significant popularity and influence in the early 1920s. Finally, the Red Scare contributed to the passage of restrictive immigration laws in the 1920s and became a weapon for opponents of reform legislation, who could now argue that efforts to increase government's role in regulating the economy or protecting workers and the poor would lead America down the same path as Russia.

Red Scare hysteria particularly focused on a number of women's groups, including those in the Women's Joint Congressional Committee and the Women's International League for Peace and Freedom, which opponents claimed were spreading bolshevism in the United States. Jane Addams in particular came in for forceful criticism. Opponents' attempts to discredit women reformers with claims that they were Bolsheviks point to a further dilemma facing women activists. Pre-eminent among the opponents of reform were right-wing women's organizations. The Women Sentinels of the Republic was a small but vocal group that opposed social reform as the forerunner of bolshevism. The Daughters of the American Revolution, initially interested in women's social reform efforts, had by mid-decade also taken up the antiradical hysteria. Women in an auxiliary of the all-male Ku Klux Klan supported some reforms such as Prohibition but, like other right-wing women's groups, promoted what was called "one-hundred-percent Americanism" and were suspicious of the liberal goals of the women's lobby. (See Primary Sources: "Women's Lobbying in the 1920s," pp. 519–27.)

With these counterpressures, then, it is not surprising that the reform agenda of women's groups stalled at the nation's capitol, and it is impressive that women activists accomplished as much as they did on the local and state levels. In the process they helped to keep the reform spirit alive, if not well, and created a crucial bridge to the social welfare reforms of the 1930s introduced by President Franklin D. Roosevelt's New Deal.

Women at Work

Although women's expanding political opportunities contributed to the sense of a New Woman in the 1920s, changes in work were equally important — and were similarly mixed in offering women genuine independence. World War I had brought short-term opportunities in a variety of jobs for women, but these opportunities were not sustained. After the war, as before, women's work was characterized by sex segregation, clustered in job categories dominated by women. In the 1920s, 86 percent of women workers concentrated into ten job classifications, jobs in which they made less money and had lower status and fewer skills than men. (See Tables 1, 2, and 4 in the Appendix.) As one historian neatly summed it up, "Women were invited into the workforce and again invited not to expect too much of it."[6]

The growing acceptance of women in the workforce is evident in the hard statistics. Their participation in paid labor grew from 21.2 percent in 1900 to 24.4 percent in 1930. Not only did more women work, but the percentage of married women in the labor force doubled, rising from 6 to 12 percent. This increase resulted in part from compulsory education laws that kept children from taking jobs to help out the family, a trend that particularly affected immigrant wives. Also contributing to the rise of working wives were new consumer standards, which required more family income.

Despite the dramatic increase in the number of married women in the labor force, only 10 percent of all wives worked outside the home during the 1920s. Yet their presence signaled a trend that would grow steadily in the future, and in the 1920s the development was significant enough to spark heated controversies. Marriage experts such as Ernest Groves announced that "when the woman herself earns and her maintenance is not entirely at the mercy of her husband's will, diminishing masculine authority necessarily follows."[7] Even observers sympathetic to working wives tended to criticize those who elected to pursue careers allegedly for personal satisfaction, as opposed to women in poorer households who were compelled to join the workforce to help make ends meet.

Married or single, as more and more women entered the labor force, the idea of women's proper place profoundly shaped their work experiences and opportunities. Factory work continued to be a major source of employment, especially among immigrant daughters, but the most rapidly expanding field was clerical work. The emergence of the modern corporation in the late nineteenth century transformed office work and office personnel. By 1910, women already held most stenographic and typing positions, and in the 1920s they increased their presence as clerks and bookkeepers. As clerical work became increasingly dominated by women, or "feminized," assumptions about these positions changed as well. While men might enter the lower rungs of white-collar work as the first stepping-stone to climbing their way up the corporate ladder, jobs that women filled rarely had the same potential for upward mobility.

Status and salaries were low within the feminized white-collar hierarchy; nonetheless, many women viewed these jobs as welcome opportunities and flocked to the commercial courses offered in the public high schools. European immigrant daughters, whose level of education was improving in part because of mandatory education laws, now had more options than factory work. Middle-class workers—who would have found factory work and domestic service demeaning—also staffed the modern office, and their high visibility helped to improve the respectability of women working. Women of color, however, faced office doors that were largely closed to them. Black women found positions only in a small number of black-owned firms. Mexican, Japanese, and Chinese American women also experienced discrimination in finding office work.

Similar patterns of sexual and racial discrimination appeared in the professions. The professional woman attracted much publicity in the 1920s as an exemplar of the New Woman, yet the percentage of working women in the professions was still small. Women professionals tended to cluster in teaching, nursing, and the expanding field of social work. Even in these increasingly feminized fields, women met with discrimination. Although eight of ten teachers were women, for example, only one in sixty-three superintendents was female. For women of color, the barriers were particularly high, and they made few inroads in this period. The percentage of black women working in the professions, for example, barely rose from 2.5 percent in 1920 to 3.4 percent in 1930.

While educated women struggled to find meaningful work in the professions, the vast majority of American women worked at far less satisfying labor. Black women had been optimistic that migration to the North would provide well-paid factory work. But even in the boom time of World War I, their jobs were the least desirable ones and usually did not last after the war had ended and soldiers had returned to the workforce. In the 1920s, some black women managed to find jobs in industries such as Chicago's packing plants and slaughterhouses, where researcher Alma Herbst found them seasonally employed in the hog-killing and beef-casing departments and working "under repulsive conditions."[8]

Most African American women, however, engaged in agricultural labor, laundry work, or domestic service. Seeking to improve control over their work lives, they increasingly refused jobs as live-in servants. The change to day work allowed these women to carve out some control over their work lives and their private time. As Mayme Gibson put it, "When I got work by the days I'd work in jobs where I'd be doing all the cleaning, my way. Nobody's be looking over your shoulder, saying what you was to do. People took daywork to finally get to work by theyself; to get away from people telling you how to do every little thing."[9] While day work offered an improvement over live-in situations, domestic work continued to be highly exploitative, with poor wages and conditions.

Like black women, Mexican American women were heavily concentrated in domestic labor. In 1930, the first date for which census figures reported people of Mexican descent separately, 44 percent of Mexican women who worked were servants. Some urban women found semiskilled factory work. A 1928 study of Los Angeles reported "that in some cases the wife or mother sought the work; in others, the young daughters. In either case, poverty was the immediate incentive." Most worked in "packing houses and canneries of various kinds, followed by the clothing, needle trades, and laundries."[10] Outside the cities, many Mexicanas and their American-born daughters worked with their families in agricultural labor. Next to black women, Japanese women were the most likely women of color to work outside the home; about 30 percent worked for wages. Most were married and, like Mexican Americans, worked either as family farm laborers or as domestic servants.

◆ Mexican American Woman at Work in Food Processing

Mexican immigrant women in the West and Southwest had the double burden of working while trying to maintain their families in harsh, substandard living conditions. In addition to working in the fields, they also packed fruits and vegetables and worked in other food processing jobs. Here, a young woman picks over pecan shells at a plant in San Antonio, Texas, in 1939. This image was captured by Russell Lee, a photographer for the Farm Security Administration (FSA) who documented the lives of poor agricultural workers throughout the nation during the Great Depression. (For more photographs commissioned by the FSA, see Primary Sources: "Dorothea Lange Photographs Farm Women of the Great Depression," pp. 535–41.) *Library of Congress, 8b21336.*

For all women of color, even the educated, the double burden of race and gender translated into few job options. In contrast, most white women, especially native-born ones who had office and professional employment, had cleaner, better paying, less demanding work. Despite these significant differences, all women faced a hierarchical labor market that devalued women's work. As Emily Blair put it at the end of the decade, summarizing her and other feminists' disappointment over women's failure to make significant economic advances in the 1920s, "The best man continued to win, and women, even the best, worked for and under him. Women were welcome to come in as workers, but not as co-makers of the world. For all their numbers, they seldom rose to positions of responsibility or power."[11]

The New Woman in the Home

As significant as changes in the public realm of politics and work were for women, the most dramatic transformation in women's lives emerged in the private worlds of home, family, and personal relationships. Contemporaries in the 1920s either celebrated or condemned what was widely viewed as a female sexual revolution. At the center of the revolution was the young, emancipated flapper with her bobbed hair, skimpy clothes, and penchant for outrageous dancing and drinking. Although the image of the flapper was glamorized in movies and in the pages of popular novelist F. Scott Fitzgerald, many young women across class and racial lines eagerly adopted the flapper clothing style and danced to jazz music their elders found alarmingly erotic. Even more unnerving was their sexual activity. Rejecting the Victorian moral code, young unmarried women increasingly engaged in "petting"—a term that encompassed a wide range of sexual play short of intercourse. And the generation who came of age in the 1920s was significantly more likely than their mothers to have engaged in premarital intercourse.

But if daughters were experimenting sexually, many of their mothers, too, were carving out new roles in what historians have called the "affectionate family." Smaller families were becoming the norm for the urban middle class, but fewer children did not mean less maternal responsibility. Modern mothers, aided by a bounty of household appliances made possible by the widespread electrification of homes in this period, were expected to maintain their homes and raise their children with new efficiency and skill. Increasingly important was their role as consumers. *Photoplay* magazine ran an ad that summed up popular opinion of the New Woman in the home: "Home Manager—Purchasing Agent—Art Director—Wife. She is the active partner in the business of running a home. She buys most of the things which go to make home life happy, healthful, and beautiful."[12] The rosy images of advertising aside, most homemakers continued to have time-consuming responsibilities. Indeed, expectations about careful shopping, cleaner homes, and healthier children may have increased, rather than lightened, women's domestic burdens. Also in the 1920s, a new emphasis emerged on the marriage partnership's being a mutually satisfying sexual relationship. A 1930 sociological study, *New Girls for Old*, encapsulated the new way of thinking: "After hundreds of years of mild complaisance to wifely duties, modern women have awakened to the knowledge that they are sexual beings. And with this new insight the sex side of marriage has assumed sudden importance."[13]

Changing ideas about female sexuality were furthered in part by the increasing availability and respectability of reliable birth control, especially the diaphragm. When reformer Margaret Sanger began her drive to legalize the dissemination of contraceptives in 1912, she initially concentrated on helping poor women to control their fertility (see pp. 441–44). By the 1920s, however, discouraged by conservative opposition to her plans for birth control clinics for the poor, she began to target elite and middle-class audiences and to emphasize the erotic potential for women by separating sex from reproduction. Sanger was instrumental in liberalizing state laws to make contraceptives more available, although the requirement that a physician dispense contraceptives meant that they were more likely to be readily available to prosperous white women.

Changing conceptions about female sexuality had been evident in the prewar years, especially among radical feminists and some urban working-class young women. By the 1920s, these new ideas had filtered to a broad middle-class audience. Crucial to the popularization of these ideas was the rapid expansion of the mass media, especially motion pictures. Popular movies featured stars like Clara Bow, who had "It" (the catchphrase for sexual appeal) and attracted audiences with displays of female flesh — bare arms and legs — and sensual love scenes. Despite heightened attention to sexuality, movies rarely condoned adultery or promiscuity. While some plots titillated with the escapades of "bad" girls, these women usually paid for their sins; the heroines who resisted temptation were rewarded at the end by marriage or a renewal of their marriage commitment.

Another way in which movies and other forms of mass media, most notably advertising, simultaneously promoted a new sexuality while limiting it was the close association drawn between sexuality and consumer goods. Advertising featured a variety of images of women, but one of the most ubiquitous was the glamorous female, made sexy by the products she purchased. The 1920s also witnessed an explosion of beauty shops and a dramatic increase in the sale of cosmetics. Thus, just as women were being encouraged to explore their sexuality, they were also being encouraged to identify it with particular standards of beauty and with the purchase of consumer goods and to see its goal as the happily adjusted marriage. In the process, the radical egalitarian potential of women's sexual liberation that earlier feminists had hoped for was muted. (See Primary Sources: "Beauty Culture between the Wars," pp. 528–34.)

There were other indications that the sexual revolution was less revolutionary than it seemed. Young women might engage in petting, for example, but prevailing norms discouraged intercourse except as a prelude to marriage between engaged couples. A double standard for men and women persisted, and women could get a reputation for being "fast," which could damage their marriage prospects. Moreover, not everyone embraced the new sexuality. Divorce case records in the 1920s reveal that some wives, traditionally reared, could not comfortably accept the new sexual code, much to the dismay of their husbands, who had anticipated a highly sexualized marriage. Among Italian immigrant daughters, a very low rate of illegitimacy

◆ **Sex at the Movies**

As this poster for the 1924 movie *Alimony*, starring Grace Darmond and Warner Baxter, suggests, movies of the 1920s emphasized sexuality. One ad for the film tantalized, "Beautiful Jazz Babies — Petting parties — Moonlight bathing parties on golden beaches — Midnight revels on costly yachts — Wine, women and song — all lead to alimony!" The major characters in the film ultimately reconcile, and the virtuous but sexy wife triumphs over the women out to seduce her husband. One reviewer was relieved to claim the movie was a "dramatic indictment of the loose lives of today." *Everett Collection.*

persisted into the 1930s, an indication that many of these young women remained outside the peer culture that sanctioned sexual activity for unmarried women.[14]

The concentration on women's sexuality in the twenties also disconcerted many women's right activists, for whom equality in matters of sexuality had never been a goal. They worried that the pursuit of sexual pleasure and recreation led women away from more serious concerns such as civic reform and women's rights.

Many older activists, who came of age in a time when homosocial bonding was especially common among educated, professional women, were also disconcerted that the new psychology of sexuality focused on the erotic dimension of close relationships between women, in part because it became increasingly common for hostile critics to dismiss militant feminists as repressed lesbians. For women more comfortable with same-sex sexuality, sophisticated urban environments gave them opportunities to live the lives they wanted, but the relentless celebration of heterosexuality may well have been disconcerting.

For many African American women reformers, who had labored for decades to protect black women from sexual exploitation and to counter the stereotype of black women as promiscuous, celebrating female sexuality was also problematic. During the Harlem Renaissance, a major cultural movement of black authors and artists who sought to articulate a distinct black contribution to American culture, some women writers such as Jessie Fauset, Nella Larsen, and Zora Neale Hurston were sensitive to the sexualized portrayal of black women. But in another major expression of black culture, female jazz and blues singers such as Bessie Smith, Ida Cox, and Ma Rainey often presented an exuberant sense of women's enjoyment of their sexuality that spoke of resistance to sexual objectification and domination by men. Some songs featured a woman demanding that her lover pay attention to her needs, such as "One Hour Mamma," in which Ida Cox reminded her partner that she wanted "a slow and easy man" who "needn't ever take the lead."[15] Others suggested lesbian desire, such as "Prove It on Me Blues," in which Ma Rainey sang, "Went out last night with a crowd of my friends / They must've been women, 'cause I don't like no men."[16]

The sexual dimension of the New Woman, like her participation in politics and the workforce, was thus complex. New developments in both public and private spheres ushered in significant changes, although these were filtered through the lens of class, race, and ethnicity and were accompanied by continued emphasis on women's roles as wives and mothers. A coalescence of factors in the 1920s — an expanding role in the workplace, new political opportunities, a more sexualized marriage, and the growing importance of the consumer culture — did not give women full economic and political equality or personal autonomy, but it did give their lives a modern contour, putting in motion the trends that would characterize women's lives for the rest of the twentieth century.

◆ DEPRESSION DECADE: THE 1930S

Although the fabled prosperity of the 1920s was never as widespread as popular memory has it, the contrast between the affluence of that decade and the economic hardships faced by Americans in the 1930s is striking. In 1933, unemployment figures had reached 25 percent and the U.S. gross national product (GNP) had been cut almost in half. A stunning stock market crash in late October 1929 had helped precipitate the Great Depression, particularly by damaging the nation's banking system, but long-standing weaknesses in the economy accounted for the Depression's length and severity. A prolonged agricultural depression and a decline in certain "sick" industries such as textiles and mining were just two points of underlying vulnerability. An unequal distribution of the nation's wealth — in 1929, 40 percent of the population received only 12.5 percent of aggregate family income, while the top 5 percent of the population received 30 percent — meant that once the Depression began, the majority of people were unable to spend the amount of money that was needed to revive the economy. The Great Depression became self-perpetuating, and for ten years it left what one observer has called "an invisible scar" running through the lives of millions of Americans.

If our most familiar female icon of the 1920s is the flamboyant flapper, then the counterpart for the Depression decade of the 1930s is Dorothea Lange's haunting photograph of Florence Owens, later Thompson, titled "Migrant Mother" (see p. 537). Thompson was part of a massive exodus of farm families from the southwestern plains states, where farmers, already suffering from low crop prices in the 1920s, were devastated by a prolonged drought in the 1930s that had created the "dust bowl" and countless family tragedies. (See Primary Sources: "Dorothea Lange Photographs Farm Women of the Great Depression," pp. 535–41.) The image potently evokes the hardships embodied in the sterile statistics of the era, a period in which overall unemployment rose as high as 30 percent, banks closed by the thousands, and hundreds of thousands of Americans lost their homes and farms. Even if a woman was not among the down-and-out, she could identify with the fear and uncertainty of the migrant woman. But just as the flapper only scratches the surface of the experience of women in the 1920s, the migrant mother was just one facet of a complex mosaic of American womanhood.

At Home in Hard Times

Even more so than in good times, class and race proved powerful determinants of women's experience in the Great Depression. While elite and middle-class families experienced downward mobility and emotional and material hardships, it was the nation's working-class and farm families who suffered most from the economic crisis. Not only did they face a greater likelihood of losing their jobs or farms, but they also had fewer resources to draw on. African Americans were among the greatest losers. They were the first fired in industrial jobs and the hardest hit among the rural southern Americans so devastated by the farm crisis. Mexican and Asian American farmers and workers in the West and Southwest also experienced high rates of unemployment and low wages. Like African Americans, they met with discrimination from city, state, and federal agencies that provided relief payments to the impoverished. Indeed, resistance to subsidizing unemployed immigrant workers led to a drive to deport Mexican immigrants, especially in Texas and California. In the 1930s, Los Angeles lost one-third of its Mexican population, many of whom were citizen children of immigrant parents. This deportation movement led to significant disruption in communities, placing heavy burdens on women and families already coping with economic dislocations.

The Depression was also a heavily gendered experience. Although women's participation in the workforce had been steadily increasing in the early twentieth century, most observers continued to regard women's proper place as the home.

Thus, policy makers, sociologists, and popular writers alike interpreted the unemployment crisis of the 1930s as primarily a male dilemma, emphasizing "the forgotten man" and worrying about the psychological impact of unemployment for American traditions of masculine individualism. Sociological studies such as *The Unemployed Man and His Family* (1940) emphasized the familial disruption that resulted when men lost jobs and often sacrificed their dominant position in the household. Observers may have been correct that the crisis was harder on men than on women. As sociologists Helen and Robert Lynd put it in their widely read 1937 study of "Middletown" (Muncie, Indiana), "The men, cut adrift from their usual routine, lost much of their sense of time and dawdled helplessly and dully about the streets; while in the homes the women's world remained largely intact and the round of cooking, housecleaning, and mending became if anything more absorbing."[17]

These tasks became more absorbing because so many women had to juggle fewer resources and become adept at making do. Magazines ran articles on cooking with cheaper ingredients, and ads aimed at female consumers touted moneysaving products and offered advice for preparing nutritious "7 cents' breakfasts." For poor women, the burdens of homemaking were exacerbated by problems of poor sanitation and substandard housing — problems especially for minority women and poor white rural women. In many social groups, homemaking was made more complicated and stressful by the presence of extended kin, as families coped with reduced income by combining households.

Other issues shaped the households women inhabited. Unemployment for men often strained marriages, especially ones that had been patriarchal. Desertion rates rose, but rates for divorce, an expensive proposition, did not. Another measure of the Depression's impact was the decline in fertility rates, dropping, for example, from eighty-nine to seventy-six live births per thousand women of childbearing age between the years 1930 and 1933. The trend toward smaller families and the use of contraception, evident among more prosperous families in the 1920s, spread to many working-class families in the 1930s, as fewer children became an economic necessity and access to legal birth control was facilitated by a 1936 decision (*United States v. One Package of Japanese Pessaries*) invalidating federal laws that had prohibited the dissemination of contraceptive information.

Women and Work

Although contemporaries viewed women's primary responsibility to be maintaining the home in hard times, women as workers constitute an important part of the Depression story. Hostility toward the idea of married women going to work intensified in the 1930s, as evidenced in public opinion polls such as the one conducted by George Gallup in 1936, which asked if married women should work if their husbands were employed; 82 percent of the respondents said no, although there was less opposition to wives in very low-income families who worked.[18] Legislation reflected this attitude. The 1932 National Economy Act required that when workforce reductions occurred, the first let go should be those who already had a family member in the government's employ. While this legislation did not specifically target women, it led to the firing of thousands of them. State and local governments echoed this trend, as did many private companies. Most school districts did not hire wives as teachers, and half of them fired women when they married. For those women who did work, wages shrank in the 1930s; women also continued to earn less than men — in 1935 they earned approximately 65 cents for every dollar of men's wages.[19]

Despite this discrimination, women's desire and need to work increased, and their participation in the workforce grew modestly, inching up from 24.4 percent in 1930 to 25.4 percent in 1940. More striking was the increase of married women workers. In 1930, 12 percent of wives worked; in 1940, 17 percent.[20] While women also experienced devastating unemployment, especially in the early hard years of the Depression, white women at least found jobs far more quickly than their male counterparts. Sex segregation in the workforce ironically assisted them. Heavy industrial jobs, the domain of men (where women counted for less than 2 percent of all workers), were the most affected by the Depression, while light industry, usually associated with female operatives, recovered more quickly as the decade progressed. More significantly, opportunities in clerical work expanded in part because the federal agencies of the New Deal designed to cope with the Depression almost doubled the number of federal employees.

In contrast to white women, black women lost jobs during the 1930s. One traditional field for black women — farm labor — constricted as hundreds of thousands of sharecroppers and wage workers were thrown out of work in the South. Mechanization further eliminated farm jobs. At the same time, opportunities in the other major area of employment for black women — domestic work — shrank and competition grew. In New York City and elsewhere, "slave markets" provided a particularly potent example of the harsh conditions. Black women would stand on street corners waiting for white women to drive by and hire them for a day's heavy labor for less than $2.00. Whatever their jobs, black women were almost certain to earn less than other groups. The average wage per week of white women in Texas factories, for example, was $7.45, while Mexican women took home $5.40 and black women only $3.75.[21]

The patterns of work in the 1930s underlined the broad trends becoming clear in the previous decade. Participation of women, especially married women, in the workforce increased, but it did so in sex-segregated labor markets that limited women's occupational mobility and income. Moreover, that market was further segregated by race and ethnicity, with white women dominating the rapidly expanding clerical workforce. Jobs in agriculture decreased, but they were still a significant source of work for women of color, as were domestic labor and semi-skilled industrial work, especially that related to garment and food processing. The restricted nature of women's job opportunities would not be challenged — and then only temporarily — until the United States entered World War II in 1941.

Women's New Deal

As American women and men coped with hard times, they sought strong political leadership. They found it in President Franklin D. Roosevelt. In 1932, as the Depression deepened, Roosevelt defeated Republican incumbent Herbert Hoover

◆ **"Make a Wish": Bronx Slave Market**

This 1938 photograph of the so-called Bronx Slave Market was part of a series shot by Robert H. McNeill, an African American who would later work for the Works Progress Administration (WPA). These two neatly dressed women and the man standing next to them seem to be merely waiting for something. But context is everything. In 1935 Ella Baker and Marvel Cooke wrote an article for *Crisis* on the demeaning process whereby impoverished black women sold their labor, mostly to Jewish housewives, in New York City's Bronx. "Rain or shine, cold or hot, you will find them there — Negro women, old and young — sometimes bedraggled, sometimes neatly dressed — but with the invariable paper bundle, waiting expectantly for Bronx housewives to buy their strength and energy for an hour, two hours, or even for a day at the munificent rate of fifteen, twenty, twenty-five, or, if luck be with them, thirty cents an hour. If not the wives themselves, maybe their husbands, their sons, or their brothers, under the subterfuge of work, offer worldly-wise girls higher bids for their time."[22] As Baker and Cooke reported, the women were largely powerless in the arrangement and were often short-changed and required to do arduous labor. The market, born of the Great Depression, lasted into the 1950s. *Smithsonian American Art Museum, Washington, DC/Art Resource, NY.*

handily and came to Washington, D.C., with a clear mandate to act forcefully to bring about recovery and relieve suffering. He brought to the presidency charisma and a willingness to experiment with programs that directly assisted the needy. Labeling these programs a "New Deal" for Americans, Roosevelt pushed an enormous amount of legislation through Congress. Roosevelt's New Deal agencies

READING INTO THE PAST

MARY MCLEOD BETHUNE
Letter to President Franklin D. Roosevelt (1940)

African American women leaders worked for women's rights in the context of the broader struggle for justice for all members of their race. Mary McLeod Bethune was in this tradition. A prominent educator, Bethune had founded Bethune-Cookman College, served as president of the National Association of Colored Women, and established the National Council of Negro Women in 1935. Bethune began her New Deal experience as an advisor to the National Youth Administration but soon became the director of the Division of Minority Affairs, later called the Division of Negro Affairs. Although the New Deal's assistance to blacks fell short of her expectations, Bethune was a loyal supporter of both Eleanor and Franklin Roosevelt. The following is a formal letter to President Roosevelt. In 1940, as the United States began mobilizing its industrial productivity anticipating the advent of war, Bethune wrote from her position as president of the National Council of Negro Women. Although not a participant in the white women's New Deal, Bethune had a strong base of power among black women's organizations.

My dear Mr. President:

At a time like this, when the basic principles of democracy are being challenged at home and abroad, when racial and religious hatreds are being engendered, it is vitally important that the Negro, as a minority group in this nation, express anew his faith in your leadership and his unswerving adherence to a program of national defense adequate to insure the perpetuation of the principles of democracy. I approach you as one of a vast army of Negro women who recognize that we must face the dangers that confront us with a united patriotism.

contributed to his immense popularity, a popularity that the efforts of his wife, Eleanor Roosevelt, enhanced. A gifted woman with a long-standing commitment to social reform, Eleanor called herself "the eyes and ears of the New Deal," perhaps an implicit reference to her husband's limited physical mobility. (He was severely crippled from polio.) She crisscrossed the nation promoting the New Deal, pushed Roosevelt to pay more attention to the plight of African Americans, and gathered around her a group of activist women particularly concerned about the hardships women and children faced during the Depression. Despite her efforts, however, most New Deal programs slighted or discriminated against women.

We, as a race, have been fighting for a more equitable share of those opportunities which are fundamental to every American citizen who would enjoy the economic and family security which a true democracy guarantees. Now we come as a group of loyal, self-sacrificing women who feel they have a right and a solemn duty to serve their nation.

In the ranks of Negro womanhood in America are to be found ability and capacity for leadership, for administrative as well as routine tasks, for the types of service so necessary in a program of national defense. These are citizens whose past records at home and in war service abroad, whose unquestioned loyalty to their country and its ideals, and whose sincere and enthusiastic desire to serve you and the nation indicate how deeply they are concerned that a more realistic American democracy, as visioned by those not blinded by racial prejudices, shall be maintained and perpetuated.

I offer my own services without reservation, and urge you, in the planning and work which lies ahead, to make such use of the services of qualified Negro women as will assure the thirteen and a half million Negroes in America that they, too, have earned the right to be numbered among the active forces who are working towards the protection of our democratic stronghold.

Faithfully yours,
Mary McLeod Bethune

SOURCE: McCluskey and Smith, *Mary McLeod Bethune*, 173–74.

QUESTIONS FOR ANALYSIS

1. What is Bethune asking of Roosevelt in this letter?
2. What claims does she make about African American women and why?
3. How does she appeal to broader national ideals in order to advance African American women at this moment of impending war?

The National Industrial Recovery Act (NIRA) reflected the way in which the New Deal reinforced existing assumptions about women's subordinate role in the workforce. Passed in 1933 and designed to stimulate recovery, this pivotal piece of legislation established codes that set wages, hours, and prices in the nation's major economic sectors. Jobs described as "light and repetitive" were those usually assigned to women, and 25 percent of the codes explicitly permitted differential wages between men and women, anywhere from 5 to 25 cents per hour. Clerical workers in many fields were excluded, and farm and domestic workers were not covered at all.

◆ Eleanor Roosevelt and Marian Anderson

Although Franklin Roosevelt's New Deal did not significantly challenge institutionalized racism, many New Dealers sought to draw attention to issues of poverty, segregation, and disfranchisement. None was more important in this regard than Eleanor Roosevelt. In 1939 she made one of her more famous interventions as First Lady when the Daughters of the American Revolution (DAR), which owned the largest concert venue in Washington, D.C., Constitution Hall, refused to lease the space for a concert by the brilliant black contralto Marian Anderson. In response, Roosevelt not only resigned from the DAR but also facilitated the use of the Lincoln Memorial for what became an iconic moment in American history when an integrated audience of 75,000 covered the length of the mall to hear Anderson's concert. The connection between the two women continued when Roosevelt attended the NAACP's convention in order to present Anderson with the NAACP's Spingarn medal, pictured here. In her comments, the First Lady noted that Anderson "had the courage to meet many difficulties. She has always had great dignity; and her modesty and her dignity together with her great gift have gained for her wide recognition. I am glad to have been chosen to give you this medal, Miss Anderson, for your achievement far transcends any question of race. It is an achievement in the field of art, and this medal is given to you in recognition of the perfection of your art."[23] *Bettmann/Getty Images.*

Despite such shortcomings, the New Deal did help some women workers, especially in its efforts to provide protection for organized labor. The 1920s had been a low point for unions, which suffered from the postwar Red Scare and corporate antiunion drives. Union membership stood at a mere 12 percent of the workforce at the end of the decade. The NIRA, however, contained provisions that legitimized unions and helped to spark hundreds of organizing drives that tapped into the widespread discontent of workers. Women were particularly active in the International Ladies' Garment Workers' Union, which conducted organizing drives in sixty cities, increasing its size by 500 percent between 1933 and 1934. When in 1935 the Supreme Court, arguing that the NIRA represented an unconstitutional delegation of power to the executive, invalidated the act, the New Deal replaced its labor provisions with the National Labor Relations Act, known as the Wagner Act. This legislation again galvanized unionization campaigns and contributed to the success of a new national union federation, the Congress of Industrial Organizations (CIO), which in 1935 had broken off from the more conservative American Federation of Labor (AFL). The CIO, influenced in part by the significant presence of Communist Party members among its organizers, many of whom were women, concentrated on mass production industries. Women especially benefited from union inroads in light industries such as tobacco and paper products manufacturing. In 1924, 200,000 women belonged to a union; by 1938, the figure was 800,000.

Women actively participated in strikes, both as workers and as wives of male strikers. In 1933, poor wages and working conditions led to a long and bitter strike by eighteen thousand cotton workers in California, most of whom were Mexicans associated with the Cannery and Agricultural Workers Industrial Union. Women participated by preparing and distributing food among the strikers, but they were also active on the picket line. They taunted strikebreakers, urging them to join the strike, yelling out in Spanish, "Come on out, quit work, we'll feed you. If you don't, we'll poison all of you." This confrontation ended in violence as many women armed themselves with knives and lead pipes.[24]

Women also played a crucial role in the 1937 Flint, Michigan, sit-down strike against General Motors. When the men sat down at their machines, their wives as well as women workers (who were not included in the occupation of the factory because of concerns about sexual propriety) organized the Women's Emergency Brigade. They fulfilled the traditional female role of providing food for the men, but then they moved beyond that role to stage a women's march of seven thousand and to create other diversions that allowed men to expand the strike to another GM plant. Brigade leader, autoworker, and socialist Genora Johnson Dollinger explained, "This was an independent move. It was not under the direction of the union or its administrators — I just talked it over with a few women — the active ones — and told them this is what we had to do."[25] (See Reading into the Past: "Genora Johnson Dollinger and the General Motors Sit-Down Strike.") The successful strike ended with GM's recognition of the United Auto Workers union. Thus, as supporters and as workers, women played an important role in the labor radicalism that shaped the 1930s.

The federal government's new involvement in protecting working-class Americans through labor legislation was matched by its unprecedented intervention

READING INTO THE PAST

Genora Johnson Dollinger and the General Motors Sit-Down Strike (1936–37)

Genora Johnson (later Dollinger) was a Socialist Party organizer who played a central role in mobilizing women in the Flint, Michigan, General Motors sit-down strike of 1936–37. Johnson created the Emergency Brigade, which armed women with clubs and blackjacks to assist the United Auto Workers (UAW) union in standing up to the violent efforts to break the strike. But Johnson also spearheaded the creation of the Women's Auxiliary, consisting mostly of wives of strikers, which aided the strike in more conventionally female ways, as she describes in this oral history account.

I should tell you how the Women's Auxiliary was formed. The last days of December 1936 were when the sit-downs began. Following that came New Year's Eve. Among working class families, everybody celebrates New Year's Eve. I was amazed at the number of wives that came down to the picket line and threatened their husbands, "If you don't cut out this foolishness and get out of that plant right now, you'll be a divorced man!" They threatened divorce loudly and openly, yelling and shouting at their husbands. I knew I couldn't go and grab each one of them to talk to them privately. So I could only watch as some of the men climbed out of the plant window up on the second floor, down the ladder to go home with their wives. These were good union members, but they were hooted and hollered at by their comrades in the plant who were holding the fort in the sit-down. This was a very dangerous turn of events because I knew how few men were inside holding that plant, and it worried many of us.

The next day, we decided to organize the women. We thought that if women can be that effective in breaking a strike, they could be just as effective in helping to win it. So we organized the Women's Auxiliary and we laid out what we were going to do.

Now remember, the UAW was still in the process of getting organized. It didn't have elected officers or by-laws or any of the rest of it. So we were free to organize our Women's Auxiliary, to elect our president, vice-president, recording secretary and heads of committees, all on our own.

We couldn't have women sitting down in the plants because the newspapers were antagonizing the wives at home by saying that women were sleeping over in the plant. In fact, GM sent anonymous messages to the wives of some of the strikers alleging that there were prostitutes in those embattled plants. But we knew we could get women on the picket lines.

So we organized a child-care center at the union headquarters, so children would have some place to go when their mothers marched on the picket line. Wilma McCartney, who had nine children and was going to have her tenth, took charge of that. At first, the women were scared to death to come down to the union, and some may have been against the union for taking away their pay check so they couldn't feed their children who were hungry or crying for milk. Then this wonderful woman, this mother of nine children who was pregnant with another, would talk to them about how it would benefit them for their husbands to participate actively. And if they won the strike, it would make all the difference in the world in their living conditions. We recruited a lot of women just through the child-care center.

We also set up a first aid station with a registered nurse in a white uniform and red union arm-band. She was a member of the Women's Auxiliary. The women in the Auxiliary also made house calls to make sure every family had enough to eat, and they gave advice on how to deal with creditors.

But that wasn't enough as far as I was concerned. Women had more to offer than just these services. So we set up public speaking classes for women. Most of the women had never even been to a union meeting. In those days, many of the men would go to union meetings and say to the women, "It's none of your damn business. Don't you mix into our affairs." So the women didn't express any of their ideas about what could be done to better their conditions.

Women came out of those classes thinking, "Well, women did play a role in the unions. We have got a right to say something." We trained them in how to get up in union meetings and what appeals to make. We gave them an outline of a speech and they practiced in the classes.

Some of the men were very opposed to having their wives at the union headquarters and a few of them never gave up their sexist attitudes. But most of the men encouraged their wives. They thought we were doing a wonderful job, making things better for them at home because their wives understood why their husbands had to be on the picket line all day long and do a lot of extra things for the union. They could talk and work together as companions. And the children were learning from their parents' discussions about the strike.

A few men still opposed women becoming active or walking the picket lines. I was often called a "dyke." Some men said that women who came down to the picket line were prostitutes or loose women looking for men. But as more married men with families became active in the strike, they kept those elements quiet.

Source: Susan Rosenthal, *Striking Flint: Genora Dollinger Recalls the 1936–37 General Motors Sit-Down Strike* (ReMarx Publishing, 2014).

QUESTIONS FOR ANALYSIS

1. How did the women's auxiliary help sustain the Flint autoworkers' community during the sit-down strike?

2. What parallels do you see between Johnson's description of the problems facing women on the picket line and those faced by the strikers described in "Parades, Picketing, and Power: Women in Public Space," pp. 462–69.

in providing relief for those made destitute by the Depression. Although most policy makers perceived the unemployment crisis as primarily a male one, an inner circle of female New Dealers, aided by Eleanor Roosevelt, insisted that the government pay attention to the "forgotten woman." A central figure was Ellen S. Woodward, who headed the Women's and Professional Projects Division of several agencies that provided federal relief for the unemployed — the Federal Emergency Relief Administration (FERA), Civil Works Administration (CWA), and Works Progress Administration (WPA). Woodward worked hard to get women included in programs that created jobs for the unemployed. A small number of professional women, such as librarians, social workers, teachers, and nurses, were accommodated in federal projects, and some artists and writers found employment in programs such as the Federal Art Project or the Federal Theater Project, headed by Hallie Flanagan. But the vast majority of women needing help (almost 80 percent in 1935) were unskilled, and for them the work-relief jobs clustered in traditional women's work of sewing, canning, and domestic labor.

In addition to offering individual employment, these programs benefited the community. Between 1933 and 1937, women made over 122 million articles that were distributed to the poor free of charge. They provided the food for highly successful free school lunch programs. Librarians created card catalogs and oversaw Braille transcription projects. Handicraft programs drew on regional variations. In Texas, women were given leather to make coats and jackets; in Arizona, Native American women fashioned copperware; in Florida, women produced hats, handbags, and rugs for the tourist industry.

Yet, despite these benefits and Woodward's promise that "women are going to get a square deal," New Deal programs were riddled with discrimination against women. Most programs focused on male unemployment and treated women as subordinate earners who ideally should be in the home. To be eligible for work relief, women needed to prove that they were heads of family, and if a husband was physically able to work, whether he had found work or not, women were unlikely to be given federal jobs. Some young women found jobs with the National Youth Administration (NYA), but they were excluded from the Civilian Conservation Corps, which put 2.5 million young men to work conserving the nation's parks and natural resources. Only after Eleanor Roosevelt intervened were similar camps set up for women, but these accommodated only eight thousand young women.

This type of discrimination provoked protest from women's groups as well as the unemployed. One woman wrote to the Roosevelts to complain: "I should like to know why it is that men can be placed so easily and not women."[26] The answer to that question lay in part with local administrators, who often resisted finding work for women, particularly work that challenged traditional notions of women's proper domestic roles. When women found positions, the jobs invariably fell into low-paying categories. New Deal agencies, then, not only followed sex segregation policies based on traditional notions of women's proper place in the home but also helped to institutionalize them.

Similarly, New Deal agencies replicated the discrimination based on race and ethnicity found in the private labor market. Relief policies were designed to help the poor, and indeed, most minority groups benefited from them to some degree. But despite official guidelines that tried to limit racial discrimination, federal agencies rarely challenged the policies of local administrators. On many Native American reservations, officials often were even more indifferent to the problem of work relief for women than to Native peoples in general. In the racially segregated South, local New Deal agencies resisted giving black women jobs during harvest periods when cheap farm labor was in demand. When African American women could get federal jobs, they were usually in segregated programs and were routinely given the most menial work. In San Antonio, a three-part caste system was in operation. African American women were formally segregated from projects that could employ white or Mexican women, but an informal process kept white and Mexican women from working together in sewing or canning rooms.

That the New Deal both assisted women especially in their family responsibilities and reinforced their inequality as wage workers was most dramatically evident in the Social Security Act of 1935. This pathbreaking legislation owed much to women reformers, especially Secretary of Labor Frances Perkins. It provided a federal pension plan and federal-state matching fund programs for unemployment assistance and for aid to dependent mothers and children. Neither domestic workers nor farmworkers — two major employment options for poor women — were covered by the program, however, and women who worked in the home as mothers and housewives were similarly excluded. A 1939 amendment to Social Security further institutionalized inequality. Married working women were taxed at the same rate as their husbands, but because there was a family limit to benefits, a wife's benefits were reduced if her wages and her husband's exceeded the family limits. In addition, widows and their children received benefits when a husband and father died, but a married woman's dependents did not. In common with other New Deal programs, then, Social Security operated under the assumption of women's subordinate place in the labor market and their primary role in the home.

Despite its mixed record in terms of racial and gender discrimination, the New Deal did assist a wide variety of Americans in coping with the devastating effects of the Great Depression. It facilitated the growth of unions, put millions of people to work, and institutionalized the modest welfare provisions of the Social Security Act. One thing it failed to accomplish was to end the Depression. The return of prosperity would not come until the advent of World War II, when the demand for war production set American factories back to work and created full employment.

◆ WORKING FOR VICTORY: WOMEN AND WAR, 1941–1945

In the late 1930s, as the militarism of Germany, Italy, and Japan rose to a crescendo, most Americans adamantly opposed being drawn into war. This remained true even after Germany, under Adolf Hitler, invaded Poland in 1939 and France and Britain, the United States's allies in World War I, declared war on the Axis powers, Germany and Italy. Despite the official neutrality mandated by Congress, the United States offered financial and other material assistance to its former allies and began its own defense buildup. Public sentiment remained high against becoming involved in the war, but December 7, 1941, shattered that resistance. When Japan, which had signed an alliance with the Axis, executed a devastating surprise air attack on the American naval base and fleet at Pearl Harbor, Hawaii, killing 2,400 Americans, Congress declared war on Japan. Within days, Germany and Italy declared war on the United States, and the United States in turn declared war on those nations. The United States entered a global conflagration being fought in Europe, Asia, and Africa that would last until 1945.

The global war and the massive mobilization it entailed had a tremendous impact on American women. By undercutting patterns of sex-segregated labor and offering women new independence and responsibilities — perfectly symbolized by the poster image of "Rosie the Riveter" — it produced significant changes, both in the workplace and in the domestic arena. (See Primary Sources: "Voices of 'Rosie the Riveter,'" pp. 542–47.) Yet to a striking degree, Americans continued to reiterate traditional notions about woman's proper sphere in the home even as they challenged these ideas in daily life. And, as was the case during the Depression, race, ethnicity, and gender discrimination continued to shape American women's experience.

Women in the Military

Despite a long tradition of exceptional American women edging their way onto the battlefield, donning the nation's uniform was a particularly male act that served to shape definitions of ideal masculinity. As the American military establishment geared up for World War II, it initially resisted incorporating women into the service. Eventually, military necessity, as well as pressure from women's groups under the leadership of Congresswoman Edith Nourse Rogers of Massachusetts, led to the acceptance of female military recruits. Thousands of men were thus made available for combat. The Women's Army Corps (WAC) attracted 140,000 recruits; 100,000 served in the navy's Women Accepted for Volunteer Emergency Service (WAVES); 23,000 were in the Marine Corps Women's Reserve (MCWR); and 13,000 enlisted with the Coast Guard Women's Reserve (SPAR: from the motto Semper Paratus, Always Ready). Another 76,000 served as army or navy nurses.

In the service, women's jobs typically followed the conventional patterns of peacetime. While some women worked as mechanics and welders and in other skilled jobs that broke the gender barrier, most filled jobs as clerks, telephone operators, and dieticians and in other routine assignments. A particularly vital role filled by women was nursing, often in exceptionally dangerous circumstances, just behind the front in all the major theaters of the war — North Africa, Europe, and Asia. While the military welcomed nurses, it resisted commissioning women as doctors — despite the severe shortage of physicians — until April 1943, fifteen months after America's entry into the war.

Black women experienced racial discrimination at the hands of the federal government's segregated military establishment. Because the navy prohibited African American men from serving in any but menial positions, it also refused to incorporate black women into its ranks until 1944, almost at the end of the war. Black nurses were commissioned in the army, and 10 percent of WACs were African American, but they lived and worked in segregated units and had less access to training and skilled jobs than white women. Black nurses were allowed to attend only to African Americans or prisoners of war, and they were often assigned to menial, not skilled, patient services.

◆ A War Job with a Future

To address a nursing shortage at home and abroad, in 1943 the U.S. Congress created the U.S. Cadet Nurse Corps to support nursing students who would pledge to "engage in essential nursing, military or civilian, for the duration of the war." This advertisement for the program appeared in *Modern Screen*. The ad emphasizes many elements of interest to women, beginning with the cadet nurses' beauty and femininity. It also reassures prospective nurses that they will not be "closing the door on romance," because they will still have time to date and even continue their training after marriage. And finally the text emphasizes that nursing offers a "job with a future." Do you think young women looking at this advertisement would have been more intrigued by the promise of a career or the glamour of serving one's country in uniform? *Media History Digital Library.*

◆ **Officer Charity Adams**

The federal government did not use images of black women in its recruitment campaigns for the Women's Army Auxiliary Corps, whose members were known as WACs (formerly WAACs). But the African American magazine *Opportunity*, which often featured black women defense and military workers, published this 1943 photograph of officer Charity Adams standing in front of a WAC poster, suggesting that black women could also "answer America's call." Adams, a former teacher, rose to the rank of major in the WAC. Her autobiography details pride in her accomplishments and the women who served with her but also harshly criticizes the segregation they experienced. *Schomburg Center, NYPL/Art Resource, NY.*

All women in the service encountered a public that was ambivalent about the gender challenges presented by women in uniform. Oveta Culp Hobby, a prominent Houston woman who became director of the WACs, had to counter pervasive rumors of sexual immorality and drunkenness among servicewomen. Although some of the rumors focused on lesbianism among recruits, referring to the "queer damozels of the Isle of Lesbos," most critics alleged promiscuity among heterosexual women.[27] The WACs distributed publicity praising the women's high moral character, but the agency also refused to distribute contraceptives to women in the service, in contrast to the policy adopted for men that was designed to prevent the spread of venereal disease. For women and men alike, the military also adopted a harsh policy toward homosexuality, making "homosexual tendencies," as diagnosed by a psychiatrist, sufficient grounds for dismissal from the service. However, although World War II military service offered many women and men opportunities to participate in a discreet lesbian and gay subculture, relatively few servicepeople were discharged on these grounds.

Equally as pressing as concerns about sexual immorality was the worry that servicewomen were sacrificing their femininity by usurping men's roles. In an effort to put these fears to rest, the *New York Times* reported in 1945 that the WAC "will always be a civilian at heart," and predicted that "the most important postwar plans of the majority of women in the WAC include just what all women want—their own homes and families."[28] Similarly, Colonel Hobby, while insisting that women in the service be treated with respect, reiterated traditional notions of women's proper place by asserting that military women were developing "new poise and charm" and that they "were only performing the duties that women would ordinarily do in civilian life."[29]

One duty that women rarely took on in civilian life was eagerly embraced by the members of the Women Airforce Service Pilots (WASPs). The U.S. government refused to militarize this agency, a measure of just how threatening the idea of women performing high-status "male" jobs was. Instead, these pilots were civil servants without military rank, privileges, or uniforms. Drawing on an eager applicant pool of over 25,000 women, the air force accepted 1,074 as WASPs, all of whom had pilot's licenses and experience, unlike most men accepted for training as military pilots. Of these, two were Mexican American, two Chinese American, and one Native American. The lone African American who applied was urged to withdraw her application by WASP director Jacqueline Cochran, who explained that she wanted to avoid controversy at a time when the program had not yet been officially put in place.

WASPs ferried and tested planes and participated in maneuvers and training. Although they did not participate in combat, thirty-eight women lost their lives on duty. The WASPs performed invaluable services, but they were disbanded in December 1944, before the end of the war, because of pressure from civilian male pilots and veterans groups, which resented potential female competition in an elite male field. WASPs were not eligible for veterans benefits until a congressional act passed in 1977 finally gave them partial recognition for what they had accomplished. In 2010, they were awarded a Congressional Gold Medal for their service.

Working Women in Wartime

Just as the military establishment was reluctant to incorporate women into the armed services, employers did not initially welcome female workers into defense industries. But by mid-1942, as more male workers were drafted into the army, the reality of labor scarcity started to erode resistance to female war workers. Women became the objects of a massive propaganda campaign to urge them to do their bit for Uncle Sam. Women responded eagerly to expanded job opportunities, not just in defense industries but in other sectors of the economy as well. After the hardships of the Depression, with some 3 million women unemployed as late as 1940, a burgeoning demand for labor put the unemployed to work and created jobs that provided new opportunities for women coming into the labor market for the first time. Between 1940 and 1945, almost 5 million new female workers entered the labor force, representing a 43 percent increase in women workers.[30] In 1944, an estimated 37 percent of adult women worked in the paid labor force. In a particularly important trend that foreshadowed postwar developments, older, married women provided the largest numbers of new workers, while there was little change in women between twenty and thirty years of age. Traditional jobs in light industry and clerical work expanded, and for white women, professional positions also became more readily available.

Women's participation in the defense industry was particularly significant because it broke down sex-segregated labor patterns, at least for the duration of the war. Women were trained in skilled high-paying jobs such as welders, riveters, and electricians. Although it was imperfectly implemented, the federal government's National War Labor Board (NWLB) issued an order in November 1942 calling for equal wages for women when the work they were doing was comparable to men's. Women's groups had pressured the NWLB, but the main motivation for the order was a desire not to undercut men's wages while women were temporarily taking on male jobs. Unions adopted a similar approach. Women's participation in unions rose from 9.4 percent of union members before the war to 22 percent in 1944. Although some left-wing unions' nondiscriminatory policies stemmed from genuinely egalitarian goals, most unions supported equal pay primarily with the goal of preserving male privileges. Moreover, older patterns of male and female classifications for jobs persisted, as well as seniority-based pay scales that served to ensure higher wages for men. Thus, a development that could have dramatically challenged sex segregation in the labor market was robbed of its more radical potential. (See Primary Sources: "Voices of 'Rosie the Riveter,' " pp. 542–47.)

For African American women, war job opportunities presented a mixed lot. Defense industries resisted hiring black women until it became absolutely necessary. In Detroit's war industries in 1943, of ninety-six thousand jobs filled by women, women of color held only one thousand.[31] Not until later that year did wartime manufacturers begin to hire black women. These possibilities for breaking into better-paying industrial work—the first since World War I—were undeniably exciting and helped to create another large migration out of the South. This time, in addition to the cities of the Midwest and North, African Americans branched out into the West, especially southern California. In this burgeoning center of defense manufacturing, as many as twelve thousand African Americans arrived monthly in the peak year of 1943.

War jobs allowed many black women to escape the drudgery and poor wages of domestic work. However, they were often denied training and, even with training, assigned to less desirable positions, such as work in foundries and outside labor gangs. Although some of the treatment black women received reflected employer racism, white women often resisted working with black women, in particular refusing to share toilet, shower, and meal facilities. In some cases, white women even went on strike over these issues, reflecting more a desire to maintain social distance between the races and a deep-seated belief that black women were "unclean" than fears about economic competition.[32]

Many black women protested the discrimination they encountered. Black organizations such as the NAACP fostered this new militancy, as did black newspapers. In Los Angeles, publisher Carlotta Bass used the pages of the *Eagle* to call for more jobs for African Americans. In concert with the NAACP, Bass organized a march in July 1942 against the local U.S. Employment Services office to insist that black women be given jobs in war industries, a tactic that eventually helped to integrate southern California defense plants. Black women also turned to the Fair Employment Practices Commission (FEPC), filing 25 percent of the complaints it received. This federal agency, charged with ensuring that defense industries and training programs did not discriminate, had been created in 1941 in response to a determined black protest and a threat to lead a march on Washington, D.C. A significant development in the history of civil rights, the FEPC nonetheless had limited success. The imperative of keeping war production up to speed meant that the FEPC had few tools for disciplining discriminating companies, and it rarely succeeded in forcing defense contractors to hire black women.

Nonetheless, black women benefited significantly from war opportunities. The percentage of black women employed in domestic service decreased from 60 percent in 1940 to 45 percent in 1944, and their participation in the industrial workforce increased from 7 to 18 percent for the same period. They also obtained more white-collar work in the federal government, especially in Washington, D.C. However, black women's low seniority usually meant that as the war wound down, they were the first fired. Margaret Wright, a skilled worker for Lockheed Aircraft, a major defense contractor, was laid off at the war's end; later she sadly recalled, "I had to fall back on the only other thing that I knew, and that was doing domestic work."[33] By 1950, some of the gains made in breaking away from domestic work had eroded: 50 percent of African American working women were still in domestic service. After the war, however, some women were able to hold on to higher-paying industrial and clerical work. Even for those who went back to domestic work, the migration from the impoverished rural South offered at least the hope for a better life.

Other women of color found expanded opportunities in the war years and faced less discrimination than African Americans. Defense industry companies as well as the government actively recruited Mexican Americans. The Office of War Information distributed posters touting "Americanos Todos" ("Americans All") that featured a Mexican sombrero and Uncle Sam's star-studded hat and proclaimed, "Americans All Let's Fight For Victory."[34] In the Midwest, Mexicans, who before the war had difficulty finding industrial work and were routinely asked for their citizenship papers, found that employers "stopped asking for proof of legalization because they needed all the workers they could find for the war effort."[35] In Los Angeles, Mexican American women flocked to the new jobs, especially in the aircraft industry. During the 1930s, as garment workers they earned $8 to $10 per week. But in war plants, as riveters, welders, inspectors, and punch press operators, they could earn as much as $40 to $60 per week. Besides taking satisfaction in better pay and increased skills, many found long-term economic and social mobility in their new jobs. As Rose Echeverria commented in an oral interview, "We felt that if we worked hard and that if we proved ourselves, we, too, could become doctors and lawyers and professional people."[36] Not only did these women secure jobs in defense industries, but they also found that the labor scarcity improved their circumstances in other industrial jobs. Food processing, which was traditionally characterized by low status and pay, was vital to the war effort, and the United Cannery, Agricultural, Packing, and Allied Workers of America union in California was able to use the war emergency to push usually resistant employers for pay concessions and other benefits, including in one instance a plant nursery for children of employees.

Native American women's employment also expanded during the war. About one-fifth of adult women on reservations left to take jobs, and those who stayed behind increased their duties, helping to maintain farming and tribal businesses such as the timber industry. The Bureau of Indian Affairs, under John Collier, a New Dealer who had constructed a more humanitarian and liberal Native American policy (though still perpetuating a patronizing attitude toward Indians), publicized Native American contributions to the war effort, as did the journals of off-reservation boarding schools, which supplied most of the young women who went into defense work.[37]

For Chinese American women, the war offered unusual opportunities. Jobs in defense industries represented a significant economic improvement over working in family businesses or in food processing or garment industries. Unlike many other groups of women, Chinese American defense industry workers were young and unmarried. Before the war, these second-generation women had found most jobs outside Chinatown closed to them, despite their American education and English language proficiency. Their improved job prospects stemmed in part from the labor scarcity but also from a reduction in the racial prejudice against the Chinese now that China was a U.S. ally in the war against Japan. Even on the West Coast, where Asian Americans were most densely populated and where prejudice ran extremely high, the Chinese became the "good" Asians. Symbolic of this change in attitude was the 1943 congressional decision to abolish the legal strictures prohibiting Chinese aliens from becoming naturalized citizens. For Chinese women and their families, then, World War II facilitated more integration into mainstream American society as well as improved economic opportunities.[38]

For most Japanese American women, especially those in the West, the situation was bleak. Following decades of anti-Japanese sentiment on the West Coast, the Japanese bombing of Pearl Harbor touched off a firestorm of suspicion directed at the Japanese in the United States. Despite the absence of any evidence of sabotage or disloyalty, President Roosevelt, encouraged by military leaders and western politicians, issued Executive Order 9066, mandating the internment of over 110,000 people of Japanese descent, more than two-thirds of whom were native-born American citizens. In ten remote camps in California, Arizona, Utah, Colorado, Wyoming, Idaho, and Arkansas, the Nisei (the Japanese term for second-generation Japanese Americans) and the Issei (their parents) lived in stark barracks behind barbed wire. Prisoners without trial, incarcerated because of race, the internees found the experience bewildering and humiliating.

Women continued as best they could with their familial duties, trying to supplement the unappetizing and inadequate food provided in the mess tent, keeping clothes clean without the benefit of running water in their barracks, and above all struggling to keep the family unit together in the face of the disruption of relocation and camp life. Ironically, internment may have offered slight benefits to young Nisei women. They worked in the camps as clerks or teachers for the same low wages as their fathers and brothers, giving them some small taste of economic equality and independence. Within the camps, peer groups exerted strong pressure as teenage girls tried to keep up with the latest fashions on the outside and socialized with young men. Club life, which had been important to urban Nisei girls and young women before the war, flourished in the camps. Groups associated with the YWCA and the Girls Scouts, for example, staged elaborate candlelight initiation ceremonies, which offered relief from the depressing camp environment and, as one historian has observed, linked the Nisei "to national organizations and the outside world from which they had been exiled."[39] The strong patriarchal authority of the Japanese household further eroded when the Nisei began to leave the camps in 1942 after the government decided that an individual Nisei's loyalty could be sufficiently investigated and determined. Some obtained permission to go to college in regions outside the West; an estimated 40 percent of those who became students were women. Others secured jobs in the Midwest and on the East

◆ Japanese Internment

Personally horrified by the internment order, Dorothea Lange nonetheless accepted a commission from the War Relocation Authority in order to document the lives of Japanese Americans and their experiences as internees. Presumably because the images showed the Japanese in such sympathetic terms, the photographs were impounded for the duration of the war. This 1942 photograph features a mother and baby in Centerville, California, in conversation with another woman while they await an evacuation bus. Posted on the wall behind them were schedules listing the names of families, the buses to which they were assigned, and the departure time. Note the tag on the parcel the woman on the left is holding. Families were identified by numbers, and their belongings and their children bore these tags as they were evacuated. Do you see any similarities between the composition here and the photographs Lange shot for the Farm Security Administration? *National Archives no. 537581.*

Coast, with the most likely type of work being domestic service, although some found employment in manufacturing. After Nisei men were urged to volunteer for military service to "prove" their loyalty, some Nisei women followed suit and became WACs or military nurses.

War and Everyday Life

Far removed from the experience of Japanese internment, most American women faced very different sorts of pressures connected to everyday life on the home front. When men went off to join the military, wives often followed them while they were in training stateside, living in makeshift accommodations and coping with a sense of impermanency and an uncertain future.[40] Other women migrated either alone or with their families in search of better-paying jobs in cities, confronting the challenges of adjustment to new surroundings. These included scarce housing in boom areas, a particularly pressing problem for black women and Mexicans, who were also subject to housing discrimination.

The new environment also could be liberating, especially for single women. New jobs offered higher income and a sense of independence that led to more sexual experimentation. As one young war worker expressed it, "Chicago was just humming, no matter where I went. The bars were jammed, and unless you were an absolute dog you could pick up anyone you wanted to." Observers worried about this trend, pointing out that it was not prostitutes but "amateurs" who were undermining morality and spreading sexually transmitted disease.[41] Although promiscuity was probably not as great as critics feared, women did experience more personal freedom. Particularly notable were opportunities for lesbian women. Leaving provincial hometowns for large cities, they found other women who identified as lesbians. A woman who called herself "Lisa Ben," an anagram of "lesbian," reported that she moved from a ranch in northern California to a job in Los Angeles, ending up in a boardinghouse occupied by young single women and asking herself, "Gee, I wonder if these are some of the girls I would very dearly love to meet." They apparently were; Ben stayed in Los Angeles after the war and became part of the discreet lesbian bar scene that emerged there and in other major cities during the war years.[42]

Despite the sexual experimentation, conventional expectations about marriage and family remained unaltered. The number of marriages escalated, with the Census Bureau estimating that between 1940 and 1943 a million more families were formed than would have been expected in peacetime. Fertility spiked as well, after the low levels of the Depression, with the birthrate rising from 19.4 per 1,000 in 1940 to 24.5 per 1,000 in 1945 (see Chart 1, p. A-17). Popular culture reiterated respect for the domestic ideal. While movie heroines were often portrayed as self-reliant and independent war workers or army nurses, the message remained that women at war were only temporarily outside their proper place of home and family.

Whether they worked or not, married women faced ongoing responsibilities in the household. Although released from the extreme restraints of making do in the hard times of the 1930s, homemakers still worked hard. Consumer goods such as sugar, meat, and shoes were rationed, and housewives had to organize their shopping carefully. Home appliances that might have lightened their load were not being produced because factories and workers were needed for war production—though manufacturers continued their advertising campaigns to keep up consumer desire. A vacuum cleaner company promised, "A day is coming when this war will be done. And on that day, like you, Mrs. America, Eureka will put aside its uniform and return to the ways of peace . . . building household appliances."[43]

For women who worked, household burdens proved particularly difficult. Limited hours for shopping after their workday ended was one source of frustration. Nor could women expect any help from absent husbands and sons during their "second shift" at home. Child care posed another problem. Some corporations, faced with high turnover and absenteeism, offered nurseries. The federal government mounted a limited program of day care centers, but these were underutilized, in part because women associated federal programs with New Deal assistance to the down-and-out and in part because of cultural resistance to the idea of strangers taking care of one's children. Most women relied on friends and family members for help with child care.

As the war drew to a close in 1945, people expressed growing fear about the long-term roles of Rosie the Riveter and her colleagues and the implications for the postwar family. Anthropologist Margaret Mead reported that soldiers contemplating their return to the United States worried, "Well, mostly we've been wondering whether it's true that women are smoking pipes at home."[44] Americans foresaw that women were in the workforce to stay, and agencies like the U.S. Department of Labor's Women's Bureau still worked to improve their wages and opportunities. But most opinion makers advocated reinstating women to their rightful place, the home, so that returning GIs could expect full employment and a stable family life. Industrial leader Frederick Crawford pronounced, "[F]rom a humanitarian point of view, too many women should not stay in the labor force. The home is the basic American institution."[45]

Surveys of women working during the war indicated that a significant number — a Women's Bureau survey reported three of four women — had hoped to continue to work outside the home after the war.[46] But with demobilization women were laid off in large numbers. Gladys Poese Ehlmann recalled the shock of her dismissal from Emerson Electric Company in St. Louis: "[T]he war was over on August 14 and we went in on the 15th. They lined us up and had our paychecks ready for us."[47] Accounting for 60 percent of the dismissals in heavy industry, women were fired at a rate 75 percent higher than men. But although women's participation in the workforce dropped, this decline was short-lived. Women lost better-paid positions and most of the high-status jobs that had challenged sex-segregated labor patterns. But within a few years of the armistice, 32 percent of women were back in the labor force, and more than half of them were married. The war had not eroded cultural ideas about women's primary role in the home and their secondary status as wage earners, but it had been a vehicle for sustaining and even accelerating a process of increased female participation in the workplace.

◆ CONCLUSION: The New Woman in Ideal and Reality

The images called up at the start of this chapter — the 1920s flapper, the 1930s migrant mother, and the 1940s Rosie the Riveter — capture the distinctive qualities of these three decades. But while the eras of prosperity, depression, and war affected women in different ways, we can still discern broad trends for the period as a whole that reveal the trajectory of twentieth-century women's lives.

Between 1920 and 1945, women worked in greater numbers, and more wives and mothers contributed to this trend, but they did so in the context of discriminatory sex-segregated labor patterns and unequal opportunities for women of color. In politics, women also witnessed important changes. Women now had the vote in all states, with the significant exception of African American women in the South, who like southern black men were largely disfranchised. In most states, women also enjoyed other legal rights — the right of married women to own property and obtain divorces and the right of all non-disfranchised women to serve on juries.

Although women did not sustain the ambitious hopes that followed the successful suffrage campaign, they could claim smaller victories. Reformers in the 1920s struggled against a repressive political climate to sustain their social justice agenda and, in the Depression years, became active and valued participants in the New Deal. Not as influential in the war years, they nonetheless left a permanent mark on public policy, especially in their Women's Bureau and Social Security activities.

Patterns in the home are less clearly defined. The Depression and war had contradictory effects on marriage, divorce, and fertility rates. Trends of the 1920s toward increased emphasis on female sexuality persisted, but they did so in the context of an abiding cultural ideal that assumed that this sexuality would be confined in the context of marriage and the home.

As Americans faced the realities of a complex postwar world, these themes of women's lives at home and in the workplace and political arena would do more than continue. They would eventually erupt in dramatic challenges to prevailing notions of women's proper place.

CHAPTER 9 REVIEW

KEY TERMS AND PEOPLE

Terms	Social Security Act	**People**
League of Women Voters	Fair Employment Practices	Dorothea Lange
Women's Joint Congressional	Commission	Alice Paul
Committee	Anti-Lynching Crusaders	Frances Perkins
Equal Rights Amendment	Woman Patriots	Mary McLeod Bethune
Sheppard-Towner Act		Eleanor Roosevelt
Women's Auxiliary, General		Marian Anderson
Motors strike		Ellen S. Woodward

REVIEW QUESTIONS

1. In terms of politics, work, and family life, what were the most significant changes for women in the 1920s? What were the greatest areas of continuity?

2. In what ways was the Great Depression a "heavily gendered experience"?

3. How did the New Deal reflect older ideas about women's conventional roles?

4. To what extent did World War II challenge gender stereotypes for women? To what extent did it reinforce them?

5. **Making Connections** The chapter concludes with the comment that despite the differing circumstances of the 1920s, Great Depression, and World War II, "we can still discern broad trends for the period as a whole that reveal the trajectory of twentieth-century women's lives." What were these trends?

PRIMARY SOURCES

Women's Lobbying in the 1920s

WHEN THE NINETEENTH AMENDMENT WAS RATIFIED in 1920, many American women eagerly looked for new opportunities to influence policies and policy. While some did so through electoral politics, others focused on lobbying around legislation on the state and national levels (see pp. 484–89). Although the maternalist social welfare reforms associated with the "women's dominion of reform" were a crucial part of women's political activism in the 1920s, other issues occupied a diverse group of women, including African American activists seeking racial justice and conservatives who drew upon the anti-Bolshevik Red Scare to challenge the extension of social justice reforms.

African American women activists were eager to use their vote to bring about significant improvements in the lives of black Americans. Although stymied in their efforts to challenge disfranchisement of African American men and women in the South, in states where they had the vote, women mobilized, mostly through the Republican Party, to help elect candidates they viewed as friendly to black interests. In the wake of a wave of race riots and violence, African American women became particularly focused on the campaign to pass a federal antilynching law. First introduced by Missouri representative Leonidas C. Dyer in 1919, the assumption behind the Dyer Bill was that a federal law would offer a means of prosecuting racial murders that local and state officials ignored. Women had been central to condemning lynching ever since Ida B. Wells began her campaign in 1892. (See Primary Sources: "Ida B. Wells: 'Race Woman,' " pp. 325–29.) Now, armed with the vote, women turned to a well-organized lobbying campaign. Although many of the women who formed the Anti-Lynching Crusaders were members of the National Association of Colored Women (NACW), which had been outspoken in its condemnation of lynching, the Anti-Lynching Crusaders was formed under the auspices of the National Association for the Advancement of Colored People (NAACP; see pp. 432–34), which had taken the lead as the premier black civil rights organization. Founded in 1922, the Crusaders committee consisted of fifteen women, headed by Mary B. Talbert, who in turn recruited seven hundred women nationally with a goal of raising $1 million, lobbying politicians, and publicizing their campaign through meetings, prayer services, press releases, and advertising. The group actively reached out to white women's groups and was successful in eliciting support from a number of prominent women.

Although the antilynching bill passed the House of Representatives in 1922, it failed in the Senate due to a filibuster by white southern Democrats.

It would be reintroduced repeatedly and unsuccessfully over the next two decades. Although the Crusaders disbanded after one year and fell far short of their hopes for uniting 1 million women and raising $1 million, the publicity they distributed undoubtedly raised consciousness among white Americans. It may well have contributed to the creation of one of the first biracial women's organization to address racial violence — the Association of Southern Women for the Prevention of Lynching (1930).

The first document below is from the NAACP's magazine, *The Crisis*. It is followed by an excerpt from an African American newspaper that reported on the founding of the organization and published its statement. Figure 9.1 is an example of the advertising that the Crusaders placed in newspapers throughout the country. What do you think was the significance on the emphasis on prayer in *The Crisis* article? What arguments did the Crusaders use in the advertisement to secure support for the Dyer Bill? How do these excerpts compare with those of Ida B. Wells?

The Anti-Lynching Crusaders (1922)

Under the leadership of Mrs. Mary B. Talbert of Buffalo and an executive committee of 15 supported by over 700 state workers, there has been started the "Anti-Lynching Crusade," the object of which is to "unite a million women to stop lynching." These crusaders are planning a short, sharp campaign beginning immediately and ending January 1, 1923. They seek to arouse the conscience of the women of America, both white and black. They are in deadly earnest and they put forward as the first fact in the lynching campaign the horrid truth that 83 American women have been lynched by mobs in the last 30 years in addition to 3,353 men. This, in part, is the prayer which the Anti-Lynching Crusaders have sent out:

"We are slain all the day long in the land of our nativity, which is the land of our loyalty and of our love. The vials of race vengeance are wreaked upon our defenseless heads. The inhuman thirst for human blood takes little heed of innocence or guilt. Any convenient victim identified with our race suffices to slake the accursed thirst. We are beaten with many stripes. Our bodies are bruised, burned and tortured and torn asunder for the ghoulish mirth of the blood-lusty multitude. Whenever such atrocity is perpetrated upon any one of our number, because of his race, it is done unto us all. Vengeance and wrath are not invoked for the fit atonement of committed crime, nor yet for the just punishment of evil doer [sic]; but the sinister aim is to cow our spirit, enslave our soul and to give our name an evil repute in the eyes of the world. . . .

We pray Thee to enlighten the understanding and nerve the hearts of our lawmakers with the political wisdom and the moral courage to pass the Dyer Bill, now hanging on the balance of doubt and uncertainty. . . .

Quicken the conscience of the people with the moral firmness and determination to demand and to uphold the effective enforcement of this measure and of all righteous laws."

SOURCE: "The Anti-Lynching Crusaders" *The Crisis* 25 (November 1922): 8.

One Million Women Are Working Like Trojans to Stop Lynching in the U.S.A. (1922)

The anti-lynching program demands: Publicity. Pressure upon Congress, Pressure upon state legislatures. Investigation. Legal processes.

The Negro has never given his cause proper publicity. It is proposed, if sufficient funds are obtained, to conduct a newspaper campaign of publicity patterned after the Red Cross and Child Welfare campaigns. A campaign where full page statements of the facts concerning lynching shall appear in every influential daily paper through the country until the general public is informed of the fact that this country is cursed with lynching.

SOURCE: "One Million Women Are Working Like Trojans to Stop Lynching in the U.S.A.," *Richmond Planet* (December 9, 1922), p. 6.

◆ **Figure 9.1** **"The Shame of America" (1922)**
Fotosearch/Getty Images.

AMONG WHITE WOMEN REFORMERS the most important agenda in the 1920s on the national level was the effort to improve the lives of women and children. Women like Florence Kelley, for example, worked hard to secure a Child Labor Amendment. Although they failed in that campaign, reformers did have modest success with the Maternity Act (the Sheppard-Towner Act of 1921), with Kelley directing much of the lobbying. Supporters had hoped that the legislation would provide some financial assistance for poor mothers, but intense resistance by the medical establishment and conservative politicians and women's groups like the Women Sentinels of the Republic limited the act to establishing a mothers' education program through the Children's Bureau and a program of visiting nurses for new mothers and infants. The act continued to be controversial and was phased out by 1929. The document below, a summary of an article by Anne Martin published in *Current Opinion* in 1920, includes the claim that medical care would be available to poor families, a provision that was cut from the final law. Martin's call to action reveals the way in which women reformers hoped to draw upon new voters to put pressure on their representatives to pass the bill. What arguments does Martin make? Why might these arguments have been effective?

American Women Urged to Vote for State Protection of Motherhood (1920)

Four million voters in 1916 were able, by concerted action, to make the national Woman Suffrage amendment a political issue in the last Presidential election, with the result that it has lately been passed by Congress. Can fifteen million women voters in the present year be persuaded to unite in behalf of governmental protection of maternity and infancy? Anne Martin, the Woman Suffrage leader of Nevada, raises the question in *Good Housekeeping* and urges that a movement be started to educate American public opinion in the matter.

Investigations carried on by the Children's Bureau in rural areas in Wisconsin, Kansas, North Carolina and Montana have revealed a higher maternal mortality rate than in the United States as a whole. "The rural districts," Miss Martin observes, "are in the greatest need of help." Imagination easily supplies pictures of women who have no trained attendance of any kind at the births of their babies; who are compelled to work until the

last moment before a birth and who are expected to resume work in their households within two or three weeks after a birth.

The bill introduced by Senator Sheppard and seconded by Representative Towner in the House is entitled "A Bill for the Public Protection of Maternity and Infancy, and Providing a Method of Cooperation between the Government of the United States and the Several States." . . . [I]t furnishes help to mothers in industrial, as well as in rural, districts—to all others, in fact. It creates a Federal Board of Maternal and Infant Hygiene, consisting of the Secretary of Labor, who shall be chairman, the Chief of the Children's Bureau, who shall be the executive officer, the Surgeon-General of the United States Public Health Service and the United States Commissioner of Education. The Federal Board is to act through State boards appointed by the various legislatures. The benefits extended are of two kinds. First, popular instruction in the hygiene of infancy and maternity and related subjects is to be supplied through public health nurses and consultation centers, and through qualified

SOURCE: "American Women Urged to Vote for State Protection of Motherhood," *Current Opinion* 68(3) (March 1920): 375.

lecturers in extension courses. Second, medical and nursing care for mothers and infants at home or at a hospital, when necessary, will be supplied.

Practically all of the leading countries, with the exception of the United States, now furnish some kind of government aid to mothers. Germany, in 1884, was the first to initiate legislation of this sort; Austria and Hungary soon followed. Italy and New Zealand took action in 1901, Great Britain in 1911, France in 1913. "When it is squarely presented to them," Miss Martin concludes, "American women voters will unite upon this great human issue. They will insist that Congress take instant action."

CONSERVATIVE WOMEN — ORGANIZED IN GROUPS like the Women Sentinels of the Republic, the Woman Patriots, Massachusetts Public Interest League, and the Daughters of the American Revolution — roundly condemned welfare reforms like the Sheppard-Towner Act. Profoundly shaped by the Red Scare, they viewed reformers, pacifists, and feminists as an unholy alliance of women determined to undermine the family and the ideals of the nation. A popular piece of evidence for their claim was the so-called Spider Web Chart (Figure 9.2). Concocted by Lucia Ramsey Maxwell, who was a librarian at the Army's Chemical Warfare Service, the convoluted diagram highlighted twenty women and seventeen organizations. Although it is difficult to read the details, how does the image below convey the supposed threat of organized women reformers?

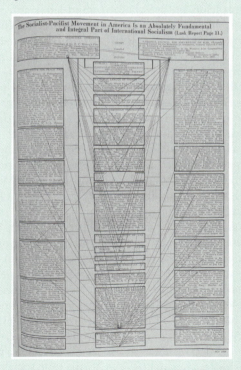

◆ **Figure 9.2 "The Spider Web Chart" (1924)**
Newberry Library, Chicago/Bridgeman Images.

CONSERVATIVE WOMEN, MANY OF WHOM had been anti-suffragists, nonetheless felt patriotic women must become activists to fight the threat of encroaching Bolshevism. In the document below, a statement that Delaware senator Thomas Bayard read into the Congressional Record, the Woman Patriots summed up the threat posed by the Sheppard-Towner Act, which in 1926 was up for renewal. Do you think the argument made here might have influenced Congress's decision to limit that renewal to only two years? Many scholars see in groups like the Woman Patriots the origins of the contemporary radical right in American politics. Do you see any similarities?

Woman Patriots Protest the Sheppard-Towner Act (1926)

SUMMARY OF GENERAL OBJECTIONS

1. The Congress and public tricked: These bills are dishonestly presented to hide their true scope and purpose. They are counterfeit legislation, organized schemes to trick the Congress and the country by pretended humanitarian, beneficent-appearing bills, masked as "welfare" and "women's" measures, and intrusted to certain women's organizations to engineer, the better to allay public suspicion, but are none the less straight imported communism. The Bolshevik wolf rarely gets to the doors of Congress except as a little Red Riding-hood.

2. Unconstitutional and unpopular: The . . . bill concerns matters over which the American people never gave their Federal Government an iota of authority. It involves the same principal of nationalized, standardized care of children and Federal interference between parent and child which the American people so sweepingly repudiated in defeating the Federal child labor amendment, on which the States, acting under popular pressure, now stand 36 to 4 for rejection. Since aroused by the campaign of information waged from Massachusetts to Oregon against the child-labor amendment, there can be no question where the people stand on Federal interference in their homes. More oppressive invasions of the private lives of citizens have recently been proposed or attempted by the encroaching Federal power than George III would have dared to impose

upon the American colonists. . . . Citizens of Massachusetts have said that they regarded the advisory referendum of 1924, against the child labor amendment, as a bloodless, second Concord, "to leave their children free" . . . from tyrannous control by Congress. . . .

3. Revolutionary conspiracy: The Federal maternity bill inextricably interlocks with the child labor amendment and the Federal Children's Bureau. They constitute, with the Federal Education Department bill, a unified agency and program of revolution by legislation. They are as deliberate a conspiracy to destroy this Republic as any plot ever hatched to overthrow a government by force and violence.

Including the creation of the Children's Bureau in 1912, they were all backed by the same open groups and "underground" by the communists, and were chiefly promoted by one woman, a Marxian socialist, Mrs. Florence Kelley, formerly Mrs. Wischnewetsky . . . pupil and translator of Friedrich Engels (coauthor with Karl Marx of the communist manifesto) and Engel's chosen lieutenant for introducing communism into "the flesh and blood of Americans" as he instructed her. . . .

The Engels-Kelley program carries in its wake as logical sequence doles for children and maternity or childbirth doles for women — "maternity benefits" — not as a help for needy mothers, but as a natural right, confirmed the socialist doctrine that maternity is "a service to the state" and that all children "legal

SOURCE: Woman Patriots, "Maternity and Infancy Act," *Congressional Record*, 69th Congress, 1st Session, July 3, 1926, 12918–52.

or illegal" and all mothers, married or unmarried, should be supported by public taxes instead of by individual husbands and fathers. This cattleizing, stock-farm, breeding proposition for replenishing the population that dehumanizes marriage and lifts responsibility for their offspring from fathers and mothers has incalculable social and moral consequences compared with which the mere cost or taxation aspect of the issues, however enormous, is relatively trivial.

An examination of Children's Bureau publications will reveal so many elaborate "studies" of illegitimacy, compared with the few short pamphlets of infant and child care, that the bureau might be considered to have a morbid interest in this subject were it not a well-known and deliberate plan of socialists, set forth at length in Engels' Origin of the Family, Private Property and the

State, and August Bebel's Woman and Socialist, to wipe out all legal, social and moral distinction between legitimate and illegitimate children. It will be shown hereafter that both of these indecent socialist books have been recommended by Mrs. Kelley as fundamental studies for social workers. . . .

With the inner ring of socialists and feminists in control throughout the country, under the Federal maternity act, of the health centers for mothers and infants (corresponding to the "shop nuclei" in factories as agitation centers in the industrial communist campaign) and of public schools and colleges under the proposed education bill, a channel of propaganda as pervasive as the circulation of the blood in the human system, the youth of the Nation would be at their mercy.

W OMEN WHO FOR THE MOST PART SHARED THE ASSUMPTIONS of reformers like Florence Kelley hoped to create a powerful national lobbying entity to promote reform and women's rights. The document below is an extract from a pamphlet written by Maud Wood Park, who was chair of the Women's Joint Congressional Committee (WJCC), founded in 1924. According to Park, what was the rationale for the WJCC? How does she counter the anti-Bolshevik type propaganda used to discredit the WJCC and its organizations?

ORGANIZED MANUFACTURERS VS. ORGANIZED WOMEN

[T]he Women's Joint Congressional Committee . . . functions as the cooperative agency of constituencies in every State of the Union; functions by conveying to members of Congress the sentiment of the women voters back home; and to those women in turn it conveys the news of what their representatives do at Washington.

USE VOTING S TRENGTH — NO FINANCIAL POWER

Nothing just like this joint committee exists for any other group of voters; certainly nothing like

it representing men's organizations as such. . . . Their corporations, their manufacturers' associations, their chambers of commerce, their fraternal orders, their mutual-benefit clubs — all these have a different history, a different concept, a different motive. They may be used for political ends, but their dependence is not upon their voting strength per se. . . .

Women's organizations — the group here considered at all events — have a social welfare purpose. They work without self-interest, for the public good. Their service is largely voluntary and unpaid. They have scant funds in their treasuries. Their influence upon public opinion and their voting strength are their sole reliance and source of power.

SOURCE: "Organized Manufacturers vs. Organized Women," *Life and Labor Bulletin* 3 (May 1925): 1–2.

USING THE TOOLS OF CITIZENSHIP

Women's propensity . . . for organization, and their instinct for social as well as family welfare, has carried them into politics as a highly organized voting force seeking certain specific things. The "women's clubs" with their great variety of local community purposes, had convened into the General Federation of Women's Clubs. Thousands and thousands of women had organized as mothers, into a National Congress of Mothers; as wage-workers into the National Women's Trade Union League; as prohibitionists into the Women's Christian Temperance Union. Others had organized as business and professional women, as consumers, as teachers, as college and university women, as church members. Two million women had been enrolled in the National American Woman Suffrage Association, which with the adoption of the Nineteenth Amendment made way for the National League of Women Voters, a full-fledged non-partisan organization of women.

The Women's Joint Congressional Committee is a piece of machinery through which at first ten and now twenty-two national organizations of women execute their programs of federal legislation. Not all of them endorse the same legislation, and the Women's Joint Congressional Committee itself, being merely a clearing house, and a cooperative machine, endorses no legislation, proposes none. Whenever any piece of legislation is called for by five or more organizations, however, a subcommittee, composed of the legislative representative of the supporting organizations, is formed for the promotion of that bill.

THE ANTIS AND THEIR ATTACKS

These lists — of measures sought and organizations seeking them — should be scanned thoroughly. There are people who insist that they conceal a plot to overthrow the Government of the United States — yes, by violence. They say it is a program dictated by Moscow, by the leaders of the Russian communist party. They say its proponents are 'Organizing Revolution through Women and Children.'" The women, they say, are dupes of their "radical" leaders, "socialists" and "communists."

The same people are saying this who used to say the suffrage leaders believed in free love. They profess to consider the Government in danger from the very women that the organized women of the country have delighted to honor. By weird distortion and artificial juxtaposition of paragraphs and phrases lifted from newspaper stories, by garbled quotations from speeches, and sometimes from fantasies or nightmares all their own, they throw out a fabric of misrepresentation to destroy, if possible, the faith of the women of America in such woman as Mrs. Carrie Chapman Catt, Miss Julia Lathrop, Miss Grace Abbott, Miss Mary Anderson, Mrs. Florence Kelley, Mrs. Harriet Taylor Upton, Mrs. Emily Newell Blair, Mrs. Raymond Robbins, Miss Jane Addams, Miss Mary McDowell, and other women who have achieved important results in fields of usefulness. With the epithet "bolshevist" or "communist" they try to discredit both the women leaders and the reforms they seek.

WOMEN MUST STAND THEIR GROUND

It is, of course, to laugh. Or rather it would be but for the fact that the credulous are too often misled by the printed word. Women therefore must firmly stand their ground, and hold their purpose.

Women organized, as voters, are seeking social legislation; the kind of legislation that considers human beings and human happiness above and before dollars and cents, or politicians' fate. Women voters care supremely about the health and education of their children, the well-being of their families, and the peace and decent conduct of their communities. They want to abolish child labor. They want an eight-hour day, a decent standard of wages, and healthful surroundings for the girls and women, as well as for the men, who work for their living. They want a square deal for women everywhere and an opportunity to share with men the responsibilities of government. And they demand that the nations of the world find some way to keep the peace.

Women have, fortunately, the courage to use their voting power to these ends. They will not be diverted or terrorized by witch-burners, or their hirelings. The question really is this:

Do the men of the country intend to leave the women to make the fight? Or will you, men and brothers, do your part to make public sentiment such that no man or woman *dare* asperse the loyalty and patriotism of your wives and sisters and daughters who believe in giving to our country, as to our homes, the kind of thought and care that puts human beings above property, social well-being above the dollar mark and commercial profit?

QUESTIONS FOR ANALYSIS

1. Despite the significant differences among the three groups of women represented here, do you see any similarities in their approaches to political activism?

2. How do these documents help explain some of the limits to women's efforts to achieve political success in the 1920s?

3. In the Woman Patriot document, why do you suppose the author invokes American Revolutionary images such as King George III and the battle of Concord?

4. Do these documents shed light on any of the political issues contemporary Americans struggle with?

Beauty Culture between the Wars

THE 1920S MARKED THE EMERGENCE of a highly commercialized beauty industry that built upon the growing interest in cosmetics of the prewar years. Cosmetic use expanded after 1900, but because such products were associated with prostitution and the seductive "painted lady," concern about respectability meant that many women were cautious about using beauty aids. As interest grew, hundreds of women operated small businesses and a handful turned cosmetics into lucrative beauty empires. Among these were Elizabeth Arden and Helena Rubenstein, who catered to white women, and Annie Turnbo Malone and Sarah Breedlove (later known as Madam C. J. Walker), who focused on African Americans. These entrepreneurs pioneered marketing techniques and the concept of using a beauty "system" of related products. They hired women as agents, demonstrators, and clerks, thus making the beauty industry largely female.

After World War I, the nature of the cosmetic industry changed for both white and black women. Beauty salons, which mostly offered hair care, multiplied dramatically, growing from five thousand in 1920 to forty thousand by 1930. At the same time, the sale of cosmetics grew an astounding 400 percent. As fears about respectability receded with the popularity of the New Woman of the 1920s, rouge, lipstick, mascara, and nail polish were added to women's makeup routines. This growth took place in the context of a modern consumer culture dominated by corporations. Although the prewar companies of Arden, Rubenstein, Walker, and Trumbo persisted, male-dominated firms increasingly took over the beauty industry. Firms that marketed to black women were run not only by men but by white men, although consumers rarely knew this. A smaller niche focused on Mexican American women, with mainstream companies like Max Factor advertising in Spanish-language newspapers.

This essay focuses on a key part of beauty culture — advertising — and explores the differences and similarities in marketing strategies directed at black and white consumers. Generous advertising budgets (mass-market magazines' expenditures for ads reached $16 million in 1930, up from $1.3 million in 1915) led to the marketing not just of products but also of an idealized beauty that emphasized youth and sexuality. Ad agencies seized on public fascination with glamorous Hollywood stars to sell products as well. The techniques we recognize today were already in place in the 1920s. All the advertisements reprinted here come from movie fan magazines and as such were primarily targeted to young and working-class women.

One of the most common themes in cosmetic advertising is what historian Kathy Peiss terms the promise to women of the "democratic" ability to remake

◆ **Figure 9.3** "Can you tell us her name?" (1926)
Media History Digital Library.

themselves, to choose and to have the resources to be beautiful.[48] How does the
1926 Tre-Jur ad in Figure 9.3, part of a series that featured beautiful unknown
women in the fan magazine *Photoplay*, demonstrate this motif? Note that although
the emphasis is on face powder, the young woman has bobbed and marcelled hair,
providing a modern look typical of the era's flappers. This ad also demonstrates the
new emphasis on attractive packaging for cosmetics that appeared as mass-market
corporations took over the industry.

◆ **Figure 9.4 "Irresistible" (1938)**
Media History Digital Library.

Despite the Great Depression, the cosmetic industry continued to flourish. "Irresistible" was a low-cost line sold in dime stores. The heavily made-up face of the woman in the dramatically colored (in reds and purples) 1938 ad in Figure 9.4 further suggests that these products were marketed to working-class women, because the trend in 1930s higher-end cosmetics was toward the "natural" look. What were the advertisers promising consumers who bought the Irresistible line?

Cosmetic ads used Hollywood stars to promote their products, with the promise that ordinary women could be as glamorous as the women they saw on the

Rita Hayworth

CO-STARRING IN "YOU WERE NEVER LOVELIER"
A Columbia Picture

Color Harmony Face Powder!

1...*it imparts a lovely color to the skin*
2...*it creates a satin-smooth make-up*
3...*it clings perfectly — really stays on*

Blondes, brunettes, brownettes, redheads..
you can add loveliness to your looks with
your Color Harmony shade of this famous
powder created by *Max Factor Hollywood.*

The very first time you make up with this remarkable face
powder you'll note how the Color Harmony shade created
for you accents all the beauty of your type. You'll note that
your skin looks more youthful, more attractive. You'll
marvel how satin-smooth your make-up appears...and
how this powder clings perfectly and really stays on. Try
your Color Harmony shade of *Max Factor Hollywood* face
powder today...make a new beauty discovery. One dollar.

★ *COMPLETE your
make-up in Color Har-
mony with Max Factor
Hollywood Rouge and
Tru-Color Lipstick.*

Max Factor ★ Hollywood

SCREENLAND

◆ **Figure 9.5 "You Were Never Lovelier" (1942)**
Media History Digital Library.

screen. Ads featuring stars often had tie-ins to their latest movie. The 1942 ad in
Figure 9.5 links Max Factor products, movie star Rita Hayworth, and her film *You
Were Never Lovelier.* Hayworth, who was born Margarita Carmen Cansino and was
of Spanish descent, had small parts in dozens of movies before she changed her
name in 1937. She also altered her hairline and dyed her hair red to look less like the
Spanish dancer she was often typecast as. Actively seeking publicity, she frequently
told the story of her makeover as a typical American success story and retained her
ethnic identity even as she rose to extraordinary stardom in the 1940s. An icon for
Mexican Americans, she was widely popular and was one of the era's most glamorous
and sexy stars. Although publicity stills showed more skin and erotic energy than the

◆ **Figure 9.6** **"Glorifying Our Womanhood" (1925)**
Madam C. J. Walker Collection, Indiana Historical Society.

image used here, in what ways does the ad stress Hayworth's sexual appeal? Do you think the phrase "beauty of your type" reflects any ethnic or racial preference?

In the prewar era, Madam C. J. Walker, highly celebrated for her financial success and commitment to civil rights, stressed the ways in which her firm represented the success of black businesses and gave employment to women agents. Competition from new white firms resulted in ad campaigns that featured beautiful black women using the Walker products, but ads featuring the company itself continued, as is evident in the 1925 ad in Figure 9.6. The "Tan-Off" product mentioned in the bottom left "note" referred to a skin-lightening cream. Walker had refused to sell whitening products, but after her death in 1919, the company kept up with the competition by offering them. Black critics lashed out at these products as well as hair-straightening processes, viewing them as attempts to emulate white notions of beauty. Manufacturers answered these complaints by insisting that their customers were not trying to be white but aiming to achieve a neat and carefully groomed appearance. Many scholars agree, and one historian has noted that while the ads might stress light skin or soft, wavy hair as a goal in beauty rituals, they nonetheless "reassured black women of their beauty when so much of American popular culture told them they were unattractive."[49] Is this argument evident in the ad? How does the ad justify its claim that the products "glorify" their users' womanhood?

Although there were not many black popular culture stars to choose from, firms marketing to black women used stars to promote their products in much the same way as white cosmetic companies did. In the ad in Figure 9.7, the white-owned firm Golden Brown features popular black recording artists and vaudeville

◆ **Figure 9.7** "Golden-Brown Beauty Preparations" (1923)

performers Hazel Meyers, Ethel Waters, Rosa Henderson, and Edna Hicks. The "Madame Mamie Hightower" referred to here was an invention, part of Golden Brown's masquerade as a "race" firm. In what other ways does the company present itself as a black firm? How does this ad compare with Figures 9.5 and 9.6?

QUESTIONS FOR ANALYSIS

1. Changes in the cosmetic industry emerged at the same time as the New Woman of the 1920s. How do these ads enhance our understanding of corporate business and popular culture's role in creating the New Woman?

2. How have ads for cosmetic products changed since the years of the ads shown here? How significant are these changes?

3. Historians disagree on whether the rise of the cosmetic industry signaled new freedoms for women to choose individual styles and play with personal appearance, or led to a higher, more impossible single standard for beauty, privileging appearance over other qualities. Is this debate still relevant? Where do you stand?

Dorothea Lange Photographs Farm Women of the Great Depression

Tʜᴇsᴇ ᴅᴏᴄᴜᴍᴇɴᴛᴀʀʏ ᴘʜᴏᴛᴏɢʀᴀᴘʜs of poor farm women provide compelling evidence of the hardships of Depression-era rural American women. The numbers of Americans involved in agricultural labor declined steadily in the twentieth century, a reflection of both the mechanization of farmwork and the growing importance of the industrial and commercial sectors of the economy. Even before the Depression, farm women and their families faced hard times, but the economic collapse made their lives even harder — especially for tenant farmers in the South and Southwest, many of whom were forced off the land and became homeless and desperate. Also suffering were farmers of the southern plains, where decades of soil neglect and years of drought turned parts of Oklahoma, Texas, and Arkansas, as well as neighboring states, into arid wastelands. Such conditions prompted over three hundred thousand to go west to California. These "Okies," as they were pejoratively called, were potent symbols of the economic collapse and its human toll.[50]

A New Deal agency called the Farm Security Administration (FSA) sought to resettle poor farmers on better land and to provide assistance to migrant farmers, primarily in the South and West. Only a small percentage of tenant farmers were actually resettled, however, and the number of temporary camps established for homeless migrant families was small — only fifteen in California — but they did provide a minimum of housing, child care, and sanitation. While the FSA programs themselves were very limited, the photographs they commissioned — at least one hundred thousand of them — had the enormous effect of creating empathy with the rural poor. These photographs shaped a visual legacy of the Great Depression that informs popular memory to this day.

The following images, produced by Dorothea Lange for the FSA, would eventually establish Lange as one of the foremost American photographers of the twentieth century. As she recorded the experiences and despair of the unemployed, Lange became part of the development of documentary photography. Although earlier photographers like Jacob Riis (see pp. 408–14) had embarked on a similar undertaking, photographers and filmmakers of the 1930s had a distinct vision of their work: they hoped to create an authentic record of the experiences of ordinary Americans.

In keeping with the concept of documentary photography as it was evolving, and in line with the FSA's desire to deflect criticism of the photography program as mere propaganda for the New Deal, the photographers were under strict orders not to manufacture scenes or alter photographs in the darkroom. Yet in many ways the photographs *were* propaganda: their purpose was to drum up sympathy for the victims of the Depression and to demonstrate the way in which the New Deal was helping them. Despite the imperatives of "documenting" the real experience, we do know that FSA photographers, including Lange, often posed their subjects and routinely cropped images to make them more dramatic.

Lange, like the other artists working for the New Deal, aligned with the social realism approach to representation. Social realism celebrated the hardworking men and women of the United States and invoked the promise of democratic values. One scholar has calculated that Lange, in keeping with her progressive values and her early experiences photographing Mexican farmworkers, featured people of color in one of three of her FSA images.[51] Yet the photographs distributed by the FSA to the print media were almost exclusively of whites, in keeping with a conscious effort to create empathy for hardworking rural white Americans, who, through no fault of their own, had become "down-and-out." This approach of the FSA reminds us of another way in which photographs do not necessarily represent "reality."

The most famous of Lange's photographs, "Migrant Mother #1" (Figure 9.8), was one of six pictures Lange took in 1936 in Nipomo, California, at a "pea pickers" camp. The next day, Lange sent the now-famous image to San Francisco papers. But the succession of photographs here reveals that Lange experimented to get the "right" picture. The long shot (Figure 9.9, "Migrant Mother #3") set the scene with the lean-to tent on the back of the truck and Florence Owens Thompson with four of her children. What does this image tell us about the family's life? Although the teenage daughter is prominent in this image (and in one other shot similar to the first), she is not present in the other four photographs Lange took. Instead, Lange experimented with close-up compositions such as Figure 9.10 ("Migrant Mother #5") that frame Thompson in a Madonna-like posture. This motif was common for Lange and other FSA photographers. Why would viewers have found this pose evocative? Why might Lange have chosen to eliminate the teenager from her photographs?

For Figure 9.8, Lange dispensed with some of the context of poverty. The symbolic empty pie tin and oil lantern disappear, and all that remains is the four figures. In what ways does the image still convey that the family is destitute? Why do you suppose Lange had the two children who stand leaning on her shoulders turn their faces away from the camera? Although most scholars emphasize that this image evokes a heroic mother-hood, one has suggested that despite the pose and the physical closeness of the children to Thompson, the lack of visual contact or engagement with her children might suggest the burdens or even the imprisonment of motherhood. What do you think?

Lange usually took a great deal of time with her subjects, but these images were shot in haste late in the day and Lange learned little about Thompson, not even her name. Years later, a more complicated story emerged. Thompson's granddaughter reported that Lange had promised that the photographs would not be published but would be used to help the migrants. (In fact, they did help the migrants: after their publication in the San Francisco newspapers, contributions of over $200,000 poured in to help the pea pickers in Nipomo, but by then Florence Thompson's family had moved on.) Decades later, Thompson resented the photograph's wide-spread distribution and the fact that she never received any money from its publication. She also felt it misrepresented her as a dust bowl "Okie." She and her family

◆ **Figure 9.8** *Migrant Mother #1* (1936)
Library of Congress, 8b29516.

◆ **Figure 9.9** *Migrant Mother #3* (1936)
Library of Congress, 8b29525.

◆ **Figure 9.10** *Migrant Mother #5* (1936)
Library of Congress, 3b06165.

◆ **Figure 9.11 "Unemployed Lumber Worker Goes with His Wife to the Bean Harvest" (1939)**
Library of Congress, 8b15572.

originally migrated to California in the 1920s. Thus, ironically, the portrait that has embodied the poor white farmers of the Great Depression era was in fact of a Native American, part of a group that the FSA largely chose to ignore.

Lange's caption for Figure 9.11 was "Unemployed lumber worker goes with his wife to the bean harvest. Note social security number tattooed on his arm. Oregon." Although the work of Lange and other FSA photographers often featured strong, heroic mothers, images of husbands and wives together rarely challenged the gender order. In what ways does the positioning and posture of the two indicate the woman's subordinate status? Lange often featured women surrounded by the implements of their household labor and showed them in their struggle to maintain cleanliness and order. What is the significance of the small table, towels, and pot in this image? Why has Lange chosen to feature the man's Social Security number? Though it is unlikely that Lange had this in mind, consider the gendered nature of the Social Security Act (p. 507) and the way in which this image seems to embody that quality.

◆ **Figure 9.12** **"You don't have to worriate so much and you've got time to raise sompin' to eat" (1938)**
Library of Congress, 8b32752.

In addition to her work on the West Coast photographing migrant farmworkers, Lange also worked in the South among sharecroppers and migrant tenants. She often photographed women at work in the fields, showing the hard, stooped labor involved in cotton and tobacco production. The close-up of a woman in Figure 9.12 working in a more domestic setting, as she sorts tobacco on a porch, perhaps minimizes the harshness of tobacco labor and the history of African American women as slave laborers in the fields (see the image on p. 125 and Chapter 3). The image is a very harmonious one that emphasizes the woman's beauty and dignity. She is placed in the center of the photograph as the stable, central figure, and the piles of tobacco on either side of her chair provide balance and symmetry. The caption read, "Near Douglas, Georgia. 'You don't have to worriate so much and you've got time to raise sompin' to eat.' The program to eliminate the risk and uncertainty of a one-crop system meets the approval of this sharecropper. She sits on the porch and sorts tobacco. (July 1938)." It's not clear what specific program Lange refers to, and in fact few African Americans received many benefits from the New Deal agricultural programs. But how might the caption explain the optimistic quality embodied in the image Lange produced?

For Figure 9.13, Lange's caption is terse: "Cotton weighing near Brownsville, Texas, August 1936." This would have been an arresting image in 1936 because it features a white woman in the cotton fields, which challenged American notions of appropriate work for white women. Yet, among poor tenant farmers and migrant workers alike, both black and white women routinely worked in the fields, in addition to carrying out their domestic and child care responsibilities. Although this image does not feature the cotton picker engaged in harsh labor, it shows the aftermath: her harvest being weighed. How does Lange's composition reflect class status between picker and weighers? At first glance the image might suggest patriarchal power, with men determining the welfare of the woman. Yet the figure in the foreground is almost certainly a woman — the hair is long and the waist is narrow. What does this suggest about the relationship between women of different classes in the farm economy?

◆ **Figure 9.13 Cotton Weighing near Brownsville, Texas (1936)**
Library of Congress, 8b38503.

Figure 9.14's caption was "Sign of the Times — Depression — Mended Stockings, Stenographer, 1934." Lange's title might only refer to how the economic downturn had forced the woman to mend her stockings and "make do." However, if Lange was suggesting that the stockings were a symbol for the nation as a whole, what do the tear — and the mending — suggest? Compare Figure 9.12 with Figure 9.15, "Feet of Negro Cotton Hoer near Clarksdale, Mississippi," which was taken in 1937. The stenographer is evidently dressed up and composed, and she is in an indoor setting, as indicated by the wood floor. In contrast, the black cotton hoer is in a natural, outdoor setting, her feet in contact with the rough ground. Her shoes are in a worn-out condition. How might the second image be a symbolic representation of the harshness of agricultural labor, and especially of black women laborers? Why did Lange choose to photograph just the feet of these two women?

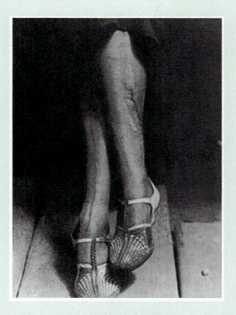

◆ **Figure 9.14 Sign of the Times—
Depression—Mended Stockings,
Stenographer (1934)**
*Copyright the Dorothea Lange Collection, Oakland Museum of
California, City of Oakland. Gift of Paul S. Taylor.*

◆ **Figure 9.15 Feet of Negro Cotton Hoer near
Clarksdale, Mississippi (1937)**
Library of Congress, 8b32076

QUESTIONS FOR ANALYSIS

1. The director of the FSA photography project, Rexford Tugwell, once commented, "You could never say anything about photography—it was a photograph, it was a picture. This was something you couldn't deny. This was evident."[52] In what ways does the work of Dorothea Lange challenge Tugwell's assessment?

2. In what ways do these photographs of diverse women support the FSA project of creating empathy with the "down-and-out" in the Great Depression?

3. What insights do these photographs give you about the lives of poor farm women in the Great Depression?

4. In many ways, the images reproduced here tell us more about Lange's intent and values than they do about the women she photographed. Today, we might consider such photography an invasion of privacy that would be embarrassing to the subject. Indeed, we know that Florence Thompson was later unhappy about becoming the face of the "migrant mother." Why do you suppose these women cooperated with Lange?

Voices of "Rosie the Riveter"

DURING WORLD WAR II, THE FEDERAL GOVERNMENT embarked on a well-organized publicity campaign to recruit women to work in the defense industry. For the most part, these efforts portrayed women's work as patriotic service and stressed that such labor would not undermine their femininity. The campaign drew extensively upon modern advertising techniques and encouraged newspapers and magazines to run stories about women defense workers. Although defense work was notable for providing new opportunities for black and Mexican American women, most government propaganda featured white women. While the most well-known image of a woman defense worker, illustrator Norman Rockwell's "Rosie the Riveter," pictured a brawny, self-assured woman, the majority of government ads and posters emphasized attractive, even glamorous women, as Figure 9.16 suggests. Portrayed in full color, the woman wears a vivid red shirt and beret, with matching red nail polish and lipstick. How does this ad compare with the one on page 509, featuring servicewomen? In what ways does it emphasize the defense worker's femininity? Compare it to the World War I posters in Chapter 8 (pp. 470–74).

While the government campaign sought to defuse anxieties about the implications of women's tackling "men's" jobs by indicating that their motives were purely patriotic, in women's contemporary accounts and oral histories a more complicated set of reasons emerges. As this set of documents makes clear, higher wages, more interesting jobs, and personal independence accompanied patriotic motives, but the motivations that shaped women's decisions were as diverse as the women themselves.

◆ **Figure 9.16 "The more women at work the sooner we win!" (1943)**
Library of Congress, 3g05600.

HORTENSE JOHNSON

For MANY AFRICAN AMERICANS, this demonstration of patriotism could also be linked to demands for full citizenship. The first document appeared in *Opportunity*, the magazine of the National Urban League, a black organization. During the war, the Urban League had a firm commitment to a campaign called the Double V, which encouraged African Americans to support the war while at the same time continuing to call for civil and economic rights at home. Hortense Johnson, who was an inspector at an arsenal in Dover, New Jersey, won first place in *Opportunity*'s contest for essays by black women war workers. Johnson was atypical in leaving what she called a well-paid business position for defense work — for most African American women, the war offered opportunities to leave poorly paid domestic and farm labor. Johnson's level of political engagement may also have been atypical, yet she offers a compelling account of the appeal of defense work for African American women. What motivates her? How might the publication of her story in the Urban League's journal have affected what she wrote?

What My Job Means to Me (1943)

Did I say my job isn't exciting, or complicated? I take that back. It may be a simple matter to inspect one box or a dozen, but it's different when you are handling them by the hundreds. The six of us in my crew sometimes inspect as many as fourteen or fifteen hundred boxes during one shift. That means two hundred and fifty apiece — an average of one every two minutes, regardless of size and not counting any rest periods. Try that sometime and see if it's a simple job! You stand at your bench all day long, with rest periods sometimes seeming years apart. You fight against the eye fatigue that might mean oversight. You probe with your fingers and tap here and there. Your back aches, your legs get weary, your muscles scream at you sometimes — groan at you all the time. But the dozen and one little operations must be carried on smoothly and efficiently if your work output is to keep up. It's exciting all right, and

it's plenty complicated — in the same way that jungle warfare must be, hard and painstaking and monotonous — until something goes off with a bang! . . .

So if it's as tough as all that — and it is! — why do you stick on the job? Why did you leave the comfortable job you held with a city business house? Why don't you go back to it and make as much money as you're making now? Why? Because it's not that easy to leave, and it's not that tough to stay! Of course the work is hard and sometimes dangerous, but victory in this war isn't going to come the easy way, without danger. And we brown women of America need victory so much, so desperately. America is a long way from perfect. We resent the racial injustices that we meet every day of our lives. But it's one thing to resent and fight against racial injustices; it's another thing to let them break your spirit, so that you quit this struggle and turn the country over to Hitler and the Talmages and Dieses [prominent white southern politicians who were ardent supporters of segregation] who will run this country if Hitler wins. America can't win this war without

SOURCE: Hortense Johnson, "What My Job Means to Me," *Opportunity*, April 1943, in Maureen Honey, ed., *Bitter Fruit: African American Women in World War II* (Columbia: University of Missouri Press, 1999), 71–75.

all of us, and we know it. We must prove it to white Americans as well—that our country can't get along without the labor and sacrifice of her brown daughters, can't win unless we *all* fight and work and save. . . .

I'm not fooling myself about this war. Victory won't mean victory for Democracy—yet. But that will come later, because most of us who are fighting for victory today will keep on fighting to win the peace—maybe a long time after the war is over, maybe a hundred years after. By doing my share today, I'm keeping a place for some brown woman tomorrow, and for the brown son of that woman the day after tomorrow. Sterling Brown [an African American poet] once wrote, "The strong men keep a-comin' on," and millions of those men have dark skins. There will be dark women marching by their side, and I like to think that I'm one of them.

BEATRICE MORALES

BEATRICE MORALES (CLIFTON), A MEXICAN AMERICAN WOMAN born in Texas, lived with her husband, Julio, and their four children when the United States entered the war. As Morales recalled in an oral history interview conducted in 1981, her husband resisted when she first decided to take a defense job. But she told him, "Well, I've made up my mind. I'm going to go to work regardless of whether you like it or not." Morales found work as a riveter at Lockheed Aircraft. At first, she was overwhelmed by the noise, the enormous size of the factory, and the challenge of learning the necessary skills, but she soon mastered her job. Although paid employment was new to her, her account makes it clear that she found her work satisfying. What was so appealing about being a Lockheed riveter? Do you think that the growth of the women's movement in the 1970s may have affected Morales's understanding of her marriage and work history? How might the fact that this interview took place so many years after her World War II experience have affected her story?

Oral Interview (1981)

As time went on, I started getting a little bit better. I just made up [my] mind that I was going to do it. I learned my job so well that then they put me to the next operation. At the very first, I just began putting little pate nuts and stuff like that. Then afterwards I learned how to dill the skins and burr them. Later, as I got going, I learned to rivet and buck. I got to the point where I was very good.

I had a Mexican girl, Irene Herrera, and she was as good a bucker as I was a riveter. She would be facing me and we'd just go right on through. We'd go to one side and then we'd get up to the corner and I'd hand her the gun or the bucking bar or whatever and then we'd come back. Her and I, we used to have a lot of fun. They would want maybe six or five elevators a day. I'd say, "let's get with it." We worked pretty hard all day until about 2:00. Then we would slack down.

I had a lot of friends there. We all spoke to each other. Most of them smoked, and we'd sit

SOURCE: Sherna Berger Gluck, *Rosie the Riveter Revisited: Women, the War, and Social Change* (Boston: Twayne, 1987), 198–219.

in the smoking areas out there in the aisle. Then, some of the girls — on the next corner there was a drugstore that served lunches. There was a white lady, she used to go, and Irene would go. We'd talk about our families and stuff like that.

Irene stayed on that same operation. I don't know why I got a chance to learn all the other jobs, but I learned the whole operation until I got up to the front, the last step. They used to put this little flap with a wire, with a hinge. I had to have that flap just right so that it would swing easy without no rubbing anywhere. I used to go with a little hammer and a screwdriver and knock those little deals down so that it would be just right. That guy that I used to work with helped me, teached me how to do it, and I could do it just like him.

New people would come in, and they would say, "You teach them the job. You know all the jobs." Sometimes it would make me mad. I'd tell them, "What the heck, you get paid for it. You show them the job." But I would still show them. . . .

I was just a mother of our kids, that's all. But I felt proud of myself and felt good being that I have never done anything like that. I felt good that I could do something, and being that it was war, I felt that I was doing my part.

I went from 65 cents to $1.05. That was top pay. It felt good and, besides, it was my own money. I could do whatever I wanted with it because my husband, whatever he was giving to the house, he kept on paying it. I used to buy clothes for the kids; buy little things that they needed. I had a bank account and I had a little saving at home where I could get ahold of the money right away if I needed it. Julio never asked about it. He knew how much I made; I showed him. If there was something that had to be paid and I had the money and he didn't, well, I used some of my money. But he never said, "Well, you have to pay because you're earning money." My money, I did what I wanted.

I started feeling a little more independent. . . . [When one of her children became ill, Morales quit working to stay home with her children, but she explained, "I wasn't too satisfied." She worked at various jobs and then in 1950 returned to Lockheed, where she worked until 1978, eventually being promoted to a "lead man," with enhanced responsibility. When the interviewer, Sherna Gluck, asked for her opinion about the women's movement, she replied as follows.]

I wouldn't want to lose my identity as a woman. I wouldn't want a man to treat me like a man, to say, "you go dig ditches. Because I dig them, you go dig them, too." There are a lot of things that a woman can do — and good — but to lose your identity completely, I just can't see that.

My life, it was changed from day to night. I'm not the person that I started when I first married Julio. The changes started when I first started working. They started a little bit, and from then on it kept on going.

SYLVIA R. WEISSBORDT, U.S. WOMEN'S BUREAU

WHEN THE FEDERAL GOVERNMENT ESTABLISHED the United States Women's Bureau within the Department of Labor in 1920, it explicitly recognized the growing importance of women in the workforce. The U.S. Women's Bureau took seriously its charge to "formulate standards and policies which shall promote the welfare of wage-earning women, improve their working conditions, increase their efficiency, and advance their opportunities for profitable employment."[53] During World War II, it particularly focused on women in the defense industry and urged employers to follow equal pay for equal work guidelines. As the war came to a close, it drew attention to the dilemma women faced when they lost the better-paid, more interesting industrial war jobs and returned to less desirable ones that were considered appropriate for women. In summarizing its findings for this 1946 study, the bureau emphasized that the vast majority of working women needed to continue working after the war and noted that women faced "a variety of postwar readjustment problems." Despite the bureau's hope that its report would lead to national policies to ease women's transition to nondefense work, it had little success in advocating for expanded opportunities for working women. According to the report, why did most women want to keep their wartime jobs?

Women Workers and
Their Postwar Employment Plans (1946)

Three conclusions of particular postwar significance stand out from the series of home interviews by representatives of the Women's Bureau with women who were employed in 10 war production areas in 1944 and 1945.

First, the war brought about great increases in the number of women employed in each of the 10 areas and in the number of women who planned to remain in the labor force in the respective areas.

Second, there were tremendous increases in the proportions of women employed in industries producing directly for war purposes, and the take-home earnings of these women considerably exceeded the take-home earnings of women employed in other industries.

Third, a high proportion of the women employed during the war period reported that they carried heavy economic responsibilities at home, and a high proportion of those who planned to continue working after the war gave economic reasons for their decision. . . .

The outstanding postwar question in any war production areas is, of course, how many of the wartime workers will want jobs and how many will want them in the same area.

SOURCE: Sylvia R. Weissbordt, *Women Workers in Ten War Production Areas and Their Postwar Employment Plans* (Washington, DC: U.S. Government Printing Office, 1946), 1–20.

That very large numbers of wartime women workers intend to work after the war is evidenced by their statements to interviewers. On the average, about 75 percent of the wartime-employed women in the 10 areas expected to be part of the postwar labor force. . . .

The highest percentage of prospective postwar workers in most areas came from the group of women who had been employed before Pearl Harbor, rather than from those who had been in school or engaged in their own housework at that time. On the average over four-fifths of the women who had been employed both before Pearl Harbor and in the war period intended to keep on working after the war. Among the war-employed women who had not been in the labor force the week before Pearl Harbor, over three-fourths of the former students expected to continue working, while over half of those formerly engaged in their own housework had such plans. . . .

The nature of postwar employment problems is influenced not only by the number of wartime workers who expect to remain in the labor force but also by their expressed desires for work in particular industries and occupations. Postwar job openings as cafeteria bus girls, for example, are not apt to prove attractive to women who are seeking work as screw-machine operators.

The bulk of the prospective postwar workers interviewed in this survey, or 86 percent, wanted their postwar jobs in the same industrial group as their wartime employment, and about the same proportion wanted to remain in the same occupational group. Postwar shifts to other industries were contemplated on a somewhat larger scale, however, among the wartime employees in restaurants, cafeterias, and similar establishments, as well as in the personal service industries in certain areas. . . .

In each of the nine areas where there were enough non-white employed women in the war period to make comparison valid, a much higher proportion of the Negro women planned to continue work than of the white women. In six areas 94 percent or more of the Negro or other non-white women who were employed in the war period planned to continue after the war. . . .

Responsibility for the support of themselves or themselves and others was the outstanding reason given by war-employed women for planning to continue work after the war. . . . Fully 84 percent of [those surveyed] had no other alternative, as this was the proportion among them who based their decision on their need to support themselves and often, other persons as well. Eight percent offered special reasons for continuing at work, such as buying a home or sending children to school; and only 8 percent reported they would

remain in the labor force because they liked working, or liked having their own money.

Virtually all of the single women and of those who were widowed or divorced (96 and 98 percent, respectively) who intended to remain in gainful employment after the war stated they would do so in order to support themselves or themselves and others, whereas 57 percent of the married wartime workers who expected to remain at work gave this reason. The remaining married prospective postwar workers interviewed offered reasons of the special purpose type, such as buying a home, about as often as those of the "like-to-work" type. . . .

That the need to work is just as pressing among some married women as among some single women was highlighted by the replies from the war-employed women on the number of wage earners in the family group. Out of every 100 married women who were living in family groups of two or more persons, 11 said they were the only wage earner supporting the family group. This was almost identical to the proportion of sole supporting wage earners among single women living with their families. The state of marriage, therefore, does not, in itself, always mean there is a male provider for the family.

QUESTIONS FOR ANALYSIS

1. Scholars have compiled a number of oral history archives documenting women's war defense work, and many have online audio files where you may listen to these fascinating firsthand accounts. Listen to some of these interviews (for example, the "Rosie the Riveter Revisited" collection, which you can find by searching online) to learn more about how different types of women interpreted their war work experiences. Compare one of the online accounts to one of the excerpts you read here.

2. How might Johnson or Morales have reacted to the ad in Figure 9.16?

3. How might Johnson or Morales have responded to the U.S. Women's Bureau report about women's postwar work plans?

NOTES

1. Dorothy M. Brown, *Setting a Course: American Women in the 1920s* (Boston: Twayne, 1987), 69.
2. Ibid., 50.
3. Paula Giddings, *When and Where I Enter: The Impact of Black Women on Race and Sex in America* (New York: Quill Press, 1988), 169.
4. Nancy F. Cott, *The Grounding of Modern Feminism* (New Haven, CT: Yale University Press, 1987), 102.
5. Kristi Andersen, *After Suffrage: Women in Partisan and Electoral Politics before the New Deal* (Chicago: University of Chicago Press, 1996); Cott, *The Grounding of Modern Feminism*, 104–8, 318–19.
6. Alice Kessler-Harris, *Out to Work: A History of Wage-Earning Women in the United States* (New York: Oxford University Press, 1982), 248.
7. Lynn Y. Weiner, *From Working Girl to Working Mother: The Female Labor Force in the United States, 1820–1980* (Chapel Hill: University of North Carolina Press, 1985), 104.
8. Jacqueline Jones, *Labor of Love, Labor of Sorrow: Black Women, Work, and the Family, from Slavery to the Present* (New York: Basic Books, 1985), 177.
9. Elizabeth Clark-Lewis, *Living In, Living Out: African American Domestics in Washington, D.C., 1910–1940* (Washington, DC: Smithsonian Institution Press, 1994), 157.
10. Paul S. Taylor, "Mexican Women in Los Angeles Industry in 1928," *Aztlan* 11 (1980): 116 (originally written in 1929).
11. Emily Newell Blair, "Discouraged Feminists," *Outlook and Independent 158* (July 8, 1931): 303.
12. *Photoplay*, February 1926, 105.
13. Phyllis Blanchard and Carlyn Manasses, *New Girls for Old* (New York: Macaulay, 1930), 196.
14. Elaine Tyler May, *Great Expectations: Marriage and Divorce in Post-Victorian America* (Chicago: University of Chicago Press, 1980); John D'Emilio and Estelle B. Freedman, *Intimate Matters: A History of Sexuality in America* (New York: Harper & Row, 1988).
15. Hazel V. Carby, " 'It Jus Be's Dat Way Sometime': The Sexual Politics of Women's Blues," *Radical America* 20 (1986): 9–22.
16. Christina Simmons, "Women's Power in Sex: Radical Challenges to Marriage in the Early-Twentieth-Century United States," *Feminist Studies 29* (Spring 2003): 188.
17. Robert S. and Helen Merrell Lynd, *Middletown in Transition: A Study in Cultural Conflicts* (New York: Harcourt, 1937), 178–79.
18. Kessler-Harris, *Out to Work*, 257.
19. Susan Ware, *Holding Their Own: American Women in the 1930s* (Boston: Twayne, 1982), 27.
20. Weiner, *From Working Girl to Working Mother*, 4–6.
21. Jones, *Labor of Love*, 209.
22. Ella Baker and Marvel Cooke, "The Bronx Slave Market," *The Crisis* 42 (November 1935): 330.
23. Blanche Wiesen Cook, *Eleanor Roosevelt: The War Years and After, 1939–1962*, vol. 3 (New York: Viking, 2016), 94.
24. Devra Weber, *Dark Sweat, White Gold: California Farm Workers, Cotton, and the New Deal* (Berkeley: University of California Press, 1994), 95–96.
25. Ware, *Holding Their Own*, 47.
26. Martha H. Swain, *Ellen S. Woodward: New Deal Advocate for Women* (Jackson: University of Mississippi Press, 1995).
27. Melissa A. Herbert, "Amazons or Butterflies: The Recruitment of Women into the Military during World War II," *Minerva* 9 (1991): 50–68.
28. Ibid., 7.
29. Susan M. Hartmann, *The Home Front and Beyond: American Women in the 1940s* (Boston: Twayne, 1982), 42.
30. Kessler-Harris, *Out to Work*, 276.
31. Karen Tucker Anderson, "Last Hired, First Fired: Black Women Workers during World War II," *Journal of American History 69* (1982): 85.
32. Eileen Boris, " 'You Wouldn't Want One of 'Em Dancing with Your Wife': Racialized Bodies on the Job in World War II," *American Quarterly* 50 (1998): 77–108.
33. Paul Spickard, "Work and Hope: African American Women in Southern California during World War II," *Journal of the West 32* (1993): 75.
34. Elizabeth R. Escobedo, *From Coveralls to Zoot Suits: The Lives of Mexican American Women on the World War II Home Front* (Chapel Hill: University of North Carolina Press, 2013), 51.
35. Richard Santillán, "Rosita the Riveter: Midwest Mexican American Women during World War II, 1941–1945," *Perspectives in Mexican American Studies 2* (1989): 132.
36. Escobedo, *From Coveralls to Zoot Suits*, 101.
37. Grace Mary Gouveia, " 'We Also Serve': American Indian Women's Role in World War II," *Michigan Historical Review* 20 (1994): 153–82.
38. Xiaojian Zhao, "Chinese American Women Defense Workers in World War II," *California History* 25 (1996): 138–53.
39. Valerie J. Matsumoto, *City Girls: The Nisei Social World in Los Angeles, 1920–1950* (New York: Oxford University Press, 2014), 158.
40. Elaine Tyler May, "Rosie the Riveter Gets Married," in Lewis A. Erenberg and Susan E. Hirsch, eds., *The War in American Culture: Society and Consciousness during World War II* (Chicago: University of Chicago Press, 1996), 128.
41. D'Emilio and Freedman, *Intimate Matters*, 261.
42. Ibid., 290.
43. Hartmann, *The Home Front and Beyond*, 200.

44. Margaret Mead, "The Women in the War," in Jack Goodman, ed., *While You Were Gone: A Report on Wartime Life in the United States* (New York: Simon and Schuster, 1946), 278.

45. May, "Rosie the Riveter Gets Married," 140.

46. Julia Kirk Blackwelder, *Now Hiring: The Feminization of Work in the United States, 1900–1995* (College Station: Texas A&M University Press, 1997), 137.

47. Nancy Baker Wise and Christy Wise, *A Mouthful of Rivets: Women at Work in World War II* (San Francisco: Jossey-Bass, 1994), 182.

48. Kathy Peiss, *Hope in a Jar: The Making of America's Beauty Culture* (New York: Henry Holt, 1998), 144–46.

49. Susannah Walker, *Style and Status: Selling Beauty to African American Women, 1920–1975* (Lexington: University Press of Kentucky, 2007), 41.

50. This essay has relied extensively on the research, analysis, and words of research assistant Sharon Park. It is also indebted to the work of Linda Gordon, *Dorothea Lange: A Life Beyond Limits* (New York: W. W. Norton, 2009); Wendy Kozol, "Madonnas of the Field: Photography, Gender, and 1930s Farm Relief," *Genders* 2 (Summer 1988); and James C. Curtis, *Mind's Eye, Mind's Truth* (Philadelphia: Temple University Press, 1991).

51. Gordon, *Dorothea Lange*, 220.

52. Kozol, "Madonnas," 4.

53. United States Department of Labor, Women's Bureau, "Our History," http://www.dol.gov/wb/info_about_wb/interwb.htm (accessed April 25, 2015).

SUGGESTED REFERENCES

General Works

Dorothy M. Brown, *Setting a Course: American Women in the 1920s* (1987).

Paula Giddings, *When and Where I Enter: The Impact of Black Women on Race and Sex in America* (1988).

Susan M. Hartmann, *The Home Front and Beyond: American Women in the 1940s* (1982).

Jacqueline Jones, *Labor of Love, Labor of Sorrow: Black Women, Work, and the Family, from Slavery to the Present* (1985).

Vicki L. Ruiz, *From Out of the Shadows: Mexican Women in Twentieth-Century America* (1998).

Judy Yung, *Unbound Feet: A Social History of Chinese Women in San Francisco* (1995).

Public Lives: Work and Politics

Julia Kirk Blackwelder, *Now Hiring: The Feminization of Work in the United States, 1900–1995* (1997).

Nancy F. Cott, *The Grounding of Modern Feminism* (1987).

Kirstin Downey, *The Woman behind the New Deal: The Life and Legacy of Frances Perkins: Social Security, Unemployment Insurance, and the Minimum Wage* (2009).

Elizabeth R. Escobedo, *From Coveralls to Zoot Suits: The Lives of Mexican American Women on the World War II Home Front* (2013).

Sherna Berger Gluck, *Rosie the Riveter Revisited: Women, the War, and Social Change* (1987).

Maureen Honey, ed., *Bitter Fruit: African American Women in World War II* (1999).

Alice Kessler-Harris, *Out to Work: A History of Wage-Earning Women in the United States*, 20th anniv. ed. (2003).

Molly Ladd-Taylor, *Mother-Work: Women, Child Welfare, and the State, 1890–1930* (1994).

Evelyn M. Monahan and Rosemary Neidel-Greenlee, *A Few Good Women: America's Military Women from World War I to the Wars in Iraq and Afghanistan* (2010).

Erica J. Ryan, *Red War on the Family: Sex, Gender, and Americanism in the First Red Scare* (2015).

Vicki L. Ruiz, *Cannery Women, Cannery Lives: Mexican Women, Unionization, and the California Food Processing Industry, 1930–1950* (1987).

Private Lives: Home, Family, Consumption, and Sexuality

Beth L. Bailey, *From Front Porch to Back Seat: Courtship in Twentieth-Century America* (1988).

Donna B. Knaff, *Beyond Rosie the Riveter: Women of World War II in American Popular Graphic Art* (2012).

Valerie J. Matsumoto, *City Girls: The Nisei Social World in Los Angeles, 1920–1950* (2014).

Melissa A. McEuen, *Making War, Making Women: Femininity and Duty on the American Home Front, 1941–1945* (2011).

Kathy Peiss, *Hope in a Jar: The Making of America's Beauty Culture* (1998).

Christina Simmons, *Making Marriage Modern: Women's Sexuality from the Progressive Era to World War II* (2009).

Susannah Walker, *Style and Status: Selling Beauty to African American Women, 1920–1975* (2007).

10

Beyond the Feminine Mystique

WOMEN'S LIVES, 1945–1965

IN DECEMBER 1955, A MIDDLE-AGED AFRICAN AMERICAN woman in Montgomery, Alabama, was arrested for refusing to give up her seat to a white passenger. Rosa Parks's protest against segregation sparked the Montgomery bus boycott, one of the pivotal events of a resurgent postwar civil rights movement. Parks's story signals the importance of women in the civil rights movement, certainly, but Parks, a department store seamstress, is also significant because she was a working woman. In the postwar era, female participation in the paid labor force expanded dramatically and became a defining characteristic of many more women's lives.

Parks's life is one indication of how the period of 1945 to 1965 was rife with tensions and contradictions. Mainstream cultural values of the "feminine mystique" emphasized women's domestic and maternal roles. Yet women worked outside the home and participated in civic activism that encompassed labor unions, politics, and civil and women's rights. Other contradictions are evident in the contrast between Americans' celebration of unprecedented prosperity and their deep anxieties about the Cold War and nuclear arms race. Cold War fears contributed to a repressive social and political climate that inhibited dissenting voices and reinforced traditional expectations about women's familial roles. Yet despite the conservative temper of this era, women activists helped to launch the civil rights movement and began to challenge the discrimination women faced in the workplace and public life.

photos: top, Photofest; bottom, NASA

◆ FAMILY CULTURE AND GENDER ROLES

Two overarching themes shaped Americans' lives in the postwar era. The first, the Cold War between the Soviet Union and the United States, led to a sense of insecurity and anxiety that encouraged conformity to political and social norms. The second, the United States's extraordinary prosperity, prompted tremendous optimism about the nation's material progress. Both anxiety and affluence contributed to a popular conception of the family as a source of social stability and prosperity and reinforced traditional notions of women's place in the home.

The New Affluence and the Family

One startling measure of the nation's post–World War II prosperity was the growth in the gross domestic product (GDP), from $213 billion in 1945 to more than $500 billion in 1960. Not everyone enjoyed this new affluence. Many Americans, but especially nonwhite minorities, continued to live economically marginalized lives, and in 1959, 22 percent of all Americans still lived below the poverty line. Yet most Americans experienced a rising standard of living, with average family income almost doubling in the years between 1945 and 1960. Veterans pursued upward mobility through the Servicemen Readjustment Act of 1944, or GI Bill, which provided federal assistance through home and student loans to returning military personnel. The GI Bill was particularly significant for assisting children of European immigrants in leaving behind the poverty of urban ethnic enclaves to become middle-class suburbanites. Although educational and economic differences still created clear class distinctions between blue-collar and white-collar workers, many of the former benefited from their unions' success in negotiating improved benefits, such as health insurance and automatic cost-of-living wage adjustments.

Affluence contributed to an emphasis on domesticity and the nuclear family. With more discretionary funds, Americans spent money on homes, raising the percentage of homeownership in the country from 43 percent of families in 1940 to 62 percent in 1960. Many of these homes

photos: top, George Rinhart/Corbis via Getty Images; middle, Walter P. Reuther Library, Archives of Labor and Urban Affairs, Wayne State University; bottom, © 1976 George Ballis/ Take Stock/The Image Works

1960	John F. Kennedy elected president
1960	Sit-ins in Greensboro, North Carolina
1960	**Ella Baker helps to found Student Nonviolent Coordinating Committee (SNCC)**
1961	Freedom Rides seek to integrate interstate bus travel
1961	**Diane Nash and others jailed during Freedom Rides**
1961	**Women Strike for Peace founded**
1961	**President's Commission on the Status of Women created**
1962	**Rachel Carson publishes *Silent Spring***
1962	**Frances Kelsey receives Distinguished Service medal for blocking American distribution of thalidomide**
1962	**Dolores Huerta and César Chávez found United Farm Workers**
1963	**Betty Friedan's *The Feminine Mystique* published**
1963	**Equal Pay Act makes wage disparities based solely on gender illegal**
1963	March on Washington draws over 250,000 civil rights activists to nation's capital
1963	John F. Kennedy assassinated; Lyndon B. Johnson assumes presidency
1964	Freedom Summer
1964	**Mississippi Freedom delegate Fannie Lou Hamer speaks at Democratic National Convention**
1964	**Casey Hayden and Mary King distribute "Women in the Movement" paper at SNCC retreat**
1965	Voting Rights Act bans literacy tests and authorizes federal intervention to enable African Americans to register and vote

551

were located in new suburban developments that created a haven for the new domesticity. However, much postwar housing remained racially segregated both by law and custom. To furnish their homes and garages, families bought electrical appliances, cars, and the exciting new form of at-home entertainment, televisions. New housing construction, road building, and consumer goods fueled the burgeoning postwar economy. Advertisers, manufacturers, and public policy makers all considered consumer purchasing power crucial to prosperity. They extolled the family as the bedrock of the nation's economic well-being and targeted women as its purchasing agent. *Life* magazine captured the essence of this understanding with a 1958 cover that featured thirty-six babies and the caption "Kids — Built-in Recession Cure."

Figures on marriage and fertility for the postwar era suggest Americans' enthusiasm for family and domestic life. Temporarily reversing the long trend since early in the nineteenth century toward fewer children, family size between the war and the early 1960s went up, creating a "baby boom" (see the Appendix, Chart 1, p. A-17). More Americans married and married younger, further spiking the birthrate. In the 1930s, women gave birth to 2.4 children on average; in the 1950s, that number increased to 3.2. More babies were born between 1948 and 1953 than had been born in the previous thirty years. In these years, the divorce rate briefly turned downward, a pattern unique in the twentieth century. Pent-up desires for traditional family life denied to many in the Great Depression and war years undoubtedly played a part, while the pervasive celebration of family life in popular culture may also have shaped young couples' decisions.

The Cold War and the Family

While prosperous families lay at the heart of America's material success, a stable family order was also credited with a crucial role in giving the United States the upper hand in the Cold War. World War II had barely ended before the two former allies, the Soviet Union and the United States, began facing off for what became a global struggle lasting almost fifty years. Representing the conflicting systems of capitalism and communism, each side attempted to achieve dominance in world geopolitics. In the United States, President Harry S. Truman articulated the doctrine of "containment," which called for resisting the spread of Communist governments in countries around the world. The Cold War became hot in Korea between 1950 and 1953, in the first major overseas armed conflict in American history not authorized by congressional declaration. The newly formed United Nations sent troops, primarily supplied by the United States, to defend the U.S.-backed government in the south of Korea against encroachment by the Communist regime in the north. The war ended with a cease-fire that left Korea divided by a demilitarized zone between North and South Korea that is still in existence. The Cold War also spawned an escalating nuclear arms race. The terrible power of atomic destruction unleashed when the United States dropped bombs on Hiroshima and Nagasaki, Japan, and became a mushrooming threat to the peoples of

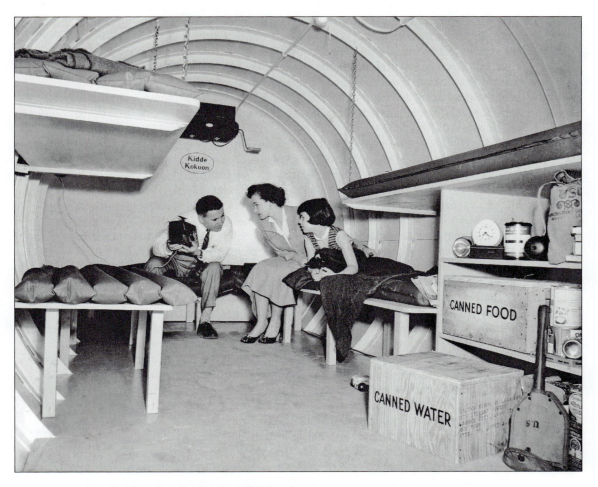

◆ Family Togetherness in the Cold War Era

As the Cold War spread fears of nuclear warfare, many Americans, encouraged by the federal government, built fallout shelters in their front and backyards. Magazines and newspapers frequently ran articles that featured pictures of 1950s families posed in their shelters, reflecting the strong emphasis on family culture in the era. This 1955 image depicts mother, father, and daughter in a "Kidde Kokoon," a shelter manufactured by Walter Kidde Nuclear Laboratories of Garden City, New York. The shelter cost $3,000 and was outfitted with such items as canned food and water, a chemical toilet, a radiation detector, and a face respirator. *Bettmann/Getty Images.*

the world as the U.S. and Soviet governments matched their militant rhetoric with competition to stockpile nuclear weapons.

The Cold War had a chilling effect on U.S. domestic politics. In the late 1940s and early 1950s, the nation was immersed in a hunt for Communists within its borders, led by the House Un-American Activities Committee (HUAC) and U.S.

Senator Joseph McCarthy. McCarthy's search for Communists in high places was more symptom than cause of the new witch hunts. Other politicians and leaders also called for purging American institutions of "internal subversives." The most notorious manifestations of the period's "Red Scare" were a federal loyalty program that scrutinized thousands of public employees and widely publicized congressional hearings held by the HUAC to investigate Communist influence in American life. Women and men lost jobs and had their civil liberties violated based on flimsy evidence.

In 1950, U.S. Representative Helen Gahagan Douglas was red-baited (accused of being a Communist) and pushed from politics because she supported causes such as rent control laws and federal regulation of oil drilling. Douglas lost a hotly contested U.S. Senate race in California to future president Richard M. Nixon, who hinted at what he thought were her pro-Communist sympathies by saying that "she was pink down to her underwear."[1] Unions and mainstream liberal organizations, including the American Association of University Women and the National Council of Negro Women, purged their membership of Communists and "fellow travelers" — people deemed sympathetic to communism. The intensity of the Red Scare began to ebb after 1954, when Senator McCarthy, overreaching by investigating the U.S. Army, was formally censured by the Senate for unbecoming conduct. But anxieties about subversion and dissent continued to shape the political climate for many years to come.

The Red Scare targeted a great many others as well. The hysterical hunt for Communists was accompanied by an attack on lesbians and gay men as alleged security risks and subversive presences in government employment. Executive Order 10450, issued in 1953, tightened the federal government's loyalty program (established in 1947) and explicitly included "sexual perversion" as grounds for dismissal. Applicants for federal jobs were asked, "Have you ever had, or have you now, homosexual tendencies?" and a rule in the Federal Personnel Manual read, "Persons about whom there is evidence that they have engaged in or solicited others to engage in homosexual or sexually perverted acts with them, without evidence of rehabilitation . . . are not suitable for Federal employment."[2] While the majority of people fired or not hired under these loyalty investigations were men, women felt the pervasive risk of exposure, too. Private employers also were unwilling to hire or retain homosexuals. Middle-class lesbians kept their sexual identity private if they wanted to keep their jobs. Those lesbians who did not want or could not afford such closeted privacy, especially working-class women, began to form an identifiable subculture in the 1950s and early 1960s. In large and midsize cities, bars known to tolerate lesbians provided a semipublic space where women could socialize and identify potential partners. On the one hand, lesbian life reflected much of the extreme emphasis on gender roles in these years. In their public presentations, lesbians mirrored the decade's insistence on clearly defined masculine and feminine roles. Often they fell into two groups: the "butches" and the "femmes." On the other hand, fifties lesbians also began to challenge the dominant heterosexual culture by insisting on their right to live and love in the open. In the face of outside threats such as police raids and hostile encounters with passersby on the streets, lesbians defended their turf. The first lesbian rights organization, Daughters of Bilitis, formed in San Francisco in 1955.

In addition to anxieties over homosexuality, the postwar era witnessed a continuation of fears about women's sexual promiscuity. The 1953 publication of Alfred Kinsey's *Sexual Behavior in the Human Female*, the follow-up to Kinsey's *Sexual Behavior in the Human Male* (1948), shocked many Americans with its statistics: 50 percent of the women surveyed admitted to premarital intercourse, 90 percent to "petting" (sexual play short of intercourse), and 28 percent to what Kinsey termed "homosexual tendencies." Kinsey's findings signaled changes in sexual behavior. Further evidence for the shift is the substantial increase in unwed pregnancies, which almost doubled during the 1940s and 1950s.

Scholars, however, do not think these changes came about as a result of an increase in promiscuity, but rather because of the cultural norm of "going steady" in the postwar years. A couple's agreement to see each other "created space within youth culture for girls to minimize stigma while sexually experimenting."[3] However much young women may have enjoyed expanded sexual experiences, in the era before legal abortion and reliable birth control, the fear of unwanted pregnancy always loomed over them. Pregnant teenagers were ousted from schools for fear they might corrupt their presumably innocent classmates. Although some married, many did not. Nor were adoption opportunities equally distributed. White girls had access to institutions for unwed mothers that funnelled the infants into adoption agencies, where they became much sought after commodities. Social workers felt that once these white women relinquished their babies, they could be rehabilitated, cured of their inappropriate sexual behavior. However, racist assumptions about black women's sexuality as somehow pathological and cultural norms that made women unwilling to give up their babies to strangers meant that relatively few options were available to women of color. They or their families usually cared for the children.

Clearly taboos against female sexuality outside of heterosexual marriage remained strong, as did a double standard that excused male sexual adventures before marriage while prizing premarital female virginity. In the face of challenges to these norms, leading experts championed early marriages to reduce premarital experimentation and firm gender roles in the home to ensure the heterosexuality of children.

Indeed, one key aspect of the postwar culture of conformity was an emphasis on the nuclear family as a bastion of social order, one that would help Americans resist the menace of communism and provide shelter in the midst of an uncertain world. Employers and returning soldiers had been eager to send women back to the home to restore traditional gender patterns. Meshing with anxieties flowing from the disruptions of World War II, Cold War fears of atomic annihilation and Soviet expansion reinforced what was a revised and revived cult of domesticity. And just as social stability presumably led to family order, family dysfunction was deemed responsible for social problems. An apparent postwar rise in crime among children, referred to as "juvenile delinquency," was blamed on working mothers and weak fathers. (See Primary Sources: "'Is a Working Mother a Threat to the Home?'" pp. 606–10.)

COSMOPOLITAN

SEPTEMBER 1953 · 35¢

SEX
BEHAVIOR
OF WOMEN

*A First Look
at Kinsey's
New Report*

SHEREE NORTH

*See "Nothing Sacred"
by James H. Street*

Another Terrific Murder
Novel by
Sebastian Blayne

◆ **The Kinsey Report**
Despite the report in Alfred Kinsey's *Sexual Behavior in the Human Female* (1953) that 50 percent of American women admitted to engaging in premarital intercourse, taboos against women's sexuality outside of marriage remained strong. At the same time, the report signaled a real change in Americans' sexual behavior. Kinsey's findings were widely publicized, as is evident in this cover of *Cosmopolitan* magazine. *Courtesy of the Hearst Corporation.*

With this concentration on the family came a strong emphasis on rigid gender roles — on men's role as breadwinners and women's as wives and mothers. Many psychologists insisted that "maturity" entailed a willing acceptance of one's biologically determined social roles. Parents who turned to the best-selling childrearing book *Baby and Child Care* (1946), by Dr. Benjamin Spock, learned that working mothers damaged their children: "If a mother realizes clearly how vital [a mother's] care is to a small child, it may make it easier for her to decide that the extra money she might earn, or the satisfaction she might receive from an outside job, is not so important, after all."[4] In educational films such as *A Date with Your Family*, high school students viewed a mother and daughter dutifully catering to men as they prepared and served a meal. And in movies such as *The Best of Everything* (1959), filmgoers followed a plot that not only depicted career women's sterile lives but also warned young women that "love, even when it's bad, is the best of everything." While some television shows pictured men struggling to control their scheming and adventuresome wives, most portrayed women as content wives and mothers. (See Primary Sources: "Television's Prescriptions for Women," pp. 590–605.)

Rethinking the Feminine Mystique

In 1963, Betty Friedan captured the essence of this postwar ideology of female domestic containment in her best-selling book *The Feminine Mystique*. Arguing that millions of American women were suffering from "the problem that has no name," a malaise brought about by the limited aspirations to which society restricted women, Friedan indicted the "feminine mystique" of popular culture. Excoriating mass media for encouraging women to develop a sense of personal creativity through the use of cake mixes and floor waxes, she similarly lambasted psychologists for prescribing tranquilizers for "neurotic" women rather than examining the social bases of their unhappiness. She criticized popular magazines for disseminating the feminine mystique at every turn, while denying that women were interested in reading about political, international, and social issues. Friedan argued that such attitudes denied women a sense of an autonomous self. *The Feminine Mystique* sold over 3 million copies, a clear indication that Friedan had tapped into many women's frustrations over their prescribed roles. Letters to Friedan, as well as interviews conducted by sociologist Stephanie Coontz, confirm the life-changing impact the book had on many American women.

Despite the impact of Friedan's book, recent critics have pointed out that she vastly overstated the pervasiveness of this restrictive domestic ideal. Rarely acknowledging that the women she described were affluent and white, she glossed over the significant differences that class, race, and ethnicity produced and neglected the increasing number of women entering the paid workforce. Among black women, working wives and mothers had long been valued and understood as virtually essential to families hoping to achieve middle-class status. Images and articles promoting the feminine mystique were largely absent from *Ebony*, the major African American popular magazine of the period. Instead, *Ebony* featured women who fought racial discrimination and achieved success in business, politics, and the arts, although it was careful to note the importance of these women's family roles and their attention "to the needs of their husbands and children."[5]

Even among middle-class white women, Friedan overstated her case. Articles in popular magazines directed at white women often depicted successful career women, including those who combined work and marriage. Writers encouraged women to be active in community affairs and held up as models women who achieved "great pride and accomplishment and the satisfaction of 'doing a job.' "[6] Moreover, in contrast to Friedan's claim that magazines ignored women's discontent, they gave extensive attention to wives' dissatisfaction with their married lives and their housework obligations. In advice columns like the *Ladies' Home Journal*'s "Can This Marriage Be Saved?" letter writers testified to the drudgery of household chores and the stresses entailed in unrelenting domesticity. Nevertheless, the advice dispensed uniformly encouraged women to find psychological tools to help them adjust to the gendered expectations of middle-class marriage, rather than challenge the expectations themselves.[7]

The most ironic corrective to Friedan's assessment is that the author was not the simple housewife and unwitting victim of domestic confinement that she claimed to be. Friedan had a background in radical politics; had been a journalist for the United Electrical, Radio and Machine Workers Union; and in the 1940s and 1950s had frequently written about racial and gender discrimination in the workforce. Thus she knew about women workers but chose not to discuss them in her book. She obscured her past probably because of the anti-Communist preoccupations of the era and because portraying herself as an angry casualty of the feminine mystique made for a more marketable book.

These limitations do not decrease *The Feminine Mystique*'s value as a historical source. Not only was the book important in the revival of feminism in the 1960s, but it also captured a crucial aspect of mainstream Cold War cultural values about women. The ideology of the feminine mystique is best understood as a prescription for female behavior promulgated by those Americans most eager to reinforce rigid gender roles as a means of creating social order. This eagerness may well have stemmed from the challenges posed by working women to conventional expectations.

Women and Work

These challenges were most evident in women's changing employment patterns. As the baby boom suggests, women embraced motherhood in the 1950s, but they also poured into the paid labor market in what many observers at the time called a revolutionary development. In 1940, 25 percent of women worked; by 1960 the figure had climbed to 35 percent (see the Appendix, Table 2, p. A-19).

More dramatic was the growth in the percentage of married women in the labor force. In 1940, only 17 percent of wives worked; by 1960, 32 percent of wives earned wages, constituting fully 61 percent of the female labor force. While all groups of women held jobs outside the home, particularly significant was the growth in wage earning of middle-class white married women, the very group assumed to be most in the grip of the feminine mystique. White wives' participation in the workforce more than doubled between 1940 and 1960, rising from 14 to 30 percent, while for black wives the increase was smaller but began at a higher level, going from 32 percent in 1940 to 47 percent in 1960. In a reversal of older patterns, educated women were more likely to work than those without high school and college degrees.

Mothers also increased their participation in the workforce. One of the most significant developments was the trend toward older women entering the workforce when their children reached school age. By having children at younger ages, mothers found themselves positioned to join the labor force. Because advances in health care meant Americans were living longer, women could expect to work for twenty or more years after their children began going to school.

The expanded availability of jobs, created by a burgeoning economy and fueled by the growth of the consumer culture, also affected women's work patterns. White-collar fields dominated by women for decades — clerical work, sales, nursing, social work, and teaching — grew dramatically. In blue-collar employment, women had lost many skilled positions in heavy manufacturing at the end of World War II, but they found other fields opening up: the lower ranks of the printing industry, positions in industrial assembly, and jobs as delivery personnel and bus and taxi drivers. Service sector jobs — so-called pink-collar work, such as food service, personal care, and beauty salon work — also multiplied and became increasingly feminized. Food service employment was especially sex-segregated. While in 1900, approximately 33 percent of the 100,000 people who waited tables were women, by 1970, 92 percent of the 1 million food servers were women. Unlike other pink-collar workers, waitresses were well represented in unions, with about 25 percent of them organized in the 1950s.

Improvements in the opportunities for women of color were particularly notable. Latinas and Chinese American and Japanese American women increased their participation in white-collar work in the postwar decade. Because of their high degree of education, Nisei (second-generation Japanese American) women also made strides in teaching, social work, and civil service. Although the absolute numbers were small, black women in the 1950s attended college at a rate higher than either white women or black men. They made modest gains in the clerical field and in the teaching and nursing professions.

For all these improvements, poor women of color still had limited options. Although the percentage of black women workers employed as domestics dropped significantly, from 60 percent in 1940 to 42 percent in 1950, a substantial minority continued to work in low-paid, devalued labor, as did many Latina and Asian women. Immigrant women, because of lack of language and other skills as well as discrimination, found few jobs available to them. In 1943, Congress repealed the Chinese Exclusion Act of 1882, in deference to America's World War II alliance with China. As a result of this and the War Brides Act of 1945 and the 1953 Refugee Relief Act, between 1948 and 1965, approximately forty thousand Chinese women immigrated to the United States. Most clustered in Chinatowns in the nation's cities, especially New York and San Francisco. There they worked in family

◆ Clerical Workers

The booming economy of the postwar era created a strong demand for office workers. Technological changes of new machines and automated processes meant that types of jobs formerly held by men became "feminized," most notably in the fields of bookkeeping. A tight labor market also made employers more willing to hire older and married women, but patterns of racial discrimination persisted. While Asian American and Mexican American women made inroads into clerical jobs, African Americans still found fewer opportunities. In 1960, for example, only 8 percent of working black women held clerical jobs compared to 34.7 percent of white working women. This 1952 photograph shows women in a New York City office building. *Bettmann/Getty Images.*

enterprises as well as the garment industry, which was a crucial source of income. Puerto Rican women, part of a vastly expanded post–World War II migration from Puerto Rico mostly to New York City, also concentrated in the garment trade, an industry that was in decline. The results were low wages, poor working conditions, and erratic employment. These poorer women's restricted options underline an important characteristic of the "revolutionary" aspect of women's work after World War II. While certainly many women of color had new opportunities, the most dramatic change was the entrance into the labor market of white married women who could take advantage of new service and clerical jobs that offered "respectable" employment.

Women's increased employment also stemmed from changes in employment practices. Well aware of the expanding labor market and concerned about finding qualified workers, employers not only willingly hired women but also dropped the "marriage bar" that had operated in many fields. Moreover, they restructured the nature of the work market by making part-time jobs widely available for the first time to tap a rich vein of labor power.

Employers who enticed married women with more flexible schedules and other incentives had encouragement from administrators in the U.S. Department of Labor, including its Women's Bureau, and other public policy makers. Maintaining economic prosperity and keeping the upper hand over the Soviet Union in the Cold War motivated employment experts to evaluate the labor market carefully. Many insisted that "womanpower" needed to be exploited efficiently as a means of promoting U.S. productivity and competitiveness. Alice Leopold, head of the Women's Bureau in the mid-1950s, emphasized the need to compete with communism by training American women in new skills. "Women," she noted, "are becoming increasingly important in the development of our country's industry, in scientific research, in the education field, and in the social sciences."[8]

This recognition framed the work of two important agencies in the 1950s. The National Manpower Council (NMC), a private group with close ties to government agencies and corporations, used conferences and publications to draw attention to women's employment. At a 1951 conference on "Women in the Defense Decade," held in the midst of the Korean War, the American Council on Education tackled the "urgent question . . . about just how and in what respects women could serve the defense of the nation,"[9] leading to the 1953 creation of the Commission on the Education of Women (CEW).

In both groups, organizers walked a tightrope between what they viewed as national needs and the dominant ideology about women's place. Sensitive to the prevailing gender norms, they took care not to be viewed as undermining traditional roles. A 1955 CEW report explicitly stated that its recommendations concerning women "must not detract from the importance of their roles as wives and mothers."[10] Yet both groups also encouraged training and education for women and criticized discriminatory labor patterns that limited full use of the nation's womanpower.

These groups legitimated married women's participation in the workforce but barely scratched the surface of the discrimination women faced. Neither the NMC nor the CEW addressed the limited economic opportunities for women of color, focusing their attention almost exclusively on white women, whose education in public schools continued to track them into traditional female occupations such as clerical work. Although Cold War imperatives called for more American engineers and scientists, women were often shunted into high school science teaching and experienced pervasive discrimination in graduate programs, corporations, and government employment. There were notable exceptions. Frances Kelsey, a pharmacologist for the Federal Drug Administration, received the government's Distinguished Service medal for her steadfast refusal in the face of pharmaceutical industry pressure to approve the sleeping pill thalidomide, which had been shown

◆ **Rachel Carson**

A year before Betty Friedan's *The Feminine Mystique* was published, another woman, Rachel Carson, published a controversial and pathbreaking best-seller. In 1962's *Silent Spring*, Carson, a well-known natural science writer, traced the devastating impact of pesticides on plant, animal, and human life. The book expressed her outrage that the pursuit of profits and the thoughtless embrace of technology and science had undermined the natural environment. Carson's work in spreading awareness of the toxicity of pesticides has led many scholars to view her as the impetus for the modern environmental movement, which gained strength in the late 1960s and 1970s and resulted in significant legislation to control chemical pollutants. Though Carson explicitly stated that she was not a "feminist," a small group of women scientists and conservation activists helped support her as she finished her book amidst trying personal circumstances, including the cancer that would take her life in 1964. Many women's organizations were among the quickest to acknowledge the significance of Carson's contribution. The press generally avoided using this image of her at a microscope, preferring the "soft" images of Carson in nature. *George Rinhart/Corbis via Getty Images.*

◆ Human Computers: Kathryn Peddrew Johnson at NASA

Beginning in World War II, women mathematicians found employment with the federal government's NACA (National Advisory Committee for Aeronautics, which became NASA in 1958), where they were crucial to airplane and later space technological research. Before the advent of electronic computers, these women performed complex calculations using conventional calculators and airplanes and later became computer programmers. Of the many hundreds of women working at NASA's Langley Memorial Aeronautical Laboratory in Hampton, Virginia, at least fifty were African American. They enjoyed satisfying work but were frustrated by limited opportunities for advancement and the indignities of racial segregation at the research facility. As Mary Jackson, who became an engineer in 1958 after a struggle to get the training she needed in the segregated educational system of Virginia, put it, "I changed what I could and what I couldn't I endured."[11] Once obscure, these women became the subject of a book and major motion picture in 2016 named, appropriately enough, *Hidden Figures*. This photograph features mathematician Katherine Peddrew Johnson sitting at her desk at NASA's Langley Research Center. The globe is a celestial navigation aid. Johnson's work was crucial to the success of astronaut John Glenn's 1962 orbit, as well as the Apollo mission of 1969. *NASA*.

to produce birth defects among European women. Kelsey came to public attention in 1962, the same year science naturalist Rachel Carson published her pathbreaking *Silent Spring*, an exposé of pesticide usage, which helped spark the modern environmental movement. Carson, who had a master's degree in zoology and had worked for sixteen years for the United States Fish and Wildlife Service, had done meticulous research and consulted with well-established scientists every step of the way. However, her critics, including the chemical industry, vigorously condemned her work with gendered terms, describing her as a "hysterical" or "emotional" woman. Hundreds of women mathematicians also found work in government agencies and research institutions, working first as "human computers" and later as computer programmers and engineers. Although crucial to the early development of computer technology and the aerospace industry, their role has only recently been acknowledged.

Despite slow-changing attitudes toward working women and the sex-segregated nature of their opportunities, women, including wives and mothers, persisted in entering the workforce. Changes in the labor market and encouragement on the part of employers and the government are crucial factors in understanding the growth in women's work outside the home, but this development was also fundamentally a question of personal choice. Scattered evidence suggests the complicated processes that undergirded these choices. Nurses, the largest category of female professional labor, described themselves as taking advantage of new work opportunities to serve their community.[12] At the same time, they emphasized that their home responsibilities came first, and it was only the flexibility of nursing that allowed them to work for wages. In contrast, many working-class women apparently felt less need to justify working, admitting that they took paid labor to get out of the house in addition to providing assistance to their families.

The degree of family need may have been the crucial factor in most married women's decisions to seek employment. Poor women of color — as they had done for decades — worked to make ends meet. For others, paid labor made life easier for their families and, in particular, enabled them to participate in the burgeoning consumer economy and enter the middle class. A survey of unionized women indicated that a significant number of them took jobs to finance their children's education or to make house payments. Contemporary observers echoed these explanations. A 1957 Ford Foundation study, *Womanpower*, reported that "the desire to achieve a richer life for the family has such widespread approval that it provides a generally acceptable reason for married women whose responsibilities at home do not absorb all their time and energy to go to work."[13] Similarly, in 1956 *Look* magazine concluded: "No longer a psychological immigrant to man's world, she works rather casually as a third of the U.S. labor force, and less toward a big career than as a way of filling a hope chest or buying a new home freezer. She gracefully concedes the top job rungs to men."[14] *Look*'s assessment fittingly summed up prevailing assumptions about women's work. Acknowledging a significant shift in labor patterns, the article minimized the impact of women's work on their role in the home, reflecting a belief that sustained the persistent discrimination that the rising tide of working women encountered.

◆ WOMEN'S ACTIVISM IN CONSERVATIVE TIMES

No matter how observers minimized the implications of women's work outside the home, it represented a potentially significant challenge to cultural norms. Still other evidence of women's engagement in the public world was the wide range of activism that flourished in the postwar era. Organized feminism remained weak, but women participated in a variety of efforts to improve their work lives and to contribute to their communities. Their activism, like women's participation in the workforce, laid the seeds for challenging the prevailing ideas of women's role in the family, the workplace, and public life.

Working-Class Women and Unions

While the increased participation of middle-class women in the labor market was one of the most striking characteristics of the postwar era, working-class women's struggle to maintain the gains they had made during World War II was an important aspect of women's activism. Unionized women in industry led the way in challenging layoffs, poor pay, restricted job opportunities, and other discriminatory policies. And in some industries, black and white women came together to challenge the racial discrimination that African American women faced in the workplace.

Women of the United Packinghouse Workers of America (UPWA) exemplified a female activism that not only sought to improve working women's opportunities in the 1950s but also laid the groundwork for working-class women's participation in the feminist movement of the 1960s. Like many other Congress of Industrial Organization (CIO) unions, the UPWA had theoretically embraced an egalitarian stance in the 1930s and 1940s and actively recruited black men and white and black women. Women, however, did not always find their union sympathetic to their concerns. As in most industries during World War II, sex-segregated labor patterns broke down in the big meatpacking houses, with women taking on heavy work formerly reserved for men. But after the war, the companies largely reverted to prewar job classifications that limited women's opportunities and wages, and union men did not challenge employers' decisions to lay off women in large numbers, regardless of their seniority rights.

Despite the UPWA's failure to support women during postwar reconversion, the national leadership had become more sympathetic by the 1950s, in part because women made up a significant percentage (approximately 20 percent) of the union. Women drew on the union's Anti-discrimination Department — which also addressed racial discrimination — to bolster their efforts at improving their work lives. This department organized women's conferences, sponsored a woman's column in the union's newspaper, and served as a clearinghouse for grievances.

African American women became some of the most militant female activists in many unions. Women like UPWA member Addie Wyatt of Chicago often built on their positions as community leaders. Wyatt recalled, "[In my church] women were always leaders. They were preachers, they were officers . . . and whatever was necessary in the church to do, women and men always did it in partnership. And I always thought that was right."[15] As Wyatt rose to prominence in the union — eventually becoming president of her local chapter — she turned her attention to the struggle for racial justice and served as a labor advisor to civil rights leader Martin Luther King Jr. Other black UPWA women were active on the local level, drawing their colleagues into drives against segregation and other discriminatory policies in their communities.

Wyatt and other black women focused in part on challenging the discrimination black women faced in the packinghouses. Joined by many white women union members, they successfully protested racial discrimination in hiring as well as the packers' policy of racially segregating departments, where white women had cleaner, better-paid positions such as bacon slicers, while black women were relegated to dirty work such as cleaning feces from sausage casings.

These women concentrated on breaking down racial barriers, but they also recognized some of their shared concerns as working women. They addressed the problems that kept women from being active in the union and made clear connections between women's domestic lives and their work lives. At a 1954 conference, UPWA leader Marian Simmons pointed out, "[M]erely satisfying the needs of women on the job would not be enough. Just now with women working in the plants and having to go home to all the household drudgery and assuming the full responsibility of taking care of children during non-working hours and providing for their keep during working hours, it is impossible for [them] to exercise [their] full freedom and equality. We have to map out a plan by which women can be free to exercise [their] full talents and inclinations."[16]

UPWA women tackled a number of issues specifically focused on women's employment concerns. They negotiated contracts calling for equal pay for equal work—a provision that affected relatively few women, however, as it applied to men and women doing the same jobs, when most women were clustered in low-paying "women's work." The next logical step in achieving better wages for women—challenging the gendered structure of the workplace—was more problematic, in part because men resisted but also because women were divided on the issue. UPWA women had long supported the concept of protective labor legislation for women and opposed the Equal Rights Amendment, which they viewed as something for elite working women that did not speak to their concerns. Slow to challenge sex-typed work, they sought instead to improve women's wages and conditions within their separate work sphere.

In the immediate postwar years, Mexican women were particularly active in organizing workers in the cannery industry in California and became leaders in a struggle between the more conservative union affiliated with the AFL's Teamster Union and the groups associated with the CIO, the Food, Tobacco, Agricultural and Allied Workers of America (FTA, formerly UCAPAWA). The FTA was among the most egalitarian of labor unions and had organized southern tobacco workers, as well as southwestern food processors, a large proportion of whom were women. The union was sensitive to women's needs and in California during the war had been successful in negotiating nurseries for workers' children. In the postwar era, the issue was union survival. Weakened from the internal struggle and recalcitrant employers, the union was further undercut by red-baiting. The FTA was branded as "Red," and the Immigration and Naturalization Service deported six of its organizers, including longtime activist Luisa Moreno, because of claims that they were Communists. As with many other unions that appeared too radical, the CIO expelled the FTA from its membership, leading to its eventual demise. However, many of its women leaders became community activists; Julia Luna Mount, for example, became a grassroots organizer around community issues in East Los Angeles.

Most women unionists in the late 1940s and 1950s concentrated on improving their work opportunities and wages, primarily in the context of jobs carved

◆ Women and Union Activism

Like women in the UPWA and the UE, women in the United Auto Workers (UAW) fought hard in the postwar era to counter discriminatory employment practices. One of the most militant groups emerged in 1947 in the Detroit area, where women created Region 1-A's Women's Committee, which spawned similar committees elsewhere. This photograph captures Region 1-A's Women's Committee conference in November 1955, a period in which tensions over the impact of automation on women was one of several issues that concerned female union leaders. Although it appears that only a few African Americans are present in this picture, black women were active in the UAW and pursued twin goals of workers' rights for African Americans and for women. *Walter P. Reuther Library, Archives of Labor and Urban Affairs, Wayne State University.*

out as women's work. They called for fair treatment as workers but rarely framed their analysis in terms of women's equality. Class more than gender was their lens for understanding their circumstances, although certainly black women had a more complicated analysis due to the racial inequality they routinely faced. But the struggles of this era and the recalcitrance of both corporate employers and male unionists would culminate in a far more activist movement for women's rights in the 1960s and beyond.

Middle-Class Women and Voluntary Associations

More affluent women were also activists in the postwar years. The cultural values that discouraged middle-class women from working outside the home sanctioned the long tradition of their participation in voluntary associations outside the domestic sphere. In the postwar era, middle-class women participated in a wide range of civic and political activities, sometimes in mixed-sex groups such as the American Civil Liberties Union (ACLU), the National Association for the Advancement of Colored People (NAACP), or Parent-Teacher Associations (PTAs), and sometimes in all-female groups such as the Young Women's Christian Association (YWCA) and the League of Women Voters (LWV). As was the case with working-class union leaders, middle-class women's organizations rarely tackled questions of women's rights, but their activism nonetheless belies the stereotype of the bored or self-satisfied housewife cut off from the larger world outside the home.

In the 1950s, many women's organizations shifted their focus away from gender issues. Cold War anxieties over communism and the domestic ideology of the 1950s put pressure on organizations to moderate their interests in women's rights and in social reform more generally. Changing demographics also fostered the retreat from previous agendas. Both the LWV and the American Association of University Women (AAUW) expanded dramatically in the postwar era, bringing an influx of suburban housewives who had less interest in women's issues than did older members. The LWV moved away from endorsing legislation and narrowed its focus to voter education and local civic issues. The AAUW membership showed less interest in an action-oriented agenda to promote women's educational advancement and focused instead on local study groups.

In other organizations, interest in promoting women's rights was redirected to a growing concern with the civil rights movement. The YWCA's long-standing concern with working-class women helped prepare it to focus on racial inequality. Spurred by black women in its ranks, it eliminated its own organizational segregation and forged alliances in support of black women's civil rights efforts. In the context of the 1950s, this modern reform activity led critics to label YWCA women as "subversive." Other organizations with religious affiliations, such as the National Council of Catholic Women and the National Council of Jewish Women (NCJW), also became involved in racial justice issues. The NCJW's interest in civil rights was particularly deepened by the shock of the Holocaust. The extermination of 6 million Jews by Adolf Hitler's Nazi regime fostered a belief that racism in all its forms needed to be combated vigorously.

The National Council of Negro Women (NCNW) also witnessed significant changes in this era. Founded during the Great Depression by Mary McLeod Bethune (see pp. 500–1) with the idea of creating a political pressure group that could agitate for black women's political and economic advancement, the NCNW fell on hard times in the 1950s. It had difficulty attracting young women, in part because it had gained the reputation of being interested only in black professional women. By the mid-1960s, the NCNW revived, but it did so by downplaying women's rights in favor of community service and civil rights.

Women also found outlets for civic activism in conventional political organizations, working for both the Democratic and Republican Parties. One important example was the National Federation of Republican Women, a group founded in 1937 that consisted of local clubs composed mostly of white middle- and upper-class women, although other women, including some African Americans, joined as well. In the postwar era, leaders emphasized women's domesticity, arguing that their concerns for home and family and religious and moral values were exactly what were needed in promoting a patriotic anticommunism that focused on what one leader called the "moral issue of a free America."[17] The federation served a vital role for the Republicans by taking over what was often called the "housework" of the party: grassroots organizing. Working in their local neighborhoods, women, mostly homemakers, became precinct workers. Their tasks included ringing doorbells, registering voters, sending out mailings, and babysitting on Election Day. In 1956, they orchestrated Operation Coffee Cup: small social gatherings in private homes that allowed women to meet local candidates or watch television together as the national ticket of Dwight D. Eisenhower and Richard M. Nixon spoke to a group of women. Although the federation consisted of both moderate and conservative women, in some areas, notably suburban southern California in the early 1960s, it became the seedbed for a militant sector of the party that sought more right-wing policies, particularly in calling for a more aggressive foreign policy and in demanding reduced federal domestic programs and expenditures. In 1964, these women and their grassroots activities were crucial to the Republican nomination of Senator Barry Goldwater, whose unsuccessful campaign historians now cite as the origin of the moderate right wing of the Republican Party (see pp. 689–96).

Other conservative women participated in new organizations such as the Minute Women of the USA, Pro-America, and Women for Constitutional Government, founded to tackle what they viewed as pervasive Communist subversion of American ideals. In their local communities, these women investigated politicians, teachers, and school boards and focused attention on international issues, including U.S. participation in the United Nations, which they viewed as undermining America's sovereignty. In the domestic political realm, they were on the lookout for liberals whom they considered too sympathetic to communism and opposed the Democrats' efforts to extend the welfare state established by the New Deal, which they called "creeping socialism." They promoted their ideas within the mainstream organizations to which they belonged, such as the PTA, and they red-baited liberal groups such as the AAUW and the YWCA. Women in these small radical groups networked with more moderate right-wing organizations such as the Daughters of the American Revolution and helped to fuel and perpetuate the Red Scare. Even after the intensity of the Red Scare abated, these women continued to be active in conservative anti-Communist groups and, like the National Federation of Republican Women, became important contributors to the growth of the right wing within the Republican Party.

◆ **Republican Women for Nixon**
Even as popular culture celebrated the 1950s "homemaker" wife and mother, many
women — liberal and conservative alike — were active in public life. Here, young women
attending the 1960 Republican convention in Chicago express their support for Richard
Nixon's presidential campaign. *AP Photo.*

On the other side of the political spectrum was a new entry in the long-
standing female pacifist tradition. Women Strike for Peace (WSP) came into the
public spotlight on November 1, 1961, when over fifty thousand American women
in at least forty communities staged a one-day peace demonstration protesting the
nuclear arms race and the Soviet Union's and the United States's proposed resump-
tion of atmospheric testing of bombs after a three-year moratorium. Over the next
year, the WSP sponsored peace vigils, petition drives, forums, and letter-writing
campaigns. Although the media often characterized WSP members as "simple
housewives and mothers," many had a long history of activism. Some had connections to the Communist Party, and many had been active in the Committee for a

Sane Nuclear Policy (SANE), an organization that had been founded to challenge the proliferation of nuclear weaponry and that had been damaged by red-baiting. Other members had abandoned the Women's International League for Peace and Freedom (see pp. 444–45), which they found too hierarchical to achieve its aims.

Despite WSP members' concerted efforts to present themselves as merely concerned middle-class mothers, their activism drew the attention of HUAC, which summoned fourteen women to a congressional hearing in December 1962. As WSP women prepared to be grilled on their political affiliations and opinions, they determined that they would not give in to any HUAC demands that they identify Communists in the organization. When the committee called its first witness, Blanche Posner, a volunteer in WSP's New York office, all the WSP women stood with her as a gesture of solidarity. Much to the consternation of the interrogators, they applauded witnesses' comments and seemed not so much defiant as slightly mocking. The women frequently suggested to their questioners that the "male mind" simply could not understand their refusal to have a structured organization with clearly defined leaders and membership lists. They repeatedly invoked their maternal role. As Posner put it, "This movement was inspired and motivated by mothers' love for their children. . . . When they were putting their breakfast on

◆ **Women Strike for Peace**

The antinuclear group Women Strike for Peace (WSP) began by literally striking — walking out of their kitchens and off their jobs. As the group's numbers swelled, women engaged in lobbying, petitioning, and picketing. This 1962 photo captures WSP members' attempt to stop atmospheric testing in Nevada. *Photo used by permission of Harvey Richards Media Archive, www.estuarypress.com. Print from Swarthmore College Peace Collection.*

the table, they saw not only the Wheaties and milk, but they also saw [radioactive traces of] strontium 90 and iodine 131. . . . They feared for the health and life of their children. This is the only motivation."[18]

The women's conduct made the hearings a media embarrassment for HUAC. Major newspapers featured articles with such titles as "Peace Gals Make Red Hunters Look Silly" and "It's Ladies Day at Capitol: Hoots, Howls and Charm."[19] The hearings strengthened rather than crippled the WSP, which in the following year claimed some credit for President John F. Kennedy's decision to agree to a limited test ban treaty with the Soviet Union. The organization went on to play an important role in the early years of the anti–Vietnam War movement, but its rhetoric of maternalism gradually subsided as WSP women felt the powerful influence of the younger activists of the women's liberation movement.

That a group with such radical political ideas could make use of rhetoric that aligned so well with the feminine mystique sheds light on the complexity and contradictions of postwar female activism. Like other working- and middle-class women activists, WSP members wielded public influence and power but did not overtly challenge the primacy of women's domestic roles. The influence of the feminine mystique, coupled with the anti-Communist climate that stifled dissent, explains why women's activism was not accompanied by feminist questioning of women's unequal position in American society.

◆ A MASS MOVEMENT FOR CIVIL RIGHTS

Women who supported the civil rights movement through their unions or through middle-class organizations like the YWCA were responding to one of the most potent movements for social change of the twentieth century, the civil rights campaign of the postwar years. Going against the tide of the era's political conservatism, black women and men fought against the system of white supremacy in the South. Joined by white liberals sympathetic to their cause, they achieved substantial gains but met with much frustration as well. Both black and white women were major activists in the civil rights movement, and, although women's rights took a backseat to the issue of race, the civil rights movement nonetheless proved a seedbed for the resurgence of feminism in the late 1960s.

As late as a week before the most famous public moment of the civil rights movement — the August 28, 1963, March on Washington, which attracted an unprecedented 250,000 black and white demonstrators — no woman had been invited to speak from the platform. At the last minute, Rosa Parks and a few other women were added to the program, but their participation was clearly an afterthought. The charismatic Martin Luther King Jr. overshadowed all other speakers, male and female, with his "I Have a Dream" speech. Historians have only recently begun to reconstruct women's substantial contributions to the postwar civil rights movement. Some were blue-collar unionists, others college and high school students; some were well-educated professionals, others illiterate sharecroppers. In their search for racial justice, they rarely focused on specific concerns of women, but their gender shaped the nature of the activism they engaged in — both creating opportunities and imposing limits — as they helped to forge the modern civil rights movement. (See Primary Sources: "Women in the Civil Rights Movement," pp. 611–19.)

Challenging Segregation

At first the movement focused specifically on the South, where widespread racial violence and economic exploitation left millions of African Americans economically, socially, and politically deprived. Racism, moreover, was institutionalized. Since the late nineteenth century, southern states had enforced Jim Crow laws establishing a rigid system of segregation where everything from water fountains to public schools was designated for either "whites" or "colored." In all southern states, the majority of African Americans were also disfranchised through poll taxes and stringent literacy requirements. This legalized apartheid system, which denied blacks virtually any protection under the law, came under relentless attack in the postwar era.

World War II helped to set the stage for radical racial change. Continuing migration out of the South, new job opportunities, and military service gave black men and women heightened expectations. By successfully lobbying the federal government to establish the Fair Employment Practices Commission in 1941, African American leaders established a beachhead, albeit one with limited impact, in the struggle to force the national government to take responsibility for enforcing the Fourteenth and Fifteenth Amendments. Further, as more African Americans moved outside the South to regions where they could finally vote, they expanded their political base and gained influence with national politicians in both parties. This influence helped to bring about the desegregation of the army during the Korean War. The Cold War, too, created a new climate, as the shocking inequities faced by African Americans became a common refrain in the Soviets' argument that American democracy was a sham.

In the immediate postwar period, national organizations, especially the NAACP and the Congress of Racial Equality (CORE, founded during World War II), battled disfranchisement and segregation, joined by unions that worked to counter economic discrimination against black people, such as the UPWA. The movement against segregation is usually dated from the 1954 Supreme Court decision in *Brown v. Board of Education of Topeka*, a case brought by the NAACP on behalf of elementary school student Linda Brown and others. The *Brown* decision effectively overturned the 1896 decision *Plessy v. Ferguson*, which had legitimized the southern pretense of a "separate but equal" system (see pp. 303–4). The *Brown* decision found that segregated schools were inherently unequal and thus violated the Fourteenth Amendment, infusing African Americans with new hope. In the aftermath, their efforts to organize resistance to the southern racial system multiplied (see the Appendix, pp. A-9 to A-10).

Thurgood Marshall, who later became the first black Supreme Court justice, led the NAACP team that won the *Brown* case. Constance Baker Motley, the first

African American woman to be appointed to the federal judiciary (1966), was the only woman on the legal team. Black women were more in the forefront of the many local struggles to compel school boards to comply with the Court's decision. Of all these confrontations, the one that drew the most national attention occurred in Little Rock, Arkansas. In 1957, with the support of the Little Rock Board of Education, nine black students, six of them young women, registered to attend the all-white Central High School. For their determination, the young people, known as the "Little Rock Nine," and their families were subjected to considerable violence. One of the young women, Melba Patillo, later recalled that she was threatened with sexual assault as she walked back from school but did not dare tell her parents for fear they would withdraw her from the desegregation effort. Arkansas governor Orval Faubus sent the state National Guard to block the black students' entry. Finally, President Dwight D. Eisenhower, concerned about the defiance of federal law, sent U.S. troops to protect the students so that they were able to enter the school. Their victory, however, was only temporary. The following year, Faubus closed the school system rather than integrate it, a tactic that was not checked by the federal courts for several years. Although parts of the Upper South desegregated their school systems voluntarily, by 1964 only 2 percent of southern blacks attended integrated schools, a measure of the deep resistance *Brown* evoked among many southern whites.

Throughout the Little Rock students' ordeal, one local woman organized their efforts and provided much-needed support. Daisy Bates was in many ways typical of black female activists throughout the twentieth century. A successful businesswoman and civic leader — she and her husband owned the local black newspaper, the *State Press* — Bates had long been active in the NAACP, serving as president of the Arkansas branch in 1953. While federal troops remained to guard the students throughout the school year, each day Bates ushered the students to their high school and provided crucial leadership within the black community (see Figure 10.13, p. 613).

Efforts to integrate higher education also were hard-fought battles in which women had high visibility. In 1956, Autherine Lucy became the first black student to be admitted to the University of Alabama, only to be expelled three days later "for her own protection" against relentless white brutality and official intransigence. Seven years later Vivian Malone, along with a black male student, succeeded in integrating that university. At the University of Georgia, Charlayne Hunter, later a nationally prominent television newswoman, broke the racial barrier of that state's higher education system in 1961.

A year after the *Brown* decision, the Montgomery, Alabama, bus boycott became the second great watershed in invigorating the postwar civil rights movement. African Americans stayed off the buses of Montgomery for 381 days until the U.S. Supreme Court struck down the city's system of segregated public buses. The boycott had its origins on December 1, 1955, when Rosa Parks refused to give up her seat to a white passenger, a daily humiliation required of black bus riders. Parks was not simply a tired woman whose arrest unwittingly sparked a massive protest. She had been active in the local NAACP for fifteen years, and her decision to make this stand against segregation was part of a lifelong commitment to racial justice. For some time local NAACP leaders had wanted to find a test case to challenge Montgomery's bus segregation in the courts. Parks, a respectable, hardworking, middle-aged woman, fit the bill perfectly (see Figure 10.12, p. 612).

On the night of Parks's arrest, a group working independently of the NAACP sprang into action. The Women's Political Caucus (WPC), consisting primarily of black professional women, had been founded in 1946 to focus on challenging disfranchisement and segregation in Montgomery. According to one member, well before Parks's arrest, "We had all the plans and we were just waiting for the right time."[20] WPC president Jo Ann Robinson used the organization's extensive network to duplicate and distribute flyers announcing a boycott. At a community meeting the evening after Parks's arrest, the boycott was formally organized and endorsed. Shortly afterward a twenty-six-year-old minister newly arrived in town, Martin Luther King Jr., was selected to head up the Montgomery Improvement Association (MIA), an agency created in response to the boycott. (See Primary Sources: "Women in the Civil Rights Movement," pp. 611–19.)

Men, particularly ministers, who traditionally were at the center of black southern leadership, predominated in the MIA, and women largely were excluded from formal leadership positions, an exclusion they rarely questioned. But women were nonetheless pivotal to the success of the boycott. They not only initiated the boycott but also formed its backbone. Ever since 1884, when Ida B. Wells (see p. 301) had challenged her ejection from a Tennessee railroad car, black women had been in the forefront of battles to desegregate public transportation. Much more than men, women depended on public transportation to travel to their jobs as domestic servants in white households. During the Montgomery bus boycott, some were able to take advantage of a carpool system created by women activists, but most walked. In addition to their personal sacrifices, other women helped the boycott by raising funds and providing food for mass meetings. As one WPC leader put it, the "grassroots support" was "a hundred percent among the women."[21]

Women as "Bridge Leaders"

Montgomery women demonstrated a pattern repeated in other civil rights activities. Men monopolized the formal leadership roles and mediated among the community, the media, and government officials. Women were far more likely to have unofficial positions, yet they served vital functions in organizing and inspiring their local communities. One scholar terms this pattern "bridge leadership."[22] The role of bridge leader became increasingly significant as the struggle took on a new trajectory. While not neglecting the older methods of pursuing legal battles in the courts and lobbying legislators, the movement increasingly became a mass movement. In boycotts, sit-ins, demonstrations, and marches, women repeatedly served as bridge leaders.

Ella Baker exemplified the bridge leader. A well-educated southerner who migrated to New York in the 1920s, Baker became active in the NAACP, eventually becoming director of the branch offices. An extraordinary woman and gifted speaker, Baker was committed to bringing about social change by mobilizing grassroots resistance. In 1957, she began to work for the Southern Christian Leadership Conference (SCLC), an organization of black ministers under the direction of Martin Luther King Jr. The SCLC reluctantly appointed Baker an "acting" executive director until a suitable male executive could be found. She accepted the position but clearly chafed at the male-dominated leadership structure and hierarchical style. She later said, "I had known . . . that there would never be any role for me in a leadership capacity with SCLC. Why? First, I'm a woman. Also, I'm not a minister."[23]

Perhaps Baker's most lasting contribution was her central role in the establishment of the Student Nonviolent Coordinating Committee (SNCC, pronounced "snick"). SNCC had emerged from yet another kind of mass protest, the sit-in movement that started in 1960 in Greensboro, North Carolina, when four black male students took seats at the "whites only" lunch counter at the local Woolworth's store, determined to "sit in" until they were served. Their protest eventually drew in hundreds of students, women and men, blacks and whites. Their goal was both economic disruption and publicity for the movement. They showcased the tactics of nonviolent resistance, a doctrine popularized by King but originating with the Indian nationalist leader Mahatma Gandhi. Students stoically withstood taunts and physical abuse in a steadfast determination to overcome oppression. The successful Greensboro sit-in sparked a wave of sit-ins in fifty-four cities that helped to desegregate many public facilities in the Upper South. The Deep South, however, especially Alabama and Mississippi, remained resistant.

In her role as SCLC acting director, Baker convened a meeting of over three hundred college students to help form an organization to orchestrate their future efforts. Following Baker's precept that strong leaders were not necessary for a strong movement, SNCC emerged as a nonhierarchical organization, with rotating officers. Although women were active in all the civil rights organizations, SNCC gave women the greatest opportunity to participate and influence the civil rights movement.

SNCC men and women participated in the Freedom Rides of 1961, which CORE organized to challenge segregated interstate bus travel and bus terminals in the South. On May 14, 1961, a group consisting of black and white men and women boarded a bus in Washington, D.C., headed to New Orleans. In Anniston and Birmingham, Alabama, the activists encountered vicious mob violence. A pivotal bridge leader in the Freedom Rides was Diane Nash, a young black SNCC activist who had earlier led the Nashville sit-ins. (See Primary Sources: "Women in the Civil Rights Movement," pp. 611–19.) After the violence in Birmingham, some SCLC leaders called for an end to the rides, but Nash interceded, insisting, "[I]f they stop us with violence, the movement is dead."[24] The rides continued. The unwillingness of Alabama's officials to protect the Freedom Riders eventually led President John F. Kennedy to send federal marshals to Alabama to protect them. He later ordered the Interstate Commerce Commission to enforce desegregation on interstate bus routes. Even though they never made it to New Orleans, the Riders had succeeded in integrating interstate bus travel.

Voter Registration and Freedom Summer

Women activists like Nash faced violence, harassment, and degrading jail conditions. By far the most challenging — and dangerous — activities were the voter organizing drives that took place deep in the rural South. In 1960, SNCC had begun a voter registration drive in Mississippi, where, although African Americans represented 45 percent of the population, only 5 percent of black adults were registered to vote. In 1962, registration efforts heated up after the SCLC, SNCC, the NAACP, and CORE established the Council of Federated Organizations (COFO) to oversee voting registration drives in Mississippi.

As they struggled to overcome the reluctance of local blacks to risk their livelihood or personal safety to register to vote, the activists also encountered stiff resistance from local whites. Viewed as outside agitators, they experienced harassment, intimidation, and deadly violence. But they were usually able to rely on a small number of local community leaders — often women — who provided shelter, moral support, and valuable personal contacts, at great personal risk to themselves. (See Primary Sources: "Women in the Civil Rights Movement," pp. 611–19.)

The most famous of these local leaders was Fannie Lou Hamer of Sunflower County, Mississippi. Hamer worked on a large cotton plantation. There, despite having only a sixth-grade education, she exhibited natural leadership capacities that eventually elevated her to a position as a kind of forewoman for her boss and an influential person in the local black community. Motivated by the desire to make blacks full citizens, Hamer joined SNCC and, after a year of effort, finally registered to vote in 1963. "We just got to stand up now as Negroes for ourselves and for our freedom," she insisted, "and if it don't do me any good, I do know the young people it will do good."[25] Despite the loss of her job and threats to her life, she became an organizer and spokeswoman for the Mississippi voter registration effort. She was renowned for her outspoken and charismatic style and for her passion and skill as an inspirational singer. Hamer was an exemplar of the rural black southern women who were pillars of the southern civil rights movement. But appreciation for their strength must not obscure the considerable personal sacrifices these women endured. Until she died in 1977, Hamer suffered both physically and emotionally from the ramifications of a brutal 1963 beating she received as punishment for her commitment to the civil rights movement.

Despite such heroism, southern black voter registration was stalled by fear, violence, and the determined resistance of white political leaders. In the spring of 1964, COFO devised a plan to import one thousand volunteers from outside the South, primarily white students, to register black voters in the Deep South. Freedom Summer, as the plan was called, was meant not only to infuse new energy into the voter registration drive but to use these white students to focus media and federal attention on southern recalcitrance. Trained in nonviolent resistance and warned about the dangers involved, the first volunteers arrived in June 1964. Violence overshadowed Freedom Summer. Four volunteers were killed, eighty beaten, and more than a thousand arrested. Thirty-seven churches were bombed and burned.

◆ **Fannie Lou Hamer**
Fannie Lou Hamer, one of the most charismatic civil rights figures, was active in SNCC in Mississippi and came to national attention as a delegate of the Mississippi Freedom Democratic Party to the 1964 Democratic National Convention in Atlantic City. Under pressure from President Johnson, the networks cut off live coverage of Hamer's passionate speech, in which she asked "Is this America?" but the speech later made network news. Standing next to Hamer are Eleanor Holmes (later Norton) and Ella Baker (far right). © *1976 George Ballis/ Take Stock/The Image Works.*

The recruitment of white northern students created tension within the movement. Some of these highly educated whites tried to assume leadership positions and had to be reminded that they had come to help, not to take charge. The presence of white women raised particular issues. A handful of southern white women had been active in the civil rights movement from the very beginning, including older women like Virginia Foster Durr and Anne Braden, who had a lifelong commitment to challenging segregation, and younger activists like Joan Browning, who was a Freedom Rider, and Casey Hayden, who was an early member of SNCC. During Freedom Summer, however, the number of white women, estimated at somewhere between one-third and one-half of the volunteers, increased dramatically. Any sort of closeness or intimacy between black men and white women constituted a highly charged trigger for white racists' anger. White women and black men had their own reasons for engaging in these flirtations and sexual liaisons, but black women often resented them, and these tensions contributed to racial divisions in the early years of the women's liberation movement.

The climax of southern voter registration efforts and Freedom Summer was a bold challenge to the all-white Mississippi Democratic Party. Mississippi blacks organized a delegation of the newly formed Mississippi Freedom Democratic Party (MFDP) to attend the Democratic National Convention (DNC) in Atlantic City in August 1964. They demanded that the DNC replace the all-white state group as the official Mississippi delegation. Hamer testified before the convention's rules committee about the violence and beatings she suffered in order to register to vote. Despite the extraordinary power of her story, the party leadership, including President Lyndon Johnson and Vice President Hubert Humphrey, with the tacit approval of more moderate black leaders, chose to seat the all-white delegation and to offer the MFDP two "at-large" seats. The MFDP rejected this proposal as a compromise that did not address the illegality of Mississippi's systematic denial of blacks' access to the political process. Deeply disillusioned, the MFDP delegates returned to Mississippi. Although Hamer and others continued their activism on behalf of southern black economic and political empowerment, the civil rights movement as a whole never recovered its optimism after the disappointment in Atlantic City.

Sexism in the Movement

When Hamer returned home in the fall of 1964, SNCC was faltering, beset by a wide range of tensions, including the influx of new white members who had stayed on after Freedom Summer and questions about the viability of nonviolent resistance in the face of relentless persecution. A discussion paper written by Casey Hayden and Mary King, two longtime, highly respected white members of SNCC, drew parallels between the subordination of blacks and the subordination of women in society. Hayden and King criticized SNCC for not "recognizing that women are the crucial factor that keeps the movement running on a day-to-day basis [or giving women] equal say-so when it comes to day-to-day decision making."[26] The paper received virtually no attention at the time, but historians now regard it as an important document linking women's participation in the civil rights movement to the women's liberation movement of the late 1960s (see Reading into the Past: "Women in the Movement").

Was SNCC sexist? Were women relegated to minor positions and not taken seriously by male leaders? Many black women had established themselves as a powerful presence in SNCC, but white women, especially the new student volunteers, were viewed, and usually viewed themselves, as playing supportive roles. In retrospect it seems that males monopolized formal leadership positions, but few women now claim that they experienced any resentment at the time. For black women, race was of utmost importance, and few acted in the context of bettering the position of black women specifically. Even those white women who criticized male domination of the movement remember above all that participating in the civil rights movement proved personally and politically liberating. Harriet Tanzman, a University of Wisconsin student who first went south during Freedom Summer, explained, "I was able to do things I never knew I could do. I mean it took the best of us, the movement, whether we were eighteen or twenty-five. It empowered our lives."[27]

READING INTO THE PAST

CASEY HAYDEN AND MARY KING
Women in the Movement

Casey Hayden (b. 1939) and Mary King (b. 1940) anonymously distributed a document titled "Position Paper: Nov. 1964" during a SNCC retreat in Waveland, Mississippi. The statement symbolizes the close connection between young white women's civil rights activism and the emergence of the women's liberation movement later in the decade.

Staff was involved in crucial [SNCC] constitutional revisions at the Atlanta staff meeting in October. A large committee was appointed to present revisions to the staff. The committee was all men.

Two organizers were working together to form a farmers league. Without asking any questions, the male organizer immediately assigned the clerical work to the female organizer although both had had equal experience in organizing campaigns.

Although there are some women in Mississippi projects who have been working as long as some of the men, the leadership group in COFO is all men. A woman in a field office wondered why she was held responsible for day-to-day decisions, only to find out later that she had been appointed project director but not told.

A fall 1964 personnel and resources report on Mississippi projects lists the number of people on each project. The section on Laurel, however, lists not the number of persons, but "three girls."

One of SNCC's main administrative officers apologizes for appointment of a woman as interim project director in a key Mississippi project area. . . .

Any woman in SNCC, no matter what her position or experience, has been asked to take minutes in a meeting when she and other women are outnumbered by men.

The names of several new attorneys entering a state project this past summer were posted in a central movement office. The first initial and last name of each lawyer was listed. Next to one name was written: (girl).

Capable, responsible, and experienced women who are in leadership positions can expect to have to defer to a man on their project for final decision-making.

A session at the recent October staff meeting in Atlanta was the first large meeting in the past couple of years where a woman was asked to chair.

Undoubtedly this list will seem strange to some, petty to others, laughable to most. The list could continue as far as there are women in the movement. Except that most women don't talk about these kinds of incidents, because the whole subject is [not] discussible — strange to some, petty to others, laughable to most. The average white person finds it difficult to understand why the Negro resents being called "boy," or being thought of as "musical" and "athletic," because the average white person doesn't realize that *he assumes he is superior.* And naturally he doesn't understand the problem of paternalism. So too the average SNCC worker finds it difficult to discuss the woman problem because of the assumptions of male superiority. Assumptions of male superiority are as widespread and deep rooted and every much as crippling to the woman as the assumptions of white supremacy are to the Negro. Consider why it is in SNCC that women who are competent, qualified, and experienced, are automatically assigned to the "female" kinds of jobs such as typing, desk work, telephone work, filing, library work, cooking, and the assistant kind of administrative work but rarely the "executive" kind. . . .

This paper is presented anyway because it needs to be made know[n] that many women in the movement are not "happy and contented" with their status. . . . What can be done? Probably nothing right away. . . . [But] maybe sometime in the future the whole of the women in this movement will become so alert as to force the rest of the movement to stop the discrimination and start the slow process of changing values and ideas so that all of us gradually come to understand that this is no more a man's world than it is a white world.

November, 1964

SOURCE: Alexander Bloom and Wini Breines, eds., *"Takin' It to the Streets": A Sixties Reader* (New York: Oxford University Press, 1995), 45–47.

QUESTIONS FOR ANALYSIS

1. What are Hayden and King's key concerns?
2. According to the authors, why is it difficult to discuss women's position in the movement?

In numerous ways, the civil rights movement was fundamental in helping to revive the feminist movement, discussed in Chapter 11. It gave middle-class white women exposure to role models of female public activism and leadership, like Ella Baker and Fannie Lou Hamer, and opportunities to envision themselves operating outside the rigid gender norms of middle-class culture. What might be called implicit feminist impulses underlay their willingness to undertake the risks of civil rights activism. Rita Schwerner Bender (the wife of Mickey Schwerner, one of four activists killed during Freedom Summer) was a member of CORE in Brooklyn before heading to Mississippi in 1964. In 1994, she recalled her decision to join the movement: "I did not see myself as saving anyone, but I did have a view of saving myself from a split-level house."[28] The empowerment that Tanzman and other women described later led many to challenge the patriarchal nature of their society.

Tensions within SNCC exacerbated by Freedom Summer and its aftermath were part of a larger change in the direction of the civil rights movement. The Atlantic City disappointment exposed the degree to which the Johnson administration temporized about protecting African Americans' constitutional rights. Repeatedly, as activists faced violence and intimidation, the Justice Department intervened only when forced by massive media exposure of violence against peaceful demonstrators. Despite years of agitation, Congress resisted passing a Civil Rights Act until 1964, when President Lyndon Johnson pushed it through as homage to the assassinated John F. Kennedy. Brutality to demonstrators in Selma, Alabama, was followed by passage of the Voting Rights Act of 1965, which threw out the literacy tests used to keep blacks out of southern Democratic parties and authorized the U.S. attorney general to intervene in counties where less than 50 percent of the black voting-age population was registered. But for many young blacks, this was too little too late. Breaking from more moderate leaders like Martin Luther King Jr. in the late 1960s, militant blacks turned from the goal of integration to "Black Power," an explicitly male-dominated phase of the civil rights movement. Rejecting the "beloved community" of black/white unity that had emerged in the heady first days of civil rights radicalism, SNCC demanded that whites leave the organization so that it could be run entirely by blacks for goals of their own choosing.

A Widening Circle of Civil Rights Activists

As African Americans mounted their civil rights struggle, Mexican Americans intensified their own drive to fight prejudice and attain legitimacy in American society. Here, too, women made significant contributions that have been obscured by the attention given to male leaders.

After World War II, Mexican Americans in Texas, California, and some states in the Midwest sought to improve their communities, increase their political influence, and challenge de facto segregation and economic and educational discrimination. One of the most dynamic organizations of the period was the Community Service Organization (CSO), founded in 1947 and based primarily in California. The CSO had wide-ranging goals of fostering civil rights, improving health care and living conditions, and developing leadership skills in urban Mexican communities. Historians estimate that close to half of the CSO's members were women, most of whom participated with their husbands. Men dominated formal leadership positions, while women played subordinate but nonetheless vital roles, including most of the clerical work. Helen Chávez, wife of César Chávez, who became the most significant Chicano activist of his time, recalled that daily she recorded in longhand her husband's dictated reports and that for meetings, "I would address all the envelopes and address the postcards."[29] Women also turned their energies to citizenship education programs, voter registration drives, and fund-raising. In the latter, their efforts reflected the gendered nature of their activism. They often raised money through sales of items such as Mexican tamales or *pan dulce* (sweet rolls). The *CSO Reporter* described another quintessential 1950s social gathering that these Mexican American women adapted to their cause: "A series of Tupper Ware parties with a percentage of sales given to CSO are being conducted under the able leadership of Ursula Gutierrez."[30]

◆ Dolores Huerta

Dolores Huerta is most famous for her role as cofounder with César Chávez of the United Farm Workers in 1962. Huerta played a leading role in organizing workers and negotiating contracts. In the late 1960s, she spearheaded a national boycott of grapes that forced growers to sign a contract with the union. Here she is shown in 1962 registering farmworkers. *Walter P. Reuther Library, Archives of Labor and Urban Affairs, Wayne State University.*

Some Mexican women worked outside these patterns of gendered activism. Dolores Huerta began her career doing volunteer work for the Mexican American community but later served as a paid lobbyist for CSO and, in 1962, cofounded the United Farm Workers with César Chávez. Another prominent woman, Hope Mendoza, had been active in the International Ladies' Garment Workers' Union and, like women in the UE and UPWA, was militant in her defense of women workers. Chairing the CSO's labor relations committee, she brought her labor expertise and extensive contacts to the CSO's efforts to support Mexican American workers. Among other things, she educated workers to the value of unions, raised funds, and interviewed politicians seeking the CSO's endorsement. Mendoza's high-profile activities were exceptional, but many other women in the CSO shared her union experience. Although most women in the organization stayed within traditional female boundaries, many more women followed the more assertive paths of Huerta and Mendoza in the late 1960s and 1970s as the Chicano movement for Mexican American empowerment gathered force (see pp. 639–40).

◆ WOMEN AND PUBLIC POLICY

While the civil rights movement forged ahead, encouraging many young women to begin to question the cultural assumptions that reinforced women's subordination, other women focused on public policy issues, especially discrimination in the workforce. The creation of the President's Commission on the Status of Women in 1961 proved a turning point. It not only focused renewed attention on the problems employed women faced but also helped to create a network of activists committed to addressing working women's rights.

The Continuing Battle over the ERA

The community of women interested in promoting women's legal rights and economic opportunities faced many obstacles in the years following World War II. With the feminine mystique holding sway over much of American culture and the Red Scare promoting conformity, the social and political climate hampered serious questioning of women's roles. Nonetheless, professional lobbyists for organizations like the YWCA, the AAUW, and the National Federation of Business and Professional Women (BPW) formed a female network attentive to policy developments in Washington that kept alive concerns over women's rights. Throughout the late 1940s and 1950s, however, these women were divided by the long-standing debate over the Equal Rights Amendment (ERA). Their division on this issue discouraged fresh approaches to questions concerning women's growing, yet fundamentally unequal, participation in the workforce.

The battle lines were similar to those of the 1920s, when the ERA was first introduced (see pp. 484–89). The National Woman's Party, with strong support from career women in the BPW, argued for the amendment as a device that would strike down all manner of laws and policies that fettered women's rights as free and equal individuals. Opposing the ERA were most of the staff of the federal Women's Bureau and the women's organizations traditionally allied with it, such as the League of Women Voters and the YWCA. Women labor union leaders formed a particularly adamant group in opposition to the ERA.

All of these opponents believed that the ERA endangered protective labor legislation, which ever since its inception in the Progressive era had emphasized women's distinctiveness, especially in their maternal function. By the 1950s, Women's Bureau leaders had retreated somewhat from their emphasis on promoting more protective legislation in the various states and had moved toward fostering equal pay laws and challenging some discriminatory policies. They no longer had to defend special minimum wage and maximum hours laws for women since the Fair Labor Standards Act of 1938 had extended these protections to men. Under the Republican administration of Dwight D. Eisenhower, Republican politicians, including many women, joined with anti-union conservative business interests to support the ERA because they viewed protective labor legislation as an intrusion of the government into the labor market. Alice Leopold, appointed by Eisenhower as the new head of the Women's Bureau, was a supporter of the amendment. Nonetheless, Women's Bureau staffers and their traditional allies continued to condemn the ERA, their commitment heightened by the anti-union climate of the 1950s and by the affiliation of some with the Democratic Party, which remained resolutely anti-ERA.

A Turning Point: The President's Commission on the Status of Women

It was in part to deflect attention away from the ERA that Esther Peterson, who became head of the Women's Bureau in 1961, proposed a commission on the status of women. Appointed by Democrat John F. Kennedy, Peterson had strong union ties and enthusiastically supported the new president's program for revived activism on the part of the federal government, especially on behalf of disadvantaged Americans. Kennedy pledged to "get this country moving again" with a "New Frontier" to continue the liberal reforms started by Franklin Roosevelt's New Deal. Peterson prevailed on Kennedy to establish the President's Commission on the Status of Women (PCSW) in late 1961, with the hope that it would particularly advance the cause of working women. (See Reading into the Past: "Esther Peterson and the President's Commission on the Status of Women.")

Eleven men and fifteen women drawn from leaders in women's organizations, unions, business, education, and politics composed the PCSW, which was chaired by former First Lady Eleanor Roosevelt. Supplementing the commission were dozens of subcommittees that brought many women activists into the process of research and deliberation on issues ranging from inequities in wage rates and limited job opportunities to the particular problems of poor black women and of working mothers. As activists like Peterson pushed an agenda to assist working

READING INTO THE PAST

Esther Peterson and the President's Commission on the Status of Women

Esther Peterson served as both the director of the Women's Bureau and the assistant secretary of labor in John F. Kennedy's administration. In 1961, President Kennedy empowered her to establish the President's Commission on the Status of Women, where she served as executive vice chairman. Former First Lady Eleanor Roosevelt chaired the committee (see pp. 585–88). In this passage from a 1977 oral history interview, Peterson recalls her work for women's labor rights in the early 1960s.

"Equal pay for equal work" became the policy of the Women's Bureau, and, through its efforts, the law of the land. To help break down that notion that women workers were somehow different on the job from men, we abolished the practice in government of designating "job male - job female." We helped win the end of sex-segregated help-wanted ads, and fostered the widespread use of day-care centers in federal facilities. Predominantly women's jobs were also added to coverage under the Fair Labor Standards Act, even domestic workers.

Our efforts at that time were concentrated on extending the Fair Labor Standards Act to cover more women workers, working for collective bargaining agreements in women-dominated industries, and seeking passage of the Equal Pay Act. We wanted equality for women, but we wanted bread for our low-income sisters first. Only after basic protection

women, many members of the commission worried lest their efforts be interpreted as undermining women's maternal roles by encouraging them to work. Indeed, the executive order creating the commission revealed the contradictions implicit in its task. The commission was responsible for "developing recommendations for overcoming discriminations in government and private employment on the basis of sex and for developing recommendations for services which will enable women to continue their roles as wives and mothers while making a maximum contribution to the world around them."[31]

Not surprisingly, the PCSW's final report, published in 1963, outlined moderate proposals for the most part. It recommended child care tax benefits for low-income working mothers and improved maternity benefits. It called for state and federal governments to promote women's education and job training and endorsed equal pay for equal work. The PCSW recommended an executive order to require such as equal pay and federal wage and hours laws were in place, were we willing to consider the Equal Rights Amendment. I wanted to get consideration of women into the warp and woof of everything. Passage of the Equal Pay Act was an initiative the commission worked on. Mrs. Roosevelt and many commission members testified on behalf of the bill, and we were delighted to secure passage in 1963.

. . . [T]he issue of comparable worth, or "quality and quantity," was hard fought at the time, and the . . . Republican women who supported the Equal Rights Amendment in 1960 were not with us. They had a part in our losing the comparable worth provisions. The commission position on the Equal Rights Amendment was a carefully worded compromise that strongly supported the principle of equality, but encouraged interest groups to seek a court case that would clarify the fourteenth amendment rather than seeking a new amendment.

SOURCE: *Rocking the Boat: Union Women's Voices, 1915–1975*, ed. Brigid O'Farrell and Joyce L. Kornbluh (New Brunswick, NJ: Rutgers University Press, 1979), 81–82.

QUESTIONS FOR ANALYSIS

1. How does Peterson explain the dilemma the Equal Rights Amendment posed for women's labor rights activists?
2. In what ways does her account help to explain the limited concrete results of the President's Commission on the Status of Women?

private employers to give women "equal opportunities," a strikingly vague mandate already established for federal employment. It proposed expanding provisions of existing legislation to improve women's Social Security benefits and bring more women under the coverage of the Fair Labor Standards Act of 1938, a change that would particularly benefit poor black and Chicana women. In keeping with the Women's Bureau's long-standing commitment to protective legislation, it endorsed a forty-hour workweek for women, with overtime pay beyond forty hours. The PCSW also addressed the need for states to repeal outdated laws that limited the rights of women to serve on juries or control their own property.

The commission did not endorse the ERA but offered as an alternative a recommendation that the Fourteenth Amendment be understood as protecting women's equal rights. Pauli Murray, an African American civil rights attorney who served on the Subcommittee on Political and Civil Rights and had long been active in promoting black and women's rights, formulated this argument for the PCSW, explicitly drawing a connection between the discrimination women faced and the civil rights movement, claiming that "arbitrary discrimination against women violated the Fourteenth Amendment in the same way racial bias did."[32] Despite Murray's insightful analysis, the commission omitted any discussion of a race-gender analogy — presumably because it was too controversial — and simply urged the Supreme Court to legitimate the Fourteenth Amendment's applicability to women, which it did within the decade.

One legacy of the PCSW was passage of federal "equal work for equal pay" legislation. The Equal Pay Act of 1963 offered significantly less than the Women's Bureau or its female union supporters had hoped for. It rejected the concept of equal pay for comparable work, substituting instead the proviso that women working in identical jobs with men — a relatively small class of workers — must be paid equally. The act also limited its applicability to those occupations already covered by the 1938 Fair Labor Standards Act, a measure that failed to include women's jobs in the agricultural and domestic service sectors. Despite its limits, the Equal Pay Act resulted in concrete gains for some women and at least theoretically committed the federal government to the recognition that women's labor had equal value to men's.

Still, few concrete results followed the commission's recommendations. Its importance was in the way in which it focused attention, however ambivalently, on the varied discriminations that women faced. It was instrumental in encouraging many activists to retreat from an interpretation that emphasized sexual difference and the need for laws to protect women toward an approach that favored equal rights and promoted the government's role in challenging discrimination against women. The PCSW's deliberations also encouraged a network of women activists interested in promoting women's rights and spawned dozens of state commissions on the status of women, which in turn created a community of women throughout the country addressing similar concerns. Pauli Murray explained, "Like-minded women found one another, bonds developed through working together, and an informal feminist network emerged to act as leaven in the broader movement that followed."[33]

◆ CONCLUSION: The Limits of the Feminine Mystique

American women in the postwar era lived in conservative times. Cold War fears stifled dissent, labeled labor unions and civil rights activity "subversive," and contained women and men in rigid gender roles to maintain family and social order. Certainly many women's lives were limited by this dominant ideology, yet women's lives were more diverse and complex than mainstream cultural prescriptions indicate. Women's place might have been in the home, but it was also in the workforce, as both public officials and employers eagerly sought to fuel American productivity and achieve the upper hand in the Cold War. Women may have been shunted into sex-segregated jobs, but participation in the workforce and the discrimination experienced there would have long-term implications for their consciousness.

Other signs that women's roles were not as constrained as popular images of the era suggest are evident in women's central role as bridge leaders in the burgeoning civil rights movement, as well as the persistent efforts of working-class union women to fight for fair treatment on the job. Middle-class women, too, in a wide range of voluntary associations and political activity represented women's desire to engage as citizens in the world outside their homes. These different forms of activism, combined with initiatives from the federal government's Women's Bureau, especially the President's Commission on the Status of Women, helped lay the groundwork for the resurgence of feminism in the late 1960s that would have a powerful impact on many women's domestic and public lives.

CHAPTER 10 REVIEW

KEY TERMS AND PEOPLE

Terms
Red Scare
Daughters of Bilitis
Kinsey Report
The Feminine Mystique
Commission on the Education
    of Women
Women Strike for Peace
Congress of Racial Equality
    (CORE)
Brown v. Board of Education

Southern Christian Leadership
    Conference (SCLC)
Student Nonviolent
    Coordinating Committee
Freedom Rides
Freedom Summer
President's Commission on the
    Status of Women
Equal Pay Act

People
Rosa Parks
Helen Gahagan Douglas
Betty Friedan
Rachel Carson
Ella Baker
Diane Nash
Fannie Lou Hamer
Casey Hayden
Mary King
Dolores Huerta

REVIEW QUESTIONS

1. Why do we need to "rethink" *The Feminine Mystique*?
2. How did women's activism in unions and voluntary associations plant the seeds for challenging the prevailing ideas of women's role in the family, the workplace, and public life?
3. What role did women take in the civil rights movement during the 1950s and 1960s? How does the concept of "bridge leadership" help us understand women's contributions?

4. What were the recommendations of the President's Commission on the Status of Women? What was the Commission's long-term significance?
5. **Making Connections** How does this chapter demonstrate that women's lives were more diverse and complex than mainstream cultural prescriptions about women's "proper" place in the home would indicate?

PRIMARY SOURCES

Television's Prescriptions for Women

Thanks to youtube and online content providers like hulu, viewers today have access to some well-known 1950s television programs and commercials. Some critics explain the popularity of these shows and advertisements by suggesting that for some present-day viewers they are camp entertainment, amusing in their outdated, unintended humor, but for others they evoke a nostalgic sense of simpler, more innocent times. Historians who study 1950s television delve more deeply into the medium and its message and, as with any other historical source, examine both the televised images and the assumptions of the people who created programming and advertising. This essay explores women and television in the 1950s by looking first at the way in which television programming and advertising targeted and understood the female viewer and second at the images of women conveyed in the decade's situation comedies. While advertising tended to reinforce key aspects of the feminine mystique, especially a relentless depiction of white middle-class women's role in the home, situation comedies of the 1950s displayed a more diverse and complex rendering of women and their families.

Television was a novelty until after World War II. Some national programming began to appear in 1947, and then during the years 1948–1950 the new medium took off: by 1951 there were 107 stations in 52 cities. Rising prosperity and a burgeoning consumer culture facilitated Americans' eager embrace of TV. By 1955, 65 percent of the nation's households had televisions, and by 1960 that figure had grown to 90 percent. National networks dominated television from the medium's inception, and network executives, along with their programs' sponsors, viewed television's purpose as the selling of products. This commercial motivation encouraged the networks to promote television as family entertainment and in the process to reinforce conventional notions of women's roles as housewives and mothers.

Many observers in the postwar years argued that television viewing would bring families together, thus stabilizing the home. Women's magazines ran articles discussing how women might integrate the "box" into their homes. While some authors addressed decorating problems that arose in making room for a large appliance, others explored the placement of the television in the context of family leisure-time patterns. They noted that the TV set was quickly displacing the piano as a source of family entertainment and that it was usurping the role of the fireplace as the focal point for social interaction. The TV had become, many argued, an electric hearth, the heart of family "togetherness."

ADVERTISEMENTS

The idea of the television as a means of bringing families together appeared in many advertisements for television sets. Figure 10.1 depicts a comfortable middle-class home with an elegant TV as part of its attractive furniture. The family clusters around the Motorola TV in a semicircle, watching a program designed for

◆ **Figure 10.1**
Advertisement for Motorola Television (1951)

family viewing, the variety show starring singer Dinah Shore (who was the television spokeswoman for Chevrolet cars, suggesting another element of the flourishing consumer market of the period). That the mother alone is standing is typical of many depictions of television viewers. Why do you think advertisers chose to show the mother standing? What does the posture and position of the woman suggest about her role in the family? How does the text above the image reinforce the television's familial function?

Although the television industry generally assumed that its family audience was white and largely middle class, manufacturers did aggressively market television sets to African Americans and routinely ran ads in *Ebony*, a popular black magazine founded in 1942. Blacks were negatively stereotyped in television programming, but they were interested in buying sets, perhaps because they could enjoy entertainment in their homes rather than suffer the indignity of segregation in public venues. Some ads were identical to those that appeared in white mainstream periodicals, such as a May 1953 advertisement in *Ebony* that featured glamorous white brides framed by an Admiral TV set, with text noting that a television made a "memorable wedding gift."

Other advertisers attempted to adapt to their black audience. Figure 10.2 is an example of one of a number of 1953 RCA Victor advertisements that featured

◆ **Figure 10.2** **Advertisement for RCA Victor Television (1953)**

African Americans watching television. Another ad in this series depicts the Dinah Shore television show (as in Figure 10.1), but this ad displays black singer Eartha Kitt, a frequent performer on network variety shows. Notice that the woman is once again standing, this time in the effort to help her husband select a station, now made easier by an automatic dial. Compare Figures 10.1 and 10.2. How do these advertisements for televisions reinforce conventional roles for male and female viewers?

Televisions were often depicted as bringing families together, but some critics worried that the new medium would create new sources of familial conflict, as parents and children and husbands and wives collided over control of the set. Television advertisers themselves often tackled this theme. Their solution, as Figure 10.3 indicates, was multiple television sets! Consider the two-part construction of this 1955 General Electric ad. Why might the advertiser have chosen to use a cartoon to portray family conflict? How does the photograph depict stereotypical gender roles?

Women's primary roles as housewives became a predominant theme for network executives and sponsors in the early years of television. They were eager to attract women viewers because of their responsibilities as family purchasing agents. One executive noted, "We're after a specific audience, the young housewife — one cut above the teenager — with two to four kids, who has to buy the clothing, the food, the soaps, the home remedies."[34] As the television industry saw it, the dilemma was whether daytime programming geared to this specific audience would be compatible with women's patterns of household labor. Unlike radio, they feared, television needed to be watched with some degree of concentration. These hesitations were finally overcome by 1952, when the networks began to offer a full range of daytime programs that included soap operas, quiz shows, and magazine-style variety shows. As the 1955 *Ladies' Home Journal* ad in Figure 10.4 indicates, they explicitly marketed their daytime lineup to women by emphasizing that the programs did not interfere with their household duties. Read the descriptions of the seven shows watched by the young housewife in a single morning. How do they attempt to persuade women that television watching hastens rather than hinders their household work? What assumptions does this advertisement make about women's domestic labor?

One program the ad in Figure 10.4 featured was *Home*, a magazine-style variety show modeled after NBC's *Today* program, which debuted in 1952, aired between 7 and 9 A.M., and offered short segments of news and entertainment designed for the whole family, plus features on fashion and homemaking directed toward women. Inspired by *Today*'s success, NBC introduced *Home*, expressly for women, in 1954. *Newsweek* noted that NBC's president, Sylvester Laflin (Pat) Weaver, sought to tap the advertising market that women's magazines enjoyed. "It is inconceivable to me," Weaver noted, "that all that advertising money spent on women's products . . . has been allowed to escape [from television]."[35] In keeping with that idea, *Home* segments were generally tied to specific sponsors and commercials, and indeed NBC described the program's set as "a machine for selling."[36]

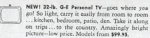

◆ **Figure 10.3** Advertisement for General Electric Television (1955)

WHERE DID THE MORNING GO?

Time for lunch already?
Where did the morning go?
The chores are done, the
house is tidy . . . but it hasn't
seemed like a terribly
tiring morning.

First there was breakfast, and that was pleasant. We all got the news from "TODAY," and Dave Garroway had some fascinating guests. The children were still laughing about J. Fred Muggs when they left for school.

Then I sat Kathy down in front of "DING DONG SCHOOL" and I didn't have to worry about her while I tidied up. Miss Frances got her interested in finger-painting, and after the program Kathy just went on playing quietly.

"WAY OF THE WORLD" had the second installment of the new story, and I couldn't miss that. It's like a magazine serial — you keep looking forward to the next episode. And beautifully acted, with new stars for every new story.

I think I started the ironing while I watched "THE SHEILAH GRAHAM SHOW". First she discussed the latest Hollywood news and gossip. Then she interviewed William Holden, and showed parts of his exciting new movie.

And I finished the ironing while I watched "HOME". I couldn't *count* the good ideas I've had from Arlene Francis and her expert assistants on health, home decorating, gardening and food. I added a few things to my shopping list.

Any morning of any day, "THE TENNESSEE ERNIE FORD SHOW" can brighten things up for me. Tennessee Ernie and his talented friends joke, sing and share the fun with everyone . . . at the studio and at home.

And then "FEATHER YOUR NEST", where that lovely couple won a living room suite, and Bud Collyer and Janis Carter were so nice to them. And I think that it's a wonderful idea that viewers at home can win prizes, too.

The morning was a pleasure instead of drudgery. And yet I have everything done . . . I haven't really wasted a second. It's the way I like to have the morning go.

EXCITING THINGS ARE HAPPENING ON

NBC TELEVISION
a service of RCA

◆ **Figure 10.4** *Ladies' Home Journal* Advertisement for NBC (1955)

◆ **Figure 10.5 Advertisement for Betty Crocker (1957)**

The line between programming and commercials was often blurred in shows geared to "Mrs. Consumer." This was evident in programs featuring Betty Crocker, General Mills' mythical spokeswoman, who was portrayed by a series of actresses on both radio and television. Figure 10.5 features actress Adelaide Hawley, who appeared in the ABC daytime programs *Bride and Groom* and *Betty Crocker Star Matinee* beginning in 1952. In the former, a couple was married on-screen and Betty gave tips to brides on fixing their grooms' favorite foods, foods that featured General Mills products. Her television appearances featured this verse:

> American homemakers
> Keepers of the hearth
> Whose hands and hearts are filled
> With the day-to-day cares and joys
> That, taken with one another
> Make homemaking a woman's
> Most rewarding life.[37]

How does Figure 10.5 illustrate this verse? What does it suggest about the relationship between popular media and the "feminine mystique"?

SITUATION COMEDIES

This section examines the depiction of women in situation comedies (sitcoms), which, in contrast to the genres discussed above, were shown in the evening and geared to the whole family. The images reproduced here, of course, do not adequately convey the dynamic medium of TV. They do not capture motion, dialogue, or laugh tracks. Missing, too, is the importance of audience familiarity with the shows' characters, another crucial aspect shaping how Americans experienced sitcoms. These photographs, mostly publicity stills, nonetheless stand as emblems of popular sitcoms' depiction of women and the family in this era. With a very few exceptions, such as *Our Miss Brooks*, a comedy starring Eve Arden as a schoolteacher, adult white women characters in sitcoms did not work outside the home and were portrayed as housewives, despite the number of married women entering the paid workforce. Beyond this common thread, these programs offered strikingly diverse images of the American family.

The networks adopted many sitcoms from successful radio programs. Two of these starred African Americans. *Beulah* aired on ABC from 1950 to 1953 and portrayed a maid and the white family she worked for, the Hendersons. Over the life of the series on radio and television, three well-known black actresses played Beulah: Louise Beavers, Hattie McDaniel, and Ethel Waters. Figure 10.6 shows Louise Beavers as Beulah. Two other black characters appeared regularly in the series: Beulah's boyfriend, Bill, an oafish man who ran a fix-it shop but seemed to spend most of his time in his girlfriend's kitchen, and Oriole, her scatterbrained friend who worked for the white family next door. Although some of the comedy derived from Beulah's persistent, yet fruitless, efforts to convince Bill to marry her, the major focus of the series was Beulah's nurturing her white family and solving their small dilemmas. A classic "mammy" figure, she was known for her catchphrase "Somebody bawl fo' Beulah?" In one episode her southern cuisine (she was described as the "queen of the kitchen") helped Mr. Henderson impress a business client. In another, she taught Donnie, the family's son, to jive dance.

◆ **Figure 10.6 Scene from *Beulah***
Photofest.

Although some African Americans took pleasure in seeing an African American star on television, other individuals and groups, including the NAACP, criticized the series for perpetuating degrading stereotypes. Does Beulah appear to be part of the family? In what ways does Figure 10.6 reinforce racial hierarchies of the day? Contrast this image with the slave nurse in Figure 4.12 (p. 216).

A more famous sitcom with black cast members was *Amos 'n' Andy* (1949–1953), which starred men but featured a number of women. On the original radio show, two white men who had created the series played the title characters, but on television the cast was all African American. Even before the show aired, the NAACP launched a protest over bringing the radio program, which many blacks found degrading because of its racist stereotypes, to television. In response to this pressure, CBS modified Amos, one of the title characters, by making him and his wife, Ruby, models of middle-class propriety. To fill the comedic void, however, the series gave enhanced attention to George ("the Kingfish") Stephens, with his fractured English and his scams to avoid work and get rich quick. The unambitious and none-too-smart Andy served as the victim of many of the Kingfish's schemes.

The major female character was the Kingfish's wife, Sapphire, played by Ernestine Wade, who had also performed the role in radio. For the most part Sapphire was a shrew, a caricature of the domineering wife who routinely threw her husband out of the house. In Figure 10.7, she is shown waiting to pounce on the Kingfish as he attempts to sneak into their home. An even more negative portrayal of black women emerged with Sapphire's large and loudmouthed mother, "Mama." As the Kingfish described her, "Andy, you take de venom of a cobra, de disposition of a alligator and de nastiness of a rhinoceros. . . . Put 'em all together dey spell Mother!"[38] Partially as a result of NAACP pressure and partly because of declining ratings, CBS canceled the show in 1953. Compare Sapphire and her husband to the loving black couple shown in Figure 10.2. What might account for the striking differences in these two popular culture depictions? After at first perpetuating negative stereotypes of black women as either mammies or shrews, sitcoms subsequently treated them as invisible. African Americans would not reappear in sitcoms for another decade, and it was not until 1968, when Diahann Carroll appeared as a nurse in *Julia*, that a black woman starred in a series.

◆ **Figure 10.7 Scene from *Amos 'n' Andy***
Everett Collection.

A number of early sitcoms featured white immigrant families, most notably *The Goldbergs* (1949–1954). CBS adopted the show from the popular radio program of the same name, which starred Gertrude Berg as Molly Goldberg. Berg also wrote the scripts for the program, which she said was modeled after the experiences of her mother and grandmother. The show explored the domestic crises of a Jewish family living in the Bronx and their circle of neighbors. Molly dominated the show, and part of the humor was her accented English and eccentric phrasing: "Enter, whoever. If it's nobody, I'll call back."[39]

A stereotypical Jewish mother, Molly eagerly turned her nurturing skills to solve friends' and family members' problems. Each show began with Molly leaning out her apartment window to shout across the airshaft, "Yoo-hoo, Mrs. Bloom." Inside the family circle, a key theme was the aspiration for assimilation and the American middle-class dream. Significantly, assimilation was often cast in terms of consumption. In one show Molly disapproves of her daughter-in-law's plan to buy a washing machine on the installment plan. "I know Papa and me never bought anything unless we had the money to pay for it," Molly says. Her son convinces her she is wrong, and by the end she is suggesting that the family buy two cars in order to "live above our means — the American way."[40]

Figure 10.8 shows Molly in her dining room, where she is serving the guest of honor, well-known television personality Arthur Godfrey. Molly is depicted as nurturing and the family as close-knit. The room's decor is old-fashioned, as is Molly for the most part. At a time when many upwardly mobile Jews were leaving the crowded cities and the ethnic neighborhoods their parents and grandparents had created, the cozy world of the Goldbergs was increasingly anachronistic. Why might this disparity contribute to the appeal of the program?

A less sentimental rendering of the urban family was *The Honeymooners* (1955–1956), in which Jackie Gleason played bus driver Ralph Kramden, a dreamer who always missed realizing his hopes for a more comfortable life. Audrey Meadows played Alice, his long-suffering and practical wife. Marital bickering between the two was a constant in the series. The stance of Alice in Figure 10.9 as she looks disapprovingly at Ralph, with their friends Norton and his wife, Trixie, in the background, conveys some of this tension. One of Ralph's catchphrases, "One of these days, Alice, one of these days, pow! Right in the kisser!" suggests even more. Plots frequently involved Alice's disappointment over their limited income and the drabness of the apartment, completely devoid of the consumer goods that most Americans were eagerly acquiring in this period. The show generally closed with a harmonious resolution, but the overarching tone was nonetheless one of male-female conflict, with Alice fighting back.

Marital disputes also served as the focal point for the humor in one of the most beloved sitcoms of early television, *I Love Lucy* (1951–1961). Lucille Ball's character, Lucy, is married to Ricky Ricardo, played by Ball's real-life husband, Cuban bandleader Desi Arnaz. In the process of the show, they have a baby, Little Ricky, whose TV birth coincided with the birth of the couple's real son. Lucy seemingly represents a stereotypical dizzy female. Childish and

◆ **Figure 10.8** **Scene from *The Goldbergs***
Photofest.

impractical, she is juxtaposed with Ricky, whose demeanor is usually mature. She constantly is forced to defer to his decisions as head of the family and resorts to wheedling, deception, and "feminine wiles" to get her way. But like the Kramdens' conflicts, the Ricardos' marital disagreements prove fodder for most plots. Lucy eternally desires a job in show business and constantly hankers for consumer items, from kitchen appliances to Parisian frocks. Ricky proves the obstacle on both counts.

Many plots focus on Lucy's schemes to get a job, yet repeatedly she humiliates herself as she fails in each attempt. A particularly revealing episode for its comments on male-female roles is the show in which Lucy and her best friend, Ethel, wager with Ricky and Ethel's husband, Fred, that men's work is easier than women's labor in the home. They trade places, and while Ricky and Fred make a mess of homemaking (Figure 10.10, top), Lucy and Ethel look for work.

◆ **Figure 10.9** **Scene from *The Honeymooners***
Photofest.

In the middle image of Figure 10.10, a clerk in an employment agency reads a
list of jobs, and the women realize they have no training for any of them except
perhaps candy making. They get jobs making chocolates, but their incompetence leads to their demotion to packing on an assembly line. They do well at
first, but they fall behind as the conveyer belt speeds up and they start eating
the chocolate instead of packing it (Figure 10.10, bottom). At the end of the
episode, both men and women agree to call the bet off and to return to their
accustomed roles.

    Some critics argue that, far from reinforcing the feminine mystique, with
its emphasis on women's roles as housewives and mothers, *Lucy* subverts it. For
if Lucy is a housewife, she is not a contented one, as her quest for employment
suggests. Conversely, others maintain that despite her aspirations, she fails at her

◆ **Figure 10.10** Scenes from *I Love Lucy*
Photofest.

forays into the workplace, and the story lines generally end with her return to her housewifery role and her acceptance of Ricky's authority. Do you think the images shown in Figure 10.10 suggest subversion or reinforcement of the feminine mystique? How do you suppose contemporary audiences interpreted the squabbles between Lucy and Ricky?

Sitcoms that featured working-class or minority families had almost disappeared by the mid-1950s. And, with the exception of *I Love Lucy*, so, too, had programs that traded on marital bickering and themes concerning domestic power. As more and more real American women went into the workforce, the networks offered up sitcoms that idealized the family and reinforced women's prescribed role in the home. Unlike Lucy, the mothers in *The Adventures of Ozzie and Harriet*, *The Donna Reed Show*, *Leave It to Beaver*, and *Father Knows Best* lead contented lives with serene marriages. Their husbands are successful breadwinners, and their homes are spacious and well furnished. They are rarely depicted as performing arduous household labor, but their immaculate houses are a reflection of their womanly skills.

Although these sitcoms were ostensibly comedies, their humor was sometimes barely discernible. Plots usually revolved around the dilemmas of childrearing as parents strove to teach children social and moral lessons. *Father Knows Best* (1954–1963), the first of this genre, led the way among sitcoms that promoted middle-class family values. Figure 10.11 shows the mother, Margaret Anderson (played by Jane Wyatt), joining in a prayer around the family dinner table. In what ways are the Andersons similar to and different from the families shown in the earlier sitcoms?

Father Knows Best was aptly named. In the episode titled "Kathy Becomes a Girl," the youngest daughter, Kathy, learns that boys do not like tomboys. As her father explains, "Being dependent — a little helpless now and then" was a sure ploy designed to win men.[41] An even more telling statement about the ideal female role came in a show that uncharacteristically featured Margaret expressing a degree of dissatisfaction with her lot. As her children and her husband are winning trophies for various activities, Margaret is forced to acknowledge that she has never received a medal for anything. To compensate, she takes up fishing and plans to compete in a tournament. Her chances are good, her coach tells her, because so few women compete. Ready for the competition, she falls, injures herself, and misses the contest. Her children seek to cheer her up with a series of tributes to her motherly skills and homemade awards, such as a frying pan emblazoned with the title "Most Valuable Mother." The episode received a 1958–59 directing Emmy.

Neither advertising nor sitcom images should be taken as an accurate reflection of American women. What they offer are insights into how television portrayed women. The inherently commercial nature of television facilitated advertising and programming that featured women's role as housewives and the purchaser of consumer goods for her family. Sitcoms, too, had close commercial links. When Molly Goldberg left her window at the start of the

◆ **Figure 10.11 Scene from *Father Knows Best***
Everett Collection.

show, she returned to her kitchen and launched into a commercial for Sanka coffee, the program's sponsor. Although early sitcoms acknowledged some diversity among Americans, with a few exceptions most women were portrayed in their domestic roles. As the example of *Lucy* indicates, tensions over these roles often served as the comedic plot. But despite the reality of women's increased participation in the workforce, by the second half of the 1950s, TV sitcoms idealized the middle-class family and the stay-at-home mother and thus served as a powerful reinforcement of the cultural prescriptions of the feminine mystique.

QUESTIONS FOR ANALYSIS

1. What messages do the spatial arrangements, figure positions, and clothing styles in the advertisements (Figures 10.1–10.5) suggest about popular perceptions of the middle-class family and women's role in it?

2. Why did advertisers think these ads would sell consumer goods and network programming?

3. To what extent do the images from the sitcoms (Figures 10.6–10.11) reflect American diversity in terms of ethnicity, race, or class?

4. In what ways have television messages about gender roles changed since the 1950s?

"Is a Working Mother a Threat to the Home?"

DURING THE 1950S, PUBLIC POLICY EXPERTS extensively studied the question of the working wife and mother. While there was a widespread assumption that the growing number of mothers in the workforce was an irreversible phenomenon, officials and experts differed as to whether this new trend would have adverse effects on children, the family, and the social order in general. Popular magazines intently followed the debate and offered extensive coverage on working wives and mothers. The gamut of responses ran from the ex–working mother who reported, "I am now a better mother. I know I am a happier one,"[42] to the office worker and mother of two who explained her decision to go back to work in part by noting, "Some vital part of me wasn't being used."[43] Men chimed in as well. One man exulted over being married to a working mother who combined a successful career with a happy home, while another insisted that the career woman "may find many satisfactions in her job, but the chances are that she, her husband and her children will suffer psychological damage, and that she will be basically an unhappy woman."[44] In 1958, the *Ladies' Home Journal* assembled a forum of experts and mothers to address the question of whether mothers of young children should work. The following is an excerpt from that forum.

Should Mothers of Young Children Work? (1958)

[MODERATOR] MISS [MARGARET] HICKEY: Traditionally, in our country, marriage and motherhood have been considered difficult, full-time jobs — as well as satisfying ones. Married women and mothers who worked outside the home did so only for really pressing reasons: because they had to support their families; because there was a war on; because they were driven by great ambition or talent.

But recently a change seems to be taking place. Women no longer are working entirely from necessity or to satisfy a driving ambition, but rather from choice. Today one out of three wives is a wage earner. And, even more startling — one out of five of the mothers of small children is now working outside the home.

This situation raises many questions, but the one most asked by mothers is the basic personal one: Should I or shouldn't I work? Mrs. Easton, will you tell us what you wrote us some time back — in one of the letters that started us thinking of this forum today?

MRS. EASTON: Well, as you said, I always thought it was out of necessity that mothers went to work. Then, looking around me, I couldn't help noticing that a lot of my neighbors didn't *have* to work, but they did. So then I began wondering,

SOURCE: "Should Mothers of Young Children Work?" *Ladies' Home Journal*, November 1958, 58–59, 154–56, 158–61.

who is right — are they or am I? Where are mothers needed? Are they needed at home or is it better to be out making some money? I want to feel I am someone who does the right thing. So I wrote to the JOURNAL. . . .

MISS HICKEY: Secretary Mitchell, what do you think the national need is — does the country need women jobholders today?

SECRETARY [OF LABOR JAMES P.] MITCHELL: Yes, it does. Our economy would suffer severely if women left the labor force. By 1965, we expect to have a population of 193,000,000 — an increase of 20,000,000 people. This means that if we are to have the standard of living we have now, and increase it, which we must, and if we are to maintain our defense, which we must, we will need a work-force increase of 10,000,000 people — half of which we expect will be women.

MISS HICKEY: So we have grown dependent on women workers. But from your statistics, Mr. Mitchell, do you think that this group will have to include the mothers of small children?

SECRETARY MITCHELL: Let me say first that I think it is very right that we in this country have freedom of choice, unlike the communist world, where there is no such thing. I would not want to say to anyone whether he or she should work or not. But it is my hope that the women workers we need will *not* be sought or encouraged to come from the group who are mothers. It seems to me that in our world a mother's place — and I hope this is not heresy in this group — is in the home.

Of course, there *are* times in a nation's history, such as war, when everyone has to be asked to work outside the home. But I believe strongly that no nation should ever forget that the very primary, fundamental basis of a free society is the family structure — the home — and the most vital job is there. . . .

[CHILD PSYCHOLOGIST] DR. [JOHN] BOWLBY: [on the impact on children whose mothers work] I don't mean to say that all small children of working mothers are necessarily deprived of mothering, but clinical evidence shows clearly that you can't bring up a child adequately if you leave him

first with this person and then with that one in the first years of his life. The trouble is that we know there are serious risks, and as yet we have too little knowledge of the safety margin.

MRS. ERNEST LEE [A STENOGRAPHER AND MOTHER OF THREE]: My children are older now, six to nine, but in the past few years I have had four different sitters with them. They have shown no bad effects. Every once in a while they say, "Mommy, I wish you were not working," but then they say, "When we get our house you won't be."

If I didn't work to help pay the rent now and to save for a home of our own later — well, we'd have to live in one of those overcrowded cramped places where there are gangs and profane language and no safe place for the kids to play. Or my husband would have to work two jobs and the children would never see him. This way at least we all have the evenings together and a decent place to live. Isn't this important? . . .

DR. BATUSKA: Well, I started out as just a career girl. In premedical school I thought I would never marry, and then, in medical school, my plans changed very drastically because I met my husband-to-be and almost before I knew it I *was* married. I was still in medical school when I had my first baby. . . . But things went well and I thought that as long as I had gotten that far, I might as well go ahead and get the state boards, so I did, and I had another child and still no trouble, so I decided I might as well get a specialty, so I did that and now I do cancer research and am a fellow in endocrinology, and have another child, and things still go along smoothly.

If the children had seemed to need me in some way really I would have just given all this up but for some reason I still cannot understand they appear well adjusted and the happiest children I know. I am amazed that it has worked out as well as it has. . . .

MRS. [ROY] DAVIS [A NURSE WHO WORKS AT NIGHT "AND RUNS HER HOUSE BY DAY"]: Until I had my first child I worked full time. Then I worked part time until I had my second child, then I retired for a while, but my husband had to let his profession slide — he is a lawyer — and take another job to supplement our income — so I went back to work.

I feel that the father is almost as important as the mother to the child, and by my working at night I saw the children in the daytime and he saw them in the later afternoon. Together we have done everything. We have not even had household help. We agreed on a ten-year plan ending in June, 1958, to get him through law school, to begin a family, and pay the ten-year mortgage on our home. Our family is here, our practice started. . . .

[SOCIOLOGIST] DR. [MIRRA] KOMAROVSKY: Unfashionable as it is today to defend women's education, I think it is on the right track. All women's colleges have courses in child psychology and in sociology of the family, and men's colleges should follow suit. I don't think it is the job of the college to teach housekeeping skills. The best preparation for family life, is, after all, a liberal-arts education. A woman has to have her own mind awakened before she can awaken the mind of her child, and I don't think that colleges devalue homemaking. In any event, they don't succeed! About 20 per cent of Barnard's seniors are married by Commencement Day. . . .

SENATOR [FRANK J.] LAUSCHE: If our way of life is to survive, we must keep the family intact. We must give it importance.

A woman needs cultivation of the mind for a unified personality. She needs a vocation to turn to in times of need. But over and above everything else, she needs to give attention and devotion to the family.

Outside jobs are the symptoms of deeper problems. We must remove the forces which break down the home. The housewife, the mother, needs more than housework to keep her occupied. She needs education, books, intellectual companionship. In short, she needs a rounded life so that she will be a good influence on her children and a helpful companion to her husband. . . .

[EVANGELIST] DR. [WILLIAM F.] GRAHAM: I think all of us would agree that we do accept some

of the principles at least of the Bible, and the most fundamental one is that the first marriage was performed by God Himself and God instituted the marriage relationship and the family relationship before the school and before the government and before any other institution.

And in instituting marriage, He also gave rules and regulations concerning marriage and the home and the family. Many of these regulations we have violated, and I think we are paying for these violations.

The Bible was not against women working outside the home; it recognized the necessity and the value of this in special cases. But the whole trend of the Bible is found in the second chapter of Titus, in which it says that a woman, a family woman, should be a keeper at home. . . .

In short, I agree with the Bible. A mother should be at home during the formative years of her children unless she is a widow or in some financial straits which make it absolutely imperative for her to earn something outside the home. . . .

DR. KOMAROVSKY: But good relationships are not incompatible with being a working mother. I asked a group of students who were children of working mothers whether they thought their relationships with their mothers were affected by her working. And one girl spoke very movingly about how proud she was that her mother was a teacher — that it made her proud to help her mother in the home care of her brother, and that it was awfully exciting when her mother came home and had fascinating things to say about what had happened to her that day. "I feel very close to my mother and we are a very close family. My ideal in life is to be like my mother," this girl said.

[PSYCHOLOGIST] MRS. [FLORIDA] SCOTT-MAXWELL: This is the type of woman who is very valiant, but I would say is perhaps distorted by having her children and her career. She creates an atmosphere of activity, of achievement, but I think it very doubtful if she could teach her daughter any deep feminine wisdom this way.

The thing that is lacking is something that is very intangible but very real, very creative, that I can only call a feminine oneness with the depths of life. It isn't something that can be organized into a lesson, but if you have had deep experiences of life, feeling experiences of its sorrow and meaning, then you are a woman and you can pass this on to your daughters, and give strength to your husband and sons.

MISS HICKEY: Mrs. Phillips, would you like to comment on this? You were trained to be a school-teacher, but you chose instead to be a mother in the home.

MRS. [CHARLES R.] PHILLIPS [A STAY-AT-HOME MOTHER OF FOUR]: Well, I do feel that as a mother there are things I can give my children that no one else can, and there are moments when if you are not with them, the moment will never come again. I am glad that I have a career they could be proud of if I had to go to work, but since I don't work, I feel that by staying home I am setting an example to my three daughters of what is right for a woman to do. . . .

[LADIES' HOME JOURNAL EDITOR] MISS [JOAN] YOUNGER: There seems to be general agreement that ideally, mothers of small children should work at home. May I ask, then, who will pay the bills for those mothers whose only choice is to go out to work or starve?

SENATOR LAUSCHE: We have an aid-to-dependent-children program paid for jointly by the states and the Federal Government for those families who are deserted or left bereft by fathers. It works quite well in my home state of Ohio.

MISS HICKEY: In many states, however, it is most inadequate. Why, in Mississippi the average monthly payment to a recipient is only $7.53. In Washington State, with the highest average payment, it is $42.49 — a little less than $10 a week. It is no wonder that some mothers waive the public assistance payment in favor of a job outside the home. I have been watching with great interest the children's allowance program in Canada. There, all parents, regardless of need, are given small allowances to aid in the care of their children, to buy shoes for school, to get medicine, that sort of thing.

SENATOR LAUSCHE: I think that basically this is regimentation. I think the more you take away from the individual the necessity of independent effort, the more you take away his character. . . .

MISS HICKEY: It is difficult to decide how many of America's working mothers would see real deprivation by staying home. There are perhaps three million mothers of young children working. The majority of these are in low-income brackets — that is, under average. But what seems like an economic necessity to one family may not to another.

[COLLEGE PROFESSOR] DR. [LYNN] WHITE: The mothers I know who work do so either for self-expression or for a certain [rise?] in their standard of living rather than out of sheer necessity. . . .

MRS. DAVIS: Like all working mothers, I am constantly asking myself if I am doing the right thing. But, with us, it seemed either to wait for children until we were too old to have them, or for my husband to work at two jobs —

DR. WHITE: Mrs. Davis, I was filled with appalled admiration as I listened to your schedule of nursing at night and housework by day. But it is not in the proper sense an economic necessity. You are seeking what for you is the ideal physical setting of life. And I suspect that no matter what we say here, a lot of people will go on seeking this thing. . . .

MRS. SCOTT-MAXWELL: Meanwhile, we have come back to the responsibility of the individual mothers. There is an enormous responsibility upon them to become conscious of the situation —

MRS. GOULD: To feel the importance of their role and the value of it —

MRS. SCOTT-MAXWELL: Women need to live their public side, and their private side, and they must have every help in find[ing] the right balance of the two.

QUESTIONS FOR ANALYSIS

1. What do critics of working mothers suggest are the most serious drawbacks of their participation in the labor market?

2. What justifications are offered for the presence of mothers in the workforce?

3. How do you reconcile the extensive attention to working mothers in this era with Betty Friedan's complaints about the "feminine mystique" (pp. 557–58)?

4. What is the significance of the discussion of aid to dependent children, and how does that discussion relate to the history of mothers' pensions discussed on pages 429–30?

PRIMARY SOURCES

Women in the Civil Rights Movement

As historians examine the lives of American women of the last half of the twentieth century, they are able to draw on a wider variety and number of sources than historians researching earlier periods can. As the documents offered here suggest, oral histories have been particularly important in capturing the experiences of activists in the civil rights movement. If oral accounts are recorded long after the events described, they are sometimes marred by faulty memories or influenced by the person conducting the interview. Nonetheless, they give invaluable insights into the experiences and feelings of historical actors whose voices are often unheard in more traditional documentary sources. In addition, we have a powerful photographic record that not only documents the actions of civil rights activists and their opponents, but also helped to sway public opinion by documenting the brutality civil rights workers encountered.

PHOTOGRAPHS

The most iconic pictures of Rosa Parks, whose arrest sparked the Montgomery bus boycott in December 1955, show her either riding a bus or being arrested. These were images widely distributed at the time. Figure 10.12, however, is relatively unknown. Taken in Summer 1955, it documents Parks's participation in a desegregation workshop at the Highlander Folk School in New Market, Tennessee, six months before her arrest. The biracial school, founded in 1938, first served as a training school for labor organizers and then, beginning in 1953, civil rights activists. In addition to its focus on desegregation tactics, the school promoted citizenship schools as part of a voter education strategy. The workshop shown here was probably being led by Septima Clark, the black woman farthest to the left in the photograph. Clark was the director of Highlander's education program and was crucial in establishing the program of citizenship schools. Other notable women civil rights activists who attended Highlander included Ella Baker and Fannie Lou Hamer. How does this image of Rosa Parks help us to understand the planning that went into such tactics as the bus boycott? Is it surprising that most of the participants pictured here were women?

Unlike the photograph of Rosa Parks, the image in Figure 10.13, from the Little Rock, Arkansas, school desegregation crisis, is well known (see p. 613). It shows sixteen-year-old Elizabeth Eckford, of the "Little Rock Nine," walking to school

◆ **Figure 10.12 Rosa Parks at a Desegregation Workshop (1955)**
Emil Willametz/Highlander Archives.

on September 4, 1957, surrounded by hostile white women and girls. Governor Orval Faubus had announced that the state's National Guard would block the black students' entry, and Daisy Bates, of Little Rock's NAACP, had provided escorts for the other students, who walked together in case of trouble. Elizabeth's family had no telephone and could not be reached so she set out on her own. The girl behind Eckford was Hazel Bryan, a fifteen-year-old, who seemed to represent the face of vicious white racism. The legacy of that photograph was traumatic for her and in the early 1960s, Bryan called Eckford to apologize. In 1997, at the fortieth anniversary of Little Rock, the two women posed together in a smiling photograph. But in 1957, Elizabeth was terrified. When the guardsmen (who are pictured on the left) raised their bayonets and blocked her entrance to the school, she was pushed into the crowd. "They moved closer and closer," she later said. "Somebody started yelling, 'Lynch her! Lynch her!' "[45] Why is this image such an iconic photograph of the civil rights movement? How does the fact that Eckford and Bryan were young teenagers impact your reading of the image?

◆ **Figure 10.13 Elizabeth Eckford, Little Rock, Arkansas (1957)**
Bettmann/Getty Images.

ORAL INTERVIEWS

As you read these extracts of interviews, consider the following questions. How does the narrator's commitment shape her recollection? Does she have an ax to grind? Is she anxious to justify or exaggerate her actions? Need we be concerned that her memory is accurate? Has the interviewer unduly influenced the narrative?

This first selection is drawn from a 1979 interview with Diane Nash (later Bevel), conducted as part of the pathbreaking documentary series *Eyes on the Prize: America's Civil Rights Years (1954–1965)*. Nash is one of the best known of the young women SNCC activists. Nash (b. 1938), an African American who left Chicago to attend Fisk University in Nashville, describes her early involvement in the movement at the Nashville sit-ins in 1960. Why is this account so powerful?

DIANE NASH

The sit-ins were really highly charged, emotionally. In our non-violent workshops, we had decided to be respectful of the opposition, and try to keep issues geared toward desegregation, not get sidetracked. The first sit-in we had was really funny, because the waitresses were nervous. They must have dropped two thousand dollars' worth of dishes that day. It was almost a cartoon. One in particular, she was so nervous, she picked up dishes and she dropped one, and she'd pick up another one, and she'd drop it. It was really funny, and we were sitting there trying not to laugh, because we thought that laughing would be insulting and we didn't want to create that kind of atmosphere. At the same time we were scared to death. . . .

After we had started sitting in, we were surprised and delighted to hear reports of other cities joining in the sit-ins. And I think we started feeling that power of the idea whose time had come. Before we did the things that we did, we had no inkling that the movement would become as widespread as it did. I can remember being in the dorm any number of times and hearing the newscast, that Orangeburg had demonstrations, or Knoxville, or other towns. And we were really excited. We'd applaud, and say yea. When you are that age, you don't feel powerful. I remember realizing that with what we were doing, trying to abolish segregation, we were coming up against governors, judges, politicians, businessmen, and I remember thinking, "I'm only twenty-two years old, what do I know, what am I doing?" And

Source: Henry Hampton and Steve Fayer, comps., *Voices of Freedom: An Oral History of the Civil Rights Movement from the 1950s through the 1980s* (New York: Bantam, 1990), 57–59, 82–83.

I felt very vulnerable. So when we heard these newscasts, that other cities had demonstrations, it really helped. Because there were more of us. And it was very important.

The movement had a way of reaching inside you and bringing out things that even you didn't know were there. Such as courage. When it was time to go to jail, I was much too busy to be afraid.

[As a SNCC activist, in 1961 Nash became involved in the Freedom Rides. Here, she describes her leadership role when violence threatened to stop the rides and Nash insisted that they go forward (see p. 576).]

A contingent of students left Nashville to pick up the Freedom Ride where it had been stopped. Some of the students gave me sealed letters to be mailed in case they were killed. That's how prepared they were for death.

The students who were going to pick up the Freedom Ride elected me coordinator. As coordinator, part of my responsibility was to stay in touch with the Justice Department. Our whole way of operating was that we took ultimate responsibility for what we were going to do. But it was felt that they should be advised, in Washington, of what our plans were. Some people hoped for protection from the federal government. I think Jim Lawson cautioned against relying on federal protection.

I was also to keep the press informed, and communities that were participating, such as Birmingham, Montgomery, Jackson, and Nashville. And I coordinated the training and recruitment of more people to take up the Freedom Ride.

[Nash later became a rider herself and was jailed in Jackson, Mississippi, in 1961.]

CIVIL RIGHTS ACTIVISTS INCLUDED whites as well as blacks. Among them were many women. Vivian Leburg Rothstein, originally from Queens, New York, grew up in a lower-middle-class Jewish family in Los Angeles. She first became active in the civil rights movement while at the University of California at Berkeley, where she participated in protests against local merchants who discriminated against black employees and customers. The Free Speech Movement at Berkeley also shaped her growing radicalism. She was only nineteen when she went south. She went on from this experience to a lifelong commitment to social activism.

In this interview conducted for the PBS documentary *People's Century*, Rothstein recounts her experiences when she was part of the contingent of northern white students who went to Mississippi in 1965. This was the second year of voter registration and school integration campaigns conducted by the Student Nonviolent Coordinating Committee and the Committee on Racial Equality. Young white activists were invited in part to draw national media attention to the violence that local activists were experiencing. Rothstein refers to several of these events, including the murder, in the summer of 1964, of three civil rights activists, two white and one black.

How does Rothstein convey her reaction to the profound segregation of the rural South, and how did the activism of young people like herself challenge that system? Why does she call it a personally transformative experience? What do you think motivated her to go south?

Vivian Leburg Rothstein

Q: You traveled across the country to Mississippi . . . what was that like?

ROTHSTEIN: I'd never traveled anyplace. I had never really seen America. I mean, I'd only gone camping with my family. This felt like we were going into a different country really. I went with my boyfriend and we were on a Greyhound bus so it happened gradually. You'd stop at the bus terminal, have something to eat. You're way out in the country. The whole physical sense of the country changed dramatically but the visible poverty that I started to see . . . particularly down in Louisiana . . . I had never seen anything like that. We'd see people living on the side of the road in shacks and it got worse and worse as we went further south. Then you'd notice that many of them were black and the blacks were separated . . . it was this gradual thing.

I don't think I was prepared. It was a lot poorer than anything I'd ever seen. I had learned about racial discrimination but I'd never seen dirt-poor

families . . . people living in shacks. That was really shocking to me. I worked in a very rural area and there had never been a white woman in any of these people's homes before. People wanted to have me in their home overnight. It was really weird. I was special to them as a white person coming to their completely segregated community.

I had never had a personal connection like that with black people or with people who were that poor. Getting to know each other as people was what the whole civil rights movement was about. You couldn't just talk about it, you had to do it. So you had these profound personal transformative experiences. I remember feeling I had to push myself to do this. When I went back 25 years later, this family still talks about me. It's just incredible. I thought I had this incredible experience, but so did they and that movement was so important to them.

Q: Was it frightening?

ROTHSTEIN: Yeah, it was . . . it was scary. It was the summer after Chaney and Goodman were killed and so we actually knew that this could be a matter of life and death. Then Mrs. Luizza was killed, the woman who was driving to Selma. She was shot. She was driving demonstrators back and forth. There had been a number of deaths but when

SOURCE: Interview with Vivian Rothstein, "Young Blood," *People's Century*, PBS, June 14, 1999, http://www.pbs.org/wgbh/peoplescentury/episodes/youngblood/rothsteintranscript.html (accessed March 19, 2015).

you're 19 years old, you think you're never going to die. It seemed worrisome but it didn't seem real.

We went down and had an orientation session at Mt. Beulah, this religious campground, and then we went to Jackson, Mississippi. SNCC and CORE decided to organize a demonstration to challenge an ordinance against parading without a permit. So within a few days of getting there we were in this demonstration with Mississippi police officers with black jacks and dogs . . . people were getting beaten up . . . that was the scariest thing I've ever been in . . . it scared me to death and there was really nothing you could do. You were part of it and you just went along . . . you just didn't know what was going to happen. That was really scary.

Then we were put in jail and we were segregated. The white women were put in the Heinz County Jail and everyone else — white men, black women and black men — were put in the country fairgrounds. We were in jail about two weeks. A parade of officials came to see us . . . they sent a rabbi who told us how bad it was for Jews in Mississippi. Once we were together in the cell, and we didn't feel like we were going to get hurt, it was both boring and exciting. We had grits for breakfast with molasses on it and biscuits and we all got hugely constipated and really sick and then they gave us huge doses of laxatives. It was your classic jail experience. We didn't think we had broken any laws . . . we thought we were . . . the innocent and righteous.

Q: Why did SNCC organizers want white college students to get involved?

ROTHSTEIN: Well, I think it focused the attention of the whole country on what was happening in Mississippi. All of us had parents and our parents voted. We had access to the press. I think they also wanted the energy and the bodies.

It was a brilliant strategy in retrospect. It broke those separations between black and white, northern and southern, rich and poor because people worked together, lived together.

I think it helped the Mississippi black community to feel it wasn't isolated, that the eyes of the world were on it because we were there helping them and of course it brought our eyes on their situation.

Q: How important was this exposure to the black civil rights struggle for white student activists?

ROTHSTEIN: Well, it was . . . it was life transforming. To be a part of the righteous social movement, fighting for something bigger than yourself . . . you were just elevated as a human being. You had incredible significance in the world . . . it was ecstasy. It's really hard to explain it. It was the music and the singing that was used to build courage because everyone was afraid. It just lifted you up.

Q: This is a letter that you wrote from jail . . .

ROTHSTEIN: Thursday, June 17th, 1965. Dear Mom, I'm in jail in Jackson, Mississippi. You've probably already read about it. We were put in here Monday at 5 P.M. for marching on a sidewalk with no permit. We were protesting unconstitutional laws against demonstrations. On Tuesday, 200 people were arrested. On Wednesday 150 more people joined us and on Friday people will come from all over the nation to demonstrate in support of our actions and will be arrested. I am perfectly all right. The food is horrible and it's boring but we're all right. They segregated the white women from the black women. We have cells, eight in a cell and four beds, while the Negro women are in a hall at the state fairgrounds lying on the concrete floors with only two meals a day. The boys are in another building at the fairgrounds, segregated of course. Gregor was arrested too. I think he's all right too. What we have to wait for now is donations for bail money. The bail is set at $100 dollars each. . . .

We really don't know how long we will be in here. Maybe by the end of next week we could get out because there's an injunction coming up in court next week to declare the laws against demonstrating unconstitutional. It is terribly boring. We have only one book and two pens. We made cards and carved soap . . . besides that we just talk and sleep. How is everything?

My finals were okay. I don't know how well I did. I'm really all right. I'll try to write again soon if this letter gets through. I love you. Don't worry please. Love, Vivian.

ORAL HISTORIES ARE PARTICULARLY VALUABLE for capturing the stories of older rural women who offered indispensable aid to the activists who came to their communities. In this selection, published in 1977, Mary Dora Jones reminisces about taking in Freedom Summer workers in Marks, Mississippi. The interviewer is the Pulitzer Prize–winning journalist Howell Raines, who later became executive editor of the *New York Times*. What does Jones's account convey about disagreements within the African American community and the dangers facing those African Americans who supported the civil rights activists?

MARY DORA JONES

MARY DORA JONES: I had about several blacks and four whites in my house, wouldn't nobody else take 'em.

RAINES: In Marks?

JONES: Right . . . they really move. They comes in, they mean business. They didn't mind dyin', and as I see they really mean business, I just love that for 'em, because they was there to help us. And since they was there to help us, I was there to help them. . . .

RAINES: Did that cause you any problems in the community . . . opening your home up?

JONES: Oh, really, because they talkin' about burnin' my house down. . . . Some of the black folks got the news that they were gonna burn it down. . . . My neighbors was afraid of gettin' killed. People standin' behind buildin's, peepin' out behind the buildin's, to see what's goin' on. So I just told 'em. "Dyin' is all right. Ain't but one thing 'bout dyin'. That's make sho' you right, 'cause you gon' die anyway." . . . If they had burnt it down, it was just a house burned down.

RAINES: That's the attitude that changed the South.

JONES: So that's the way I thought about it. So those kids, some of 'em from California, some of 'em from Iowa, some of 'em from Cincinnati, they worked, and they sho' had them white people up there shook up.

RAINES: . . . [Y]oungsters that came in, particularly the white ones from outside the South, did they have a hard time adjusting . . . ?

JONES: They had a hard time adjustin' because most all of the blacks up there didn't want to see 'em comin' . . . said they ain't lettin' no damn civil rights come. "If they come up here to my house, I'm gon' shoot 'em."

See this is what the black folks were sayin', and those kids had went to the preachers' houses, they had done went to the deacons' houses, they had done went to the teachers' houses, all tryin' to get in. Some of 'em come in around five o'clock that evenin', landed in my house. I give 'em my house, "My house is yo' house." I was workin' for a man, he was workin' at the Post Office, and he and his wife was beggin' me everyday, "Don't fool with them Communists."

RAINES: The white people?

JONES: That's what they was tellin' me, those kids was Communists. I said, "Well, I tell you what. I don't think they no more Communist than right here where I am, because if they Communists, then you Communists. They cain't hurt me no mo' than I already been hurt." Anything that helped the peoples, then I'm right there. So I didn't stop, although I got him scared to fire me. He would have fired me, but I got him scared to fire me. . . .

RAINES: This was your white boss?

JONES: This was my white boss I was working for. His wife was sick, and every day the wife

SOURCE: Howell Raines, *My Soul Is Rested: Movement Days in the Deep South* (New York: Putnam, 1977), 279–81.

would talk to me about those people, askin' me where they lived. I said, "Well, they ain't livin' at yo' house. Why you want to know where they live?" So she said, "They ain't livin' with you?" And I said, "Well, I'm payin' the last note on the house," just like that. And I never did tell her.

Finally one day she brought me home, and it was a car sittin' there in my driveway, and two white men was in there, and there were some sittin' on the porch. She put me out and she went on back. When I went to work the next morning,

she say, "Mary, was them, ah, civil rights people at yo' house?" I said, "Now when you turned around and stopped and they were sittin' there, you oughta been askin' 'em what they was. They'da told you."

And I never did tell 'em anything. So it went on some, she said, "Ain't but one thing I hate about it, this intermarriage." And I said, "Well, ain't no need in worryin' about that, because if you wanna worry about that, you oughta been talkin' to your granddaddy."

Earline boyd of Hattiesburg, Mississippi, had been involved in the NAACP in her community even before civil rights activists came to her town for the voter registration drive. In this interview, conducted in 1991 by Dr. Charles Bolton of the University of Southern Mississippi's Civil Rights in Mississippi Oral History Project, she describes some of the harassment African Americans active in civil rights faced. What insights does she offer about women's participation in the movement?

Earline Boyd

EARLINE BOYD: There was the pressure on people about jobs or they would try and intimidate them in different ways.

I remember one man lost his job. He had been working for one of the white funeral homes here and his wife was very active in it. When they found out that she was marching that day going to the courthouse — that's where we were marching to that particular day — when he went back to work the people — I don't remember exactly what they said to him, but I do know that she his wife told him just to give that job up and not to go back anymore. So evidently they had said things to him, had made him know that they did not want him. He didn't go; it was his wife who was doing the marching and was active in the movement.

So it was hard on people and a lot of people was afraid, you know, to take a step towards trying to work with the movement. I don't remember where I was working then, but it didn't have any effect on me, on my job at the time. And I would just go whenever they had it and it was kind of hard. Now some people probably, well, the ones that was working for people who didn't want them to go, I'm sure they gave them a lot of hard times. So that was my way of getting started in the movement.

DR. CHARLES BOLTON: Were a lot of women involved? It sounds like the women maybe were more involved than the men.

BOYD: There were more women involved than men in the movement.

BOLTON: Why do you think that is?

BOYD: Well, I guess the man was the person who was really head of the household and needed a job. Women worked but I guess they felt like it would be easier for them to go and not lose their job than for men. Even so, like I said about this

SOURCE: "Civil Rights in Mississippi Digital Archive," Mississippi Oral History Program of the University of Southern Mississippi, interview conducted August 29, 1991, http://anna.lib.usm.edu/%7Espcol/crda/oh/ohboydrp.html (accessed January 29, 2003).

man who lost his job when the person that he was working for found out that his wife was going, then he started talking to him. And of course, his wife was working for herself and had her own day care center. So it wouldn't bother her. And he stopped working there, and I don't know where he went to work after that. But later on I do remember that he started working for himself too.

QUESTIONS FOR ANALYSIS

1. What insights do these sources offer about the distinct experiences of women in the civil rights movement?

2. What kinds of leadership skills did these movement women display?

3. Can you find specific examples in the interviews that suggest any of the pitfalls historians face in drawing upon remembrances as sources?

4. To what extent do these documents reveal the obstacles facing civil rights activists?

5. What clues do these documents provide as to the relationship between the civil rights movement and the emergence of the feminist movement in the late 1960s?

NOTES

1. James T. Patterson, *Grand Expectations: The United States, 1945–1974* (New York: Oxford University Press, 1996), 223.

2. David K. Johnson, *The Lavender Scare: The Cold War Persecution of Gays and Lesbians in the Federal Government* (Chicago: University of Chicago Press, 2004), 196.

3. Amanda H. Littauer, *Young Women, Sex, and Rebellion before the Sixties* (Chapel Hill: University of North Carolina Press, 2015), 125.

4. Jessica Weiss, *To Have and to Hold: Marriage, the Baby Boom, and Social Change* (Chicago: University of Chicago Press, 2000), 57.

5. "Wright Girls Combine Careers and Marriage," *Ebony*, January 1951, 74.

6. Joanne Meyerowitz, "Beyond the Feminine Mystique: A Reassessment of Postwar Mass Culture, 1946–1958," in Joanne Meyerowitz, ed., *Not June Cleaver: Women and Gender in Postwar America, 1945–1960* (Philadelphia: Temple University Press, 1994), 240.

7. Eva Moskowitz, " 'It's Good to Blow Your Top': Women's Magazines and a Discourse of Discontent, 1945–1960," *Journal of Women's History* 8 (Fall 1996): 66–98.

8. Alice Kessler-Harris, *Out to Work: A History of Wage-Earning Women* (New York: Oxford University Press, 1982), 304.

9. Susan M. Hartmann, "Women's Employment and the Domestic Ideal in the Early Cold War Years," in Meyerowitz, *Not June Cleaver*, 88.

10. Ibid., 90.

11. Beverly E. Golemba, *Human Computers: The Women in Aeronautical Research* (1994), 43, https://crgis.ndc.nasa.gov/crgis/images/c/c7/Golemba.pdf (accessed July 3, 2017).

12. Susan Rimby Leighow, "An 'Obligation to Participate': Married Nurses Labor Force Participation in the 1950s," in Meyerowitz, *Not June Cleaver*, 37–56.

13. Weiss, *To Have and to Hold*, 55.

14. Sara M. Evans, *Born for Liberty: A History of Women in America* (New York: Free Press, 1989), 254.

15. Bruce Fehn, "African-American Women and the Struggle for Equality in the Meatpacking Industry, 1940–1960," *Journal of Women's History* 10 (Spring 1998): 50.

16. Ibid., 58–59.

17. Catherine E. Rymph, *Republican Women: Feminism and Conservatism from Suffrage through the Rise of the New Right* (Chapel Hill: University of North Carolina Press, 2006), 117.

18. Amy Swerdlow, *Women Strike for Peace: Traditional Motherhood and Radical Politics in the 1960s* (Chicago: University of Chicago Press, 1993), 110.

19. Ibid., 117.

20. Belinda Robnett, *How Long? How Long? African-American Women in the Struggle for Civil Rights* (New York: Oxford University Press, 1997), 59.

21. Ibid., 67.

22. Ibid., 17–32.

23. Ibid., 94.

24. Ibid., 104.

25. Clayborne Carson, *In Struggle: SNCC and the Black Awakening of the 1960s* (Cambridge: Harvard University Press, 1995), 74.

26. Sara Evans, *Personal Politics: The Roots of Women's Liberation in the Civil Rights Movement and the New Left* (New York: Knopf, 1979), 86–87.

27. Debra L. Schultz, *Going South: Jewish Women in the Civil Rights Movement* (New York: New York University Press, 2001), 83.

28. Ibid., 9.

29. Margaret Rose, "Gender and Civic Activism in Mexican American Barrios in California: The Community Service Organization, 1947–1962," in Meyerowitz, *Not June Cleaver*, 181.

30. Ibid., 190.

31. Patricia G. Zelman, *Women, Work, and National Policy: The Kennedy-Johnson Years* (Ann Arbor: UMI Research Press, 1982), 28.

32. Linda Kerber, *No Constitutional Right to Be Ladies* (New York: Hill and Wang, 1998), 192.

33. Alice Kessler-Harris, *In Pursuit of Equity: Women, Men, and the Quest for Economic Citizenship in Twentieth-Century America* (New York: Oxford University Press, 2001), 234.

34. William Boddy, *Fifties Television: The Industry and Its Critics* (Urbana: University of Illinois Press, 1990), 20.

35. *Newsweek*, March 15, 1954, 93.

36. Lynn Spigel, *Make Room for TV: Television and the Family Ideal in Postwar America* (Chicago: University of Chicago Press, 1992), 83.

37. Jim Hall, *Mighty Minutes: An Illustrated History of Television's Best Commercials* (New York: Harmony, 1984), 47.

38. Melvin Patrick Ely, *The Adventures of Amos 'n' Andy* (New York: Free Press, 1991), 211.

39. Rick Mitz, *The Great TV Sitcom Book* (New York: Richard Marek, 1992), 14.

40. George Lipsitz, "The Meaning of Memory, Family, Class and Ethnicity in Early Network Television Programs," in Lynn Spigel and Denise Mann, eds., *Private Screenings: Television and the Female Consumer* (Minneapolis: University of Minnesota Press, 1992), 78.

41. Susan J. Douglas, *Where the Girls Are: Growing Up Female with the Mass Media* (New York: Times Books, 1994), 36.

42. Violet Brown Weingarten, "Case History of an Ex-Working Mother," *New York Times*, September 20, 1953, p. 54.

43. Gerry Murray Engle, "I Chose Work," *Good Housekeeping*, November 1953, 299.

44. David Yellin, "I'm Married to a Working Mother," *Harper's*, July 1956, 34–37; Robert Coughlan, "Modern Marriage," *Life*, December 24, 1956, 116.

45. Quoted in Daisy Bates, *The Long Shadow of Little Rock: A Memoir* (Little Rock: University of Arkansas Press, 2014), Kindle edition.

SUGGESTED REFERENCES

General Works

Rochelle Gatlin, *American Women since 1945* (1987).

Joanne Meyerowitz, ed., *Not June Cleaver: Women and Gender in Postwar America, 1945–1960* (1994).

Deborah Gray White, *Too Heavy a Load: Black Women in Defense of Themselves, 1894–1994* (1999).

Marriage, Family, and Cold War Culture

Wini Breines, Young, *White, and Miserable: Growing Up Female in the Fifties* (1992).

Stephanie Coontz, *A Strange Stirring:* The Feminine Mystique and American Women at the Dawn of the 1960s (2011).

Lillian Faderman, *Odd Girls and Twilight Lovers: A History of Lesbian Life in Twentieth-Century America* (1991).

Amanda H. Littauer, *Bad Girls: Young Women, Sex, and Rebellion before the Sixties* (2015).

Elaine Tyler May, *Homeward Bound: American Families in the Cold War Era* (1988).

Jessica Weiss, *To Have and to Hold: Marriage, the Baby Boom, and Social Change* (2000).

Women and Work

Julia Kirk Blackwelder, *Now Hiring: The Feminization of Work in the United States, 1900–1995* (1997).

Dorothy Sue Cobble, *The Other Women's Movement: Workplace Justice and Social Rights in Modern America* (2004).

Vicki L. Ruiz, *Cannery Women, Cannery Lives: Mexican Women, Unionization, and the California Food Processing Industry, 1930–1950* (1987).

Margot Lee Shetterly, *Hidden Figures: The American Dream and the Untold Story of the Black Women Mathematicians Who Helped with the Space Race* (2016).

Women's Activism

Vicky L. Crawford, Jacqueline Anne Rouse, and Barbara Woods, eds., *Women in the Civil Rights Movement: Trailblazers and Torchbearers, 1941–1965* (1993).

Constance Curry et al., *Deep in Our Hearts: Nine White Women in the Freedom Movement* (2000).

Sara Evans, *Personal Politics: The Roots of Women's Liberation in the Civil Rights Movement and the New Left* (1979).

Susan Lynn, *Progressive Women in Conservative Times: Racial Justice, Peace, and Feminism, 1945 to the 1960s* (1992).

Danielle L. McGuire, *At the Dark End of the Street: Black Women, Rape, and Resistance — a New History of the Civil Rights Movement from Rosa Parks to the Rise of Black Power* (2010).

Michelle M. Nickerson, *Mothers of Conservatism: Women and the Postwar Right* (2012).

Belinda Robnett, *How Long? How Long? African-American Women in the Struggle for Civil Rights* (1997).

Leila J. Rupp and Verta Taylor, *Survival in the Doldrums: The American Women's Rights Movement, 1945 to the 1960s* (1987).

Catherine E. Rymph, *Republican Women: Feminism and Conservatism from Suffrage through the Rise of the New Right* (2006).

11

Modern Feminism and American Society

1965–1980

IN 1966, A GROUP OF SIXTEEN WOMEN MET IN WASH-INGTON, D.C., to create the National Organization for Women (NOW) to "bring women into full participation in the mainstream of American society." Two years later, Alice Peurala, who worked for U.S. Steel in Chicago, was denied a higher-paying job in the mill; after her boss told her, "We don't want any women on these jobs," she filed an antidiscrimination suit with a government agency, a case she won in 1974.[1] In 1968, members of a guerrilla street group staged a dramatic protest at the Miss America pageant, in which they crowned a live sheep and tossed symbols of women's oppression — curlers, bras, and makeup — into a "freedom trash can." That same year, African American women formed the Black Women's Liberation Committee. In 1970, Chicana activists created the Comisión Femenil Mexicana with the purpose of "organizing women to assume leadership positions within the Chicano movement and in community life."[2]

These disparate events highlight the emergence of a multifaceted feminism that flourished in the late 1960s and 1970s. The feminism of women associated with NOW took inspiration from the civil rights movement and was rooted in the early 1960s activism that had focused on women's employment rights. Different visions of feminism stemmed from the protest movements of the 1960s in which young men and women took to the streets to demand an end to the war in Vietnam while others demanded racial justice through a variety of nationalist power movements. Exhilarated to be part of the ambitious activism of the period but frustrated by their exclusion from its leadership, women had begun by 1968 to insist that equality and liberation should characterize the relations between the sexes, as well as among races and nations. As African American writer and activist Toni Cade (later Bambara) put it, "mutinous cadres of women" in all sorts of protest organizations were "getting salty about having to . . . fix the coffee while the men wrote the position papers and decided on policy."[3]

Out of this combination of excitement and frustration came "women's liberation," a new kind of feminism rooted in 1960s experiences and perspectives. Initially concentrated on gaining equality for women within the protest movements of Black Power, Chicanismo, and the New Left, women's liberation soon challenged the condition of women in the larger society. In conjunction with NOW, women's liberation made feminism into a mass movement. Sometimes called the "second wave" (the "first wave" having been the feminism associated with the woman suffrage movement of the Progressive era — see pp. 440–44), this modern feminism outlived its 1960s origins to become one of the most important social and political forces of the late twentieth century.

◆ ROOTS OF SIXTIES FEMINISM

In 1960, "feminism" was often a term of derision or contempt, if it was used at all. By decade's end, Americans were hearing a great deal about it. A diverse group of women — young and old, working class and privileged, heterosexual and lesbian, white and of color — all contributed to a resurgent feminism. Rooted in the social upheavals surrounding the civil rights movement, the Vietnam War, and the counterculture, the new feminism that emerged in the second half of the 1960s signaled the beginning of a transformative era in women's history.

photos: top, Phelan M. Ebenhack/AP Photo; middle, Lester Sloan; bottom, AP Photo/Houston Chronicle, Sam C. Pierson Jr.

1972 Congress passes Equal Rights Amendment; Phyllis Schlafly founds STOP-ERA

1972 Title IX of Education Amendments Act bans sex discrimination in federally funded education

1972 Shirley Chisholm seeks Democratic Party nomination for president

1972 Sally Preisand becomes first woman rabbi

1972 Stewardesses for Women's Rights founded

1973 Supreme Court rules in *Roe v. Wade* that women's right to abortion constitutionally protected

1973 Paris Peace Accords end U.S. participation in war in Vietnam

1973 OPEC oil embargo leads to economic recession

1974 Watergate scandal forces Nixon's resignation

1974 Coalition of Labor Union Women (CLUW) founded

1975 United Nations sponsors first International Women's Conference in Mexico City

1976 Jimmy Carter elected president

1977 Eleanor Holmes Norton appointed to head Equal Employment Opportunity Commission (EEOC)

1977 National Women's Conference held in Houston

1978 Mexican American women lose the forced sterilization lawsuit *Madrigal v. Quilligan* against California hospitals

The Legacy of the Civil Rights Movement

The revival of feminism in the 1960s first emerged clearly among a group of women associated with the National Organization for Women (NOW), founded in 1966. This version of feminism owed much to the civil rights movement and a dramatic legislative milestone: the passage of the Civil Rights Act of 1964. Pressure from the civil rights movement had led to a call for an omnibus federal act forbidding discrimination on the grounds of race. While Congress was debating the legislation, members of the National Woman's Party encouraged U.S. Representative Howard Smith of Virginia, a supporter of the Equal Rights Amendment (ERA), to propose an amendment to the bill that would extend federal civil rights protection to women. Smith did so, in large measure because as a white southerner he opposed the Civil Rights Act and thought the inclusion of sex would undermine support for the legislation. Once the bill was introduced in the House, however, the few women congressional representatives, notably Martha Griffiths of Michigan, backed it, with support from many women activists such as African American lawyer Pauli Murray, who saw the amendment as a way of fighting both "Jim Crow" and "Jane Crow."

The Women's Bureau staff, led by Esther Peterson (see pp. 585–88), initially withheld support for the amendment not only because they worried that if the Civil Rights Act applied to women it would undermine state protective legislation, but also because they feared damage to the African American cause, which the bureau viewed as the more serious form of discrimination. Once the measure went to the Senate, however, President Lyndon B. Johnson backed the amendment to assure the entire bill's swift passage, and Peterson and Women's Bureau allies came on board. Title VII of the Civil Rights Act of 1964, prohibiting employment discrimination based on race, sex, national origin, or religion, became law.

The Equal Employment Opportunity Commission (EEOC), the agency established to implement Title VII, estimated that in the first year of its operation, grievances about sex discrimination constituted an unexpected 37 percent of its complaints. Women, many of them rank-and-file union members, complained about unequal benefits and pay, discrimination in hiring and firing, restrictive state protective legislation, and separate union seniority lists. The commission, however, concentrated on racial discrimination and gave little priority to women's complaints, making the EEOC an ineffective tool to counter sexual discrimination in the workplace.

NOW and Liberal Feminism

Discontent with the failures of the EEOC erupted in the 1966 Third Annual Conference on the Status of Women. By then, a groundswell of women, whose growth began among the President's Commission on the Status of Women and the state commissions and was reinforced by labor union and civil rights activists, had emerged to insist on women's equal rights. Their consciousness had also been raised by the 1963 publication of Betty Friedan's *The Feminine Mystique* (see pp. 557–58). As a result, sixteen women held an impromptu meeting to create an outside pressure group; thus the National Organization for Women was founded with Friedan as its first president. Although NOW is often described as a white middle-class organization, African Americans, such as Pauli Murray and Aileen Hernandez (who was NOW's second president), participated from the very beginning. In addition, labor union members such as Dorothy Haener of the United Auto Workers were crucial to the organization's success (see Reading into the Past: "Women's Bill of Rights").

The creation of NOW put women's civil rights on the political map. Consciously modeling their organization after the National Association for the Advancement of Colored People, the founders expected NOW to act primarily as a lobbying and litigating group to promote women's political and economic rights, but its goals gradually expanded. In 1967, for example, the organization endorsed women's right to reproductive freedom. The breadth of NOW's agenda was symbolized by its national Women's Strike for Equality on August 26, 1970. Commemorating the fiftieth anniversary of the Nineteenth Amendment granting woman suffrage, the strike focused on drawing attention to abortion rights, child care, and equal educational and economic opportunity. By 1974, NOW boasted seven hundred chapters, forty thousand members, and an annual budget of $300,000. Especially outside of large cities and college towns, women — inspired by the growing media visibility of women's liberation in the early 1970s — turned to the only organization they could find, NOW, and in the process broadened it from a lobbying group to a mass membership organization.

Other liberal organizations were also important in spreading the feminist message. In 1968, women who described themselves as "less radical" than the feminists in NOW — primarily because of their unwillingness to support abortion rights — created the Women's Equity Action League (WEAL). WEAL focused on discrimination in education and the workforce and lobbied extensively in Washington, D.C. Dozens of older women's organizations, such as the National Council of Jewish Women, the National Council of Negro Women, and the American Association of University Women, also supported specific legislative campaigns. Women in labor unions continued their commitment forged in the postwar years to improving working-class women's job opportunities. Many were active in NOW and, in 1974, they founded the Coalition of Labor Union Women (CLUW) to bring women's issues to the forefront of the labor movement. A host of mixed-sex organizations, with a strong interest in social justice causes, including the American Civil Liberties Union, the Young Women's Christian Association, and the National Council of Churches, also helped bring feminism to the mainstream.

Historians often describe NOW and groups that supported much of its agenda as representing "liberal" feminism because it focused on bringing about women's formal equality through legal and political means, a process that paralleled other

READING INTO THE PAST

NATIONAL ORGANIZATION FOR WOMEN
Women's Bill of Rights

At its 1967 convention, a year after its founding, NOW issued its "Women's Bill of Rights in 1968."

   I. Equal Rights Constitutional Amendment
  II. Enforce Law Banning Sex Discrimination in Employment
 III. Maternity Leave Rights in Employment and in Social Security Benefits
 IV. Tax Deduction for Home and Child Care Expenses for Working Parents
  V. Child Day Care Centers
 VI. Equal and Unsegregated Education
VII. Equal Job Training Opportunities and Allowances for Women in Poverty
VIII. The Right of Women to Control Their Reproductive Lives

We Demand:

   I. That the United States Congress immediately pass the Equal Rights Amendment to the Constitution to provide that "Equality of rights under the law shall not be denied or abridged by the United States or by any State on account of sex" and that such then be immediately ratified by the several States.
  II. That equal employment opportunity be guaranteed to all women, as well as men by insisting that the Equal Employment Opportunity Commission enforce the prohibitions against sex discrimination in employment under Title VII of the Civil Rights Act of 1964 with the same vigor as it enforces the prohibitions against racial discrimination.
 III. That women be protected by law to insure their rights to return to their jobs within a reasonable time after childbirth without loss of

twentieth-century liberal reform movements. These groups continued many of the issues and approaches that previous phases of feminism had begun, and many of their members had been working on women's issues for decades. By contrast, the feminism known as "women's liberation" drew on a younger generation and considered itself revolutionary, seeking changes that went beyond civil rights and formal equality to cultural transformation.

seniority or other accrued benefits and be paid maternity leave as a form of social security and/or employee benefit.

IV. Immediate revision of tax laws to permit the deduction of home and child care expenses for working parents.

V. That child care facilities be established by law on the same basis as parks, libraries and public schools adequate to the needs of children, from the pre-school years through adolescence, as a community resource to be used by all citizens from all income levels.

VI. That the right of women to be educated to their full potential equally with men be secured by Federal and State legislation, eliminating all discrimination and segregation by sex, written and unwritten, at all levels of education including college, graduate and professional schools, loans and fellowships and Federal and State training programs, such as the job Corps.

VII. The right of women in poverty to secure job training, housing and family allowances on equal terms with men, but without prejudice to a parent's right to remain at home to care for his or her children; revision of welfare legislation and poverty programs which deny women dignity, privacy and self respect.

VIII. The right of women to control their own reproductive lives by removing from penal codes the laws limiting access to contraceptive information and devices and laws governing abortion.

Source: https://en.wikisource.org/wiki/N.O.W._Bill_of_Rights (accessed August 20, 2017).

QUESTIONS FOR ANALYSIS

1. What does the statement reveal about the impediments facing women's equality, and how does it propose to address them?

2. What is the significance of terming the statement a "bill of rights"?

◆ WOMEN'S LIBERATION AND THE SIXTIES REVOLUTIONS

All of the upheavals collectively known as the "sixties revolutions" played a role in the emergence of women's liberation. The counterculture of youthful radicals who defied conventional norms of sexual behavior and criticized both the nuclear family and the middle-class ethos of success helped to fuel feminist critiques of the subordinate status of women within the family and their call for a feminist sexual revolution. At the same time, the political ferment ignited by Black Power advocates and other groups that promoted nationalist movements in opposition to the white-dominated power structure of American life offered women's liberationists a model for challenging male power. Finally, the antiwar movement directed against U.S. involvement in Vietnam mobilized tens of thousands of Americans to challenge the federal government and gave impetus to radical feminists' calls for taking on another kind of authority by dismantling patriarchy.

Sexual Revolution and Counterculture

The introduction in 1960 of the birth control pill, along with the confidence that modern medicine could cure any sexually transmitted disease (proved tragically wrong by the AIDS epidemic that began two decades later), forged a conviction that sexual relations no longer had unwanted consequences and could be indulged in casually and freely. The sixties atmosphere of sexual liberation pushed women past the expectations of earlier generations that marriage and motherhood were both their goal and their fate. But the ethic of sexual liberation set different sorts of restraints on women. What sexual liberation meant before women's liberation is captured in images of women in miniskirts and go-go boots, with exaggerated eye makeup and long straight hair, signaling their availability to men. Women were not supposed to be sexual adventurers themselves so much as rewards for the men who crashed through the barricades of respectability.

By the late 1960s, young people had expanded sexual liberation into a broader challenge to the very foundations of their parents' way of life. The "counterculture," as this diffuse phenomenon was known, went beyond the "hippie" lifestyle of sex, drugs, and rock 'n' roll to experiment with new forms of living. Instead of following in the path of the idealized, hardworking, male-headed, nuclear family of the 1950s, the counterculture encouraged the creation of "communes," groups determined to find different forms of intimacy and interdependence. These deliberately created communities (latter-day versions of the utopian communities of the 1830s and 1840s — see pp. 238–40) retained more of the gender divisions of the larger society than they cared to admit. Nonetheless, the countercultural ambition to replace the traditional middle-class family with a radically different alternative set the stage for an explicitly feminist revolt against expected norms of domesticity and motherhood.

Black Power and SNCC

Changes in the civil rights movement also had an impact on the emergence of women's liberation. African Americans, deeply frustrated by the slow federal response to their demands, were further dispirited by a wave of black ghetto riots in the summer of 1965. Then, when Martin Luther King Jr. was assassinated in

Memphis, Tennessee, in April 1968, the nonviolent phase of the modern civil rights movement died with him. The assassination in June that year of Robert Kennedy, whose campaign for the Democratic presidential nomination championed African American and Chicano civil rights, also traumatized black leaders, many of whom now turned away from the goal of racial integration and concentrated instead on cultivating black leadership, sensibility, and mass empowerment. Their spirit of militant collective antiracism spread to other communities of color. Young Mexican American civil rights advocates created the era of Chicano nationalism. Mostly urban Native Americans formed the American Indian Movement in 1969, and Asian Americans established a Pan Asian movement. Coming together under the term "third world" — borrowed from the term for developing countries outside the Cold War orbits of the first world (highly developed industrialized Western nations) and the second world (the Soviet Union and other Communist nations) — these radical activists saw themselves as part of a larger uprising against America's traditions of white supremacy.

Of all these forms of militant antiracism, the most influential was Black Power. In contrast to earlier, southern-based civil rights activism, the Black Power movement thrived in northern cities. Black Power advocates adopted a black nationalist philosophy, which, although it did not call for an independent state, did seek to consolidate a sense of peoplehood among African Americans. A major inspiration for Black Power was the philosophy of Malcolm X, a renegade leader of the Nation of Islam (whose members were commonly known as Black Muslims) who challenged the goal of integration and the message of black inferiority it subtly conveyed. He was assassinated in 1965. In 1966, the Student Nonviolent Coordinating Committee (SNCC) became a Black Power organization, voting to expel its white members and embracing the goal of black self-determination. That same year, the Black Panther Party was formed in Oakland, California, and quickly became known for insisting on the right to community self-defense, with weapons if necessary, against police abuse.

The impact of the Black Power movement on the emergence of women's liberation was complex. Black Power had a decidedly masculine cast, in contrast to the earlier phases of civil rights activism, in which African American women had been prominent as local leaders (see pp. 573–75). Black nationalism tended to cast women as mothers of a new peoplehood rather than as political actors themselves. Black men were to lead and defend their people; black women were to give birth to and nurture them. Nonetheless, there were significant female figures in the Black Power era, notably Angela Davis, a philosophy professor who went underground to escape FBI charges that she had aided a black prisoner revolt in Marin County, California. Yet Black Power's emphasis on self-determination rather than integration, on the group rather than the individual, provided the model for the emerging women's liberation movement. Black Power ideas inspired women's liberation by insisting that true freedom could be won only when the oppressed and the activist were one and the same, when subordinate people sought to liberate themselves rather than look to powerful saviors.

◆ **Angela Davis**

The face of Angela Davis, framed by the halo of her natural Afro hairstyle, is one of the signature female images of the era. Her early engagement in the Black Power movement led to a lifelong commitment to challenging what she called the prison industrial complex in the United States. Here, she speaks at a rally against the death penalty at the state capitol in Raleigh, North Carolina, in July 1974. *The Granger Collection, New York.*

The War in Vietnam and SDS

Even more than sexual liberation and Black Power, however, the U.S. war in Vietnam provided the immediate context for the appearance of the women's liberation movement. The presence of U.S. armed forces in Vietnam began to escalate in 1961, as part of President John F. Kennedy's decision to intervene in the civil war there between a Communist government in the north and an anti-Communist regime in the south. In 1965, President Lyndon B. Johnson began sending ever-larger numbers of combat troops and ordered the bombing of Hanoi, the capital of North Vietnam. By the time U.S. forces withdrew in 1973, approximately 2.8 million Americans had served in Vietnam. Of these, an estimated seven thousand were women. Among the approximately sixty thousand Americans who died in Vietnam were eight military nurses and fifty-six women working with organizations ranging from the Red Cross to the CIA.

In general, however, the Vietnam War—fighting in it or fighting against it—was an intensely male experience. The U.S. armed forces had been deliberately "remasculinized" after World War II. At the time of the Vietnam War, the military was operating under a gender quota allowing only 2 percent of active-duty personnel to be female.[4] By the mid-1960s, the possibility of being called up through the draft hung like a cloud over the lives of nearly all young men in the United States. As opposition against the war grew, men could pursue alternative forms of heroism: by refusing to be drafted, by publicly burning their draft cards, or by leaving the United States. Women who opposed the war were their supporters. "Hell no, we won't go" was the slogan of men in the draft resistance movement. "Girls say yes to guys who say no" was the female equivalent. In the many giant demonstrations against the Vietnam War, women were fully half of the rank and file.

The major organization behind the antiwar protests was Students for a Democratic Society (SDS). Formed in 1962 by forty college students meeting in Port Huron, Michigan, SDS protested against America's hypocritical claim to be the bastion of democracy. Impatient with what they regarded as the outdated, class-based politics of the previous generation of left-wing activists (the "Old Left"), SDS activists declared themselves the "New Left." After white students left SNCC, many joined SDS.

Even more than SNCC, SDS tended strongly to reserve leadership roles for men. By 1967, largely in response to SDS men's hostility to women's issues, SDS women began to meet separately from men, following the model of the Black Power movement. "Women must not make the same mistake that blacks did at first of allowing others . . . to define our issues, methods and goals," an anonymous group of women SDSers announced. "The time has come for us to take the initiative in organizing ourselves for our own liberation."[5]

By 1969, an estimated 2 million Americans, women and men, had taken to the streets in cities all over the country to protest the war. In the spring of 1970, antiwar demonstrations closed down many college campuses. Tragically, in May 1970 National Guard troops killed four students, two of whom were women, and wounded nine others at Kent State University in Ohio; later that month, two young men at Jackson State University in Mississippi were killed by local police. Rebellion at home combined with mounting American casualties in Vietnam to increase the pressure on President Richard Nixon to find some way out of what now appeared to be an unwinnable war, although the United States would not withdraw from Vietnam until 1973.

Significantly, the first national political event at which the radical women's liberation movement made its appearance was a women's antiwar demonstration, organized in January 1968 by Women Strike for Peace (WSP). Named the "Jeannette Rankin Brigade" in honor of the first woman elected to the U.S. Congress, who had cast her vote against both world wars, the Washington, D.C., demonstration drew five thousand women, including eighty-seven-year-old Rankin. A group of younger women, determined to leave behind older traditions of female activism, organized a protest within the protest. They criticized the WSP for the link between pacifism and motherhood on which it relied. "You have resisted our roles of supportive girlfriends and tearful widows," read the leaflet they distributed. "Now you must resist approaching Congress playing these same roles that are synonymous with powerlessness."[6]

◆ **Women against War**

Although the most common images of antiwar protesters in the Vietnam era focus on
college students, Americans of all sorts protested the war in Indochina. Among the first
were members of Women Strike for Peace (WSP), a group that had taken up the antinuclear
cause in the 1950s (see pp. 570–72). This photograph of an April 1972 "die-in" in New York
City captures the dramatic techniques prevalent in antiwar demonstrations of the 1960s
and 1970s. Here, WSP women are protesting President Nixon's bombing of Cambodia while
specifically targeting International Telephone & Telegraph because of its defense contracts
with the military. *Dorothy Marder Collection, Swarthmore College Peace Collection.*

◆ IDEAS AND PRACTICES OF WOMEN'S LIBERATION

Women's liberationists approached the challenge of greater freedom for women in a manner radically different from that which NOW had laid out two years before. Well educated, confident of an affluent future, politically alienated, and disdainful of sexual restraints, many young people in the 1960s had no faith in the older generation's ability to create a better world. "We want something more, much more, than the same gray, meaningless, alienating jobs that men are forced to sacrifice their lives to," wrote Robin Morgan in criticism of NOW's goal of integrating women into the American mainstream.[7] The young women who had come through the movements of the sixties envisioned a different kind of emancipatory politics for their sex, and they offered new theories and new approaches to that emancipation. Their goal — and in many ways their achievement — was to revolutionize consciousness and culture, not to reform law and public policy. Determined to bring about a dramatic shift in the fabric of history, they did not form a single overarching organization but rather declared themselves a "movement."

Consciousness-Raising

These new activists wanted to transform consciousness, and they did so even with the term "feminism." Viewing it as too old-fashioned and circumscribed to describe their movement, they adopted a term of their own making: "women's liberation." This term pointed to freedom for women without limits and without pragmatic considerations of what was politically feasible. Small women's liberation groups surfaced in 1968 and 1969 in many places throughout the country. Much has been written about New York City, but early and influential groups emerged as well in smaller (often college) towns such as Chapel Hill, North Carolina; Iowa City; and Gainesville, Florida. Women's liberation periodicals published in Seattle and Baltimore were read in Los Angeles and Boston. Spontaneity and the lack of centralized direction or national organization were hallmarks of women's liberation.

A key component of women's liberation was a practice called consciousness-raising, which consisted of small groups of women — perhaps a dozen women meeting weekly — sharing personal and private aspects of their lives in order to understand female subordination. Accumulating their personal experiences into collective truths could free women from the belief that their lives were abnormal or that they were to blame personally for their alienation from norms of femininity. Ultimately, consciousness-raising rested on the conviction that "the personal is political," that the massive power inequities from which women suffered could be found in the tiniest details of daily existence. No longer was it trivial that husbands refused to change the baby's diapers, that construction workers harassed women on the streets, or that women felt inhibited from telling their boyfriends what they wanted sexually.

Groups of women's liberationists also worked to raise consciousness among a larger female public through dramatic public actions. They picketed and sat in at magazines from *Playboy* to *Ladies' Home Journal* in protest of their perpetuation

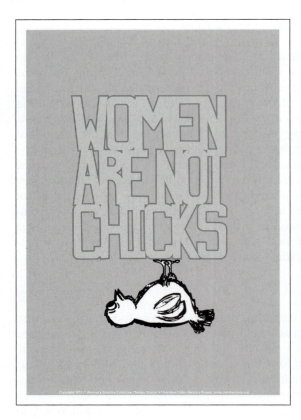

◆ **Women Are Not Chicks**
Founded in 1970, the Women's Graphic Collective, part of the Chicago Women's Liberation Union, created compelling, witty feminist posters that graced the walls of many a liberated woman's home or apartment. This widely distributed poster depicted a key issue of concern to feminists — sexism in everyday language. Women are not chicks (or any other kind of animal), this consciousness-raising poster made clear. The images were not signed because anonymity reinforced the sense of the collective feminist identity of the artists. Now the term "chick" referring to women and girls is commonly used in popular culture, with such phrases as "chick lit" or "chick flick" part of the language. Should today's women take offense? *Copyright © 1972 by Chicago Women's Graphics Collective, www.cwluherstory.org.*

of degrading stereotypes of women. The most famous such protest took place in Atlantic City, New Jersey, at the 1968 Miss America pageant, the site of a notorious "bra-burning" episode that has come down through history as a symbol for women's liberation. In reality, no bras were actually burned at the demonstration.

Lesbianism and Sexual Politics

Of all the changes in women's lives that came out of these consciousness-raising efforts, perhaps the most pervasive was the revisioning of sexuality from a thoroughly female point of view. No longer were feminist women willing to regard their own sexuality solely in terms of how sexy they appeared to men. Instead they concentrated on exploring their own desires. They suggested that intercourse might not be as good a way for women to experience sexual pleasure as it was for men. Rejecting widespread diagnoses of female frigidity, women's liberation celebrated the possibilities of the clitoris. "What we must do is redefine our sexuality," wrote Anne Koedt in her widely read article "The Myth of the Vaginal Orgasm"[8] (see pp. 682–83). Masturbation, long a favorite topic among young men, now became a subject of experimentation and discussion among women.

The most radical change in sexual thinking and behavior centered on lesbianism. The powerful new assertion of women's sexual desires, coupled with the exploration of the richness of women's relationships, encouraged many women's liberationists to pursue sexual relations with each other. "We were putting our energy into each other and slowly falling in love with each other," explained Marilyn Webb of Washington, D.C.[9] At the 1970 Congress to Unite Women in New York City, a group of lesbians took over the meeting, proudly declared themselves the "Lavender Menace" feminists had warned against, and challenged the women in the audience to acknowledge, accept, and even explore same-sex love. The legitimization of lesbianism within women's liberation was facilitated by the argument that loving women was as much a political identity as a sexual one. "Feminism is the theory, lesbianism is the practice," declared New Yorker Ti-Grace Atkinson.[10]

These feminist-inspired developments coincided with changes in lesbian communities (see pp. 552–57). A gay power movement exploded on the scene alongside women's liberation. Instead of acquiescence to a police raid on a New York City working-class gay bar, the Stonewall, on June 27, 1969, men and a small number of women fought back with beer cans and bottles. During the subsequent two days of demonstrations, the protesters chanted "gay power," a slogan modeled after "Black Power." The results were electrifying. The gay liberation movement spread quickly throughout the nation's cities; public demonstrations were often held in conjunction with protests against the Vietnam War.

In the early 1970s, many young lesbians worked from within the feminist movement, arguing that the root of discrimination against lesbians could be found in the oppression of women, and that an ideological commitment to women loving women was the only way to quash patriarchal power and achieve female liberation. Novelist Rita Mae Brown expressed this view powerfully: "I became a lesbian because the culture that I live in is violently anti-woman. How could I, a woman, participate in a culture that denies my humanity? . . . To give a man support and love before giving it to a sister is to support that culture, that power system."[11] With their passionate commitment to creating a "lesbian nation," these radicals advocated lesbianism on the basis of political ideology. This ideology, which reflected the growth of a style of politics based on group identity, sometimes led to conflict between heterosexual and lesbian feminists, even as it strengthened lesbian communities. Lesbians and gay men were also sometimes wary of each other and organized separately until the AIDS crisis of the 1980s led to a new era of collaboration.

Lesbian separatism manifested itself in women-only community institutions, small businesses, public spaces, and collective living environments. In cities from Dayton to Washington, D.C., women who wished to live, love, work, and play separately from men founded lesbian-oriented bookstores, cafés, women's softball leagues, and community centers. A thriving women's music scene generated a national recording company and annual summer festivals that drew thousands of women (the preferred term, eliminating the incorporation of "men," was "womyn"), creating the context for later artists.

The feminism of the 1970s was critical of the "butch" and "femme" roles lesbians had assumed in earlier times. It was also not particularly tolerant of transgender people and saw those who wanted to live their lives as and change their bodies to the other sex as embracing the very gender stereotypes that their movement opposed. And yet some transgender people understood themselves to be following the logic of women's and gay liberation — that gender is a social construction and that society should not dictate sexual expression — to its ultimate conclusion. Reconciliation between the lesbian movement and transgender people began to take place decades later, in the 1990s.

Transgender people participated in the early events of the gay liberation movement. In 1966, at Compton's Cafeteria in San Francisco, they led a fight back against police harassment that was much like the Stonewall event three years later. Transgender people were also affected by new medical procedures that were becoming available in the 1960s to allow for what was then called "sex reassignment surgery." While these could and were applied to infants with "ambiguous genitals" who were in no position to make decisions for themselves, they were also welcomed by adults who longed for ways to transition to the gender they understood themselves to be.

By the end of the 1970s, "out of the closet" lesbians were proceeding in two simultaneous directions: seeking to enter the mainstream and reasserting their radicalism. Local efforts to outlaw discrimination on the basis of sexual preference produced political attacks from the right (most famously in Florida, led by former beauty queen Anita Bryant, in 1977). These attacks in turn inspired gay and lesbian people to pursue political office. In Massachusetts in 1975, Elaine Noble became the first openly gay person elected to a state legislature. At the same time, gay men and lesbians transformed words, symbols, and behaviors once associated with contempt and shame into assertions of pride and confidence. Corps of lesbians on motorcycles, proudly styling themselves "dykes on bikes," led Gay Pride parades in San Francisco, New York City, and elsewhere. By the end of the decade, "queer" no longer signaled homosexual inferiority or self-hate; as a publicly claimed term of pride, it signaled the embrace of an ever-wider range of sexual identity and behavior.

Although the link between women's liberation and lesbianism is strong in popular memory, most women's liberationists remained heterosexual. Indeed, women's liberation encouraged utopian ambitions for revolutionizing intimate relations so that men and women could be genuine and full partners. One goal was that women would no longer need to choose between their own needs and ambitions and their love of men. Some marriages were shattered by the rise of women's liberation, but others were initiated or remade on an explicit basis of equality and mutuality. The women's liberation practice of women not taking their husband's names upon marriage began to spread among women in general.

Radical Feminist Theory

As women attempted to put into practice the ideas that emerged from consciousness-raising, feminists devised radical liberation theories. The central project was to understand the structures of universal male dominance. "Our society, like all other historical civilizations, is a patriarchy," declared feminist writer Kate Millett in *Sexual Politics* (1970).[12] One of the boldest statements came from Shulamith

Firestone, a twenty-four-year-old whose book *The Dialectic of Sex: The Case for Feminist Revolution* (1970) became an international best-seller. Like many radical feminists, Firestone worked from a left-wing framework garnered from her background as a student radical. Marxist theorists spoke of the dialectic, or contradiction, of class; Firestone wrote of the "dialectic of sex." The most basic human conflict was not economic but sexual, she contended, and its roots were nothing less than the biological distinction between the sexes.

Other theorists took the opposite tack, challenging the idea that differences between men and women were rooted in nature and thus fundamentally unchangeable. They documented the different ways that various societies formulated this distinction and how vigorously our own society worked to teach young children to be appropriately masculine or feminine. Part of the problem, they observed, lay with the word "sex" itself. Because it referred both to the biological capacity for human reproduction and the behavioral and psychological differences of men and women, it confused what was anatomical and what was social. To distinguish the two, women's liberation writers revived the obscure grammatical term "gender" for what anthropologist Gayle Rubin described in 1975 as "a set of arrangements by which the biological raw material of human sex and procreation is shaped by human, social intervention."[13]

◆ DIVERSITY, RACE, AND FEMINISM

Concerns with racial and ethnic diversity also reflected the influence of the civil rights movement on the first generation of women's liberation activists. Early anthologies such as *Sisterhood Is Powerful* (1970) included selections from African American, Latina/Chicana, and Asian American women to substantiate the claim that sisterhood was all-inclusive. Nonetheless, there was little cross-racial organizing within women's liberation. While white women withdrew from New Left groups to form their own all-female collectives, women of color tended to remain within mixed-sex (but racially separatist) organizations, unwilling to give up personal and political alliances with besieged male allies. As historians have begun to explore the feminism of other women of color more deeply, it is clear that Latinas, Asian American women, and Native American women, as well as black women, challenged sexism within their own organizations and promoted issues of particular concern to women, especially reproductive rights and access to community welfare services. Although many women of color associated with predominantly white organizations, those associated with racial nationalist groups felt ambivalent about allying with mainstream feminist women.

African American Women

For African American women, the concentration on male-female unity was especially strong in response to the 1965 publication of a federal report, "The Negro Family: A Case for National Action," authored by Daniel Patrick Moynihan, then assistant secretary in the U.S. Department of Labor. The Moynihan Report characterized the competence and power of African American women, in their families and in their communities, as "pathological," a holdover from slavery still affecting black Americans. The report was intended to aid in the advancement of African Americans, but written as it was before the emergence of women's liberation, it did so by blaming black women for single-parent households and rising male unemployment. Here was a federally authorized report calling for greater male authority in the black community as a way to bring it into line with the larger society.

But the Moynihan Report alone would not have had such a powerful impact if it had not been for long-standing strains of racial antagonism within the history of American feminism, reaching back through the white-dominated women's movement of the early twentieth century to the Reconstruction-era split over black suffrage (see pp. 436–37 and 292–94). Further exacerbating relations with white women was black women's resentment at sexual relations between black men and white women in the civil rights movement. Put simply, many African American women did not trust white advocates of women's liberation to be truly inclusive in their struggle for freedom for women. One of the major challenges confronting the revived feminist movement was to face this history, overcome this distrust, and create a more inclusive, diverse women's freedom movement.

Despite their mistrust of white women's liberationists, women of color shared an interest in many feminist issues. Within the women's caucuses that they formed in their mixed-sex groups, they discussed and wrote about male chauvinism, reproductive freedom, and sexual exploitation. Simmering resentments about the treatment of women within SNCC led to the formation of the Black Women's Liberation Committee in 1968. "We can't talk about freedom and liberation," explained one of the committee's founders, Frances Beal, "and talk about putting women down."[14] The group later expanded to include Puerto Rican and Asian American women and renamed itself the Third World Women's Alliance.

One of African American women's most distinctive contributions to the activism of the period focused on the struggle for welfare rights. State welfare recipients had risen significantly in the postwar era, and most states, fueled by racially charged (and false) stereotypes that most women receiving Aid to Dependent Children (ADC) were black single mothers of illegitimate children, had cut benefits and tried to force women into the labor force (48 percent of ADC recipients in 1961 were African American).[15] In many places local agencies instituted humiliating home visits and "morals" tests. In protest against poverty and the indignities of public assistance, women, the majority of whom were African American, created local welfare rights organizations such as Los Angeles Aid to Needy Children (ANC), Mothers Anonymous, and Milwaukee's Welfare Rights Organization. In 1966, the same year NOW was founded, these groups staged protests in twenty-five cities (including Chicago, Newark, Los Angeles, Louisville, New York, and Columbus, Ohio), and later that year were brought together as the National Welfare Rights Organization (NWRO), which had both male and female leadership. Eventually women in the NWRO, spurred on by sexism within the organization and a desire to give poor working women more voice, became explicitly more defined as feminist.

Latina Activism

When Chicanas began to explore feminist ideas, they felt unwelcome in white-dominated women's groups but were charged by male comrades with being *vendidas* (traitorous sellouts) for allegedly following Anglo ideas. Chicanas particularly resented the argument that the truly authentic and politically devoted Mexican American woman was one who remained focused on her family and also complained about sexual harassment from their male colleagues. Many criticized what they saw as the Chicano movement's emphasis on *machismo*, arguing that it undermined women's ability to participate in the struggle for racial pride and justice. As Leticia Hernández explained it, "The men felt that they should be the ones to make the statements and they should be the ones to write the papers and that the women should be the ones to type the papers and women should be the ones who serve the coffee on the side and make everything nice and comfy for them when they come home from the 'war.'"[16]

To draw attention to women's issues, Anna NietoGomez and other Chicanas, including Hernández, at California State University at Long Beach founded the Hijas de Cuauhtémoc (Daughters of Cuauhtémoc, an Aztec emperor) in 1971, named after a 1911 Mexican women's rights group that the Cal State students rediscovered. Later that year the Hijas de Cuauhtémoc and six hundred other Chicanas from all over the country gathered in Houston for the first National Chicana Conference, crowding into workshops with titles such as "Sex and the Chicana" and "Marriage Chicana Style." Although productive, the conference also highlighted the tensions surrounding Chicana feminism: a significant number of delegates walked out, claiming that the organizers were too closely allied with white feminists. This tension was never really resolved for Chicana activists. Writing in 1973, Nieto-Gomez commented on the intimidation faced by "people who define themselves as Chicana feminists." They were frustrated by the belief that "if you're a Chicana you're on one side, if you're a feminist, you must be on the other side. They say you can't stand on both sides."[17] Not surprisingly, most Chicanas worked from within the larger Chicano movement in organizations such as the paramilitary Brown Berets and the student group Movimiento Estudiantil Chicano de Aztlán (MEChA) on behalf of welfare rights, reproductive freedom, and community control of social services.

Women in the Puerto Rican Young Lords Party had an agenda similar to that of other Latina activists and were unusually successful in pressuring their organization to take their concerns seriously. Anger over sexism in the movement in 1970 prompted them to make the personal political by calling for a "no-sex strike" against male leaders with whom they had personal relations until their demands were met. The result was that the Young Lords' central committee passed

◆ **Anna NietoGomez**

Anna NietoGomez, shown here at a conference in 1973, emerged as a Chicana leader at California State University at Long Beach. In 1969, she was elected to the presidency of the campus's MEChA. She persisted despite hostility from some of the male members, including an incident where she was hanged in effigy. In response to their frustration with sexism within the Chicano movement, Long Beach women, led by NietoGomez, founded Hijas de Cuauhtémoc in 1971, the Long Beach, California, Chicana feminist organization. In the 1970s, as a professor at California State University at Northridge, NietoGomez pioneered a Chicana Studies curriculum. Although she was denied academic tenure in a controversial decision, her contributions to the field were long-lasting. *Courtesy of Anna NietoGomez.*

a resolution that explicitly endorsed women's rights.[18] In 1971, the following statement appeared in a Young Lords' publication: "Third World women have an integral role to play in the liberation of all oppressed people. In the struggle for national liberation they must press for the equality of women. The woman's struggle is the revolution within the revolution."[19]

Asian American Women

Asian American women's activism was forged in Asian American groups that emerged in the 1960s around the issues of racial pride, identity, and particularly the Vietnam War. Women formed a number of local organizations, especially in Los Angeles and the San Francisco area, but mostly worked from within the broader Asian American movement. They were especially adamant about challenging insidious stereotypes of Asian women. The first issue of *Gidra*, a Los Angeles Asian

American movement newspaper, featured an article by Dinora Gil in which she insisted, "It is not enough that we must 'kow tow' to the Yellow male ego, but we must do this by aping the Madison Avenue and Hollywood version of *White* femininity. All the peroxide, foam rubber, and scotch tape will not transform you into what you are not. . . . Whether this is a conditioned desire to be white, or a desperate attempt to attain male approval, it is nothing more than Yellow Prostitution."[20]

Native American Women

Native American women participated extensively in the militant activism of their people in the late 1960s and 1970s. In 1969, a group of Native Americans began a two-year occupation of an abandoned federal penitentiary on Alcatraz Island in San Francisco Bay to protest the policies of the Bureau of Indian Affairs and to draw attention to the historic oppression of Native Americans. One of the main leaders to emerge was LaNada Means, a Shoshone-Bannock, who had also been active in antiwar demonstrations in Berkeley. Wilma Mankiller, who later became the first female principal chief of the Cherokee Nation, initially became involved in the Native American movement during the occupation of the island. Then, in 1973, reservation-based activists at the Pine Ridge Reservation, supported by the urban-based American Indian Movement (AIM), organized against local corruption. Women were particularly prominent. Ellen Moves Camp, a local activist, asked, "Where are our Men? Where are our defenders?"[21] Within days, they had occupied the Wounded Knee Trading Post, at the site of a devastating massacre in 1890, remaining for seventy-one days; however, the activities of women tended to be obscured by high-profile male AIM leaders.

Some women activists did speak out against the sexism they encountered within groups such as AIM, but others emphasized men and women working together within the movement against white oppression. Although most remained aloof from the women's movement, many Native American women were active in the 1977 National Women's Conference (see pp. 656–58). In the South, for example, Native women participated extensively in the state conferences that preceded the national meeting. In Texas, Choctaw Owanah Anderson chaired that state's executive committee, and in Louisiana, Native women called for an end to "coerced sterilization, hysterectomy, and other experimental practices on the bodies of women, especially poor, minority, and Third World women."[22] (See Reading into the Past: "Forced Sterilization.") Only 17 of the 2,916 delegates at the national meeting were Native Americans, but they nonetheless influenced a reproductive rights plank that condemned compulsory sterilization and others that called for federal policies to ensure tribal rights and sovereignty and to improve Native American health and education. They brought an emphasis on spirituality to the feminist movement by invoking the traditional power of "American-Indian and Alaskan Native women," pointing out that they "have a relationship to the Earth Mother and the Great Spirit as well as a heritage based on the sovereignty of Indian peoples."[23] (See pp. 649–52.)

READING INTO THE PAST

Forced Sterilization

By the late 1970s, resistance to the coercive sterilization of poor women became part of the larger feminist agenda of reproductive rights. This extract is from an article by Jean Horan that appeared in the radical feminist periodical Off Our Backs *in 1977. Drawing on materials from CESA (Committee to End Sterilization Abuse), Horan summarizes several court cases involving blacks, Native Americans, and Chicanas.*

Norma Jean [a Native American woman who was sterilized without her knowledge and who lost custody of her children because she was living with a black man] is bringing to trial a women's right to control her own body, to live with whom she chooses, and to raise her own children. She is fighting the power of racist welfare bureaucracies who control the lives of welfare recipients. Norma Jean is not an isolated case. There are numerous other cases of sterilization abuses:

Rosalind Johnson, a 20-year-old black prisoner sterilized without her consent in New York City. "They told me that it was a temporary form of birth control which could be undone. . . . At no time was I told that if I had either a tubal ligation or any sort of hysterectomy I would never be able to become pregnant again. . . . I try not to think about the fact that I've been sterilized but every once in a while it hits me. . . . [T]hen I get very upset."

Eleven Chicana women have filed a class action suit against hospital and state health officials charging that they were either coerced

Women of Color

Walking a careful line between embracing and challenging the premises of women's liberation, between promoting and criticizing their own communities and cultures, women of color raised fundamental issues. They asked in what way white women wanted to be equal, and to whom. The Third World Women's Alliance posed the following question: "Equal to white men in their power and ability to oppress Third World people?"[24] While women's liberation theory emphasized the overwhelming role of patriarchal power in the subordination of women, women of color insisted that the reality of inequality was more complex and that their lives were shaped by the intersections of race, class, and sex. This idea later gave rise to the term "intersectionality," first coined by civil rights activist Kimberlé Williams Crenshaw in 1989.

or deceived into being sterilized. Some of the women were presented with consent forms while in labor. Others never signed forms at all, learning later that they had been sterilized. One woman wore an IUD unnecessarily for two years because she had not been told that she had been sterilized.

Two black sisters in Alabama, aged 12 and 14, were sterilized in 1973 in a federally funded family planning program. Consent was given by their mother by making an X on a form she could not read.

Norma Jean's suit is important for many reasons, but underlying it is the fundamental and elementary principle that, as women, we have the right to control our own destiny.

SOURCE: Jean Horan, "Condition: Socio-Economic — Treatment: Sterilization," *Off Our Backs* 6 (January 1977): 6.

QUESTIONS FOR ANALYSIS

1. How does Horan's use of stories of specific individuals strengthen the impact of her argument?
2. How does she link the sterilization issue to the broader themes of feminism?
3. How does this excerpt review the influence of women of color feminism on agendas for reproductive rights?

The feminism of women of color took a major step toward articulating this notion of intersectionality with the publication in 1977 of "A Black Feminist Statement," authored by the Combahee River Collective, a Boston-based group of African Americans, many of them lesbians. They insisted that their "sexual identity combined with their racial identity to make their whole life situation and the focus of their political struggles unique."[25] They named their approach, which focused on their own oppression rather than the suffering of others, "identity politics." Their formulation encouraged a multiplicity of feminist voices, reflecting a diversity of women's experiences, rather than the unitary statement of a single, common "women's oppression" that had characterized the early white-dominated women's liberation years. Over time, these new, diverse approaches to women's lives and demands helped to shift the center of feminist energy and authority away from the white middle-class women with whom it had begun.

◆ **"We Cannot Live without Our Lives," Combahee River Collective Members**
This April 1979 photograph includes three founding members of the Combahee River Collective — Barbara Smith, Beverly Smith, and Demita Frazier — participating in the Coalition for Women's Safety Protest, which protested the murders of six (later twelve) black women in Boston and what they viewed as police indifference to the crimes. In a widely distributed pamphlet, collective members also criticized black men for addressing the crimes in terms of only race. The women insisted, too, that women should work collectively to protect themselves and not rely on men or the state for their safety. In words that clearly reflected the Combahee River Collective Statement, the pamphlet insisted that "As Black women who are feminists we are struggling against all racist, sexist, heterosexist and class oppression. We know that we have no hopes of ending this particular crisis and violence against women in our community until we identify *all* of its causes, including sexual oppression."[26] *Tia Cross.*

◆ THE IMPACT OF FEMINISM

As the ideas and experiences of women of color suggest, there were multiple forms of feminism and tensions among women activists over race, class, sexual orientation, and ideology. None of these tensions were ever completely resolved, but by the early 1970s at least women's liberation and NOW had moved closer to form a common feminist movement, with the former contributing the issues and the militant stance and the latter the organizational structure and focus on institutional and legislative change. By the end of the decade, feminists could point to significant improvements in women's lives, especially in their economic and educational opportunities and their ability to exercise more control over their bodies and reproductivity.

Challenging Discrimination in the Workplace

Feminist lobbying resulted in a raft of important federal actions on women's rights issues in the early 1970s, including legislation clarifying the inclusion of women in earlier civil rights legislation such as the 1963 Equal Pay Act and Title VII of the 1964 Civil Rights Act, which had created the Equal Employment Opportunity Commission (EEOC). An important piece of economic legislation was the 1974 law that "prohibited discrimination on the basis of sex or marital status during credit transactions."[27] And in 1978, Congress passed the Pregnancy Discrimination Act, which recognized the increased participation of mothers in the workforce and gave pregnant women explicit protection against workplace discrimination under the Civil Rights Act. Another valuable tool in the fight for equality emerged in 1971 when the Republican administration of President Nixon issued guidelines for federally contracted employment that went beyond banning discrimination by race and gender to authorize "affirmative action" in hiring. This process of expanding women's rights received crucial reinforcement when the Supreme Court began to rule that legal discrimination by gender was unconstitutional, including in cases where the law favored women over men. The first of these cases, *Reed v. Reed* (1971), involved an Idaho state law that gave fathers preference over mothers in control over the estate of a deceased child. The court found this discrimination by gender irrelevant to the purposes of the law and ruled it unconstitutional. (See the Appendix, pp. A-11 to A-12.)

With the Civil Rights Act's inclusion of discrimination against women clarified by further legislation, NOW, WEAL, and feminist lawyers both inside and outside of government increased their pressure on the EEOC. NOW's Legal Defense and Education Fund assisted women in bringing lawsuits against their employers. Women were also helped by the Women's Rights Project of the American Civil Liberties Union, cofounded by future Supreme Court justice Ruth Bader Ginsburg. The most notable successes included challenges to the steel and airline industries, to AT&T, and to Sears, Roebuck, and Company, where the focus was primarily on overturning patterns of sex-segregated labor that kept women clustered in low-paying jobs. (See Primary Sources: "Feminism and the Drive for Equality in the Workplace," pp. 660–71.)

Symbolic of the change in attitude of the EEOC was the appointment in 1977 of Eleanor Holmes Norton to head the commission. Norton, an African American attorney who was a protégée of Pauli Murray (see pp. 587–88) and a seasoned activist in the civil rights and feminist movements, pushed the EEOC to even greater efforts on behalf of minorities and white women. She was responsible for establishing guidelines against sexual harassment in the workplace so that finally in 1985 the Supreme Court agreed that harassment violated women's civil rights. One historian summed up her accomplishments as follows: "By the time Norton left the EEOC, American workplaces looked and felt very different than they had in 1964 when Title VII passed."[28]

As significant as national efforts were, local activists were central to the campaign against discrimination: they organized demonstrations against companies, picketed newspapers that ran sex-segregated help-wanted ads, and staffed telephone hotlines to offer advice about workplace discrimination. Some of these activities were sponsored by women's liberation groups. For example, the Chicago Women's Liberation Union sponsored both the Action Committee for Day Care to promote public support for child care for working women and Women Employed to help clerical workers organize for better pay, wider job opportunities, and general respect as workers.

Activism also emerged in the workplace when women coworkers came together to share grievances. This consciousness-raising led them to demand change, ranging from the right to wear pants to work to an end to what became known as the "glass ceiling" against advancement. As one historian has put it, "Women were organizing in steel plants and auto factories, in banks and large corporations, in federal and university employment, in trade unions and professional associations, and in newspaper offices and television networks."[29] Among the most highly publicized activist groups was the *New York Times* Women's Caucus, started in 1972. Not only did the women employees draw up a list of grievances concerning discrimination in pay, promotion, and opportunities, but they also challenged the sexist language in the newspaper. Eventually the *Times* agreed to establish an affirmative action program and to compensate women workers for past pay inequities. Similar grassroots organizing allowed women to break ground in other white-collar professions, as well as in skilled blue-collar jobs. (See Primary Sources: "Feminism and the Drive for Equality in the Workplace," pp. 660–71.)

Another approach to challenging workplace discrimination sought to address the concerns of poor women that had been raised by the national welfare rights organizations. In cities throughout the United States, women established organizations such as Wider Opportunities for Women (Washington, D.C.) and Advocates for Women (San Francisco) to help poor women break into the male domain of construction work by taking advantage of federal funds for job-training programs. Women of color provided leadership as well as the clientele for many of these organizations. In 1979, over ninety of these employment centers came together to create the Women's Force Network, which in turn established the Construction Compliance Task Force.

The gains for working women were nonetheless not as dramatic as the lawsuits, agitation, and organizations fighting against discrimination might suggest. Although sex segregation in the labor force declined and newspapers stopped running ads for sex-segregated jobs, patterns of sex segregation, especially in low-paying service and clerical work, did not disappear, and women at the lowest rungs of clerical work saw fewer of the gains. Women made inroads into skilled blue-collar work in the 1970s and even more in the 1980s. Despite some incursions into fields such as mining, firefighting, and construction work, however, many jobs traditionally associated with masculinity nonetheless remained resistant to women's employment. (See Primary Sources: "Women's Liberation," pp. 672–85.) Elite professionals experienced the most improvement in the 1970s: the number of female lawyers more than quadrupled between 1970 and 1980, while the number of physicians and surgeons more than doubled. Women also significantly improved their representation in middle-class professional and managerial positions.

Ironically, as some women achieved success in employment, women as a whole were worse off financially in the 1970s, primarily because of a worsening economic climate. After decades of prosperity and international dominance, the U.S. economy faltered in the 1970s, because of the high cost of the Vietnam War as well as rising competition from Japan and Europe. An energy crisis, prompted by the 1973 Middle East embargo on oil imports to nations that supported Israel, further eroded the economy, bringing in its wake high inflation and repercussions for automakers and related industries. As jobs disappeared, heavy industry regions, especially in the Midwest, began a process that scholars term "deindustrialization." The inflationary crisis, accompanied by increased unemployment (which reached 9 percent in 1975), led to hard times for many American families and was a crucial factor in bringing more working wives and mothers into the workforce (see the Appendix, Table 1, p. A-18).

Another factor that profoundly affected women economically was the rise in the percentage of female-headed households, which was in turn a reflection of higher divorce rates and an increase in the numbers of single mothers. Because of long-standing patterns of workplace discrimination, women heads of households generally had far fewer economic resources and options than men: "In 1976, one out of every three families headed by women was living below the officially defined poverty level, compared with only one of eighteen husband-wife families."[30] The position of African American women who headed households was far worse than white women's. In 1981, 52.9 percent of black women lived in poverty, while 27.4 percent of white women's households did. Dubbed the "feminization of poverty" in the 1970s, this reality indicated the difficulties feminists faced in addressing the deep structural and institutional problems that kept women unequal in the economy.[31]

Equality in Education

One way to promote long-term economic benefits for women was to improve their educational opportunities. In 1972, feminists succeeded in introducing Title IX of the Education Amendments Act, which prohibits sex discrimination in federally funded educational programs. Title IX passed with very little fanfare and took several years to become effective, but eventually led to a revolution in education, especially in high school and college athletics, by requiring that women's sports be funded at equivalent levels to men's sports. Title IX, as well as pressure placed on institutions of higher learning to adopt affirmative action policies, also brought tangible results in graduate programs. Between 1972 and 1980, the proportion of women among students who earned PhDs expanded from 16 to 30 percent, while the percentages of women in medical school and law schools grew, respectively, from 10 to 34 percent and from 11 to 26 percent (see the Appendix, Table 3, p. A-20).[32]

But equally important as challenges to discrimination in the schools, the content of education reflected the impact of feminism, especially the women's

◆ Women College Athletes

This 2016 photograph shows Autumne Franklin of Harvard at the NCAA championship preliminary event for the women's 400 meter hurdles. The passage in 1972 of Title IX, which prohibits sex discrimination in federally funded programs, transformed the world of female athletics. In 1972, only one in twenty-seven girls participated in high school athletics, but by 2012 two in five high school girls were athletes. In universities and colleges, women's team participation increased sixfold. Despite these developments, women's programs still lag behind men's: a 2012 study indicated that women's athletic programs at NCAA Division I institutions received only 39 percent of the school's athletic budgets even though women represented close to half of the schools' student athletes. *Phelan M. Ebenhack/AP Photo.*

liberation movement. Charging that the standard college curriculum ignored women's presence, women faculty and students laid the basis for a different sort of education. Time-honored generalizations were reexamined for their applicability to women. "Did women have a Renaissance?" asked historian Joan Kelley Gadol. (The answer was no.) Examination of entire disciplines revealed hidden assumptions about the gendered nature of reason and intellectual authority. The natural and physical sciences were found to be particularly unfriendly to women. To challenge the existing canon of appropriate topics for study, in the early 1970s graduate students began writing doctoral dissertations on the history of women, comparative anthropology of sex roles, and forgotten women writers and artists. Simultaneously, Title IX of the federal Education Amendments Act increased pressure on university administrations to hire women to remedy the colossal gender inequity in faculty staffing. Women's studies programs were established, initially on the very margins of legitimate academic study. The first such programs were founded in 1969 at Cornell University and San Diego State University. By 1973, there were over eighty programs and one thousand courses around the country.

Women's Autonomy over Their Bodies

The feminist movement also significantly transformed women's ability to exercise control over their own bodies. Determined to implement fundamental changes in gender relations, women's liberation groups sought to address the long-standing but unacknowledged oppression of women in their relationships with men and in the family. They particularly addressed women's health and reproductivity as well as the issues of abuse and violence.

One major concern was to bring rape and other sorts of violence against women dramatically into public light. Before women's liberation, rape victims were often suspected of dressing or behaving in provocative ways, and their testimony was distrusted by police and courts. Husbands were legally sheltered from rape prosecution on the grounds that sexual service was a wife's conjugal obligation. As women broke the silence around rape, it soon became clear how many sexual assaults went unreported. Women's liberationists held "speak-outs," in which they went public with their own experience as rape victims, and established crisis centers to help other women find support. They undertook state-by-state campaigns to make sexual assault within marriage a crime. They established shelters for wives who were battered and exposed the common police practice of keeping the lid on domestic violence.

Another indication of women's determination to uproot patriarchy emerged in their protest against the medical system's treatment of women. The authority of physicians, roughly 90 percent of whom were male, routinely went unchallenged, and women's complaints were often treated as psychological rather than physical. Focusing less on women becoming doctors and more on wresting the control of women's health from the hands of professionals altogether, some women's liberationists learned the skills of midwifery and encouraged women to give birth at home, not in obstetrical wards. Carol Downer of Los Angeles specialized in teaching women how to do safe self-abortions at early stages of pregnancy. The Boston Women's Health Collective, none of whose members were doctors, became expert on the topics of women's bodies and needs and produced a short book, *Women and Their Bodies* (1970), which eventually became the large, multiedition *Our Bodies, Ourselves*. Its foundational belief was that "women's experiences not clinical research by physicians represented the most empowering, most liberating source of knowledge."[33] The approach proved so successful that the book outgrew the resources of the original collective and was turned over to a commercial publisher for broader distribution. Now in its fourth edition, it is still in print.

The campaign to give women more control over their bodies also focused on the newest dimension of feminism, women's quest for sexual self-determination and in particular its relationship to abortion. Since no form of contraception was 100 percent reliable (the birth control pill came close, but the side effects posed significant complications), legal and safe access to abortion was important to heterosexually active women who wanted to have full control over whether, when, and how often they became pregnant. Although many states allowed doctors to perform what were called "therapeutic" abortions, in the postwar years access to these procedures had become increasingly cumbersome and expensive. By 1970, when it was estimated that 1 million American women a year had illegal abortions, an abortion reform movement surfaced that sought to widen the legal loophole that allowed doctors to perform medically necessary abortions.[34] The feminist movement aimed to go further, insisting that abortion was not a matter of medical practice or criminal law but a highly personal decision that belonged only to the woman who was pregnant. The movement to reform abortion laws was thus transformed by the rising tide of feminism into the movement to repeal them.

Starting in 1967 in Colorado, some states began to liberalize their abortion laws, and in 1971, New York State completely decriminalized abortion in the first six months of pregnancy. But as the majority of state legislatures resisted these changes, abortion activists turned to the federal courts to challenge abortion laws. Norma McCorvey, a young, single pregnant mother, was willing to be the plaintiff in such a case, even though it meant she would have to carry her pregnancy to term. She took the pseudonym "Jane Roe" and with her lawyers challenged the highly restrictive abortion laws of Texas. They won at the lower level, but the State of Texas appealed the decision to the U.S. Supreme Court.

On January 22, 1973, the Supreme Court ruled seven to two in favor of Jane Roe (see the Appendix, pp. A-12 to A-13). *Roe v. Wade* was the most important Supreme Court case concerning women's rights since *Minor v. Happersett*, a century before (see the Appendix, p. A-6). The decision effectively threw out as unconstitutional all state laws making abortion a crime. But the decision was not without its troubling aspects and effectively invited the states to rewrite their laws to restrict abortion more narrowly after the first trimester of pregnancy. With this inviting loophole, the battle for abortion rights began in earnest (see pp. 690–95).

Meanwhile, women of color were beginning to draw attention to another aspect of the problem of reproductive freedom. Throughout the 1960s and early 1970s, many poor women, especially those dependent on government aid, were subject to tremendous pressure from physicians and social workers to allow themselves to be sterilized by tubal ligation, often while lying on the delivery table in the midst of labor. The procedures were usually funded by Medicaid, a federal program for health services for the poor and were a source of profits for doctors and hospitals. Among women on welfare, on Native American reservations, and in the U.S. colony of Puerto Rico, sterilization statistics reached as high as one-third of women of childbearing age, a figure that activists equated to racial genocide.

The issue came to public attention in a series of lawsuits brought against hospitals that routinely sterilized poor women. In California, a group of Mexican American women sued University of Southern California/Los Angeles County General for nonconsensual sterilizations in the 1978 case *Madrigal v. Quilligan*. A doctor who testified on behalf of the women claimed that in the period 1968–70, elective hysterectomies at the hospital had increased by 742 percent, and tubal ligations by 470 percent. A medical student also supported the women's claim,

◆ Fighting for Reproductive Rights

By the mid-1970s, feminists' understanding of reproductive rights had moved beyond access to contraception and abortion to encompass the campaign against coercive sterilization, an abuse with its origins in public health officials' desire to control the childbearing of women in the welfare system. As this poster suggests, unwanted sterilization especially affected women of color: Native Americans, blacks, Puerto Ricans, and Chicanas. Because of the efforts of groups like the Committee for Abortion Rights and Against Sterilization, the U.S. Department of Health, Education, and Welfare created guidelines that eventually halted these practices. *Artist: Rachael Romero, SF Poster Brigade.*

describing, "an entrenched system of forced sterilization based on stereotypes of Mexicans as hyperbreeders and Mexican women as welfare mothers in waiting."[35] Although the women lost their case, their suit, as well as others brought by African American and Native American women, fueled the efforts of activists in groups like NWRO, the Committee for Abortion Rights and Against Sterilization Abuse, and Women of All Red Nations. Pointing out the irony that many states were willing to fund sterilization of poor women but were not willing to provide crucial health care for their families, activists linked the issue to their broader demands for community control of social services, including health, welfare, and education.

In response to the groundswell of complaints about coerced sterilization, in 1974 the Department of Health, Education, and Welfare issued guidelines requiring a three-day waiting period between granting consent and getting the operation. Even so, a great deal of patient advocacy at the local level was necessary to ensure that women understood the situation and had granted truly informed consent. The fight against sterilization abuse was important in clarifying that women must be able to make their own choices about their reproductive lives rather than have decisions forced on them by public regulations, institutional policy, or economic exigency. The campaign enlarged the abortion repeal movement into something larger and more basic, a movement for comprehensive reproductive rights for all women. Despite the early successes of this campaign, a drive to reverse the movement toward reproductive freedom began almost immediately and would fuel the rise of conservative politics in the late 1970s and 1980s (see pp. 702–3).

◆ CHANGING PUBLIC POLICY AND PUBLIC CONSCIOUSNESS

Just as feminism helped to improve women's opportunities and secure their rights to reproductive control and self-determination, it also made its mark on American politics and on public consciousness. In their drive to change public policy, feminists engaged as political actors in lobbying, demonstrations, and lawsuits, but they also sought more explicit influence in national party politics and mounted a massive campaign to pass the Equal Rights Amendment. At the same time, both in the patterns of daily life and in the content of popular culture, we can track the ways in which feminism entered the mainstream of American society in the 1970s.

Women in Party Politics

Women's political activism in the 1970s needs to be understood in the context of the tumultuous national politics of the era. Richard Nixon had been elected president in 1968 (and reelected in 1972) by promising to achieve "peace with honor" in Vietnam. Nixon simultaneously negotiated with and bombed the North Vietnamese, but his actions only deepened protests at home. In 1973, the troops began to come home through a negotiated cease-fire with the North Vietnamese. Nixon had also won support by playing upon the resentment that many white middle Americans — a group he called the "silent majority" — harbored toward the disruptions of the 1960s. A potent backlash was forming against youth radicalism, antiwar protest, the counterculture, and racial nationalism. Many voters north and south resented programs like affirmative action and busing to end segregated schooling. Still others balked at the monetary cost of the "Great Society" social welfare programs established by President Johnson. At the same time, Americans were coping with the failure in Vietnam, the energy crisis, and economic decline.

Despite being a candidate who promoted "law and order," Nixon contributed to a sense of disorder by plunging the country into a constitutional crisis. In 1972, Nixon's Committee to Reelect the President (known by the acronym CREEP) arranged for a covert break-in at the Democratic National Committee's headquarters in the Watergate apartment complex in Washington, D.C. The Watergate burglars were arrested, and, when they went on trial, evidence of high-level involvement in the episode, as well as a host of political "dirty tricks," began to accumulate. Despite the administration's cover-up efforts, in the summer of 1974 Congress began to draw up articles of impeachment. To avoid this fate, Richard Nixon resigned, becoming the only American president to do so during his term in office.

The lasting legacies of the Watergate scandal were profound, including both widespread public distrust of government and recognition of the political power wielded by the news media. Thus the women's movement of the 1970s bucked a trend of conservatism and pessimism. It was remarkable for its successes and for its optimism about the possibilities for social change, even as its successes helped fuel backlash politics.

To facilitate women's more equal participation in the political process, in 1971 a diverse group of women, including NOW stalwarts such as Betty Friedan, congressional representatives Bella Abzug and Shirley Chisholm, and civil rights activist Fannie Lou Hamer (see p. 577), came together to create the National Women's Political Caucus (NWPC). Its purpose was the election of women to political office and the use of political influence to affect public policy. Its ambitious goals were to eliminate "racism, sexism, institutional violence and poverty through the election and appointment of women to public office, party reform, and the support of women's issues and feminist candidates across party lines."[36] The caucus attracted a diverse group of women, including African Americans, Chicanas, Native Americans, and Puerto Ricans, and although they were not always in accord on specific agenda items, the group was responsible for significant gains in women's representation.

Pressured by the NWPC, the 1972 Democratic National Convention had three times as many women delegates as in 1968 and included numerous women's demands in its platforms, including support for the ERA and national funding for child care. Women Republicans to a lesser extent also saw their influence increase within their party. The NWPC chose to support liberal Democrat George McGovern in the hope that his successful candidacy would result in significant gains for women. They also vigorously backed an impressive but unsuccessful effort to give Texan Frances "Sissy" Farenthold the vice presidential nomination. The NWPC, however, lost an opportunity to make a dramatic statement in support of women officeholders when it failed to back New Yorker Shirley Chisholm, who had been elected in 1968 as the first African American woman representative to the U.S. Congress and now mounted a serious campaign for the Democratic nomination for president, the first woman and the first African American to do so. On the national level, the NWPC helped to increase women's influence in both political parties, especially the Democratic National Committee, but met with little immediate success in terms of electing women to public office.

The Reemergence of the ERA

Among the most potent political issues for feminists in the 1970s were the Equal Rights Amendment (ERA) and reproductive rights. The ERA, which sought to amend the Constitution to prohibit the denial of legal equality on the basis of gender discrimination, had first been proposed in 1923 (see pp. 484–89). Organized labor had long opposed the ERA for endangering protective labor legislation, but in the wake of the feminist upheaval of the sixties, the composition of the forces for and against the ERA changed dramatically. In 1973, urged on by female labor activists, the American Federation of Labor–Congress of Industrial Organizations (AFL-CIO) formally switched its position to support the ERA. In the wake of this change, working women became a mainstay of the pro-ERA movement.

This switch in labor's attitude toward the ERA flowed directly from profound changes in the place and prospects of women in the labor force. (See Primary Sources: "Feminism and the Drive for Equality in the Workplace," pp. 660–71.) Equal access to all occupations and equal pay for equal work were the most widely supported elements of the feminist agenda, and the ERA appeared to be just the tool to ensure economic justice for women. In 1972, the ERA easily passed both houses of Congress, and within a year thirty of the necessary thirty-eight states had ratified the amendment. As victory seemed imminent, few could foresee the long and protracted battle over the ERA and how it would lead to the emergence of an antifeminist movement (see pp. 689–90).

Feminism Enters the Mainstream

Although we may chart concrete developments spurred on by the feminist movement — especially those related to public policy — evaluating changes in women's consciousness, women's private lives, and public opinion is far more difficult. Nonetheless, demographic changes for the 1970s are striking. In contrast to the trend of the 1950s, women in the 1970s married later and had children later. Divorce rates rose dramatically in this era (from 2.2 per thousand marriages in 1960 to 4.8 per thousand in 1975).[37] The number of children born to single women increased significantly (for the period 1960–1964 premarital first-child births constituted 10.3 percent of all first births, while for the period 1975–1979 the figure was more than double, at 25.7 percent), and the number of couples cohabitating outside of marriage more than quadrupled between

1970 and 1984.[38] Survey data also suggest a rise in premarital sex, as well as an expanded repertoire of sexual behavior. At the same time as these changes in family structure emerged, women's participation in the workforce continued its twentieth-century upward trajectory, growing in the decade of the 1970s from 43.5 to 51.1 percent. Even more striking was the increase in the percentage of mothers in the workforce (40.8 to 50.1 percent).[39]

But to what extent may these changes be credited to feminism? Most scholars argue that the rise in women's participation in the workforce was prompted in part by the nation's economic decline of the era. Divorce increases may have been promoted by the feminist ideological critique of the family but were also influenced by many women's increased wage-earning capacity and to liberalization in state divorce laws. Similarly, changes in sexuality must be understood in part as a result of the technology of the birth control pill as well as the related sexual revolution.

Nonetheless, feminism undoubtedly sparked many changes in personal life. In 1972, *Life* magazine featured a cover story on feminist Alix Kate Shulman's marriage contract, in which she and her husband agreed, among other things, that both "had an equal right to his/her own time, work, values, and choices." The article was later reprinted in *Redbook*, and by 1978, according to one historian, "even *Glamour* magazine was explaining how to write your own marriage contract."[40] Opinion polls conducted during the 1970s and early 1980s also suggested that many Americans had changed their views on working mothers and embraced more egalitarian notions of household responsibilities. Moreover, by 1970, 40 percent of American women were willing to say to pollsters that they favored "efforts to change and strengthen women's status in society."[41] Working women particularly favored changes, and African American women were twice as likely as white women to be supportive.

What two scholars have termed the epoch's "cultural validation of erotic pleasure"[42] may well have spread to women in general through feminist arguments about sexual double standards and women's sexual empowerment. As one young woman said, "I may have had an unusual upbringing, but . . . I have the same needs and moods as a man, and I am not going to let some chauvinist pig stifle them."[43] One measure of this legitimation of women's sexuality was the popularity of fiction that presented women's erotic lives in explicit language from a decidedly feminist point of view. Erica Jong's novel *Fear of Flying* (1973) featured a woman's "uninhibited odyssey," which one critic characterized as a "decidedly new way of thinking about women."[44] The feminist and gay power movements also were instrumental in the decisions of homosexual couples to live openly together and to begin the campaign for legal access to civil union and gay marriage.

Another way of gauging feminism's impact is to examine its permeation of mainstream popular culture. One major breakthrough was the emergence of *Ms.*, a glossy, mainstream national feminist magazine that began publication in 1972. The term "Ms." was revived by feminists in the 1970s so that women would no longer need to advertise their marital status by having to choose between the appellations "Miss" and "Mrs." and was itself a reflection of the way in which feminism would

help to challenge unnecessarily gendered language. Under the editorship of journalist Gloria Steinem, *Ms.* magazine matured to feature high production values
and commercial advertisements carefully chosen for their nonexploitive portrayal
of women.

Elsewhere in the media, early feminist agitation often met with condescending
coverage with women's liberation activists' more radical critiques of patriarchy sensationalized or trivialized. Yet there were sympathetic treatments of the movement,
especially concerning liberal feminists' attention to economic discrimination. In
1970, an eleven-hour sit-in at the offices of the *Ladies' Home Journal* forced that
magazine to run an eight-page spread on the movement, with articles written by
feminists themselves. Later in the 1970s, *McCall's* featured a column titled "Betty
Friedan's Notebook" as well as a regular series titled "The Working Woman." However, critics have noted that even sympathetic treatments of feminist issues in the
mainstream magazines tended to dilute the feminist message by stressing women's
need to change from within rather than to focus on challenging patriarchy or
changing society.

A similar process may be seen in television. Sitcoms of the 1950s primarily
featured white middle-class families and the happy (usually) homemaker. In the
1970s, those shows' characters were still largely white and middle class but offered
broader possibilities in their representations of women that reflected the influence
of contemporary feminist issues. In *Maude* (1972–1978), Bea Arthur played a
middle-aged feminist who in many ways was a caricature that antifeminists loved to
hate: loud, domineering, and opinionated. However, the most controversial episode,
aired in the 1972–73 season, featured a sympathetic portrayal of Maude's decision
to get an abortion. By far the most popular "new woman" on television in the 1970s
was Mary Richards of the *Mary Tyler Moore Show* (1970–1977). Richards was a single thirty-ish career woman who settled in Minneapolis, determined, as the show's
theme song put it, to "make it on her own." One of the series' writers described the
writers' assumption that Mary "represented a new attitude, that you could be single
and still be a whole person, that you didn't need to be married to have a complete
life."[45] The show explicitly touched on feminist themes, including the centrality of
Mary's friendship with her neighbor, Rhoda, and Mary's chagrin that, although she
got the job as associate producer of a TV news program, her pay was less than the
man who preceded her. Despite this sympathetic treatment, it is easy to overstate
the feminist sensibilities of the *Mary Tyler Moore Show*. Although Mary didn't have
a husband or children, she was consistently nurturing and other-directed in her
relationships with her coworkers. The show's modern approach to the single career
woman allowed the producers (and advertisers) to tap into a young, sophisticated
viewing audience without seriously challenging traditional notions of womanly
virtues. Shows like *Mary Tyler Moore* thus reflected aspects of feminism but also
co-opted its more radical potential. Despite these limits, the media reflects the way
in which modern feminism became increasingly mainstream in the 1970s.

The growing influence of feminism in the mainstream was also evident in the
National Women's Conference held in Houston in 1977. The meeting, a follow-up
to the first International Women's Conference held in Mexico City in 1975,

◆ National Women's Conference in Houston

In 1977, the U.S. government authorized funds for a National Women's Conference, which was held in Houston the same year. The conference brought together a diverse range of participants: one-third were women of color, and one-fifth were conservative women. The conference passed the comprehensive National Women's Agenda calling for ratification of the ERA, reproductive freedom, lesbian rights, support for the rights of women of color, and action against violence and rape. Here U.S. Representative Barbara Jordan, of Houston, gives the keynote address. From left to right, the other women in the front row on the platform are former U.S. Representative Bella Abzug, then First Lady Rosalynn Carter, and former First Ladies Betty Ford and Lady Bird Johnson. A noted orator, Jordan was active in the civil rights movement and in 1996 received the Presidential Medal of Freedom. *AP Photo/ Houston Chronicle, Sam C. Pierson Jr.*

received funding from the federal government, and two former First Ladies, Lady Bird Johnson and Betty Ford, as well as then First Lady Rosalynn Carter, presided over the opening services. Gloria Scott, national president of the Girl Scouts of America, also made opening remarks. African American congressional representative Barbara Jordan's keynote address similarly reflected feminism's incorporation into the mainstream. Jordan noted, "None of the goals stated in this conference are incompatible with the goals of America. The goals of this conference, as a matter of fact, sound like stanzas to 'America the Beautiful.' "[46]

Jordan overstated the case. Many of the ideas presented at the conference were still radical to many, if not most, Americans. An important event in the development of American feminism, the conference brought together a diverse range of attendees: one-third were women of color. The high point of the meeting was the approval of the comprehensive National Women's Agenda, which called for action against domestic violence and rape, ratification of the ERA, reproductive freedom and lesbian rights, and a unified statement of the importance of rights for women of color. Coretta Scott King offered a hopeful vision of the future, declaring, "Let the message go forth from Houston . . . and spread all over this land. There is a new force, a new understanding, a new sisterhood against all injustice that has been born here. We will not be divided and defeated again."[47]

But even as feminists celebrated, they recognized that the Houston meeting also exposed a growing threat to feminist goals. As the various states elected representatives to the conference, conservative forces, including anti-abortion and anti-ERA activists, had mobilized and managed to secure about 20 percent of the delegates. At the same time, right-wing activist Phyllis Schlafly, who in 1972 had founded the group STOP-ERA (see pp. 689–90), organized a counter-convention in Houston and founded a new conservative coalition she dubbed the "Pro-Family movement." The counterconvention at Houston did not disrupt the National Women's Conference, but its attendees' activities were a harbinger of a resurgent conservatism that would transform the American political climate in the next two decades.

◆ CONCLUSION: Feminism's Legacy

The 1960s and 1970s proved an era of extraordinary ferment for women. Politically and culturally, the radical movements of the sixties and early seventies — from Black Power, the counterculture, and the antiwar movement to Chicano, Native American, and Asian American nationalism — were fundamental to women's history, reigniting a long-dormant feminist tradition and encouraging a new generation to rethink the meaning of freedom for women. Despite divisions and disappointments, the various strands of feminist activism led to improvements in many women's economic and political equality and changed the consciousness of millions who in turn challenged conventional notions about women's role in the home, family, and workplace. It might seem that feminism caused the deep economic and social changes in American women's lives, but it is more accurate to say that it resulted from them. Feminism gave millions of women a framework for interpreting their lives and served as a catalyst for mobilizing women for social and political change. Above all, from the special perspective of this book — revisioning American history through women's eyes — the modern feminist revival marked a tremendous increase in women's determination to take an active, conscious role in the shaping of American society.

CHAPTER 11 REVIEW

KEY TERMS AND PEOPLE

Terms

National Organization for
    Women (NOW)
Equal Rights Amendment
    (ERA)
Women's Equity Action
    League (WEAL)
Coalition of Labor Union
    Women (CLUW)
Lavender Menace
Third World Women's Alliance

National Welfare Rights
    Organization
National Chicana Conference
National Women's Conference
Combahee River Collective
Title IX of the Education
    Amendments Acts
Roe v. Wade
Madrigal v. Quilligan

People

Angela Davis
Anna NietoGomez
Eleanor Holmes Norton
Shirley Chisholm
Barbara Jordan

REVIEW QUESTIONS

1. What is liberal feminism? In what ways does NOW represent this version of feminism? How does it compare with women's liberation?

2. How did women of color participate in the women's movement of the 1960s and 1970s?

3. What was the impact of feminism on the workplace, education, and reproductive rights and sexuality?

4. In what ways did the goals of feminism of the 1960s and 1970s become part of mainstream American life?

5. **Making Connections** The text states on page 658, "It might seem that feminism caused the deep economic and social changes in American women's lives, but it is more accurate to say that it resulted from them." What were those changes and how did they impact the development of 1960s feminism?

PRIMARY SOURCES

Feminism and the Drive for Equality in the Workplace

DURING WORLD WAR II, ALTHOUGH WOMEN entered the workforce in large numbers and took on high-skilled blue-collar jobs that had formerly been closed to them, no feminist movement existed to rally women in sustaining their gains or in defense of their economic rights. When increasing numbers of women, including mothers of young children, continued their march into the workforce in the postwar years, sex-segregated labor patterns returned and women's work continued to be devalued. In the 1960s, however, the liberal women's movement associated with NOW and WEAL became a crucial engine for challenging deeply rooted discriminatory patterns, especially sex segregation, in the workplace. Women did not benefit equally or at the same rate of change, but legal challenges as well as consciousness-raising about women's rights and capabilities produced a dramatic expansion of their employment opportunities. As witness to these changes, photographs abounded in the 1970s that graphically documented the transformation in women's work. This essay explores a selection of these images. They record areas in which women achieved significant success as well as those in which change came far more slowly.

One of the most powerful tools for women seeking equal rights as paid laborers was Title VII of the 1964 Civil Rights Act (see pp. 645–47), but it was of little use until feminists put pressure on the Equal Employment Opportunity Commission (EEOC) to take seriously the constant stream of complaints women began filing as soon as the commission was established. Among the early challengers were flight attendants who faced demeaning circumstances in which they were treated as servants. But bread-and-butter issues tied to sex segregation in what one critic called a "pink-collar ghetto" were the most potent concerns. Airlines hired women exclusively and placed strict limits on weight, appearance, and age. They also refused to hire women of color and married women. Discontented flight attendants recognized that employment practices that defined a job as appropriate only to young, unmarried women devalued their work and provided justification for poor wages and disrespectful treatment. In 1968, the EEOC finally ruled in favor of an attendant who had filed suit against American Airlines for mandatory retirement. Other discriminatory practices were also disallowed over a period of years, and finally, in 1971, the U.S. Court of Appeals ruled that "female-only" hiring practices of the airlines were discriminatory.

Although these legal successes changed the face of the flight attendant workforce dramatically in the 1970s, opening up the career to women of color and to men, the profession still suffered from low wages, long hours, and recalcitrant airlines, problems that increased flight attendants' union activism and helped spur the growth of pink-collar unions in this era. Flight attendants also continued their complaints about airlines' advertising campaigns that sexualized them. A National Airlines series enticed passengers with the slogan "I'm Debbie [or Susan or Betty], Fly Me." (National also required attendants to wear buttons that said "Fly Me.") Even worse, Continental Airlines ads featured stewardesses who promised that "we really move our tail for you."[48] Frustration with this sexual objectification led to the creation of Stewardesses for Women's Rights (SFWR) in 1972. Reflecting the influence of women's liberation, the group announced that it hoped to "raise the consciousness of stewardesses" to their " 'slut-in-service-to-America' status." They vowed "to fight the demeaning treatment to which 35,000 stewardesses are subjected by airlines, crews, and male passengers[;] . . . to enforce airline compliance with Federal affirmative action guidelines[;] . . . to improve the economic status of stewardesses[;] . . . [and] to increase the promotional opportunities for stewardesses."[49]

The two images in Figure 11.1 are from *Newsweek*'s 1974 article on SFWR, which focuses on the organization's campaign to draw attention to health problems faced by flight attendants, including excessive fatigue and exposure to hazardous cargo. The image on the left shows members of SFWR, and the one on the right shows "Stews on the Job." What might have been *Newsweek*'s goal in juxtaposing these images? What does the photograph on the left suggest about the breadth of the influence of feminism in the early 1970s?

Other major targets of discrimination suits were the nation's phone companies. The major focus of complaint was sex-segregated labor policies that excluded women from highly skilled and better-paid jobs and funneled them into poorly

Photos by Lester Sloan—Newsweek

Stews on the job and on the march

◆ **Figure 11.1 Flight Attendants Protest Discriminatory Practices (1974)**
Lester Sloan.

◆ **Figure 11.2 AT&T Advertises for Telephone Operators**
Courtesy of the AT&T Archive and History Center.

rewarded positions, such as operators and clerks. Lorena Weeks, a working mother and a nineteen-year veteran telephone operator employed at Southern Bell in Georgia, was refused her 1966 request to be transferred to a better job as a "switch-man": she filed a complaint with the EEOC. In court, when the company claimed that state law barred women and minors from lifting more than thirty pounds, "Weeks pointed out that her typewriter, which supervisors made her move, weighed more than that."[50] She won the case in 1971, when the U.S. Court of Appeals observed that Title VII of the Civil Rights Act prohibits such "stereotyped characterization" and "rejects just this type of romantic paternalism as unduly Victorian and instead vests individual women with the power to decide whether or not to take on unromantic tasks."[51]

◆ **Figure 11.3 AT&T Promotes Women Installers**
Courtesy of the AT&T Archive and History Center.

Especially far-reaching was the success of women who challenged the behemoth AT&T, which employed more women than any other company in the country. A twenty-five-thousand-page government study concluded that the Bell system was "without a doubt, the largest oppressor of women workers in the United States."[52] By 1973, the company had agreed to significant restitution ($38 million to thirteen thousand women of all races and to two thousand minority men) and had transformed its hiring policies. Even before the settlement was finalized, AT&T embarked on an advertising campaign that emphasized affirmative action. Consider the 1972 advertisements in Figures 11.2 and 11.3. The first one explains that AT&T wants to hire male operators and the second shows a woman in a job formerly reserved for men. What clues do the images provide to indicate the kind of employment climate the company wishes to project? At the time, both of these ads would have been startling to many viewers. Do they have any shock value today? Does one seem more jarring than the other? If so, why do you think that is?

Other women challenged the sex segregation of one of the most dangerous fields of employment—mining. In the seventeenth century, Virginia slave women apparently engaged in some mine work, and labor shortages during the Great Depression and World War II gave some women opportunities in Appalachian coalfields. But in general, mining was historically one of the most jealously protected male occupations. Many states had laws prohibiting women's work as miners, and unions, employers, and male miners all resisted women's entrance into this male-dominated job category. In addition, notions of women's proper place in the home were particularly rigid in Appalachian community culture, where mining was a significant part of the economy. Beginning in the early 1970s, some individual women successfully challenged companies that refused to hire them. Then, in 1978, a group of Tennessee women created the Coal Employment Project and, working with NOW, won a massive class action suit against the coal operators for sex discrimination. As a result, individual women received financial compensation and over 830 women were hired in the mines. By 1980, there were 3,871 women miners, but this number represented only 3 percent of the total miners in the nation.

Although the numbers were small, these women provide insights into the experiences of women who sought to break down employment barriers in this era. Because working-class women were excluded from the only significant skilled-labor job in the Appalachian coal-mining areas, they had few job options beyond domestic work or low-paid service employment. Many poor women were on welfare. Most of the women who bucked community disapproval to become miners did

◆ **Figure 11.4 Women in the Coal Mines**
www.earldotter.com.

so because the job paid the best wages available in their region, and they recognized that the sex-segregation patterns of the mining industry limited their ability to earn a living wage. Even though mining jobs brought in more income, women who did become employed in the mines faced hostility and sexual harassment underground. They also found themselves relegated to low-level work that offered few options for advancement. Although many women worked well together and created bonds of friendship, sometimes across racial lines, their limited numbers and the nature of their jobs made it difficult to create women's work communities that could mitigate some of the hardships of their labor.

The photograph in Figure 11.4 was taken by labor photographer Earl Dotter in 1976 in Vansant, Virginia. Many of Dotter's images emphasize the hardship and danger of coal work, but this one strikes a different tone. What do the women's expressions and bearing suggest concerning their feelings about their work? Does the photograph give any clues as to why it was so difficult for women to challenge the sex segregation of coal mining? How might their reactions have been different if there had only been one of them?

Firefighting, a job as arduous and dangerous as mining, also saw small but symbolically significant challenges to male monopoly in the 1970s. Some women served as firefighters in the face of severe labor shortages during World War II, but for several decades after the war fire departments did not employ women as career personnel. According to one account, Arlington County, Virginia, hired the first woman career firefighter, Judith Livers, in 1974. The following year, a handful of cities followed suit and small numbers of women found jobs as firefighters throughout the country.

Figure 11.5 features the first women to graduate from the New York City Fire Department Training Academy. (They are, top row from left: Eileen F. Gregan, Catherine A. Riordan, Lorraine Cziko, Judith Murphy, Marianne McCormack, Janet M. Horan, and Maureen T. Harnett. Front row, from left: Brenda Berkman, Patricia A. Fitzpatrick, Zaida Gonzalez, and JoAnn Jacobs.) The city, as well as the all-male Uniformed Firefighters Association, had resisted hiring women. In 1977, Berkman and five hundred other women passed the written test of the Fire Department of New York (FDNY), but afterwards the FDNY instituted new requirements for the physical part of the exam. Berkman, an attorney, filed a complaint, and a New York District Court ruled that the FDNY policy discriminated against women and violated the 1964 Civil Rights Act.

After the court ruling, new physical tests were put in place, and forty-one women, eleven of whom were African American, qualified for a position in the FDNY in 1982. JoAnn Jacobs was the first black women firefighter in New York City. Unlike many of her female colleagues, Jacobs had a supportive chief in her first assignment and also benefited from the mentoring offered her by the Vulcan Society, an organization of black firefighters. Jacobs was particularly conscious of her status as a role model for young black women. She commented that her job "brought me a lot of respect. I loved wearing my uniform, especially as a black woman. You know? I'd walk down the street in my uniform and feel really special. Otherwise, you know—you know—they think you're a maid or a nanny or—you know because of the perceptions in this city and this society. . . . I felt that it was a higher calling in terms of letting young girls, especially, see me in uniform."[53]

After joining the department, Berkman founded the United Women Firefighters, an organization that mentored women in the city's firehouses, and she continued to be a leader in the fight against gender discrimination in firefighting. Although she had a successful career, eventually achieving the high rank of captain, Berkman faced continual hostility from male firefighters.

Tensions over women firefighters continued to disrupt engine companies across the nation into the twenty-first century. The employment barriers remain high to this day, and women still constitute a tiny percentage of professional firefighters (3.7 percent in 2013). Does the photograph offer any indication of how these pioneering New York women felt about becoming firefighters?

For many women in white-collar work, the struggle to break down sex-segregated labor patterns was just as difficult as that undertaken by blue-collar workers. Women

◆ **Figure 11.5 New York City Firefighters**
AP Photo/David Bookstaver.

were traditionally shunted into low-level office work, while men monopolized management positions. In many instances in the 1970s, office workers met with significant success in unionizing to gain some power in negotiations with employers and in their struggle to open up managerial positions to women. One of the most intransigent sectors, however, proved to be the banking industry, which became the site of one of the most publicized strikes mounted by women during the 1970s.

Like other banks throughout the nation, Citizens National Bank of Willmar, Minnesota, routinely kept women out of high-status and well-paid work in the bank: only one woman was a bank officer (and she made $4,000 less annually than the men she supervised), while no men were tellers or clerks. In 1977, when the bank passed over its experienced women workers to hire a man with no training at a salary higher than all but one of the women employees, the women protested to their employers, to no avail. Like countless other women workers, they filed a complaint with the EEOC and sought the assistance of the local NOW chapter. At the same time, they created their own union, the first bank employees' union

◆ **Figure 11.6 The Willmar Eight**
Photo by Jim McTaggart, Star Tribune, Minnesota, MN, © 1977.

in the state. The bank, however, was adamant in its refusal to engage in collective bargaining or address the women's concerns. In response, eight women employees went out on strike and organized a picket line in the freezing Minnesota winter. Their strike garnered publicity from all over the world, and they received letters from other women who pleaded, "You can't stop, you can't stop. Please understand you're doing this for all of us." As one striker, Ter Wisscha, proudly recalled, "It wasn't very long before it wasn't our strike anymore."[54]

In the end, after two long years, the strike failed. As a result of the EEOC's recommendation, the women received a small economic settlement in return for an agreement not to sue, but the National Labor Relations Board did not endorse the strikers' demand for reinstatement of their jobs. The bank rehired only one of the strikers at a job that paid less than the one she had left. Nor did the strike or subsequent unionizing efforts elsewhere make significant progress for women in banking or undercut the industry's sex-segregation patterns. Today, women represent 75 percent of the banking industry, but only 10 percent of all banking officers. Yet the strike, which became the subject of a moving documentary, *The Willmar Eight*, is viewed as important in part for its demonstration of the broad impact of feminism in the 1970s, even among women who did not call themselves feminists. Does Figure 11.6 offer any clues as to why the strike became so well-known? How does this picket line of white-collar workers compare to the striking textile workers depicted on page 463? Do their picket signs offer us any sense of how they view themselves as workers?

During the first decade of the feminist movement, women workers made perhaps the most significant gains when they broke down barriers that had largely excluded them from professional occupations such as law and medicine. Less numerous but nonetheless noteworthy pioneer professionals were women who became ordained as rabbis or ministers in this era. As the seventeenth-century story of Anne Hutchinson indicates (see pp. 64–67), women have been spiritual leaders throughout American history, but rarely have they become leaders in organized religion. During the 1970s, feminist theologian Mary Daly urged women to leave their patriarchal churches and create new communities of religious women. But most women sought change from within. Black and white women were active within the National Council of Churches of Christ and its allied group Church Women United, which agitated for more women leaders and attention to women's issues within the churches. The struggle to gain acceptance for female clerics met with mixed success. Catholic women failed in their 1975 call (and subsequent calls) for women's acceptance into the priesthood. However, as early as 1970, some Lutheran denominations ordained women, and in 1976 the Episcopalian church bowed to pressure and agreed to women's ordination.

Jewish women as a group were highly attracted to the feminist movement, and it is not surprising that they would exert pressure for change within Judaism. Especially among Reform and Conservative congregations, the two largest wings of American Judaism, and in the smaller group of Reconstructionists, feminists succeeded in bringing women's issues into their congregations and religious practices. Conservative women established Ezrat Nashim in 1972 to press for equality in Jewish religious observance, but it was not until 1985 that Conservatives began to ordain women. The movement for female ordination had to counter a three-thousand-year-old tradition of male leadership in which the rabbi was revered above all for his great learning. In 1972, Sally Preisand, a Reform Jew who studied at Hebrew Union College in Ohio, became the first American woman to be ordained as a rabbi. Preisand did not start her quest for ordination from an explicitly feminist perspective, but she became a central figure among Jewish feminists who sought equality within the Jewish faith.

◆ **Figure 11.7 Rabbi Sally Preisand**
© *TopFoto/The Image Works.*

Figure 11.7 is a photograph of Preisand in 1972. The power of this photograph might not be immediately

◆ **Figure 11.8** "Hire him. He's got great legs."
Legal Momentum, the Women's Legal Defense and Education Fund (formerly NOW LDEF).

evident to anyone not familiar with Judaism. It shows Preisand with the central ritual object of Jewish practice, the first five books of the Old Testament, handwritten on a parchment scroll. The rabbi's job is to teach the contents of the Torah and the long interpretive tradition that accompanies it. Why might some religions have been easier to integrate at the clerical level than others? Is the image of a woman presiding over public religious practice still somewhat shocking?

Everywhere Americans turned in the 1970s, they saw images that challenged conventional notions of women's proper place, especially women's proper place in the workforce. A final example of this challenge comes from NOW's Legal Defense and Education Fund (LDEF), which in the early 1970s mounted an advertising campaign to raise public consciousness about the employment discrimination women faced. With the help of free creative services from J. Walter Thompson and other advertising agencies, in 1973 the LDEF ran a series of print ads that appeared in mainstream magazines such as *Time*, *Saturday Review*, and *BusinessWeek*, as well as thirty-second television commercials. In both cases the advertisements appeared as free-of-charge public service ads. Midge Kovacs, head of the Image

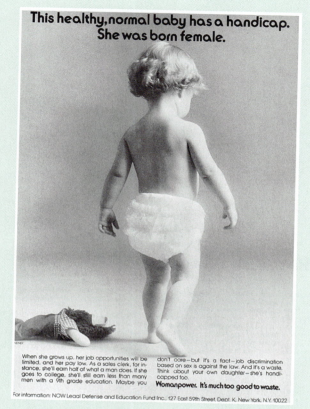

This healthy, normal baby has a handicap. She was born female.

When she grows up, her job opportunities will be limited, and her pay low. As a sales clerk, for instance, she'll earn half of what a man does. If she goes to college, she'll still earn less than many men with a 9th grade education. Maybe you don't care—but it's a fact—job discrimination based on sex is against the law. And it's a waste. Think about your own daughter—she's handicapped too.

Womanpower. It's much too good to waste.

For information: NOW Legal Defense and Education Fund Inc., 127 East 59th Street, Dept. K, New York, N.Y. 10022

◆ **Figure 11.9** "This healthy, normal baby has a handicap. She was born female."
Legal Momentum, the Women's Legal Defense and Education Fund (formerly NOW LDEF).

Committee of NOW, was responsible for the campaign; she commented, "We hope it will make all Americans aware of the limited aspirations of girls and the limited opportunities for women, and that they will act to do something about both."[55]

The two print ads reproduced in Figures 11.8 and 11.9 take two different approaches. What point is being stressed in "Hire him. He's got great legs"? How is that point different from the one stressed in the ad featuring the baby? In what ways and for whom would the two ads have been effective? Kovacs later commented that she regretted that the initial ad series contained no images of women of color. Several years later, the LDEF ran the advertisement in Figure 11.10. Besides the race of the two children, what are the differences in the ways in which Figures 11.9 and 11.10 attempt to convey their messages? One of the rationales behind the LDEF campaign was to counter the pervasive sexism in advertising, including those that devalued women's work. How successful do you think these advertisements were in meeting this challenge?

◆ **Figure 11.10** "When I grow up, I'm going to be a judge, or a senator or maybe president."
Legal Momentum, the Women's Legal Defense and Education Fund (formerly NOW LDEF).

QUESTIONS FOR ANALYSIS

1. How do these images convey the changing nature of women's work in the 1970s?

2. To what extent do these images reflect the impact of feminism?

3. This essay has emphasized change. Taking into account the chapter's analysis of women's work in this period, what other sorts of images would be necessary to convey the broad contours of women's paid labor, especially in those areas where change was less dramatic?

Women's Liberation

W̲OMEN'S LIBERATION ACTIVISM̲ produced an immense amount of feminist literature, most of which was published in organizational journals and newsletters. The late 1960s and 1970s saw an explosion of these periodicals, with eighty-five debuting in 1970 alone. Many of these were modeled after the underground newspapers that had been the staple of the New Left and were the result of New Left women's frustration over the control and content of these newspapers. One of the most famous of the early feminist salvos, Robin Morgan's "Goodbye to All That," grew out of this anger. Morgan detailed how women engineered the takeover of the New York newspaper *Rat*, whose sometimes pornographic articles, graphics, and advertising were demeaning to women. She explained, "No more, brothers. No more well-meaning ignorance, no more co-optation, no more assuming that this thing we're all fighting for is the same: one revolution under man, with liberty and justice for all."[56]

These alternative periodicals spread feminist ideology, with its commitment to collective rather than individual identity and to the elimination of hierarchical structures. As one scholar has noted, the writers "were not communicating about something outside themselves, as mass media journalists might. They were communicating about their own ideas, activities, and the growing movement among women."[57] Fortunately, much of the early, ephemeral women's liberation literature survives in major archives with online access. These archives include Duke University's Documents from the Women's Liberation Movement and the Chicago Women's Liberation Herstory Project. Their survival is in part a result of feminists' recognition that they were making history, a point evident in the comments of the editors of *Notes from the First Year*, a publication of New York Radical Women: "We needed a movement periodical which would expand with the movement," and "reflect its growth accurately, and in time become a historical record, functioning politically as much as did Stanton's and Anthony's Revolution exactly a century ago."[58]

The documents excerpted here demonstrate some key themes of the early women's liberation movement: its roots in New Left politics and racial and ethnic nationalist movements, the critique of patriarchy, the ambivalence of women of color toward white feminists, the ideology of political lesbianism, the call for women to exert control over their sexuality, the technique of consciousness-raising, and the recognition that the "personal is political." Women's liberationists are often termed "radical feminists," in part to distinguish them from the liberals associated with NOW. As you read these documents, all written between 1969 and 1971, consider why they might have been considered radical when they were published. Do they still seem radical today? Why or why not?

WOMEN BEGAN TO ABANDON THE New Left in early 1969, frustrated with male leaders' unwillingness to take gender issues and sexism seriously. Scores of organizations sprang up, from the Redstockings in New York City to the Chicago Women's Liberation Union to Gainesville Women's Liberation in Florida. In theorizing about feminism, women's liberationists articulated a feminist ideology that reflected both their socialist roots and their innovative critique of patriarchy. This selection by Jo Freeman, from the first issue of Chicago's newsletter *Voice of the Women's Liberation Movement*, explicitly challenges men in the New Left (referred to as "the Movement"). What are her criticisms of male leaders of the left? Why does she think women need to organize?

JO FREEMAN
What in the Hell Is Women's Liberation Anyway? (1968)

To list all the ways in which our society exploits women would be overwhelming and unnecessary. There are so many, and they are so endemic to our social organization, that women can be liberated only with a total restructuring of this society. Likewise, because this exploitation is so intrinsic, restructuring of society can be significant only in so far as it incorporates the changes necessary for women to be liberated.

Women's liberation does not mean equality with men. Mere equality is not enough. Equality in an unjust society is meaningless. Inequality in a just society is a contradiction in terms. We want equality in a just society. And this means the encouragement and opportunity of all individuals to be fully themselves to explore, express and develop their human potentials to the greatest extent possible unconfined by the narrow bounds of societal stereotypes. . . .

Altho women in the Movement have long been aware of their secondery [*sic*] status within and without the movement it is only recently that they have begun to do something about it. Since a small group of women began their first searching meetings last fall the movement for women's liberation has grown to a nationwide network of women who recognize the interdependence of radical change and women's liberation.

Our political awareness of these twin concerns has developed as we sought to apply the principles of justice, equality, mutual respect and dignity which we learned from the movement to the lives we lived as part of the movement only to come up against the solid wall of male chauvinism.

It is time that Movement men realized that they cannot speak the languages of freedom while treating women in the same dehumanizing manner as their establishment peers. It is time Movement women realized this is a social problem of national significance not at all confined to our struggle for personal liberation within the Movement and that, as such, must be approached politically.

The time has come for us to take the initiative in organizing ourselves for our liberation, and in organizing all women, around issues which directly affect their lives, to see the need for fundamental social change.

As women radicals we are involved with political issues because we realize that we cannot be

SOURCE: Jo Freeman, "What in the Hell Is Women's Liberation Anyway?" *Voice of the Women's Liberation Movement*, March 1968, 1, 4, The CWLU Herstory Website Archive, https://www.uic.edu/orgs/cwluherstory/CWLUArchive/voice.html (accessed March 17, 2015).

free until all people are free. But as radical women we are not interested in forming a women's auxiliary to the Movement. Our interest is in thoroughly integrating that movement particularly its leadership and policymaking positions. To this end we feel it is necessary to create women's groups to organize other women into the Movement and to organize ourselves to take power.

THE THIRD WORLD WOMEN'S ALLIANCE emerged from an earlier organization, the Black Women's Alliance, founded by Frances Beal and other women in SNCC (see pp. 575–76). The term "third world" was drawn from the language of geopolitics to characterize underdeveloped nations and peoples who were outside the "first world / second world" antagonisms of the Cold War. As the following statement indicates, the group changed its title and broadened its focus when Puerto Rican and Asian women joined. The organization, probably numbering about two hundred, had members in Cambridge, Massachusetts, and New York City and lasted through the 1970s. Like later organizations founded by women of color, it emphasized the intersection of race, class, and gender in understanding the oppression they experienced. Why does the statement stress the myth of the black matriarchy (see pp. 637–39)? What criticisms does it make of white feminists? What premises do the statement's authors share with white feminists?

THIRD WORLD WOMEN'S ALLIANCE
Statement (1971)

The Third World Women's Alliance started about December, 1968. Within SNCC (Student Nonviolent Coordinating Committee) a Black women's liberation committee was established and a number of women who had been meeting over a period of a few months decided that we would be drawing in women from other organizations, and that we would be attracting welfare mothers, community workers, and campus radicals — so we decided to change the name to the Black Women's Alliance. As of now, the organization is independent of SNCC and at the same time SNCC has decided to retain its women's caucus.

We decided to form a Black women's organization for many reasons. One was and still is, the widespread myth and concept in the Black community of the matriarchy. We stated that the concept of the matriarchy was a myth and that it has never existed. Our position would be to expose this myth. There was also the widespread concept that by some miracle the oppression of slavery for the Black woman was not as degrading, not as horrifying, not as barbaric [as for men]. However, we state that in any society where men are not yet free, women are less free because we are further enslaved by our sex.

Now we noticed another interesting thing. And that is, that with the rise of Black nationalism and the rejection of white middle class norms and values, that this rejection of whiteness — white cultures, white norms and values — took a different

SOURCE: Rosalyn Baxandall and Linda Gordon, eds., *Dear Sisters: Dispatches from the Women's Liberation Movement* (New York: Basic Books, 2000), 65.

turn when it came to the Black woman. That is, Black men defined the role of black women in the movement. They stated that our role was a supportive one; others stated that we must become breeders and provide an army; still others stated that we had kotex power or pussy power. We opposed these concepts also stating that a true revolutionary movement enhances the status of women.

Now one of the changes that have taken place in the organization, is that we recognize the need for Third World solidarity. That is, we could not express support for Asia, Africa and Latin America and at the same time, ignore non-Black Third World sisters in this country. We found that we would be much more effective and unified by becoming a Third World Women's organization. So our group is opened to all Third World sisters because our oppression is basically caused by the same factors and our enemy is the same. The name of the organization has been changed to reflect this new awareness and composition of the group—THIRD WORLD WOMEN'S ALLIANCE.

Some women in the movement cannot understand why we exclude whites from our meetings and programs. The argument that we are all equally oppressed as women and should unite as one big family to confront the system is as artificial as the argument that Third World women should be fighting on only one front.

And to the white women's liberation groups we say . . . until you can deal with your own racism and until you can deal with your OWN poor white sisters, you will never be a liberation movement and you cannot expect to unite with Third World peoples in common struggle.

Most white women involved in liberation groups come from a middle-class and a student thing. They don't address themselves to the problem of poor and working class women, so there is no way in the world they would be speaking for Third World women. There are serious questions that white women must address themselves to. They call for equality. We answer, equal to what? Equal to white men in their power and ability to oppress Third World people?

It is difficult for Third World women to address themselves to the petty problems of who is going to take out the garbage, when there isn't enough food in the house for anything to be thrown away. Fighting for the day-to-day existence of a family and as humans is the struggle of the Third World woman. We are speaking of oppression, we don't need reforms that will put white women into a position to oppress women of color or OUR MEN in much the same way as white men have been doing for centuries. We need changes in the system and attitudes of people that will guarantee the right to live free from hunger, poverty, and racism. Revolution and not reform is the answer.

To some extent, Chicanas' feminism was similar to that of African Americans in that it was rooted in the nationalist movement of Chicanos and Chicanas that flourished in the late 1960s and 1970s. Here, too, women were leery of associating with white feminists yet felt frustrated by the sexism they experienced from Chicano men. In 1969, at a women's workshop at the Chicano Youth Liberation Conference in Colorado, Chicanas issued a statement, saying, "It was the consensus of the group that the Chicano woman does not want to be liberated." Although subsequent scholarship has suggested that these women were primarily concerned with indicating that they did not want to identify with white feminism, the statement proved highly controversial among Chicanas and helped to generate an upsurge in Chicana feminism. Two years later in Houston, at the first national conference of Chicanas, the tone had changed dramatically. In the following selection, Mirta Vidal, an Argentinean-born socialist, describes the issues raised at the Houston conference. "La Raza," which literally means "the race," is the term militant Chicanos and Chicanas invoked to describe the unity of people of Mexican descent. How did Chicanas describe the nature of the oppression they experienced? How did they get beyond the charge that women's liberation was a "white woman's thing"?

Mitra Vidal
New Voice of La Raza: Chicanas Speak Out (1971)

At the end of May 1971, more than 600 Chicanas met in Houston, Texas, to hold the first national conference of Raza women. For those of us who were there it was clear that this conference was not just another national gathering of the Chicano movement.

Chicanas came from all parts of the country inspired by the prospect of discussing issues that have long been on their minds and which they now see not as individual problems but as an important and integral part of a movement for liberation.

The resolutions coming out of the two largest workshops, "Sex and the Chicana" and "Marriage — Chicana Style," called for "free, legal abortions and birth control for the Chicano community, controlled by *Chicanas*." As Chicanas, the resolution stated, "we have a right to control our own bodies." The resolutions also called for "24-hour child-care centers in Chicano communities" and explained that there is a critical need for these since "Chicana motherhood should not preclude educational, political, social and economic advancement."

While these resolutions articulated the most pressing needs of Chicanas today, the conference as a whole reflected a rising consciousness of

Source: Alma M. Garcia, ed., *Chicana Feminist Thought: The Basic Historical Writings* (New York: Routledge, 1997), 21–24.

the Chicana about her special oppression in this society. . . .

In part, this awakening of Chicana consciousness has been prompted by the "machismo" she encounters in the movement. . . .

This behavior, typical of Chicano men, is a serious obstacle to women anxious to play a role in the struggle for Chicano liberation. The oppression suffered by Chicanas is different from that suffered by most women in this country. Because Chicanas are part of an oppressed nation if they are subjected to the racism practiced against La Raza. Since the overwhelming majority of Chicanos are workers, Chicanas are also victims of the exploitation of the working class. But in addition, Chicanas, along with the rest of women, are relegated to an inferior position because of their sex. Thus, Raza women suffer a triple form of oppression: as members of an oppressed nationality, as workers, *and* as women. Chicanas have no trouble understanding this. At the Houston Conference 84 percent of the women surveyed felt that "there is a distinction between the problems of the Chicana and those of other women."

On the other hand, they also understand that the struggle now unfolding against the oppression of women is not only relevant to them, but *is* their struggle. Because sexism and male chauvinism are so deeply rooted in this society, there is a strong tendency, even within the Chicano movement, to deny the basic right of Chicanas to organize around their own concrete issues. Instead they are told to stay away from the women's liberation movement because it is an "Anglo thing."

We need only analyze the origin of male supremacy to expose this false position. The inferior role of women in society does not date back to the beginning of time. In fact, before the Europeans came to this part of the world women enjoyed a position of equality with men. The submission of women, along with institutions such as the church and the patriarchy, was imported by the European colonizers, and remains to this day part of Anglo society. Machismo — in English, "male chauvinism" — is the one thing, if any, that should be labeled an "Anglo thing."

When Chicano men oppose the efforts of women to move against their oppression, they are actually opposing the struggle of every woman in this country aimed at changing a society in which Chicanos themselves are oppressed. They are saying to 51 percent of this country's population that they have no right to fight for their liberation.

Although women in radical movements often challenged men for the sexism evident in the movements they led, much feminist literature was meant for women and was specifically designed to raise their consciousness concerning sexism. Bread and Roses, a socialist feminist group founded primarily by white women in Boston in 1969, was one of the earliest women's liberation organizations. The name refers to the history of working women's struggles in the United States and highlights the historical consciousness that accompanied the growth of women's liberation (see pp. 633–37). The following document is a leaflet distributed at a pro–child care demonstration in Boston in 1970. Bread and Roses women supported community child care, so how do you explain their critique of the demonstration? What do the words they offer as starting points for discussions with friends suggest about their perspectives?

BREAD AND ROSES
Outreach Leaflet (1970)

Sisters

We are living in a world that is not ours — "it's a man's world." We feel our lives being shaped by someone or something outside ourselves; because we are females we are expected to act in certain ways and do certain things whether or not it feels right to *us*. We have had to teach ourselves to run off our real feelings and real desires — to be "realistic" — in other words, to accept the place we have been given in the world of men.

But it's no good — deep in our guts we know this. Cooking and cleaning and children have not given us the fulfillment the ladies' magazines promise even after we've followed all their recipes. Our most honest selves know there is more to it than being hung-up when our emotions fight against a [male partner's] casual sexual affair. Why have we always assumed it was *our* fault if the "new morality" wasn't satisfying us? What does it mean when men whistle at us on the street?

We are waking up angry and shocked, amazed that we didn't realize before. Women

SOURCE: Baxandall and Gordon, *Dear Sisters*, 35.

begin to name enemies: men, capitalism, families, neurosis, technology, etc. And in various ways we start trying to make changes. Some women — such as those who have expressed themselves in the platform of this march — look to the state and federal legislation to give us the unrestricted humanity which has been denied us for so long. They have decided to "work within the system." In other words, they say, "Let us into the world you men live in. Give us your education and your jobs and your public positions. Free us with childcare programs designed in your offices." Is this really what we want? How about female generals in Vietnam?

DO WE WANT EQUALITY IN THE MAN'S WORLD, OR DO WE WANT TO MAKE IT IN A NEW WORLD?

Women being ourselves and believing in ourselves, women finding the strength to live how we feel, *powerful* women, can lead the way to create a new kind of politics, a new life.

To join the Women's Liberation Movement, begin by talking with friends. Here are some words which might help to get started:

date-bait community-controlled childcare centers fathers my boss castrating woman *Playboy* rape fashions marriage high school abortions doctors pretending orgasms masculinity self-reliance

---

F OR MANY FEMINIST THEORISTS, one persistent problem was how to analyze the oppression of women in a way that clarified that the problem was not individual men, but rather the larger structure of patriarchy. In this abridgment of an article published in 1970, Boston activist Dana Densmore takes on the simplistic critique that feminists are men-haters who think that men are the enemy. If men are not the enemy, who or what is? What is your analysis of her advice to women for overcoming their oppression?

DANA DENSMORE
Who Is Saying Men Are the Enemy? (1970)

The question "Are men the enemy?" has always struck me as a curious one.

If enemies are perceived as that force against which one does battle and against whom (having killed off sufficient numbers) one wins, the concept is obviously inappropriate.

It is clear to me that in its form "I object to your attitude that men are the enemy" the issue is a dishonest one: it is an attempted smear or a

defensive counterattack against the force of our analysis. . . .

It makes it appear that if we do anything but embrace all men, whatever their individual attitude, as our friends and allies, treating them as allies however they treat us, if we so much as speak of men generally as "our oppressors," then it must be that we regard them as "enemies" in the sense of an opponent so all-powerful and implacable that he must be killed in order to be neutralized.

Of course we couldn't kill off all men if we wanted to, but the point is that it isn't necessary and we know it. It is the situation men and women find themselves in, the structures of society and

SOURCE: Dana Densmore, "Who Is Saying Men Are the Enemy?" excerpt from *A Journal of Female Liberation*, issue 4, April 1970.

the attitudes of women, that make it *possible* for men to oppress.

Given power and privileges, told by society that these are not only legitimate but the essence of his manhood, it is not surprising that a man should accept an oppressor's role. But if women refused to cooperate, and if they demanded changes in the structures, institutions and attitudes of society, then men, whatever their desires, could not and therefore would not oppress women. . . .

The distinction is often made in the female liberation movement between an "enemy" and an "oppressor." The real enemy, I think we all agree, is sexism and male supremacy; a set of attitudes held by men and women and institutionalized in our society (and in all societies throughout history). . . .

If the minds of the women are freed from these chains, no man will be able to oppress any woman. No man can, even now, in an individual relationship; all the woman has to do is walk out on him. And ironically enough, that is exactly what would force the men to shape up fastest. Not very many men could tolerate being deserted, especially over a political issue. And all that's needed is for the woman to learn enough respect for herself to be unwilling to live with a man who treats her with contempt.

Men are not our "enemies" and we should refuse to play "enemy" games with them. If they ridicule us or try to smear us or isolate us, we must laugh and walk out. "Winning rounds" with individual men will not bring our final victory closer and cannot change contempt and terror into a generous respect. Challenges by individual women to individual men have always been met the same way: threats, ridicule, smears, repression. These are the prescribed ways for men to defend their "manhood" against "castrating females."

Although many lesbians participated in the gay liberation front spearheaded by the Stonewall Rebellion in 1969, many lesbian activists worked within the women's liberation movement. In articulating an ideology of lesbian feminism, they not only shaped lesbians' feminism but contributed to heterosexual feminists' critique of patriarchal power and to the notion that the bonds of sisterhood link women together. Radicalesbians evolved from a group calling itself Lavender Menace, in reference to the disparaging term used by NOW leader Betty Friedan in 1970. Later that year the group electrified the Second Congress to United Women by taking over open microphones, removing their shirts to reveal T-shirts emblazoned with "Lavender Menace," and distributing their manifesto, "The Woman Identified Woman." The document makes few references to sexual intimacy between women and instead emphasizes "political lesbianism" (see pp. 634–36). How does the document explain lesbianism as a political choice? Why do Radicalesbians consider the woman identified woman essential to feminism?

RADICALESBIANS
The Woman Identified Woman (1970)

What is a lesbian? A lesbian is the rage of all women condensed to the point of explosion. She is the woman who, often beginning at an extremely early age, acts in accordance with her inner compulsion to be a more complete and freer human being than her society — perhaps then, but certainly later — cares to allow her. These needs and actions, over a period of years, bring her into painful conflict with people, situations, the accepted ways of thinking, feeling and behaving, until she is in a state of continual war with everything around her, and usually with her self. She may not be fully conscious of the political implications of what for her began as personal necessity, but on some level she has not been able to accept the limitations and oppression laid on her by the most basic role of her society — the female role. The turmoil she experiences tends to induce guilt proportional to the degree to which she feels she is not meeting social expectations, and/or eventually drives her to question and analyze what the rest of her society more or less accepts. She is forced to evolve her own life pattern, often living much of her life alone, learning usually much earlier than her "straight" (heterosexual) sisters about the essential aloneness of life (which the myth of marriage obscures) and about the reality of illusions. To the extent that she cannot expel the heavy socialization that goes with being female, she can never truly find peace with herself. For she is caught somewhere between accepting society's view of her — in which case she cannot accept herself — and coming to understand what this sexist society has done to her and why it is functional and necessary for it to do so. Those of us who work that through find ourselves on the other side of a tortuous journey through a night that may have been decades long. The perspective gained from that journey, the liberation of self, the inner peace, the real love of self and of all women, is something to be shared with all women — because we are all women.

It should first be understood that lesbianism, like male homosexuality, is a category of behavior possible only in a sexist society characterized by rigid sex roles and dominated by male supremacy. Those sex roles dehumanize women by defining

Source: Radicalesbians, "The Woman Identified Woman," http://scriptorium.lib.duke.edu/wlm/womid (accessed July 31, 2017).

us as a supportive/serving caste *in relation to* the master caste of men, and emotionally cripple men by demanding that they be alienated from their own bodies and emotions in order to perform their economic/political/military functions effectively. Homosexuality is a by-product of a particular way of setting up roles (or approved patterns of behavior) on the basis of sex; as such it is an inauthentic (not consonant with "reality") category. In a society in which men do not oppress women, and sexual expression is allowed to follow feelings, the categories of homosexuality and heterosexuality would disappear.

But lesbianism is also different from male homosexuality, and serves a different function in the society. "Dyke" is a different kind of put-down from "faggot," although both imply you are not playing your socially assigned sex role . . . are not therefore a "real woman" or a "real man." The grudging admiration felt for the tomboy, and the queasiness felt around a sissy boy point to the same thing: the contempt in which women — or those who play a female role — are held. And the investment in keeping women in that contemptuous role is very great. Lesbian is a word, the label, the condition that holds women in line. When a woman hears this word tossed her way, she knows she is stepping out of line. She knows that she has crossed the terrible boundary of her sex role. She recoils, she protests, she reshapes her actions to gain approval. Lesbian is a label invented by the Man to throw at any woman who dares to be his equal, who dares to challenge his prerogatives (including that of all women as part of the exchange medium among men), who dares to assert the primacy of her own needs. To have the label applied to people active in women's liberation is just the most recent instance of a long history; older women will recall that not so long ago, any woman who was successful, independent, not orienting her whole life about a man, would hear this word. For in this sexist society, for a woman to be independent means she *can't be* a woman — she must be a dyke. That in itself should tell us where women are at. It says as clearly as can be said:

women and person are contradictory terms. For a lesbian is not considered a "real woman." And yet, in popular thinking, there is really only one essential difference between a lesbian and other women: that of sexual orientation—which is to say, when you strip off all the packaging, you must finally realize that the essence of being a "woman" is to get fucked by men. . . .

Women in the movement have in most cases gone to great lengths to avoid discussion and confrontation with the issue of lesbianism. It puts people up-tight. They are hostile, evasive, or try to incorporate it into some "broader issue." They would rather not talk about it. If they have to, they try to dismiss it as a "lavender herring." But it is no side issue. It is absolutely essential to the success and fulfillment of the women's liberation movement that this issue be dealt with. As long as the label "dyke" can be used to frighten women into a less militant stand, keep her separate from her sisters, keep her from giving primacy to anything other than men and family—then to that extent she is controlled by the male culture. Until women see in each other the possibility of a primal commitment which includes sexual love, they will be denying themselves the love and value they readily accord to men, thus affirming their second-class status. As long as male acceptability is primary—both to individual women and to the movement as a whole—the term lesbian will be used effectively against women. Insofar as women want only more privileges within the system, they do not want to antagonize male power. They instead seek acceptability for women's liberation, and the most crucial aspect of the acceptability is to deny lesbianism—i.e., to deny any fundamental challenge to the basis of the female. It should also be said that some younger, more radical women

have honestly begun to discuss lesbianism, but so far it has been primarily as a sexual "alternative" to men. This, however, is still giving primacy to men, both because the idea of relating more completely to women occurs as a negative reaction to men, and because the lesbian relationship is being characterized simply by sex, which is divisive and sexist. On one level, which is both personal and political, women may withdraw emotional and sexual energies from men, and work out various alternatives for those energies in their own lives. On a different political/psychological level, it must be understood that what is crucial is that women begin disengaging from male-defined response patterns. In the privacy of our own psyches, we must cut those cords to the core. For irrespective of where our love and sexual energies flow, if we are male-identified in our heads, we cannot realize our autonomy as human beings. . . .

It is the primacy of women relating to women, of women creating a new consciousness of and with each other, which is at the heart of women's liberation, and the basis for the cultural revolution. Together we must find, reinforce, and validate our authentic selves. As we do this, we confirm in each other that struggling, incipient sense of pride and strength, the divisive barriers begin to melt, we feel this growing solidarity with our sisters. We see ourselves as prime, find our centers inside of ourselves. We find receding the sense of alienation, of being cut off, of being behind a locked window, of being unable to get out what we know is inside. We feel a real-ness, feel at last we are coinciding with ourselves. With that real self, with that consciousness, we begin a revolution to end the imposition of all coercive identifications, and to achieve maximum autonomy in human expression.

O NE OF THE MOST COMPELLING IDEAS to emerge from women's liberation was the notion that the "personal is political." Nowhere was this more explicit than with respect to women's sexuality. In consciousness-raising groups, women exchanged intimate details and recounted daily experiences, in the hopes of realizing that many of the experiences that women thought were unique to them (and about which they may have been embarrassed or ashamed) were actually part of a larger pattern of intimate sexism. By assessing the ways in which societal pressures shaped sexual behavior and reinforced male domination over women, women's liberationists situated the private world of sexuality in the political context of male/female inequalities. At the same time, they encouraged women to move beyond a mentality of victimization and to empower themselves sexually and otherwise.

Anne Koedt, a member of New York Radical Women, published "The Myth of the Vaginal Orgasm" in 1970. Freudian psychology had long insisted that women's orgasms were either good — to the degree that they were the direct result of intercourse — or bad — because they came from clitoral stimulation. Scientific studies of the way that women actually achieve orgasms challenged the idea of two different female orgasms, one generated in the vagina and the other in the clitoris. Koedt drew on this research in the essay excerpted here. How did the physiological experience of women's sexual climax fit with the women's liberation agenda? How did it coincide with growing interest in lesbianism? Why do you think this article made such a powerful impression when it was published?

ANNE KOEDT
The Myth of the Vaginal Orgasm (1970)

Whenever female orgasm and frigidity are discussed, a false distinction is made between the vaginal and the clitoral orgasm. Frigidity has generally been defined by men as the failure of women to have vaginal orgasms. Actually the vagina is not a highly sensitive area and is not constructed to achieve orgasm. It is the clitoris which is the center of sexual sensitivity and which is the female equivalent of the penis.

I think this explains a great many things: First of all, the fact that the so-called frigidity rate among women is phenomenally high. Rather than tracing female frigidity to the false assumptions about female anatomy, our "experts" have declared frigidity a psychological problem of women. Those women who complained about it were recommended psychiatrists, so that they might discover their "problem" — diagnosed generally as a failure to adjust to their role as women.

The facts of female anatomy and sexual response tell a different story. Although there are many areas for sexual arousal, there is only one area for sexual climax; that area is the clitoris. All orgasms are extensions of sensation from this area. Since the clitoris is not necessarily stimulated sufficiently in the conventional sexual positions, we are left "frigid."

Aside from physical stimulation, which is the common cause of orgasm for most people, there is also stimulation through primarily mental processes. Some women, for example, may achieve orgasm through sexual fantasies, or through fetishes. However, while the stimulation may be psychological, the orgasm manifests itself physically. Thus, while the cause is psychological, the effect is still physical, and the orgasm necessarily takes place in the sexual organ equipped for sexual climax, the clitoris. The orgasm experience may also differ in degree of intensity — some more localized, and some more diffuse and sensitive. But they are all clitoral orgasms.

SOURCE: Anne Koedt, "The Myth of the Vaginal Orgasm," in Baxandall and Gordon, *Dear Sisters*, 158.

All this leads to some interesting questions about conventional sex and our role in it. Men have orgasms essentially by friction with the vagina, not the clitoral area, which is external and not able to cause friction the way penetration does. Women have thus been defined sexually in terms of what pleases men; our own biology has not been properly analyzed. Instead, we are fed the myth of the liberated woman and her vaginal orgasm — an orgasm which in fact does not exist.

What we must do is redefine our sexuality. We must discard the "normal" concepts of sex and create new guidelines which take into account mutual sexual enjoyment. While the idea of mutual enjoyment is liberally applauded in marriage manuals, it is not followed to its logical conclusion. We must begin to demand that if certain sexual positions now defined as "standard" are not mutually conducive to orgasm, they no longer be defined as standard. New techniques must be used or devised which transform this particular aspect of our current sexual exploitation.

CALLING ATTENTION TO WOMEN'S ROLE in the family, and especially their responsibility for child care and housework, was another compelling way in which feminists demonstrated that the personal is political and brought their critique of patriarchy close to home. Pat Mainardi penned a witty critique of male privilege in the home for the journal *Redstockings* in 1970. How did she combine down-to-earth advice to women in their daily struggles over who would wash the dishes or change the diapers with an analysis of the power struggles between women and men? Do you think her critique is still valid today? Why or why not?

PAT MAINARDI
The Politics of Housework (1970)

Though women do not complain of the power of husbands, each complains of her own husband, or of the husbands of her friends. It is the same in all other cases of servitude; at least in the commencement of the emancipatory movement. The serfs did not at first complain of the power of the lords, but only of their tyranny.
— JOHN STUART MILL,
On the Subjection of Women

Liberated women — very different from Women's Liberation! The first signals all kinds of goodies, to warm the hearts (not to mention other parts) of the most radical men. The other signals — HOUSEWORK. The first brings sex without marriage, sex before marriage, cozy housekeeping arrangements ("I'm living with this chick") and the self-content of knowing that you're not the kind of man who wants a doormat instead of a woman. That will come later. After all, who wants that old commodity anymore, the Standard American Housewife, all husband, home and kids? The New Commodity, the Liberated Woman, has sex a lot and has a Career, preferably something that can be fitted in with the household chores — like dancing, pottery, or painting.

On the other hand is Women's Liberation — and housework. What? You say this is all trivial?

SOURCE: Pat Mainardi, "The Politics of Housework," CWLU Herstory Project, https://www.cwluherstory.org/classic-feminist-writings-articles/the-politics-of-housework (accessed July 30, 2017).

Wonderful! That's what I thought. It seemed perfectly reasonable. We both had careers, both had to work a couple of days a week to earn enough to live on, so why shouldn't we share the housework? So I suggested it to my mate and he agreed — most men are too hip to turn you down flat. You're right, he said. It's only fair. Then an interesting thing happened. I can only explain it by stating that we women have been brainwashed more than even we can imagine, [p]robably too many years of seeing television women in ecstasy over their shiny waxed floors or breaking down over their dirty shirt collars. Men have no such conditioning. They recognize the essential fact of housework right from the very beginning. Which is that it stinks.

Here's my list of dirty chores: buying groceries, carting them home and putting them away; cooking meals and washing dishes and pots; doing the laundry; digging out the place when things get out of control; washing floors. The list could go on but the sheer necessities are bad enough. All of us have to do these things, or get someone else to do them for us. The longer my husband contemplated these chores, the more repulsed he became, and so proceeded the change from the normally sweet, considerate Dr. Jekyll into the crafty Mr. Hyde who would stop at nothing to avoid the horrors of housework. As he felt himself backed into a corner laden with dirty dishes, brooms, mops and reeking garbage, his front teeth grew longer and pointier, his fingernails haggled and his eyes grew wild. Housework trivial? Not on your life! Just try to share the burden.

So ensued a dialogue that's been going on for several years. Here are some of the high points: "I don't mind sharing the housework, but I don't do it very well. We should each do the things we're best at." MEANING: Unfortunately I'm no good at things like washing dishes or cooking. What I do best is a little light carpentry, changing light bulbs, moving furniture (how often do you move furniture?). ALSO MEANING: Historically the lower classes (black men and us) have had hundreds of years experience doing menial jobs. It

would be a waste of manpower to train someone else to do them now. ALSO MEANING: I don't like the dull, stupid, boring jobs, so you should do them.

"I don't mind sharing the work, but you'll have to show me how to do it." MEANING: I ask a lot of questions and you'll have to show me everything every time I do it because I don't remember so good. Also don't try to sit down and read while I'M doing my jobs because I'm going to annoy hell out of you until it's easier to do them yourself."

"We used to be so happy!" (Said whenever it was his turn to do something.) MEANING: I used to be so happy. MEANING: Life without housework is bliss. No quarrel here. Perfect Agreement. . . .

"Housework is too trivial to even talk about." MEANING: It's even more trivial to do. Housework is beneath my status. My purpose in life is to deal with matters of significance. Yours is to deal with matters of insignificance. You should do the housework.

"This problem of housework is not a man-woman problem. In any relationship between two people one is going to have a stronger personality and dominate." MEANING: That stronger personality had better be me.

"In animal societies, wolves, for example, the top animal is usually a male even where he is not chosen for brute strength but on the basis of cunning and intelligence. Isn't that interesting?" MEANING: I have historical, psychological, anthropological and biological justification for keeping you down. How can you ask the top wolf to be equal?

"Women's liberation isn't really a political movement." MEANING: The revolution is coming too close to home. ALSO MEANING: I am only interested in how I am oppressed, not how I oppress others. Therefore the war, the draft and the university are political. Women's liberation is not.

"Man's accomplishments have always depended on getting help from other people, mostly women. What great man would have accomplished what he did if he had to do his own housework?" MEANING: Oppression is built into the system and I, as the white American male, receive the benefits of this system. I don't want to give them up.

Participatory democracy begins at home. If you are planning to implement your politics, there are certain things to remember.

1. He is feeling it more than you. He's losing some leisure and you're gaining it. The measure of your oppression is his resistance.

2. A great many American men are not accustomed to doing monotonous, repetitive work which never issues in any lasting, let alone important, achievement. This is why they would rather repair a cabinet than wash dishes. If human endeavors are like a pyramid with man's highest achievements at the top, then keeping oneself alive is at the bottom. Men have always had servants (us) to take care of this bottom stratum of life while they have confined their efforts to the rarefied upper regions. It is thus ironic when they ask of women — Where are your great painters, statesmen, etc.? Mme. Matisse ran a military shop so he could paint. Mrs. Martin Luther King kept his house and raised his babies.

3. It is a traumatizing experience for someone who has always thought of himself as being against any oppression or exploitation of one human being by another to realize that in his daily life he has been accepting and implementing (and benefiting from) this exploitation; that his rationalization is little different from that of the racist who says, "Black people don't feel pain" (women don't mind doing the shitwork); and that the oldest form of oppression in history has been the oppression of 50 percent of the population by the other 50 percent.

4. Arm yourself with some knowledge of the psychology of oppressed peoples everywhere, and a few facts about the animal kingdom. I admit playing top wolf or who runs the gorillas is silly but as a last resort men bring it up all the time. Talk about bees. If you feel really hostile bring up the sex life of spiders. They have sex. She bites off his head. The psychology of oppressed peoples is not silly. Jews, immigrants, black men and all women have employed the same psychological mechanisms to survive; admiring the oppressor, glorifying the oppressor, wanting to be like the oppressor, wanting the oppressor to like them, mostly because the oppressor held all the power. . . .

5. Beware of the double whammy. He won't do the little things he always did because you're now a "Liberated Woman," right? Of course he won't do anything else either. . . .

I was just finishing this when my husband came in and asked what I was doing. Writing a paper on housework. Housework? he said. Housework? Oh my god how trivial can you get? A paper on housework.

QUESTIONS FOR ANALYSIS

1. In what ways do these documents suggest the diverging concerns of white feminist women and feminist women of color? What similarities do they indicate?

2. Women's liberation pioneered the concept of consciousness-raising for feminists. What do these documents suggest about the themes addressed in consciousness-raising?

3. Compare the writings of these feminists to those of the early twentieth century on pages 475–79. To what extent are they similar, and in what ways do they differ?

NOTES

1. Nancy MacLean, *Freedom Is Not Enough: The Opening of the American Workplace* (Cambridge, MA: Harvard University Press, 2006), 130.

2. Francisca Flores, "Conference of Mexican Women in Houston — Un Remolino," in Alma M. Garcia, ed., *Chicana Feminist Thought: The Basic Historical Writings* (New York: Routledge, 1997), 160.

3. Toni Cade, ed., *The Black Woman: An Anthology* (New York: New American Library, 1970), 107.

4. Cynthia Enloe, *Nimo's War, Emma's War: Making Feminist Sense of the Iraq War* (Berkeley: University of California Press, 2010), 159.

5. "To the Women of the Left," in Rosalyn Baxandall and Linda Gordon, eds., *Dear Sisters: Dispatches from the Women's Liberation Movement* (New York: Basic Books, 2000), 29.

6. "Burial of Weeping Womanhood," in Baxandall and Gordon, *Dear Sisters*, 25.

7. Robin Morgan, ed., *Sisterhood Is Powerful: An Anthology of Readings from the Women's Liberation Movement* (New York: Random House, 1970), xxxv.

8. Anne Koedt, "The Myth of the Vaginal Orgasm," in Baxandall and Gordon, *Dear Sisters*, 158.

9. Quoted in Alice Echols, *Daring to Be Bad: Radical Feminism in America, 1967–1975* (Minneapolis: University of Minnesota Press, 1989), 212.

10. Ibid., 238.

11. Quoted in Lillian Faderman, *Odd Girls and Twilight Lovers: A History of Lesbian Life in Twentieth-Century America* (New York: Columbia University Press, 1991), 207.

12. Kate Millett, *Sexual Politics* (New York: Avon, 1970), 25.

13. Gayle Rubin, "The Traffic in Women: Notes on the 'Political Economy' of Sex," in Joan W. Scott, ed., *Feminism and Theory* (New York: Oxford University Press, 1996), 111.

14. Quoted in Benita Roth, *Separate Roads to Feminism: Black, Chicana, and White Feminist Movements in America's Second Wave* (New York: Cambridge University Press, 2004), 90.

15. Premilla Nadasen, *Welfare Warriors: The Welfare Rights Movement in the United States* (New York: Routledge, 2005), 7.

16. Maylei Blackwell, *¡Chicana Power! Contested Histories of Feminism in the Chicano Movement* (Austin: University of Texas Press, 2011), 69.

17. Roth, *Separate Roads to Feminism*, 157.

18. Jennifer Nelson, *Women of Color and the Reproductive Rights Movement* (New York: New York University Press, 2003), 120.

19. Michael Abrahamson, *Palante: Young Lords Party* (New York: McGraw-Hill, 1971), 117.

20. Susie Ling, "The Mountain Movers: Asian American Women's Movement in Los Angeles," *Amerasia* 15 (1989): 56.

21. Paul Chaat Smith and Robert Allen Warrior, *Like a Hurricane: The American Indian Movement from Alcatraz to Wounded Knee* (New York: New Press, 1996), 199.

22. Meg Devlin O'Sullivan, "Engaged in the Struggle for Liberation as They See It: Indigenous Southern Women and International Women's Year," in Tim Garrison and Greg O'Brien, eds., *The Native South: New Histories and Enduring Legacies* (Lincoln: University of Nebraska Press, 2017), 226.

23. Beatrice Medicine, "The Native American Woman: A Perspective," *ERIC/CRESS* (March 1978): 95.

24. Third World Women's Alliance, "Statement" (1968), in Baxandall and Gordon, *Dear Sisters*, 65–66.

25. Combahee River Collective, "A Black Feminist Statement," in Dawn Keetley and John Pettegrew, eds., *Public Women, Public Words: A Documentary History of American Feminism* (Madison, WI: Madison House, 2002), 3:77.

26. "Why Did They Die?" *Radical America* 13 (1979): 46.

27. Rita J. Simon and Gloria Danziger, *Women's Movements in America: Their Successes, Disappointments, and Aspirations* (New York: Praeger, 1991), 149.

28. MacLean, *Freedom Is Not Enough*, 145.

29. Nancy MacLean, "The Hidden History of Affirmative Action: Working Women's Struggles in the 1970s and the Gender of Class," *Feminist Studies* 25, no. 1 (Spring 1999), online at ProQuest (accessed July 16, 2007).

30. Winifred D. Wandersee, *On the Move: American Women in the 1970s* (Boston: Twayne, 1988), 133.

31. Ibid., 136.

32. Mary Ann Millsap, "Sex Equity in Education," in Irene Tinker, ed., *Women in Washington: Advocates for Public Policy* (Beverly Hills: Sage, 1983), 116.

33. Wendy Kline, *Bodies of Knowledge: Sexuality, Reproduction, and Women's Health in the Second Wave* (Chicago: University of Chicago Press, 2010), 42.

34. Flora Davis, *Moving the Mountain: The Women's Movement in America since 1960* (Urbana: University of Illinois Press, 1999), 158.

35. Alexandra Minna Stern, "Sterilized in the Name of Public Health: Race, Immigration, and Reproductive Control in Modern California," *American Journal of Public Health* 95 (July 2005): 1135.

36. Sara M. Evans, *Tidal Wave: How Women Changed America at Century's End* (New York: Free Press, 2003), 62.

37. Gerald C. Wright and Dorothy M. Stetson, "The Impact of No-Fault Divorce Law Reform on Divorce in American States," *Journal of Marriage and the Family* 40 (1978): 575.

38. *Statistical Abstract of the United States, 2000*, Allcountries.org, http://www.allcountries.org/uscensus/146_marital_status_of_women_15_to.html (accessed July 31, 2017); Sara R. Rix, *The American Woman 1987–1988: A Report in Depth* (New York: W. W. Norton, 1987), 74.

39. Rix, *The American Woman 1987–1988*, 107–8.

40. Stephanie Coontz, *Marriage, a History* (New York: Viking Press, 2005), 255.

41. Cited in Myra Marx Ferree and Beth B. Hess, *Controversy and Coalition: The New Feminist Movement across Three Decades of Change*, 3rd ed. (New York: Routledge, 2000), 8.

42. John D'Emilio and Estelle B. Freedman, *Intimate Matters: A History of Sexuality in America* (New York: Harper and Row, 1988), 337.

43. Ibid., 336.

44. Susan M. Hartmann, *From Margins to Mainstream: American Women and Politics since 1960* (New York: Knopf, 1989), 70.

45. Bonnie J. Dow, *Prime-Time Television: Television, Media Culture, and the Women's Movement since 1970* (Philadelphia: University of Pennsylvania Press, 1996), 25.

46. Donald R. Martin and Vicky Gordon Martin, "Barbara Jordan's Use of Language in the Keynote Address to the National Women's Conference," *Southern Speech Communication Journal* 49 (1984): 322.

47. Evans, *Tidal Wave*, 141.

48. Dorothy Sue Cobble, *The Other Women's Movement: Workplace Justice and Social Rights in Modern America* (Princeton, NJ: Princeton University Press, 2004), 209, 210.

49. Kathleen M. Barry, *Femininity in Flight: A History of Flight Attendants* (Durham, NC: Duke University Press, 2007), 192.

50. MacLean, *Freedom Is Not Enough*, 124.

51. Ibid.

52. Ibid., 132.

53. Interview with JoAnn Jacobs, "Sisters in the Brotherhood: Working Women Organizing for Equality in New York City," http://www.talkinghistory.org/sisters/oh_transcripts/joann_jacobs_interview_2004.pdf (accessed July 31, 2017).

54. Minnestoa AFL-CIO, "Workday Minnesota," http://wayback.archive-it.org/1837/20111012215735/ http://www.workdayminnesota.org/index.php?article_1_70 (accessed July 31, 2017).

55. *New York Daily News*, February 10, 1973, p. 14.

56. Baxandall and Gordon, *Dear Sisters*, 53.

57. Martha Allen, "The Development of Communication Networks among Women, 1963–1983," Women's Institute for Freedom of the Press: History of Women's Media, http://wayback.archive-it.org/1837/20111012215735/ http://www.workdayminnesota.org/index.php?article_1_70 (accessed April 3, 2015).

58. Ibid.

SUGGESTED REFERENCES

General Works

Maylei Blackwell, *¡Chicana Power! Contested Histories of Feminism in the Chicano Movement* (2011).

Sara M. Evans, *Tidal Wave: How Women Changed America at Century's End* (2003).

Estelle B. Freedman, *No Turning Back: The History of Feminism and the Future of Women* (2002).

Ruth Rosen, *The World Split Open: How the Modern Women's Movement Changed America*, 2nd ed. (2007).

Christine Stansell, *The Feminist Promise: 1792 to the Present* (2010).

Feminist Movements

Rosalyn Baxandall and Linda Gordon, eds., *Dear Sisters: Dispatches from the Women's Liberation Movement* (2000).

Patricia Hill Collins, *Black Feminist Thought: Knowledge, Consciousness, and the Politics of Empowerment* (2000).

Alice Echols, *Daring to Be Bad: Radical Feminism in America, 1967–1975* (1989).

Sara Evans, *Personal Politics: The Roots of Women's Liberation in the Civil Rights Movement and the New Left* (1979).

Lillian Faderman, *Odd Girls and Twilight Lovers: A History of Lesbian Life in Twentieth-Century America* (1991).

Elizabeth Lapovsky Kennedy and Madeline D. Davis, *Boots of Leather, Slippers of Gold: The History of a Lesbian Community* (1993).

Cherríe Moraga and Gloria Anzaldúa, eds., *This Bridge Called My Back: Writings by Radical Women of Color* (1979).

Premilla Nadasen, *Welfare Warriors: The Welfare Rights Movement in the United States* (2005).

Jennifer Nelson, *Women of Color and the Reproductive Rights Movement* (2003).

Benita Roth, *Separate Roads to Feminism: Black, Chicana, and White Feminist Movements in America's Second Wave* (2004).

Susan Stryker and Stephen Whittle, eds., *The Transgender Studies Reader* (2006).

Impact of Feminism

Carrie N. Baker, *The Women's Movement against Sexual Harassment* (2008).

Dorothy Sue Cobble, *The Other Women's Movement: Workplace Justice and Social Rights in Modern America* (2004).

Stephanie Coontz, *Marriage, a History* (2005).

Bonnie J. Dow, *Prime-Time Television: Television, Media Culture, and the Women's Movement since 1970* (1996).

Wendy Kline, *Bodies of Knowledge: Sexuality, Reproduction, and the Women's Health Movement* (2010).

Rebecca M. Kluchin, *Fight to Be Tied: Sterilization and Reproductive Rights in America, 1950–1980* (2011).

Nancy MacLean, *Freedom Is Not Enough: The Opening of the American Workplace* (2006).

12

U.S. Women in a Global Age

1980–PRESENT

I**N 1993, PRESIDENT BILL CLINTON NOMINATED** corporate lawyer Zoe Baird to be the first woman attorney general of the United States. But Baird's nomination foundered when it was discovered that she and her husband had employed an undocumented immigrant couple from Peru, Lillian and Victor Cordero, to serve as nanny and driver and that they had failed to pay Social Security taxes for the couple. After a media firestorm, Baird withdrew her name from consideration, and Janet Reno, a single woman with no children or household help, became America's first woman attorney general instead.

The fate of Baird's nomination suggests the dramatic change in women's professional and political opportunities since the 1960s. That Baird, unlike male cabinet appointees, was grilled about her child care providers also reveals that a double standard exists about parental responsibility, despite women's widespread entrance into the workplace. Finally, the fact that Baird paid Lillian Cordero $250 a week while her own household income was $600,000 a year indicates the wide disparity among working women's experiences and highlights the centrality of immigrant women to the functioning of millions of prosperous American households.

◆ FEMINISM AND THE NEW RIGHT

Some of the hostility Baird encountered stemmed from innuendos that she was too ambitious and had foisted her child care responsibilities onto hired help. The backlash against feminism was a major theme of the late twentieth century and contributed significantly to the strength of the conservative "New Right" in American politics. As of 1968, the obstacles faced by insurgent feminism stemmed mostly from traditional beliefs and long-established sexism. Within a decade, however, a much more determined and organized resistance began to surface, concentrated especially on stopping ratification of the Equal Rights Amendment (ERA) and reversing the 1973 Supreme Court decision in *Roe v. Wade*. The political gains of antifeminism were reinforced by a cultural and media backlash that questioned the desirability of feminist life choices. This antifeminism was part of a broader movement of religious and other conservatives against the social and cultural transformations fueled by the events of the 1960s and 1970s.

The STOP-ERA Campaign

Opposition to the ERA in the 1970s and early 1980s came primarily from the far right of the Republican Party. Throughout the 1950s and 1960s, right-wing leaders had dedicated themselves to halting the spread of communism. Starting in the early 1970s, however, a self-proclaimed New Right (a kind of mirror image of the New Left of the 1960s) switched to domestic issues and contested the dramatic gains of the civil rights and feminist movements (and later the gay rights movement). The Republican Party, eager to break out of its image as the party of the rich, found this focus on social issues useful in attracting new adherents. The New Right was important to the election of Republican Ronald Reagan (1981–1989) and played a vital role in presidential politics through the presidency of George W. Bush (2001–2009).

Antifeminism was critical in the conservative offensive that marked American political life starting in the late twentieth century. The activist core of the antifeminist movement was primarily women. Mostly white, devoutly Christian, and married with children, they rose in defense of

2000 Highly contested presidential election resolved by Supreme Court in favor of George W. Bush

2001 Terrorists destroy New York's World Trade Center and attack Pentagon on September 11

2003 United States and allies invade Iraq

2004 Gay marriages begin in California and Massachusetts

2004 George W. Bush reelected president

2005 Condoleezza Rice becomes first African American woman secretary of state

2006 Immigration rights protest marches in cities throughout the United States

2006 Nancy Pelosi becomes first woman Speaker of the House of Representatives

2008 Barack Obama elected first African American president

2009 Sonia Sotomayor becomes first Hispanic and third woman Supreme Court justice

2011 "Don't ask, don't tell" military policy repealed

2013 Defense of Marriage Act ruled unconstitutional in *United States v. Windsor*

2013 Black Lives Matter movement founded

2014 *Burwell v. Hobby Lobby* Supreme Court ruling permitting private businesses whose owners had religious objections to withhold health insurance coverage for contraception and abortion

2015 *Obergefell v. Hodges* rules that no state can deny same-sex couples the right to marry

2016 Hillary Clinton loses presidential election to Donald Trump

2017 Nationwide anti-Trump women's marches among the largest protest demonstrations ever held in the United States.

traditional gender roles and family values. Ironically, the antifeminist movement, like the feminist movement that it condemned, pushed concerns about women's social role and status to the forefront of American politics. Indeed, the prominence of women in the conservative movement is one of the most striking measures of the changing place of women in American life in the late twentieth century.

Activist Phyllis Schlafly almost single-handedly put New Right antifeminism on the political map. One of the most important conservative leaders in U.S. history, she first made a name for herself when she wrote *A Choice Not an Echo* in support of Republican presidential candidate Barry Goldwater in 1964. Schlafly argued that elite Republicans, who controlled the party, had abandoned its principles of limited government and strong national defense. Goldwater was trounced by Lyndon B. Johnson in the election, but grassroots efforts on his behalf continued and were crucial to the election of Ronald Reagan in 1980.

Beginning in 1972, Schlafly used the ERA issue and a new antifeminist approach to help galvanize grassroots support for her conservative goals. She formed an organization, STOP (Stop Taking Our Privileges)-ERA, into which she recruited women who felt personally marginalized by feminist gains and were convinced that feminists threatened the moral and social order of the nation. They viewed the battle against the ERA as a fight against secular values that they felt were undermining the family.

A lawyer, an author, and the mother of six, Schlafly maintained a highly public career that contradicted her message that American society was best served and women were happiest when they remained full-time housewives and mothers (see Reading into the Past: "What's Wrong with 'Equal Rights' for Women?"). She claimed that ratification of the ERA would wreak social chaos by eroding fundamental gender distinctions. She insisted that instead of ending sex discrimination, the ERA would deprive women of crucial privileges such as the expectation of economic support from their husbands. Schlafly's claims put the pro-ERA forces on the defensive. Ironically, many of her concerns, such as women being fully integrated into the armed services, came to pass despite the defeat of the ERA.

By lobbying forcefully in crucial state legislatures, STOP-ERA slowed the pace of ratification to a crawl. The National Organization for Women (NOW) vainly fought back by urging feminists to boycott states that refused to ratify the ERA. In 1982, the ERA went down in defeat, three states short of ratification, with both pro- and anti- forces exhausted but also battle strengthened (see Map 12.1). The contest contributed to a growing cultural divide in American politics between those with conservative social values, especially concerning women and the family, and those who emphasized individual choice, social diversity, and the importance of federal government protection against discrimination.

The Abortion Wars

The campaign to undo *Roe v. Wade* has lasted longer and has been more contested than STOP-ERA. Although it has so far failed to recriminalize abortion completely, it has made the procedure much more difficult to obtain — in some cases

◆ **Map 12.1　The Battle over the ERA**
The ERA quickly won support in 1972 and 1973 but then stalled. ERAmerica, a coalition of women's groups formed in 1976, lobbied extensively, especially in North Carolina, Florida, and Illinois, but failed to sway the conservative legislatures in those states. After Indiana ratified it in 1977, the amendment still lacked three states' votes toward the three-fourths majority required for a constitutional amendment. Subsequent efforts to revive the ERA were unsuccessful.

completely impossible — in many U.S. states. The impact of the "abortion wars" on the larger political climate has been enormous. To those in the anti-abortion movement, the legalization of abortion represents the triumph of untrammelled individualism over women's sacred social role of motherhood. They stake their ground on the rights of the fetus, framing the women who seek abortions either as murderously selfish or victimized by abortion advocates. Nonetheless, popular support for abortion has not appreciably waned over the last four decades.

To indicate the larger issues its leaders believed to be at stake, the anti-abortion movement renamed itself "pro-life" — prompting the pro-abortion-rights forces to christen themselves, in equally expansive language, "pro-choice." Although many of the more visible leaders of right-to-life organizations are male, women constitute as much as three-quarters of the grassroots membership. In 1995, the movement secured a tremendous public relations victory when Norma McCorvey, the Roe of *Roe v. Wade*, renounced her support for abortion (see p. 650).

The anti-abortion movement got its start in 1971 when the Catholic Church sponsored the formation of the National Right to Life Committee. A sophisticated

READING INTO THE PAST

PHYLLIS SCHLAFLY
What's Wrong with "Equal Rights" for Women?

Phyllis Schlafly (1924–2016) began her conservative activism in the 1950s when she fervently embraced the anti-Communist campaign. In the 1970s, she took up the cause of antifeminism and founded the organization STOP-ERA. In this 1972 article published in her own newsletter, The Phyllis Schlafly Report, *Schlafly details her objections to the Equal Rights Amendment and feminism.*

In the last couple of years, a noisy movement has sprung up agitating for "women's rights." Suddenly, everywhere we are afflicted with aggressive females on television talk shows yapping about how mistreated American women are, suggesting that marriage has put us in some kind of "slavery," that housework is menial and degrading, and — perish the thought — that women are discriminated against. New "women's liberation" organizations are popping up, agitating and demonstrating, serving demands on public officials, getting wide press coverage always, and purporting to speak for some 100,000,000 American women.

It's time to set the record straight. The claim that American women are downtrodden and unfairly treated is the fraud of the century. The truth is that American women never had it so good. Why should we lower ourselves to "equal rights" when we already have the status of special privilege?

The proposed Equal Rights Amendment states: "Equality of rights under the law shall not be denied or abridged by the United States or by any state on account of sex." So what's wrong with that? Well, here are a few examples of what's wrong with it.

This Amendment will absolutely and positively make women subject to the draft. Why any woman would support such a ridiculous and un-American proposal as this is beyond comprehension. Why any Congressman who had any regard for his wife, sister, or daughter would support such a proposition is just as hard to understand. Foxholes are bad enough for men, but they certainly are *not* the place for women — and we should reject any proposal which would put them there in the name of "equal rights." . . .

Another bad effect of the Equal Rights Amendment is that it will abolish a woman's right to child support and alimony, and substitute what the women's libbers think is a more "equal" policy, that "such decisions should be within the discretion of the Court and should be made on the economic situation and need of the parties in the case."

Under present American laws, the man is *always* required to support his wife and each child he caused to be brought into the world. Why should women abandon these good laws — by trading them for something so nebulous and uncertain as the "discretion of the Court"?

The law now requires a husband to support his wife as best as his financial situation permits, but a wife is not required to support her husband (unless he is about to become a public charge). A husband cannot demand that his wife go to work to help pay for family expenses. He has the duty of financial support under our laws and customs. Why should we abandon these mandatory wife-support and child-support laws so that a wife would have an "equal" obligation to take a job?

By law and custom in America, in case of divorce, the mother always is given custody of her children unless there is overwhelming evidence of mistreatment, neglect or bad character. This is our special privilege because of the high rank that is placed on motherhood in our society. Do women really want to give up this special privilege and lower themselves to "equal rights," so that the mother gets one child and the father gets the other? I think not. . . .

Many women are under the mistaken impression that "women's lib" means more job employment opportunities for women, equal pay for equal work, appointments of women to high positions, admitting more women to medical schools, and other desirable objectives which all women favor. We all support these purposes, as well as any necessary legislation which would bring them about.

But all this is only a sweet syrup which covers the deadly poison masquerading as "women's lib." The women's libbers are radicals who are waging a total assault on the family, on marriage, and on children.

SOURCE: William H. Chafe et al., *A History of Our Time: Readings on Postwar America*, 6th ed. (New York: Oxford University Press, 2003), 211–13. Original source: *The Phyllis Schlafly Report* 5, no. 7 (February 1972).

QUESTIONS FOR ANALYSIS

1. What are Schlafly's reasons for opposing the ERA?
2. How do Schlafly's ideas reflect those of the emerging "New Right"?

media campaign, including films of late-term fetuses in utero and photographs of tiny fetal hands, built popular support. Pro-abortion forces retaliated with the image of a wire coat hanger to symbolize deaths from illegal abortions, but many young women no longer understood the reference. Starting in the late 1970s, leadership of the anti-abortion movement shifted to fundamentalist Protestants and then relocated at the very center of the Republican Party.

Starting in the mid-1970s, anti-abortion protesters gathered outside the clinics that had sprung up since *Roe v. Wade*. They intended to dissuade women from having abortions and to intimidate physicians from providing them. Across the country, pro- and anti-abortion activists engaged in angry face-to-face encounters. Eventually, the heightened rhetoric of the anti-abortion forces, which characterized legalized abortion as a "holocaust" of unborn babies, spilled into physical violence, as clinics were bombed and abortion providers murdered. Between 1976 and 2015, there were 227 bombing and arson attacks on clinics, including eight murders of medical providers. Threats have accelerated in response to heinous false rumors based on a doctored video produced by anti-abortion advocates that abortion clinics were selling fetal body parts.

Anti-abortion activists have also exerted significant political muscle. They have successfully sponsored numerous state laws making abortions difficult or even impossible to obtain. These laws require underage girls to obtain parental permission for an abortion, deny public funds for abortion, and mandate waiting periods and elaborate counseling. Doctors who wish to perform abortions are required to have medical privileges at local hospitals, a privilege often denied them. Thirty-nine states have attempted to prohibit a late-term abortion procedure known as intact dilation and extraction (but called "partial-birth abortion" by opponents), intended to help pregnant women unable to terminate their pregnancies earlier. Since 2011, more state-level restrictions have been established than in the entire previous decade. As a result, in 2017, only 30 percent of women between the ages of 15–44 lived in states where abortion rights are supported. As a current abortion rights defender insists, "[A]lthough abortion has been legal for four decades, . . . for many women in America it might as well not be. It is inaccessible—too far away, too expensive to pay for out of pocket, and too encumbered by restrictions and regulations and humiliations."[1]

Cases challenging these laws have made their way through the court system. In the 1989 *Webster v. Reproductive Health Services* and the 1992 *Planned Parenthood v. Casey* cases, the Supreme Court stopped short of overturning *Roe v. Wade* but ruled that states could prohibit the use of public facilities and public funds for abortions (see pp. A-14 to A-15). In the 1992 *Casey* decision, the Court reaffirmed the regulation of abortion when the fetus is at the point of extrauterine "viability," which it lowered to twenty-three weeks. Justice Anthony M. Kennedy, writing for the Court, commented that the "respect for human life finds an ultimate expression in the bond of love the mother has for her child," noting that "some women come to regret their choice to abort the infant life they once created and sustained."[2] Twenty-four-hour waiting periods to ensure "informed consent" and the requirement of parental consent for minor girls were also ruled constitutional.

◆ The Abortion Controversy

Few issues in recent American political life have been more divisive than a woman's right to choose an abortion. Rallies for and against abortion often provoke heated confrontations. Here demonstrators face off in Washington, D.C., in 2005. *Win McNamee/Getty Images.*

In 2016, in a surprise 5–3 decision, the Court (which was still short one justice) ruled that a Texas law requiring abortions to be performed in surgical facilities was unconstitutional. Nonetheless, the U.S. Supreme Court remains a shaky bastion of abortion rights.

Antifeminism Diffuses through the Culture

During this same time, popular culture also began to feature a more diffuse anti-feminism. In her best-selling 1991 book, *Backlash: The Undeclared War against American Women*, Susan Faludi explored claims that circulated widely about the unhappiness and disappointment allegedly suffered by women who had chosen feminist lifestyles. One particularly inflammatory study reported in *Newsweek* magazine in 1986 stated that if a woman was over forty and single, her chances for marriage were less than her chances of being killed by a terrorist.[3] Exaggerated statistics and news stories also appeared about the economic costs to women of the rising divorce rate and widespread psychological depression among unmarried career women. Not only were there no remaining tasks for feminism, according to the backlash mentality, but the movement's achievements had cost women dearly.

Television was particularly striking for the very mixed messages it was giving to its female audience. Programs directed at an adult female demographic featured strong, independent, career women characters. The most watched show of the decade, *Roseanne,* featured one of the most unusual TV heroines ever — a working-class, overweight, often unpleasant wife and mother, who worked in a factory and as a waitress. Among its plots were the following: the grandmother of Roseanne having had two abortions; Roseanne's sister being a single parent; Roseanne's best friend being a lesbian, one of the first regular lesbian characters on TV. Meanwhile, programs directed at a younger female demographic featured ambitious female characters — Ally McBeal is often cited — who were nonetheless preoccupied with their weight, boyfriends, and clothes. Cultural critic Susan Douglas characterized this as a combination of notions of equality apparently accepted and "embedded" in the culture with a subtle and updated sexism "enlightened" by the recognition that overt inequality no longer plays well.[4]

◆ FEMINISM AFTER THE SECOND WAVE

Public opinion and social pundits alike insisted that feminism was a thing of the past — its goals accomplished and its passion outdated. Nonetheless, feminist motivations, activism, awareness, and challenges were continuing to disperse throughout U.S. society and culture. In the response to the antifeminist "backlash," feminism revived in the 1990s and into the twenty-first century, in a movement known as third-wave feminism. Younger generations of women have found their way into a wide variety of movements, including attention to women's concerns, female leadership, and broad social justice goals, such as antiviolence and ecofeminism movements.

Third-Wave Feminism

In addition to the feminist impact on these and other social justice movements, young women in the early 1990s returned to specifically feminist activism. They called themselves the "third wave," a characterization that drew on the distinction between the first wave of women's rights between 1848 and 1920 and the women's liberation movement of the 1960s and 1970s, known as the second wave. Third wavers criticized their second-wave predecessors — not always accurately — for emphasizing women's victimhood over their empowerment, for not speaking to the concerns of women of color, and for a general cultural conservatism when it came to sexuality, appearance, and entertainment.

Third-wave anthologies, most of them personal accounts that hark back in genre to the consciousness-raising essays of the 1970s, flourished. The Third Wave Foundation, founded in 1992, worked to identify and fund new-generation feminist organizations. This generation of young women also brought feminist agendas into popular culture, especially in the worlds of punk and hip-hop music. Unafraid to be outrageous, new feminist magazines like *Bitch* and *Bust* appeared, supplemented by inexpensively reproduced small-run magazines ("zines") and Web pages self-published by young women and devoted to women's issues.

Women Stand Up to Violence

Young women spearheaded a widespread movement against sexual assault on college and university campuses in 2013. (Estimates are that one in five undergraduates have been assaulted, usually by someone they know.) In 1990 Congress attempted to address this endemic problem by passing the Clery Act, named for a woman who had been raped and murdered in her dorm room. The law requires that institutions report statistics on campus sexual assaults to federal authorities, but it has proven inadequate. In 2013, several assault survivors from prestigious institutions like Amherst College, the University of North Carolina, and Occidental College went public with the stories of their institutions' failure to address their cases adequately. Using social media, organizations such as Know Your IX and End Rape on Campus encouraged students to file complaints with the U.S. Department of Education and to put pressure on their institutions to improve their policies. Their efforts also influenced provisions in the 2013 reauthorized Violence Against Women Act that improved complaint procedures. The next year, President Barack Obama created a White House task force on college sexual assault.

Attention to domestic violence was part of second-wave feminism and continues to be an important issue for women activists pursuing social justice. Many of these address the problems faced by immigrant women. For example, Sakhi, an organization for New York South Asian women, founded in 1989, focuses on encouraging women to break the silence about domestic violence within their community. It describes its key aim as creating "a safe place with a full range of culturally-sensitive, language-specific information, support, services, and advocacy for South Asian women facing abuse in their lives."[5]

Native American women have also organized against domestic violence in organizations such as the National Indigenous Women's Resource Network and the South Dakota Coalition Ending Domestic and Sexual Violence. Estimates from 2008 are that 39 percent of Native women on reservations have been sexually assaulted, making them three times more likely to be victims than women of other races. Non-Indian men commit the vast majority of these assaults, reflecting in part the large percentage of Native women married to non-Native men. Native lobbying efforts led to provisions in the reauthorized Violence Against Women Act[6] that brought assault against women by non-Native men on tribal lands under the jurisdiction of tribal authorities, which supporters hope will provide greater ability to prosecute more cases and stem the tide of violence.

Black women have been at the forefront of addressing another aspect of pervasive violence in American society. Three African American community organizers, Alicia Garza, Patrisse Cullors, and Opal Tometi, created the Black Lives

Matter (BLM) movement in 2013 as a response to the acquittal of Floridian George Zimmerman who killed a black teenager, Trayvon Martin. A year later, when police in Ferguson, Missouri, killed eighteen-year-old Michael Brown, hundreds of members of BLM descended on the city for a nonviolent demonstration, and the movement grew dramatically. Brilliantly using social media, BLM generated hundreds of protests throughout the nation that persisted as more police-related deaths occurred. Most of those publicized were of young men, though the case of Sandra Bland who died in police custody in Texas in 2015, was a notable exception.

Yet BLM leaders, many of whom are LGBTQ, have insisted that the issues go beyond the deaths of black males. According to one scholar, the organization's success is based on the feminist theory of "intersectionality" (see p. 642) that calls "for a united focus on issues of race, class, gender, nationality, sexuality, disability, and state-sponsored violence. It argues that to prioritize one social issue over another issue will ultimately lead to failure in the global struggle for civil and human rights."[7] Another significant movement that embraced intersectionality emerged from the African American Policy Forum, which created #SayHerName, a social media-driven campaign to "help ensure that Black women's stories are integrated into demands for justice, policy responses to police violence, and media representations of victims of police brutality."[8]

◆ **#SayHerName**
As protestors marched to draw attention to antiblack police violence in the second decade of the twenty-first century, activists called for recognizing that the movement should recognize that women, too, were routinely victims of violent tactics. Here at a 2014 New York demonstration against police violence, two women hold up a banner featuring black women with the message, "Say Their Names. Remember Their Faces." *Viviane Moos/Corbis via Getty Images.*

Ecofeminism

One of the first social justice concerns to be reinvigorated by feminism was the environmental movement. Ecofeminism emerged in the mid-1970s to contend that "the domination of women and the domination of nature are fundamentally connected."[9] In its earliest phases, ecofeminists emphasized women's close relationship to nature's rhythms, theoretically allying with "essentialist" feminists, who held that gender differences are inherent. Subsequently, ecofeminism has become increasingly activist. It has contributed significantly to the "green" movement. It has also shifted attention to the ways in which environmental degradation has a heavy impact on poor women of color and their communities. Native American women have spoken out forcefully and appeared in large numbers in the ongoing protests over the Dakota Access Pipeline (DAPL), which would cut through Native American lands in the Dakotas. The demonstrations at Standing Rock Reservation began in April 2016 and attracted thousands of protesters, many of them from the Dakotas, Lakotas, and Nakotas tribes. Native women have invoked traditional concerns of indigenous people, claiming that they aim "to peacefully and prayerfully defend our rights, and rise up as one to sustain Mother Earth and her inhabitants." (See Reading into the Past: "The Meaning of the Standing Rock Protests.")

Ecofeminist activism has also drawn attention to global inequalities in access to the world's resources and capitalist shortsightedness in their use. Such approaches have proved attractive to women of the global South, for whom economic modernization policies have proved profoundly disempowering. Indian scientist Vandana Shiva has become an international biodiversity champion, insisting that the agency of women and their traditional agricultural practices are crucial to creating sustainable development policies. Kenyan activist and 2004 Nobel Peace Prize winner Wangari Maathai developed her environmentalism in response to the difficulty African women were experiencing in finding adequate fuel and safe drinking water.

Peace Activism

Peace activism — and American women's prominent role in it — has continued to grow alongside U.S. military interventions abroad. Despite the increasing integration of women into military service (see Primary Sources: "Gender and the Military," pp. 725–33), women continue to play a major role in peace activism. Beginning in the 1990s, women in cities throughout the United States held vigils as part of an international movement called Women in Black, which grew out of protests against the Israeli occupation of the West Bank and Gaza. Wearing the traditional color of mourning, Women in Black criticized militarism in its many forms from an explicitly feminist perspective, writing on their Web site: "We have a feminist understanding: that male violence against women in domestic life and in the community, in times of peace and in times of war, is interrelated. Violence is used as a means of controlling women."[10]

READING INTO THE PAST

LaDonna Brave Bull Allard
The Meaning of the Standing Rock Protests

Allard, who was instrumental in creating the anti-DAPL protest, puts the recent controversy into the context of Native history by relating the story of the 1863 Invan Ska (Whitestone) Massacre, where over three hundred Sioux were killed by the U.S. Army.

As my great-great-grandmother Mary Big Moccasin told the story, the attack came the day after the big hunt, when spirits were high. The sun was setting and everyone was sharing an evening meal when Sully's soldiers surrounded the camp on Whitestone Hill. In the chaos that ensued, people tied their children to their horses and dogs and fled. Mary was 9 years old. As she ran, she was shot in the hip and went down. She laid there until morning, when a soldier found her. As he loaded her into a wagon, she heard her relatives moaning and crying on the battlefield. She was taken to a prisoner of war camp in Crow Creek where she stayed until her release in 1870.

Where the Cannonball River joins the Missouri River, at the site of our camp today to stop the Dakota Access pipeline, there used to be a whirlpool that created large, spherical sandstone formations. The river's true name is Inyan Wakangapi Wakpa, River that Makes the Sacred Stones, and we have named the site of our resistance on my family's land the Sacred Stone Camp. The stones are not created anymore, ever since the U.S. Army Corps of Engineers dredged the mouth of the Cannonball River and flooded the area in the late 1950s as they finished the Oahe dam. They killed a portion of our sacred river.

I was a young girl when the floods came and desecrated our burial sites and Sundance grounds. Our people are in that water.

This river holds the story of my entire life.

I remember hauling our water from it in big milk jugs on our horses. I remember the excitement each time my uncle would wrap his body in cloth and climb the trees on the river's banks to pull out a honeycomb for the family — our only source of sugar. Now the river water is no longer safe to drink. What kind of world do we live in?

Look north and east now, toward the construction sites where they plan to drill under the Missouri River any day now, and you can see the old Sundance grounds, burial grounds, and Arikara village sites that the pipeline would destroy. Below the cliffs you can see the remnants of the place that made our sacred stones.

Of the 380 archeological sites that face desecration along the entire pipeline route, from North Dakota to Illinois, 26 of them are right here at the confluence of these two rivers. It is a historic trading ground, a place held sacred not only by the Sioux Nations, but also the Arikara, the Mandan, and the Northern Cheyenne.

Again, it is the U.S. Army Corps that is allowing these sites to be destroyed.

The U.S. government is wiping out our most important cultural and spiritual areas. And as it erases our footprint from the world, it erases us as a people. These sites must be protected, or our world will end, it is that simple. Our young people have a right to know who they are. They have a right to language, to culture, to tradition. The way they learn these things is through connection to our lands and our history.

If we allow an oil company to dig through and destroy our histories, our ancestors, our hearts and souls as a people, is that not genocide? . . .

We are the river, and the river is us. We have no choice but to stand up.

Today, we honor all those who died or lost loved ones in the massacre on Whitestone Hill. Today, we honor all those who have survived centuries of struggle. Today, we stand together in prayer to demand a future for our people.

SOURCE: *Yes!* Magazine "Why the Founder of Standing Rock Sioux Camp Can't Forget the Whitestone Massacre," http://www.yesmagazine.org/people-power/why-the-founder-of-standing-rock-sioux-camp-cant-forget-the-whitestone-massacre-20160903 (accessed July 22, 2017).

QUESTIONS FOR ANALYSIS

1. What are the reasons Allard gives for protesting the pipeline?
2. Why does Allard view the building of the pipeline as "genocide"?

Another antiwar group, Code Pink, started in 2003 on the eve of the Iraq invasion, uses the color pink as an ironic commentary on both the traditional "girlish" color and the Bush-era practice of coding terrorist threat levels as yellow, orange, or red. Code Pink's demonstrations draw on the confrontational protest tradition of early twentieth-century suffrage militants (see p. 435).

◆ WOMEN AND POLITICS

While the backlash against feminism has put the women's movement on the defensive, feminist activism has kept women's issues a vital part of national politics for more than forty years. Republicans and Democrats radically differed over, but were equally attentive to, issues of concern to women, from economic inequality to abortion rights to gender violence. Despite the expansion of the New Right's conservative power, women's political influence continued to grow, and the number of women in Congress, the presidential cabinet, and the Supreme Court grew. The dramatic impact of the September 11, 2001, attacks and the subsequent "war on terror" intensified political implications for women at home and abroad.

The 1980s: Carter and Reagan

Feminists were lukewarm to the 1977–1981 presidency of Democrat Jimmy Carter. A social conservative and evangelical Christian, Carter was unsympathetic to the pro-choice movement and supported the law banning the use of federal funds for abortions. But Carter also appointed feminist Bella Abzug to head the planning commission for the 1977 National Women's Conference in Houston, Texas, and his wife, Rosalynn, was an active proponent of the ERA. His appointment of civil rights veteran Eleanor Holmes Norton (see p. 645) to head the Equal Employment Opportunity Commission (EEOC) rescued that agency from irrelevance and led to a significant increase in the federal government's ability to challenge workplace discrimination by gender and race.

The election of Ronald Reagan in 1980 raised greater obstacles to women's concerns on the national stage. Reagan had campaigned with the promise "to get the government off our backs." His administration trimmed federal agencies' resources by 12 percent, dramatically shrinking federal programs that assisted poor women and children. The cuts also affected specifically feminist programs, for instance, the Women's Education Action Project, which addressed gender discrimination in education. For the crucial position of head of the EEOC, President Reagan chose Clarence Thomas, an African American lawyer who believed that affirmative action programs eroded the self-confidence of their supposed beneficiaries.

Among Reagan's many friendly gestures to the anti-abortion movement was the 1988 Emancipation Proclamation of Preborn Children, an executive order that deliberately played off of Abraham Lincoln's 1863 Emancipation Proclamation by equating abortion with slavery. His administration cut public funding for abortions for poor women and blocked organizations that received federal funds for reproductive counseling if abortion was mentioned. Abortion opponents received public funds for their "pregnancy crisis clinics," designed to convince women to forgo abortion in favor of carrying their pregnancies to term. Now that the ERA had failed, Reagan endorsed a pro-life amendment that would have made abortion unconstitutional.

Ironically, in 1981 President Reagan appointed the first woman justice — Sandra Day O'Connor — to the Supreme Court. Over her long tenure on the bench, O'Connor was regularly the swing vote in abortion cases, accepting the constitutionality of numerous restrictions on the practice while upholding *Roe v. Wade* itself.

Anita Hill and Clarence Thomas

In 1991, Reagan's successor, President George H. W. Bush, named Clarence Thomas to fill the Supreme Court seat vacated by the African American civil rights leader Thurgood Marshall. During the nomination process, Anita Hill — like Thomas, an African American lawyer — charged that Thomas had sexually harassed her when they worked together at the EEOC. Television audiences sat riveted while Hill testified before the all-white, all-male Senate Judiciary Committee about the intimate and embarrassing details of Thomas's unwanted sexual advances. Thomas angrily denied the charges and claimed that he was being subjected to a "high-tech lynching for uppity blacks." The senators, unwilling to appreciate the gravity of Hill's charges, narrowly approved the nomination. Thomas's term on the Court has been marked by unwavering support for conservative decisions and a stubborn unwillingness, presumably born of the trauma of his nomination process, to join the other justices in openly addressing cases while the Court is in session.

The Thomas-Hill incident catapulted the issue of sexual harassment into public consciousness. In the wake of the hearings, national polls found that four out of ten women said they had experienced sexual harassment on the job. The Thomas-Hill incident also contributed to the growing power and assertiveness of women in electoral politics. In the 1992 elections, the number of women elected to the U.S. Senate increased from three to seven. Carol Moseley Braun, an Illinois state legislator, became the first African American woman elected to the Senate. As of 2017, women holding office in the U.S. Congress include twenty-one senators (21 percent) and eighty-four congressional representatives (19.3 percent). Three senators and thirty-four representatives are women of color. The state of California takes the lead in women in Congress, including, once again, both of its senators.

Behind the increasing numbers of women officeholders were women voters, many of them influenced by feminist perspectives. By the 1980s, more than sixty years after women won the right to vote, a female voting bloc had finally emerged.

◆ **Anita Hill Testifies before the Senate Judiciary Committee**
Anita Hill's 1991 testimony against Clarence Thomas's Supreme Court nomination set off
a media firestorm. The Senate at that time had only two women members, and the Senate
Judiciary Committee that heard Hill's testimony was entirely male. While the committee
did not give much weight to her account of the sexual harassment she endured, Hill's
story brought the issue to wide public notice, helping to transform workplace policies and
procedures. It also stimulated women's political engagement in electoral politics. *Ernie Cox
Jr/KRT/Newscom.*

Women were more likely to vote Democratic than men. "The gravitation of men
and women to different political camps appears to be the outstanding demographic
development in American politics over the past twenty years," claimed the *Atlantic
Monthly* in 1996.[11] Women of color are disproportionately responsible for American women's Democratic Party leanings. Not only did men and women evidence
basic differences over feminist issues such as reproductive choice and wage equity,
but women were more favorably inclined to an enhanced role of government in
extending social services.

The "woman's bloc" was enabled by an increasingly sophisticated network of
female fund-raising. The National Women's Political Caucus, established in 1971,
promoted women candidates regardless of party. In 1984, the National Political
Congress of Black Women was founded to address political issues of specific concern to African Americans. In 1985, Ellen Malcolm founded Emily's List to provide
seed money for female, Democratic, pro-choice candidates. "Emily" is an acronym
for "Early Money Is Like Yeast." It is now one of the most important political action
committees in American politics.

The Clinton Years

In the 1992 election, women helped elect Democratic candidate Bill Clinton over Republican incumbent George H. W. Bush as president. During his first administration, Clinton's strength among women voters grew. Among the women he appointed to prominent federal offices was Madeleine Albright, who as secretary of state became the highest-ranked female cabinet member ever. For the Supreme Court, Clinton chose women's rights litigator Ruth Bader Ginsburg. In the 1996 presidential election, the female vote for a second Clinton administration was eleven points higher than the male vote.

Hillary Rodham Clinton was America's first First Lady to have worked full-time for a living. Modeling herself after Eleanor Roosevelt (see pp. 498–508), she sought to use her position to enact political change. She was charged with primary oversight of her husband's efforts to pass national health care legislation. When it failed, she was ridiculed and maligned for overstepping her role, in a right-wing attack that has continued to this day. In 1995, she played a major role at the United Nations International Women's Conference, held in Beijing, China. Aligning herself with "world attention on issues that matter most in the lives of women and their families," she gave voice to and became publicly associated with the global feminist slogan "women's rights are human rights."[12]

Then, in 1998, President Bill Clinton became embroiled in a scandal over a sexual affair with a twenty-two-year-old White House intern named Monica Lewinsky. On the grounds that he had publicly lied about the relationship, he became the only president since Andrew Johnson in 1868 to be tried on articles of impeachment. Feminism played a complicated, even ironic, role in this episode. Although many previous presidents had been notorious adulterers, thirty years of feminism had called into question the long-standing assumption that men in power could engage in extramarital sex with impunity, and the proponents of impeachment made ample use of this new revulsion at the double standard. Nonetheless, many feminist groups stood by Clinton because of his defense of abortion rights and other feminist issues.

George W. Bush

Bill Clinton was followed into the presidency by George W. Bush, who shared the right wing's commitment to narrowing abortion rights. However, the most dramatic historic events of his presidency were the September 11, 2001, al-Qaeda attacks on the World Trade Center and the Pentagon and the military response he authorized.

Even more than Republican predecessors George H. W. Bush and Ronald Reagan, George W. Bush allied himself with the religious right and the "pro-family" lobby. He wore away at abortion rights, withdrawing $34 million in congressionally authorized funds from United Nations family planning programs on the grounds that the money would facilitate the availability of abortions worldwide. He also opposed research involving stem cells derived from fetal tissue. (In contrast to this, it should be noted that his administration provided unprecedented levels of funding to tackle AIDS in Africa.) His appointments of John Roberts and Samuel Alito greatly increased the conservative and pro-life strength on the U.S. Supreme Court. Yet at the same time, he named numerous women to high positions, most notably Condoleezza Rice as secretary of state, the highest national political position ever held by an African American woman.

A new epoch in American history began on September 11, 2001, when extremists from the al-Qaeda terrorist group hijacked four commercial airliners. Two of the planes destroyed the World Trade Center towers in New York City, another seriously damaged the Pentagon, and a fourth crashed in a Pennsylvania field. Among the more than three thousand people who died were of course many women. Flight attendants CeeCee Lyles and Debbie Welsh helped bring down the fourth plane before it could be flown into the White House or the Capitol. The United States went to war against Afghanistan in October 2001 because the ruling group, the Taliban, had harbored al-Qaeda leaders. This became the longest-running war in American history.

Two years later, President George W. Bush announced a preemptive strike on Iraq, claiming, falsely as it turned out, that the nation had "weapons of mass destruction" and intimate links to al-Qaeda. Within a few months, Bush proclaimed an end to major combat operations there, but actual victory remained elusive. The Iraq War continued, becoming a bloody battle between U.S. forces and insurgents, and helped fuel a continuing civil war among Iraqis.

Bush's enhanced status as a leader in the war against terror helped him win a second term in 2004. Within two years, however, discontent over the war in Iraq and the federal government's incompetence in the face of Hurricane Katrina in 2005 led to midterm election victories for Democratic candidates. In 2007, Californian Nancy Pelosi became the first woman majority leader and Speaker of the House of Representatives, second in the line of presidential succession.

The Election of 2008: A Historic Presidential Choice

Despite the significant successes of women in politics, the presidency and vice presidency remained elusive. In 1972 Shirley Chisholm had been the first African American and the first woman to make a meaningful bid for her party's presidential nomination, and in 1984 Geraldine Ferraro had run for vice president, but until 2008 neither party had seriously considered nominating a woman for president. Hillary Clinton changed this. Breaking out of the limitations of the First Lady role, she was elected senator from New York in 2000. By 2007, she had become the presumed front-runner for the 2008 Democratic Party presidential nomination.

Then Hillary Clinton's chances at the nomination were challenged by Barack Obama, a charismatic first-term African American senator from Illinois. Clinton and Obama fought a contentious battle through a long and suspenseful primary season. Although Clinton began the campaign with little emphasis on her gender, she was the object of sexist attacks from commentators who concentrated on her clothing and criticized her emotional responses, charging her with lack of emotion in some cases and too many tears in others. These attacks precipitated a revived feminist awareness among younger women who thought that such explicit misogyny was a thing of the past. When Obama finally secured a majority of delegates, Clinton endorsed Obama and belatedly acknowledged the historic significance of her candidacy. Referring to the number of popular votes cast on her behalf, she movingly told her supporters, "Although we weren't able to shatter that highest, hardest glass ceiling this time, thanks to you, it's got about 18 million cracks in it."[13]

The 2008 campaign then took a surprise turn when Republican nominee John McCain selected Alaska governor Sarah Palin as his running mate, hoping that she might attract women voters disappointed by Clinton's exit from the race. Photogenic and charismatic, Palin characterized herself as an ordinary "hockey mom." She did not attract the majority of women voters, but she did prove enormously successful with the right-wing conservative base. She was resolutely anti-abortion, played to traditional "family values," and staunchly advocated Republicans' anti-government, anti-tax concerns. She played a major role in catalyzing a grassroots insurgency that called itself the Tea Party and considered the party's establishment insufficiently conservative. It would go on to play a major role in subsequent elections.

The Obama Years

The 2008 election was a clear victory for Barack Obama. His success stemmed from his exceptionally well-organized grassroots campaign and his appeal to young and nonwhite voters. He also pledged to end the wars in Iraq and Afghanistan. He brought enough Democrats into office with him to secure impressive albeit temporary majorities in both houses of Congress. Entering office amid the dire political fallout of an economic recession that had begun in December 2007, he was able to reverse the alarming banking and mortgage crisis, a steep decline in the stock market and housing values, and a sharp spike in unemployment.

Michelle Obama, a high-powered professional woman with a strong personality, might have been expected to follow in Hillary Clinton's footsteps as First Lady, but as an African American woman, she faced different challenges. Invoking long-standing negative stereotypes, critics characterized her as "an angry black woman." In response, she worked to soften her public persona, successfully balancing activism and traditionalism. She was outspoken and passionate about her projects — military families and childhood obesity — which stayed within a relatively conventional female sphere of interest. She became enormously popular for her elegance, forthright advocacy of her husband's priorities, and the admirable family of two daughters she raised in the White House spotlight.

President Obama appointed a significant number of women to high-level positions, fourteen to cabinet-level posts alone. He also named Hillary Clinton as secretary of state. The third woman to hold that office, she served successfully for the entirety of his first administration and, in contrast to her subsequent career, became one of the most admired women in American public life. Privileged with two opportunities for Supreme Court appointments, the president named women to both: Sonia Sotomayor, the first Hispanic justice, and Elena Kagan. The court now had an unprecedented four women.

In President Obama's first few days in office, he reversed the ban on funding for international family planning programs imposed by his predecessor. He also signed the Lilly Ledbetter Fair Pay Act, which repealed restrictions on filing an equal pay lawsuit. But Obama's greatest domestic achievement, the reform of the national health care system, had the most profound implications for women and their families. Ever since Harry Truman, American presidents had sought to reform national health care. Obama succeeded, though not without many compromises. The 2010 Patient Protection and Affordable Care Act (ACA), which the Right nicknamed "Obamacare," left the employer-based private insurance system intact while phasing in a network of state "health exchanges" and federal supplemental funds to assist those who could not otherwise afford health care and insurance. As a disproportionate percentage of the uninsured poor, women — and their children — would have far more reliable access to health care. In addition, the law required insurance plans to provide specific preventive treatments, such as mammograms, for women.

The public's response to the ACA was contradictory. Many elements were popular, for example, regulations requiring the maintenance of insurance coverage for those with "previously existing conditions." And in states that cooperated with the federal law, the number of people with health coverage increased dramatically. But conservatives made political capital of the law by decrying it as a government intrusion into private life, and they used this issue to help make a clean sweep in Congress in the midterm elections of 2010. They successfully eliminated the law's coverage of abortions and challenged the requirement that as part of a basic standard of health, women must receive access to birth control. In 2014, in *Burwell v. Hobby Lobby,* the Supreme Court agreed that private businesses whose owners had religious objections were not required to provide contraception coverage to their employees. Nonetheless, two years later, thanks in part to intense divisions among Republicans, President Obama secured reelection. The controversy surrounding the ACA would go on to make it one of the most politically significant pieces of legislation in many years and promised to play a major role in post-Obama politics.

The Long War on Terror

Obama's pledge to end the Afghan and Iraq wars contributed to his successful run for president. Over the course of his presidency, U.S. forces in Afghanistan were steadily drawn down from 180,000 to less than 10,000 at the end of 2014, but military departure from Iraq proved more difficult. In August 2010, President Obama announced that the United States was ending its official combat mission there, but subsequent developments made the drawdown impossible to complete.

Beyond the staggering financial price tag of these two wars, the human costs have been enormous. By 2016, almost 6,000 Americans troops had been killed in the two wars, approximately 160 of them women. Compared to the number of Americans killed in the Vietnam War, the death numbers are relatively low in part because care of those wounded on the battlefield has been intense and aggressive. However, the high number of survivors has meant that tens of thousands of severely wounded and traumatized veterans have returned to the United States, only to find the U.S. Veterans Administration unprepared and unable to provide them with adequate and timely care. Current estimates of civilian deaths among Afghans number 31,000. Figures for Iraq are harder to determine, but one reliable source puts the number of civilians close to 200,000.[14]

Iraqi and Afghan women have been deeply affected by these wars. Part of the rationale for going to war in Afghanistan was the Taliban's barbaric treatment of Afghan women, to which women's groups in the United States had been trying to draw attention for decades. Some gains for Afghan women emerged during the U.S. war in Afghanistan as education levels improved and political representation expanded though only in urban areas; isolated rural areas continue to be hostile environments for women. In contrast, the situation for women in Saddam Hussein's Iraq had been nowhere near as dire before the war and was made worse as a result of the conflict. The post-Hussein regime was heavily influenced by Muslim fundamentalists, who increased pressure on women to leave their jobs and education for subordinate positions in the home. The new constitution in Iraq permitted local religious sects to oversee family courts, which alarmed many women's rights advocates. The war created instability and danger in Iraq, particularly for women fearing rape, kidnapping, and even murder at the hands of religious extremists.

Far from countering terrorists, U.S. action in Iraq seems to have destabilized the region and created a power vacuum that allowed even more extreme terrorists to flourish. In the summer of 2014, a startling new threat to peace in the region emerged. A radical Islamic terrorist group, more sophisticated and brutal than al-Qaeda, made significant inroads into controlling parts of Syria and Iraq. The Islamic State of Iraq and Syria, known as ISIS, uses social media to recruit new fighters and produces videos with high production values that feature horrific beheadings. ISIS announced that its policy toward women considered infidel or disloyal would include rape, enslavement, and forced marriage.

ISIS has gone on to declare itself a virtual Islamic Empire, a "Caliphate." Although it has suffered increasing losses of territory on the ground, ISIS has stepped up its dramatic international terrorist attacks, especially in Europe. Numbers of women have joined its ranks to become suicide bombers, ISIS's primary weapon of terror. Fear of this escalating international war of terrorism played a significant role in the election of 2016.

The Election of 2016

The election of 2016 will surely be one of the most disturbing and consequential in modern American history. When the campaign began, a full two years before the November 2016 election, Hillary Clinton seemed a sure bet for the Democratic

◆ **Hillary Clinton and the 2016 Campaign**
Observers have noted that although Hillary Clinton did well among women voters as a whole in the 2016 election, Donald Trump had greater success with white women without college degrees. Clinton performed well among women of color. Her most impressive showing was among young women. She carried 63 percent of those between 18 and 29 years old. This photograph at a Nevada rally features Clinton with actress Eva Longoria, Chelsea Clinton, and actress America Ferrera. *Mike Nelson/Epa/REX/Shutterstock.*

nomination. She sought to address growing income inequality by increasing corporate taxes and also campaigned against unregulated private funds pouring into American politics. Protecting and extending women's rights and working toward equal pay for equal work were important parts of her platform. She promised to build on and protect the gains of the Obama administration, most notably the Affordable Care Act.

The Republican field began with sixteen candidates, but gradually real estate mogul and reality television star Donald Trump knocked off all the others. Trump ran an antiglobalization and extremely nationalistic campaign. He promised to withdraw the United States from global free trade agreements and to dramatically limit immigration from Mexico, which he claimed was responsible for American workers' economic problems, and to target Muslim immigration for national security reasons. In particular, he promised to halt the immigration of Muslims completely and to build a wall across the southern border of the United States to halt what he claimed was massive illegal immigration from Mexico.

Republicans concentrated a barrage of attacks on Clinton, focusing on her years as secretary of state. As Trump rose to the top of the field, he alleged that, by using a nonsecure email server, Secretary Clinton had put national security at risk. Claiming that her behavior rose to the level of criminality, he regularly incited his audiences to chant "Lock Her Up!" Meanwhile, Clinton faced an equally unlikely primary challenge from Senator Bernie Sanders of Vermont, self-described socialist, who pressed for much more aggressive income equalization measures. The expectation was that Clinton would ride the support of women to the nomination and then the presidency, but both Trump and Sanders attracted sectors of the female electorate (young women in Sanders's case and noncollege educated white married women in Trump's). Strong evidence of Trump's long-term sexual harassment of women, which was expected to undercut white women's support for him, seemed to make little difference. Clinton's strength among women voters remained strongest among women of color. Despite Sanders's strong showing, Clinton captured the Democratic Party's nomination. In the election, Trump won the Electoral College, aided by narrow victories in a half dozen crucial states although Clinton won the popular vote by over three million votes. Riding on Trump's coattails, Republicans retained narrow control of the Senate and significantly increased their control of the House. The horrified reaction of millions of women to the election led to demonstrations the day after Trump's inauguration all over the country and on all seven continents. By many counts, the January 21, 2017, women's marches were the largest protest demonstrations ever held in American history.

Trump's egregious sexual predation contributed to the emergence, nine months into his presidency, of the willingness of more and more sexual assault victims, beginning in Hollywood but spreading much more widely, to go public and name the powerful men who were their assailants. In an exceptionally activist expression of the capacity of social media, accusations began to accumulate under the Twitter sign #MeToo, and the public began to take greater notice than ever before of the sexual violence faced by women.

Even before Election Day, evidence was beginning to accumulate of intrusion into the voting process by computer hackers almost certainly with the knowledge and support of Russian president Vladimir Putin. In the months just after the election, congressional committees and an officially charged special federal prosecutor began investigating these charges although President Donald Trump refused to give them credence.

Trump has approached the presidency with an unprecedented disdain for the traditional protocol of the office — refusing to release his tax returns, questioning the integrity of the media, and denigrating his predecessor President Obama. His casual misogyny was much on display during the campaign, and for the most part, women play a small role in his administration. There are two exceptions. His daughter Ivanka Trump, who sometimes acts as counsel to her father, often supplants his much less visible third wife, Melania, in the public eye. And in July 2017, Sarah Huckabee Sanders became White House press secretary. An aspect of the Trump presidency that is still unfolding concerns investigations into whether the Trump presidential campaign colluded with Russia to undermine Hillary Clinton's

◆ **Women's March, Washington, D.C., January 21, 2017**
The shock of Hillary Clinton's unexpected defeat by Donald Trump, a well-documented sexual harasser, generated a spontaneous, widespread call for women to gather together and protest. Gathering steam on social media, protest leaders quickly determined to be genuinely intersectional, so that all races, ethnicities, and sexualities would be equally represented and visible. The marches, spreading to most major American cities and beyond, were marked by clever, daring signs and slogans; and by ubiquitous, pink "pussy hats," hand-knitted by participants to satirize the president-elect's proud boast that he could grab women by "the pussy" with impunity. *Mario Tama/Getty Images.*

campaign and whether Trump obstructed justice when he fired FBI Director James Comey, who was investigating the possibility of Russian intervention in the election.

Beyond "Russiagate," the first year of the new administration was marked by four key developments. When Supreme Court Justice Antonin Scalia died in the last months of the Obama administration, Republicans in the Senate refused to allow the sitting president to fill the seat. Soon after Trump took office, he nominated and the Republican Congress ratified Neil Gorsuch, who was expected to strengthen the right wing of the Court, including on abortion cases. In addition to its ability to shape the Supreme Court, with control of all three branches of government, the Republican Congress seemed to be perfectly situated to fulfill Trump's and the party's campaign promises to undo the Affordable Care Act, which would have devastating consequences for poor women and children. This promise, however, has proved difficult to fulfill. Acting solely through executive action, the president has sought to fulfill a second campaign pledge, to draw a virtual halt to Muslim immigration, which he has said threatens the nation with terrorism. Massive popular demonstrations and quick court actions stayed the president's anti-immigration orders, until, in July 2017, the Supreme Court ruled that parts of the order could remain in force. Undocumented families, discussed below, also became targets of anti-immigration policy. Again, vulnerable families are the most deeply affected by this radical shift in national policy. In December 2017, Trump achieved arguably his only legislative success when Congress passed on overhaul of the federal tax system, one that primarily benefited wealthy Americans. Other dramatic changes in American politics and standing in the world no doubt are to come. (For a view of American politics from the perspective of its first Somali America woman elected to public office, see Reading into the Past: "First Muslim Somali American Lawmaker.")

◆ WOMEN'S LIVES IN MODERN AMERICA AND THE WORLD

While feminism and the conservative backlash against it provide an essential framework for understanding the recent history of American women, there have been other engines of change in women's lives, especially the maturation of the female labor force and corresponding shifts in American marriage patterns in family life and sexual choices, as well as changing immigration patterns.

Inequalities — Old and New — in the Labor Force

Consistent with long-running developments, women currently constitute nearly half of paid labor, and working mothers are now the norm (see the Appendix, Table 2, p. A-19). This development has occurred in the context of a dramatic increase in national wealth inequality, making the United States the most economically stratified industrial nation in the world. Women at the turn of the twenty-first century could be found on both extremes of the labor force.

From one perspective, many women workers are moving in the direction of greater opportunity, better wages, and increasing equality with men. The median wage for full-time women workers increased from 59 percent of men's average earnings in 1970 to approximately 80 percent in 2015. White and Asian women are earning 75 percent and 85 percent, respectively, of the average white male wage, while black and Hispanic women earn much less, 63 percent and 54 percent, respectively.[15]

In the professions, the infusion of women has been especially stunning. The percentage of medical degrees awarded to women jumped from 7 percent in 1966 to 46 percent in 2016, and the percentage of law degrees increased from 4 percent to 47 percent in that same period. By the turn of the twenty-first century, women were the majority of graduates in veterinary medicine and pharmacy programs.

READING INTO THE PAST

ILHAN OMAR
First Muslim Somali American Lawmaker

Although the big political news in 2016 was the election of Donald Trump, who ran a campaign hostile to immigrants, Muslims, women's reproductive freedom, and LGBT rights, there were also progressive victories. Ilhan Omar, a Somali refugee, worked as a Minneapolis city council policy analyst before running for election to Minnesota's state legislature in 2016. Building on a coalition of students, immigrants, and progressives, she unseated a forty-four-year incumbent and became the first Somali American lawmaker in the nation. In January 2017, she graced the cover of Time *magazine as one of the "women who are changing the world." The passages below are from her Web site.*

Meet Ilhan

Ilhan Omar is an experienced Twin Cities policy analyst, organizer, public speaker, and advocate. She was recently elected as the Minnesota House Representative for District 60B, making her the highest-elected Somali American public official in the United States. Ilhan is the Assistant Minority Leader, with assignments to three house committees: Civic Law and Data Practices Policy, Higher Education and Career Readiness Policy and Finance, and State Government Finance. In addition to serving in the legislature, Ilhan is a mother of three and the Director of Policy Initiatives at Women Organizing Women, where she empowers East African women to take civic leadership roles in their community. Born in Somalia, Ilhan and her family fled the country's civil war when she was eight. The family spent four years in a refugee camp in Kenya before coming to the United States in the 1990s.

Fighting for Equity and Justice

Rep. Ilhan Omar is the first Somali American Muslim legislator elected to a state legislature in the United States. She proudly represents district MN-60B, including University of Minnesota, Augsburg, Prospect Park, Seward, Como, Cedar Riverside neighborhoods.

Our campaign's vision is rooted in co-governance, equity, and justice and we are committed to training the next generation of organizers to create grassroots, progressive change throughout our district and state from the ground up.

Advancing Equity for All

As a woman, immigrant, and person of color, I am an intersectional progressive who works to build power within our community. In order to do so, I am dedicated to advancing an agenda focused on economic, social, racial, and environmental justice.

When elected, I will be both the first Muslim woman and Somali American woman to hold office in the United States. However, women leaders and leaders of color have been drawn to our campaign not because we have sought them out as a politically expedient, but because the campaign represents the changes in our community and district that are bringing underrepresented people into the political process. I am proud of the leadership roles women and people of color play in my campaign — leading our finance team, communications, field outreach, organizing conventions, and crafting policy in favor of social justice. My work in the community and my campaign demonstrates that we as Minnesotans do better when we all do better.

I am the only candidate endorsed by OutFront Minnesota Action and Stonewall DFL. I was humbled and honored to be part of our state's historic victories for marriage equality in 2012 and 2013. However, there is still a great deal of work to do in the struggle for LGBT inclusion. Many LGBT community members have endured bullying, homelessness, lack of opportunity, and discrimination. I realize that these struggles are the same struggles many new immigrants face. I understand civil rights issues are human rights issues. Discrimination is harmful no matter who you are; all people deserve respect and equity under the law. I will be a steadfast advocate for all underrepresented communities at the Capitol. It is not our job to judge one another, but to welcome and serve everyone.

I want to help build a world where chances of birth don't define people's lives. I want my daughters to be judged not by their gender or skin color, but by their contributions to our community.

I unequivocally support women's reproductive rights and I am the current Vice President of the DFL Feminist Caucus. I have fought my entire life for human rights and as your representative, I will continue that fight.

Source: https://www.ilhanomar.com

QUESTIONS FOR ANALYSIS

1. How do Omar's experiences compare to those of earlier immigrant women?
2. What does her election suggest about the changing role of women of color in American politics?

◆ **Positive Images for Female Achievement**
In 2013, Sheryl Sandberg, chief operating officer at Facebook, published *Lean In: Women, Work, and the Will to Lead*. Her fundamental message was that ambition in women was denigrated as unfeminine and that women colluded with this by holding themselves back instead of marshaling their talents to advance into top leadership positions. Some feminists criticized Sandberg for focusing on individual corporate success rather than on the social conditions of most working women. Others appreciated her recognition that the larger culture made it difficult for women to see themselves as accomplished leaders. This photograph of a young girl deeply engaged in the male-dominated world of technology was part of a Lean In project to provide more accurate and attractive representations of working women to mainstream advertisers, magazines, and newspapers. *Peter Cade/ Getty Images.*

Even in the corporate world, female executives quintupled from 5 percent in 1970 to 26 percent in 2014. Still, at the highest professional and corporate levels women remained underrepresented.

These achievements contrast sharply with the experience of working women at the low end of the labor market. The majority of women continue to work in female-dominated jobs that paid a fifth to a third less than those in male-dominated sectors. In 2010, 75 percent of clerical and administrative support jobs, 91 percent of private household labor, and almost 90 percent of institutional health care service work continued to be performed by women. These underpaid sectors of the labor force provide for much of the continuing disparity between men's and women's earnings. For the experience of the majority of working women to improve, this continuing sexual division of labor must change.

Combating Discrimination

The traditional tool of workers, union membership, has declined sharply in this era. At the same time, women's representation in organized labor has risen dramatically from 19 percent in 1962 to 46 percent in 2014. As one scholar has noted, "Labor feminists increased their numbers and leadership in a class movement that was rapidly declining in power and prestige."[16]

Labor unions have served as a resource for women, especially in female-dominated industries such as the clerical and service sectors. Groups of female workers who had never been previously considered candidates for unionization surprised male labor leaders by forming militant unions. The Association of Flight Attendants, formed in 1973, successfully fought demeaning age and weight requirements and the title of "airline hostess" (see Figure 11.1, p. 661). In the 1980s and 1990s, service sector and public employee unions benefited from women members and a new generation of women leaders. In 1988, the Harvard Union of Clerical and Technical Workers won a seventeen-year battle against Harvard University.

Today, the most vital area of labor organization is among immigrant workers, many of whom are women in the low-wage sectors of food preparation, cleaning-service work, and in-home health care. In 1985, the Service Employees International Union created the Justice for Janitors campaign to organize the cleaning personnel who work in office buildings and hotels in major cities. Unions have been active in living wage campaigns, which also address the concerns of immigrant workers. These programs bring together low-wage workers with community, religious, women's, and labor organizations to campaign for increases in municipal minimum wage rates.

In addition to turning to unions, women seeking to break through labor market segmentation have made use of two important legal tools. In class action suits, based on the Equal Pay and Civil Rights Acts of the 1960s (see pp. 582 and 588), instead of one person's seeking to prove individual discrimination, a group of people (the "class") establishes a pattern of job segregation and underpayment. In the first decade of the twenty-first century, at least five hundred of these actions were settled in favor of the women litigants. The other tool is the voluntary affirmative action program, by which employers undertake plans to qualify more women and minorities for employment in areas in which they are underrepresented. Affirmative action campaigns have opened up not only professional work, such as university employment, but also jobs in steel factories, construction trades, and police and fire departments.

A measure of the impact of these programs has been the political and legal reaction against them. Characterizing affirmative action programs as "reverse discrimination," Republican candidates vowed to dismantle them. The Supreme Court's 1978 ruling in *University of California Regents v. Bakke* was a major blow to affirmative action (see the Appendix, p. A-14). In 2011, the Supreme Court also dealt a major blow to class action antidiscrimination suits. In *Walmart v. Dukes*, a group of women suing the largest retail employer of women in the

◆ **Los Angeles Latinas Strike for Justice**
Organized in 1985, the Justice for Janitors movement has drawn attention to the issues of low
wages, poor benefits, and difficult working conditions among service workers in cities all over
the country. The campaign has had notable successes in Los Angeles, Houston, Miami, and
Cincinnati. This image is from an October 2005 rally protesting California governor Arnold
Schwarzenegger's anti-union initiatives. The majority of the protesters were Latino, and the rally
included large numbers of women. Many of the speakers, including veteran farm labor activist
Dolores Huerta, spoke in Spanish. The women chanting in the foreground are Janitors for Justice
members Martina de Maroana (right) and Ana Castro (left). What do their expressions and
body language suggest about how they view their labor activism? *David McNew/Getty Images.*

country was found to be too varied and diverse to be able to stand as a "class" and
thus to sue. The decision will have far-reaching consequences for antidiscrimination suits that come from groups of people rather than individuals.

◆ CHANGES IN FAMILY AND SEXUALITY

Much like the bifurcation of the female labor experience into high-end achievement and low-end economic decline, the changes in family life are very much
affected by class and income differences. The increased presence, new demands,
and political gains of gay, lesbian, and transgender people constitute another

historic development in family and personal life. Similarly, attention to sexual assaults on America's college campuses, like similar developments in the military (see Primary Sources: "Gender and the Military," pp. 725–33), opens up a new front in American women's struggles for sexual dignity and freedom.

Changing Marriage Patterns

By the late twentieth century, lifelong marriage had become far less common as an experience for women than ever before. With women's increasing capacity for self-support and the widespread acceptability of cohabitation among unmarried couples, the marriage rate has declined. In 2016, only one out of five households in the United States included a married couple with children. Women married at later ages — an average of twenty-seven in 2016. Currently, perhaps as many as half of all first marriages end in divorce. One historian refers to this development as the "disestablishment" of the institution of marriage in favor of the "pluralization" of sexual and familial arrangements.[17]

In one area, marriage seems to be thriving in the twenty-first century. By the mid-1990s, religious leaders were sanctifying gay unions, and corporate practices and state law were beginning to grant marriage-like recognition to "domestic unions." Seeking to halt this development, congressional conservatives passed and President Bill Clinton signed the 1996 Defense of Marriage Act, which denied federal recognition of gay marriages and prohibited married gay couples from having the benefits attached to marriage, such as tax and Social Security benefits.

Marriage regulation, however, has always been a matter of state law, which in many states was becoming more liberal. Ground zero for the battle over gay marriage became California. Antigay marriage forces were able to pass a state constitutional amendment stating that "only marriage between a man and a woman is valid or recognized in California." Two gay couples took the California amendment to the Supreme Court, joining a case from New York. In 2013, the Court ruled that the Defense of Marriage Act was unconstitutional (see the Appendix, pp. A-15 to A-16). Dramatically, in June 2015, in the case of *Obergefell v. Hodges*, the Supreme Court ruled that no state can deny same-sex couples the right to marry.

Parenting

Childbearing and childrearing have also undergone significant change. American women have fewer children, have them later, have more of them outside of marriage, and are more likely never to have them at all. Single motherhood is one of the most dramatic statistical changes in women's lives over the last half century, rising from 5 percent of births in 1960 to 40 percent in 2014. Racial differences are equally dramatic, with 70 percent of African American mothers single, compared with 66 percent of Native Americans, 53 percent of Hispanics, and 29 percent of whites. Although much attention has been paid to pregnancies among unmarried teens, their numbers have been declining while the numbers of adult single mothers have been rising.

The experience of single mothers differs significantly by class. At the upper-income levels, single women have been able to support themselves, become homeowners, and

◆ **Edith Windsor, Plaintiff in *United States v. Windsor***

New Yorkers Edith Windsor and Thea Spyer had been together for thirty years when, in 2007, they traveled to Canada, where gay marriage was legal, to have their union made official. Two years later, Thea died and left Edith a large inheritance. However, because of the 1996 Defense of Marriage Act, the federal government refused to recognize their marriage and denied Edith a spousal inheritance tax exemption. She brought her case to the court system, and lower courts found the relevant section of DOMA unconstitutional. In this 2013 photograph, Windsor (center) and her lawyer celebrate on the steps of the U.S. Supreme Court, which had just reaffirmed the lower courts' findings, a decision that marked a turning point in the legalization of gay marriage throughout the United States. *Jewel Samad/AFP/Getty Images.*

have children. For most single mothers, however, this has not been the case. In 2015, 36 percent of all homes headed by working single mothers fell below the poverty line. For women at the lower end of the income scale, cuts in social services have made single motherhood even more difficult. Aid for Families with Dependent Children, known colloquially as "welfare," had been under attack since the Reagan years. Finally, in 1996, President Clinton signed the Personal Responsibility and Work Opportunities Act, claiming to "end welfare as we know it." The law limited to five years the time that poor women and children could receive federal welfare assistance. By 2000, the welfare rolls had been cut in half. The impact of this step was blunted until the economy collapsed a decade later. Poor single mothers were now required to take any job available to them, no matter how low the pay; most of these jobs lacked any health benefits to replace the federal programs from which these families had been removed.

For all working women, mothering is challenging. The problem of balancing home and work life is now arguably the most persistent and difficult personal dilemma for American women. In contrast to the mothers of the 1950s, who were discontent because they spent too much time at home raising children, twenty-first-century mothers worry about their divided lives, about not having enough time with their children, and about falling behind in the workplace. The United States is the only major industrial country in which new mothers do not have rights to paid leave.

Because early feminist calls for publicly funded child care went unheeded, well-paid women turned to low-wage women to care for their children, clean their homes, and tend to their aging parents. At the lower end of the labor force, the children of working mothers were cared for by family members or in informal and too often unlicensed family day care facilities. A 2007 survey found most commercial child care to be of fair or poor quality.[18] Although feminist groups continue to call for publicly supported child care, noting, for instance, that the armed forces provide this benefit, there is no significant political support for extending it to society at large. By comparison, publicly supported child care, staffed by licensed educators, is available in all the European Union countries. No demand of second-wave feminism has fallen off the political radar more steeply than the call for child care support to working mothers.

Gay, Lesbian, Bisexual, and Transgender Rights

The early twenty-first century saw two very important gains in gay rights: the normalization of gays in the military and the growing legalization of gay marriage. Nonetheless, the movement for an expansion of civil rights has been limited by the significant backlash against gays and continuing violence, especially against gay and lesbian youth.

The increasing visibility and demands of transgender people have added a major new element to the battle for recognition and rights of gay and lesbian people and the radically shifting territory of American sexuality. Throughout American history, there have been women living as men who have fought in wars, done men's work, or married women (to a lesser extent, men have also lived as women). In the 1950s, physicians became involved, and highly publicized examples of people who surgically changed their bodies brought new recognition to people seeking to be transgender. Transgender people were always part of the gay and lesbian movement, but in the 1990s they became more prominent.

Transgender issues simultaneously pose a challenge to feminism and extend its basic premises. If one of the goals of feminism is to increase the range and variety of ways to be a woman (and a man), some feminists have argued that physically changing sex reinscribes rigid gender distinctions. Proponents of a growing transgender movement have argued differently—that the feminist principle that gender roles are a matter of social construction and individual choice should be extended to one's fundamental designation as male or female. Moreover, they ask, in a society that accepts bodily modifications such as tattoos and breast modification and the use of hormones for contraceptive purposes, why are these practices suspect for the purposes of transitioning between male and female?

The twenty-first century has seen many transgender firsts in politics, entertainment, and academia. Many government bodies now allow transgender individuals to change their official sexual designation on birth certificates, on passports, and in Social Security records, and some government and business antidiscrimination practices have been extended to transgender persons. In contrast to these gains, violence against vulnerable transgender people, such as teens, prisoners, and sex workers, is a serious problem. Some states have also begun efforts to limit transgender rights. Although it later repealed the bill after extensive public protest and boycotts, North Carolina in 2016 enacted legislation that prohibited transgender individuals from using public bathrooms for the sex they identified with and in addition placed limits on the state's antidiscrimination laws.

Women and the New Immigration

Changes in both women's work and family lives highlight the large, significant presence of immigrants (see the Appendix, Table 5, p. A-21). The 1965 Immigration and Nationality Act opened up gates of immigration that had been closed since 1924; it also shifted from quotas based on countries of origin to categories based on occupational skills, family ties, and political refugee status. Many in the flood of new immigrants lacked formal immigration papers, either because they overstayed temporary visas or because they crossed into the country without papers in the first place. Instead of coming from eastern and southern Europe as in the early twentieth century, half of the new immigrants came from Latin America and a quarter from Asia. From a gendered perspective, late twentieth-century immigration also differed dramatically because women were now in the majority. They immigrate to the United States as part of an international labor market of low-waged women.

The boom in immigration has been accompanied by considerable anti-immigrant sentiment, much of it focused on immigrants' reliance on publicly funded social services. Women and children are the special targets of these attacks because they made much greater use of educational, health, and welfare services than men did. Laws in southwestern border states have attempted to ban immigrants from public services but have generally failed in the courts, giving way instead to congressional legislation on this fundamentally federal issue. In 1996, the federal Illegal Immigration Reform and Immigrant Responsibility Act barred immigrants, even those with legal status, from federal welfare programs for five years after their arrival. The law also mandated the addition of new federal officers to patrol the borders.

While the economic downturn in the United States and the moderate improvement in conditions south of the border have reduced the number of illegal immigrants, those who still try to cross the border do so at greater risk. The Obama administration drastically increased deportation, in 2013 estimated at four hundred thousand cases per year. Despite increasing public activism on the part of the growing Latino population, national politics has refused to ease the path to citizenship for the estimated 10 million undocumented immigrants currently in the United States, an increasing number of them parents of U.S.-born, hence citizen, children. Observers expect the situation will become more problematic because of the election of Donald Trump to the presidency in 2016. In his campaign he promised not only to deport millions of undocumented immigrants, but also to build a wall on the U.S.-Mexico border. It is too early in his presidency, however, to evaluate the long-term impact of his policies, but their immediate effect has been to spread fear and mobilize action among undocumented children and their parents.

Immigrant women constitute approximately 17 percent of the female labor force. It may be surprising to realize that one-third of immigrant women hold professional or managerial jobs, such as the many Filipina and Korean nurses. Undoubtedly, immigrant women flow into the lowest rungs of the female labor force ladder, making services and manufactured goods affordable for middle-class Americans. In the garment industry, the majority of workers are Latina and Asian women. Low pay, long hours, and dangerous working conditions recall the immigrant sweatshops of a century ago. Immigrant women also pour into the booming service sector. Cooking and cleaning in hospitals and hotels, they usually do the dirtiest work and have the least desirable working shifts. Immigrant women also constitute the overwhelming number of private domestic workers. The low cost of immigrant women's labor has made it easier for middle-class women to hire other women to work in their homes while they take demanding outside jobs. We began this chapter with the story of Zoe Baird, one such woman.

The importance of immigration in the United States is part of "globalization," the process by which massive international businesses have grown in size and power, exacerbating inequalities both within and between nations. The end of the Cold War and the collapse of the Soviet Union in 1989 left international capitalism an unchallenged system, thus accelerating globalization. Manufacturing jobs have been exported abroad, particularly in the wake of free trade policies such as the North American Free Trade Agreement signed in 1994 by Canada, Mexico, and the United States. In foreign factories run by or subcontracted to companies with familiar brand names like Nike and Gap, garments are produced at a fraction of the wages paid to American workers and then shipped to the United States for sale. The workers are preponderantly female, many of them mothers whose earnings are crucial to their families' well-being. In this way, women who work for American corporations abroad — across the Mexican border making clothing, in China making children's toys, and in Vietnam making athletic shoes — need to be considered part of the history of the United States through women's eyes.

◆ CONCLUSION: Women in the Twenty-First Century

Just as the political and cultural upheavals of the 1960s profoundly influenced women's lives and gave rise to second-wave feminism, broad historical developments over the last forty years have had an enormous impact on women's experiences. In part fueled by a backlash against feminism, conservatism has eroded some of the advances forged by the women's movement, especially in the realm of reproductive freedom. Yet despite the culture wars and political conflicts that have so divided the nation, the conventional patterns by which women were subordinated in the family have continued to change. Women have also continued to make concrete gains in their quest for political and economic equality.

Growth in the labor force, accelerating inequality, and transformation in family and sexual experience — some of these changes long-standing and others new and unexpected — have made women's lives in the twenty-first century very different from their lives fifty years ago. Patterns of globalization have significantly shaped American women's economic opportunities and will continue to do so in the future. Women are crucial to the expansive immigration that has been one of the defining demographic developments of these years.

We cannot predict the extent to which the twenty-first century will be an era of "progress" for women or what that progress might specifically entail. Yet, as noted in this book's introduction, Mary Ritter Beard, whose book inspired ours, insisted in 1933 upon the need to understand women's role in "the development of American society — their activity, their thought about their labor, and their thought about the history they have helped to make or have observed in the making." *Through Women's Eyes* has extended Beard's charge, to look not only at the profound changes in women's lives but also at the way in which historians recognize the centrality of women's experiences for understanding the nation's past, up to and through the twenty-first century.

CHAPTER 12 REVIEW

KEY TERMS AND PEOPLE

Terms
STOP-ERA
third-wave feminism
Clery Act
Violence Against Women Act
(2013)
Black Lives Matter
#SayHerName
ecofeminism

Emily's List
Burwell v. Hobby Lobby
Justice for Janitors campaign
Defense of Marriage Act
Obergefell v. Hodges
Personal Responsibility and
Work Opportunities Act
United States v. Windsor

People
Phyllis Schlafly
Anita Hill
Condoleezza Rice
Hillary Clinton
Michelle Obama

REVIEW QUESTIONS

1. What was the "New Right," and how did it seek to counter feminism?
2. What were the most significant developments among feminists and social justice activists after the second wave?
3. Describe the advances made by women in politics since the Thomas-Hill hearings in 1991. What limitations still exist? How do you account for them?

4. What role do immigrant women play in today's economy? What challenges do they face?
5. Describe the most important changes to family life in the last thirty years. How do you account for them?
6. **Making Connections** In what ways have the experiences of American women's lives been affected by patterns of globalization in the recent past?

PRIMARY SOURCES

Gender and the Military

IN THE DECADES AFTER THE VIETNAM WAR, feminists became interested in the American military in two very different ways. On the one hand, the doors to service, training, and military benefits were opened wider to women, and many took advantage of the rich array of educational and job opportunities, as well as the adventure, mobility, and patriotic expression the military offered. On the other hand, the long and deep history of military masculinism and misogyny remained a powerful force, and the growing number of women in the ranks faced serious gender discrimination, rampant sexual harassment and abuse, and sex-based limits on the combat capacities in which they could serve. We trace the history of these opposing forces in this essay, through military recruitment devices, firsthand experiences of servicewomen, and direct evidence of gender discrimination and sexual abuse.

In 1973, the draft was effectively ended. (Though men continue to register for service, this is a formality and they have never been called up on this basis.) The widespread conscription of the U.S. male population had arguably been a major incitement for the anti–Vietnam War movement. Replacing a "citizen's army" with an "all volunteer" force would, it was hoped, keep future wars from affecting the entire population and limit the impact to those who, for whatever reason, chose to serve. The other consideration in setting aside the draft was the emergence of the women's liberation movement. As American society became increasingly aware of the breadth and consequences of gender discrimination, an all-male draft no longer seemed politically feasible. Yet drafting women was opposed by both family traditionalists and pacifist feminists and would never have been acceptable in the United States.

Small and brief U.S. military actions took place in the 1970s and 1980s in Panama and the small Caribbean nation of Grenada. Then, in 1991, in response to the Iraqi invasion of Kuwait, President George H. W. Bush took the United States into a six-month war, ultimately involving over seven hundred thousand U.S. troops. Military recruitment for the new "all volunteer" army was directed at those for whom service, even with the risks that war incurred, might constitute an attractive opportunity: the unemployed and underemployed, African Americans and Latinos, and women. Over the six months of the war, forty thousand women served, constituting 11 percent of U.S. troops. Fifteen women died in combat, approximately 10 percent of official combat deaths.

This brief and seemingly successful war, followed by what looked like a stable U.S.-dominated world peace, brought a great deal of attention to American military women. Women, no longer limited to nursing and support functions, served in many of the same positions as men and were exposed to the same dangerous conditions as men. Admitted into the college-based Reserve Officer Training Corps in the early 1970s and the military academies in 1980, women were being trained for leadership positions as well as being relied upon as rank-and-file forces. For women in the military, the emphasis was no longer on how to reconcile their femininity with military participation (and then demobilize back into civilian life), as it had been in the first and second world wars, but on how to use military service as an expression of and route to gender equality (see pp. 508–11).

Jennifer Bailey, portrayed in Figure 12.1, joined the marines in the aftermath of the first Gulf War. She decided to take advantage of new opportunities and train to be a marine drill sergeant, a notoriously harsh and aggressive job. This picture of her was initially featured in a 1999 Marine Corps recruiting publication. Several years later, a fellow drill sergeant used the same image of her to create his own unofficial version of a female-specific recruiting poster, shown in Figure 12.1.

We don't promise you a rose garden either.

THE FEW, THE PROUD, THE WOMEN MARINES

◆ **Figure 12.1 "We don't promise you a rose garden either." (1999)**
SGAC, Inc.

He modified the slogan that the marines used, "We never promised you a rose garden," to highlight women's role. Do you think that this fake poster was meant to celebrate or ridicule women in the armed forces? How does the slogan, normally used on posters of tough male marines, change meaning when linked to a servicewoman? And finally, given that the volunteer army and the women in it were disproportionately drawn from people of color, how do you interpret the racial dynamic that this image represents?

After the apparently successful use of female troops in the first Gulf War, the longstanding prohibition against women in direct combat roles came in for criticism. The increasing technological sophistication of American military performance, the enormous role that various sorts of technological and support staff played in connection with ground forces, and the growing reliance on war from the air rather than on the ground made distinctions between combat and non-combat positions difficult, even arbitrary. In the early 1990s, feminists, politicians, and military leaders began to reconsider the prohibitions limiting women's combat service. For the most part, military figures, recognizing the deployment advantages of having more women in the military and more flexibility in assigning them, supported these changes. Politicians were divided, with conservatives opposing any changes, and congresswomen, their numbers beginning to increase, supporting them.

In the wake of the 1991–1992 war, President George H. W. Bush established an official commission to recommend new policies on women in combat. Torn between liberals and conservatives, it narrowly voted to decrease rather than increase women's access to combat roles. In response, Shirley Sagawa and Nancy Duff Campbell of the National Women's Law Center issued the following report, outlining the flaws and myths in arguments for combat restrictions. The feminist movement, which had first appeared in conjunction with the anti–Vietnam War effort, was changing gears.

Which of the objections to women in wider combat roles do you believe are justified, and which do you believe are not? How successful was the Women's Law Center in refuting the policy? Why do you think that integrating women fully into combat has been such a long, slow process? How does the way in which the military recruited women in the 1990s compare to the way in which the several military services recruited women during World War II?

SHIRLEY SAGAWA AND NANCY DUFF CAMPBELL
Women in Combat (1992)

Serious attention has focused on women's roles in the military since the end of the [first] Persian Gulf War. As a result of women's performance in Desert Storm, Congress repealed the law barring women from combat aircraft assignments and established a Presidential Commission on the Assignment of Women in the Armed Forces to study whether additional positions should be opened to women. This paper outlines the law as it currently pertains to women's assignability, provides arguments against and in favor of opening combat positions to qualified women, [and] discusses the work of the Presidential Commission. . . .

Although no law bars women from *engaging* in combat, women are excluded from half of all military positions. . . . No statute prevents women from serving in ground combat units. Army and Marine Corps policy, however, excludes women from assignments to units that are likely to become engaged in direct combat. In addition, a "risk rule" . . . provides that "risks of exposure to direct combat, hostile fire, or capture are proper criteria for closing noncombat positions or units to women. . . ."

Because assignment of women is limited by military policy, the military uses a quota system that limits the number of women who may enlist or be admitted to ROTC or the service academies. As a result less qualified men are taken over more qualified women. Currently, about 11 percent of

SOURCE: Shirley Sagawa and Nancy Duff Campbell, "Women in Combat," National Women's Law Center, 1992, www.nwlc.org/sites/default/.../Combat.pdf.

military personnel are women. Despite their small numbers, military women now serve with distinction in every service. . . . Among the women who served in Operation Desert Storm were women who flew planes into enemy territory, fired weapons, commanded combat support units, ferried troops in to the combat zone and carried them fuel and supplies. . . .

[A]rguments raised by opponents of opening positions to women in Congressional debate and before the Presidential Commission include:

- Women are physically weaker than men and therefore standards would have to be lowered and unit effectiveness jeopardized;
- The presence of women in units leads to fraternization, sexual harassment, and sexual assault;
- Women lose a disproportionate share of time due to pregnancy, which would undermine unit readiness;
- Combat would take women away from their families, which would have harmful psychological effects on the children;
- If combat units are open to women, women would have to be drafted; and
- The presence of women in combat units would adversely affect unit cohesion and undermine the morale of men who do not want to work with women. . . .

In the Persian Gulf War, 13 women were killed, two were taken prisoner of war, and many more were injured. But when women who serve in the Gulf come up for promotions, they may be passed over because current policies deny women the experience that provides a route to higher-level jobs. . . .

Studies show that sexual harassment is most common in nontraditional jobs with low numbers of women. In the military, barriers to assignability have led to a quota system limiting the number of women at all levels including senior positions. They also have created a climate in which it is acceptable to treat women as inferior. . . . Making assignments based on ability rather than gender would go a long way toward ending second-class status and abuse of women in the military.

The incorrect perception that military women lose a disproportionate share of work time, primarily due to pregnancy, has also been used to justify unequal treatment. . . . Men are more likely to lose time due to discipline problems—drug or alcohol use, fighting, etc. As for concerns about parenting responsibilities, the great majority of single parents in the military are fathers, and more male personnel than women have children at home. . . .

The presence of women in a unit does not undermine cohesion. Experience and research has demonstrated that cohesion is found in mixed-gender units as well as male-only units in the military. With good leadership, a group of dissimilar individuals can bond based on their commonality of experience, regardless of the gender make-up of the group. In fact, evidence suggests that mixed-gender units may actually communicate and work better than single gender units performing similar tasks.

GENDER RESTRICTIONS CONTINUE TO EXIST in the military, especially in high-profile, high-skilled divisions such as the Navy Seals and the Army Rangers. In *G.I. Jane,* a 1997 movie riding the wave of women's greater military participation, Demi Moore played a woman determined to become a Navy Seal. However, despite many people's expectations, the ban was not terminated, and such service by women is still not fully authorized. Nonetheless, although women are not yet allowed to become Navy Seals, Navy Seals can apparently become women. This was the lesson of the highly publicized case of Chris Beck, a decorated veteran. This former Navy Seal announced in 2013 that she was transgender and had transitioned to become Kristin, a woman (Figure 12.2). What do you think the relationship was between Beck's experiences with the hypermasculine Navy Seals and as a transgender person?

Women in this new era of American military life encountered obstacles other than discrimination in service and advancement. Gradually it became apparent that sexual assault of military women by the men with whom they were serving was a major problem. Initially unrecognized and even deliberately hidden, the issue first surfaced in 1991 in the notorious Tailhook scandal.

Tailhook, a voluntary association of naval and marine aviators, holds an annual professional and social meeting, where in 1991 dozens of women and a handful of men were sexually assaulted in a drunken hazing ritual. The account below is the official Department of Defense report, issued in May 1992, nine months after the incident. Despite the copious detail in the report, the

◆ **Figure 12.2 Kristin Beck (2013)**
Nicholas Kamm/AFP/Getty Images.

result was that only two lower-ranking officers were disciplined. Objections, including those from Assistant Secretary of the Navy Barbara Pope, ultimately led to the resignation of the secretary of the navy. However, since Tailhook '91, sexual assault in the military has become, if anything, an ever more serious problem. By some accounts, as many as one-third of women serving have either experienced or been threatened by unwanted sexual encounters. The Veterans Administration now officially considers rape a cause of post-traumatic stress disorder.[19]

As you read the following report, consider the distinction, accepted as such by the investigators and made by male observers, between women who willingly entered the hallway where the attacks took place, known as "the gauntlet," and those who were assaulted. On what basis was this distinction made, and is it a valid distinction? According to the report, what distinguishes an assault from a woman's willing participation? Of the female witnesses, only one, Paula Coughlin, is named and quoted directly. Why do you think this was the case? As the report suggests, her persistence finally brought the sexual assaults of Tailhook '91 to light.

INSPECTOR GENERAL, DEPARTMENT OF DEFENSE
Tailhook '91 (1992)

According to most descriptions, Tailhook conventions in earlier years were largely "stag" affairs. . . . The nature of the gauntlet activities apparently changed some time in the mid to late 1980's when the gauntlet started to involve males touching women who walked through the hallway. . . . Our investigation disclosed that gauntlet-related indecent assaults dated back to at least Tailhook '88. Ten women reported to us that they were assaulted when they attended Tailhook conventions between 1988 and 1990. The women reported they had been grabbed on the breasts, buttocks and/or crotch area. None of the women are known to have reported their assaults to authorities until after Tailhook '91. . . . A significant number of witnesses reported that women went through the gauntlet and seemed to enjoy the attention and interaction with the aviators. Those witnesses, . . . both men and women, generally stated they could tell the women were enjoying themselves because, despite being grabbed and pushed along through the crowd, they were smiling and giggling. . . .

Our investigation also revealed a much more sinister aspect to the gauntlet at Tailhook '91 which involved assaults on unsuspecting women. . . . [As a] couple who appeared to be in their mid to late 60's . . . walked through the gauntlet, a passageway opened up to let the couple through. . . . He recalled that one woman started down the gauntlet and became irate when she was apparently pinched. He said she turned around and threw a beer at a man standing 3 to 4 feet away, hitting him in the face and head with the beer. The man retaliated by throwing his beer on the woman. The woman hit the man on his jaw and the man then struck the side of the woman's head with a closed hand and the witness thought the woman might have fallen to her knees. . . . He noted that in previous years he also took part in the

gauntlet. . . . He opined that the gauntlet is more of a melee than an organized event. . . .

The officer's spouse provided a somewhat different perspective of the same incidents. . . . She said it appeared that some signal had been given that the "gauntlet" was about to start, and all the men in the hallway began lining the halls rather than milling about, as though suddenly organized. . . . Regarding the incident described by her husband in which a man and a woman struck each other in the gauntlet, she said that she was personally shocked by the force of the blow the man used. It appeared to her that the man put his full strength behind the blow. Unlike her husband, she did not see any women lining up to get pinched or patted, but rather it seemed to her that they were simply trying to get through the hallway. . . .

The gauntlet was also vividly described to us by several victims. One female civilian victim . . . told us that, as she walked up the hallway, at least seven men suddenly attacked her. They pulled down her "tube top" and grabbed at her exposed breasts while she attempted to cover herself with her arms. She fell to the ground and the assault continued. She bit several of her attackers in an attempt to stop their assault. After a few moments, they stopped their attack and she was allowed to get up from the floor. She turned and looked back down the hallway and observed another woman screaming and fighting her way down the hallway as she too was attacked. . . . The victim later told her boyfriend, a Navy officer, about the attack but he advised her not to tell anyone about it because they would think she was a "slut. . . ."

One victim, a 32-year old female, reported that she attended Tailhook '91 with her spouse, a Navy officer, her mother, and two of her mother's female friends. As the group walked through the hallway the victim, who was wearing a formal cocktail dress, was suddenly grabbed around the waist and lifted above the crowd by two men. The men lifted the skirt of her dress above her waist and pushed

SOURCE: Inspector General, Department of Defense, *Tailhook '91* (May 1992).

their hands between her legs in an attempt to get their fingers inside her panties. Our investigation revealed that the victim's mother as well as one of her mother's friends were also indecently assaulted as they walked through the hallway.

LT Paula Coughlin, the Navy officer who first publicly revealed allegations of impropriety at Tailhook '91, told us that she entered the third floor hallway at the Hilton Hotel and, as she walked up the hallway and into a crowd of men, someone began to yell "Admiral's Aide!" She was grabbed on the buttocks from behind with such force that she was lifted up off the ground. As she turned to confront the man, another man behind her grabbed her buttocks and she was pushed from behind into a crowd of men who collectively began pinching her body and pulling at her clothing. One man put both his hands down the front of her tank top, inside her brassiere and grabbed her breasts. LT Coughlin told us that she crouched down and bit the man on his forearm and on his right hand. As the man released his grip on her breasts, another man reached up under her skirt and grabbed her panties. She then kicked at her attackers. She stated, "I felt as though the group was trying to rape me." LT Coughlin told us that she saw one of the men in the group turn to walk away so she "reached out and tapped him on the hip, pleading with the man just let me get in front of him." The man turned around to face her, raised both his hands, and placed them on her breasts.

ANOTHER ISSUE AFFECTING SERVICEWOMEN is that of military parenthood. Aggressive recruitment of young enlistees was insufficient to meet the demands of the armed forces, especially once the United States officially went to war in Iraq in 2003. Military reservists made up the difference. These were usually older adults, both women and men, many of them with children and spouses. As terms of service were extended, the pressure on military families intensified, undermining the military's efforts to isolate the majority of the public from people whose lives were affected by serving in the armed forces. Those whose spouses were serving found themselves raising their children and managing their households alone for extended periods of time. With large numbers of servicemen returning home with post-traumatic stress disorder, domestic abuse also became a problem.

As for women service members, a significant number of mothers of young children entered the ranks. An estimated one hundred thousand mothers, 50 percent of all active women in the military, were serving in 2009. Single mothers are not allowed to enlist, but those who are reservists can be called up and face especially intense challenges.[20] Military mothers are a specific subset of working mothers. The military has been no more successful than other employers in balancing antidiscrimination policies with support policies for working mothers.

Motherhood has long infused people's understandings of women's relationship to war. This has been the case whether mothers objected to sacrificing their boy children or whether they supported their soldier sons out of patriotic pride. Americans' increasing awareness that many mothers, most of them with young children, are themselves serving in the theaters of war brings mothers' dilemmas right into the heart of warfare.

Below is a review, written for young readers, of *Hero Mom*, a 2013 picture book for young children of military mothers, written by Melinda Hardin and illustrated by Bryan Langdo. The cover of the book (which you can find online) features a drawing of a black woman in desert fatigues about to board a helicopter, reaching out to her young son, who reaches back to her; both smile. As you consider this book and the review, ask yourself: What approach does the author take to the problem of military mothers? What other issues are not discussed? What policies might the military have undertaken to deal with the issues faced by military mothers and fathers and their children? Do you think that mothers of young children should be allowed to serve or should be prohibited from serving? Why?

TRACY MOORE
Review of Hero Mom (2013)

In *Hero Mom*, a diverse range of children discuss how proud they are of their military moms and the ways in which the women resemble heroes or superheroes for their courage and skill during deployment.

Hero Mom takes a difficult subject — family separation during deployment — and presents it as a point of pride for children, who can explain to others that their mothers are gone but are doing something extremely important, whether they're transporting cargo, repairing aircraft, or leading a

Source: Tracy Moore, review of *Hero Mom*, by Melinda Hardin, Common Sense Media, https://www.commonsense-media.org/book-reviews/hero-mom (accessed March 23, 2015).

battalion. The book makes a point of showing the way moms who are deployed show love for their children with letters or by email or video chat. And the soft watercolor illustrations give the book an expressive, sentimental feel.

For kids missing their moms overseas, *Hero Mom* can help instill a sense of pride in their moms' line of work. For parents, this can be a way to broach a tender subject and open up a dialogue about managing the separation.

Families can talk about separation. Have you been separated from your mom or dad for a period of time due to their work, travel, or deployment? How did it make you feel?

How do you stay in touch when your mom or dad has to leave for a period of time?

FINALLY, THE ISSUE OF GAYS IN THE ARMED FORCES has affected women service members. In 1993, President Bill Clinton instituted the "don't ask, don't tell" policy. Gay and lesbian servicepeople were counseled to remain discreet and private about their sexual orientation, which, if discovered, still subjected them to involuntary discharge. In practice, the policy actually increased the pressure on them because of the threat of exposure and dismissal, and rather than diffusing the issue, intensified it.

According to a careful study, from the late 1990s on, women and men of color became increasingly likely to be investigated and discharged with violating the "don't ask, don't tell" policy.[21] The disproportionate impact on lesbians is especially interesting because it flies in the face of straight men's fear of being exposed to male homosexuality, which has played such a major role in public anxiety over gay people's serving. Criticism of the policy grew among politicians, including President Obama, and military leaders, including former secretary of state General Colin Powell. Finally, in 2010, Congress repealed the policy. Gay men and women are now welcomed into military service without any restrictions.

◆ **Figure 12.3 Major Margaret Witt Gets Married (2012)**
Nate Gowdy Photography.

While debate over the policy was still going on, gay servicepeople who had been victims of "don't ask, don't tell" challenged their dishonorable discharges in court. One of these was Margaret Witt, an air force major and nurse, who was discharged in 2007. Her crime was that she was discovered to be living in a long-term lesbian relationship. She had been extremely cautious but was turned in to her superiors by the ex-husband of a woman she had dated. Witt claimed that her Fourteenth Amendment rights to due legal process had been violated. After a lower court decided against her, an appeals court agreed with her, ruling that the air force could not simply assume that her actions interfered with "unit cohesion and morale," but had to prove this, which it did not do. After the "don't ask, don't tell" policy was repealed, Witt was allowed to retire with full benefits.

Why do you think lesbians suffered disproportionately under "don't ask, don't tell"? Figure 12.3 is a photograph of Witt marrying her partner, a civilian, the year after the air force reversed its action against her. Why do you think the issue of military service has had such a ripple effect on other rights of gays and lesbians?

QUESTIONS FOR ANALYSIS

1. With the ban against women's serving in the military ending, what are the new obstacles that military service poses to women?

2. How do you think the increase in the number of women in military service will affect society's attitude to gender difference and equality?

NOTES

1. Katha Pollitt, *Pro: Reclaiming Abortion Rights* (New York: Picador, 2014), 25.

2. Quoted in "Supreme Court Upholds Federal Abortion Ban, Opens Door for Further Restrictions by States," *Guttmacher Policy Review* 10 (Spring 2007), http://www.guttmacher.org/pubs/gpr/10/2/gpr100219.html (accessed July 24, 2007).

3. Eloise Salholz, "The Marriage Crunch," *Newsweek*, June 2, 1986, 55.

4. Susan J. Douglas, *The Rise of Enlightened Sexism: How Pop Culture Took Us from Girl Power to Girls Gone Wild* (New York: St. Martin's, 2010), 15.

5. SAKHI, "Mission and History," http://www.sakhi.org/about-sakhi/mission-and-history (accessed August 12, 2017).

6. Rebecca A. Harts and M. Alexander Lowther, "Honoring Sovereignty: Aiding Tribal Efforts to Protect Native American Women from Domestic Violence," *California Law Review* 96, no. 1 (February 2008): 188–89.

7. Herbert Ruffin, "Black Lives Matter: The Growth of a New Social Justice Movement," http://www.blackpast.org/perspectives/black-lives-matter-growth-new-social-justice-movement (accessed July 27, 2017).

8. The African American Policy Forum, "#SAYHERNAME," http://www.aapf.org/sayhername (accessed August 12, 2017).

9. Cathleen McGuire and Colleen McGuire, "Ecofeminist Visions" (1991, 1993, 2003), reproduced by Eve Online, http://eve.enviroweb.org/what_is/main.html (accessed March 24, 2015).

10. "Who Are Women in Black?" Women in Black, http://womeninblack.org/pagina-ejemplo (accessed March 24, 2015).

11. Steven Stark, "Gap Politics," *Atlantic Monthly*, July 1996, 71–80.

12. Hillary Rodham Clinton, Remarks for the United Nations Fourth World Conference on Women, Beijing, China, September 5, 1995, http://www.americanrhetoric.com/speeches/hillaryclintonbeijingspeech.htm (accessed March 20, 2014).

13. Hillary Rodham Clinton, "Yes, We Can" (speech on ending her presidential candidacy), *Guardian*, June 7, 2008, http://www.theguardian.com/commentisfree/2008/jun/07/hillaryclinton.uselections20081 (accessed November 3, 2014).

14. http://www.iraqbodycount.org; http://watson.brown.edu/costsofwar/costs/human/civilians/afghan (accessed July 27, 2017).

15. AAUW, "The Simple Truth about the Gender Pay Gap" (Spring 2017), http://www.aauw.org/research/the-simple-truth-about-the-gender-pay-gap (accessed July 27, 2017).

16. Dorothy Sue Cobble, *The Other Women's Movement: Workplace Justice and Social Rights in Modern America* (Princeton, NJ: Princeton University Press, 2004), 222.

17. Nancy Cott, *Public Vows: A History of Marriage and the Nation* (Cambridge, MA: Harvard University Press, 2000), 212.

18. Jonathan Cohn, "The Hell of American Day Care," *New Republic*, April 15, 2013, http://www.newrepublic.com/article/112892/hell-american-day-care (accessed March 24, 2015).

19. Cynthia Enloe, *Nimo's War, Emma's War: Making Feminist Sense of the Iraq War* (Berkeley: University of California Press, 2010), 175.

20. Lizette Alvarez, "Wartime Soldier, Conflicted Mom," *New York Times*, September 26, 2009, http://www.nytimes.com/2009/09/27/us/27mothers.html?pagewanted=all&_r=0 (accessed March 24, 2015).

21. Gary J. Gates, "Discharges under the Don't Ask, Don't Tell Policy: Women and Racial/Ethnic Minorities," Williams Institute, September 2010, http://williamsinstitute.law.ucla.edu/research/military-related/discharges-under-the-dont-ask-dont-tell-policy-women-and-racialethnic-minorities-2 (accessed March 24, 2015).

SUGGESTED REFERENCES

General

Dorothy Sue Cobble, Linda Gordon, and Astrid Henry, *Feminism Unfinished: A Short, Surprising History of American Women's Movements* (2014).

Gail Collins, *When Everything Changed: The Amazing Journey of American Women from 1960 to the Present* (2009).

Sarah M. Evans, *Tidal Wave: How Women Changed America at Century's End* (2003).

Estelle B. Freedman, *No Turning Back: The History of Feminism and the Future of Women* (2002).

Ruth Rosen, *The World Split Open: How the Modern Women's Movement Changed America*, 2nd ed. (2007).

Feminism and the New Right in American Politics

Mary Frances Berry, *Why ERA Failed: Politics, Women's Rights, and the Amending Process of the Constitution* (1986).

Donald T. Critchlow, *Phyllis Schlafly and Grassroots Conservatism: A Woman's Crusade* (2005).

Susan J. Douglas, *The Rise of Enlightened Sexism: How Pop Culture Took Us from Girl Power to Girls Gone Wild* (2010).

Susan Faludi, *Backlash: The Undeclared War against American Women* (1991).

Rebecca E. Klatch, *Women of the New Right* (1987).

Katha Pollitt, *Pro: Reclaiming Abortion Rights* (2014).
Rickie Solinger, ed., *Abortion Wars: A Half Century of Struggle, 1950–2000* (1998).

Third-Wave Feminism, Women Stand Up to Violence, Ecofeminism, and Peace

Jennifer Baumgardner and Amy Richards, eds., *Manifesta: Young Women, Feminism, and the Future*, rev. ed. (2010).
Cynthia Cockburn, *Antimilitarism: Political and Gender Dynamics of Peace Movements* (2012).
Irene Diamond and Gloria Orenstein, eds., *Reweaving Feminism: The Emergence of Ecofeminism* (1990).
Rory Dicker and Alison Piepmeier, eds., *Catching a Wave: Reclaiming Feminism for the 21st Century* (2003).
Barbara Ehrenreich, *Blood Rites: Origins and History of the Passions of War* (1997).
Barbara Findlen, ed., *Listen Up: Voices from the Next Feminist Generation,* 2nd ed. (2001).
Daisy Hernández and Bushra Rehman, eds., *Colonize This! Young Women of Color on Today's Feminism* (2002).
Vivien Labaton and Dawn Lundy Martin, eds., *The Fire This Time: Young Activists and the New Feminism* (2004).
Catriona Sandilands, *The Good-Natured Feminist: Ecofeminism and the Quest for Democracy* (1999).
Sonia Shah, *Dragon Ladies: Asian American Feminists Breathe Fire* (1997).
Keenanga-Yamahtta Taylor, *From #BlackLivesMatter to Black Liberation* (2016).

Women in Politics

Lauren Berlant and Lisa Duggan, eds., *Our Monica, Ourselves: The Clinton Affair and the National Interest* (2001).
Nancy L. Cohen, *Delirium: How the Sexual Counterrevolution Is Polarizing America* (2012).
Beverly Guy-Sheftall and Johnnetta Betsch Cole, eds., *Who Should Be First? Feminists Speak Out on the 2008 Presidential Campaign* (2010).
Anne E. Korblut, *Notes from the Cracked Ceiling: Hillary Clinton, Sarah Palin, and What It Will Take for a Woman to Win* (2009).

Toni Morrison, ed., *Race-ing Justice, En-Gendering Power: Essays on Anita Hill, Clarence Thomas, and the Construction of Social Reality* (1992).

Women in the Military

Cynthia Enloe, *Nimo's War, Emma's War: Making Feminist Sense of the Iraq War* (2010).
Evelyn M. Monahan and Rosemary Neidel-Greenlee, *A Few Good Women: America's Military Women from World War I to the Wars in Iraq and Afghanistan* (2010).
Judith Hicks Stiehm, *It's Our Military, Too! Women and the U.S. Military* (1996).

Modern Life, Work, and Family

Randy Albelda and Chris Tilly, *Glass Ceilings and Bottomless Pits: Women's Work, Women's Poverty* (1997).
David Boies and Theodore B. Olson, *Redeeming the Dream: The Case for Marriage Equality* (2014).
Dorothy Sue Cobble, *The Other Women's Movement: Workplace Justice and Social Rights in Modern America* (2004).
Stephanie Coontz, *Marriage, a History* (2005).
Barbara Ehrenreich, *Nickel and Dimed: On (Not) Getting By in America* (2001).
Arlie Russell Hochschild with Anne Machung, *The Second Shift*, rev. ed. (2003).
Nancy MacLean, *Freedom Is Not Enough: The Opening of the American Workplace* (2006).
Judith Stacey, *Brave New Families: Stories of Domestic Upheaval in Late-Twentieth-Century America*, rev. ed. (1998).
Susan Stryker, *Transgender History* (2008).

Immigration

Teri L. Caraway, *Assembling Women: The Feminization of Global Manufacturing* (2007).
Barbara Ehrenreich and Arlie Russell Hochschild, eds., *Global Woman: Nannies, Maids, and Sex Workers in the New Economy* (2003).
Miriam Ching Yoon Louie, *Sweatshop Warriors: Immigrant Women Workers Take On the Global Factory* (2001).

APPENDIX
DOCUMENTS
Seneca Falls Declaration of Sentiments and Resolutions

I N 1848, ELIZABETH CADY STANTON, Lucretia Mott, and Martha Coffin Wright, among others, called a meeting in Stanton's hometown of Seneca Falls, New York, to discuss "the social, civil and religious condition of Woman." Over three hundred men and women attended, and one hundred signed a comprehensive document that detailed the discriminations women endured and demanded women's rights, most controversially the vote. The "Declaration of Sentiments" was forthrightly modeled on the Declaration of Independence, which is telling evidence of the Seneca Falls signers' understanding that the liberties and rights promised by the American Revolution had not been extended to the female half of the population.

DECLARATION OF SENTIMENTS

When, in the course of human events, it becomes necessary for one portion of the family of man to assume among the people of the earth a position different from that which they have hitherto occupied, but one to which the laws of nature and of nature's God entitle them, a decent respect to the opinions of mankind requires that they should declare the causes that impel them to such a course.

We hold these truths to be self-evident: that all men and women are created equal; that they are endowed by their Creator with certain inalienable rights; that among these are life, liberty, and the pursuit of happiness; that to secure these rights governments are instituted, deriving their just powers from the consent of the governed. Whenever any form of government becomes destructive of these ends, it is the right of those who suffer from it to refuse allegiance to it, and to insist upon the institution of a new government, laying its foundations on such principles, and organizing its powers in such form, as to them shall seem most likely to effect their safety and happiness. Prudence, indeed, will dictate that governments long established should not be changed for light and transient causes; and accordingly all experience hath shown that mankind are more disposed to suffer, while evils are sufferable, than to right themselves by abolishing the forms to which they were accustomed. But when a long train of abuses and usurpations, pursuing invariably the same object evinces a design to reduce them under absolute despotism, it is their duty to throw off such government, and to provide new guards for their future security. Such has been the patient sufferance of the women under this government, and such is now the necessity which constrains them to demand the equal station to which they are entitled.

The history of mankind is a history of repeated injuries and usurpations on the part of

SOURCE: Susan B. Anthony, Elizabeth Cady Stanton, and Matilda Joslyn Gage, eds., *History of Woman Suffrage* (Rochester, NY: S. B. Anthony, 1889).

man toward woman, having in direct object the establishment of an absolute tyranny over her. To prove this, let facts be submitted to a candid world.

He has never permitted her to exercise her inalienable right to the elective franchise. He has compelled her to submit to laws, in the formation of which she had no voice. He has withheld from her rights which are given to the most ignorant and degraded men — both natives and foreigners.

Having deprived her of this first right of a citizen, the elective franchise, thereby leaving her without representation in the halls of legislation, he has opposed her on all sides.

He has made her, if married, in the eye of the law, civilly dead.

He has taken from her all right in property, even to the wages she earns.

He has made her, morally, an irresponsible being, as she can commit many crimes with impunity, provided they be done in the presence of her husband. In the covenant of marriage, she is compelled to promise obedience to her husband, he becoming, to all intents and purposes, her master — the law giving him power to deprive her of her liberty, and to administer chastisement.

He has so framed the laws of divorce, as to what shall be the proper causes, and in case of separation, to whom the guardianship of the children shall be given, as to be wholly regardless of the happiness of women — the law, in all cases, going upon a false supposition of the supremacy of man, and giving all power into his hands.

After depriving her of all rights as a married woman, if single, and the owner of property, he has taxed her to support a government which recognizes her only when her property can be made profitable to it.

He has monopolized nearly all the profitable employments, and from those she is permitted to follow, she receives but a scanty remuneration. He closes against her all the avenues to wealth and distinction which he considers most honorable to himself. As a teacher of theology, medicine, or law, she is not known.

He has denied her the facilities for obtaining a thorough education, all colleges being closed against her.

He allows her in Church, as well as State, but in a subordinate position, claiming Apostolic authority for her exclusion from the ministry, and, with some exceptions, from any public participation in the affairs of the Church.

He has created a false public sentiment by giving to the world a different code of morals for men and women, by which moral delinquencies which exclude women from society, are not only tolerated, but deemed of little account in man.

He has usurped the prerogative of Jehovah himself, claiming it as his right to assign for her a sphere of action, when that belongs to her conscience and to her God.

He has endeavored, in every way that he could, to destroy her confidence in her own powers, to lessen her self-respect, and to make her willing to lead a dependent and abject life.

Now, in view of this entire disfranchisement of one-half the people of this country, their social and religious degradation — in view of the unjust laws above mentioned, and because women do feel themselves aggrieved, oppressed, and fraudulently deprived of their most sacred rights, we insist that they have immediate admission to all the rights and privileges which belong to them as citizens of the United States.

In entering upon the great work before us, we anticipate no small amount of misconception, misrepresentation, and ridicule; but we shall use every instrumentality within our power to effect our object. We shall employ agents, circulate tracts, petition the State and National legislatures, and endeavor to enlist the pulpit and the press in our behalf. We hope this Convention will be followed by a series of Conventions embracing every part of the country.

RESOLUTIONS

WHEREAS, The great precept of nature is conceded to be, that "man shall pursue his own true and substantial happiness." [William] Blackstone in his *Commentaries* remarks, that this law of Nature being coequal with mankind, and dictated by God himself, is of course superior in obligation to any other. It is binding over all the globe, in all countries and at all times; no human laws are of any validity if contrary to this, and such of them as are valid, derive all their force, and all their validity, and all their authority, mediately and immediately, from this original; therefore,

Resolved, That such laws as conflict, in any way, with the true and substantial happiness of woman, are contrary to the great precept of nature and of no validity, for this is "superior in obligation to any other."

Resolved, That all laws which prevent woman from occupying such a station in society as her conscience shall dictate, or which place her in a position inferior to that of man, are contrary to the great precept of nature, and therefore of no force or authority.

Resolved, That woman is man's equal — was intended to be so by the Creator, and the highest good of the race demands that she should be recognized as such.

Resolved, That the women of this country ought to be enlightened in regard to the laws under which they live, that they may no longer publish their degradation by declaring themselves satisfied with their present position, nor their ignorance, by asserting that they have all the rights they want.

Resolved, That inasmuch as man, while claiming for himself intellectual superiority, does accord to woman moral superiority, it is preeminently his duty to encourage her to speak and teach, as she has an opportunity, in all religious assemblies.

Resolved, That the same amount of virtue, delicacy, and refinement of behavior that is required of woman in the social state, should also be required of man, and the same transgressions should be visited with equal severity on both man and woman.

Resolved, That the objection of indelicacy and impropriety, which is so often brought against woman when she addresses a public audience, comes with a very ill-grace from those who encourage, by their attendance, her appearance on the stage, in the concert, or in feats of the circus.

Resolved, That woman has too long rested satisfied in the circumscribed limits which corrupt customs and a perverted application of the Scriptures have marked out for her, and that it is time she should move in the enlarged sphere which her great Creator has assigned her.

Resolved, That it is the duty of the women of this country to secure to themselves their sacred right to the elective franchise.

Resolved, That the equality of human rights results necessarily from the fact of the identity of the race in capabilities and responsibilities.

Resolved, therefore, That, being invested by the Creator with the same capabilities, and the same consciousness of responsibility for their exercise, it is demonstrably the right and duty of woman, equally with man, to promote every righteous cause by every righteous means; and especially in regard to the great subjects of morals and religion, it is self-evidently her right to participate with her brother in teaching them, both in private and in public, by writing and by speaking, by any instrumentalities proper to be used, and in any assemblies proper to be held; and this being a self-evident truth growing out of the divinely implanted principles of human nature, any custom or authority adverse to it, whether modern or wearing the hoary sanction of antiquity, is to be regarded as a self-evident falsehood, and at war with mankind.

[Signers, in alphabetical order]

Caroline Barker
Eunice Barker
William G. Barker
Rachel D. Bonnel
   (Mitchell)
Joel D. Bunker
William Burroughs
E. W. Capron
Jacob P. Chamberlain
Elizabeth Conklin
Mary Conklin
P. A. Culvert
Cynthia Davis
Thomas Dell
William S. Dell
Elias J. Doty
Susan R. Doty
Frederick Douglass
Julia Ann Drake
Harriet Cady Eaton
Elisha Foote
Eunice Newton Foote
Mary Ann Frink
Cynthia Fuller
Experience Gibbs
Mary Gilbert

Lydia Gild
Sarah Hallowell
Mary H. Hallowell
Henry Hatley
Sarah Hoffman
Charles L. Hoskins
Jane C. Hunt
Richard P. Hunt
Margaret Jenkins
John Jones
Lucy Jones
Phebe King
Hannah J. Latham
Lovina Latham
Elizabeth Leslie
Eliza Martin
Mary Martin
Delia Mathews
Dorothy Mathews
Jacob Mathews
Elizabeth W. M'Clintock
Mary M'Clintock
Mary Ann M'Clintock
Thomas M'Clintock
Jonathan Metcalf
Nathan J. Milliken

Mary S. Mirror
Pheobe Mosher
Sarah A. Mosher
James Mott
Lucretia Mott
Lydia Mount
Catharine C. Paine
Rhoda Palmer
Saron Phillips
Sally Pitcher
Hannah Plant
Ann Porter
Amy Post
George W. Pryor
Margaret Pryor
Susan Quinn
Rebecca Race
Martha Ridley
Azaliah Schooley
Margaret Schooley
Deborah Scott
Antoinette E. Segur
Henry Seymour
Henry W. Seymour
Malvina Seymour
Catharine Shaw

Stephen Shear
Sarah Sisson
Robert Smallbridge
Elizabeth D. Smith
Sarah Smith
David Spalding
Lucy Spalding
Elizabeth Cady Stanton
Catharine F. Stebbins
Sophronia Taylor
Betsey Tewksbury
Samuel D. Tillman
Edward F. Underhill
Martha Underhill
Mary E. Vail
Isaac Van Tassel
Sarah Whitney
Maria E. Wilbur
Justin Williams
Sarah R. Woods
Charlotte Woodward
S. E. Woodworth
Martha C. Wright

Major U.S. Supreme Court Decisions Through Women's Eyes

T HE FOLLOWING BRIEF EXCERPTS of Supreme Court decisions, carefully abridged from the full opinions delivered by the Court, have been selected for their particular importance to the history of women in the United States. Not all of them deal solely or primarily with gender discrimination. Those decisions concerning racism and the legacy of slavery, beginning with the 1856 *Dred Scott* case, have profound implications for women. Read one after another, these decisions give evidence of both the continuity of judicial reasoning and the dramatic shifts in judicial conclusions that have characterized the nation's highest court.

Dred Scott v. Sandford involved a slave couple who claimed they had gained freedom by virtue of residence for many years on free soil. The case took almost ten years to arrive before the Court, where a seven-to-two majority ruled that the Scotts remained slaves. In his last major opinion, Chief Justice Roger Taney not only dismissed the Scotts' claims but sought to intervene in the raging national political debate over slavery by declaring that any federal intervention in slavery, including the 1820 Missouri Compromise (which had banned slavery from the territories in which the Scotts had lived), was unconstitutional.

Dred Scott v. Sandford (1856)

It is difficult at this day to realize the state of public opinion in relation to that unfortunate race, which prevailed in the civilized and enlightened portions of the world at the time of the Declaration of Independence, and when the Constitution of the United States was framed and adopted. . . .

They had for more than a century before been regarded as beings of an inferior order, and altogether unfit to associate with the white race, either in social or political relations; and so far inferior, that they had no rights which the white man was bound to respect; and that the negro might justly and lawfully be reduced to slavery for his benefit. . . . We refer to these historical facts for the purpose of showing the fixed opinions concerning that race, upon which the statesmen of that day spoke and acted. It is necessary to do this, in order to determine whether the general terms used in the Constitution of the United States, as to the rights of man and the rights of the people, was intended to include them, or to give to them or their posterity the benefit of any of its provisions.

[T]he right of property in a slave is distinctly and expressly affirmed in the Constitution. . . . This is done in plain words — too plain to be misunderstood. And no word can be found in the Constitution which gives Congress a greater power over slave property, or which entitles property of that kind to less protection than property of any other description. . . .

Upon these considerations, it is the opinion of the court that the act of Congress which prohibited a citizen from holding and owning property of this kind in the territory of the United States north of the line therein mentioned, is not warranted by the Constitution, and is therefore void; and that neither Dred Scott himself, nor any of his family, were made free by being carried into this territory.

T HE FOURTEENTH AMENDMENT, which was designed to overturn the *Dred Scott* decision by defining national citizenship broadly enough to include the ex-slaves, became the constitutional basis for challenging both race and gender discrimination. Soon after its ratification in 1868, woman suffragists saw the amendment as a potential resource. The National Woman Suffrage Association contended that, inasmuch as women were citizens, their rights as voters were automatically secured. Accordingly, Virginia Minor tried to vote in her hometown of St. Louis, Missouri, and then sued the local election official who refused her ballot. Chief Justice Morrison Waite delivered the Court's unanimous opinion that although the Fourteenth Amendment did indeed grant women equal citizenship with men, it did not make them voters. His contention, that suffrage was not a civil right but a political privilege outside the amendment's intended scope, was underscored by the passage of the Fifteenth Amendment in 1870, which was addressed explicitly to voting. Waite's reasoning applied to all citizens, not just women. After the *Minor* decision, suffragists realized they needed a separate constitutional amendment to secure women's political rights.

Minor v. Happersett (1874)

The argument is, that as a woman, born or naturalized in the United States and subject to the jurisdiction thereof, is a citizen of the United States and of the State in which she resides, she has the right of suffrage as one of the privileges and immunities of her citizenship, which the State cannot by its laws or constitution abridge.

There is no doubt that women may be citizens. They are persons, and by the fourteenth amendment "all persons born or naturalized in the United States and subject to the jurisdiction thereof" are expressly declared to be "citizens of the United States and of the State wherein they reside." . . .

If the right of suffrage is one of the necessary privileges of a citizen of the United States, then the constitution and laws of Missouri confining it to men are in violation of the Constitution of the United States, as amended, and consequently void. . . . It is clear, . . . we think, that the Constitution has not added the right of suffrage to the privileges and immunities of citizenship as they existed at the time it was adopted.

It is true that the United States guarantees to every State a republican form of government. . . . No particular government is designated as republican, neither is the exact form to be guaranteed, in any manner especially designated. . . .

[I]t is certainly now too late to contend that a government is not republican, within the meaning of this guaranty in the Constitution, because women are not made voters.

I NVOKING THE FOURTEENTH AMENDMENT three decades later, Homer Plessy argued that he had been denied equal protection of the law when a Louisiana statute forced him to travel in a separate all-black railroad car. By a vote of eight to one, the Court ruled against his claims and found the emerging system of state-sponsored racial segregation that was settling on the postslavery South to be fully constitutional. Writing for the majority, Justice Henry Brown argued that because a system of segregation affected both black and white, it was not discriminatory. The famous phrase by which this argument has come to be known — "separate but equal" — appears in the brave, dissenting opinion of Justice John Harlan. Note how the Court's ruling treats racial distinction and black inferiority as facts of nature that any legal decision must recognize.

Plessy v. Ferguson (1896)

A statute which implies merely a legal distinction between the white and colored races — a distinction which is founded in the color of the two races, and which must always exist so long as white men are distinguished from the other race by color — has no tendency to destroy the legal equality of the two races. . . .

The object of the [fourteenth] amendment was undoubtedly to enforce the absolute equality of the two races before the law, but, in the nature of things, it could not have been intended to abolish distinctions based upon color, or to enforce social, as distinguished from political, equality, or a commingling of the two races upon terms unsatisfactory to either. Laws permitting, and even requiring, their separation, in places where they are liable to be brought into contact, do not necessarily imply the inferiority of either race to the other. . . .

We consider the underlying fallacy of the plaintiff's argument to consist in the assumption that the enforced separation of the two races stamps the colored race with a badge of inferiority. If this be so, it is not by reason of anything found in the act, but solely because the colored race chooses to put that construction upon it. The argument necessarily assumes that if, as has been more than once the case, and is not unlikely to be so again, the colored race should become the dominant power in the state legislature, and should enact a law in precisely similar terms, it would thereby relegate the white race to an inferior position. We imagine that the white race, at least, would not acquiesce in this assumption. The argument also assumes that social prejudices may be overcome by legislation, and that equal rights cannot be secured to the negro except by an enforced commingling of the two races. We cannot accept this proposition. . . . Legislation is powerless to eradicate racial instincts, or to abolish distinctions based upon physical differences, and the attempt to do so can only result in accentuating the difficulties of the present situation.

I N *MULLER V. OREGON*, Curt Muller challenged the constitutionality of an Oregon law setting a maximum ten-hour working day for women employees. Starting in the 1880s, the Court had turned away from the Fourteenth Amendment's original purposes to emphasize its guarantee of the individual's right of contract in the workplace, free from state regulation. This reading made most laws setting limits on the working day unconstitutional. Arguing on behalf of Oregon, Louis Brandeis, lead counsel for the National Consumers' League, successfully pressed an argument for the law's constitutionality on the ground that it was directed only at women. Brandeis's argument circumvented the Fourteenth Amendment by contending that the federal government's constitutionally authorized police power, which permitted special regulations for the national good, allowed legislation to protect motherhood and through it "the [human] race." The Court ruled unanimously to uphold the Oregon law, with Justice David Brewer delivering the opinion. As in the *Plessy* decision, the Court held that physical difference and even inferiority are facts of nature that the law may accommodate and that are compatible with formal legal equality. Yet the decision here was hailed by many women reformers as a great victory. Brandeis was appointed to the Supreme Court in 1916, the first Jewish member of the Court.

Muller v. Oregon (1908)

We held in *Lochner v. New York* [1903] that a law providing that no laborer shall be required or permitted to work in bakeries more than sixty hours in a week or ten hours in a day was not as to men a legitimate exercise of the police power of the state, but an unreasonable, unnecessary, and arbitrary interference with the right and liberty of the individual to contract in relation to his labor, and as such was in conflict with, and void under, the Federal Constitution. That decision is invoked by plaintiff in error as decisive of the question before us. But this assumes that the difference between the sexes does not justify a different rule respecting a restriction of the hours of labor. . . .

That woman's physical structure and the performance of maternal functions place her at a disadvantage in the struggle for subsistence is obvious. This is especially true when the burdens of motherhood are upon her. Even when they are not, . . . continuance for a long time on her feet at work, repeating this from day to day, tends to injurious effects upon the body, and, as healthy mothers are essential to vigorous offspring, the physical well-being of woman becomes an object of public interest and care in order to preserve the strength and vigor of the race. . . .

Even though all restrictions on political, personal, and contractual rights were taken away, and [woman] stood, so far as statutes are concerned, upon an absolutely equal plane with [man], it would still be true that she is so constituted that she will rest upon and look to him for protection; that her physical structure and a proper discharge of her maternal functions — having in view not merely her own health, but the well-being of the race — justify legislation to protect her from the greed as well as the passion of man. The limitations which this statute places upon her contractual powers, upon her right to agree with her employer as to the time she shall labor, are not imposed solely for her benefit, but also largely for the benefit of all.

T HE IRONY OF THE *MULLER* DECISION in favor of maximum hours laws to benefit women workers on the basis of their maternal dependency is underlined by the *Adkins* case, decided fifteen years later. *Adkins v. Children's Hospital* involved a congressionally authorized procedure for setting minimum wages for women workers in the District of Columbia. Writing for a five-to-three majority (Justice Brandeis had recused himself from the case), Justice George Sutherland found the maximum hours law unconstitutional on two major grounds. First, while maximum hours laws were constitutionally sanctioned public health measures, minimum wage laws were unacceptable restraints on free trade. Second, the ratification of the Nineteenth Amendment granting woman suffrage in the years since the *Muller* decision made protections of women on the basis of their need to be sheltered by men outdated. Thus, whereas in the earlier case the Court used an appeal to nature to sustain special labor laws that benefited women, in *Adkins,* the Court relied on an evolutionary approach to overturn such regulations.

Adkins v. Children's Hospital (1923)

In the *Muller* case, the validity of an Oregon statute, forbidding the employment of any female in certain industries more than ten hours during any one day was upheld. . . . But the ancient inequality of the sexes, otherwise than physical, as suggested in the *Muller* case has continued "with diminishing intensity." In view of the great — not to say revolutionary — changes which have taken place since that utterance, in the contractual, political and civil status of women, culminating in the Nineteenth Amendment, it is not unreasonable to say that these differences have now come almost, if not quite, to the vanishing point. . . .

[W]e cannot accept the doctrine that women of mature age, *sui juris* [able to act on their own behalf legally], require or may be subjected to restrictions upon their liberty of contract which could not lawfully be imposed in the case of men under similar circumstances. To do so would be to ignore all the implications to be drawn from the present day trend of legislation, as well as that of common thought and usage, by which woman is accorded emancipation from the old doctrine that she must be given special protection or be subjected to special restraint in her contractual and civil relationships.

I N THE WATERSHED CASE of *Brown v. Board of Education of Topeka,* the Supreme Court reversed its 1896 *Plessy v. Ferguson* decision to find state-sponsored racial segregation a violation of the Fourteenth Amendment guarantee of equal protection of the laws. The unanimous ruling was written by Earl Warren, newly appointed chief justice. Linda Brown was the plaintiff in one of several cases that the court consolidated, all of which challenged the constitutionality of racially segregated public schools. The case bears certain similarities to *Muller v. Oregon.* Both made use of sociological evidence, with *Brown* relying on research into the negative impact of segregation on young black children. Also as in *Muller,* the successful lead counsel in the *Brown* decision, NAACP lawyer Thurgood Marshall, ultimately was appointed to the Supreme Court, where he became the first African American justice.

Brown v. Board of Education of Topeka (1954)

The plaintiffs contend that segregated public schools are not "equal" and cannot be made "equal," and that hence they are deprived of the equal protection of the laws. . . .

Does segregation of children in public schools solely on the basis of race, even though the physical facilities and other "tangible" factors may be equal, deprive the children of the minority group of equal educational opportunities? We believe that it does. . . .

To separate them from others of similar age and qualifications solely because of their race generates a feeling of inferiority as to their status in the community that may affect their hearts and minds in a way unlikely ever to be undone. . . .

We conclude that, in the field of public education, the doctrine of "separate but equal" has no place. Separate educational facilities are inherently unequal. . . .

Because these are class actions, because of the wide applicability of this decision, and because of the great variety of local conditions, the formulation of decrees in these cases presents problems of considerable complexity.

ESTELLE GRISWOLD, executive director of the Planned Parenthood Federation of Connecticut, was arrested for providing a married couple with birth control instruction in violation of an 1879 state law forbidding any aid given "for the purpose of preventing conception." Writing for a seven-to-two majority, Justice William O. Douglas held the law unconstitutional, developing an innovative argument for the existence of a "zone of privacy" not specifically enumerated in the Constitution but found in the surrounding "penumbra" of specified rights. Note Douglas's lofty language about the nature of marriage.

Griswold v. Connecticut (1965)

This law . . . operates directly on an intimate relation of husband and wife and their physician's role in one aspect of that relation. . . .

[S]pecific guarantees in the Bill of Rights have penumbras, formed by emanations from those guarantees that help give them life and substance. . . . Various guarantees create zones of privacy. The right of association contained in the penumbra of the First Amendment is one, as we have seen. . . . The Ninth Amendment provides: "The enumeration in the Constitution, of certain rights, shall not be construed to deny or disparage others retained by the people." . . .

The present case, then, concerns a relationship lying within the zone of privacy created by several fundamental constitutional guarantees. And it concerns a law which, in forbidding the use of contraceptives rather than regulating their manufacture or sale, seeks to achieve its goals by means having a maximum destructive impact upon that relationship. Such a law cannot stand in light of the familiar principle, so often applied by this Court, that a "governmental purpose to control or prevent activities constitutionally subject to state regulation may not be achieved by means which sweep unnecessarily broadly and thereby invade the area of protected freedoms." . . .

We deal with a right of privacy older than the Bill of Rights — older than our political parties, older than our school system. Marriage is a coming together for better or for worse, hopefully enduring, and intimate to the degree of being sacred. It is an association that promotes a way of life, not causes; a harmony in living, not political faiths; a bilateral loyalty, not commercial or social projects.

L IKE THE *GRISWOLD* CASE two years earlier, *Loving v. Virginia* concerns the marriage relationship and government intrusion into it. Richard Loving was a white man who married Mildred Jeter, a black woman, in 1958 in Washington, D.C. When they moved to Virginia a year later, they were found guilty in state court of violating a 1924 Virginia law forbidding white people from marrying outside of their race, a crime known as "miscegenation." They appealed their conviction to the U.S. Supreme Court. Speaking for a unanimous Court, Chief Justice Earl Warren found this and similar laws in fifteen other states unconstitutional under the Fourteenth Amendment. The Court's rejection of the argument that antimiscegenation laws were constitutionally acceptable because they rested equally on all races echoes the logic of its ruling in *Brown v. Board of Education,* in which intent to discriminate is crucial despite the superficially neutral language of the law.

Loving v. Virginia (1967)

This case presents a constitutional question never addressed by this Court: whether a statutory scheme adopted by the State of Virginia to prevent marriages between persons solely on the basis of racial classifications violates the Equal Protection and Due Process Clauses of the Fourteenth Amendment. . . .

In upholding the constitutionality of these provisions, . . . the state court concluded that the State's legitimate purposes were "to preserve the racial integrity of its citizens," and to prevent "the corruption of blood," "a mongrel breed of citizens," and "the obliteration of racial pride," obviously an endorsement of the doctrine of White Supremacy. . . . [T]he fact of equal application does not immunize the statute from the very heavy burden of justification which the Fourteenth

Amendment has traditionally required of state statutes drawn according to race. . . .

Over the years, this Court has consistently repudiated "distinctions between citizens solely because of their ancestry" as being "odious to a free people whose institutions are founded upon the doctrine of equality." At the very least, the Equal Protection Clause demands that racial classifications, especially suspect in criminal statutes, be subjected to the "most rigid scrutiny." . . .

Marriage is one of the "basic civil rights of man," fundamental to our very existence and survival. . . . Under our Constitution, the freedom to marry, or not marry, a person of another race resides with the individual and cannot be infringed by the State.

T HE *REED V. REED* CASE involved the mother of a deceased child contesting an Idaho law mandating that preference be given to the father in designating an executor for a dead child's estate. Sally Reed's case was argued by then American Civil Liberties Union lawyer Ruth Bader Ginsburg. Ginsburg revived elements of the argument made in the 1874 *Minor* case, that the Fourteenth Amendment's guarantees of equal protection before the law applied in cases of discrimination against women. This time the Court accepted the argument. The unanimous opinion was written by Chief Justice Warren Burger. Like Brandeis and Marshall, Ginsburg was later a pathbreaking appointee to the Supreme Court, the second woman (after Sandra Day O'Connor) to serve.

Reed v. Reed (1971)

[W]e have concluded that the arbitrary preference established in favor of males by . . . the Idaho Code cannot stand in the face of the Fourteenth Amendment's command that no State deny the equal protection of the laws to any person within its jurisdiction.

In applying that clause, this Court has consistently recognized that the Fourteenth Amendment does not deny to States the power to treat different classes of persons in different ways. . . .

The Equal Protection Clause of that amendment does, however, deny to States the power to legislate that different treatment be accorded to persons placed by a statute into different classes on the basis of criteria wholly unrelated to the objective of that statute. A classification must be reasonable, not arbitrary, and must rest upon some ground of difference having a fair and substantial relation to the object of the legislation, so that all persons similarly circumstanced shall be treated alike.

J ANE ROE WAS THE PSEUDONYM of Norma McCorvey, an unmarried pregnant woman whose name headed up a class action suit challenging an 1879 Texas law criminalizing abortion. In *Roe v. Wade,* the Court ruled seven to two in Roe's favor. Justice Harry Blackmun wrote the lead opinion, relying on the concept of privacy developed in the *Griswold* case. His opinion included a detailed history of laws prohibiting abortion to show that these were of relatively recent vintage, an approach that contrasted with the antihistorical arguments of nineteenth-century cases such as *Dred Scott* and *Minor v. Happersett.* The *Roe* decision very carefully avoids declaring that a woman's right to abortion is absolute. The limits placed on women's choice — consultation with a physician, government interest in fetal life in the third trimester — opened the way for attempts to reinstitute limits on abortion.

Roe v. Wade (1973)

We forthwith acknowledge our awareness of the sensitive and emotional nature of the abortion controversy. . . . One's philosophy, one's experiences, one's exposure to the raw edges of human existence, one's religious training, one's

attitudes toward life and family and their values, and the moral standards one establishes and seeks to observe, are all likely to influence and to color one's thinking and conclusions about abortion.

In addition, population growth, pollution, poverty, and racial overtones tend to complicate and not to simplify the problem. . . .

The Constitution does not explicitly mention any right of privacy. In a line of decisions, however, . . . the Court has recognized that a right of personal privacy, or a guarantee of certain areas or zones of privacy, does exist under the Constitution. . . .

This right of privacy . . . is broad enough to encompass a woman's decision whether or not to terminate her pregnancy. The detriment that the State would impose upon the pregnant woman by denying this choice altogether is apparent. Specific and direct harm medically diagnosable even in early pregnancy may be involved. Maternity, or additional offspring, may force upon the woman a distressful life and future.

Psychological harm may be imminent. Mental and physical health may be taxed by child care. There is also the distress, for all concerned, associated with the unwanted child, and there is the problem of bringing a child into a family already unable, psychologically and otherwise, to care for it. In other cases, as in this one, the additional difficulties and continuing stigma of unwed motherhood may be involved.

[A]ppellant [in this case Jane Roe] . . . [argues] that the woman's right is absolute and that she is entitled to terminate her pregnancy at whatever time, in whatever way, and for whatever reason she alone chooses. With this we do not agree. . . . [A] State may properly assert important interests in safeguarding health, in maintaining medical standards, and in protecting potential life. At some point in pregnancy, these respective interests become sufficiently compelling to sustain regulation of the factors that govern the abortion decision. The privacy right involved, therefore, cannot be said to be absolute. . . .

The appellee . . . argue[s] that the fetus is a "person" within the language and meaning of the Fourteenth Amendment. . . . If this suggestion of personhood is established, the appellant's case, of course, collapses, for the fetus' right to life would then be guaranteed specifically by the Amendment. . . .

The Constitution does not define "person" in so many words. . . . [T]he word "person," as used in the Fourteenth Amendment, does not include the unborn.

In view of all this, we do not agree that, by adopting one theory of life, Texas may override the rights of the pregnant woman that are at stake. We repeat, however, that the State does have an important and legitimate interest in preserving and protecting the health of the pregnant woman, . . . and that it has still *another* important and legitimate interest in protecting the potentiality of human life. . . .

With respect to the State's important and legitimate interest in the health of the mother, the "compelling" point, in the light of present medical knowledge, is at . . . the end of the first trimester. . . . [F]rom and after this point, a State may regulate the abortion procedure to the extent that the regulation reasonably relates to the preservation and protection of maternal health. Examples of permissible state regulation in this area are requirements as to the qualifications of the person who is to perform the abortion; as to the licensure of that person; as to the facility in which the procedure is to be performed. . . .

[T]he attending physician, in consultation with his patient, is free to determine, without regulation by the State, that, in his medical judgment, the patient's pregnancy should be terminated. If that decision is reached, the judgment may be effectuated by an abortion free of interference by the State.

With respect to the State's important and legitimate interest in potential life, the "compelling" point is at viability. This is so because the fetus then presumably has the capability of meaningful life outside the mother's womb. State regulation protective of fetal life after viability thus has both logical and biological justifications.

Affirmative action programs were initially developed in the 1960s to aid African Americans to achieve greater educational and economic opportunity. President Richard Nixon urged them as a moderate response to the demands of militant civil rights activists. Nonetheless, these programs came under fire. In 1976, Allan Bakke, a white man, filed suit when his application for admission was rejected by the University of California at Davis Medical School. He argued that affirmative action was the problem. His claim, based on the Fourteenth Amendment, became known as the "reverse discrimination" argument. The Court was sharply divided, four justices believing that Bakke was the victim of reverse discrimination, four justices believing that the Davis Medical School's affirmative action policy offered a reasonable approach to eradicating the effects of a long history of racial injustice. Justice Lewis Powell forged a five-to-four majority by writing an opinion that took both positions into account. An educational affirmative action plan premised on the goal of racial diversity could be constitutional if the system used was less rigid, less "quota"-like, than that of the Davis Medical School. The Court ordered Bakke admitted to the university's medical school.

University of California Regents v. Bakke (1978)

The Medical School of the University of California at Davis (hereinafter Davis) had two admissions programs for the entering class of 100 students—the regular admissions program and the special admissions program. . . . A separate committee, a majority of whom were members of minority groups, operated the special admissions program. The 1973 and 1974 application forms, respectively, asked candidates whether they wished to be considered as "economically and/or educationally disadvantaged" applicants and members of a "minority group" (blacks, Chicanos, Asians, American Indians). . . . Special candidates, however, did not have to meet the 2.5 grade point cutoff and were not ranked against candidates in the general admissions process. . . . Without passing on the state constitutional or federal statutory grounds the [lower] court held that petitioner's special admissions program violated the [Fourteenth Amendment] Equal Protection Clause. . . . Racial and ethnic classifications of any sort are inherently suspect and call for the most exacting judicial scrutiny. While the goal of achieving a diverse student body is sufficiently compelling to justify consideration of race in admissions decisions under some circumstances, petitioner's special admissions program, which forecloses consideration to persons like respondent, is unnecessary to the achievement of this compelling goal and therefore invalid under the Equal Protection Clause.

A series of cases followed *Roe v. Wade* that both upheld and limited a woman's right to seek an abortion. The plaintiff in *Webster v. Reproductive Health Services* was attorney general for the State of Missouri, appealing a lower court ruling that found restrictions on a woman's right to abortion unconstitutional, including the requirement that a woman seeking a second- or third-trimester abortion must have a test to make sure that the fetus was not viable (could not live outside the womb). The lower court ruled that the law violated the Supreme Court's *Roe v. Wade* decision. The Supreme Court overturned this ruling. Chief Justice William Rehnquist wrote for the five-to-three majority that, while the *Roe* decision had recognized the state's obligation to protect potential life, it had been too rigid in establishing the point at which this became paramount. From Rehnquist's perspective, it was permissible for the state to act to favor childbirth even while preserving the woman's formal right to abortion.

Webster v. Reproductive Health Services (1989)

In *Roe v. Wade,* the Court recognized that the State has "important and legitimate" interests in protecting maternal health and in the potentiality of human life. During the second trimester, the State "may, if it chooses, regulate the abortion procedure in ways that are reasonably related to maternal health." . . .

[But] the rigid trimester analysis of the course of a pregnancy enunciated in *Roe* has resulted in . . . making constitutional law in this area a virtual Procrustean bed. . . . [T]he rigid *Roe* framework is hardly consistent with the notion of a Constitution cast in general terms, as ours is, and usually speaking in general principles, as ours does. . . .

[W]e do not see why the State's interest in protecting potential human life should come into existence only at the point of viability, and that there should therefore be a rigid line allowing state regulation after viability but prohibiting it before viability. . . . [W]e are satisfied that the requirement of these tests permissibly furthers the State's interest in protecting potential human life, and we therefore believe [the article] to be constitutional.

Both appellants and the United States as *amicus curiae* [filing a brief sympathetic to the parties that appealed the decision] have urged that we overrule our decision in *Roe v. Wade.* The facts of the present case, however, differ from those at issue in *Roe.* Here, Missouri has determined that viability is the point at which its interest in potential human life must be safeguarded. . . . This case therefore affords us no occasion to revisit the holding of *Roe.*

THE DEFENSE OF MARRIAGE ACT (DOMA) WAS PASSED by a Republican-dominated Congress and signed by President Bill Clinton in 1996. It limited federal conjugal benefits, ranging from income tax deductions to Social Security, to marriages between "a man and a woman." Although gay marriage was not yet legal anywhere in the United States, the political capital poured into the passage of DOMA suggests that antigay marriage forces were beginning to feel themselves on the defensive. Subsequently, states began to formally legalize gay marriages, beginning with Vermont in 2000.

In 2013, a case challenging DOMA, *United States v. Windsor* from New York, came before the U.S. Supreme Court. By this time, the Obama administration's Department of Justice had registered its own objections to DOMA by announcing that it would not defend the law before the courts.

Nonetheless, the Court's decision ruling crucial sections of DOMA unconstitutional was largely unexpected. Indeed, many proponents of gay marriage had been concerned that bringing the law before the court would give conservative justices the opportunity to rule against them. The five-to-four decision was delivered on June 26, 2013, by Justice Anthony Kennedy, joined by the three female justices — Ruth Bader Ginsburg, Elena Kagan, and Sonia Sotomayor — and by Justice Stephen Breyer.

The constitutional essence of the decision is the assertion that legal regulation of marriage and family life has always been a matter of state rather than federal law. Underlying this, the decision registers a strong moral objection to the use of federal law to visit "indignity" rather than new rights upon a select class of American citizens.

United States v. Windsor (2013)

DOMA is unconstitutional as a deprivation of the equal liberty of persons that is protected by the Fifth Amendment. . . . By history and tradition the definition and regulation of marriage has been treated as being within the authority and realm of the separate States. Congress has enacted discrete statutes to regulate the meaning of marriage in order to further federal policy, but DOMA, with a directive applicable to over 1,000 federal statutes and . . . the whole realm of federal regulations, has a far greater reach. Its operation is also directed to a class of persons that the laws of New York, and of 11 other States, have sought to protect. Assessing the validity of that intervention requires discussing the historical and traditional extent of state power and authority over marriage.

The State's decision to give this class of persons the right to marry conferred upon them a dignity and status of immense import. But the Federal Government uses the state-defined class for the opposite purpose — to impose restrictions and disabilities. The question is whether the resulting injury and indignity is a deprivation of an essential part of the liberty protected by the Fifth Amendment, since what New York treats as alike the federal law deems unlike by a law designed to injure the same class the State seeks to protect.

◆ **Chart 1**
U.S. Birthrate, 1820–2010 (Number of Births per 1,000)

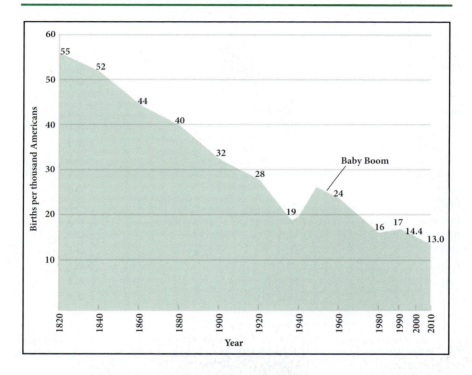

Source: Data from *Historical Statistics of the United States, Colonial Times to 1970* (1975); U.S. Census Bureau, *Statistical Abstract of the United States, 2001* (Washington: GPO, 2001); *U.S. Census Bureau Statistical Abstract* (2011).

◆ Table 1
U.S. Women and Work, 1820–2015

Year	Percentage of Women in Paid Employment	Percentage of Paid Workers Who Are Women
1820	6.2	7.3
1830	6.4	7.4
1840	8.4	9.6
1850	10.1	10.8
1860	9.7	10.2
1870	13.7	14.8
1880	14.7	15.2
1890	18.2	17.0
1900	21.2	18.1
1910	24.8	20.0
1920	23.9	20.4
1930	24.4	21.9
1940	25.4	24.6
1950	29.1	27.8
1960	34.8	32.3
1970	43.3	38.0
1980	51.5	42.6
1990	57.4	45.2
2000	59.9	46.5
2010	58.6	46.9
2015	57.7	46.7

Source: U.S. Census Bureau, *Historical Statistics of the United States, Colonial Times to 1970* (Washington: GPO, 1975); *Statistical Abstract of the United States, 2002* (Washington: GPO, 2002); *U.S. Census Bureau Statistical Abstracts* (2017), table 1.

◆ **Table 2**
Participation Rate in the Female Labor Force, by Family Status, 1890–2015

Year	Single	Widowed/ Divorced	Married	Mothers*
1890	41	30	5	—
1900	41	33	6	—
1910	48	35	11	—
1920	44†	— †	9	—
1930	46	34	12	—
1940	48	32	17	28
1950	51	36	25	33
1960	44	37	32	37
1970	57	40	41	40
1980	64	44	50	56
1990	67	47	58	67
2000	69	49	61	73
2010	63	49	61	71
2015	57.8	44.1	56.3	70

*Mothers of children under age eighteen.

†Single women counted with widows and divorced women.

Sources: Lynn Weiner, *From Working Girl to Working Mother: The Female Labor Force in the United States, 1820–1980* (Chapel Hill: University of North Carolina, 1985), 6; U.S. Bureau of Labor Statistics, "Labor Force Participation Rates of Women by Presence and Age of Children, March 1980–2000," U.S. Department of Labor, "Women in the Labor Force: A Databook" (2011 and 2017), tables 4 and 7.

◆ **Table 3**
Degrees Granted to Women, 1950–2017

	Bachelor's Degrees		Doctoral Degrees	
	Number	% of Total	Number	% of Total
1950	103,217	23.9	616	9.6
1960	136,187	35.0	1,028	10.5
1970	343,060	41.5	3,976	13.3
1980	456,000	49.0	9,672	29.7
1990	560,000	53.2	14,000	36.8
2000	707,000	57.0	19,780	44.0
2010	920,000	60.0	25,200	49.1
2017	1,057,000	59.9	37,100	55.5

Source: National Center for Education Statistics, *Digest of Education Statistics, Selected Years 1869–70 to 2016–17*, table 258.

◆ **Table 4**
Occupational Distribution (in Percentages) of Working Women Ages Fourteen Years and Older, 1900–2000*

	1900	*1910*	*1920*	*1930*	*1940*	*1950*	*1960*	*1970*	*1980*	*1990*	*2000*
Professional, Technical, and Kindred Workers	8.2	9.6	11.7	13.8	12.8	12.2	12.5	15.2	13.6	18.5	21.8
Managers, Officials, and Proprietors	1.4	2.0	2.2	0.7	3.3	4.3	0.6	3.5	7.2	11.1	14.3
Clerical and Kindred Workers	4.0	9.2	18.7	20.9	21.5	27.4	29.1	34.2	33.6	27.8	23.5
Sales Workers	4.3	5.1	6.3	6.8	7.4	8.6	7.8	7.3	11.3	13.1	13.0
Craftsmen, Foremen, and Kindred Workers	1.4	1.4	1.2	1.0	1.1	0.5	1.2	1.8	2.4	2.2	2.2
Operatives and Kindred Workers	23.8	22.9	20.2	17.4	19.5	20.0	16.2	14.9	10.1	8.0	6.4
Laborers	2.6	1.4	2.3	1.5	1.1	0.9	0.6	1.0	2.0	0.5	0.4
Private Household Workers	28.7	24.0	15.7	17.8	18.1	8.9	7.9	3.8	1.3	1.0	1.3
Service Workers (Not Household)	6.7	8.4	8.1	9.7	11.3	12.6	13.5	16.5	17.8	16.8	16.4
Farmers and Farm Managers	5.8	3.7	3.2	0.4	1.2	0.7	0.5	0.2	0.3	0.3	0.3
Farm Laborers	13.1	12.0	10.3	6.0	2.8	2.9	1.2	0.6	0.6	0.7	0.4

*Data beginning in 1990 are not directly comparable with data for earlier years because of the introduction of a new occupational classification system. The occupational classification system changed again in 2003, reducing the number of major categories to five. The 2015 statistics on percentages of working women by occupation are: management, professional, and related occupations: 4.4 percent; service occupations: 19.8 percent; sales and office occupations: 30.1 percent; natural resources, construction, and maintenance occupations: 1.0 percent; and production, transportation, and material moving occupations: 5.1 percent.

Source: U.S. Census Bureau, *Historical Statistics of the United States*, part 1, table D, 182–232; *Statistical Abstract of the United States, 1985* (Washington: GPO, 1984), table 673; 1991 (Washington: GPO, 1991), table 652; 2000 (Washington: GPO, 2001), table 593; "Employed Persons by Major Occupation, Sex, Race, and Hispanic Origin, Annual Averages, 1983–2002," U.S. Department of Labor Statistics, "Women in the Labor Force: a Databook" (2017), table 11.

◆ **Table 5**
Immigration to the United States, 1900–2015

Years	Female Immigrants to the United States	Total Immigrants to the United States
1900–1909	2,492,336	8,202,388
1910–1919	2,215,582	6,347,156
1920–1929	1,881,923	4,295,510
1930–1939	386,659	699,375
1940–1949	454,291	856,608
1950–1959	1,341,404	2,499,286
1960–1969	1,786,441	3,213,749
1970–1979	2,299,713	4,366,001
1980–1989	3,224,661	6,332,218
1990–1999	4,740,896	9,782,093
2000–2010	6,227,291	11,351,447
2011–2015	1,659,045	3,084,224

Source: U.S. Census Bureau, *Historical Statistics of the United States, Colonial Times to 1970* (Washington: GPO, 1975), Series C 102–114; U.S. Department of Justice, *1978 Statistical Yearbook of the Immigration and Naturalization Service* (Washington: GPO, 1978), table 10; *1984 Statistical Yearbook of the Immigration and Naturalization Service* (Washington: GPO, 1987), table I M M 4.1; *1988 Statistical Yearbook of the Immigration and Naturalization Service* (Washington: GPO, 1989), table 11; *1994 Statistical Yearbook of the Immigration and Naturalization Service* (Washington: GPO, 2002), table 1; *2003 Statistical Yearbook of the Immigration and Naturalization Service* (Washington: GPO, 2004), table 6; *2004 Statistical Yearbook of the Immigration and Naturalization Service* (Washington: GPO, 2005), table 7; *2005 Statistical Yearbook of the Immigration and Naturalization Service* (Washington: GPO, 2006), table 8; *2006 Statistical Yearbook of the Immigration and Naturalization Service* (Washington: GPO, 2007), table 9; *2007 Statistical Yearbook of the Immigration and Naturalization Service* (Washington: GPO, 2008), table 9; *2011 Statistical Yearbook of the Immigration and Naturalization Service* (Washington: GPO, 2012), table 8; *2012 Statistical Yearbook of the Immigration and Naturalization Service* (Washington: GPO, 2013), table 8; *2013 Statistical Yearbook of the Immigration and Naturalization Service* (Washington: GPO, 2014), table 8; *2014 Statistical Yearbook of the Immigration and Naturalization Service* (Washington: GPO, 2015), table 8; *2015 Statistical Yearbook of the Immigration and Naturalization Service* (Washington: GPO, 2016), table 8.

Acknowledgments

Chapter 2: Mrs. Agatha Stubbings, Prenuptial Agreement (1645), excerpted from Susie M. Ames, ed., *County Court Records of Accomack-Northampton, Virginia, 1640–1645* (Charlottesville: University of Virginia Press, 1973), 433–34. Copyright © 1973 by the Virginia Historical Society. Reprinted by permission of the Virginia Historical Society.

Eliza Lucas Pinckney, "To Miss Bartlett" and excerpt from 1740 letter, from *The Letterbook of Eliza Lucas Pinckney, 1739–1762*, ed. Elise Pinckney. Copyright © 1997. Reprinted by permission of the University of South Carolina Press.

Chapter 3: Benjamin Rush, "Thoughts upon Female Education" (1787), from *Essays on Education in the Early Republic*, edited by Frederick Rudolph (Cambridge, MA: The Belknap Press of Harvard University Press). Copyright © 1965 by the President and Fellows of Harvard College. Reprinted by permission of the publisher.

Phillis Wheatley, "To Arbour Tanner," May 19, 1772, and "To Rev. Samson Occom," March 11, 1774, from *The Poems of Phillis Wheatley*, edited and with an introduction by Julian D. Mason Jr. Copyright © 1966 by the University of North Carolina Press, renewed 1989. Used by permission of the publisher. www.uncpress.unc.edu.

Chapter 4: Advertisements for Wet Nurses, from Stephanie Jones-Rogers, " '[S]he Could . . . Spare One Ample Breast for the Profit of Her Owner': White Mothers and Enslaved Wet Nurses' Invisible Labor in American Slave Markets," *Slavery & Abolition* 38, no. 2 (2017): 337–55. https://doi.org/10.1080/0144039X.2017.1317014. Copyright © 2017. Reprinted by permission of Taylor & Francis Ltd., http://www.tandfonline.com.

Chapter 5: "Narrative of Mrs. Rosalia Leese, Who Witnessed the Hoisting of the Bear Flag in Sonoma on the 14th of June, 1846," from Rose Marie Beebe and Robert M. Senkewicz, trans. and eds., *Testimonios: Early California through the Eyes of Women, 1815–1848*. Copyright © 2006 by Rose Marie Beebe and Robert M. Senkewicz. Reprinted by permission of the University of Oklahoma Press.

Chapter 7: Excerpt from "Indian Schools," Sarah Winnemucca quoted in *Silver Slate*, July 9,

1886); excerpt from "We are referred . . . ," Sarah Winnemucca quoted in *Daily Alta California*, July 24, 1886, from *The Newspaper Warrior: Sarah Winnemucca Hopkins's Campaign for American Indian Rights, 1864–1891*, edited by Cari M. Carpenter and Carolyn Sorisio. Copyright © 2015 by the Board of Regents of the University of Nebraska. Reprinted by permission of the University of Nebraska Press.

Chapter 9: Susan Rosenthal, "Genora Johnson Dollinger and the General Motors Sit-Down Strike" (1936–37), from *Striking Flint: Genora (Johnson) Dollinger Remembers the 1936–37 General Motors Sit-Down Strike* (1996; repr., ReMarx Publishing, 2014). Copyright © 1996 Susan Rosenthal, UAW. Reprinted by permission of ReMarx Publishing.

Hortense Johnson, "What My Job Means to Me," *Opportunity*, April 1943, excerpted from Maureen Honey, ed., *Bitter Fruit: African American Women in World War II*. Copyright © 1999 by The Curators of the University of Missouri, University of Missouri Press, Columbia, Missouri 65201. Reprinted by permission.

Sherna Berger Gluck, "Beatrice Morales Clifton, Oral Interview" (1981), from *Rosie the Riveter Revisited: Women, the War, and Social Change*. Copyright © 1987 by Sherna Berger Gluck. Reprinted by permission of Sherna Berger Gluck.

Chapter 10: Esther Peterson and The President's Commission on the Status of Women, excerpt from 1977 oral history interview, from "The Twentieth Century Trade Union Woman: Vehicle for Social Change" oral history project at the Bentley Historical Library, University of Michigan. Copyright © Bentley Historical Library, University of Michigan.

Interview with Diane Nash, excerpted from *Voices of Freedom: An Oral History of the Civil Rights Movement from the 1950s through the 1980s* by Henry Hampton and Steve Fayer. Copyright © 1990 by Blackside, Inc. Used by permission of Bantam Books, an imprint of Random House, a division of Penguin Random House LLC. All rights reserved. Any third-party use of this material, outside of this publication, is prohibited. Interested parties must apply directly to Penguin Random House LLC for permission.

Interview with Vivian Leburg Rothstein, student activist, excerpted from "People's Century: Young Blood," *People's Century* #114, June 14, 1999, http://www.pbs.org/wgbh/peoplescentury /episodes/youngblood/rothsteintranscript .html (accessed March 19, 2015). Copyright © 1998–2017 by WGBH Educational Foundation. Reprinted with permission.

Interview with Mary Dora Jones, from *My Soul Is Rested: Movement Days in the Deep South* by Howell Raines. Copyright © 1977 by Howell Raines. Used by permission of G. P. Putnam's Sons, an imprint of Penguin Publishing Group, a division of Penguin Random House LLC, and by permission of Russell & Volkening as agents for the author. All rights reserved. Any third-party use of this material, outside of this publication, is prohibited. Interested parties must apply directly to Penguin Random House LLC for permission.

Interview with Earline Boyd, conducted by Dr. Charles Bolton, September 29, 1992. Held in the Civil Rights in Mississippi Digital Archive. Reprinted by permission of the Center for Oral History and Cultural Heritage at The University of Southern Mississippi.

Casey Hayden and Mary King, Position Paper: November 1964, from "SNCC Position Paper: Women in the Movement," November 1964. Reprinted by permission of Casey Hayden and Mary King.

"Should Mothers of Young Children Work?," *Ladies' Home Journal*®, 75, November 1958. Copyright © 1958. All rights reserved. Reprinted by permission of the Meredith Corporation.

Chapter 11: Anne Koedt, "The Myth of the Vaginal Orgasm" (1970), from *Dear Sisters: Dispatches from the Women's Liberation Movement* by Rosalyn Baxandall and Linda Gordon. Copyright © 2000. Reprinted by permission of Basic Books, an imprint of Hachette Book Group, Inc.

Jean Horan, "Forced Sterilization," excerpted from Jean Horan, "Condition: Socio-Economic — Treatment: Sterilization," *off our backs* 6, no. 10 (January 1977). Reprinted by permission.

"Women's Bill of Rights," 1968. Reprinted by permission of the National Organization for Women.

Jo Freeman, "What in the Hell Is Women's Liberation Anyway?," excerpt from *Voice of the Women's Liberation Movement* 1, no. 1 (March 1968), 1, 4. Copyright © 1968 by Jo Freeman. Reprinted by permission of the author.

Statement from the Third World Women's Alliance (1971), from *Dear Sisters: Dispatches from the Women's Liberation Movement* by Rosalyn Baxandall and Linda Gordon. Copyright © 2000. Reprinted by permission of Basic Books, an imprint of Hachette Book Group, Inc.

Mirta Vidal, "New Voice of La Raza: Chicanas Speak Out," from *Chicanas Speak Out: Women, the New Voice of La Raza*; originally published in the *International Socialist Review,* October 1971. Copyright © 1971 by Pathfinder Press. Reprinted by permission.

Dana Densmore, "Who Is Saying Men Are the Enemy?," from *A Journal of Female Liberation,* Issue 4, April 1970. Copyright © 1970 by Dana Densmore. Reprinted by permission of the author.

Radicalesbians, "The Woman Identified Woman" (1970). Copyright © 1970 by Radicalesbians. Reprinted by permission. All rights reserved.

Chapter 12: Ilhan Omar, "First Muslim Somali-American Lawmaker," excerpted from Ilhan Omar's Web site ("Meet Ilhan"; "Fighting for Unity and Justice"; "Advancing Equity for All"), at https://www.ilhanomar.com. Copyright © Ilhan Omar. Reprinted by permission.

Phyllis Schlafly, "What's Wrong with 'Equal Rights' for Women?," *The Phyllis Schlafly Report* 5, no. 7 (February 1972). Copyright © 1972. Reprinted by permission.

LaDonna Brave Bull Allard, "The Meaning of the Standing Rock Protests," from "Why the Founder of Standing Rock Sioux Camp Can't Forget the Whitestone Massacre," *YES! Magazine,* September 3, 2016, http://www .yesmagazine.org/people-power/why-the-founder-of-standing-rock-sioux-camp-cant-forget-the-whitestone-massacre-20160903. Copyright © 2016. Reprinted by permission of Positive Futures Network.

Shirley Sagawa and Nancy Duff Campbell, "Women in Combat," excerpted from "Women in Combat," National Women's Law Center, 1992, https://www.nwlc.org/wp-content/uploads /2015/08/Combat.pdf. Copyright © 1992 by the National Women's Law Center. Reprinted with permission.

Tracy Moore, Review of *Hero Mom*, from *Common Sense Media,* https://www .commonsensemedia.org/book-reviews/hero-mom (accessed March 23, 2015). Copyright © 2013. Reprinted by permission of Common Sense Media.

INDEX

Letters in parentheses following pages refer to the following:
- *(b)* for boxed excerpts
- *(d)* for documents
- *(i)* for text illustrations
- *(v)* for visual sources
- *(m)* for maps
- *(c)* for charts and graphs

Area ceded by
the United States
to Great Britain,
1818

WASHINGTON
★ Olympia

Columbia R.

Salem ★

OREGON COUNTRY
*Agreement with Britain,
1846*

OREGON

★ Boise
IDAHO

Snake R.

Helena ★
MONTANA

Missouri R.

NORTH DAKOTA

Bismarck ★

SOUTH DAKOTA

Pierre ★

WYOMING

LOUISIANA
PURCHASE
From France, 1803

N. Platte R.

NEBRASKA

Cheyenne ★

Platte R.

Sacramento R.

★ Salt Lake
City

Carson City ★

Sacramento ★

NEVADA

UTAH

S. Platte R.

Denver ★
COLORADO

KANSAS

San Joaquin R.

MEXICAN CESSION
1848

Colorado R.

CALIFORNIA

PACIFIC
OCEAN

ARIZONA

Santa Fe ★

NEW
MEXICO

Red R.

TEXAS
Annexed, 1845

Phoenix ★

TEXAS

GADSDEN PURCHASE
from Mexico, 1853

Rio Grande

ARCTIC OCEAN

RUSSIA

ALASKA
*Purchased from
Russia, 1867*

CANADA

Yukon R.

Bering
Sea

Gulf of
Alaska

Juneau ★

HAWAII
*Annexed,
1898*

Honolulu ★

PACIFIC
OCEAN

0   250   500 miles

0   250   500 kilometers

0   50   100 miles

0   50   100 kilometers

MEXICO

ceded by
at Britain,
1818

Areas ceded by Britain, 1842
(Webster-Ashburton Treaty)

CANADA

St. Lawrence R.

MAINE

Lake Superior

VERMONT

★ Augusta

Lake Huron

Montpelier ★

★ Concord · N.H.

NEW YORK

★ Boston

St. Paul ★

WISCONSIN

Lake Michigan

MICHIGAN

Lake Ontario

Albany ★

MASS.

Connecticut R.

Hudson R.

★ Providence

MINNESOTA

Lansing ★

Hartford ★

RHODE
ISLAND

Madison ★

Lake Erie

PENN.

Delaware R.

CONNECTICUT

IOWA

INDIANA

OHIO

Trenton ★

NEW JERSEY

Des
Moines ★

ILLINOIS

Columbus ★

Harrisburg ★

Dover ★

DELAWARE

Indianapolis ★

WEST
VIRGINIA

Susquehanna R.

Potomac R.

Annapolis ⊛

MARYLAND

Springfield ★

THE ORIGINAL THIRTEEN COLONIES

WASHINGTON, D.C.

Jefferson
City ★

Frankfort ★

Charleston ★

Proclamation Line of 1763

*Chesapeake
Bay*

Ohio R.

James R.

Richmond ★

MISSOURI

KENTUCKY

VIRGINIA

*Gained by treaty
with Britain, 1783*

NORTH
CAROLINA

Cumberland R.

Raleigh ★

ARKANSAS

Nashville ★

Tennessee R.

TENNESSEE

Cape Fear R.

ATLANTIC
OCEAN

Arkansas R.

SOUTH
CAROLINA

OKLAHOMA

Little
Rock ★

Columbia ★

Atlanta ★

Savannah R.

Mississippi R.

ALABAMA

MISSISSIPPI

GEORGIA

LOUISIANA

Montgomery ★

Jackson ★

Tallahassee ★

Baton
Rouge ★

FLORIDA

*Areas taken
from Spain,
1810 and 1813*

*FLORIDA
Treaty with Spain,
1819*

U.S. Territories

*ATLANTIC
OCEAN*

*VIRGIN
ISLANDS
Acquired from
Denmark,
1916–1917*

San
Juan ★

BAHAMAS

*PUERTO RICO
Acquired from
Spain, 1898*

Gulf of Mexico

*Caribbean
Sea*

0   50   100 miles

0   50 100 kilometers

0   150   300 miles

0   150   300 kilometers

About the Authors

ELLEN CAROL DuBOIS (PhD, Northwestern University) is retired Professor Emerita of History and Gender Studies at the University of California, Los Angeles. She is the author of *Feminism and Suffrage: The Emergence of an Independent Women's Movement in America, 1848–1869; Harriot Stanton Blatch and the Winning of Woman Suffrage* (winner of the 1998 Joan Kelly Memorial Prize in Women's History from the American Historical Association); and *Woman Suffrage and Women's Rights*. With Vicki L. Ruiz she was coeditor of the influential anthology *Unequal Sisters: A Multicultural Reader in U.S. Women's History*. With Vinay Lal, she was coauthor of *A Passionate Life: Writings By and About Kamaladevi Chattopadhyay*. Her newest book, *Suffrage: Women's Long Road to the Ballot Box*, will appear in 2020, the first comprehensive history of the American woman suffrage movement to be published in a half century.

Scarlett Freund

LYNN DUMENIL (PhD, University of California, Berkeley) is Robert Glass Cleland Professor of American History, Emerita, at Occidental College. She has written *The Second Line of Defense: American Women and World War I, The Modern Temper: American Culture and Society in the 1920s*, and *Freemasonry and American Culture: 1880–1930*. Her articles and reviews have appeared in the *Journal of American History*, the *Journal of American Ethnic History, Reviews in American History*, and the *American Historical Review*. Dumenil's current book project is *American Working Women in World War II: A Brief History with Documents*.

Lee Brubaker

SHARLA FETT (PhD, Rutgers University) is Professor of History at Occidental College. She is the author of *Working Cures: Healing, Health and Power on Southern Slave Plantations* and *Recaptured Africans: Surviving Slave Ships, Detention, and Dislocation in the Final Years of the Slave Trade*. Her work also appears in *Slavery and Abolition* and the edited collections *New Studies in the History of American Slavery* and *Paths of the Atlantic Slave Trade*. Fett has been a teaching partner and created digital exhibits with *Colored Conventions: Bringing Nineteenth-Century Black Organizing to Digital Life*.

John S. Rogers

Key to the Cover Images

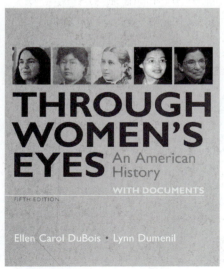

Left to right:
Dolores Huerta
Mary Tape
Susette La Flesche
Rosa Parks
Ruth Bader Ginsberg

Cathy Murphy/Hulton Archive/Getty Images (Huerta); Smith Collection/Gado/ Getty Images (Tape); National Portrait Gallery, Smithsonian Institution (La Flesche); Photo12/Universal Images Group/Getty Images (Parks); Terry Ashe/The LIFE Images Collection/Getty Images (Ginsberg)